W9-BNT-320

From
Joanie
xMas 1997

Golf Travel's
Guide to the
World's Greatest
Golf Destinations

FIRST EDITION

GOLF TRAVEL

GOLF TRAVEL'S GUIDE TO THE WORLD'S GREATEST GOLF DESTINATIONS

FIRST EDITION

THE ULTIMATE RESOURCE FOR
THE DISCRIMINATING GOLFER

BY TERENCE SIEG
AND THE EDITORS OF GOLF TRAVEL

BROADWAY

Broadway Books titles may be purchased for business or promotional use or for special sales. For information, please write to: Special Markets Department, Bantam Doubleday Dell Publishing Group, Inc., 1540 Broadway, New York, NY 10036

Library of Congress Cataloging-in-Publication Data
Sieg, Terence, 1942–
Golf travel's guide to the world's greatest golf destinations : the ultimate resource for the discriminating golfer / by Terence Sieg and the editors of Golf Travel.—1st ed.
p.   cm.
Includes index.
ISBN 0-7679-0029-4
1. Golf courses—Directories.
2. Golf resorts—Directories.
I. Golf travel.   II. Title.
GV975.S54   1997
796.352′025—dc21
97-11917   CIP

FIRST EDITION

Designed by Spinning Egg Design Group

97 98 99 00 01 10 9 8 7 6 5 4 3 2 1

ACKNOWLEDGMENTS

When working on a book project such as this one that has relied upon the talents of so many people, you quickly come to appreciate the dynamics of a true team effort. This book is a reality rather than just an idea, thanks to the smart, selfless, and enthusiastic work of a dedicated group of people. Regarding authorship, emphasis should be placed upon the editors of GOLF TRAVEL rather than myself. As with any sports team, it is quickly apparent who the true team players are—those who are there at the very end, when (finally!) the very last revision of the manuscript has been hauled away by Federal Express. Special thanks to my wife, Barbara, who has been such a consistent, committed partner in her tireless editing and always tasteful art direction. Her unwavering dedication to the highest quality has made this a much better book. My deep appreciation goes to our team of editors here at GOLF TRAVEL, particularly Tracy Davis and Bill Irwin, who worked tirelessly from the beginning of the project until its completion. Thanks to our two daughters—Ashley, who gracefully captured the exotic essence of the Asian pieces of this book, and Kendall, who kept the office going during the craziness of this creative process. Also thanks to Adam Butler, who did much of the quarterbacking on the project. The folks at Broadway Books have been perfect partners throughout—thanks to Bill Shinker, always the complete gentleman, for his wise encouragement from the very beginning; Suzanne Oaks, our superb "steel magnolia" editor; her always engaging assistant, Ann Campbell; and Yash Egami, our first editor. Yet more thanks to the most supportive agent imaginable—Rafe Sagalyn.

Concluding, I would like to express deep appreciation to Mike Klemme, who contributed the majority of the photos included in this book. In our opinion, Mike is the best in the world at doing what is so difficult—namely, taking distinctive and memorable photographs of golf courses. Thanks also to his diligent assistant, Margaret Wright, who was such a help in pulling the images together.

CONTENTS

Contents

Contents

INTRODUCTION

The very fact that you're holding this book and reading these words shows that, to some degree, you subscribe to the idea that one of life's greatest joys is traveling and playing golf—wherever it may be. We all know that traveling to the British Isles and playing golf is as natural as going to New York City and visiting Central Park, but what about a day of golf while visiting Paris, Seattle, Milan, Chicago, Sydney, or Dallas. In the middle of a week of sightseeing or business, five hours on the links could be just what the doctor ordered—an instant escape to gorgeous scenery, fresh air, mental and physical rejuvenation, and the renewal of the love affair with the game itself. This book will help you do just that, whether it be fitting in a round while in Dallas to see a client or planning your dream two-week golfing expedition to Australia.

The game of golf knows no boundaries. It is played with the same unabashed gusto in the Land of the Midnight Sun, the Land of the Rising Sun, the Land of the Setting Sun, and Down Under. But, of course, not all great golf destinations are located in exotic and far-distant places. Many of the world's best golf facilities are right here close to home. They are in the Arizona desert, all over California, the Pacific Northwest, the Rockies, the Northeast, the Carolinas, Florida, the Midwest—anywhere and everywhere.

GOLF TRAVEL's *Guide to the World's Greatest Golf Destinations* springs from a newsletter we have published since November of 1992—GOLF TRAVEL: *The Ultimate Guide to Great Golf Getaways*. In this exploding world of golf, where new golf courses are being built every day—not only in the United States but all over the world—and where more and more people are reaching beyond the provincial horizons of their home course in order to explore the magnificent golfing opportunities throughout the world, we saw a clear need to provide accurate, animated, and absolutely honest assessments about the golf travel scene. Like the newsletter it springs from, GOLF TRAVEL's *Guide to the World's Greatest Golf Destinations* is for those golfers who not only want to play the very best courses in the world but who, at the end of the day, also want to savor their round over a fine dinner and a good bottle of wine. Our goal, always, is to help you avoid the mediocre and enjoy the exalted!

This book is about the very *best* golfing destinations throughout the world. it includes information about the must-see, must-play courses, as well as extremely helpful non-golfing activities that will round out your trip for you and your family. Some of the destinations included here are obvious, such as the Monterey Peninsula, Scottsdale, and Ireland, yet this book also covers places you would not expect, such as an Apache reservation in New Mexico, the Lake Como region of Italy, and the environs of Paris—just to name a few. As you know, Paris has extraordinary cuisine, some of the world's best shopping, the Louvre, Notre-Dame, and the Musée d'Orsay but, as you may not know, it also happens to have five wondrous, private golf courses that you, as a visitor, can play during the week.

In the four years of compiling information for this book, we have traveled roughly 495,000 air miles and played more than six hundred golf courses. Sure, we came across our share of vastly overrated courses, but the good news is that we also discovered a great many wonderful and truly memorable courses—some virtually unknown and hidden away, while others are hugely famous.

As we take you along on our travels, we offer our candid impressions, frank evaluations, and up-to-date information so that you won't miss a beat at these golfing destinations. The material compiled within these pages will help you plan your trip from beginning to end—from deciding exactly where and when to travel, to how to arrange a tee time on courses that restrict public access, to which courses do and do not accept credit cards, to whether or not to take your meals at the resort's dining room or two miles down the road at that intimate jewel of a dining spot known only to the locals. Each and every review in this book is based upon a completely anonymous visit. We have experienced each destination—its golf courses, hotels, and restaurants—just as you would in your travels. Wherever we have traveled, we have paid full fare, just as you would be expected to do. This is the very best way of insuring that our experience will mirror yours.

This book is intended to be a helpful, user-friendly guide—not a book to be placed on a coffee table but one meant to help you enjoy your every golf trip more. Put it in your suitcase; write in it; earmark the pages. While traveling, you can use this as a reference for the essentials such as phone and fax numbers, addresses, prices, and other pertinent data or simply browse through the historical tidbits and local lore at the breakfast table in your hotel the morning of your first game. There are eighty-three destinations listed here and more than three hundred golf courses reviewed, more than half of which are in the United States and Canada. Our book includes some courses that, although ostensibly private, can be accessed by the public; we will tell you how. And are there some world-class courses not listed here? Sure there are. But we are confident that no other guidebook in publication provides the inside scoop on a broader range of destinations than what we have arranged here for you.

As you read and use this book you will get the very strong sense that we are concerned with much more than just course layout, yardage, and difficulty. The aesthetics and setting of a golf course are equally, if not more, important to us. Appreciating the inherent beauty of a golf course and its surroundings is, for us, one of the great joys of playing the game. Those who make the mistake of focusing *solely* upon the game—their score, a deteriorating backswing, another lost ball—risk coming away from the golf course exhausted rather than rejuvenated, having missed the grandeur of the scene, the artfulness of the layout, and the pleasure of playing, regardless of how well. At Pebble Beach, for example, we can all either become deeply distraught at having hooked another ball into the domain of a sea otter *or* we can savor the fresh salt air, observe the sweeping Pacific swells moving across Carmel Bay, and delight in the chorus of barking sea lions amid the breaking waves.

We vividly remember the awe we felt playing Royal Cinque Ports, a true links course along the English Channel, where every single hole offers some view of this brooding, slate-gray, historical body of water where the guns of England faced toward France to ward off Nazi attacks. An incessant, invigorating wind was our constant companion. We recall with equal clarity playing, on the other side of the channel, the sixth hole of the Omaha Beach Course straight out to the cliffs, with the menacing World War II bunkers and the beaches below where so many died in the invasion.

Whether it is the Reynolds Plantation Course with its intriguing land tentacles reaching out to Lake Oconee, or the Pete Dye River Course following the lovely Sheboygan River at Kohler, Wisconsin, or the Jackson Hole Course with the spectacular Grand Teton as a backdrop, the point of playing these glorious courses is missed if *all* you are concerned about is your performance.

One cannot help but appreciate the poetry and artistry of golf courses. Does this mean that course architects are artists? Without question. Some courses deserve to be hung in the Louvre, while others should be packed away in the attic. Fortunately, golf course architecture is a thriving art. Tom Morris, Donald Ross, Alister Mackenzie, Stanley Thompson, Tom Simpson, and all the other old masters have passed the torch to a current generation of course architects who would make their predecessors proud: Tom Fazio, Pete Dye, Jack Nicklaus, Jay Morrish, and the sons of Robert Trent Jones, the gifted maestro who spans both generations. All of these men have done much that is truly inspired within the last twenty-five years. While playing an absolutely memorable golf course and experiencing an almost spiritual sensation, one can feel the presence of the architect, not unlike walking through a van Gogh exhibit at the National Gallery and feeling the spirit of that crazed Dutch genius.

Everyone loves scoring systems, and we are certainly no exception. In GOLF TRAVEL's *Guide to the World's Greatest Golf Destinations*, we score The Golf, Golf Services, Lodging, Restaurants, and Non-Golf Activities each on a scale of 1 to 20, with a total possible cumulative score of 100 for the destination itself. As you will see, in this book we have given only seven destinations a score of 20 for The Golf—St. Andrews, Pebble Beach, Royal Dornoch in Scotland, the magical courses of Liverpool, Scotland's Cruden Bay, and the wondrous courses of Northern Ireland and Melbourne, Australia. A course receiving a score of 17 is one that a golfer should definitely play if in the area, a course receiving an 18 has great fascination and few faults, and courses earning a score of 19 or 20 are worth making a special trip to experience. Apply the same standards of scoring to the other areas we rate. For a quick reference to all five features according to rank, consult the appendices at the back of the book.

Finally, we would like to make clear that this is not a book written solely for the deadly serious, low handicapper. Rather, this is a book written for people who love the wonder of golf, the opportunity to go and see new places, and the thrill of a glorious walk in some special, new, emerald-green world. Our hope is that you will delight in each of these destinations as much as we have. *Bon voyage!*

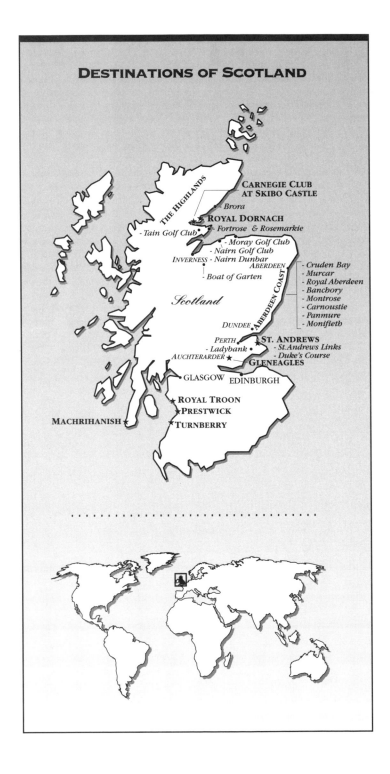

DESTINATIONS OF SCOTLAND

THE HIGHLANDS

CARNEGIE CLUB
AT SKIBO CASTLE

- *Brora*
ROYAL DORNACH
- *Fortrose & Rosemarkie*
- *Tain Golf Club*
- *Moray Golf Club*
- *Nairn Golf Club*
INVERNESS - *Nairn Dunbar*
ABERDEEN
- *Boat of Garten*

Scotland

ABERDEEN COAST
- *Cruden Bay*
- *Murcar*
- *Royal Aberdeen*
- *Banchory*
- *Montrose*
- *Carnoustie*
- *Panmure*
- *Monifieth*

Dundee
PERTH   ST. ANDREWS
- *Ladybank*   - *St.Andrews Links*
AUCHTERARDER ★   - *Duke's Course*
GLENEAGLES

GLASGOW   EDINBURGH

ROYAL TROON
★PRESTWICK
MACHRIHANISH ★   ★TURNBERRY

SCOTLAND

SCOTLAND

How straight it flew, how long it flew,
It cleared the rutty track
And soaring disappeared from view
Beyond the bunker's back—
A glorious, sailing, bounding drive
That made me glad I was alive.

—Sir John Betjeman

Religion, politics, and golf are the three great citadels of Scottish culture, so when an ecclesiastical figure of no less stature than the Dean of the Dornoch Cathedral takes it upon himself to define the difference between golf in America and golf in Scotland, then we best prick up our ears. Members of the clergy, by the way, are among the most passionate and thoughtful practitioners of golf in all of Caledonia.

"Americans believe in essential fairness," the dean once philosophized. "They expect a good tee shot to find a lovely tuft of turf in the fairway.

"However, the Scots know that there are bad breaks and bad bounces, that you do not always get what you deserve, in golf as in life itself. And therein lies the hope for redemption in both pursuits—the opportunity to make a fine recovery from a poor lie."

Bobby Jones sensed a very similar phenomenon during his first visit to St. Andrews: "I remember being puzzled when our shots from ordinary fairway lies were greeted with perfect silence, only occasionally broken by a discreet 'well played' when the ball stopped close to the hole. But when one of us from a tricky lie brought up a shot with a spoon or brassie, our gallery became quite enthusiastic."

Golf in Scotland mirrors the national character. It is a trip back through the mists of time to courses that may be two or three hundred years old. And, for the most sensitive and perceptive pilgrim, to play golf in Scotland is to achieve a spirit of unity or oneness with all golfers—past, present, and future—who have trod the links before them or will one day make the journey.

The game made famous in Scotland, the real game created there and exported across the globe, is almost always a seaside experience played over linksland, a special land of dune ridges, sand hills, resilient grasses, and flaming gorse bushes that, quite literally, links the sea with the more fertile agricultural plains that may be only a few hundred yards away. Balmy days—like those that prevailed during the 1996 Open Championship when Tom Lehman routed the field—are rare. True links golf is a battle with the elements. "Anyone who has ever been stranded at the far end of a links as rain, driven on a strong wind, sweeps in from the sea will know what desolate places they can be. Mighty men can be turned into midgets as the knack of flighting shots low becomes vital to survival," architect Donald Steel, the designer of the fine Carnegie Club at Skibo Castle, has written.

Links golf simply calls for more improvisation than we are accustomed to in America. Over these less perfectly manicured courses, you hit the shots you can, not the shots you want. High, lofted balls are treated with contempt by swirling winds. Much of the game, instead, is played on the ground, with long running approaches up banks and down hollows, with lots of chipping and putts of amazing length. Far from considering wind a nuisance, the Scottish golfer conceives of it as a spice that intensifies the true flavor of the game.

The visitor will discover that Scotland may be neatly subdivided into three chief golfing regions: the west coast, the east coast, and the Highlands.

The best courses on the west coast include the Ailsa and Arran courses at Turnberry, Royal Troon and the Portland Course at Troon, Prestwick, underrated Western Gailes, and remote Machrihanish, located on the southern tip of the Mull of Kintyre, with the greatest opening hole in the world of golf.

A few of the best golfing venues on the east coast include monstrously difficult Carnoustie, six golf courses in the city of St. Andrews, Panmure and Montrose, both within thirty minutes of Carnoustie, and the legendary Gleneagles resort, with its three great parkland layouts only an hour's drive from Edinburgh.

Up north in the Highlands you will find incomparable Royal Dornoch, the Carnegie Club at Skibo Castle, two championship layouts in Nairn, the eccentric Moray Golf Club (also known as Lossiemouth) where Royal Air Force bombers fly over the links at low altitude, spectacular Cruden Bay north of Aberdeen, and Royal Aberdeen, located just outside Aberdeen's city center.

All of these golf courses are part of private clubs that welcome public play. Certain clubs impose more stringent conditions for public access than others; most have handicap limits, and you must remember to bring your handicap certificate and a letter of introduction from your home professional. Although you will likely be greeted graciously by the golf course staff and many of the club members, keep in mind that the membership of a few of the most exclusive Scottish clubs have justifiably earned a reputation for their disdain of invading foreign holiday players. Also keep in mind that golf in Scotland has traditionally been the exclusive province of adult males. Women and juniors may still encounter a bit of discomfort or discrimination. We say this by way of warning and also add that for the most part you will be warmly received and made to feel at home. The endearing qualities of the Scots will cheer your soul, especially at clubs that are a bit off the beaten path.

No single—or sane—golfing trip could encompass the entire roster of Scottish golf course masterpieces. Readers are advised to visit Scotland between May and September, find a comfortable base of operation (see our hotel recommendations), and tackle one or two regions at most, especially if contemplating a trip of ten days or less. Scotland's windswept coastline, rugged Highlands, brooding moors, and dark and forbidding castles do not appeal to everyone. Family activities include pony trekking and visiting magnificent medieval castles, abbeys, great houses, and prehistoric ruins. You can take a canal tour along Scotland's three longest lakes and try to catch a glimpse of "Nessie," the legendary monster of Loch Ness. When the weather cooperates, the Highlands and lake region are stunningly beautiful. If you have arrived in late August or early September, consider heading to the Edinburgh Festival, one of the most elaborate arts festivals in Europe.

How much you enjoy your trip to Scotland's historic golf links may well depend on the weather and how long it takes you to adjust to such drastically unfamiliar golf conditions. First-time travelers to St. Andrews usually have no appreciation for how different the game will be on the Old Course—it is a taste that, for many players, must definitely be acquired. Also, you will have to walk these courses—nature never intended golf courses to be littered with golf carts. Expert caddies can, however, make a significant difference in your round; by all means, take advantage of their vast local knowledge.

As for the notorious and unpredictable weather, expect the worst and pray for something better. Always bring your cold-weather gear and your waterproof clothing. If the Scottish skies turn and you encounter miserable conditions, bear it the best you can and comfort yourself that this is how the game has always been played here. We are fond of telling GOLF TRAVEL subscribers that if you approach Scottish golf with the proper attitude, you will want to go back for more! And finally, do not forget the important fourth citadel of Scottish culture—single-malt whiskey, which may be freely enjoyed in the comfort of the clubhouse after your round is complete.

►ST. ANDREWS

THE HIGHER GAME

	The Golf	Golf Services	Lodging	Restaurants	Non-Golf Activities	Total
Rating	20	18	18	18	18	92

St. Andrews, Scotland

The outward dignity, quiet calm, and surface serenity of St. Andrews—the golfers coming up the eighteenth fairway dressed in the classic style of Walter Hagen and Gene Sarazen, the windblown university students tramping the city's cobblestones with bags of clubs hitched casually over their shoulders, the ghostly ruins of the medieval cathedral and castle overlooking the sea, the aristocratic mien of the Royal and Ancient Golf Club (where the rules of golf are made), the obvious pride and propriety of the townspeople, the resort air of St. Andrews and its spirit of muscular Christianity—all of this, all of the poise, tradition, gentility, and unmistakable elegance of the place, all of it vanishes utterly as you prepare to take up your position on the first tee of the Old Course and send your small white ball into space. Only then, as the adrenaline takes complete charge of your body, as the crowd of spectators (the vast crowd!) stands in respectful silence behind you, only then will you discover the true soul of St. Andrews. You will also discover at that moment, quite possibly, something important within yourself.

People here take seriously the "Saint" in St. Andrews. The decorous manner and upright conduct of residents seem to spring from the dictates of some higher code. It's almost as if the Rules of Golf, created and administered in St. Andrews by the R. & A., has significant moral carryover in the town's civic proceedings. You will count every mis-hit and penalty stroke on the Old Course—and have to look hard on the pristine streets of St. Andrews for a single shred of litter. Honesty, fair play, and personal integrity are the values shared in common in the kingdom, values that impact and subtly elevate every visitor to this place.

Yet raw human drama has always lain at the heart of St. Andrews history, both ancient and present-day. Patrick Hamilton, a university student with unfashionable religious views, was burned at the stake in the city streets in 1527. His initials, P.H., painted on the cobbles of North Street, mark the spot of his martyrdom. John Knox, who led the Reformation in Scotland, preached his first fiery sermons in St. Andrews in the sixteenth century, when the game of golf was at least 150 years old here. The sermons, delivered when St. Andrews was the ecclesiastical capital of Scotland, brought results. They led to the dismantling of the St. Andrews cathedral, the foundation of Presbyterianism, and the eventual union of Scotland with England.

The golfer saturated with adrenaline who tees it up on the Old Course today faces a fate more benign than that of Patrick Hamilton. Disasters aplenty lurk beyond that critical first drive, but the worst that can happen, the St. Andrews equivalent of excommunication, is the quite real possibility of being ejected from the course for slow play. The scorecard clearly states: "Rangers have the power to order slow play offenders off the course." Single players traveling thousands of miles to St. Andrews also face the daunting fear that they may not get on the Old Course at all since starting times are not accepted from singles. For details on securing a starting time, see below.

Once you tee off and quickly acclimate yourself to the brisk pace of St. Andrews play, however, other associations, both spontaneous and surprising, may then seize your imagination and fill it with involuntary visions. You may well picture golfers who walked this turf before you, from Mary, Queen of Scots, who played here just days after the murder of her husband, Darnley; to Shivas Irons, the mystical hero of Michael Murphy's *Golf in the Kingdom*, who scored a hole in one in the middle of the night on the thirteenth hole of the "Burningbush Links" by striking a featherie with a carved shillelagh; to Fred Couples, who drove the green of the 370-yard first hole in the 1984 Open by bouncing his ball over Swilcan Burn. After that there is an even higher realm of St. Andrews speculation, talk—inspired by the shimmering sea air, the crashing waves, and the thousand-year-old landscape—of the holiness and mystery of the Old Course, the haunted holes and bunkers, the banshee-infested gorse, the transforming power of the links, and the spiritual odyssey from world to world and hole to hole. Such talk is part of the magic of St. Andrews. And only here is it truly credible.

THE GOLF

20

The throng clustered behind the first tee of the **Old Course** summons nautical imagery from the 1930s. Certain ocean liners departing Liverpool harbor on maiden crossings undoubtedly were sent off with less fanfare. Part of the crowd is leaving, part is waving them good-bye, while a few indecent souls may be expecting to see the ship go down with all hands on board. The sketch by H. M. Bateman—"The Man Who Missed the Ball on the First Tee of St. Andrews"—does not overstate the case. There

are quiet clumps of anxious golfers who have arrived well in advance of their tee times, dozens of seasoned caddies awaiting their assignments, the dapper officials of the St. Andrews Links Management orchestrating play, scores of townsfolk and sightseers watching the action or strolling toward West Sands, and heaven only knows how many members of the R. & A. sipping their whiskey and surveying the scene from

Clubhouse, St. Andrews

leather armchairs behind the big bay windows of the venerable clubhouse. The fourball before us arrived with its own, quite sizable, cheering section. But absolutely everyone—every man, woman, toddler, and grandmother—holds their breath in unison when it comes your turn to face the fairway and approach the ball. Try to remember, if you can, to hit it left.

St. Andrews is both the soul and symbol of Scottish golf, but play on the Old Course is thoroughly international. Our own four-ball included an Australian lawyer, a Canadian schoolteacher, and an enormously polite Japanese whose entire English consisted of one affable line, always punctuated with an exclamation mark: "Good show!" Yet the artificial barriers of language and nationality were swept away in the face of an awesome shot. Two steps up the fairway we collapsed into one another's arms, comrades forever, bound by our mass baptism in St. Andrews' fire.

Now heading away from town, the distinct harmony of the Old Course gradually unfolds and wraps you in its full embrace. One is struck by the intimacy of golfer and caddie, the eight golfers and caddies huddled tightly together against the wind on the tee box, the religious adherence to the rules of the game, and the deafening takeoffs of Harrier and Phantom jets from the nearby NATO base at Leuchars across the Eden Estuary. Even by the second hole, the shared fairways congested with golfers walking and playing into one another look like recipes for impending doom, runways at an eccentric airport where planes take off and land at the same time. Then comes the inevitable unraveling. Our strong Canadian, the best player among us, took a ten or eleven on the seventh hole after his second shot landed in Shell Bunker, one of the most notorious on the course. Three times he tried to clear the eight-foot embankment before giving up and retreating to the rear—with a powerful blast into deep gorse. Another great challenge, or reversal of fortune, lurks on the legendary 461-yard seventeenth, the decisive Road Hole, the most famous hole in golf and the most dreaded par four in the world. Jack Nicklaus calls it "a par four and a half." A bogey is excellent play on the Road Hole; a par will live with you until your dying day. The conservative tee shot here again plays left of center (a slice sends you onto the roof of the Old Course Hotel) followed by a big three iron to the undulating green.

"The only holes that really matter on the Old Course are the first and last," our caddie said facetiously as we approached the eighteenth tee, for the entire last hole, like the first, is another public spectacle, a citywide event. No other course, including the others in St. Andrews, holds a candle to the Old because no other starts and finishes before the front terrace of the Royal and Ancient. Your last tee shot soars high above the city skyline; you cross the old stone bridge above the burn (the Scottish word for "stream") and stop to have your caddie snap your photograph. It is an exhilarating feeling. Family, friends, and a throng of tourists have gathered to watch your return. If you pulled off a big drive for the crowd on number one, this is your opportunity to choke on the eighteenth green. But even if you do, you will leave the Old Course knowing one thing with certainty—that St. Andrews has made you a better golfer.

A word or two about the caddies of St. Andrews. Like the waiters in the three-star restaurants of Paris, they are almost a professional class. Especially for first-time players on the Old Course, a caddie is worth his weight in lost balls alone. Our caddie, kindly George Stewart, took eight to ten strokes off our game. It is hard for us to think of the Old Course now without picturing George. Sports psychologist, golf instructor, and St. Andrews historian in equal measure, George's advice and club selection helped make our day. Indeed, every caddie in our group was sane, sober, and smart. Our Australian colleague sunk three amazing putts from fifty to seventy feet. On each occasion he leaped into the air and blessed his caddie for supplying the line.

St. Andrews is a small town. If you take a taxi to a restaurant, the same driver is likely to collect you later that evening. Likewise, your caddie may moonlight as the night porter behind the reception desk at your hotel. You will see the same faces again and again in St. Andrews, and they will call you by name. If you have not arranged for a particular caddie, like George, in advance, apply to

The Old Course

the caddie manager adjacent to the starter's box on the Old Course thirty minutes or so prior to your tee time. The current fee is £22 ($39), and the customary tip for a top-drawer caddie today is £10 ($18). Also, do not be surprised if your caddie invites you for a drink after the round (and make no mistake—you are buying). The Jigger Inn, the wonderful "caddie's pub" at the Old Course Hotel, is frequently filled with happy, windswept golfers from around the world lunching with their caddies and savoring their day together. It's a lovely scene.

Play is more relaxed, more a stroll in the park, on the other St. Andrews courses. After the Old, you will want to play the **New,** the **Jubilee,** and the **Eden** courses— in that order. The New and the Jubilee are nearly as extraordinary in their own way as the Old Course, but they lack the drama of its start and finish in the city center and the great treachery and danger of its hidden bunkers. Do not feel bad if you cannot fit Eden into your schedule; it has been much altered in recent years and is considered by far the least interesting course in St. Andrews. The New Course (opened in 1895) is actually longer and tighter than the Old and may, in fact, offer a stiffer challenge. The Jubilee (1897) can be a little scruffy in appearance—it is the course nearest the sea and frequently has sand on the greens and seashells on its fairways. However, it has several beautiful holes, like the gorgeous eighth with its sea view and the magical sixteenth with its blind tee shot over the dense yellow gorse. There are yet three other courses in St. Andrews: the **Duke's,** a handsome new parkland course owned by the Old Course Hotel; **Balgove,** the nine-hole beginners' course; and **Strathtyrum,** a 5,094-yard layout that opened in 1993. Strathtyrum has not been well received in certain quarters. Bobby Burnet, the noted writer and former official historian of the R. & A., calls it "insultingly short." All of the golf courses, with the exception of the Duke's, are owned and managed by the city of St. Andrews and not, as many mistakenly assume, by the Royal and Ancient Golf Club.

Practical matters. If you plan to stay at one of the two choice hotels—either the Old Course or Rusacks—the extremely competent golf staffs at both establishments will book your advanced tee time on the Old Course or see to it that your name is entered in the daily ballot. This great service is one of the hidden advantages of staying at either hotel, for the burden of arranging a tee time is then lifted from your shoulders. But if you prefer to do it yourself, advanced reservations for the Old Course can be made by telephone or fax and require full payment of your greens fee. Unreserved times are made available in the daily ballot. The ballot is drawn after 2 P.M. for play the next day. To enter the ballot golfers should give the names in their party to the Old Course reservation center prior to 2 P.M. the day before they wish to play. Singles are not permitted to book or ballot for starting times. They should simply show up on the first tee, look around for a friendly two- or three-ball, and ask to join their company. We met many single golfers in St. Andrews, and every one got on the Old Course in this fashion with no difficulty whatsoever. The Old Course is closed on Sundays, the first two weeks of March, and the last two weeks of November. Due to competition commitments, very few advanced starting times are available in September and early October. The current greens fee for the Old Course is £70 ($123). *Important note:* All golfers wishing to play the Old Course must arrive with a current handicap certificate and a letter of introduction from a bona fide golf club.

Getting on the New, the Jubilee, and the Balgove is a much simpler matter. Unreserved times are allotted on a first-come, first-serve basis. In other words, just show up and play. The Eden, Jubilee, and Strathtyrum courses have their own twenty-four-hour booking system for starting times, but otherwise, the order of play here is also determined by the arrival of golfers on the first tee.

Finally, another excellent golf course in the area that welcomes visitors without restriction is **Ladybank,** one of Scotland's finest and most beautiful inland courses. An Open qualifying course, Ladybank is twenty minutes west of St. Andrews. The greens fee is £28 ($49) for a round.

St. Andrews Links. Pilmour Cottage, St. Andrews, Fife KY16 9SF Scotland. Tel: 011-44-1334-475757. Fax: 011-44-1334-477036. Credit cards accepted.

  • *The Old Course.* Circa 1400. Designer: Old Tom Morris. Par 72. 6,566 yards. Greens fee: £70 ($123). Caddies can be arranged. No carts. Handicap limit: men 28; women and juniors 36. Closed: Sunday; two weeks in November and March. Season: year-round.

  • *The New Course.* 1895. Designers: W. Hall Blyth, Old Tom Morris. Par 71. 6,640 yards. Greens fee: £30 ($53). Caddies can be arranged. Carts available for seniors and those with medical disabilities. Season: year-round.

  • *The Jubilee Course.* 1897. Designers: Willie Auchterlonie, Donald Steel. Par 72. 6,805 yards. Greens fee: £25 ($43). Caddies can be arranged. No carts. Season: year-round.

  • *The Eden Course.* 1914/1990. Designers: H. S. Colt, Alister Mackenzie/Donald Steel. Par 70. 6,315 yards. Greens fee: £20 ($35). Caddies can be arranged. No carts. Season: year-round.

  • *Strathtyrum.* 1993. Designer: Donald Steel. Par 69. 5,094 yards. Greens fee: £15 ($26). Caddies can be arranged. Carts available for seniors and for those with medical disabilities. Season: year-round.

  • *Balgove.* 1993. Designer: Donald Steel. Par 30. 1,530 yards. Greens fee: £7 ($12). Caddies can be arranged. Two carts available for persons with medical disabilities. Season: year-round.

Duke's Course. Craigton, St. Andrews, Fife KY16 8NS Scotland. Tel: 011-44-1334-479947. (Course run by Old Course Hotel. Tel: 011-44-1334-474371. Fax: 011-44-1334-477668.) Credit cards accepted.

  • 1995. Designer: Peter Thomson. Par 72. 7,220 yards. Greens fees, round: £55 ($96), day ticket: £70 ($123). Walking permitted. No caddies. Carts. Season: year-round.

Ladybank Golf Club. Annsmuir, Ladybank, Cupar, Fife KY7 7RA Scotland. Tel: 011-44-1337-830814. Fax: 011-44-1337-831-505. Credit cards accepted.

  • 1879. Designer: Old Tom Morris. Par 72. 6,800 yards. Greens fees, round: £28 ($49), day ticket: £38 ($66). No caddies. Two carts available.

 GOLF SERVICES

The St. Andrews driving range (near the first tee of the Eden Course) requires golfers to have their own shag balls. Since most international visitors do not travel with shag balls, you will find that the short nine-hole Balgove layout is a perfect place to warm up for your outing on the Old Course.

The best place to prepare for the Old Course greens is the Himalayas, the famous eighteen-hole putting course in West Sands, so named because of the huge changes in elevation on the undulating putting surface. Do not miss the Himalayas, one of the most absorbing golf pastimes in St. Andrews and ideal for the entire family. The admission price is £1 ($1.75).

 LODGING

There is a tremendous variety of fine lodging options in St. Andrews, from inexpensive but very comfortable bed-and-breakfasts, to charming older hotels, to super-luxurious world-class establishments. Standout properties in each category are described below.

The "secret" place where St. Andrews insiders stay is **Waldon House.** This stately and elegant bed-and-breakfast has an unmistakable air of exclusivity—it is, in fact, owned and operated by that most aristocratic organization, the Royal and Ancient Golf Club. When the eight bedrooms with private baths at Waldon House are not occupied by members of the R. & A. (which is most of the time), they are made available to the public. Waldon House has a wonderful location next door to Rusacks Hotel. It overlooks the eighteenth fairway of the Old Course and is literally a two-minute walk from the first tee. Single rooms with breakfast are £38 ($67), and doubles are £70 ($123). The best room is the spacious Captain's Suite (£130/$228), which is reserved for the R. & A. captain whenever he is in St. Andrews on official business. When he is not in residence, you may rent it and stay there yourself. Pat Cheslere, of the R. & A.'s membership department, handles bookings for Waldon House. Her telephone number is 011-44-1334-472112. Be sure to request a room at the front overlooking the golf course and the beach beyond. The helpful management of Waldon House assists with restaurant reservations and all manner of shopping and sightseeing tips.

Another outstanding St. Andrews bed-and-breakfast is **Lindores** at 6 Murray Place, about an eight-minute walk from the Old Course. Lindores is a particularly intriguing choice for serious golfers because owner Gerald Donlon is an excellent golfer himself (a six handicap) who will gladly caddie for guests of his establishment who arrange for his services well enough in advance. Gerald is good company on the course and knows everything about golf in St. Andrews. Lindores may be the perfect place to stay for three or four golfing friends who are traveling together on a tight budget. Gerald will arrange tee times on the Old Course for your party and assemble other seasoned caddies as needed. Mrs. Donlon runs their bed-and-breakfast with obvious pride, and the establishment is spic-and-span. The three bedrooms (with two or three beds per room) have their own private baths. The cost is a very modest £25 ($44) per person per night, breakfast included, of course.

Old-fashioned Rusacks and the spectacularly renovated and expanded Old Course Hotel are the two traditional rivals at the top end of the St. Andrews hotel market.

The strengths of **Rusacks** are its superior location (within easy walking distance of everything in St. Andrews), its friendly staff, and its famous lounge at the back of the hotel with its unsurpassed view of the first and last holes of the Old Course. Unfortunately, however, Rusacks has several serious shortcomings. Owner Forte Hotels has made its investment in the handsome public areas, which are well maintained, but the guest rooms have not been so recently renovated and can be terribly disappointing, particularly at such prices (about £125/$219). We stayed in number 328, which the receptionist said was one of the best rooms in the hotel. Despite a fine view of the Old Course, the furnishings in the room were worn and drab, the mattresses were uncomfortably soft, and the entire room actually seemed quite dirty with dust and debris on dresser tops and windowsills. We also were not favorably impressed with the restaurant at Rusacks. The restaurant itself is attractive and the service good, but the cooking is bland, uninspired, and, again, expensive for what you get. The aura and spirit of St. Andrews can be found in this old Victorian hotel, but overall the place feels a little shabby.

Not so the **Old Course Hotel,** stunningly renovated in 1990 and occupying a magnificent site on the seventeenth hole (the Road Hole) with commanding views of all the St. Andrews golf courses, the ancient city's skyline, and the sea. An international consortium with very deep pockets (Japanese and American interests, plus the R. & A.) spared no expense to make this one of the greatest resort destinations in all of Scotland. The Old Course Hotel is costly (a standard double goes for

£235/$412), but you get great facilities and tremendous luxury for your money here. There is a glistening new spa complex with exercise rooms and an indoor swimming pool, four delightful restaurants, an extremely competent golf staff, and perhaps the most handsome golf pro shop in the city. The Old Course Hotel is the consensus favorite among upscale visitors to St. Andrews. During our stay it was filled to capacity with well-dressed Japanese guests and a large group of happy American radiologists on a Scottish golfing junket. The guest bedrooms would satisfy anyone. They are spacious, tastefully decorated, and equipped with luxurious gray marble baths and every conceivable amenity. Two of the hotel's biggest assets are the Road Hole Bar and the Jigger Inn. The Road Hole Bar, on the fourth floor of the hotel, is very dressy and the perfect spot for a drink before or after dinner. It has a great selection of single-malt whiskeys and an incomparable view of the R. & A. clubhouse, which is beautifully lit at night. The Jigger Inn is the single best place in all St. Andrews for lunch. Even if you don't stay at the Old Course Hotel, be certain to stop in these two absolutely wonderful spots. Special low-price golf packages are frequently available at the Old Course Hotel. Inquire in advance when booking.

Waldon House. The Links, St. Andrews, Fife KY16 9JB Scotland. Tel: 011-44-1334-472112. Fax: 011-44-1334-477580. 8 rooms. Doubles cost £70 ($123). Credit cards accepted.

Lindores. 6 Murray Place, St. Andrews, Fife KY16 9AP Scotland. Tel: 011-44-1334-477628. No fax. 3 rooms. Doubles cost £25 ($44). No credit cards.

Rusacks. Pilmour Links, St. Andrews, Fife KY16 9JQ Scotland. Tel: 800-225-5843 or 011-44-1334-474321. Fax: 011-44-1334-477896. 50 rooms from £125 to £175 ($219 to $307). Credit cards accepted.

Old Course Hotel. St. Andrews, Fife KY16 9SP Scotland. Tel: 800-327-0200 or 011-44-1334-474371. Fax: 011-44-1334-477668. 125 rooms and suites. Doubles range from £235 to £285 ($412 to $500). Credit cards accepted.

RESTAURANTS   18

You will not exhaust the area's supply of excellent restaurants even if you golf in St. Andrews for a week or more. The celebrated **Peat Inn,** a whitewashed cottage in open countryside five miles south of St. Andrews, heads the culinary list. This very elegant hideaway—tapestries hanging on white stuccoed walls, classic table settings, and extremely attentive service—is one of only four restaurants in all of Scotland to be awarded a Michelin star. Chef/owner David Wilson serves real Scottish food fashioned seductively in the French manner—six courses at dinner and four at lunch. Dinner commences in the sophisticated front lounge with a drink before the roaring fire. The dining rooms have lovely views of rolling farmland at the rear. Specialties include spring lamb with rosemary, wonderful smoked haddock, breast of pigeon, fresh seafood, and wild duck with blueberries. The wine list has been carefully assembled. Two prix fixe dinner menus are available at £34 ($60) and £44 ($77) per person. Advanced booking is essential. The Peat Inn also operates eight very stylish guest rooms and suites priced from £100 to £140 ($175 to $245), delicious gourmet breakfast included. The dining room is closed Sundays and Mondays in low season.

    The Cellar is the best seafood restaurant in the St. Andrews area, well worth the twenty-minute drive to the adorable fishing village of Anstruther, home of the interesting Scottish Fisheries Museum. The Cellar is located on a back street in an old factory where ship sails were once produced. The original sewing tables—set on stone floors with fireplaces in every corner of the room—now accommodate diners. Chef Peter Jukes is a large man with a kindly demeanor. He buys from the small boats that dock in Anstruther and cooks the fish simply and quickly. It is superb. We enjoyed the herring appetizer, the fresh langoustine and crab, and the wonderful sea bass. There is an excellent selection of wines, sweet service by friendly young waitresses, and a beef selection always available for those who do not care for fish. Expect to spend £65 ($114) for two at dinner, wine and tip included. Closed Sundays and Mondays.

The Grange Inn is an old, very friendly, and wonderfully atmospheric country pub (low beamed ceilings, ancient stone walls, and roaring fires) with an equally wonderful and informal dining room decorated with photographs of golfing subjects from the nineteenth century. Just two miles south of St. Andrews, the Grange Inn is set on a high hillside with a panoramic view of the city, St. Andrews Bay, and the Tay Estuary. If weather permits, dine outside in the garden and take full advantage of the view. The appealing menu offers smoked Tay salmon, Perthshire venison, and local beef and lamb. Expect to spend about £50 ($88) for two at dinner. Highly recommended. The Grange also has two very simply furnished, twin-bedded guest rooms.

The very best hotel dining room in the city of St. Andrews is the grand **Road Hole Grill** on the fourth floor of the opulent Old Course Hotel. This bright and formal room with black tie service is oriented toward the open grill at the rear, where chefs are busily at work. Those seated toward the front of the room enjoy the stupendous view of the golf courses and the sea. This is a great place to celebrate after a round on the Old Course. With the entire golf course at your feet, you can replay almost every shot just by looking out the window. The cooking at the Road Hole Grill may not be as interesting as David Wilson's at the Peat Inn, but it is extremely satisfactory and the setting is unsurpassed. You cannot go wrong here with big platters of smoked salmon, Scottish beef, roasted chicken, and lamb. Like everything at the Old Course Hotel, dinner is expensive, about £75 ($132) for two, wine and service included.

The aforementioned **Jigger Inn** pub, truly a St. Andrews institution, is a good choice for lunch at the Old Course Hotel.

Afternoon tea at charming **Rufflets Country House** makes a pleasant outing. Rufflets is a St. Andrews favorite of Jack Nicklaus, who has rented the entire place (twenty rooms) for family and friends during British Opens in the past. The guest rooms at Rufflets are starting to look a little run-down these days (we do not recommend your staying here), but the hotel has idyllic gardens at the rear overlooking a stream. Rufflets is located in a quiet setting a mile and a half west of town on the B939.

The Peat Inn. Peat Inn by Cupar, Fife KY15 5LH Scotland. Tel: 011-44-1334-840206. Fax: 011-44-1334-840530. Credit cards accepted.

The Cellar. 24 East Green, Anstruther, Fife KY10 3AA Scotland. Tel: 011-44-1333-310378. Fax: 011-44-1333-312544. Credit cards accepted.

The Grange Inn. Grange Road, St. Andrews KY16 8LJ Scotland. Tel: 011-44-1334-472670. Fax: 011-44-1334-472604. Credit cards accepted.

Road Hole Grill and **Jigger Inn,** Old Course Hotel, St. Andrews, Fife KY16 9SP Scotland. Tel: 011-44-1334-474371. Fax: 011-44-1334-477668. Credit cards accepted at Road Hole Grill. No credit cards at Jigger Inn.

Rufflets Country House. Strathkinness Low Road, St. Andrews, Fife KY16 9TX Scotland. Tel: 011-44-1334-472594. Fax: 011-44-1334-478703. Credit cards accepted.

NON-GOLF ACTIVITIES

In a town where the largest cab company is called Golf City Taxis, many non-golfing activities still involve the sport that made it famous.

Shopping in St. Andrews, for example, is dominated by golf, and the golf shops here are among the most famous in the world, great for buyers or browsers. The legendary Tom Morris Shop, overlooking the eighteenth green, is no longer owned by the Morris family, but its selection of equipment and memorabilia remains superb. The same is true of the old Auchterlonie Golf Shop around the corner on Golf Place; new owners have maintained its character while upgrading the inventory. Serious golfers who know St. Andrews well, however, prefer Jim Farmer's Golf Shop on St. Mary's Place. Mr. Farmer is a highly regarded teacher and professional, and his equipment prices are the lowest in town.

Collectors of golf antiques will have a field day in St. Andrews. The Old St. Andrews Gallery at 10 Golf Place has the best selection in Scotland of antique golf prints and old and rare golf books. This gallery also sells the exquisite persimmon woods handmade by Peter Broadbent. The ultimate experience for the collector may be the Hickory Sticks Golf Company at 4 Church Square, a manufacturer of beautiful reproduction golf clubs from the nineteenth century, in addition to play-quality featheries and gutta-percha balls. Thus equipped—and decked out in tweed knickers purchased from the Woollen Mill—you can play the Old Course as they did a hundred years ago.

Rainy-day activities include the award-winning British Golf Museum across the street from the R. & A. clubhouse, the St. Andrews Museum (free admission) off Double Dykes Road, and tours of nearby castles, gardens, and stately homes like Falkland Palace, Earlshall Castle, and Kellie Castle. The St. Andrews Sea Life Centre is an ideal activity for a family with small children.

GETTING THERE: St. Andrews is approximately an hour north of downtown Edinburgh. Cross the Firth of Forth going north by way of the Forth Bridge, connect with the A92 at Dunfermline heading northeast until you reach Kirkcaldy, and then take the A915 past Leven and Largoward into St. Andrews.

▶GLENEAGLES

AUCHTERARDER

	The Golf	Golf Services	Lodging	Restaurants	Non-Golf Activities	Total
Rating	19	18	18	15	20	90

Many great golf resorts in America are the darlings of specific regions, but only a select few share the universal recognition and acclaim that is enjoyed by Gleneagles within the United Kingdom. Gleneagles, run by the Guinness Corporation (see also the Equinox in the Northeast section), is in the lexicon of every London drawing room. For generations it has been known as the country's premier luxury destination. "The Palace in the Glen" opened in 1924. It has its own railway station on the London to Inverness line, its own bank, and its own elegant shopping arcade, consisting of smart London retailers like N. Peal (the cashmere king), Burberrys, and Harvey Nichols, plus 830 private acres of world-class facilities for great riding, shooting, salmon fishing, lawn tennis, and much else. Gleneagles may look rather austere and forbidding as you come up the driveway—remember, this is Scotland, the fountainhead of Calvinism as well as golf—but a celebratory air rules this classic, family-oriented resort.

THE GOLF

The two great, rolling, moorland courses at **Gleneagles**—much more so than the seaside links at Turnberry and St. Andrews—will initially impress American golfers for their similarities to courses back home. We say "initially" because these two lyrically beautiful, indeed poetic, golf courses—the **King's** and the **Queen's,** de-signed by five-time British Open champion James Braid—are full of picturesque idiosyn-crasies and unforgettable surprises. The Queen's is the more charming and jewellike of the two; the King's is longer, steeper, tougher, and more majestic. Both are fringed with pine and golden gorse, offer views of the stark Ochil Hills to the west and the Grampian Mountains to the east, and are virtual nature sanctuaries with their abundance of wild deer, pheasant, grouse, red squirrels, and rabbits roving the grounds and songbirds, crows, and hawks hovering at the treetops. Both are one-of-a-kind sporting experiences.

Gleneagles

The front nine of the Queen's marches directly into strong prevailing winds; most of the holes play far longer than their posted yardage. At the turn, however, the Queen's really gets interesting, with several holes in succession that, on paper, appear quite weak: two par threes in a row, the thirteenth and fourteenth, along a small loch (lake), followed by a 251-yard par four. But this fifteenth hole, in fact, makes for one of the most daunting and challenging drives on the course—from an elevated tee across forbidding terrain to a narrow green with forest on the left and a plunging ravine on the right. You will lower your score on the back side, but this short final nine is dominated by strategy and ever-changing wind directions. Other great holes on the Queen's include the seventh, a downhill, 491-yard par five into the wind with a view of the wild Ochil Hills; the 337-yard eighth with its blind tee shot around the gorse; and a great finishing hole with the wind at your back that carries your drive over the creek below and back toward the clubhouse.

The King's makes its most lasting impression on the front side, with an inspira-tional opening hole that heads uphill away from the pro shop terrace, the utterly magical third hole with its blind approach shot over a steep ridge (be sure to ring the bell when leaving the green) and number five, one of the most famous par threes in Scotland. All of the holes on the King's and Queen's are named as well as numbered. Number five is called *Het Girdle* (hot griddle or skillet), meaning your ball may not stick to the well-protected plateau green and if it slides off, trouble awaits. The best advice here is simply: "be up." The fourteenth hole, *Denty Den*, mirrors the quirky fifteenth on the Queen's. It is a 260-yard par four that requires a long, laser-guided drive. If you can deliver, a birdie might be in the cards. This handsome golf course hosts the Bell's Scottish Open every year. Come prepared for quick play: we finished our round at each course in under three and a half hours.

The truly controversial project at Gleneagles is the enormous new **Monarch's Course** designed by Jack Nicklaus that opened for play in 1993. A few of the local

Gleneagles golf members told us over a beer or two in the stunning new Dormy House that the Nicklaus course, in their estimation, is an awful abomination, a rude slap in the face of traditional Scottish golf. The Nicklaus course, you see, is the first golf course ever to be built in Scotland with installed cart paths. These serious Scotsmen like to walk, consider carts the refuge of the old and the infirm, and resent the great distance (up to a quarter mile) between green and tee on some of the new Nicklaus holes. The hearty local lads will not even call the course by its name. They disparagingly refer to it as "the Nicklaus Course." The best they can say is that it draws some of the heavy hotel traffic off their beloved King's and Queen's courses.

Indeed, the Monarch's displays none of the secret, diminutive charms of the King's and Queen's and only a few of their unique bunkering characteristics. It looks—in its barren, new course condition with baby trees and shrubs and an unfortunate view of a busy motorway—like a big American resort layout dropped incongruously amid the moors of Scotland. We were surprised and disappointed that Nicklaus brought such a dull sensibility—and a cookie-cutter approach—to the heritage and setting of Gleneagles. We also have to say that driving around Gleneagles even in a partially enclosed golf cart will be a frigid experience save for intervals in midsummer.

The Gleneagles golf staff has high hopes for the Monarch's Course. Gleneagles is moving toward the future and the Monarch's is it, whether you like cart paths or not. The Monarch's, by the way, has been built on land once occupied by the hotel's erstwhile Prince's and Glendevon courses. There are, in fact, a total of five golf courses today at Gleneagles if you include the pitch-and-putt course on the immediate hotel property and the cute **Wee Course,** a scaled-down moorland nine ideal for a lighthearted game with the children. The greens fees are £70 ($123) for the three championship courses and £15 ($27) for the Wee Course.

Gleneagles. The Gleneagles Hotel, Auchterarder, Perthshire PH3 1NF Scotland. Tel: 800-223-6800 or 011-44-1764-663543. Fax: 011-44-1764-694383. Play restricted to hotel guests. Credit cards accepted.

  • *King's Course.* 1919. Designer: James Braid. Par 68. 6,828 yards. Greens fee: £70 ($123). Caddies. No carts. Season: year-round.
  • *Queen's Course.* 1919. Designer: James Braid. Par 68. 5,695 yards. Greens fee: £70 ($123). Caddies. No carts. Season: year-round.
  • *Monarch's Course.* 1993. Designer: Jack Nicklaus. Par 72. 7,081 yards. Greens fee: £70 ($123). Walking permitted. Caddies. Carts. Season: year-round.
  • *Wee Course.* 1928. Designer: George Alexander. Par 27. 1,481 yards. Greens fee: £15 ($27). Caddies. No carts. Season: year-round.

 GOLF SERVICES

The highly professional golf operation at Gleneagles hinges around the handsome new Dormy House, which opened in 1992. It houses two lovely restaurants, a handsome bar, and spacious new locker facilities with saunas. The golf shop is well equipped with apparel and rental clubs and is staffed by friendly young pros who will give you a lesson (£65/$114) or actually play a full round with you for £200 ($351) on any of the Gleneagles courses. Guests can also avail themselves of the Golf Academy, which opened in 1994. The driving range and practice area are excellent, too, with plenty of complimentary balls.

Good caddies are always available at Gleneagles (£27/$47 per round) but—unlike Turnberry and the Old Course—a caddie is not a necessity for the first-time player because of the excellent pocket course guides published by the resort.

LODGING

⑱

Guest accommodations at the **Gleneagles Hotel** (234 rooms, including eighteen suites) are luxurious, exquis- itely decorated, and stunningly expen- sive. We were kindly bumped up to one of the better rooms over the hotel en- trance, number 176, a lavish fantasy of English designer fabrics with heavy bro- cade curtains, chintz-covered armchairs, mahogany furniture, high molded ceil- ings, a luxurious marble bath, in-room bar, writing desk, plenty of closet space, and cable television. The even pricier rooms and suites are still more spacious and have splendid views of Perthshire;

The Gleneagles Hotel

less costly rooms can be quite small and overlook the hotel buildings at the rear. Room prices range from £250 to £345 ($438 to $605) with suites starting at £395 ($692). Spe- cial two-night packages including room, dinner, breakfast, and two rounds of golf are offered year-round and are priced from £370 to £546 ($649 to $957) per person.

Gleneagles is dressy; jackets and ties are mandatory in the evening. Guests are as well manicured as the flower beds. This is one hotel where you will see private heli- copters coming and going and a long queue of Rolls-Royces by the front door. Service is excellent throughout the hotel, its restaurants, and the vast sporting facilities. We especially enjoyed meeting friendly Billy Lynch, the proud hall porter, here for thirty years, who greeted us by name whenever we passed his station.

A final note: Be sure to book tee times when making your room reservations.

The Gleneagles Hotel. Auchterarder, Perthshire PH3 1NF Scotland. Tel: 800-223- 6800 or 011-44-1764-662231. Fax: 011-44-1764-662134. 234 rooms and suites. Double rooms from £250 to £345 ($438 to $605). Credit cards accepted.

RESTAURANTS

⑮

When you stay at a large, self-enclosed facility like Gleneagles you are more or less held captive by the resort's dining options. The cuisine here is not as good as that at Turnberry, yet it is even more expensive. The prix fixe dinners (£40/$70 per person, excluding beverage) in the show- case **Strathearn Dining Room** are, frankly, quite dull. We loved being "piped in" to dinner by the Highland bagpiper in full military regalia, and the dining-room pi- anist was chock-full of Andrew Lloyd Webber. Unfortunately, however, the menu features a predictable assortment of dishes, some cooked tableside with flames reaching the ceiling. Wines, too, are served with great fanfare, but if you cut through the showmanship you are left with a mediocre meal and a large tab.

We much preferred the wonderful high tea served in the **front drawing room** (large platters of smoked salmon, beautiful pastries, and scones); the sturdy bar lunches served in the new **Dormy House** overlooking the eighteenth greens of both the King's and Queen's; and the informal, far less expensive dinners served in the poolside **Brasserie** at the Gleneagles Country Club: gourmet pizzas, salads, and Cal- ifornia-inspired pastas. Room service is available around the clock.

The restaurants at the Gleneagles Hotel. Auchterarder, Perthshire PH3 1NF Scotland. Tel: 800-223-6800 or 011-44-1764-662231. Fax: 011-44-1764-662134. Credit cards accepted.

NON-GOLF ACTIVITIES 20

A cornucopia of non-golf activities awaits guests at Gleneagles. We have not visited a golf resort that offers more for the non-golfer, save, perhaps, Disney World. The roster of individuals who direct the sports programs at Gleneagles says a lot about the overall caliber of the facilities. Virginia Wade runs the "Tennis Break" (on three grass and three all-weather courts), Mark Phillips (the former royal husband) orchestrates clinics for the high-powered equestrian program, and Jackie Stewart directs the shooting school, which provides clay targets for all levels of expertise. Members of the British Olympic team have trained at the spectacular Equestrian Center, with its two large indoor arenas, outdoor ring, fine stable of horses and ponies, outstanding instruction for everyone, from beginners to expert riders, plus carriage driving and trail rides over the moors. All riding attire is provided by Gleneagles (and it is first-rate), so there is no need to pack your own.

The resort also has a lovely and vast country club and health spa complex with an indoor pool shaped like a tropical lagoon, squash courts, saunas, Turkish baths, and every imaginable form of massage and aqua therapy. Guests can fish for salmon on the hotel's private "beats" on the famous River Tay, one of the best salmon rivers in Scotland. Trout fishing can be arranged on a private loch to which hotel guests have exclusive access. Gleneagles is even home to the British School of Falconry. Small children will delight in the many supervised activities at the resort, including croquet and snooker (a game similar to pool). And, finally, there are wonderful shops on site that offer everything from high fashion to Scotch whiskey.

GETTING THERE: The Gleneagles resort is located in Auchterarder, approximately one hour northwest of downtown Edinburgh. Cross the Firth of Forth going north by way of the Forth Bridge, connect with the A91 heading west at Milnathort, and turn right onto the A823 at Muckhart. Follow the A823 until you reach Gleneagles.

▶THE ABERDEEN COAST

	The Golf	Golf Services	Lodging	Restaurants	Non-Golf Activities	Total
Rating	**20**	**16**	**17**	**16**	**17**	**86**

Other regions of Scotland may be more legendary and may lure greater numbers of golfers to their seaside links, but the northeast coast of Scotland—the one hundred miles of rugged shoreline to the north and south of the dignified and recently reborn city of Aberdeen—offers golf courses and non-golf attractions that are second to none in this beautiful and always hospitable region.

For one reason or another, American golfers who know Scotland best always seem to come to Cruden Bay and Carnoustie last. The clusters of courses around Troon, St. Andrews, Muirfield, and Royal Dornoch always get penciled onto the travel wish list first. Only Machrihanish on the remote and largely inaccessible Mull of Kyntyre and Machrie on the solitary Isle of Islay see less traffic than these great courses just to the north and south of Aberdeen.

For example, when we visited Cruden Bay in June—at the very height of the golfing season—we had the course largely to ourselves. And during the same eventful week, we arrived at Carnoustie after a long automobile drive and actually walked on without having booked an advanced tee time. We paid the modest £50 ($88) greens fee and marched off into a frigid, thirty-five-mile-per-hour breeze, the perfect antidote to many hours spent behind the wheel. Of course, arriving at Carnoustie in mid-June without a tee time is a very bad idea, and at almost any other championship course in Scotland the starter would tell you to come back sometime next year.

Many potential visitors to this region are put off by Aberdeen's less-than-refined reputation. Thanks, however to the discovery of North Sea oil, the Granite City has seen enormous improvement during the past twenty-five years. While still true to its honest, working-class origins, Aberdeen is no longer a dreary town stymied by high unemployment. Financially healthy Aberdeen now displays a real majesty in its rows of granite houses and its spotlessly clean city streets. *Local Hero,* the wonderful movie filmed near Aberdeen starring Burt Lancaster, is a delightful portrait of this community and makes excellent viewing prior to your own visit here.

The golf traveler will not only find Aberdeen a convenient and central location (just an hour's drive north to Cruden Bay and seventy minutes south to Carnoustie, with many other courses in between) but comfortable and interesting as well. An extremely attractive hotel we recommend with enthusiasm, the Marcliffe at Pitfodels, located in Aberdeen's pleasant western suburbs (see Lodging, below), will further enhance your visit. The Marcliffe is head and shoulders better than any other hotel in the region.

In addition, you will discover much more than golf to occupy your time. Just west of Aberdeen in Royal Deeside, near the pretty towns of Banchory, Aboyne, Ballater, and Braemar, the salmon and trout fishing is incomparable. A number of spectacular castles located near Aberdeen are open to the public: Slains, which inspired Bram Stoker, the creator of *Dracula*; Craigievar, which was the model for the castle at Disneyland; and Crathes, voted the most beautiful castle in Scotland. For those who are interested in distilleries, the signposted Malt Whiskey Trail along Speyside will take you to Glenfiddich and Glenlivet. And, of course, wonderful shopping for Scottish woolens and tweeds abounds. Exquisite cashmere goods may be purchased at reasonable prices at Johnstons of Elgin, which operates several stores throughout the region.

THE GOLF

The three most sublime golf courses along the Aberdeen coast are—in descending order of greatness—Cruden Bay, Carnoustie, and Royal Aberdeen. All three of these courses are historic, and all three are outstanding seaside links, but that is where the similarity between them ends. We were overjoyed and amazed that three courses along the same shoreline could be so incredibly distinct.

We rate **Cruden Bay** the best because of the naturalness of its routing, the haunting beauty of its setting, and the extraordinary scenic qualities of the course and the surrounding landscape. The view from the tenth tee at Cruden Bay is simply one of the greatest views in the entire world of golf. Cruden Bay is not only one of the most beautiful courses we have ever laid eyes on, but it is also one of the most underrated. It is as whimsical and idiosyncratic as Lahinch (see article in the Ireland chapter) and just as much fun to play, but it is longer and tougher than Lahinch, and—we hope our friends in Ireland will forgive us—it is also more majestic. In addition, Cruden Bay has a three-hole sequence—eight, nine, and ten—that ranks among the most intriguing three consecutive holes in golf. The soul of Cruden Bay rests in its collection of short par fours and unusual par threes, including one incredible par three, number fifteen, whose blind tee shot from the ocean's edge passes over a giant sand dune to a hidden green 239 yards from the tee.

A stark beauty marks the drive from Aberdeen to Cruden Bay—the slate-colored sea dotted only by a few oil rigs towering offshore in the distance, the treeless hills, the vast empty spaces. Both the sweet little village of Cruden Bay and the Cruden Bay golf course, which is less than a mile from town, are located directly on the North Sea. The golf clubhouse sits up high above the ocean and presents commanding views of a lonely, isolated, and windswept beach and the ruins of an ancient castle that stands sentinel on a hilltop on the horizon. The golf course itself skirts the full length of the crescent beach and weaves its way up and down through the natural contours of the undulating duneland. Cruden Bay is steep walking; you will feel it in your haunches when you are done.

We were fortunate enough to play Cruden Bay in the company of a friendly local member and his very unusual dog, the best trained Doberman we have ever seen. This member happened to be American, a former navy frogman who came to Scotland years ago to work the oil rigs, then married a local girl, and now lives in a village house and plays Cruden Bay almost every day of the year. It's a good life. His amazing companion has been trained with exceptional results to retrieve balls from the hip-high rough. He found our balata in the thick rough on the third hole in about three seconds after being commanded to do so by his master. This unique Doberman—welcome on the course but banished from club tournaments because he gives his owner an unfair advantage—is a well-known fixture at Cruden Bay and has even been profiled in the Scottish golfing press.

We cannot leave Cruden Bay without describing a few of its holes. The third, for instance, is one of those short (286 yards) par fours where local knowledge counts for everything. All you need to do on three is punch an iron off the tee into the narrow fairway and then hit a short approach to the green. If you hit the ball over the green on three you will end up in the Water of Cruden, a tidal river unseen from the fairway that flows into the North Sea.

The memorable eighth at Cruden Bay (par four, 258 yards) looks easy but is not. We have yet to figure it out, but some form of optical illusion is at work on eight. Thanks to the massive size of the bowl-shaped dunes that frame the green, the pin actually looks much closer to the tee than it really is. After that great hole you walk virtually straight uphill to the ninth (462 yards), another hole that could appear only in Scotland. The drive is blind over the slope and between two big traps. If you strike it well, your ball could hit the down side of the slope and roll to within a short iron of the green.

Then you move to the amazing panorama from the elevated tenth tee. We would gladly travel to Cruden Bay again just for that view—the waves pounding the crescent beach, the farmland on the right, and the tenth fairway far below at your feet. The tenth also requires strategic thinking, especially difficult in such inspiring circumstances. A winding burn crossed by two wooden bridges protects the green, about 290 yards from the tee. But big hitters—thanks to the steeply elevated tee—are capable of putting a good three wood into the burn. No one on God's green earth can hit over the burn on the fly, so the smart drive on ten is another layup in front of the burn.

But the fun is not yet over. When the wind is at your back, the 320-yard par four twelfth at Cruden Bay is reachable from the tee. Unfortunately, the green is so hard to read on twelve that your potential eagle can quickly revert to par. Then there are the two fabulous par threes—fifteen and sixteen. Sixteen is fifty-seven yards shorter than fifteen (182 yards versus 239) but harder to hit because the tee shot is straight into the wind. Again like Lahinch, Cruden Bay is not overly long. It measures a manageable 6,395 yards from the tips, and the greens fee is an amazingly low £30 ($53) for a day ticket. This is one of the best deals in all of golf.

Carnoustie

Carnoustie, the site of the 1999 British Open Championship, has already hosted the Open five times and is considered to have one of the toughest finishes in golf. James Braid—the designer of the King's and Queen's courses at Gleneagles—was responsible for the present layout, although a few minor alterations have been made in recent years. Situated in a bright village full of appealing golf shops with a seaside resort air, Carnoustie is a monster, 6,936 yards long.

Royal Aberdeen is neither as intimidating as Carnoustie nor as lyrically beautiful as Cruden Bay, but it is a more traditional links layout than both. This is a welcoming and historic club (founded in 1780) with marvelous views—particularly on the front nine that plays along the North Sea—and tight fairways always threatened by a riot of blooming gorse in that incredible hue of burnt yellow. Royal Aberdeen is just one mile north of the city center and actually within sight of the city highrises. The testing links at Royal Aberdeen are 6,372 yards in length. During the week the greens fee is £40 ($70) per round or £60 ($105) for a day ticket.

In addition to Cruden Bay, Carnoustie, and Royal Aberdeen, there are many, many more golf courses within easy driving distance of Aberdeen that rival these three most famous links. Carnoustie may have a worldwide following, but other fine layouts within the region are still true jewels to the residents, members, and golfing insiders who know and love them.

For example, you can play an amazing stretch of six courses that run one after another along the North Sea coastline. South of Carnoustie and just outside Dundee—at the western extremity of this chain of golf links—is **Monifieth Golf Links,** where golf has been played since 1639. Monifieth is as unpretentious a golf club as you will find. The locals play the club's two courses in blue jeans, and the club members will round up someone's son to caddie for you if you like. The "pro shop" is a simple hut where an elderly gent takes your greens fee (£24/$42 on weekdays) and sells a couple of sleeves of balls. **Panmure,** which abuts Monifieth on one side and Carnoustie on the other, is a proper old club, established in 1845 (the golf course was built in 1890) and a marvelous links course set among giant sand dunes. The three courses of the Carnoustie Links complete this sublime strand of adjacent golf tracks.

Just up the coast from Carnoustie lies one of the oldest clubs in the world, **Montrose,** founded centuries ago, in 1562. When we asked the club secretary who the original designer of the course was, she replied without hesitating a moment, "Mother Nature herself." And just a mile north of Royal Aberdeen you'll find lovely **Murcar,** a dramatic James Braid design. Many golfers swear that the course at Murcar not only equals that of Royal Aberdeen but also ranks as one of the finest links in Scotland.

There are also many parkland courses nearby for those who tire of ocean vistas. One cute little parkland layout is **Banchory,** certainly not a championship affair at just 5,775 yards but a pretty course that runs alongside the River Dee and features one of the strangest par threes we have ever seen. Hole number fourteen—called "Doo'cot"—measures just eighty-eight yards but is blind and plays straight uphill. Big hitters will need a full wedge or nine iron to reach the green, and, if you can hold your line, you just might be rewarded with a hole in one.

Cruden Bay Golf Course. Aulton Road, Cruden Bay, Peterhead, Aberdeenshire AB42 0NN Scotland. Tel: 011-44-1779-812285. Fax: 011-44-1779-812945. Credit cards accepted.

• 1899. Designers: Herbert Fowler, Thomas Simpson. Par 70. 6,395 yards. Greens fee: day ticket £30 ($53). Caddies available. No carts. Season: year-round.

Carnoustie Links. Links Parade, Carnoustie, Angus DD7 7JE Scotland. Tel: 011-44-1241-853789. Fax: 011-44-1241-852720. Credit cards accepted.

• *Championship Course.* 1842/1867/1926. Designers: Allan Robertson/Old Tom Morris/James Braid. Par 72. 6,941 yards. Greens fee: £50 ($88). Walking permitted. Caddies available. Carts. Handicap limit: men, 28; women, 36. Season: year-round.

Royal Aberdeen. Balgownie Links, Bridge of Don, Aberdeen, AB2 8AT Scotland. Tel: 011-44-1224-702221 (-70251 for the clubhouse). Fax: 011-44-1224-826591. Credit cards accepted.

• 1893. Designer: Willie Park, Sr. Par 70. 6,372 yards. Greens fees: weekday: round: £40 ($70), day ticket: £60 ($105), weekend round: £50 ($88). Caddies available. No carts. Handicap must be 20 or under. Season: year-round.

Monifieth Golf Links. The Links, Monifieth, Angus DD5 4AW Scotland. Tel: 011-44-1382-535553. No fax. No credit cards.

• *Championship Course.* 1890. Designers: local members. Par 71. 6,459 yards. Greens fees: weekday: £24 ($41), weekend: £28 ($48). Caddies can be arranged. No carts. Restrictions: no public play on Saturday. Season: year-round.

Panmure Golf Club. Burnside Road, Barry, Angus DD7 7RT Scotland. Tel: 011-44-1241-855120. Fax: 011-44-1241-859737. Credit cards accepted.

• 1899. Designers: local members. Par 70. 6,317 yards. Greens fees: round: £28 ($48), day: £42 ($71). Caddies can be arranged. One cart available. Restrictions: no public play on Saturday. Season: year-round.

Montrose Links. Trail Drive, Montrose, Angus DD10 8SW Scotland. Tel: 011-44-1674-672932. Fax: 011-44-1674-671800. Credit cards accepted.

• *Championship Course.* 1562. Designer: unknown (remodeled by Willie Park, Jr., c. 1905). Par 71. 6,470 yards. Greens fees: weekday: £20 ($35), Sunday: £28 ($48). No caddies. No carts. Restrictions: no public access on Saturday. Season: year-round.

Murcar Golf Club. Bridge of Don, Aberdeen AB23 8BD Scotland. Tel: 011-44-1224-704354. Fax: 011-44-1224-704354. No credit cards.

• 1906/1909. Designer: Archie Simpson/James Braid. Par 69. 5,809 yards. Greens fee: weekday: £28 ($48), weekend: £43 ($75). No caddies. No carts. Restrictions: limited public play on weekends. Season: year-round.

Banchory Golf Club. Kinneskie Road, Banchory AB31 5TA Scotland. Tel: 011-44-1330-822365. Fax: 011-44-1330-822447. Credit cards accepted.

• 1905. Designer: unknown. Par 69. 5,775 yards. Greens fees: weekday: £17 ($30), Sunday £21 ($37). Caddies and carts can be arranged. Restrictions: no public play on Saturday. Season: year-round.

GOLF SERVICES 16

The golf services along the Aberdeen coast of Scotland are rudimentary, but part of the appeal of these courses lies in their marvelous simplicity. What could be better than pulling into the parking lot at a course like Monifieth, teeing up, and heading down the first fairway with no further ado?

Practice ranges are also uncommon, but several of the courses mentioned—like Cruden Bay and Royal Aberdeen—have shorter "second" courses that can make for a great warm-up prior to your round on the championship links.

We did not see a single riding cart at any of the courses we played (Carnoustie reputedly has a few and several courses can arrange a cart for golfers who need one for medical reasons), but pull-carts are available everywhere. Be sure to bring a bungee cord with you in order to attach your bag firmly to the "trolley." Caddies can be few and far between as well, unless you request one when booking your tee time. Caddies cost from £18 to £24 ($32 to $42) depending upon the club; the standard caddie tip is about £5 ($9).

The pro shops in Scotland are not nearly as well stocked as their counterparts in the U.S. and the prices for everything—from balls and gloves to shoes and rain suits—are easily 50 percent more expensive than in America. So buy all your supplies at home and come to Scotland overequipped rather than underequipped. The wonderful sweaters embossed with the club logos that are available in the shops make great souvenirs.

 L O D G I N G

Aberdeen is the natural place to stay when touring these courses because it is located midway between Cruden Bay to the north and Carnoustie to the south. Aberdeen is also the perfect gateway for an exploration of picturesque Royal Deeside to the west. As noted above, the finest hotel in Aberdeen—by a wide margin—is the **Marcliffe at Pitfodels,** which opened in 1994. Aberdeen's premier hoteliers, Stewart and Sheila Spence, own and manage the Marcliffe, which is beautifully decorated in traditional tartans. Lavish public areas, lovely sitting rooms, a wonderful bar with over one hundred malt whiskeys, two very fine restaurants, and a friendly and accommodating staff who are always happy to book all your golf tee times make this a truly unforgettable hotel.

The Marcliffe consists of thirty-eight rooms and four suites. All are spacious and comfortably furnished and come equipped with cable television and large baths. The best room in the house is the large and impressive Gorbachev Suite, named for the suite where the former Soviet chief stayed when visiting Scotland. Rates at the Marcliffe range from £115 to £165 ($202 to $289).

Another interesting but much less expensive place to stay is **Raemoir House,** a traditional sporting country-house hotel set amid its own 3,500 acres of highland scenery seventeen miles west of Aberdeen and three miles from the quaint village of Banchory. Run by an incredibly engaging grandmother-daughter-granddaughter team who could not be more pleasant, Raemoir House has a wonderful family atmosphere, although some of the guest rooms and public areas of the hotel are in need of renovation. The best room in the house (where we stayed) is the "Old English room" with an ancient, four-hundred-year-old, four-poster bed. The cost of a double ranges from £100 to £125 ($175 to $219) and includes breakfast.

The Marcliffe at Pitfodels. North Deeside Road, Pitfodels, Aberdeen AB1 9YA Scotland. Tel: 011-44-1224-861000. Fax: 011-44-1224-868860. Forty-two rooms and suites. Doubles from £115 to £165 ($202 to $289). Credit cards accepted.

Raemoir House. Raemoir, Banchory AB31 4ED Scotland. Tel: 011-44-1330-824884. Fax: 011-44-1330-822171. 24 rooms and suites. Doubles from £100 to £125 ($175 to $219). Credit cards accepted.

RESTAURANTS 16

The best dining in Aberdeen can be found at the **Marcliffe at Pitfodels,** where you will discover two options; the informal **Conservatory Restaurant,** which is ideal for breakfast and lunch, and the dressier **Invery Room.** With an excellent wine list that offers better than two hundred possibilities and a menu that highlights local produce cooked by a team of Scottish chefs, the Invery Room is perfect for dinner. Like everything else at the Marcliffe, the dining experience is first-rate.

All of the golf clubs noted above prepare lunch for visitors—generally a sandwich, salad, and a beer—served in a very congenial setting amid newfound friends. The clubhouse at Royal Aberdeen is the oldest and most handsome of the lot. There are several good pubs within walking distance of the clubhouse at Carnoustie. By the time you read this, a new clubhouse may be under construction at Cruden Bay.

If you find yourself exploring the pretty countryside west of Aberdeen, two good restaurants in the area include the dining rooms at **Raemoir House** in Banchory and the **Banchory Lodge Hotel,** which is situated along the banks of the River Dee.

The restaurants at the Marcliffe at Pitfodels. North Deeside Road, Pitfodels, Aberdeen AB1 9YA Scotland. Tel: 011-44-1224-861000. Fax: 011-44-1224-868860. Credit cards accepted.

Raemoir House. Raemoir, Banchory AB31 4ED Scotland. Tel: 011-44-1330-824884. Fax: 011-44-1330-822171. Credit cards accepted.

Banchory Lodge Hotel. Banchory AB31 3HS Scotland. Tel: 011-44-1330-822625. Fax: 011-44-1330-825019. Credit cards accepted.

NON-GOLF ACTIVITIES 17

Activities include salmon and trout fishing in some of the world's legendary rivers, hunting, pony trekking, exploring fishing villages along the coast like Peterhead, north of Cruden Bay, and touring historic castles and some of the lesser-known whiskey distilleries like Singleton and Glengarioch. You can take the Malt Whiskey Trail by following the signs in the area. The dearth of traffic on the roads in this part of Scotland makes touring especially pleasant.

GETTING THERE: Aberdeen is served by its own airport and has several flights daily to and from London. Driving time to Aberdeen from St. Andrews is approximately three hours. Cruden Bay is forty minutes north of Aberdeen on the A975. Carnoustie is approximately seventy-five minutes south of Aberdeen on the A930, just off the A92.

▶TURNBERRY

SCOTLAND AT ITS FINEST, GOLF AT ITS MOST CHALLENGING

	The Golf	Golf Services	Lodging	Restaurants	Non-Golf Activities	Total
Rating	18	17	19	16	18	88

We arrived on a rainy, windy Saturday at the spectacular Turnberry Hotel—magnificently renovated and enlarged in 1992 by new Japanese owners—and got settled into our stunning room overlooking the golf courses and the sea. We then stepped out eagerly into the elements on the elevated hotel terrace to absorb the fabled view, to taste the sea air after a long journey, and to pay our respects to the Ailsa Course before our game the following morning. We found that eyes accustomed to the keener contours of American golf courses, even from this close proximity, blink two or three times in the face of Turnberry and yet find little that is recognizable among the duneland layout, save for golfers waist-high in sea grass marching slowly into the wind. The land and seascape beyond the course are far more certain: the

Turnberry

football-shaped geological oddity called Ailsa Craig, eight miles off the mainland, dark storm clouds fast approaching from Ireland to the west, the stark lighthouse built upon the ruins of Robert Bruce's castle, the dim outline of mountains on the Isles of Arran and Kintyre, container ships steaming in the whitecaps of the Firth of Clyde, and miles of isolated shoreline. We saw something else, too, a phenomenon that would directly impact our game here. Big seabirds headed into the wind were stock-still, flapping their wings in vain, suspended in air for a moment before the wind turned them upside down and whisked them away like so many sheets of paper. Turnberry winds, we were to learn, treat lofted golf shots with equal contempt.

A seventy-minute drive south from the Glasgow Airport—a ride that becomes increasingly pleasant as the thorny traffic of the Glasgow suburbs gives way to the dramatic west coast scenery of Troon, Prestwick, and Robert Burns country—takes you to historic Turnberry. Built in 1907 but now newly reborn, Turnberry has clearly taken aim at the top spot of the Scottish golf and resort market. The dapper assistant manager who greeted us put it rightly: "The hotels in St. Andrews have no control over the golf courses, and some people will prefer us to Gleneagles because we are half the size and more personal." Then he added, importantly: "And we have the money now."

Indeed. Since its acquisition by the Japanese company Nitto Kogyo, more than £15 million ($26.3 million) has been invested in the hotel and its overwhelmingly beautiful new spa complex. This sterling spa, which is ingeniously linked to the hotel by an underground corridor that runs beneath the hotel access road, compares favorably with any in the world. It provides guests with a needed extra dimension for the non-golfer; it is also a luxurious haven for golfers after a game or when weather makes play impossible (which is often), and it has turned Turnberry, more or less overnight, into a family destination, not just a place where the boys can escape for a few days of bonding on the links. The Japanese investment in Turnberry continues. A huge new clubhouse overlooking the eighteenth green was built in 1994, when Turnberry last hosted the British Open.

 THE GOLF

Your experience on either the Ailsa (the championship course) or the Arran (Turnberry's excellent second layout) course will be flavored by your caddie and dominated by the weather. Although our toothless and inebriated caddie boasted that he could walk the Ailsa Course blindfolded at midnight, by the sixth hole he had twice tripped over the bag and finally fallen face-first into soft turf with a dull thud. His nonstop chatter after this alarming incident became indecipherable. We had not considered requiring our caddie, at eight-thirty on a Sunday morning, to take a Breathalyzer exam!

The rain had stopped, but the wind was a steady thirty-five miles per hour with gusts to sixty. Nearly everyone tried to hit a low ball off the first tee; hence, half the first shots hit that day were badly topped and went nowhere. Our caddie swore that conditions were just about ideal, that we should see the course when the wind was really howling.

It is important to remember what the weather was like when Tom Watson and Jack Nicklaus were hurling those sixty-fives at each other in the 1977 British Open on the **Ailsa Course:** Scotland was in the midst of a serious drought, the insanely difficult rough was burned flat, and the wind was as still as a summer day in Kansas. Turnberry, simply, was not itself. When Greg Norman won the '86 Open here under normal conditions, his composite score was twenty strokes more than Watson's winning total. We say this in advance simply because Ailsa can be a brutal course and because even outstanding players will enjoy it most if they reject the notion of scoring well the first time out. With their tear ducts in high gear from the blasting wind, many Americans may have trouble just seeing the fairways, which are hidden behind dunes and shrouded in heather. Also, don't get too excited if you score well on the famous front nine, which traces the edges of the sea and gives Ailsa its nickname, the "Pebble Beach of Scotland." The wind is at your back on the front side, and the ball carries for miles. One player in our group drove his ball to within a chip of the 378-yard second hole.

All this changes, however, as you make the turn. From the eleventh hole onward, you play every shot into the teeth of the wind. Those 390-yard par fours require three substantial shots to reach the green, and the par fives look as if you should drive there—by car. Yet nothing is predictable at Turnberry, not even the winds. A ball struck in compensation for the wind can fail utterly when the wind stops on your backswing. Turnberry will also require you to hit shots that you just do not see at home, from deep bunkers over towering mounds onto tiny greens. A good short game—and a sense of humor—will help.

There is much to console you when your score deteriorates: the sea view, the chatter (or incoherent babble) of your caddie, the long, frequently fruitless searches for your ball in the impenetrable rough, an ancient cairn in the middle of the ninth fairway, an overgrown runway left over from World War II, when the golf course was converted into an Allied air force base, and a stone memorial to pilots who perished in the war on the twelfth hole. There is amazing natural variety—and a mystical quality that many have noted—in this treeless linksland. You half expect to see a Scottish tribal chieftain appear on horseback around the next bend in the fairway. Prior to our game the fellow in the pro shop told us we should take at least eight balls with us on Ailsa. Although we played the course at least ten strokes above our handicap, ours was a successful outing indeed: we lost just three.

The **Arran Course,** on the other side of the disused runway from Ailsa, is pooh-poohed by locals as short, flat, and easy. It is not as well conditioned as Ailsa and lacks Ailsa's commanding sea views, but it features many exquisite holes. Greens fees for the Ailsa Course are £70 ($123) for hotel guests and £100 ($175) for nonguests. A round on the Arran Course costs £35 ($61)/£45 ($79). Caddies (with tip) are about £25 ($44). Pull carts are available on the Arran Course only.

There is yet another golfing jewel on the immediate hotel property: the absolutely enchanting twelve-hole pitch-and-putt course with its difficult, Ailsa-style bunkers and elevated greens. The holes are just fifty or sixty yards long, but this wonderful little course replicates in miniature the pure magic—and great challenge—of Turnberry.

Three other outstanding seaside links courses nearby that welcome the fee-paying public are **Western Gailes** (Tel: 011-44-1294-311649) and **Royal Troon** and **Prestwick** (see below), and all are within a forty-minute drive of Turnberry.

Turnberry. Ayrshire KA26 9LT Scotland. Tel: 800-223-6800 or 011-44-1655-331000. Fax: 011-44-1655-331706. Credit cards accepted.

• *Ailsa Course.* 1909. Designers: Willie Fernie, Mackenzie Ross (1948). Par 70. 6,976 yards. Greens fees: hotel guests: £70 ($123), public: £100 ($175). Caddies available. No carts. Season: year-round.

• *Arran Course.* 1909. Designer: Willie Fernie. Par 68. 6,014 yards. Greens fees: hotel guests: £35 ($61), public: £45 ($79). Caddies available. No carts. Season: year-round.

GOLF SERVICES

Golf services at Turnberry are good despite the fact that the practice area requires that you retrieve your own shag balls. But the basics—like the good course bar, where you can meet friendly local members and exchange Ailsa horror stories—are in place, and a modern practice range is in the works for 1998. The fine pro shop offers lessons from six full-time professionals, club rentals, handsome Turnberry-embossed sweaters and golfwear, and every possible golfing accessory that you may have forgotten, lost, or destroyed. The attitude of the golf course employees, strained a bit thin by the vast number of golfers descending upon the place, is helpful and interested. They are proud of Turnberry and make you glad to be there.

LODGING 19

As Turnberry's assistant manager generously indicated, Gleneagles, the cavernous hotel and multifaceted golf complex in picturesque Auchterarder, has led the Scottish resort scene for decades. Whenever we fell into conversation with fellow guests at the **Turnberry Hotel,** they, too, were forever comparing Turnberry with its renowned rival to the east. "Gleneagles," one said, as if he really could not believe his own words, "is no better than this."

Gleneagles has much to recommend it, but in our opinion, based upon recent visits to both, the accommodations at Turnberry are more attractive. Turnberry has such a personal tone and has been so tastefully refurbished in shades of beige and pale yellow that the entire establishment virtually shines. The baronial public areas on the ground floor are paneled in oak and decorated with wonderful antique golfing scenes. (Be sure to take a good look at the spectacular miniatures of the Ailsa Course in the long corridor to the dining room.) The elegant bar is stocked with a superb collection of old single malts. A big, bright, formal lounge for high tea presents views of the courses and the sea, and a series of elegant reading rooms and cozy lounges further cater to the guest's comfort. Turnberry also offers an unobtrusive gift shop or two, plus a classy billiards room with two handsome antique tables and leather Chesterfield sofas. A wonderful touch: every evening just before dinner a Highland bagpiper in full regalia makes a circuit of the hotel grounds and enchants everyone, especially the children who spill outside to follow him.

Nothing comes cheap at Turnberry, however. Rooms at the back of the hotel without the sea view cost £235 ($412); sea-view rooms at the front are £275 ($482), but prices do include a great Scottish breakfast and lodging tax. Our room at the front, number 256, was sensational. The large yellow bedroom has big windows overlooking the ever-changing coastline view, a complete library of reading material, plus the customary stocked bar and cable television. The large marble bathroom has a Jacuzzi tub, separate shower, heated towel bar, and all the amenities. All the fixtures and decorative features are new, and everything was to our liking.

A word, also, must be added concerning the service. The Scots are naturally warmhearted and willing to talk. Wherever you travel in this country—from spotless bed-and-breakfasts to luxury establishments like Turnberry—you will encounter kindness and consideration. Turnberry's setting on its cliffside above the sea is magical stuff. But we may retain even longer our memory of certain staff members, especially Lorna at the front desk, who made us feel so welcome and at home.

The Turnberry Hotel. Ayrshire KA26 9LT Scotland. Tel: 800-223-6800 or 011-44-1655-331000. Fax: 011-44-1655-331706. 132 rooms and suites. Doubles from £235 to £275 ($412 to $482). Credit cards accepted.

RESTAURANTS 16

Christopher Rouse, who has been with the Turnberry Hotel for nearly twenty years, manages the complex with grace and distinction. This expertise is especially evident in the two big restaurants, the **Turnberry Restaurant** in the hotel and the **Bay at Turnberry,** located on the second floor above the new spa complex. The other dining option at Turnberry is the restaurant in the new clubhouse.

The two principal restaurants are dressy and expensive. The five-course fixed-price dinners in the Turnberry Restaurant are good and served with a flourish but fall short of real culinary excellence. One evening in the very traditional Turnberry Restaurant was enough to satisfy our interest. We much preferred our experience in the spa restaurant the next evening. The evening began in the beautifully decorated bar overlooking the sea with a peaty, sixteen-year-old Lagavulin suggested by the waiter. The à la carte menu at the Bay at Turnberry features strictly natural cuisine (no red meat) and excellent dishes like the baked goat cheese salad and the wonderful fillet of fresh salmon. A fine assortment of wines may be ordered by the bottle or the glass. Service is outstanding. Dinner with wine will cost about £50 ($88) per person.

The restaurants at the Turnberry Hotel. Ayrshire KA26 9LT Scotland. Tel: 011-44-1655-331000. Fax: 011-44-1655-331706. Credit cards accepted.

NON-GOLF ACTIVITIES 18

The gorgeous spa, staffed by an attentive team dressed in immaculate whites, opened in January of 1992 and offers so much luxurious pampering that any non-golfing spouse will be kept happily absorbed here for at least two or three full days. The guest can try out esoteric skin treatments, water therapies, and several varieties of massage. In addition to an incredibly well equipped exercise room, the spa complex includes all-glass squash courts, exercise classes, an elegant beauty salon, saunas and plunge baths, luxurious showers and changing facilities, plus a truly spectacular indoor swimming pool with underwater music and strong countercurrent jets for serious swimmers. A great experience.

Other activities that can be arranged by the concierge include pony trekking along the beaches and riding at nearby stables, sea and river fishing, and trap and rough shooting. The hotel has two (largely unused) tennis courts. Historic sights of interest in the area are Culzean Castle, just five minutes from Turnberry, and Robert Burns's cottage in Ayr, twenty minutes to the north.

GETTING THERE: The Turnberry Hotel is located seventy minutes south of Glasgow Airport. From the airport, take the M8 south to the A726 and then connect with the A77 south, past Kilmarnock and Ayr into Turnberry. The hotel will be on your right.

▶MACHRIHANISH
GEM OF THE MULL OF KINTYRE

	The Golf	Golf Services	Lodging	Restaurants	Non-Golf Activities	Total
Rating	18	16	14	16	17	81

Savor the name as you say it. *Machrihanish*. Like the first sip of a strong and complex single malt, let the word take the slow, delightful trip down the entire length of your tongue. If you care to be truly authentic in your pronunciation, roll the r and hold the *ish* with special emphasis. And when you return from Machrihanish and mention its almost mystical name to your golfing chums back home in the States, be sure to say it with a twinkle in your eye.

The most geographically remote of all the great courses in the British Isles, Machrihanish is a true trophy course for the golf traveler who has seen it all. If you are avid enough to have made it all the way to Machrihanish—five hours from Glasgow on tortuous but spectacular mountain and lochside roads that are frequently blocked by herds of snowy white sheep—then beyond question you qualify for membership in the exclusive ranks of golf's most passionate pilgrims.

Recently we attended the funeral of a friend and spoke with the longtime golfing companion of the deceased. For decades, these two pals had traversed the world playing golf, but the most magical golf course they ever experienced together, as the friend mentioned to us with pleasure, was Machrihanish. Indeed, it felt appropriate and soothing to utter the name of Machrihanish and bring forth its associations of brooding duneland and quiet isolation on that difficult occasion.

Besides its remoteness, Machrihanish is known for possessing the greatest opening hole in the entire world of golf. Castle Harbour in Bermuda also claims the game's best first hole, but now, having played both Castle Harbour and Machrihanish, we have no choice but to give the connoisseur's award to the gem of the Mull of Kintyre. This is clearly the most unforgettable and dramatic first tee shot in all of golf. After a long automobile ride, with no warm-up, in front of Ken Campbell's humble pro shop perched above the beach, you must drive the ball over the crashing waves of Machrihanish Bay (if the tide is in), a carry of some two hundred yards. It is a heroic, adrenaline-charged shot. You can cut it as close to the left as you dare and perhaps end up on the rocky beach (which is in-bounds), or you can play it safe and easy over to the right. A daring, full-blooded drive across the waters, however, will put you in exquisite position to make par, or even birdie, on this famous, 423-yard first hole.

Equally sublime is the fact that the fees for playing this course are so incredibly low: a membership at Machrihanish is less than £170 ($295) per year, with no waiting list. An eighteen-hole round costs £21 ($37), and a daily ticket costs £28 ($49) Sunday through Friday and £36 ($63) on Saturday. For some, Machrihanish is paradise.

Machrihanish has several other striking characteristics. First and foremost, despite the low fees and famous opening shot, you will see virtually no other golfers on the course. We played on two consecutive, lovely autumn afternoons and counted just three or four groups of golfers each day. Second, you will note that almost everyone hereabouts is named Campbell, from the club pro to the fourteen-time club champion. Machrihanish is just five miles from Campbeltown, a singularly drab, unappealing, and economically depressed little city that once boasted thirteen distilleries and the highest rate of alcoholism in Scotland. And third, given the low standard of nearby accommodations (see Lodging, below), it is likely that Machrihanish will remain off the beaten track for many years to come. In other words, golfers have to put up with some discomfort and inconvenience in order to play here.

The east coast of Scotland has a stark, majestic beauty, but for sheer drama the rocky west coast is in a class by itself. The Mull of Kintyre has spectacular scenery, yet, oddly, it is one of the least visited parts of Scotland. The long journey from Glasgow to Machrihanish is remarkable, past gorgeous towns like Inveraray and Crinan and along a storm-tossed shoreline with Islay, Jura, and the Gigha islands offshore to the west and the Isle of Arran to the east. By the time you arrive at Machrihanish you are ready for a game of golf. April through October is the optimum time to visit.

THE GOLF ⑱

"The Almighty has designed Machrihanish for playing golf," declared Old Tom Morris, who descended from St. Andrews to design **Machrihanish** in 1876. J. H. Taylor, a British Open champion, redesigned the course in 1914, and Sir Guy Campbell made further alterations after World War II.

Like many great links courses in the United Kingdom from the cliffs of Dover to the Highlands of Scotland, Machrihanish was taken over during the war years by the Royal Air Force, and a massive vestige from that period remains to this day. The longest airport runway in Britain is contiguous with the Machrihanish golf links, although during our forty-eight hours here, we did not see one landing or takeoff. Machrihanish is not like Lossiemouth, where the military jets fly over the course at alarmingly low altitudes. Loganair, the regional Scottish carrier, makes the thirty-minute Glasgow to Campbeltown flight twice daily.

Machrihanish defines golf on the Mull of Kintyre south of Tarbert. The club also operates a nine-hole course that abuts the championship course. There is an eighteen-hole course in the area and one other nine-hole layout farther to the south, but with no other outstanding courses in the region, Machrihanish is a destination in its own right. Of course, you may plan a non-golfing excursion to visit ex-Beatle Paul McCartney, who has a sheep farm on the extreme southern tip of the Mull of Kintyre.

At bottom, it is the smart simplicity of Scotland that Americans fall in love with, and so it is with the whitewashed clubhouse at Machrihanish—modest, but warm and welcoming. Across the road from the clubhouse you will see Ken Campbell's little pro shop and the famous first tee of Machrihanish, a grassy terrace exposed to the elements and overlooking the crescent-shaped beach. As you walk across the street from the clubhouse to the pro shop, the enormity of that first drive over the rocky beach begins to sink in.

Not only is the first hole exceptionally outstanding at Machrihanish, but so is number two. In fact, Machrihanish may have the best first two holes in golf. The second hole is a 395-yard par four. A long drive will still leave you short of the tidal river that flows into the sea and bisects the fairway. The green is highly elevated (all you can see is the top of the flag) and protected by deep bunkers. Consequently, the second shot on two is another make-it-or-break-it affair. This second hole at Machrihanish is pure majesty.

In many ways, of course, Machrihanish is typical of Scotland. It supplies awkward stances and blind shots in abundance and tests your ability to play with the wind and rain as constant companions. The wind is at your back, in your face, and swirling from side to side. You will get soaked in a misty shower but then blown dry by the wind just as quickly. In such respects, Machrihanish is familiar territory for the experienced Scottish hand. At 6,228 yards, Machrihanish is not especially long, so it can be easy to score on when the wind and rain cooperate.

The uniqueness of this course lies in its collection of par threes. The fourth hole is Machrihanish's version of Royal Troon's Postage Stamp; it's a 123-yard par three with the prevailing winds at your back. So much depends upon selecting the right club. A big bunker guards the front of a very hard green that only reluctantly receives the ball and seldom stops it like the watered greens back home in the States. Here at Machrihanish, the ball can hit the green hard and skid past. The eleventh hole is 197 yards long, but the enormous green can be reached with less club than you think thanks to the elevated tee and the strong gusts behind you. Number fifteen is 167 yards, but you will need two extra clubs because now you are hitting into the wind. In our view, sixteen, a 233-yard par three, is the toughest hole. Even when big hitters launch a perfect drive into the full fury of the wind, they still come up short of the green. One of the toughest par threes in Scotland, especially when the wind is up, the sixteenth is a classic.

The two final holes are also beauties. Seventeen requires a drive from an elevated tee into the wind and over a stream to a narrow fairway. Any shot hit left onto the Campbeltown course is O.B., so aim right, toward the second fairway. The eighteenth hole is a short par four (just 315 yards), but uphill and into the wind.

Machrihanish's nine-hole course is also worth a look. With its square greens and tees that are on level ground with the fairway, this little golf course is as simple as they come.

Machrihanish Golf Club. Machrihanish, Britain Argyll PA28 6PT Scotland. Tel: 011-44-1586-810-277 (-213 for the clubhouse). Fax: 011-44-586-10-221. Credit cards accepted.

• 1876/1914. Designer: Old Tom Morris/J. H. Taylor. Par 70. 6,228 yards. Greens fees: Sunday-Friday: round: £21 ($37), day ticket: £28 ($49). Saturday: day ticket £36 ($63). Caddies can be arranged. No carts. Season: year-round.

 ### GOLF SERVICES

Golf services at Machrihanish are more than satisfactory. There are no caddies hanging around the pro shop waiting for a game, but they can be arranged if booked in advance. Hand carts, however, are readily available for rent. The locker room in the clubhouse is small and aged, but functional. The pro shop sells all the necessities, and there is a practice range and putting green. Ken Campbell and his staff could not be more welcoming to visitors.

 ### LODGING

The village of Machrihanish is no more than a single street with a straight row of twenty or thirty houses—plus one grocery store and one hotel—overlooking Machrihanish Bay. The hotel, called **Ardell House,** looks like a large, comfortable, middle-class home, and it has the advantage of being located two hundred yards from the Machrihanish club-house. Golfers can sleep at Ardell House, roll out of bed and head over to the club-house for meals, and spend all day on the golf course. The non-golfer, however, would likely not be very happy with this arrangement given the isolation of Machri-hanish. Ardell House has ten rooms, a dining area, and very reasonable rates, rang-ing from £24 to £30 ($42 to $53) per person per night, breakfast included.

Many visitors to Machrihanish stay in nearby Campbeltown, yet the accommo-dations there appear derelict. Your best bet might be the more distant **Crinan Ho-tel,** which has a spectacular setting in a gorgeous fishing village, an excellent restaurant, pleasant service, and a very good bar. The Crinan Hotel, however, has two disadvantages that must be stated from the outset. Being ninety minutes north of Machrihanish, the Crinan is a long haul from the golf course, and its guest rooms, while fairly comfortable, are far past their last remodeling. As we say, the hotel sit-uation on the Mull of Kintyre is far from ideal, but Crinan is a memorable place to stay because the tiny village itself, with just fifty-eight residents, is unique and ap-pealing. There is a dramatic view across Loch Crinan, with private yachts tucked in the little harbor, the picturesque Crinan Canal, and the comings and goings of a fleet of fishing vessels past the lighthouse. We stayed in room 34, which has two single beds, television, and a nice bath with shower.

Ardell House. Machrihanish, Campbeltown, Argyll PA28 6PT Scotland. Tel: 011-44-1586-810235. Fax: 011-44-1586-55-3006. 10 rooms. Doubles from £48 to £60 ($84 to $106), breakfast included. Closed November through mid-February. Credit cards accepted.

Crinan Hotel. Crinan, Lochgilphead PA31 8SR Scotland. Tel: 011-44-1546-830261. Fax: 011-44-1546-830292. 22 rooms. Double rooms priced from £200 to £240 ($351 to $421) in high season, breakfast and dinner included. Credit cards accepted.

RESTAURANTS 16

The agreeable restaurant in the Machrihanish clubhouse serves break-fast, lunch, and dinner. There is a nice bar adjoining the restaurant where you will want to have a lager after your round and strike up a friendly conversation with a member.

Lock 16, the seafood restaurant in the Crinan Hotel, is excellent. The very pleas-ant dining room features commanding views of the sea and a fine menu of fresh fish that changes daily. Specialties include smoked salmon, grilled fresh trout, and giant prawns served in the shell, which, according to the menu, were "landed at 4:40 P.M." A complete dinner for two with wine costs approximately £100 ($175). Guests of the Crinan Hotel can dine at Lock 16 for a £15 ($26) per person supplement to their room bills. A jacket and tie are recommended at dinner.

Lock 16. Crinan Hotel. Crinan, Lochgilphead PA31 8SR Scotland. Tel: 011-44-1546-830261. Fax: 011-44-1546-830292. Credit cards accepted.

NON-GOLF ACTIVITIES 17

There is wonderful shopping for tweeds and tartans, plus intriguing sightseeing, in the beautiful town of Inveraray, located midway between Glasgow and Lochgilphead. Other activities include excursions by car ferry to the islands of Islay and Jura, world-famous for their local single malts like Bowmore and Lagavulin.

GETTING THERE: The remoteness of Machrihanish—located on the southern tip of the Mull of Kintyre—is part of its enormous appeal. The golf course is approximately a five-hour drive from Glasgow Airport. From the airport, drive north across the River Clyde and connect with the A82 toward Dumbarton. Stay on the A82, passing the waters of Loch Lomond on your right, and connect with the A83 at Tarbet. Stay on the A83 past Inveraray and Lochgilphead all the way south to Campbeltown, just six miles east of Machrihanish on the B843.

▶ROYAL TROON AND PRESTWICK

TRADITION AND HISTORY ON THE WEST COAST OF SCOTLAND

	The Golf	Golf Services	Lodging	Restaurants	Non-Golf Activities	Total
Rating	19	18	17	16	16	86

You know you have arrived at the world's most peerless golfing grounds on Scotland's west coast when you are able to gaze beyond the links and catch a glimpse of that round geological curiosity called Ailsa Craig. Rising dramatically from the sea eight miles offshore, Ailsa Craig can produce hallucinations, especially after a day or two of exhilarating, wind-lashed sport on the game's most hallowed links. There are those moments when Ailsa Craig begins to resemble a gigantic, half-submerged golf ball driven into the water and left there by a race of golfing giants who played the game eons ago. Or, the somewhat more whimsical thought might cross your mind that Ailsa Craig is the cumulative size and weight of all the golf balls ever pounded into the Firth of Clyde.

Golf truly has no single highest temple. Many regions around the world have equal claim to this crown—the east coast of Scotland, Ireland's west coast, the Monterey Peninsula, Augusta, Hawaii, and many of America's finest private clubs. Yet no golfing region anywhere has greater distinction than the west coast of Scotland, the historic and tradition-bound area within sight of that enchanted landmark, Ailsa Craig. No course or collection of golf courses has a more colorful past and greater ambience, nor does any pose a challenge that is stiffer. No single region we know, save perhaps Myrtle Beach or Palm Springs, offers a larger number of courses to the golfing public. Twelve courses are clustered together near the twin towns of Troon and Prestwick, and nearly thirty lie in the larger twenty-five-mile stretch between Turnberry and Kilmarnock. In effect, the golfing fanatic could stay at the Turnberry Hotel (or one of the far less expensive hotel options recommended below) for nearly a month and play a different course every day without driving more than an hour in any one direction.

Royal Troon and Prestwick are just twenty minutes up the coast from Turnberry, but they are worlds apart in terms of atmosphere. Turnberry, owned by a Japanese conglomerate and patronized by high rollers from across the globe, is one of the world's best full-service resorts and is operated, as resorts tend to be, for the exclusive use of its guests and visitors. Royal Troon and Prestwick, on the other hand, are venerable private clubs run in frequently cantankerous fashion by club members who open the course to visitors only on selected days. The first British Open was played at Prestwick in 1860, and the course today has the air of an unrestored Bentley discovered in the recesses of great-grandmama's garage. There is an austerity and antiquity about this ancient place, as well as a universally acknowledged eccentricity. Royal Troon is more rarefied and less peculiar than Prestwick. At Troon—Royal Troon, mind you—they take their aristocratic association to heart. You will notice a distinct swagger, indeed, perhaps a snobbism, among its members.

We regret to say that we experienced a major discrepancy at both Royal Troon and Prestwick between the attitude of club employees, who welcomed us warmly and treated us with decency, and the actual club members themselves, who gave us a cold shoulder and clearly regarded us as gate-crashers. It was all a bit theatrical and absurd. Stories about the snobbism of certain Scottish clubs, Royal Troon and Prestwick in particular, are the stuff of legend. Today's members clearly believe they have an important obligation to maintain this tradition.

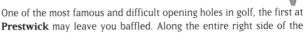

THE GOLF 19

One of the most famous and difficult opening holes in golf, the first at **Prestwick** may leave you baffled. Along the entire right side of the narrowing fairway and not far from the tee is a stone wall and busy railroad tracks where high-speed trains whiz by every ten or twelve minutes; along the left side is unplayable rough, hip-high in places. The group of Americans playing off before us ill-advisedly used drivers from the first tee, and we watched them fade ball after ball over the low stone wall onto the railway line. At Prestwick, forget about your driver until the sixth hole; on number one, all you want is a free and easy two hundred yards.

An outing at Prestwick is an excursion to a vast outdoor golf history museum. As you walk the course and take in the landscape—the mountains on the Arran Islands, the sailboats in the Firth of Clyde, the quality of light and dark that makes Prestwick look like an old movie filmed in black and white—you will be struck by the uniqueness and obvious antiquity of your surroundings. You will be impressed with the age and size of the vast Cardinal bunker, which has been in play on the third hole for over 130 years, and you will be diverted by the attire of Prestwick's members, who are reminiscent of characters from the golfing tales of P. G. Wodehouse as they stride purposefully along the fairways wearing neckties, V-neck sweaters, and flat caps.

The heart of the course is seven through ten, the great series of long par fours that range from 430 to 454 yards in length. The tenth, Prestwick's number one handicap and the meanest of the lot, is uphill, into the wind, and requires a long tee shot that carries the stream and steers clear of high grass to the left. You will definitely need your driver here. If ten is Prestwick's toughest, seventeen is its most famous hole. Seventeen (The Alps) is the only hole at Prestwick that remains entirely unaltered from the time of Willie Park, Sr.'s Open Championship in 1860. Your blind approach shot to the green on seventeen must carry a mountain of heather. Prestwick is 6,544 yards long, and par is seventy-one.

At Prestwick Golf Club, have a sandwich in the visitors' room after your morning game, then head elsewhere for sightseeing or an afternoon round, but plan to spend an entire day at **Royal Troon,** which offers the visiting golfer one of the best package deals in the entire British Isles. For a very reasonable £100 ($175) you are entitled to play two rounds of golf—one on the great Championship Course (also called the Old Course and the site of the 1997 British Open Championship) and one on the fine Portland Course—and in between you are served a good buffet lunch in Royal Troon's handsome, oak-paneled clubhouse, which is lined with magnificent trophies and oil portraits of great golfers both ancient and modern. The club secretary of Royal Troon is Mr. J. D. Montgomerie, sire of the great Scottish champion Colin Montgomerie.

As far as we are concerned, this golf-lunch-golf operation has only one small glitch. To arrive at the luncheon buffet after your morning round you must walk the entire length of the historic clubhouse, past the trophies, portraits, and the jovial members' bar. However, the club attendants do not allow you to walk there alone. They insist upon escorting you, as if they half expect you to steal the silver. And, of course, you are not permitted to mingle with the members. A special visitors' room has been set aside for your luncheon, and there you will meet amiable golfers from across America, likewise excluded from the members' rooms.

If you can, arrange to play the **Portland Course** in the morning, for it is a superb warm-up for the more meaty and scenic Championship layout. The Portland Course is much shorter than the Old Course (6,274 yards versus 7,096), with far fewer bunkers and fairways that are substantially more generous. Located across the street from the clubhouse, the Portland Course is an extremely pleasant, straightforward affair—it is used as a qualifying course when the Open is staged at Troon—but it lacks Royal Troon's intricacy and unforgettable magic.

The **Championship Course** at Royal Troon opens with a succession of great holes along the sea (numbers one through six), followed by interesting number

Royal Troon

seven with its green tucked into the hillside, then by number eight, the Postage Stamp, perhaps the most famous par three in golf and the one most copied by contemporary architects. Royal Troon's motto, *"Tam Arte Quam Marte"* ("As much by skill as by strength"), is perhaps best exemplified by this 126-yard beauty with its tiny green not much bigger than a postage stamp. We visited Troon on a sunny and uncharacteristically windless day and played the Postage Stamp with a nine iron. If the wind is up you might need as much as a five. You had better score well on these opening holes, for the back nine only gets longer and harder.

From the eighth hole you head into the undulating sand hills and heavy air traffic from Prestwick Airport (DC-10s, 747s, and assorted military aircraft) looming overhead at very low altitudes. The airport's landing lights, in fact, begin just behind the tenth tee on the Old Course. The ninth hole, a dogleg right, measures 423 yards; the tenth, with its celebrated blind tee shot, is 438 yards; eleven (The Railway) is an uphill 421 yards; twelve is 427 yards; and thirteen, named Burmah, is 465 yards long. This is the most demanding stretch of golf at Royal Troon, especially since each of these holes is a par four. The eighteenth hole finishes in dramatic fashion in front of the clubhouse. Prior to the 1989 Open (won by Mark Calcavecchia), a new back tee was added to the eighteenth because the hole was considered too short. It now measures 452 yards. Other Open winners at Royal Troon include Tom Watson (1982), Tom Weiskopf (1973), Arnold Palmer (1962), and young Justin Leonard in 1997.

Prestwick Golf Club. 2 Links Road, Prestwick, Ayrshire KA9 1QG Scotland. Tel: 011-44-1292-671020. Fax: 011-44-1292-477255. Credit cards accepted.

• 1851/1883. Designer: Old Tom Morris. Par 71. 6,544 yards. Greens fees: round: £50 ($88), day ticket: £75 ($131). Walking permitted. Caddies available. No carts. Restrictions: public excluded Saturday, Sunday, and Thursday afternoons. Handicap limit: men, 24; women, 28. Season: year-round.

Royal Troon. Troon, Ayrshire KA10 6EP Scotland. Tel: 011-44-1292-311555. Fax: 011-44-1292-318204. Credit cards accepted.

- *Championship Course.* 1900. Designer: Willie Fernie. Par 72. 7,096 yards.
- *Portland Course.* 1905. Designers: Charles Hunter, Willie Fernie. Par 70. 6,274 yards.
- Greens fee: £100 ($175) includes rounds on both courses and a lunch buffet. Walking. Caddies available. No carts. Restrictions: public play on Monday, Tuesday, and Thursday only. Women and juniors allowed only on Portland Course. Season: year-round.

GOLF SERVICES

Brian Anderson's pro shop at Royal Troon is one of the most beautiful and best stocked of any we have seen in the world. There are wonderful sweaters and logo items galore, plus a huge selection of fascinating and fairly priced golf antiques. The service is warm and outgoing, as is the service in the pro shop at Prestwick. Both clubs have practice facilities and offer clubs for rent.

Caddies are available in abundance at both Prestwick and Royal Troon, but those at Prestwick appeared to have begun their drinking earlier in the day than those at Troon. Caddies at both clubs should be requested in advance and cost £20 ($35). The standard tip is around £5 ($9). It would be nearly impossible for the first-time player to find his way around either course without a caddie.

The Scottish caddie is more than just someone to carry your bag and point the way across the heather. After your round your caddie can become your ready-made drinking companion, an all-night carouser, an antiestablishment buddy who rails against the world in spectacular local idiom, and a friend who will love you as long as you pay for the brew. If you wish to part company after the game and go off on your own, you are perfectly free to do so. But at least once, do yourself a favor and go enjoy a drink or two with your caddie.

LODGING

Three hotels in the Troon/Prestwick area are worth noting. If location is your greatest consideration, look no further than the **Marine Highland Hotel,** which adjoins the seventeenth and eighteenth holes of Royal Troon's Championship Course. If you stay at the Marine Highland you may easily walk from your hotel room to the first tee. Yet despite its location and a very pleasant main dining room, the Marine Highland is not the most desirable hotel in the area by any stretch of the imagination, for the entire property is in less than pristine condition and looks years past its last remodeling.

A much more attractive lodging option—by far the best in the region—is the newly remodeled **Lochgreen House,** a stately home set in lovely private gardens and located midway between Troon and Prestwick, no more than a five-minute drive from all the golf courses. Guests of Lochgreen House are accommodated in seven very attractive, traditionally decorated rooms in the main house, seven other rooms of equal standard in the courtyard, and one cottage. The best room in the house is the very spacious Lord Morton Suite. Lochgreen House also has a very fine restaurant run by owner/chef Bill Costley, who is highly regarded on the Ayrshire coast for both his cuisine and his hospitality. You can count on friendly service throughout. Lochgreen House is highly recommended. Room rates are £140 ($245), double occupancy with breakfast.

The third lodging choice is **Highgrove House,** a lovely, unpretentious little hotel whose only liability is its distance from the links, about twenty minutes. Highgrove House was owned and run by Bill Costley before he made the move to Lochgreen House in 1993. Highgrove House is set on a hill and provides superb views of the sea and Ailsa Craig in the distance. The best room is number 2. Double rooms with breakfast are £85 ($149).

Marine Highland Hotel. 8 Crosbie Road, Troon, Ayrshire KA10 6HE Scotland. Tel: 011-44-1292-314444. Fax: 011-44-1292-316922. 72 rooms and suites. Doubles are £114 to £135 ($200 to $237), breakfast included. Credit cards accepted.

Lochgreen House. Monktonhill Road, Southwood, Troon KA10 7EN Scotland. Tel: 011-44-1292-313343. Fax: 011-44-1292-318661. 15 rooms priced at £140 ($245), breakfast included. Credit cards accepted.

Highgrove House. Old Loans Road, Troon KA10 7HL Scotland. Tel: 011-44-1292-312511. Fax: 011-44-1292-318228. 9 rooms priced at £85 ($149) per room, breakfast included. Credit cards accepted.

RESTAURANTS

Bill Costley's cuisine is another reason to stay at charming **Lochgreen House,** for his restaurant is the best in the Prestwick/Troon area. Chef Costley's specialties include superb salmon, sole, local lamb, and home-made pâté. A complete dinner for two in the quite formal, cherry-paneled dining room costs approximately £70 ($123). An excellent selection of wine complements dinner.

As noted above, Prestwick Golf Club and Royal Troon serve lunch to visitors. **Prestwick** features two dining rooms: the **main dining room,** for men only, where the dress code of jacket and tie is strictly enforced, and the **Cardinal Room,** where women and children are welcome and a variety of hot and cold dishes are available. Lunch at **Royal Troon** is a large hot and cold buffet, included in the price of your day ticket or otherwise available for £10 ($17). On days when the public is invited to play at Royal Troon, the club also serves a five-course dinner. Be sure to book in advance, and expect to pay about £20 ($34) before beverages.

Lochgreen House. Monktonhill Road, Southwood, Troon KA10 7EN Scotland. Tel: 011-44-1292-313343. Fax: 011-44-1292-318661. Credit cards accepted.

Prestwick Golf Club. 2 Links Road, Prestwick, Ayrshire KA9 1QG Scotland. Tel: 011-44-1292-671020. Fax: 011-44-1292-477255. Credit cards accepted.

Royal Troon. Troon, Ayrshire KA10 6EP Scotland. Tel: 011-44-1292-311555. Fax: 011-44-1292-318204. Credit cards accepted.

NON-GOLF ACTIVITIES

The west of Scotland offers many activities for the non-golfer. The Ayrshire coast is Robert Burns country, and the poet's birthplace in Ayr is open to the public. Magnificent Culzean Castle is also worth a visit. Lochgreen House offers tennis and pitch-and-putt golf, and arrangements can be made for fishing and pony-trekking trips.

GETTING THERE: Royal Troon and Prestwick are located an hour south of Glasgow Airport. From the airport, take the M8 south to the A726 and connect with the A77 heading south and pass Kilmarnock. Just north of Ayr you will first come to the village of Troon; Prestwick is about ten minutes farther on.

▶THE HIGHLANDS

ROYAL DORNOCH, NAIRN, TAIN, BRORA, AND LOSSIEMOUTH

	The Golf	Golf Services	Lodging	Restaurants	Non-Golf Activities	Total
Rating	**20**	**18**	**16**	**16**	**18**	**88**

[Royal Dornoch] is the most natural course in the world. We in America are just beginning to appreciate that no golfer has completed his education until he has played and studied Royal Dornoch. It conveys to the modern golfer the evocation of golf at its best.

—Herbert Warren Wind

Easily the finest course in the world. The absolute number one. I am not going to tell anyone about Royal Dornoch. I want to keep it to myself and come back every year until I die.

—"A Dream by a Scottish Shore" by Peter Dobereiner

The Clubhouse at Royal Dornoch

By the time you finally reach Inverness you are already far north, perhaps as far north as you have ever been before. In May and June daylight makes its first startling appearance through the window shades shortly after four o'clock in the morning. Even at 11 P.M. there is still enough light out-of-doors to follow easily the flight of a golf ball as its sails across the gray, cloud-flecked sky. Inverness, after all, is just 750 miles south of the Arctic Circle.

To get to Dornoch, a cathedral city with medieval origins and a famous golf course dating from the sixteenth century, you must continue even farther northward beyond Inverness. You cross the Moray Firth over the modern suspension bridge that links Inverness with the upper Highlands, drive the full length of Black Isle, cross the Cromarty Firth with its tall oil rigs sitting idly at low tide but destined for duty in the North Sea, and then traverse a final body of water, Dornoch Firth, before catching your first glimpse of the quaint village. The feeling of romantic isolation intensifies as you drive northward and leave Inverness farther and farther behind. North of Inverness the landscape is taken over by humble sheep farms with stone cottages and old stone walls, mature forests of thick pine laid out in rectangular grids, and barren mountain peaks to the west covered with snow even in June. As your caddie will tell you, Dornoch is a little town (population 1,000) with none of the urban difficulties facing metropolitan Inverness (population 38,000).

In the Highlands, almost every village of any size along the coast has its own village links. Many of these little-known links are worth a visit, like challenging Tain, just across the Firth from Dornoch, or enchanting Fortrose and Rosemarkie on Black Isle just across the Moray Firth from Nairn. The list continues with remote Brora, north of Dornoch; tough Moray Old, contiguous with the alarmingly close and busy RAF base at Lossiemouth; and, of course, famous Nairn itself, which some believe to be every bit as great as Dornoch. There are actually two courses in the tidy resort community of Nairn: the Nairn Championship Course west of the village center and Nairn Dunbar on the village's eastern outskirts. Both are outstanding, and both played host to the British Amateur in 1994. For those who grow tired of traditional seaside links, a lovely, scenic, and quite tricky parkland layout—Boat of Garten—lies to the south of Inverness in the mountains of Aviemore.

So come up to the Highlands and stay a while. Royal Dornoch has the greatest mystique and allure among the Highland courses, but the area abounds with many other wonderful golfing opportunities.

THE GOLF

20

Despite its splendid isolation, **Royal Dornoch** certainly can no longer be called undiscovered. Once you finally arrive there, do not expect to find the first tee empty and the course entirely to yourself. Especially during the busy spring and summer months, the little clubhouse will be clogged with animated golfers from Sweden, Germany, France, and America who have made the identical pilgrimage far north into the Highlands. In fact, for the segment of the American golfing population that most relishes the Scottish game, Royal Dornoch may be the most popular track in the entire country. The course was so filled with Americans that our recent round took four and a half hours, an eternity by Scottish standards. (The members, of course, always blame slow play on visitors from overseas.)

This Dornoch-America connection goes back a long way. The father of American golf course design, Donald Ross, was born in Dornoch and learned the game here. Later, Ross moved to America and designed Pinehurst Number 2, Seminole, and more than five hundred other courses using Royal Dornoch as his model and inspiration. Donald Ross of Dornoch was to American golf course architecture what Bill Gates is to software: he virtually created the medium. In essence, therefore, a visit to Dornoch, Scotland, is a visit to the birthplace of American golf.

After St. Andrews (1552) and Leith (1593), Dornoch is the oldest course in Scotland. Golf was introduced to Dornoch by transplanted clergy who came to the Dornoch Cathedral from St. Andrews. The first nine holes at Dornoch were in use no later than 1616. In the late nineteenth century, Old Tom Morris of St. Andrews was invited to Dornoch to revise the existing nine and to build nine additional holes. In later years, Old Tom's layout was substantially enlarged by John Sutherland. Like other courses of great antiquity, Dornoch is not the work of any one man, but those who took part in its evolution—Old Tom Morris, Donald Ross, and others—are among the most famous in the history of the game.

Today at Dornoch you will find more burnt-yellow gorse than on any other course in Scotland, acres upon acres of the thorny stuff, huge fields and amazing hillsides full of it. You will also find a traditional out-and-back layout with both upper and lower holes. The eight lower holes run directly along the beach. The remaining holes on higher ground frequently present spectacular views of the course and the coastline. Bring your camera, for photo opportunities abound, especially from the elevated fifth and seventh tees.

Like St. Andrews, Royal Dornoch is located on the edge of town; you can easily walk to the cathedral from the clubhouse. Also like the Old Course, your first tee shot at Dornoch is witnessed by a large gallery of onlookers—golfers, spouses, idle spectators, adolescent caddies, and club members sitting in the second-floor bar loudly analyzing your swing while sipping their second or third pint of bitter.

Aside from the fresh ocean air, the views, and the fields of golden gorse, Dornoch's strength lies in its collection of par fours, ranging from 323 to 465 yards in length. Holes such as these can be found nowhere else on the planet. Tom Watson's favorite hole at Dornoch is the dramatic fifth, 357 yards steeply downhill and birdie material for long hitters. Drive it down in front of the green, pitch it up close, and putt once. The eighth hole starts on the high ground and ends at the beach. The blind tee shot on eight must be struck far left, for a valley of gorse lurks unseen over the hill to the right.

The back side of Royal Dornoch features the toughest hole on the course, *Foxy*, number fourteen, as well as the three exhilarating finishing holes, all par fours and all distinctly Dornoch. High Hole, the unusual sixteenth, is a long march straight uphill; Valley, number seventeen, presents another blind tee shot down to the fairway below; and Home, the 461-yard eighteenth, requires two big hits if you wish to reach the green in regulation. These three holes are an unforgettable conclusion to a memorable round.

The Royal Dornoch Golf Club operates a second course, **Struie,** originally the ladies' course, which measures 5,438 yards from the back tees versus 6,581 yards for the championship course. And finally, before leaving Dornoch, we must mention the truly spectacular **Carnegie Club at Skibo Castle,** located four miles from Royal Dornoch. Skibo Castle was steel magnate Andrew Carnegie's private home, and it has been recently restored by Peter de Savary. The Carnegie Club's new eighteen-hole layout, designed by Donald Steel, is a handsome parkland course that adds another dimension to the already rich golfing scene in Dornoch. Tee times for nonmembers and nonresort-staying guests are restricted to 11 A.M. to noon Monday through Friday and can be arranged only after filling out a written application before your visit.

Other superb courses within an hour's drive of Inverness include the following:

Fortrose and Rosemarkie, located on Black Isle, is a welcoming and low-key golf club that occupies an amazing site: its own narrow peninsula jutting out into the waters of the Moray Firth. Measuring just 5,858 yards, this course is a breather when compared with the rigors of nearby Nairn and Dornoch, but it is, nonetheless, appealing with its superb views and blooming gorse.

The **Moray Golf Club** at Lossiemouth (the club is also referred to as Lossiemouth) has two traditional seaside links that are both circular in design: **Moray Old** (6,600 yards), laid out by Old Tom Morris in 1889, is the outer loop of the circle, and **Moray New** (6,005 yards), designed by Sir Henry Cotton, is the inner loop. For RAF pilots at Lossiemouth, the Moray Golf Club is the final approach to the airfield. A sign on the eighth green reads, "Beware sudden aircraft noise." Military aircraft can terrify the uninitiated by flying over the course at an altitude of less than one hundred feet!

The **Tain Golf Club** in the lovely village of Tain, twenty minutes south of Dornoch, is another Tom Morris layout. Wonderful in its simplicity, this 6,311-yard course plays along the sea and the River Tain.

Brora is thirty minutes north of Dornoch. Designed by Open champion James Braid (who also designed the King's and Queen's courses at Gleneagles), Brora is a seaside links with waves breaking on the shore, windswept views of the sea and barren hills, marvelous greens, and a burn (stream) winding through the course. This golfing duneland is one of the few Braid tracks that remains exactly as he designed it. During June it is possible to squeeze in three rounds of play on a day ticket owing to the region's long hours of daylight; the club even holds a "midnight" tournament to celebrate the summer solstice.

Both the **Nairn Golf Club** and **Nairn Dunbar** are generally kept in exquisite condition. Of the two, Nairn is the longer, tougher, and more majestic. Seven holes at Nairn run along the sea with the balance on higher ground. The large, new clubhouse at Nairn is comfortable if somewhat sterile in appearance. The Nairn Golf Club will host the 1999 Walker Cup.

Boat of Garten is located south of Inverness in the snow-covered Cairngorm Mountains. Designed by James Braid, this challenging 5,866-yard layout is one of the most picturesque parkland courses in the Highlands.

Royal Dornoch Golf Club. Golf Road, Dornoch, Sutherland IV25 3LW Scotland. Tel: 011-44-1862-810219. Fax: 011-44-1862-810792. Credit cards accepted.

• *Royal Dornoch.* 1876. Designers: Old Tom Morris, J. H. Sutherland. Par 70. 6,581 yards. Greens fees: weekday: £43 ($75), weekend: £50 ($88). Caddies available. No carts.
• *Struie.* 1986. Designer: Donald Steel. Par 69. 5,438 yards. Greens fees: round: £12 ($21), day ticket: £18 ($31). Caddies can be arranged. No carts.

Carnegie Club at Skibo Castle. Skibo Castle, Skibo, Dornoch IV25 3RQ Scotland. Tel: 011-44-1862-894600. Fax: 011-44-1862-894601. Credit cards accepted.

• 1994. Designer: Donald Steel. Par 71. 6,671 yards. Greens fees: resort guests: unlimited golf included in room rates, public: £100 ($174). Caddies can be arranged. Carts available for persons with medical needs. Restrictions: public access by approval of pro (fax for application); public tee times limited to the hours of 11 A.M. and noon, Monday through Friday. Season: year-round.

Fortrose and Rosemarkie Golf Club. Ness Road East, Fortrose, Ross-shire IV10 8SE Scotland. Tel: 011-44-1381-620733. Fax: 011-44-1381-620733. Credit cards accepted.

• 1938. Designer: James Braid. Par 71. 5,858 yards. Greens fees: weekday: £16 ($28), weekend: £22 ($38). No caddies. No carts. Season: year-round.

Moray Golf Club. Stotfield Road, Lossiemouth IV31 6QS Scotland. Tel: 011-44-1343-812018. Fax: 011-44-1343-815102. Credit cards accepted.

• *Moray Old.* 1889. Designer: Old Tom Morris. Par 70. 6,600 yards. Greens fees: weekday: £25 ($44), weekend: £35 ($61).
• *Moray New.* 1978. Designer: Sir Henry Cotton. Par 69. 6,005 yards. Greens fees: weekday: £17 ($30), weekend: £25 ($44).
• Day ticket (a round on each course): weekday: £30 ($53), weekend: £40 ($70). Caddies available. No carts. Season: year-round.

Tain Golf Club. Chapel Road, Tain, Ross-shire IV19 1PA Scotland. Tel: 011-44-1862-892314. No fax. Credit cards accepted.

• 1890. Designer: Old Tom Morris. Par 70. 6,311 yards. Greens fees: weekday: £20 ($35), weekend: £24 ($42). No caddies. No carts. Season: year-round.

Brora Golf Club. Golf Road, Brora, Sutherland KW9 6QS Scotland. Tel: 011-44-1408-621417. Fax: 011-44-1408-621124. Credit cards accepted.

• 1923. Designer: James Braid. Par 69. 6,110 yards. Greens fees: round: £18 ($31), day ticket: £24 ($41). Caddies available. No carts. Season: year-round.

The Nairn Golf Club. Seabank Road, Nairn IV12 4HB Scotland. Tel: 011-44-1667-453208. Fax: 011-44-1667-456328. Credit cards accepted.

• 1887/1889. Designers: Archie Simpson/Old Tom Morris (remodeled in 1938 by James Braid). Par 72. 6,745 yards. Greens fees: weekday: £40 ($70), weekend: £50 ($88). Caddies can be arranged. No carts. Season: year-round.

Nairn Dunbar Golf Club. Lochloy Road, Nairn IV12 5AE Scotland. Tel: 011-44-1667-452741. Fax: 011-44-1667-456897. Credit cards accepted.

• 1899. Designer: club members. Par 72. 6,712 yards. Greens fees: weekday: £23 ($40), weekend: £28 ($49). Caddies can be arranged. No carts. Season: year-round.

Boat of Garten Golf Club. Boat of Garten, Inverness-shire PH24 3BQ Scotland. Tel: 011-44-1479-831282. Fax: 011-44-1479-831523. Credit cards accepted.

• 1932. Designer: James Braid. Par 69. 5,866 yards. Greens fees: day ticket: weekday: £20 ($35), weekend: £25 ($44). Caddies can be arranged. No carts. Restrictions: limited public tee times on weekends. Season: March through October.

 ## GOLF SERVICES

When caddies are available at the aforementioned clubs, they must always be requested in advance. Caddie fees vary from course to course (usually £15 to £25/$26 to $43); check with the starter at each club to determine the standard tip. Hand carts are always available, and a good pub is without exception close at hand. We also have to add the important fact that Americans will be warmly welcomed at every one of these clubs. Nothing about golf in the Scottish Highlands will disappoint.

 ## LODGING

Now for the less exciting side of the story: the quality of accommodations in the Highlands, while good, is certainly not great. There is no standout luxury establishment in the region—save for the Carnegie Club at Skibo Castle—that even approximates the standards of a hotel like Turnberry.

There is, however, one hotel in the Highlands that we can recommend with confidence—**Culloden House,** just outside Inverness. We visited the most highly touted hotels in the region from Dornoch to Nairn, and only Culloden House met our criteria.

First, Culloden House is centrally located within reasonable distance of all the courses. Second, if you stay at Culloden House, the staff will be delighted to make your tee times—an important bonus. Third, Culloden House is a stately home with history and a true Highland flavor. A bagpiper in full regalia com-

Culloden House

pletes a circuit of the grounds every evening around seven o'clock. And fourth, the guest rooms are attractive, comfortable, and spacious. We stayed in room 16 and would recommend it to anyone. The vast public areas of this historic hotel look run-down in places, but the guest rooms have been more recently remodeled. Culloden House has the added advantage of being located six miles from Inverness Airport, which is just ninety minutes from London Heathrow via British Airways. Rooms and suites at Culloden House are priced from £185 to £2,240 ($324 to $3,926) and include a full Scottish breakfast.

The **Carnegie Club at Skibo Castle** is one of the world's most magical private clubs and has the most luxurious guest rooms imaginable. The Carnegie Club welcomes the public to stay at a daily rate of £550 ($964) which includes room, all meals, full use of the club's sporting facilities, and unlimited golf. Very expensive but highly recommended.

Culloden House. Inverness IV1 2NZ Scotland. Tel: 011-44-1463-790461. Fax: 011-44-1463-792181. 16 rooms and suites. £185 to £240 ($324 to $421). Credit cards accepted.

Carnegie Club at Skibo Castle. Skibo Castle, Dornoch, Sutherland IV25 3RQ Scotland. Tel: 011-44-1862-894600. Fax: 011-44-1862-894601. 40 rooms. Double occupancy rooms cost £550 ($964), which also includes all meals and beverages, unlimited golf, and full use of the club's sporting facilities. Credit cards accepted.

RESTAURANTS

All of the clubs serve lunch and drinks to visiting golfers, so plan on a bite to eat between rounds or at the end of the day. In particular, the second-floor bar at **Royal Dornoch** can be a wonderful scene; lunch costs about £5 ($9), and a dinner will run about £12 ($21). Dinner at **Culloden House** (£35/$61 per person) is a formal affair commencing with drinks in the lounge and culminating with a four-course meal in the elegant dining room. Culloden House has an excellent wine list. Cuisine at the Carnegie Club is outstanding but is available only to the club's guests.

Royal Dornoch Golf Club. Golf Road, Dornoch, Sutherland IV 25 3LW Scotland. Tel: 011-44-1862-810219. Fax: 011-44-1862-810792. No credit cards.

Culloden House. Inverness IV1 2NZ Scotland. Tel: 011-44-1463-790461. Fax: 011-44-1463-792181. Credit cards accepted.

NON-GOLF ACTIVITIES 18

Non-golfing activities in the Highlands are virtually without limit: tours of nearby Loch Ness with its monster, Cawdor Castle, the Clava Cairns, Culloden Battlefield, Inverewe Gardens, distillery tours, salmon and trout fishing, tours of the famous Findhorn gardens, and much more.

GETTING THERE: Dornoch is seventy minutes north of Inverness, and Inverness, in turn, is an hour's flight from London Heathrow. From the Inverness airport, take the A9 north all the way into Dornoch.

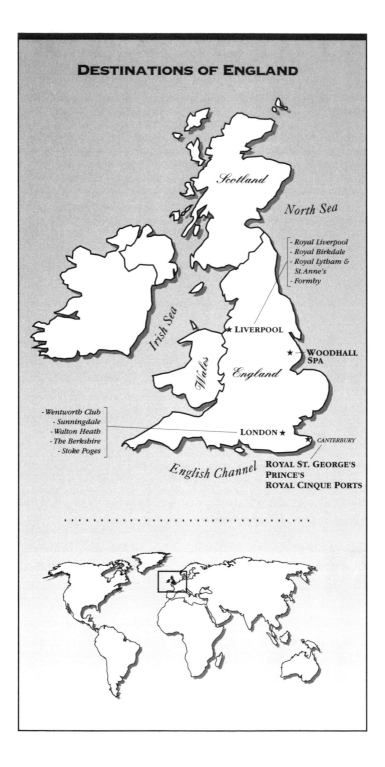

DESTINATIONS OF ENGLAND

Scotland

North Sea

- Royal Liverpool
- Royal Birkdale
- Royal Lytham & St. Anne's
- Formby

Irish Sea

★ **LIVERPOOL**

★ **WOODHALL SPA**

Wales

England

- Wentworth Club
- Sunningdale
- Walton Heath
- The Berkshire
- Stoke Poges

★ **LONDON**

★ *CANTERBURY*

English Channel

ROYAL ST. GEORGE'S
PRINCE'S
ROYAL CINQUE PORTS

ENGLAND

ENGLAND

It is almost impossible to remember how tragic a place the world is when one is playing golf.

—Robert Lynd, Irish author and journalist

The philosopher who said that all people who have a history have a paradise or a golden age may well have had the English and golf in mind. History is never far from golf in England, and English golf is not far from paradise. When we think of England in its golden age we think of the seat of a glorious and powerful empire. But at the very time the British Empire flourished, the English lavished their most noble sentiments on nature and the landscape. The English invented modern landscape architecture, so it comes as no surprise that England is home to many of the world's most gloried golf courses and golf course architects.

One of the utter joys of a golfing trip to England is the chance to explore the nation's rich history and cultural heritage. Once you have completed your round of golf, take your family motoring through the countryside's rolling hills and pasturelands. Visit stately castles and great houses on your route. Some of the mansions open to the public date back to the 1400s. If you prefer more modern history, you can tour the haunts of the Beatles in Liverpool. London, of course, is the jewel of all England. A good place to start your history lesson in London is at the British Museum, where you will get a feel for the true magnificence of the British Empire. Visit Westminster Abbey, join the multitudes at Trafalgar Square, set your watch to Big Ben, supervise the guards at Buckingham Palace, take in a play at one of London's innumerable theaters, go shopping at Harrods, and drop in at a proper establishment for traditional English tea. In England there is a never-ending wealth of activities to keep you busy when you are not playing golf.

This is not to say that golf must take a backseat to other activities. England's premier golf courses rank among the best in the world and may be found in three distinct clusters: in the Southeast hard by the English Channel, in the Northwest outside the city of Liverpool, and to the west and south of the city of London.

The three great courses in the Southeast are all seaside links that between them have hosted the Open Championship sixteen times. Royal Cinque Ports (also known as "Deal") is one of the windiest and most difficult courses in the world; Royal St. George's is aristocratic and famous for its massive bunkers; and Prince's offers twenty-seven excellent holes of golf. The cathedral city of Canterbury is a convenient base of operation for golfers touring the Southeast.

In the Northwest, within an hour and a half of the international airport in Manchester, you will find Royal Birkdale, Royal Liverpool (a.k.a. "Hoylake"), and Royal Lytham & St. Anne's, three incomparable links, although only Royal Liverpool has a sea view (Royal Birkdale and Royal Lytham & St. Anne's are set back from the shore). The elegant, half-timbered city of Chester is an excellent base for playing the courses of Northwest England.

London golf is "parkland" (or inland) golf. The three greatest clubs around London are Wentworth, Sunningdale, and Walton Heath. Wentworth, with its three golf courses, and Sunningdale with two, are both west of London near Heathrow Airport.

Historic Walton Heath is to the south, about twenty minutes from Gatwick Airport. London greens fees are expensive, however, and the courses can be difficult to access from central London hotels.

Woodhall Spa, the number-one-rated parkland course in the entire United Kingdom, is south of the city of Lincoln, a four-and-a-half-hour drive from London.

With only a few exceptions, you can count on a warm reception at the most exclusive and historic clubs in this noble land. There really is no equivalent in America, where the great golf courses of private clubs remain, sadly, the exclusive province of the few fortunate members. In England, the club members are happy to share their links and parklands with visitors from across the big pond. The only restriction most clubs place on public play is that men play to a handicap of twenty-eight or less and women thirty-six or less. Anyone golfing in England should carry a valid handicap certificate and a letter of introduction from his or her home pro.

England's courses are walking courses. Generally, golf carts are available only to people with medical needs who arrange them in advance. Use the phone and fax numbers we provide to secure your tee times well in advance of your visit—the most famous courses book up quickly in summer, and it would be a shame to travel so far to miss out on even one course. As a rule, July and August are the busiest and most inconvenient times to golf in England. May and June and September and October are our preferred months to play.

England's weather is much maligned, but this is largely a bad rap. Sure you will encounter fog, and most likely rain as well, but if you come during the peak tourist season between mid-April and mid-October you will rarely see a downpour. The summer heat is also a bit more tolerable than the stifling stretches of heat and humidity so common in America. Your biggest problem is likely to be the unpredictability of the weather and the wind. When the gales kick up off the sea, even a moderate summer day can feel bone-chillingly uncomfortable on a links course. Whatever you do, do not forget your rain gear and umbrella.

▶LONDON

	The Golf	Golf Services	Lodging	Restaurants	Non-Golf Activities	Total
Rating	18	18	19	17	20	92

London is one of the most civilized and agreeable cities on earth, and golfers on holiday can be assured of finding all they could wish for, namely, outstanding golf courses located just west and south of the city, wonderful hotels both in Central London and its outer environs, as well as truly memorable restaurants. GOLF TRAVEL's London sojourn was a dream week, full of absolutely brilliant golf at seven world-class courses, combined with remarkable dining, lodging, and non-golf activities. But let us note at the outset, London luxury these days comes with a significant price tag.

Several of the outstanding hotels and restaurants reviewed below qualify as excellent values, relatively speaking at least, but local greens fees in the London region are about as costly as golf gets anywhere in Europe. Typical London greens fees at the best courses average £100 ($175), yet these still compare favorably with Pinehurst Number Two ($200), Mauna Lani ($170), and Pebble Beach ($320).

High costs, however, do absolutely nothing to deter what can be described only as an overwhelming turnout of cleated, club-wielding sportsmen. These golf courses, in fact, may be the busiest we have seen anywhere. Each one was filled to capacity, even Wentworth, which we had the misfortune to play during a torrential downpour. Every hole that miserable May afternoon was packed with soggy foursomes in cumbersome rain gear trudging along the puddle-flecked fairways. Not a soul missed his or her appointed tee time. So be advised to book your games far in advance or you will not play at all, rain or shine.

Wentworth has three golf courses, the West, the East, and the Edinburgh; Sunningdale has two courses, the Old and the New; and Walton Heath has two, also known as the Old and the New. These are the three most famous and historic golf venues in all of London. Of course, there are other excellent places to play nearby—like the Berkshire and Stoke Poges, also noted herein—but Wentworth, Sunningdale, and Walton Heath are in an elite class of their own. Knowledgeable sources interminably debate the relative merits of each layout, but after the hairsplitting comparisons are complete, we must say that all seven courses at these three remarkable golf clubs are lovely to behold and enormously challenging.

By reputation, the West Course is considered Wentworth's best, while the Old Courses at both Sunningdale and Walton Heath are deemed their best. Sunningdale Old, in fact, is rated the second-best inland or nonlinks course in Great Britain (Woodhall Spa is rated first); the West at Wentworth holds down eighth place; and Walton Heath Old is rated eleventh. Another joy: these three celebrated golf courses, however close geographically, bear absolutely no physical resemblance to one another. The London golf scene, therefore, offers tremendous variety as well as outstanding sport.

A few quick notes about what to expect:

- The genius of Wentworth, Sunningdale, and Walton Heath lies at least partly in the fact that they are set in the full beauty of the English countryside despite their proximity to Central London. Urban sprawl certainly exists in Britain, but it is not the terrible blight on the landscape that we sadly experience on our own shores. These courses are just an hour from London, yet they are remarkably isolated, delightfully rural in feeling, and protected by the rich, suburban greenbelt that surrounds the city center.

- London golf, as already noted, is upscale golf. The parking lots at these golf clubs are filled with vintage Aston Martins, Bentleys, and Rolls-Royces. The villages of Sunningdale and Wentworth are among the most affluent in Britain. Huge, spectacular, private mansions, often enclosed by high stone walls, dominate the area. And the clubhouses themselves are among the most historic and elegant in golf. The Wentworth experience, in particular, is in a realm of its own when it comes to breathtaking luxury. Its huge and wonderfully crenelated clubhouse is filled with dapper members dressed in impeccable Savile Row pinstripes drinking and dining to their hearts' content.

- The Wentworth and Sunningdale golf clubs are virtual next-door neighbors and just five minutes apart to the west of London on the A30, not far from Windsor, Ascot, and Heathrow Airport. You may drive your rental car or take a taxi to either club from your hotel, or you may take the train from Paddington Station in Central London directly to the station in Sunningdale. Walton Heath is south of London, just inside the M25 London orbital road, about twenty minutes from Gatwick Airport.

- Traffic congestion in and around London means you should allow plenty of time to arrive at each course.
- There are several good hotel options if you do not care to stay in Central London. Cliveden is a remarkable luxury hotel about thirty minutes from Wentworth and Sunningdale. Alexander House is the best hotel within reasonable driving distance of Walton Heath. These hotels and others are described below.

Important note: When golfing anywhere in the British Isles it is critical always to have in your possession a *current handicap card* and a *letter of introduction* from your own head professional. Most golf clubs do not insist on inspecting such documents, but it is a good idea to play it safe and always have them with you.

THE GOLF

Between them, Wentworth and Sunningdale comprise one extremely high-powered golf destination in the west of London. Despite the fact that you can just about walk from one to the other, no two golf clubs make for a greater contrast in terms of overall atmosphere.

Perfumed and polished, **Wentworth** is ultraglamorous and intensely social. The gorgeous crenelated clubhouse, with its stunning and vast interior rooms filled with club members who dress far more formally than any in America, can conspire to make you feel somewhat self-conscious if your own attire does not quite match the grandeur of the scene. Those who want to enjoy refreshments after playing golf are advised to bring a conservative jacket and tie

East Course, Wentworth Club

so as to avoid feeling conspicuously underdressed in Wentworth's beautifully appointed bar and dining room. Just to give you an idea of the overall tone of the place, Bernard Gallacher, former captain of Europe's Ryder Cup team, is Wentworth's head golf pro and actually gives lessons at Wentworth. Nick Faldo, the reigning star of English golf, lives in one of the great mansions along Wentworth's West Course. We played Wentworth a week before the Volvo European PGA Championship and the club was abuzz with Volvo people putting their cars on display, even as scores of maintenance men prepared the course and hordes of ordinary golfers clogged up the registration desk and the rather cramped visitors' locker room. Wentworth is as much about prestige and social clout as it is about golf. For some visitors, the preening at Wentworth may be a bit much, but we must say we fully enjoyed the spectacle.

After Wentworth, **Sunningdale** is Olde England, far more warm, comfortable, and familiar in appearance, with packs of rapscallion, shifty-looking caddies chain-smoking, joking incoherently, and hanging about in the shadows of the fine, old, whitewashed clubhouse (versus Wentworth, where the caddies are hidden from view until summoned by the caddie master). Sunningdale's clubhouse and pro shop are plain and old-shoe when compared with Wentworth's spectacular castle, but the commanding hillside location has dramatic views of both golf courses and the famous oak tree behind the eighteenth green. Sunningdale provides a handsome, majestic setting for golf that looks distinctly American with its rolling fairways and towering pines. Indeed, ever since Bobby Jones brought fame to Sunningdale with a "perfect" round of sixty-six in a 1926 British Open qualifier, this course has been known far and wide as the most American in all of Britain. Wentworth is a multi-faceted club that serves a membership with many interests. Sunningdale is as fashionable in its way as Wentworth—and some would argue that it is the more genuinely classy of the two. Here golf, first and foremost, comprises the club's heart and soul.

All three courses at Wentworth take off from the central clubhouse and wend their way through the thick forests of the Wentworth estate. Both the **East Course,** built in 1924, and the **West Course,** which opened in 1926, were designed by the prolific H. S. Colt, the architect behind Pine Valley, Muirfield, and Royal County Down. The **Edinburgh Course** (also known as the South) was designed by John Jacobs, Gary Player, and Bernard Gallacher and was officially opened by the Duke of Edinburgh in 1990. The West hosts the PGA Championship and is known as the Burma Road because it is tight, twisting, and of exhausting length, but the newer Edinburgh track is actually slightly longer: 6,979 yards from the back tees versus 6,957 yards for the West. The East is the shortest and easiest; it measures 6,176 yards from the tips and carries a par rating of sixty-eight. The West (greens fee £140/$245) and the East (greens fee £85/$149) see the most action because the majority of members and guests want to play one of the Colt originals. The Edinburgh (greens fee £85/$149) carries the least traffic. All three, however, are tight, forest-fringed, and beautifully maintained.

The best holes on the West are its four fine finishing holes: fifteen, a 466-yard, long, beautiful, par four that doglegs to the right; sixteen, a short par four that really plays as a driver and a wedge; and seventeen and eighteen, two par fives, 571 and 502 yards respectively, one that bends to the left and the other a gentle dogleg to the right. Par on Wentworth's West Course is seventy-three.

The Edinburgh Course has a memorable collection of par threes. The seventeenth wins the picture-postcard award. This 156-yard par three demands a drive over a lovely little lake. Par for the Edinburgh is seventy-two.

Although later revised by Colt, Sunningdale's **Old Course** was designed by Willie Park, Jr., and opened for play in 1901. The **New Course,** dating from the 1920s, is another Colt design that has been altered over the years by Tom Simpson and Ken Cotton. While Wentworth is tight, Sunningdale is more wide open. A three wood can at times be used off the tee at Wentworth, but at Sunningdale you can air out your driver. The Old Course measures 6,609 yards with a par of 70. The New Course is 6,210 yards with a par of 70. The greens fee of £100 ($175) includes a round on each course.

Walton Heath has an even more illustrious history than Wentworth or Sunningdale. Designed by Herbert Fowler, the **Old Course** at Walton Heath opened in 1904 with an exhibition match between James Braid, the club's newly appointed golf pro, Harry Vardon, and J. H. Taylor—a triumvirate that dominated golf for twenty years spanning the nineteenth and twentieth centuries. Mr. Braid, who won the British Open five times and designed some of the United Kingdom's greatest courses (like the King's at Gleneagles), stayed on as head pro at Walton Heath for forty-five years, and today the charming clubhouse is filled with fascinating Braid memorabilia. The **New Course,** another Fowler design, opened in 1913. Walton Heath's Old won the ultimate accolade in 1981 when it hosted the Ryder Cup. The Old Course measures 6,801 yards against 6,609 yards for the New; each plays to a par of seventy-two. The greens fee on weekends and weekdays before 11:30 A.M. is £65 ($114) a round.

Walton Heath is an unusual blend. It has an elevated setting high up on the very windy North Downs but also the severe, no-frills look of a flat and open seaside links course. Indeed, the serious profile of Walton Heath brings Hoylake (Royal Liverpool) immediately to mind. Bernard Darwin wrote that there is no place "where the sky seems bigger" than at Walton Heath. The greens are large, the grassy tops of

Old Course, Walton Heath

the bunkers are left shaggy and uncut, and the atmosphere at the club is as friendly and cordial as you can find. Thanks to the wind and the flat terrain, members play links-style golf at Walton Heath. The low, bump-and-run shot over the firm ground and onto the green is always favored over the soft lob, which can easily be blown off course. The only liability here is the busy highway that separates the shingled clubhouse from most of its holes. The first hole on the Old is played on the clubhouse side and the remaining holes on the other side of the highway. And that first hole is a test: a 235-yard par three guarded by large bunkers to a mercifully large green.

Golf at the **Berkshire** is among the best to be found inland anywhere in Britain. Rated just two spots behind Walton Heath, in thirteenth place, among all inland courses in the United Kingdom, the Berkshire is classic heathland golf with marvelous challenges over the **Red** and **Blue** courses, both designed and built in 1928 by Herbert Fowler. The Red Course measures 6,369 yards, with a par of seventy-two, while the Blue Course is 6,260 yards, with a par of seventy-one. The greens fee for each course is £50 ($88), and a day ticket is £65 ($114). The Berkshire is located in Ascot, less than twenty minutes from Heathrow Airport and less than fifteen minutes from Sunningdale.

Even closer to Heathrow is **Stoke Poges,** founded in 1908. This is an H. S. Colt–designed course, with an utterly spectacular Palladian clubhouse, remarkable gardens designed by Capability Brown, and super-friendly members who seem delighted to lead visitors from America around the course. Measuring 6,670 yards from the back tees with a par of seventy-one and charging a greens fee of £45 ($79) for a round on weekdays and £100 ($175) on weekends, Stoke Poges is near Slough in south Buckinghamshire and is rated thirty-sixth among the best inland courses in England.

Wentworth Club. Wentworth Drive, Virginia Water, Surrey, GU25 4LS England. Tel: 011-44-1344-842201. Fax: 011-44-842804. Credit cards accepted.

   • *West Course.* 1926. Designer: H. S. Colt. Par 73. 6,957 yards.
   • *East Course.* 1924. Designer: H. S. Colt. Par 68. 6,176 yards.
   • *Edinburgh Course.* 1990. Designers: John Jacobs, Gary Player, Bernard Gallacher. Par 72. 6,979 yards.
   • Greens fees: West: £140 ($245), East: £85 ($149), Edinburgh: £85 ($149). Caddies available. No carts. Restrictions: public access weekdays only. West Course closed two weeks every May and October. Season: year-round.

Sunningdale Golf Club. Ridgemont Road, Sunningdale, Ascot, Berkshire SL5 9RR England. Tel: 011-44-1344-26064. Fax: 011-44-1344-24154. Credit cards accepted.

   • *Old Course.* Designer: Willie Park, Jr. Par 70. 6,609 yards.
   • *New Course.* 1922/1935/1950s/1920s. Designers: H. S. Colt/Tom Simpson/Ken Cotton. Par 70. 6,210 yards.
   • Greens fee: day ticket: £100 ($175) includes round on each course. Caddies available. No carts. Restrictions: public access Monday–Thursday only. Handicap limit: men, 18; women, 20. Season: year-round.

Walton Heath Golf Club. Tadworth, Surrey KT20 7TP England. Tel: 011-44-1737-812380. Fax: 011-44-1737-814225. Credit cards accepted.

- *Old Course.* 1904. Designer: Herbert Fowler. Par 72. 6,801 yards.
- *New Course.* 1913. Designer: Herbert Fowler. Par 72. 6,609 yards.
- Greens fees: weekdays before 11:30 and weekends: £65 ($114), weekdays after 11:30: £55 ($96). Caddies available. No carts. Season: year-round.

The Berkshire. Swinley Road, Ascot, Berkshire SL5 8AY England. Tel: 011-44-1344-21496. Credit cards accepted.

- *Red Course.* 1928. Designer: Herbert Fowler. Par 72. 6,369 yards.
- *Blue Course.* 1928. Designer: Herbert Fowler. Par 71. 6,260 yards.
- Greens fees: round: £50 ($88), day ticket: £65 ($114). Walking permitted. Caddies. A few carts. Restrictions: no public play on weekends or holidays. Season: year-round.

Stoke Poges. Park Road, Stoke Poges, Buckinghamshire SL2 4PG England. Tel: 011-44-1753-717171. Fax: 011-44-1753-717181. Credit cards accepted.

- 1908. Designer: H. S. Colt. Par 71. 6,670 yards. Greens fees: weekday round: £45 ($79), day ticket: £65 ($114), weekend round: £100 ($175). Walking permitted. Caddies can be arranged. Carts. Season: year-round.

GOLF SERVICES 18

Golf services at all the aforementioned clubs are outstanding. All have fascinating, commodious clubhouses with excellent dining, drinking, and locker facilities, as well as thoroughly outfitted pro shops and good practice areas. Caddies are available at all of the courses but must be arranged when you reserve your tee time. Caddie costs vary from club to club but are in the range of £20 to £25 ($35 to $44) plus a tip of £5 ($9). Of the big three, we experienced the best overall service at Walton Heath; an especially warm and outgoing employee in its pro shop made us feel particularly welcome. Sunningdale's employees proved just as friendly as Walton Heath's, but Wentworth's personnel, while polite and professional, appeared generally more hardened and uninterested. A final tip: two hundred yards down the lane past the Walton Heath clubhouse you'll find a wonderful little pub called the Blue Ball.

LODGING  19

Cliveden is the very best hotel within reasonable driving distance (about thirty minutes) of Wentworth and Sunningdale—and truly one of the most exceptional hotels in all of England. Cliveden, a stately home overlooking the Thames, is set in 376 acres of National Trust gardens and parkland. It is in a special category when it comes to lodging, far more impressive and grand than even the most luxurious of hotels. Having been the home of three dukes, the Prince of Wales, and the Astor family, it did not become a hotel until 1984. Cliveden is probably best known as the place where the seductive Christine Keeler, already the mistress of a Soviet agent, met defense minister John Profumo, thereby creating a juicy sex scandal that eventually destroyed Harold

Macmillan's government. A pencil drawing of the exquisite Ms. Keeler hangs in Waldo's, Cliveden's one-star restaurant (reviewed below).

Cliveden is a treasure trove of art, antiques, and original furnishings. John Singer Sargent's magnificent oil portrait of a vivacious Nancy Astor hangs in Cliveden's Great Hall, which is decorated with French tapestries, suits of armor, enormous Oriental carpets, overstuffed sofas, and all the trappings and symbols of traditional English elegance. Butlers and footmen dressed in white tie and tails stand at attention in each corner of the room, waiting in readiness to bring a guest an old cognac or to light properly the Cuban cigar that has been selected from the humidor.

We had the good fortune to spend two nights at Cliveden and stayed in an extraordinary room called "the Sutherland," whose enormous canopy bed, original furniture, and artwork dates from the Duke of Sutherland's tenure at Cliveden in the seventeenth century. The duke even had a portrait set into the elaborately carved marble fireplace mantel. This is honestly one of the most remarkable rooms we have ever enjoyed. Little extras abound, like crystal decanters on the drinks tray filled to the top with whiskey, vodka, and gin; a brass nameplate on the front door with your name inscribed in calligraphy; and more mundane modern amenities like a television.

The new Pavilion building at Cliveden houses a beautiful indoor pool, saunas, steam bath, massage rooms, and a beauty salon. In the small but well-equipped indoor gymnasium, cordial and attractive personal trainers are on hand to help with your workout. Guests may also avail themselves of an indoor tennis court, plus two more outdoors; horseback riding; and two stunning, fully restored river launches from the Edwardian period that ply up and down the River Thames. Cliveden also has four restaurants, Waldo's (with just seven tables), the French Room, the Terrace Dining Room, and a less formal spot in the Pavilion that serves lunch.

We have only one caveat concerning Cliveden: it opened as a hotel thirteen years ago and looks a little frayed around the edges, with some worn carpeting in the corridors and chipped paint. It is time for the owners to freshen up the interior.

Alexander House is a convenient base for both Walton Heath and Gatwick Airport. This extremely comfortable country-house hotel—at about half the price of Cliveden—has lovely gardens, an attractive series of public rooms and lounges, excellent service, and an ideal setting in the Sussex countryside. We stayed in one of the least expensive rooms at Alexander House and found it more than agreeable. There is a tennis court on the grounds, a fine bar, and an elegant restaurant in the hotel. Room rates range from £99 ($172) for a single, £135 ($235) for a standard double, and £225 ($391) for the most expensive suites in the hotel, which include a four-poster bed and separate drawing room.

As frequent visitors to London for the past twenty-five years, we have stayed in scores of the city's best, most beautiful, and most overrated of Central London hotels. Today, a new hotel trend is sweeping London. The grand hotels of Mayfair have lost a meaningful percentage of their traditional clientele to a collection of smaller, more stylish, and far less costly hotels in Chelsea and Knightsbridge, the utterly charming red-brick neighborhoods surrounding Harrods department store and Sloane Square. The big hotels—the Dorchester, Claridges, the Connaught, and the Savoy—are all as good, or better, than ever, but more and more sophisticated and value-conscious travelers have discovered new London addresses for themselves. One of the best of this new breed of hotels is the **Franklin,** with its forty-seven beautifully appointed rooms in adjoining town houses on Egerton Gardens, just a five-minute walk to Harrods, a three-minute jaunt down Brompton Road to the Victoria and Albert Museum, and a five-minute stroll to Bibendum, one of London's premier restaurants. The Franklin's charm lies in its intimacy of scale, the lovely gardens behind the hotel, the imaginative linkage of the two brick town houses, the appealing decor, and the relatively small but very well equipped guest rooms. The best—and most costly—rooms in the house have garden views. Room rates range from £165 ($289) for a standard double to £275 ($482) for a luxury garden suite—rates that are approximately $150 per night less than the big-name hotels in Mayfair. The old Etonian who owns the Franklin is also the proprietor of the charming **Egerton House Hotel,** located just around the corner from the Franklin.

Another choice hotel in Central London is the **Stafford,** which stands just around the corner from that great classic, the recently renovated **Dukes Hotel** in St. James's. In addition to outstanding service, the Stafford has arguably the finest location in London—on a quiet cul-de-sac but just steps from the fine shops in Jermyn Street. The Stafford also has perhaps the best hotel bar in all of London, the American Bar run by a great character, Mr. Charles. The Stafford has finally completed a long overdue face-lift, and its eighty rooms are now being comfortably and luxuriously appointed. Prices range from £185 to £375 ($324 to $657) for a one-bedroom master suite with sitting room.

Cliveden. Taplow, Buckinghamshire SL6 0JF England. Tel: 800-223-6800 or 011-44-1628-668561. Fax: 011-44-1628-661837. 27 rooms. Doubles range from £245 to £398 ($429 to $698). Credit cards accepted.

Alexander House. East Street, Turner Hill, West Sussex RH10 4QD England. Tel: 011-44-1342-714914. Fax: 011-44-1342-717328. 15 rooms and suites. Doubles range from £135 to £225 ($235 to $392). Credit cards accepted.

The Franklin. 28 Egerton Gardens, Knightsbridge, London SW3 2DB England. Tel: 011-44-171-5845533. Fax: 011-44-171-5845449. 47 rooms and suites. Doubles range from £165 to £275 ($289 to $481). Credit cards accepted.

Egerton House Hotel. Egerton Terrace, Knightsbridge, London SW3 2BX England. Tel: 800-473-9492. Tel: 011-44-171-5892412. Fax: 011-44-171-5846540. 28 rooms from £170 to £210 ($298 to $368). Credit cards accepted.

The Stafford. St. James's Place, London SW1A 1NJ England. Tel: 800-525-4800 or 011-44-171-4930111. Fax: 011-44-171-4937121. 80 rooms and suites. Doubles range from £205 to £245 ($359 to $429). Credit cards accepted.

Dukes Hotel. St. James's Place, London SW1A 1NY England. Tel: 800-381-4702 or 011-44-171-4914840. Fax: 011-44-171-4931264. 64 rooms and suites. Doubles from £175 to £215 ($307 to 378). Credit cards accepted.

 RESTAURANTS (17)

The best restaurants in London are frequently those that do not win the highest accolades in the gastronomic press. Indeed, the restaurants in London with three Michelin stars have almost always disappointed us. Le Gavroche badly disappointed us on previous visits to London (it has since been demoted to two stars), and, on this trip, the Waterside Inn, forty-five minutes from Central London but just ten minutes from Cliveden, struck us as one of the most absurdly overrated and overpriced places to dine in the entire world. In addition to the Waterside Inn, London has one other three-star restaurant: Pierre Koffman's La Tante Claire, which is far superior to the Waterside Inn.

The Roux brothers are London institutions. Albert Roux founded Le Gavroche in

1967, and brother Michel created the **Waterside Inn.** Both quickly won three stars for their establishments, which served as the training ground for hundreds of young chefs who eventually went on to transform the culinary landscape of Britain. We tip our hat to the Rouxs for their accomplishments.

But aside from its gorgeous view of the Thames, there is little reason to visit the Waterside Inn. The interior is quite ordinary with dull paintings along the walls, and the cuisine is unremarkable save for its prices. A complete dinner for two with cocktails, wine, and tip costs approximately £228 ($400). Save yourself a bundle and avoid the Waterside Inn.

At **La Tante Claire** Pierre Koffman's creative cuisine—with interesting combinations of humble and highbrow ingredients—exalts his Gascon roots. La Tante Claire features a stylish and bright decor, a sophisticated clientele, and impeccable service. A complete dinner for two with wine and tip costs approximately £175 ($307). The three-course luncheon at £25 ($44) is very good value.

Noisy, fun, and fashionable, **Bibendum** is one of London's most entertaining restaurants and is uniquely situated in one of the city's most enchanting buildings—the former Michelin Tire warehouse on Fulham Road. Bibendum is the name of the fat Michelin Tire man, and his happy image is everywhere, on the ashtrays, china, the antique posters, and the fabulous stained-glass windows. Simple French cuisine is Bibendum's culinary focus. Specialties include wonderful soups, seafood, and lamb, and an excellent wine list complements the food. Dinner for two runs about £100 ($175). Strongly recommended. Reserve far in advance.

Owned by the urbane actor Michael Caine, **Langan's Brasserie** is one of London's greatest restaurant scenes. A vast, brightly lit room full of glamorous commotion every evening at dinner, Langan's boasts a somewhat masculine decor that includes racing and boating motifs in addition to daring Klimt nudes hanging from the mustard-colored walls. In this wonderfully hectic environment, the front-desk telephone never stops jangling; the staff, although harried, is friendly; and a well-groomed crowd continues to pour through the front door until, by 9 P.M., the place is filled to capacity. Specialties include bangers and mash (sausages and mashed potatoes) with a white onion sauce, roasted rack of lamb, fillet of salmon, and a choice of over twenty desserts. There is a fine selection of wines, too, from inexpensive house wines to far more costly Meursaults and Pauillacs. About £80 ($140) for two at dinner.

Waldo's is the *very* cozy, quiet, and refined restaurant at Cliveden; the haute cuisine dining room has earned a one-star rating from Michelin. Our prix fixe dinner (£40/$70) included superb Cornish crab, grilled red mullet, roasted quail, and cheese. Two other set dinners are offered at £47 ($82) and £60 ($105).

The Waterside Inn. Ferry Road, Bray, Berkshire SL6 2AT England. Tel: 011-44-1628-20691. Fax: 011-44-1628-784710. Credit cards accepted.

La Tante Claire. 68 Royal Hospital Road, Chelsea SW3 4HP England. Tel: 011-44-171-351-0227. Fax: 011-44-171-352-3257. Closed Saturdays and Sundays. Credit cards accepted.

Bibendum. Michelin House, 81 Fulham Road, London SW3 6RD England. Tel: 011-44-171-581-5817. Fax: 011-44-171-823-7925. Credit cards accepted.

Langan's Brasserie. Stratton Street, London WX1 5FD England. Tel: 011-44-171-493-6437. Fax: 011-44-171-493-8309. Closed Sunday. Credit cards accepted.

Waldo's. Taplow, Buckinghamshire, SL6 0JF England. Tel: 011-44-1628-668561. Fax: 011-44-1628-661837. Credit cards accepted.

NON-GOLF ACTIVITIES 20

"The man who is tired of London is tired of life," Samuel Johnson wrote in the eighteenth century, a remark far more appropriate today. London's top ten sights include the British Museum, the National Gallery, Madame Tussaud's, the Tower of London, the Tate Gallery, St. Paul's Cathedral, the Natural History Museum, the Science Museum, the Victoria and Albert, and the Royal Botanic Gardens at Kew, and these are just for starters. London has the best theater in the world, the most literate newspapers, and the most polite cabdrivers. For men, London offers the best shopping anywhere, with establishments that have catered to gentlemen for centuries, like Swaine Adeney Brigg (leather goods and umbrellas), Anderson & Sheppard (Savile Row tailors), Floris (men's toiletries), James Lock (hats), James Purdy (shotguns), and Turnbull & Asser (shirts). Then there is the London "season" every June with its fancy dress, strawberries and cream, and traditional sporting events like the Royal Ascot, the Henley Regatta, and the All-English Championship at Wimbledon. Possible excursions from London include easy day trips to Oxford and the Cotswolds.

GETTING THERE: To make your way by rental car into Central London from Heathrow Airport, look for A4 heading east (if, however, you are leaving from Terminal 4, you must first take A30 to get to A4). Follow A4 until it turns into Great West Road heading in the direction of Hammersmith. From Great West Road, follow the road as it turns into first Talgarth Road, then Cromwell Road, and then Brompton Road. From here you are not far from a number of the Central London hotels we recommend.

►SOUTHEAST ENGLAND

THE "TRINITY" OF SOUTHEAST ENGLAND:
ROYAL ST. GEORGE'S, PRINCE'S, AND ROYAL CINQUE PORTS

	The Golf	Golf Services	Lodging	Restaurants	Non-Golf Activities	Total
Rating	19	17	16	16	18	86

Thanne longen folk to goon on pilgrimages,

from every shire

of Engelond to Caunterbury they wende.

—Chaucer

Geoffrey Chaucer summed up humankind's passion for travel in the first few lines of *The Canterbury Tales.* Folks, the poet said, are inspired to embark upon a pilgrimage every so often, but especially in spring when the breeze is fresh and the lark's song fills the air.

In a similar spirit of discovery, increasing numbers of golfing pilgrims from America are finding that Chaucer's home territory, the southeast coast of England, is more than worth the journey—that this windy little corner of Britain jutting out into the English Channel is an excellent alternative to the more famous golfing venues in Scotland that can lure hordes of players from across the globe. In other words, the golf courses that are less than an hour's drive from Canterbury are not only outstanding, they are also somewhat off the beaten track and they welcome visitors with relish.

Using Canterbury, one of the most beautiful and historic cities in England, as an overnight base, the overseas visitor on a golfing pilgrimage will find a cluster of three great courses nearby, all within easy driving distance. Between them, these three utterly superb links have hosted the British Open a total of sixteen times.

The most aristocratic and famous of the three is Royal St. George's, the site of the British Open no fewer than twelve times since 1894, most recently in 1985, when it was won by Sandy Lyle, and again in 1993 when Greg Norman claimed the claret jug. The course with the most relaxed and friendliest atmosphere of the three is Prince's, with its twenty-seven holes of golf, where Gene Sarazen won the Open title in 1932. By far the toughest and most brutal of the lot is Royal Cinque Ports, also known as "Deal," which has played host to the Open twice, in 1909 and 1920. Royal Cinque Ports, we would hazard to guess, has not been selected for the Open since 1920 because its windy back nine would make too many great professional players look like ordinary Sunday hackers. If these three great seaside links courses are not enough to satisfy your appetite, then you can also play the nearby Canterbury Golf Club, a tidy parkland layout located on the outskirts of Canterbury's massive city walls.

Between courses you will find much else to occupy your time and interest in this fascinating and picturesque part of County Kent. This is one trip the non-golfing companion will not want to miss. The completion of the new Eurotunnel at Dover (just thirty minutes from Canterbury) means you can now literally go to France for lunch. Even if you do not dine in France, you can nearly always see the gray outline of its distant shore while walking the links at Prince's or Royal Cinque Ports. The sightseeing in the area is absolutely extraordinary: Leeds, Deal, and Dover castles, all nearby, are among the most spectacular structures in Britain. Before you tee up, you can pray for your soul and your swing in another fantastic edifice, the Canterbury Cathedral, home of Anglicanism and the Archbishop. You may also visit the exquisite and historic towns between Canterbury and the golf links, like charming Wingham, which has over one hundred landmark buildings, and sleepy Sandwich, hard to believe now but once the busiest port in all of England. Shopping abounds in the region, especially for antiques, but Canterbury is filled with choice bookshops and other fine stores. Central London and Heathrow Airport are but a two-hour drive from Canterbury.

THE GOLF

Of all the golf courses in the southeast corner of England, prestigious **Royal St. George's,** founded in 1887, boasts the greatest reputation and the most influential membership. Situated on the gray English Channel at Sandwich, Royal St. George's actually abuts Prince's golf courses, located just over the fence, at several points along the course. The club's stately clubhouse is surrounded by mature gardens, and there is also a lovely, thatched-roof starter's shed. Since it is closed to visitors on weekends and certain other days throughout

Royal St. George's

the year for club events, Royal St. George's can be difficult to get on. Be certain to call far in advance to secure your tee time. You must have a current handicap card in your possession, and, in order to play Royal St. George's, your handicap must be no higher than eighteen. High handicappers who have a tendency to slow down play are not permitted on this beauty. The greens fee is £80 ($140) for a day ticket and £60 ($105) for a round. Although this is an all-gentleman's club, women with low handicaps are welcome to play the course. Caddies are available if reserved in advance. Royal St. George's is very similar in feel to Prince's, but its terrain is more undulating, its dunes and bunkers are higher and more dramatic, and level lies can be tougher to find. Royal St. George's measures 6,860 yards; par is seventy.

Prince's, located on a haunting, isolated, and treeless stretch of road along the English Channel, suffers from a bit of an image problem. Prince's strives for greater recognition from the golfing world—and it truly deserves far more praise than it gets—but it is continually upstaged by its majestic next-door neighbor, Royal St. George's. Management at Prince's fully believes that this course is up to hosting the Open once again, but whenever the officials of British golf search for a site by the English Channel, they always think of Royal St. George's first. Hence, there is more than just a friendly rivalry going on here. In fact, as in most things British, this rivalry goes back a long way. During World War I, Prince's was converted into a machine-gun range. During World War II, the military requisitioned it once again and converted it into a practice ground for tanks preparing for the D-Day invasion of Normandy, just across the channel. All the while Royal St. George's, with its large roster of prosperous and influential members, remained completely intact.

After World War II nothing really remained of the original Prince's, so Sir Guy Campbell created two wonderfully simple nines, **Shore** (3,492 yards) and **Dunes** (3,455 yards), that run parallel to the channel, as well as the enchanting **Himalayas** (3,321 yards), a magical nine-hole layout full of character and appeal. Like all linksland courses, wind is a constant factor at Prince's. You play with or against the wind on alternate holes all day long. It is also easy to lose balls hit just off the fairway into the knotty and bottomless rough.

The second hole on the Himalayas is perhaps the most beautiful of the entire course, a lovely, 417-yard dogleg left to an elevated green. Number six may be the toughest; this 570-yard par five plays straight into the wind and requires a driver, fairway wood, and long iron in order to reach the green. The wind is at your back on number eight, but on nine you play into it again. A lovely finishing hole, the ninth is a very tough, 379-yard par four with huge bunkers guarding your approach to the green. The Himalayas has a bit of everything, even a shared green serving the fourth and eighth holes. The day ticket at Prince's ranges from £30 to £55 ($53 to $96).

Royal Cinque Ports (or **Deal**), which teamed up in 1997 with Royal St. George's to host the British Amateur, has proven to be one of the most unique and challenging golf courses in the world. Strong winds blow at your back for the entire front nine, but they are fully in your face for the long march home. Deal is a Jekyll and Hyde if there ever was one. The front nine—really the first ten holes—lulls you to sleep with consistent opportunities to score well. The truly spectacular sixth hole, with its green hidden behind high dunes, 317 yards from the tee, is actually reachable off the tee for long hitters given the mighty assistance of the wind.

But then the final eight holes really kick you in the teeth. As one of Deal's friendly young professionals told us: "The idea is to establish your score on the front nine and merely to protect it on the back." But protecting your front nine score is not a likely possibility for most visitors to Deal.

Built in 1892, Deal is all magnificence. The splendid site directly on the channel looking across to France, the stark beauty of the ancient linksland, the uncompromising winds, the concrete gun emplacements left over from World War II, the casual, informal air around the clubhouse, folks riding their horses and walking their dogs along the course—for Anglophiles and connoisseurs of the British game, Deal simply has it all. The atmosphere is unlike anything that can be found in America.

Deal, which plays to a par of seventy-two and measures 6,785 yards from the back tees, forms an out-and-back arrangement along the gray and windswept channel. Number three, a 494-yard par five, is arguably the most scenic hole on the course with its distinct landing areas for your drive and second shot that are set amidst the rough. The eighth, a 166-yard par three, can be hit with a well-struck nine iron given the prevailing winds. Number ten at Deal is another great hole, a 367-yard par four that swings slightly to the left over a field of thick rough and that tempts you to cut the corner with your tee shot.

Coming back, the par fours and fives are long enough already—408, 441, 423, 453, 508, and 412 yards—but the wind throws you off balance, screws up your alignment, and devastates your promising front nine score. The finishing hole at Deal is another gem: you drive over intimidating masses of rough and play your second shot into the wind and over a stream toward the green. By the time you have finished your round at Deal, your cheeks will be as ruddy as any Englishman's.

Royal St. George's Golf Club. Sandwich, Kent CT13 9PB England. Tel: 011-44-1304-613-090. Fax: 011-44-1304-615-236. Credit cards accepted.

• 1887. Designer: Dr. Laidlaw Purvis. Par 70. 6,860 yards. Greens fee day ticket: £80 ($140), round: £60 ($105). Walking. Caddies available if booked in advance. A few carts. Restrictions: open to public Monday through Friday. Handicap limit: 18 or under. Season: year-round.

Prince's Golf Club. Sandwich Bay, Sandwich, Kent CT13 9QB England. Tel: 011-44-1304-613-797. Fax: 011-44-01304-612-000. Credit cards accepted.

• *Shore Nine.* Par 36. 3,492 yards.
• *Dunes Nine.* Par 36. 3,455 yards.
• *Himalayas Nine.* Par 35. 3,321 yards.
• 1905/1949. Designers: Sir Guy Campbell/John Morrison. Greens fee day ticket: £30 to £55 ($53 to $96). Walking permitted. Caddies available if booked in advance. A few carts available; book in advance. Season: year-round.

Royal Cinque Ports (Deal). Golf Road, Deal, Kent CT14 6RF England. Tel: 011-44-1304-374-170. Fax: 011-44-1304-379-530. Credit cards accepted.

• 1892. Designer: Tom Dunn. Par 72. 6,785 yards. Greens fees: weekday day ticket: £45 ($79) and £35 ($61) after 1 P.M.; 18 holes on weekends: £55 ($96) and £45 ($79) after 1 P.M. Walking permitted. Caddies available if booked in advance. A couple of carts. Season: year-round.

GOLF SERVICES

Golf services are excellent at all the clubs. We were especially struck by the genuine warmth of our extraordinary welcome at Prince's.

Given the heavy rain squalls that sweep this part of England, all the clubs have "drying rooms" where you may store your soaked shoes and clothing. A rainsuit, waterproof shoes, extra gloves, an umbrella, and a plastic bag cover are *essential* accessories here.

Caddies are always available if booked in advance and cost around £20 ($35) plus tip.

LODGING

There are three excellent hotels in the area from which to choose, one priced for every budget—a luxury hotel in the countryside, a comfortable and moderately priced hotel in the center of Canterbury, and an appealing and inexpensive establishment in the historic community of Sandwich, very close to all the golf courses.

The luxury hotel we suggest is **Eastwell Manor,** a country-house hotel built in 1926 and set in 3,000 acres of private grounds. Eastwell Manor is located in Ashford, a bit distant from the links at Sandwich and Deal (about seventy-five minutes), but this is the only true luxury establishment within reasonable striking distance of the golf. The spacious guest rooms are elegantly decorated in traditional English taste with chintz fabrics and wall coverings. Be sure to dine at least one night in the manor's fine restaurant. Eastwell Manor is a popular weekend getaway for well-heeled Londoners, so be certain to book far in advance.

The **County Hotel** in Canterbury is perfectly suited for golfers touring the links around Sandwich. This simple and comfortable hotel is located in the center of Canterbury on a pedestrian street within a three-minute walk of the cathedral and Canterbury's other sights and shops. The staff is accustomed to accommodating golfers from America and will be happy to book your tee times at all the area courses. We stayed in room 72, a single room with a decent private bath and nice furnishings that is reasonably priced at £85 ($149). The hotel has a convenient (and secure) parking garage, a pleasant restaurant (Sully's), and a welcoming little bar. The County Hotel is a bit hard to locate at first, given the circuitous traffic routing in Canterbury, but it is worth the effort.

For those who want the cute and the quaint—plus very close proximity to the links—we heartily recommend the **Bell Hotel** in Sandwich, no more than ten minutes from Royal St. George's and Prince's. Occupying a lovely site overlooking the river at Sandwich, this old and picturesque thirty-three-room hotel is truly charming.

Eastwell Manor. Boughton Lees, Ashford, Kent TN25 4HR England. Tel: 011-44-1233-219-955. Fax: 011-44-1233-635-530. 23 rooms and suites. Doubles from £160 to £225 ($280 to $447), breakfast included. Credit cards accepted.

County Hotel. High Street, Canterbury, Kent CT1 2RX England. Tel: 011-44-1227-766-266. Fax: 011-44-1227-451-512. 73 rooms. Doubles from £90 to £110 ($158 to $193). Credit cards accepted.

The Bell Hotel. The Quay, Sandwich, Kent CT13 9EF England. Tel: 011-44-1304-613-388. Fax: 011-44-1304-615-308. 33 rooms and suites. Doubles range from £90 to £140 ($158 to $245), breakfast included. Credit cards accepted.

R E S T A U R A N T S

Lunch and drinks are available in the golf clubs. Royal St. George's has the finest facility, while Prince's all-too-modern clubhouse is the simplest, yet the meals are more than agreeable.

Elegant **Eastwell Manor** has a fine, formal dining room and a rich wine list. Complete dinners for two with wine and tip cost approximately £90 ($158). Dover sole, one of the traditional dishes of the region, is a house specialty.

Sully's at the County Hotel is not an especially attractive room, but the cooking and service are quite good—excellent smoked salmon, Dover sole, and a nice assortment of wines. The *Michelin Guide* ranks Sully's as the best restaurant in Canterbury.

Another good place to dine in Canterbury is **Tuo e Mio,** a lively Italian spot that specializes in fresh seafood and pasta dishes and is located just behind the cathedral. About £60 ($105) for two, wine and tip included.

The dining room at Eastwell Manor. Boughton Lees, Ashford, Kent TN25 4HR England. Tel: 011-44-1233-219-955. Fax: 011-44-1233-635-530. Credit cards accepted.

Sully's. County Hotel, High Street, Canterbury, Kent CT1 2RX England. Tel: 011-44-1227-766-266. Fax: 011-44-1227-451-512. 73 rooms. Credit cards accepted.

Tuo e Mio. 16 The Borough, Canterbury, Kent, England. Tel: 011-44-1227-761-471. Credit cards accepted.

N O N - G O L F A C T I V I T I E S

Non-golf activities in the region, as noted above, are exceptional. Day trips to France via the Eurotunnel, shopping excursions into the countryside for antiques, tours of Leeds, Dover, and Deal castles, and, of course, explorations of the nooks and crannies of Canterbury are all viable excursions for the non-golfer.

GETTING THERE: Canterbury, the ideal base of operations for the golfer touring southeast England, is a two-hour drive from Central London or Heathrow Airport. Take the A2 east all the way into Canterbury.

▶CENTRAL ENGLAND

LINKS OF LIVERPOOL

	The Golf	Golf Services	Lodging	Restaurants	Non-Golf Activities	Total
Rating	20	17	17	17	16	87

The happy traveler touring the links of Great Britain by motorcar with a bag of golf clubs tucked away in the boot (trunk) will discover another cluster of breathtaking courses within an hour's drive of Liverpool, birthplace of the Beatles. No collection of golf courses anywhere in the world is more challenging and celebrated than this one.

Royal Birkdale

Royal Birkdale and Royal Lytham & St. Anne's are located roughly an hour north of Liverpool, and Royal Liverpool—also known as Hoylake—is situated in attractive countryside about forty minutes west of Liverpool's grimy and far-from-idyllic urban center. Each of these three historic courses has hosted the Open Championship on more than one occasion. In fact, the Open has been held at these great venues a total of nineteen times, six at Royal Birkdale (Ian Baker-Finch was the last winner here in 1991), five at Hoylake, and eight at Royal Lytham & St. Anne's (where Seve Ballesteros won in 1979 and 1988 and Tom Lehman in 1996).

The quality and character of these courses, combined with their rich tradition and long association with the game's best players, make them second to none in the United Kingdom. And, an important additional bonus awaits the traveler today— these spots see far fewer overseas visitors (especially Americans) than the better-known links of Scotland to the north. We played these three during the very height of the summer season and encountered only light to moderate traffic.

If you stay just south of Liverpool in the exquisite, half-timbered city of Chester—and patronize one of the two fine hotels we recommend below—your marvelous sporting experience on the links will be enhanced by excellent accommodations, fine food and service, outstanding shopping, scenic diversions, and other agreeable activities during non-golfing hours. While the golf courses themselves happen to be scattered to the north and west of the dreary city of Liverpool, there is no compelling reason to explore the innards of Liverpool itself. Driving north from Chester to Southport and Lytham & St. Anne's, you bypass the city entirely, and driving northwest to Hoylake you skirt Liverpool's port area, but fortunately you are routed around the congested city center.

THE GOLF

At **Royal Lytham & St. Anne's** we were paired with both the club captain and the club historian, completed our round in three hours fifteen minutes, and lunched together afterward in the grand Victorian clubhouse.

So much for the supposed snobbism of British golf. At what club in America, we ask, would unknown visitors be invited to join a game with the club president and the chairman of the greens committee. This incident gives you a good example of the

Royal Lytham & St. Anne's

warmth and friendliness you will encounter at Royal Lytham & St. Anne's.

Royal Lytham & St. Anne's was founded in 1886 and was awarded the "Royal" prefix in 1926, the year Bobby Jones won his first British Open and the first time Lytham hosted the event. A plaque in the rough on the left side of the brutal seventeenth hole commemorates the spot from which Jones hit his brilliant approach shot that secured the victory. Club members still come out to the plaque late on summer evenings with a pocketful of balls and attempt the same shot for themselves. The seventeenth hole is an amazing challenge: a 462-yard par four with nineteen bunkers, a dogleg left with two landing areas, one for the drive and another in front of the green to receive the second shot. Royal Lytham is a veritable museum of Jones memorabilia. On display in the clubhouse you will find the same wooden-shafted mashie Jones employed on that shot at seventeen, a famous oil portrait of Jones, and an emotional letter to the club secretary from Jones, who was always a gifted writer, expressing his love and admiration for Royal Lytham & St. Anne's. Besides Jones, Lehman, and Ballesteros, other Open winners here include Bobby Locke (1952), Peter Thomson (1958), Bob Charles (1963), Tony Jacklin (1969), and Gary Player (1974). The Ryder and Curtis cups have also been played here.

Like St. Andrews, play at Royal Lytham begins more or less as a public event in front of the busy clubhouse. The first hole is a tricky par three that plays longer than it looks. The ninth green marks the farthest point on the course, and the eighteenth finishes in front of the clubhouse, where a pleasant lunch is served as part of your £80 ($140) greens fee. The most unusual holes, however, are eight through ten, which are surrounded by shops and houses and resemble a village green. Standing on the ninth tee you watch the townsfolk across the way going about their business in the bank and the drugstore. But make no mistake, the toughest hole at Royal Lytham is the fifteenth, which Henry Longhurst called "a hole for giants." This 468-yard par four is slightly uphill, into the wind, and with thick rough on either side of the narrow fairway. And eighteen is a great finishing hole. As at Troon and St. Andrews, you putt out on the last green while members scrutinize your stroke from the safe sanctuary of the leather-upholstered clubhouse.

We played **Royal Liverpool** (or Hoylake) with a thin, bolt-upright, seventy-eight-year-old member who carried his own bag (one wood, four irons, and a putter) and who merely shrugged off our congratulations after scoring an eagle two on the seventeenth hole by running a seven iron up to the green that just rolled and rolled and then finally rolled its way into the cup. His style of play, typical of the Hoylake membership, taught us a thing or two about how to handle the terrain. Local knowledge dictates that you take only intelligent risks here; instead of taking a full swing, push the ball up the middle of the fairway with a three-quarter swing and let it run along forever. Three such shots and even the octogenarians of the club are very close to the hole.

Meanwhile, the brawny Americans are hitting it hard and high and into the rough. While the rough looks innocent enough, it is tightly knit and twists the club in your hand before the club face can make clean contact, often sending the ball careening into even deeper trouble. Hoylake's havoc-producing rough is the chief reason members play it short and straight with their free-and-easy swings. As it says in understated British fashion in the Hoylake course guide, "Any loose shot will be severely punished."

Royal Liverpool, formed in 1869, is steeped in history. The very traditional and masculine flavor here—the barren, nineteenth-century linksland and knickers, flat cap, and tobacco atmosphere—is so thick you could cut it with a knife. Hoylake is also a club of many firsts. The first Amateur Championship was played here in 1885, and the first match between Britain and America, which led to the first Walker Cup match the following year, was played at Hoylake in 1921. Royal Liverpool was the home of great players like John Ball, who won the Amateur eight times, and Harold Hilton, the first golfer to hold amateur titles on both sides of the Atlantic in the same year. The current royal patron of Hoylake is Prince Andrew, the Duke of York, the ex-husband of Fergie and an avid golfer. British Open champions crowned here include Arnaud Massy (1907), the only Frenchman ever to win the Open, Harry Vardon (1914), Bobby Jones (1930, the year Jones won the Grand Slam), Peter Thomson

(1956), and Roberto de Vicenzo in 1967, when he defeated Jack Nicklaus on the decisive sixteenth hole.

Royal Liverpool looks dead flat and featureless until you get out amid the dunes, the River Dee, and the island in the river. Even so, there are very few trees taller than four or five feet anywhere on the course, so your perspective is askew and distances are hard to judge, particularly on your first round. The course's eccentricities and peculiarities, like the practice field set in the center of the golf course that is surrounded by a low wall, which acts as a hazard for golfers playing the first and sixteenth holes, also lend Royal Liverpool its character.

Some of the best holes at Hoylake include the memorable first with its tough second shot onto the green, the great fifth with the landing area for your tee shot above a gully, number six with its blind drive over the gorse, the elegant ninth along the River Dee with its bowl-shaped mound behind the green, the long and difficult 560-yard sixteenth that plays back toward the clubhouse, and the very tricky seventeenth, which our young-at-heart friend eagled, with out-of-bounds threatening along the right side. From the back tees Hoylake measures a daunting 7,110 yards; the course plays at an only slightly more manageable 6,821 from the member tees. The greens fee is £55 ($96) per round on weekdays and £65 ($114) on weekends; day ticket prices are £75 ($131) and £95 ($167), respectively. Prices rise for the month of July, when play is busiest.

Royal Birkdale is located along the coast in Southport, just a few miles past the point where the congestion of the Liverpool dockyards finally gives way to open countryside. No holes are actually within sight of the sea at Royal Birkdale, but you can smell the salt air and see the big seabirds wheeling over the golf course. The handsome Art Deco clubhouse, styled after a ship at sea, completes the nautical flavor of this legendary club.

Royal Birkdale

There are no golf courses anywhere in the world that are more welcoming than these three. The hospitable tone at Royal Birkdale—an outgoing attitude that filters down to everyone you will encounter here—is set by head pro Richard Bradbeer and his assistants in the elegant and well-stocked pro shop.

Royal Birkdale was formed in 1889, received the "Royal" designation in 1951, and has hosted the Open, the Ryder, the Curtis, and the Walker cups. The course was originally designed by George Lowe, Jr. but was later modified by Fred Hawtree and J. H. Taylor. Like the Bobby Jones plaque at Royal Lytham & St. Anne's, Royal Birkdale has a commemorative plaque of its own, this one honoring Arnold Palmer, who made a dazzling shot from the right rough on the sixteenth hole that was instrumental in his Open victory of 1961.

Royal Birkdale, site of the 1998 Open Championship, has the massive dunes, the deep pot bunkers, and the blind shots of a traditional links, but it also has thickets of forest, particularly on the tougher back nine. Holes that you will recall long after your visit to Royal Birkdale include the sixth, the 476-yard dogleg to the right; the ninth, with its blind tee shot; the long fifteenth, and the two very fine finishing holes: seventeen, with its two massive mounds obstructing the fairway, and eighteen, a 456-yard, bunker-riddled march back home. Royal Birkdale measures 6,690 yards from the member tees. The greens fee is £75 ($131) per round and £95 ($167) for a day ticket.

If these three courses are not enough for you, there is a fourth exceptional links nearby—**Formby,** another famous old course on the Lancashire coast. Formby offers an enticing golf package, which includes accommodations (for gentlemen only, however) in Formby House (four single rooms and three twin rooms), a full English breakfast, and two rounds of golf for only £80 ($141). You can stay overnight and play your second round the following morning! Considering the daily greens fee is regularly £50 ($88), this is quite a deal.

Important information: Many of the clubs have restrictions on outside play. See below for details. The best way to secure a tee time is to call well in advance of your visit. Also, it is always best to carry a handicap certificate and letter of introduction from your club pro when traveling in the United Kingdom.

Royal Lytham & St. Anne's. Links Gate, FY8 3LQ England. Tel: 011-44-1253-724206. Fax: 011-44-1253-780946. Credit cards accepted.

• 1897. Designers: George Lowe, Jr., Charles Hawtree. Par 71. 6,892 yards. Greens fees: round: £80 ($140), day ticket: £95 ($167), including lunch. Caddies. No carts. Restrictions: no public play on weekends and Tuesday mornings. Season: year-round.

Royal Liverpool (Hoylake). Meols Drive, Hoylake, Merseyside L47 4AL England. Tel: 011-44-1516-323101. Fax: 011-44-1516-326737. Credit cards accepted.

• 1869/1912, 1920. Designer: George Morris and Robert Chambers, Jr./H. S. Colt. Par 72. 7,110 yards. Greens fees: weekday round: £55 ($96), day ticket: £75 ($131). Weekend round: £65 ($114), day ticket: £95 ($167). Caddies. No carts. Season: year-round.

The Royal Birkdale Golf Club. Southport, Merseyside PR8 2LX England. Tel: 011-44-1704-567920. Fax: 011-44-1704-562327. Credit cards accepted.

• 1889/1932. Designers: George Lowe, Jr./F. G. Hawtree, J. H. Taylor. Par 72. 6,690 yards. Greens fees: weekday: £75 ($131), weekend: £95 ($167), day ticket (weekday only): £95 ($167). Caddies. No carts. Restrictions: course is open to visitors Mondays, Tuesday afternoons, 11:30–12:00 on Sunday mornings, and certain Wednesdays and Thursdays. Season: year-round.

Formby. Golf Road, Formby L37 1LQ England. Tel: 011-44-1704-874273. Fax: 011-44-1704-833028. No credit cards.

• 1884/1937. Designers: Willie Park, Jr., with Willie Park, Sr./H. S. Colt. Par 72. 6,993 yards. Greens fee: day ticket £50 ($88). Caddies. No carts. Restrictions: No visitors before 9:30 A.M., and availability is severely limited to visitors on Wednesday and Saturday. Caddies available if booked well in advance. No carts. Season: year-round.

 GOLF SERVICES ⑰

Golf services are very good at all the clubs. Caddies are always available but must be reserved *in advance* at each course. Hand trolleys may be rented for a nominal sum, but there are no riding carts at any of the courses. Each club has a practice range. The interior of the clubhouse at Royal Birkdale has been recently remodeled and now has elegant lockers and dramatic photos of Baker-Finch winning the '91 Open.

LODGING

The key to the perfect enjoyment of these courses is your choice of hotel. You can make a critical error and stay near Liverpool, or you can create a memorable holiday by reserving a room in one of the two hotels we recommend in stunning Chester, either the Chester Grosvenor, located in the heart of the historic city, or Crabwall Manor, a sixteenth-century country-house hotel about three miles outside the city. Both have their advantages.

Of these two addresses, however, we recommend the **Chester Grosvenor** with greater enthusiasm. The guest rooms at the Grosvenor have been remodeled to a higher standard than those at Crabwall Manor, and its location means that there are wonderful sights, shops, and other diversions just outside the front door. Chester is a delightful city for evening strolling after a good dinner; the Grosvenor is well situated for this and other activities. Crabwall Manor, by contrast, may be somewhat isolated.

We stayed in an elegant standard room at the Grosvenor, number 218, which was spacious, comfortable, and equipped with luxury amenities like minibar, cable television, Floris toiletries in the bath, and other thoughtful touches. The Grosvenor features two very nice restaurants (the Arkle restaurant has earned a Michelin star), a very active bar popular in the evening with upscale residents of Chester, a small exercise room, and a very attentive staff that is more than willing to book your tee times at the aforementioned golf courses.

We enjoyed **Crabwall Manor,** too. Our room at Crabwall, number 27, was large but looked somewhat over-the-hill. It had peeling wallpaper, worn carpeting, water-stained ceilings, and cracked tiles in the shower. These minor blemishes are more than offset by Crabwall Manor's assets, which include tastefully decorated public rooms, a wonderful restaurant, and a fine, hardworking staff, which booked our tee times for us and helpfully drew detailed road maps to all the courses. Rates range from £100 to £170 ($175 to $298).

Chester Grosvenor. 56 Eastgate, Chester CH1 1LT England. Tel: 011-44-1244-324024. Fax: 011-44-1244-313246. 86 rooms and suites. Doubles range from £140 to £250 ($245 to $438). Credit cards accepted.

Crabwall Manor. Parkgate Road, Mollington, Chester CH1 6NE England. Tel: 011-44-1244-851666. Fax: 011-44-1244-851400. 48 rooms and suites. Doubles from £100 to £170 ($175 to $298). Credit cards accepted.

RESTAURANTS

All the golf clubs serve lunch to visitors in atmospheric surroundings. Although the food—like the unusual cheese and pickle sandwich at Hoylake—can sometimes be a little peculiar, dinner at both the Grosvenor and Crabwall Manor is excellent. The Michelin-starred **Arkle Room** at the Grosvenor features lobster ravioli with Dublin Bay prawns and basil vinegar, roasted pigeon with wild mushrooms, and a wine list with over nine hundred selections. Dinner for two at the Arkle (closed Sundays) costs about £100 ($175). The second restaurant at the Grosvenor is the Parisian-style **Brasserie,** less formal and less expensive than the Arkle but still very good. Specialties in the lovely **conservatory dining room** overlooking the gardens at Crabwall Manor include smoked salmon, medallions of Scottish beef, and a fine vanilla-flecked crème brûlée. Dinner for two at Crabwall costs approximately £85 ($149).

The restaurants at Chester Grosvenor. 56 Eastgate, Chester CH1 1LT England. Tel: 011-44-1244-324024. Fax: 011-44-1244-313246. Credit cards accepted.

The dining room at Crabwall Manor. Parkgate Road, Mollington, Chester CH1 6NE England. Tel: 011-44-1244-851666. Fax: 011-44-1244-851400. Credit cards accepted.

NON-GOLF ACTIVITIES

Wonderful activities for non-golfers can be found in the truly enchanting city of Chester. The Chester Castle, Cathedral, and Roman Gardens are open year-round. Chester's finest shops can be found in the Rows, an architectural feature of the city center since the Middle Ages. There is also good shopping in Hoylake, particularly for antique furniture at the Jon David shop on Market Street. Non-golfers may easily make day trips to nearby Wales and the Lake District.

GETTING THERE: To get to the Chester Grosvenor Hotel from the Manchester Airport, get onto M56. Follow signs for North Wales/Chester. Get onto M53. Turn right onto Chester's Ring Road. Follow signs for City Centre Hotels.

►WOODHALL SPA

	The Golf	Golf Services	Lodging	Restaurants	Non-Golf Activities	Total
Rating	17	17	16	16	16	82

Petwood House Hotel

For the informed British golfer, Woodhall Spa is known as one of England's most acclaimed—and most isolated—golf courses. For a very special segment of the American golfing population, however, Woodhall Spa enjoys cult status.

American connoisseurs of golf in the British Isles whisper the name of Woodhall Spa with a certain awe. The American devotee of Woodhall Spa will agree without a moment's hesitation that many other famous United Kingdom courses, like Hoylake, Royal Troon, Turnberry, and St. Andrews, are all worthy of their exceptional, even great, reputations. But a shrug of the shoulders from the Woodhall Spa veteran will betray another unspoken sentiment, that these big-name courses on the busy thoroughfare of British and Scottish golf have lost some of their mystique because too many golfers from around the world have played them.

Woodhall Spa, these Anglophiles will declare, is another matter altogether—a travel destination solely for the genuine golfing insider. It is the ne plus ultra of English golf. "Oh, been to Royal St. George's, have you? That's wonderful. I've played Woodhall Spa." In other words, there is also a certain undeniable snobbism surrounding Woodhall Spa.

Rated the number one parkland (or nonlinks) course in the entire United Kingdom by both *Golf World* and *Following the Fairways*, little-known Woodhall Spa surpasses some pretty famous competition on "the best" lists, magnificent places to play such as Sunningdale, Wentworth, Walton Heath, and the King's Course at Gleneagles.

Like other cult courses we have visited, however, Woodhall Spa is not only highly regarded for its golf, it also requires an incredible effort just to find the place. For golfers, Woodhall Spa is a true trophy course. The long journey to play it proves the golfer's utter devotion to the game, confirms his or her sense of adventure, and illustrates yet again that golf is not a game but a quest.

Woodhall Spa is located in a part of England so out of the way that even the English are largely unfamiliar with it. Lincolnshire is known—if at all—for its flat, often marshy, agricultural land, called *fens*, and its majestic Lincoln Cathedral, which has been described by the BBC as "a small hill in a flat land."

We had the good fortune to visit Woodhall Spa in Lincolnshire during the fiftieth anniversary celebrations of V-E Day and learned that the region has brilliant Royal Air Force associations. During World War II, Lincolnshire's flat terrain was put to good use by several extraordinarily heroic RAF squadrons, including the famous dam busters, who actually stayed in Petwood House (see Lodging, below) in Woodhall Spa.

Four and a half hours northeast of Heathrow Airport by car—a drive that becomes quite grueling after you exit the M1 motorway and head east on tortuous country roads—the village of Woodhall Spa proves worthy of the trek. Lovely and quiet Woodhall Spa has been officially designated as one of the prettiest villages in England. Located eighteen miles south of the city of Lincoln, the village of 2,500 inhabitants consists of little more than two main streets lined with charming, red-brick, Victorian storefronts. The old spa, which attracted travelers from as far away as London in the nineteenth century, has long since closed down. It is the golf course that lures visitors these days, and this lure is likely to become more pronounced in the near future as important developments take shape at the Woodhall Spa Golf Club.

THE GOLF

In the meantime, before these grand changes are implemented, **Woodhall Spa** remains one of the most eccentric and resolutely uncommercial golf clubs in the United Kingdom. For example, as if getting to Woodhall Spa weren't difficult enough, try finding the golf course—a task that proves remarkably difficult for a village so small. We never spotted a single sign for the course and finally found the tree-shaded entrance road after having driven past it two or three times. The club's driveway is just one hundred yards beyond the Golf Hotel. The big (unmarked) parking lot in front is your clue.

Then, once you arrive at the pleasant little clubhouse, a friendly young assistant will point out that there are no course guides available and no yardage markers on any of the fairways. You are sent out to play with a scorecard. Period.

Founded in 1905, Woodhall Spa was originally laid out by Harry Vardon, although substantial alterations were made later by the golf club's longtime owner, Colonel S. V. Hotchkin. Neil Hotchkin, the colonel's son, in turn, owned the course for more than thirty years, making Woodhall Spa one of the few great privately owned golf courses anywhere in the world.

This unusual epoch of eccentric private ownership—Mr. Hotchkin's occasionally cantankerous behavior having been the subject of much local lore—has now passed. Woodhall Spa was recently sold to the English Golfing Union, which plans to add a second eighteen-hole layout (designed by Donald Steel) and a golf school, all to be completed by early 1998. The English Golfing Union is the leading amateur association in Britain, and Woodhall Spa will become its "National Center of Excellence." Big changes, therefore, loom on the horizon for this quiet little town.

Despite the flat farmland of surrounding Lincolnshire, Woodhall Spa has all the characteristics of a classic parkland or heathland layout: sandy subsoil, heather running riot, and glorious tree-lined fairways. Typically, you are required to hit your tee shot over a waste area awash with heather into a clearly designated driving area. Do not hit it too far, however, for more heather lurks beyond, and try to keep it straight because the tight fairways are lined with mature oak, yew, pine, and flaming gorse. The greens are protected by deep bunkers on either side, but the fronts are bunker free, giving you the option of running the ball up. Lob shots to the pin are out of the question anyway, given the unreceptive firmness of the greens. There is no noise on the golf course, no artificial intrusions, only a wonderful sense of isolation and the occasional pheasant fluttering past. Woodhall Spa is long, 6,976 yards and par seventy-three from the championship tees and 6,552 yards with a par of seventy from the medal tees.

Yet is Woodhall Spa the best parkland course in the United Kingdom? No, not in our experience, and not by a considerable margin. We had a wonderful time at Woodhall Spa and would gladly visit and play again, but we found the course in questionable, even disturbing, condition. The fairways were virtually hardpan, and the ball ran on forever. The second shot onto the greens, even on Woodhall Spa's very long par fours, played as an eight iron, nine iron, or wedge all day. Only on the par five ninth hole was a full second shot required, a five iron onto a green 551 yards from the tee. It is not a disagreeable experience to reach a long par five in two, but it should not be quite so easy. The course, therefore, played far shorter than its posted yardage. Aside from the rock-hard conditions, we have no other complaint with Woodhall Spa. New ownership may eliminate some appealing quirks, but we hope it brings real benefits to the course's condition.

The routing at Woodhall Spa is an out and back arrangement, with the back nine being tougher than the front. You play into the wind and through the forest on the back side; hence, you want to make your score on the easier front side and simply hold it on the back.

Outstanding holes include number six, a 463-yard par four and Woodhall Spa's number one handicap hole; the seventh, one of just two doglegs on the course; the eighth, a very tough, 189-yard par three; and the aforementioned ninth, the long par five. Memorable holes on the back side include number eleven, a 409-yard par four; number seventeen, a short, 315-yard par four that calls for a draw off the tee; and eighteen, a long, 443-yard par four that finishes in front of the clubhouse.

Woodhall Spa. The Broadway, Woodhall Spa, Lincolnshire LN10 6PU England. Tel: 011-44-1526-352511. Fax: 011-44-1526-352778. Credit cards accepted.

• 1905/1922. Designers: Harry Vardon/S. V. Hotchkin. Par 73. 6,976 yards. Greens fees day ticket: £65 ($114), round: £40 ($70). Restrictions: Handicap limit: men, 20; women, 30. Walking permitted. Caddies available if booked in advance. No carts. Season: year-round.

GOLF SERVICES

There is a nice little pro shop at the Woodhall Spa Golf Club, plus the pleasant clubhouse with restaurant, bar, and locker rooms. Service throughout the club could not be more agreeable. Caddies are available only if booked in advance and cost £20 ($35), tip included. Hand carts are available, but riding carts are not. The club has just opened a new twenty-bay driving range, which means you need not buy your own shag balls—a rarity in the British Isles!

LODGING

There are several small hotels in the village of Woodhall Spa, but by far the best and most charming place to stay is **Petwood House,** a Tudor-style, stately home dating from the 1920s that is welcoming, well maintained, and surrounded by thirty acres of lovely gardens with lakes and footpaths. Elegant but not super-posh, Petwood House boasts a handsome interior with a very pleasant restaurant, a paneled lounge, a comfortable bar, and spacious guest rooms. The public rooms are decorated with fascinating memorabilia from the 617th Squadron, the heroic dam busters who flew their Lancaster bombers deep into Nazi Germany. The hotel served as the officers' mess for the 617th Squadron during the war years, and "Rule, Britannia" and other military tunes are still favorites today on the hotel's sound system.

Petwood House is also an extraordinary buy. Our room, including dinner and breakfast, cost just £57 ($100) per person per night, which was the special "golfing rate." The room we stayed in, number 220, is not one of the hotel's best, but we found it large and comfortable. The most luxurious accommodations are the rooms with four-posters. The service throughout Petwood House is friendly and professional.

Petwood House is located about a half mile from the Woodhall Spa golf course. The **Golf Hotel** is located right next door to the course, but it is not as attractive or pleasant as Petwood House.

Petwood House. Woodhall Spa, Lincolnshire. Tel: 011-44-1526-352411. Fax: 011-44-1526-353473. 46 rooms from £57 to £78 ($100 to $136) per person, including breakfast and dinner. Credit cards accepted.

The Golf Hotel at Woodhall Spa. The Broadway, Woodhall Spa, Lincolnshire, LN10 6SG England. Tel: 011-44-1526-353535. Fax: 011-44-1526-353096. 50 rooms. Singles cost £49 ($86), and doubles cost £40 ($70) per person, full English breakfast included. Credit cards accepted.

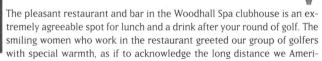

RESTAURANTS

The pleasant restaurant and bar in the Woodhall Spa clubhouse is an extremely agreeable spot for lunch and a drink after your round of golf. The smiling women who work in the restaurant greeted our group of golfers with special warmth, as if to acknowledge the long distance we Americans had traveled in order to arrive there.

Petwood House has a very delightful dining room as well, ideal for breakfast and dinner. The breakfasts are traditional and hearty, and dinner consists of excellent smoked salmon, beef, and fine seafood. Petwood House also has a more than adequate wine list. Dinner for two, excluding wine and tip, will cost about £35 ($61).

Woodhall Spa clubhouse. The Broadway, Woodhall Spa, Lincolnshire LN10 6PU England. Tel: 011-44-1526-352511. Fax: 011-44-1526-352778. Credit cards accepted.

The dining room at Petwood House. Woodhall Spa, Lincolnshire LN10 6QF England. Tel: 011-44-1526-352411. Fax: 011-44-1526-353473. Credit cards accepted.

NON-GOLF ACTIVITIES

Although non-golf activities are somewhat limited in the quiet region around Woodhall Spa, the Lincolnshire Wolds—including the charming villages of Somersby (the birthplace of Alfred, Lord Tennyson), Horncastle, and Louth—rival the Cotswolds for tranquillity and rural beauty. A visit to Lincoln Cathedral is a must, and many fine antique shops are in the area. The Battle of Britain Memorial Flight Museum is located in the nearby village of Tattershall.

GETTING THERE: Woodhall Spa is located in remote Lincolnshire, approximately four and a half hours northeast of Central London by way of the M1 motorway. The Woodhall Spa Golf Club is located just on the edge of the village of Woodhall Spa, only one hundred yards beyond the entrance to the Golf Hotel. The village itself is eighteen miles south of the city of Lincoln.

DESTINATIONS OF IRELAND

- Castlerock - Portstewart ROYAL PORTRUSH

Northern Ireland

BELFAST

ROYAL COUNTY DOWN

DUBLIN *Irish Sea*

Republic of Ireland

LAHINCH

SHANNON AIRPORT

• *LIMERICK*

BALLYBUNION

★ • *Adare Manor*

★ TRALEE

CORK

St. George's Channel

IRELAND

IRELAND

Some of the Irish links, I was about to write, stand comparison with the greatest courses in the world. They don't. They are the greatest courses in the world, not only in layout but in scenery and atmosphere and that indefinable something which makes you relive again and again the day you played there.

—Henry Longhurst, esteemed British golf journalist

Golf in Ireland is completely free of the intimidation, the austerity, and the trepidation sometimes experienced by the overseas visitor who approaches for the first time the gray stone portals of famous Scottish clubs like Royal Troon and Muirfield. In Ireland, where relaxation and playfulness lie at the heart of the game, you are welcomed like friends of the family, even at great clubs like Royal County Down, where local members may well greet you on the first tee and ask you to join their four-ball, or where, in the absence of freckle-faced local lads, a young assistant pro may volunteer to serve as your caddie. The much easier atmosphere in Ireland can also have a tonic effect on your game. A locked-up golf swing full of hitches, twitches, thoughts, and afterthoughts can suddenly, in these happy Irish environs, turn buttermilk-smooth. There is nothing to worry about in Ireland, no critical crowd to impress, no one to outgun. The Irish are as serious about the game as their Scottish brethren across the Irish Sea, but their appreciation of golfing pleasure may be more profound.

No serious golfing visitor to Ireland should omit—for whatever reason or irrational fear—the two great courses of Northern Ireland, Royal County Down and Royal Portrush, perhaps the two finest links courses in the British Isles. Located far afield from "the troubles" that plague the inner cities of Belfast and Londonderry, Royal County Down, "where the mountains of Mourne sweep down to the sea," is certainly one of the two or three most beautiful links in the world. Royal Portrush, within sight of the Giant's Causeway, was the site of the only British Open ever contested in Ireland and has one of the world's most infamous par threes, Calamity Corner, its fourteenth hole.

The west coast of Ireland is packed with great courses and hotels far finer than can be found in the North. Ballybunion, Lahinch, and Tralee are generally the first links to be ticked off on the visitor's wishlist, but others just off the beaten track await your exploration (and ours—in another book), wonderful courses like Rosses Point, Waterville, and Killarney.

Around Dublin you will find another famous cluster: Portmarnock, Royal Dublin, and County Louth, all north of the city, and the European Club, an hour south.

Ireland is smaller than the state of Maine. A carefully routed trip from course to course and from one hotel to another will keep driving times to a delightful minimum. All along the way you will marvel at the lushness of the countryside and its emerald-green hue. This is largely due to the wetness of the climate. Notice the clouds looming overhead. When the sun breaks through—most of Ireland receives an average of six hours of sunshine a day between May and August—the light will intensify the vivid colors of the landscape even further. Chances are, however, that the clouds that yielded up the sun will take it prisoner again before too long. The daily temperature range in Ireland in July and August is fifty-seven to seventy-five degrees. Spring may be the best time to visit—it is the driest season, and the golf courses and hotels are less crowded than in summer.

For a family on vacation, Ireland is a most hospitable place. The Irish may be the world's most naturally gracious people. Wherever you go—whether it's to the great private golf courses, a family-run hotel, or an automobile service station—you are made to feel welcome. The Irish seem to take a personal stake in maximizing your enjoyment of their fair land. Take every chance to get to know these wonderfully expressive people. Follow their advice on which monasteries and castles to visit, on which beaches to go to, and where to take your daily hike. Spend a day at a working farm, go pony trekking with a guide, watch performances of traditional Celtic music and dancing, listen to an Irish storyteller. We promise you will bring back equally warm memories of the wonderful golf and people of Ireland.

►THE WEST COAST

LAHINCH, BALLYBUNION, AND TRALEE

	The Golf	Golf Services	Lodging	Restaurants	Non-Golf Activities	Total
Rating	19	17	18	16	18	**88**

There is such an easygoing freedom to the game here that even the most uptight hacker with the world's most restricted backswing is certain to loosen up within a day or two of arrival and start to hit the ball with wondrous satisfaction. Relaxation, at bottom, is the tonic effect of golf on this bright-green, indeed, this emerald-colored island, and relaxation, as we all know, is the cornerstone of golfing happiness. Magically, in Ireland, it is almost as if relaxation were as much in the air as it is in the Guinness. Yes, golf in Ireland is transforming. Whatever it is that habitually locks you up at home—jitters on the first tee, the familiar faces expecting all-too-familiar results, or an unhealthy preoccupation with low numbers—all this can mercifully disappear on the wild turf of Ireland. It is easy to lose your old self and find a new one here. The shaggy landscape (Irish golf courses all look like Irish wolfhounds), the bracing ocean breezes, the myths, fables, legends, and lore that surround certain courses, and the musical lilt of the wizened caddie by your side with the leprechaun's twinkle in his eye—heady ingredients such as these can help you forget the golfer you left at home. With luck, you might even acquire a fuller, easier golf swing as a lasting and very valuable souvenir of your Irish golfing holiday.

The west of Ireland, as Sir John Betjeman wrote, has a flavor all its own:

Ah! seaweed smells from sandy caves

And thyme and mist in whiffs,

In-coming tide, Atlantic waves

Slapping the sunny cliffs,

Lark song and sea sounds in the air

And splendour, splendour everywhere.

There are dozens of great golf courses on the west coast of Ireland, some less famous than others, including Connemara, Westport, Rosses Point, Enniscrone, Cork,

Killarney, and Waterville. In fact, there is even a very fine course at Shannon Airport that adjoins one of the principal runways. While waiting to catch a flight back home, the true golf fanatic can squeeze in a final round in Ireland actually within sight of the airport terminal.

The three greatest courses on Ireland's wonderful west coast are Tralee, where ancient Gaelic warriors are said to have waged war more than a thousand years ago; Ballybunion, from which, legend has it, the strange Vision of Killsaheen can appear; and lovable Lahinch, where a pack of goats are employed to predict the weather.

Golfers and non-golfers alike will be equally intoxicated by this Irish sojourn. The literary traveler, the lover of castles, ruins, pubs, antiques, crystal, or tweeds and lace, and the hiker, the rider, the bicyclist, the fisherman, and the idler—all will find something in Ireland to love. The seductiveness of the country lies in its simplicity of scale, the tidy garden by the small stone cottage, the vivid folkways, and the charming, world-famous loquacious hospitality of your Irish hosts.

THE GOLF
⑲

Among them, Lahinch, Ballybunion, and Tralee possess the most famous—and some of the most idiosyncratic—holes of golf in Ireland: the extraordinary fifth and sixth holes at Lahinch, called Klondyke and the Dell; the great collection of par threes at Ballybunion; the eleventh at Ballybunion along the sea, which is one of the most beautiful golf holes on earth; and the notorious seventeenth at Tralee with its green perched on an amazing precipice overlooking the ocean, known as Ryan's Daughter because David Lean's movie was filmed on this site. In fact, "you have to see it to believe it" is an expression that aptly describes the entire back nine at Tralee. And Ballybunion has been ranked among the world's top fifteen courses for years and remains Tom Watson's favorite Irish links. Lahinch, Ballybunion, and Tralee constitute a logical minitour on Ireland's west coast. No more than ninety minutes apart by car, they represent three very different—and absolutely unforgettable—golfing experiences.

Of the three, **Lahinch's Championship Course** is the shortest, the most historic, the most eccentric, and, quite likely, the most fun. No one would ever attempt to build such a course today. Designed and then revised by two of golf's greatest minds—Old Tom Morris of St. Andrews and Dr. Alister Mackenzie of Cypress Point and Augusta National—Lahinch remains full of fascinating quirks that defy the logic of contemporary golf course architecture. For example, the fifth and eighteenth fairways actually cross over one another. An ominous-looking disclaimer printed in bright-red letters on the Lahinch scorecard states: "The golf committee wishes to inform all players that they will not accept liability for accidents at the crossing of the 5th and 18th fairways."

Lahinch

The only Old Tom Morris holes at Lahinch left entirely unaltered by Mackenzie are genuine curiosities from a bygone era, the aforementioned fifth and sixth—Klondyke, a short par five, and the Dell, a wonderful par three. Golfers come to Lahinch from across the globe in order to take a firsthand look at these two engaging oddballs. Your drive on Klondyke lands in a fairway no more than fifteen yards wide and hemmed in on both sides by massive, grassy dunes. Then you are required to fire a blind second shot over another even more massive dune that stands between you and the green. On the tee of the Dell you may momentarily think you are lost if this happens to be your first round at Lahinch. The green on this 142-meter (155-yard) hole is hidden between two enormous dunes. Take your cue from the white stone marker atop the mound, pitch the ball over with a nine iron, and hope for the best. Don't be surprised if you score a hole in one on the Dell, especially if you play with a caddie. Since the hole is blind, caddies act as forecaddies here and are known to occasionally place a ball into the cup with the hope of securing an especially generous tip later on. The eighth hole at Lahinch—which requires you to hit your drive directly over the seventh green from an elevated tee—is another unusual challenge. Lahinch is short, only 6,123 meters (6,696 yards) from the blue tees, 5,890 (6,441 yards) from the whites, and 5,721 (6,256 yards) from the reds.

We did not see the goats of Lahinch, which meant that the weather would be fine. It was. If the goats are huddled around the clubhouse, it means that rain is approaching. The goats, we were informed, nearly always have it right. Another Lahinch tradition is Robert McCavery's pro shop. Mr. McCavery, the pro for better than twenty years, took over from his father, who was head professional here for more than sixty years. Part museum, part retail store, the shop is filled with interesting memorabilia.

Lahinch is open every day to visitors without restriction, but you should have a current handicap card in your possession, and men must play to a handicap of twenty-eight or less and women to thirty-six or less. The greens fee is £40 ($65). A second course at Lahinch, the **Castle Course,** measures a scant 5,138 meters (5,619 yards) and is not in the same league as the Championship Course. The greens fee for the Castle Course is £25 ($40).

The **Old Course** at **Ballybunion,** straight south down the jagged coast from Lahinch, poses a stiffer challenge. It is tougher, longer, and more intimidating than Lahinch in nearly every detail. While more majestic and clearly a greater layout than Lahinch, Ballybunion is not without eerie, Lahinch-like characteristics and idiosyncrasies. After all, this is the mythical land of Ireland, where some still believe you can ruin a farmer's luck forever by burying a dead cat in his field. Ballybunion, for example, is home to the Vision of Killsaheen, a murky vision of a woman selling her wares on an eternal bridge that stretches across the sea. Beware of seeking out this vision, however, because tradition holds that whoever sees it will die within seven years. On top of this, a stark, haunted-looking graveyard looms beside the first tee. A caddie can prevent the first-time visitor from literally getting lost on the course. The oddly located fourth tee, for instance, requires that you hit your drive straight over the flagstick on the third green.

Ballybunion's back nine is as great a nine-hole sequence as exists in golf. Eleven is the 453-yard masterpiece along the ocean; twelve is the perilous, uphill par three reachable only with a wood; fifteen is a stunning, 216-yard par three that plays back toward the sea; sixteen is a magnificent dogleg-left with a drive over

Ballybunion

the dunes and a second shot up the narrow chute to the elevated green; the lovely seventeenth brings you down to the beach; and the tough eighteenth hole plays back uphill through a virtual tunnel of gigantic dunes to the luxurious, new, California-style clubhouse that was completed at Ballybunion in 1994.

Ballybunion measures 6,593 yards from the blues, 6,241 yards from the white tees, and 5,965 from the reds. The course is open every day to visitors, but tee times booked in advance are essential, as are current handicap cards for all golfers. The greens fees are £45 ($73) for a round and £65 ($105) for a day ticket, which includes a round on both the Old Course and the **Cashen Course,** the second course at Ballybunion (designed by Robert Trent Jones, Sr., in 1984), which is much more highly regarded than the second course at Lahinch. Despite its beauty and good reputation, the Cashen Course is rarely busy except on weekends in midsummer.

Purists should not be put off by the fact that **Tralee** is the newest course (1984) among this triumvirate and the only one designed by an American, Arnold Palmer. As a designer, Palmer may not get high marks on all his work, but there is no question that he absorbed the essential Irishness of the situation at Tralee. The site is spectacular. British writer and designer Peter Dobereiner has said: "Robert Louis Stevenson got it wrong when he described the Monterey Peninsula as the finest conjunction of land and sea this earth has to offer. As a spectacle, Tralee is in a different class!"

Tralee is an odyssey as much as a game of golf. Just when you think you have seen it all on the first nine holes—the incredible ocean views, the grandeur, the holes that fit so neatly into the odd landscape—you arrive at Tralee's back nine, where every green is protected by a yawning chasm and located on the edge of a cliff. Tralee's final nine holes look like that series of humorous prints depicting greens perched on top of the World Trade Center beneath a lava-spewing volcano and across the opposite side of a glacier. At Tralee, however, the hazards are real. Take the twelfth hole—the 417-meter (456-yard) par four and number one handicap—as an example. If your second shot does not clear the chasm to the left, your chances of even finishing the hole will be in serious jeopardy. The thirteenth, a 145-meter (159-yard) par three, is just as frightening, and the panoramic view from the seventeenth green is simply amazing.

Finally, if you wish to contrast the traditional Irish links courses with a modern, inland course, reserve a tee time at the new Robert Trent Jones, Sr., course at **Adare Manor Golf Club.** Conveniently located at Adare Manor (see Lodging, below), this highly regarded, 7,138-yard, American-style course features a large man-made lake that comes into play throughout the front nine. The meandering River Maigue lends a picturesque challenge to the back side.

Tralee

Lahinch Golf Club. Lahinch, County Clare, Ireland. Tel: 011-353-65-81003. Fax: 011-44-353-65-81592. Credit cards accepted.

• *Championship Course.* 1892/1928. Designers: Old Tom Morris/Alister Mackenzie. Par 73. 6,123 meters.

• *Castle Course.* 1971. Designer: John Harris. Par 70. 5,138 meters (5,619 yards).

• Greens fees: Championship Course: £40/$65; Castle Course: £25/$40. Caddies can be arranged. No carts. Restrictions: Championship Course handicap limit: men, 28; women, 36. Season: year-round.

Ballybunion Golf Club. Ballybunion, County Kerry, Ireland. Tel: 011-353-68-27146. Fax: 011-353-68-27387. Credit cards accepted.

• *Old Course.* 1893. Designer: unknown. Par 72. 6,593 yards.
• *Cashen Course.* 1984. Designer: Robert Trent Jones, Sr. Par 72. 6,216 yards.
• Greens fees: round: £45 ($73) (Old Course), £30 ($48) (Cashen Course); day ticket: £65 ($105) (includes one round on each course). Caddies available. No carts. Season: year-round.

Tralee Golf Club. West Barrow, Ardfert, County Kerry, Ireland. Tel: 011-353-66-36379. Fax: 011-353-66-36008. Credit cards accepted.

• 1984. Designer: Arnold Palmer. Par 71. 6,252 meters (6,837 yards). Greens fees: weekday: £30 ($48), weekend: £40 ($64). Caddies can be arranged. No carts. Season: April 1 to November 1; closed to public Wednesdays from June to August.

Adare Manor Golf Club. Adare Manor, Adare, County Limerick, Ireland. Tel: 800-462-3273 or 011-353-61-396566. Fax: 011-353-61-396124. Credit cards accepted.

• 1995. Designer: Robert Trent Jones, Sr. Par 72. 7,138 yards. Greens fees: hotel guests: £35 ($56), public £40 ($64). Caddies available. No carts. Season: year-round.

GOLF SERVICES · 17

Generally speaking, the services at Irish golf courses—with the exception of Ballybunion and its glamorous new clubhouse facility—are rudimentary by American standards. At each of the courses noted above, however, caddies are a necessity and always available. Caddie fees are £15 ($24) at each course. Customary tips are £3 to £5 ($5 to $8). Rental clubs and pull carts are also on hand at each location. So what more does one need? Only Guinness, that magical black elixir, always readily available in every clubhouse bar.

LODGING · 18

The little resort towns of Lahinch, Ballybunion, and Tralee offer only very modest accommodations—tidy bed-and-breakfasts and humble hotels—but absolutely nothing for those who seek first-class lodgings. The discerning traveler, therefore, must search for a fine hotel, but one within reasonable distance of all three golfing venues.

For several years now the stately **Adare Manor,** in its own eight-hundred-acre park, has been the hotel of choice for upscale golfers visiting the west of Ireland. Adare Manor is located in the beautiful village of Adare just south of Limerick and has luxurious guest rooms and lovely service. There is also an eighteen-hole golf course located immediately next door to the hotel. We have stayed in this vast castle/hotel on two occasions, once in spectacular room 302, the very best room at Adare Manor, and more recently in room 315, located in the somewhat sterile new wing at the rear. We like the fact that nearly everyone employed at Adare Manor plays golf. Jerry, a wonderfully friendly barman with whom we always enjoy talking, is a ten handicap and member of Lahinch, and Sean, a young baggage boy and carhop, sneaks in a round at the Adare Manor Golf Club next door whenever he gets the chance.

Unfortunately, Adare Manor's prices have risen into the stratosphere (to as much as £315/$508 for a double room), without a corresponding rise in quality. This discrepancy is perhaps most evident in the restaurant. The dining room with its stone arches is still an attractive room, but our recent dinner was costly and lackluster. Our dinner here during a previous visit was a vastly more exciting event. Adare Manor has a fine new Robert Trent Jones, Sr., golf course on the hotel grounds (see Golf, above), but the public Adare Golf Club next door is a rinky-dink affair. Recently expanded from nine to eighteen holes and squeezed into an all-too-small plot of land, this course has some scenic characteristics but is really not worth the effort.

There are, however, three hotels we can recommend with real enthusiasm: Sheen Falls Lodge, Gregans Castle, and the bargain-priced Dunraven Arms.

Sheen Falls Lodge gets our vote as the best hotel in all of Ireland today. This exquisite and romantic country-house hotel has forty extremely handsome guest rooms (a new extension will add twenty more rooms in 1997) and is set on the banks of a salmon river surrounded by three hundred acres of private woodlands laced with enchanting footpaths. Sheen Falls Lodge opened in 1991 after an $18 million renovation. Activities include trout and salmon fishing (the hotel staff will even smoke them for you), horseback and pony riding, a fitness center with exercise equipment, and a fully equipped spa. Guest rooms range in price from £210 to £305 ($338 to $491). There are nine suites at £360 ($580) during high season. The only liability of Sheen Falls Lodge is its distance—two hours or more—from Ballybunion and Lahinch. Sheen Falls is perfectly situated for a tour of the Ring of Kerry and Dingle Peninsula. It is forty minutes from the two golf courses at Killarney, seventy-five minutes from Waterville, ninety minutes from Tralee, and just one mile from the brand-new eighteen-hole layout at Kenmare.

Gregans Castle Hotel, which we highly recommend, is located in a beautiful part of County Clare, between beguiling Ballyvaughan and Lisdoonvarna. The hotel lies twenty minutes north of the golf courses at Lahinch in a fascinating region called the Burren and is not far from the famous Cliffs of Moher. This very elegant and appealing older hotel has spectacular views of the strange Burren limestone fields and is run in sophisticated fashion by the attractive Moira Haden. The enormous and luxurious O'Loughlin Suite is the best room in the house. The hotel, which closes from late October to late March, has twenty-two rooms.

The very well-known **Dunraven Arms Hotel** is located in the village of Adare directly across the street from Adare Manor. This cozy and comfortable hotel aims to deliver value rather than opulent luxury. Well run, charming, and with a good restaurant on the premises and a lovely garden to the rear, the Dunraven Arms will particularly suit those who seek a relaxed and low-key atmosphere. This accommodation would be perfect for a family traveling with children. Dunraven Arms has sixty-six rooms and suites, with doubles priced at £110 ($177) and suites starting at £140 ($225).

Adare Manor. Adare, County Limerick, Ireland. Tel: 800-462-3273 or 011-353-61-396566. Fax: 201-425-0332 or 011-353-61-396124. 64 rooms and suites. Doubles from £200 to £315 ($322 to $508), includes Irish breakfast. Credit cards accepted.

Sheen Falls Lodge. Kenmare, County Kerry, Ireland. Tel: 800-221-1074 or 011-353-64-41600. Fax: 011-353-64-41386. 40 rooms. Doubles range from £210 to £305 ($338 to $491). Credit cards accepted.

Gregans Castle Hotel. Ballyvaughan, County Clare, Ireland. Tel: 011-353-65-77005. Fax: 011-353-65-77111. 22 bedrooms. Doubles cost £120 ($194). Credit cards accepted.

Dunraven Arms Hotel. Adare, County Limerick, Ireland. Tel: 011-353-61-396633.

Fax: 011-353-61-396541. 66 rooms and suites. Doubles cost £110 ($177). Credit cards accepted.

R E S T A U R A N T S

There are pleasant restaurants and bars in the clubhouses at Lahinch, Ballybunion, and Tralee, where you will want to take a pint of Guinness, a bowl of soup, and a hearty sandwich after your morning round. The restaurant in the enormous, newly completed clubhouse at Ballybunion is especially nice, with a view of the eighteenth hole.

If you stay in the village of Adare at either Adare Manor or the Dunraven Arms, be sure to have dinner one evening at the popular **Mustard Seed,** located in a cozy, thatched cottage directly across the road from the Dunraven Arms. Traditional Irish dishes—hearty stews, game, and seafood—dominate the menu. There is a pleasant little bar at the front, agreeable service, and an informal atmosphere (neckties are not required). Dinner costs £28 ($45) per person.

By far the best hotel dining room we visited in Ireland was the refined and quite dressy **La Cascade** restaurant at Sheen Falls Lodge, a lovely room with sweeping views of the floodlit Sheen waterfalls. Chef Fergus Moore uses only local produce and the best ingredients to create his "modern Irish" cuisine. Specialties include tortellini of lobster with caviar butter sauce, fillets of black sole with a red-wine butter sauce, and hot chocolate soufflé with pistachio ice cream. There are more than four thousand bottles in the restaurant's wine cellar. The prix fixe dinner is £37 ($60) per person.

The very comfortable dining room at **Gregans Castle Hotel** offers good cuisine, fine service, and splendid views of the Burren. Expect to spend $100 for two at dinner, wine and service included. Dinner at the **Dunraven Arms** is very satisfying if somewhat unsensational (£50/$80 for two). The far more expensive dining experience (£80/$129 for two) at **Adare Manor** can be a disappointment.

Mustard Seed. Ballingarry, County Limerick, Ireland. Tel: 011-353-69-68508. Fax: 011-353-69-68511. Credit cards accepted.

La Cascade. Sheen Falls Lodge. Kenmare, County Kerry, Ireland. Tel: 800-221-1074 or 011-353-64-41600. Fax: 011-353-64-41386. Credit cards accepted.

Gregans Castle Hotel. Ballyvaughan, County Clare, Ireland. Tel: 011-353-65-77005. Fax: 011-353-65-77111. Credit cards accepted.

Dunraven Arms. Dunraven Arms Hotel, Adare, County Limerick, Ireland. Tel: 011-353-61-396633. Fax: 011-353-61-396541. Credit cards accepted.

Adare Manor. Adare, County Limerick, Ireland. Tel: 800-462-3273 or 011-353-61-396566. Fax: 011-353-61-396124. Credit cards accepted.

NON-GOLF ACTIVITIES ⑱

Your non-golf activities will be determined largely by your choice of hotel. If you splurge and stay at Sheen Falls Lodge, you will find a wealth of sports and other activities on the hotel premises, in addition to tours of the magnificent Dingle Peninsula and the Ring of Kerry. If you stay at Gregans Castle Hotel you will want to visit the Cliffs of Moher, which plunge four hundred feet straight down into the Atlantic, take a walking tour of the Burren, and tour the utterly charming resort village of Ballyvaughan with its wonderful craft and woolens shops. If you stay in centrally located Adare, do not forget that nearby Limerick is filled with good shops. There is even a branch of Bewley's—the famous Dublin café—on Cruises Street in Limerick. The best golf antique shop we visited is on Main Street in Ballybunion, in the center of town about a mile from the course. Owned by Noel O'Hara, it is filled with interesting antique golf prints and is worth a visit.

GETTING THERE: Lahinch, Ballybunion, and Tralee are all located within two hours of Shannon Airport. Lahinch is thirty minutes west of Ennis on the T70, just south of the Cliffs of Moher. Ballybunion is thirty minutes west of Listowel on the R553. The Tralee Golf Club is twenty minutes west of the village of Tralee. The Sheen Falls Lodge is about a two-and-a-half-hour drive from Shannon Airport. Take the N18 past Limerick, look for signposts to Tralee, take the N20 for a short distance and then the N21 to Killarney. Follow signposts to Killarney and exit onto the N71 to Kenmaire, home of the lodge.

▶NORTHERN IRELAND

THE MAGIC AND MAJESTY OF ROYAL COUNTY DOWN AND ROYAL PORTRUSH

	The Golf	Golf Services	Lodging	Restaurants	Non-Golf Activities	Total
Rating	20	19	16	16	14	85

It has long been my contention that the Irish—North or South—are the custodians of the genuine spirit of golf. They like to sling the bag across the shoulder and have at it, without fuss or formality.

—Peter Dobereiner

If given the chance to play golf in any one country of the world, we might very well opt for a trip to Ireland and hop on the next Aer Lingus flight to Shannon Airport in County Clare, near Limerick. That is, unless we were offered the opportunity to golf in the province of Northern Ireland instead. Yet, very happily, since the Republic of Ireland and the U.K. division of Northern Ireland share one middle-sized island between them, golfers on holiday need not choose one or the other. Both Ireland and Northern Ireland can easily be visited as part of the same golfing expedition. Any golfer who goes to Ireland and omits, for whatever reason, an excursion of two or three days to Northern Ireland is making a mistake. The more serious the golfer, the more serious this particular omission would be.

The golf courses in the North, although not nearly as numerous, are actually superior to those you will find in the South, and the hospitality of the people in Northern Ireland is virtually without peer. The warmth of your greeting here, in fact, simply borders on the amazing. The residents of Northern Ireland fully appreciate that you crossed a psychological divide when you entered their land, and they go to remarkable lengths to express their gratitude and make you welcome. Those employed in the hospitality trade (at the golf courses, hotels, and restaurants) treat you like family, but even the gas station attendants we met made a point of wishing us well on our holiday. Everyone we shook hands with in Northern Ireland was frustrated by politics, but they did their best to counteract it with honest friendship.

Many travelers, of course, never make it to Northern Ireland because of the decades of bad press concerning "the troubles," the sectarian bloodshed between Republicans and Loyalists that is restricted almost entirely to certain neighborhoods within the two cities of Belfast and Londonderry. Golf, as we all know, exerts a benign influence wherever it is played, and the golf communities of Northern Ireland stand well outside the realm of violence and are as peaceful and pleasant as any golf venues we have visited. Politics and religion are eschewed as topics of conversation on the golf course. If you choose to come to Northern Ireland, you will be perfectly safe. Making the initial commitment to travel, in fact, will likely be the toughest part of your entire trip.

We are operating under no illusion that this article will reverse travel patterns into Northern Ireland. Those of you who choose to go, however, will be rewarded. Northern Ireland's two great links, Royal County Down and Royal Portrush (both of which are ranked among the world's twenty-five best golf courses by *Golf Digest*), two of the most memorable golf links we have laid eyes on in our lifetime, were both dead empty during our visit at the very height of the golfing season in late June. We played thirty-six holes a day on each without pause; we had these two great beauties almost to ourselves. If you put aside the "risk" and visit Northern Ireland, you will doubtless be rewarded with an unparalleled experience both in hospitality and the sporting arena.

It is natural, however, to experience a bit of anxiety about your entry into Northern Ireland, particularly if you have not visited before. So what can you expect? Our crossing into the North by car from the Republic recalled the entrance to East Berlin years ago via Checkpoint Charlie. The border is forbidding and heavily fortified, yet in this case we were just waved through without any questions. As we proceeded up the coastal road toward the city of Newcastle and the location of Royal County Down Club, we saw armed troops in camouflaged fatigues at several spots along the route. Soldiers also waved us through a few random checkpoints on the way, but that was the extent of our inconvenience and difficulty. No one even asked to see our passports.

Royal County Down is located on the east coast in the community of Newcastle, while Royal Portrush is located on the extreme northern coast in the resort town of Portrush. The courses are approximately two and a half hours apart by car. These private clubs welcome public play more or less without restrictions. Arrange your game in advance using the phone or fax numbers below, and bring your handicap certificate. If you stay at our recommended hotels (see Glassdrumman Lodge and Bushtown House, below), the staff at each will gladly book your tee times when hotel reservations are made, thus sparing you the burden of doing it yourself. There are no other truly magnificent golf courses within close proximity of Royal County Down, but within fifteen minutes of Royal Portrush you will find a couple of other outstanding courses.

THE GOLF

"Where the mountains of Mourne sweep down to the sea"—these famous lyrics from songwriter Percy French describe **Royal County Down,** which is set at the foot of the Mourne Mountains, a location so legendary and frequently photographed that it ranks—along with the silhouette of the R. & A. clubhouse at St. Andrews and the profile of the lighthouse at Turnberry—among the most recognized symbols of golf in the British Isles. Certain links courses, when examined from a distance, can appear almost featureless, their subtle charms hidden from view until you walk the course from hole to hole and experience the various nuances. Royal County Down, on the other hand, is a mad raving beauty from any point of view, whether from afar or up close. Peter Dobereiner has said: "The links of Royal County Down are exhilarating even without a club in your hand." From an aesthetic viewpoint, we would put Royal County Down up against any golf course in the world. Add to this the hospitality of head pro Kevan Whitson and his staff (see Golf Services, below) and you have the golf experience of a lifetime.

Founded in 1889, Royal County Down is the second oldest golf club in Northern Ireland (Royal Portrush is but one year older). It was designed by Old Tom Morris at a total cost of £4.20 ($7), and alterations were made later by Harry Vardon. Royal County Down, unlike Prestwick in Scotland, for example, essentially remains faithful to Old Tom's original plan.

Royal County Down

The majesty of Royal County Down derives from its views of Dundrum Bay (you can see the Isle of Man across the water on a clear day), the Mourne Mountains, and the purple peaks of Slieve Donard and Slieve Bearnagh, but also from the sense of isolation you feel among the thick gorse and high duneland and the moody skies of Northern Ireland, always threatening a shower and often delivering. Another distinctive physical feature is the long grassy shag that is left uncut on the fringe of the bunkers, giving them the look of Highland cattle.

If you hear quibbles about Royal County Down's difficulty and fairness, then the conversation will certainly be centered on its five blind tee shots. Not only are five drives blind, a number of approach shots to the greens are also at least partially obscured. So make no mistake: unless you are playing with a member willing to lead you around the course, a good caddie is essential for a successful round at Royal County Down. Your tee shots on the blind holes are indeed guided with white stone markers placed into the hillsides, but at times the markers are actually somewhat off-kilter. We found ourselves being directed by our caddie to drive left of the markers on nearly every occasion.

Despite the evasive pins, Royal County Down creates one ecstatic moment after another, starting with the first hole, a 500-yard par five whose fairway grows progressively narrower as it moves between a mountain of prickly gorse and the sandy beach on Dundrum Bay. Number nine, however, is the most amazing hole on the course, requiring you to drive your ball over a high wall of gorse down to the fairway eighty feet below. From the top of this hill there is a memorable view of the ninth fairway, the mountains of Mourne, and the town of Newcastle ringing the sea. The blind tee shot on number eleven seems even more precipitous. When you stand on the tee you are faced with a huge heather-covered dune directly in front and not a hundred yards away; a low-trajectory drive may clear it, but only by a foot or two. The same holds true for the thirteenth hole, the famous dogleg-right, where you want to be left in the fairway to open up your shot to the beautiful green hidden within a grove of trees. Number sixteen simply fascinated us with its 265-yard par four that plays from an elevated tee, over a fairway tucked below in a gully, to an elevated green defended by woods on the left and deep bunkers everywhere else. This hole can play two ways: as a five iron into the fairway or as a driver into the fat part of the green.

Royal County Down is a long course, far longer than Prestwick or Lahinch, two other Old Tom Morris creations, measuring 6,969 yards from the back tees. There is a second course at Royal County Down abutting the Championship Course, a very short, 4,000-yard affair that makes an excellent practice area and that is utilized by children and by families playing in the evening after work.

Royal Portrush is a pursuit for purists. The feeling of remoteness around Portrush coupled with the relative dearth of good hotels and restaurants nearby (see below) means that the golfers who come here do so purely for the sport itself. Royal Portrush is no walk in the park, either. Although considered generally more fair than Royal County Down, we found it a bear. The course has hosted the Senior British Open the last several years, and it was in tournament condition when we played it, with drastically tightened fairways and knee-level rough. Royal Portrush looked flat-out intimidating. Fortunately, the stark and serious profile of the golf course is somewhat deceiving, for the golf club itself has one of the friendliest atmospheres of any in the world. The relaxed flavor is due largely to the delightful Norman Gallagher, the utterly cordial meeter-and-greeter at Royal Portrush who makes all visitors feel so much at home.

The **Dunluce Links Course** at Royal Portrush was designed by H. S. Colt (the architect of Wentworth and Sunningdale in England and the Eden at St. Andrews) and remains the only course outside of Scotland, England, and Wales to host the British Open (1951). Playing here feels like a magical mystery tour. The course starts out simply and straightforwardly enough from the terrace of Dai Stevenson's tidy pro shop, but by the fourth hole you begin to get lost in the distinctive music of Royal Portrush. Legend has it that primitive armies led by the Irish chief of Dunluce and the Viking king of Norway fought on this misty, windswept ground twelve centuries ago. As anyone who has been here will tell you, there is a strange and haunted quality to the landscape.

The holes you will remember most at Royal Portrush on the front side are four (Fred Daly's), with its narrow chute to the green, and five (White Rocks), which demands a massive tee shot over the rough and a most precise approach to the famous cliffside green. After you putt out on five, take a minute and look across the water. From this spectacular vantage point you can see the Giant's Causeway, the celebrated rock formation and geological oddity of Northern Ireland. Greater drama awaits on the back side with number thirteen, which requires two full shots uphill into the wind, and number fourteen, Calamity Corner, the 213-yard par three (you will need at least a three wood to reach it in the wind) with its green perched on the edge of a precipice. Calamity Corner is the most notorious hole at Royal Portrush and easily one of the world's most treacherous and spectacular-looking par threes. Once played, never forgotten. Purgatory, the fifteenth hole, is very tough as well; its fairway drops off the left side into never-never land. And then there's seventeen, which features one of the most comically oversized bunkers we have ever seen situated smack in the middle of the fairway.

Royal Portrush's second layout, the lovely **Valley Course,** is shorter and far less complicated than the club's championship course, yet it nonetheless merits your consideration. Two additional jewels in the immediate vicinity are Portstewart and Castlerock. **Portstewart** has not garnered the royal prefix, but, thanks to the recent completion of seven new holes in the huge sand hills, it is fast emerging from the shadows cast by its more lauded neighbor, Royal Portrush. Portstewart hosted the Irish Amateur in 1992. **Castlerock** is also fine, although its terrain is no match for the drama of Royal Portrush and Portstewart. The most famous hole at Castlerock is the Leg of Mutton, a 200-yard par three with out-of-bounds on the right (a railway line) and on the left (a stream that cuts across the fairway).

Royal County Down Golf Club. 36 Golf Links Road, Newcastle, County Down BT33 0AN Northern Ireland. Tel: 011-44-13967-23314. Fax: 011-44-13967-26281. Credit cards accepted.

• 1889/1908, 1919. Designer: Old Tom Morris/Harry Vardon. Par 73. 6,969 yards. Greens fees: weekday: £60 ($105), weekend: £70 ($123). Caddies. No carts. Restrictions: no public play Saturday, Wednesday after 9 A.M., Sunday before 1 P.M. and after 2:30 P.M. Season: year-round.

• *Annesley Links.* 1995. Designer: Donald Steel. Par 66. 4,681 yards. Greens fees: weekday: £15 ($26), weekend: £20 ($35). Caddies available. No carts. Restrictions: No public play Saturday, Wednesday after 9 A.M., Sundays before 1 P.M. and after 2:30 P.M. Season: year-round.

Royal Portrush Golf Club. Dunluce Road, Portrush, County Antrim BT56 8JQ Northern Ireland. Tel: 011-44-1265-822311. Fax: 011-44-1265-823139. Credit cards accepted.

• *Dunluce Links Course.* 1932. Designer: H. S. Colt. Par 73. 6,782 yards. Greens fees: weekday: £50 ($88), weekend: £60 ($105). Caddies must be arranged in advance. No carts. Season: year-round.

• *Valley Course.* 1932. Designer: H. S. Colt. Par 70. 6,273 yards. Greens fees: weekday: £20 ($35), weekend: £28 ($49). Caddies can be arranged. No carts. Season: year-round.

Portstewart Golf Club. 117 Strand Road, Portstewart, County Londonderry BT55 7PG Northern Ireland. Tel. 011-44-1265-832015. Fax: 011-44-1265-834097. No credit cards.

1907/1991. Designers: A. Gow/Des Giffin. Par 72. 6,752 yards. Greens fees: weekday: £35 ($61), weekend: £50 ($88). Caddies can be arranged. No carts. Restrictions: No public play Saturday; limited tee times on Sunday, Wednesday, and Thursday.

Castlerock Golf Club. 65 Circular Road, Castlerock, County Londonderry BT51 4TJ Northern Ireland. Tel: 011-44-1265-848314. Fax: 011-44-1265-848314. No credit cards.

1901. Designer: Ben Sayers. Par 73. 6,500 yards. Greens fees: weekday: £20 ($35), weekend: £30 ($54). No caddies. No carts. Restrictions: limited public tee times on Friday, Saturday, and Sunday.

GOLF SERVICES

The Emerald Isle is our favorite golfing destination for a slew of reasons, but hospitality might be chief among them. Golf is certainly glorious in Scotland, but there you might be denied access to the clubhouse, or restricted to certain visitors' rooms, or regarded as a reptile by club members. The Irish have a line for everything, and they have a description of golf in Scotland, too: "They want your revenue, but they don't want to let you on the golf course."

At Royal County Down and Royal Portrush we were approached by members and cordially invited to join their games. Royal Portrush allowed us the complete run of the clubhouse—the bar, the restaurant, even the billiards room. Royal County Down's head pro Kevan Whitson and his enthusiastic assistants overwhelmed us with kindness. And at Royal Portrush Norman Gallagher took us under his wing and regaled us with stories of football coach Mike Ditka's memorable visit (Ditka, it seems, used the eighteenth green for putting practice). This generosity of spirit is what you will remember for years to come.

Terrific caddies are always available at Royal County Down, but they need to be arranged in advance at Royal Portrush. We had a less fortunate experience at Royal Portrush, where our older caddie, a tremendously colorful character, uttered some of the most original and obscene material ever to scorch our ears on a golf course. Caddies get £20 ($35), plus a tip of £2 or £3 ($4 or $5). The pro shops at both clubs are modest by PGA West standards but are fully stocked with souvenir shirts and all the necessities. Remember: golf balls are double the U.S. price, so bring as many as you can.

LODGING

A proper tour of these golf courses requires that you spend the night in two different hotels: one near Royal County Down and one near Royal Portrush. As a rule, accommodations in Northern Ireland are not especially good, but based upon our recent visit there are two special hotels that we can recommend with great enthusiasm.

Glassdrumman Lodge is the very best hotel near Royal County Down—and in our opinion the finest hotel in all of Northern Ireland. This enchanting establishment is located about eight miles (twenty minutes) south of the golf course in a quiet country setting near Annalong. This small but truly sophisticated and luxurious ten-room inn is located in a stylishly renovated farmhouse with a fine view of the sea. Glassdrumman Lodge is an ideal sanctuary that offers not only very elegant guest rooms but also the very best cuisine in the entire region. In addition to these accolades, the service staff is so cordial you really must experience it firsthand in order to believe it. The team of polite young women employed at Glassdrumman Lodge could not work harder to make you comfortable. They are truly an impressive group. We stayed in Knockchree, one of the hotel's best rooms, and recommend that you request it. It is large, with a fireplace, lovely sea views, and a large and luxurious private bath. At £125 ($219) per night with breakfast included, it is also a great bargain. Dinner is a special event. You dine at a long communal table and get to know your fellow guests, many of whom are golfers. Owner Joan Hall puts together a five-course dinner every night with a specially selected wine for each course.

The old Slieve Donard Hotel, the famous red-brick pile that actually adjoins the

Royal County Down golf course in Newcastle, must be avoided. During our visit this hotel was overrun with two or three wedding parties and was filled to overflowing. The Slieve Donard also is not in particularly good condition.

Bushtown House in Coleraine does not match the splendor of Glassdrumman Lodge, but it is a reasonable, although far less charming, alternative in the Portrush-Portstewart area. Bushtown House provides friendly service, a decent restaurant, and good proximity to the golf. The best room in Bushtown House is number 17, which goes for £85 ($149) per night. Management will gladly make your tee times at the local courses.

Glassdrumman Lodge. Annalong, County Down, BT34 4RH Northern Ireland. Tel: 011-44-13967-68451. Fax: 011-44-13967-67041. 10 rooms and suites ranging from £95 to £135 ($167 to $237), includes breakfast. Credit cards accepted.

Bushtown House. 283 Drumcroone Road, Coleraine, County Londonderry, Northern Ireland. Tel: 011-44-1265-58367. Fax: 011-44-1265-320909. 40 rooms. Doubles from £70 to £90 ($123 to $158), includes breakfast. Credit cards accepted.

RESTAURANTS

We recommend Glassdrumman Lodge and Bushtown House in part because these two inns also have the best restaurants in their locales. The cuisine at **Glassdrumman Lodge** is sophisticated and ambitious: excellent salmon, turbot, chicken, beef, and fine local cheeses. The five-course dinner costs £28 ($48) per person. The cooking at the two restaurants at Bushtown House, however, is considerably more basic. The menu at the **Grill Bar** features chicken and sirloin steak; dinner here costs £17 ($30) per person. **Stables** is the hotel's à la carte restaurant and features pork ribs and smoked salmon.

Glassdrumman Lodge. Annalong, County Down, BT34 4RH Northern Ireland. Tel: 011-44-13967-68451. Fax: 011-44-13967-67041. Credit cards accepted.

The restaurants at Bushtown House. 283 Drumcroone Road, Coleraine, County Londonderry, Northern Ireland. Tel. 011-44-1265-58367. Fax: 011-44-1265-320909. Credit cards accepted.

NON-GOLF ACTIVITIES

The Northern Ireland Tourism Board prints many elaborate travel brochures for the region, but the fact is that the non-golf activities in the area are not particularly good. Dare we say that if the weather turns bad the non-golfer might be bored? Hiking in the Mourne Mountains is a popular pastime, but Newcastle, despite its friendly residents, does not have much appeal. In the Portrush area the Giant's Causeway and Dunluce Castle are interesting sights. The beach in the Portrush area extends for two miles. Other popular activities include pony trekking and paragliding.

GETTING THERE: Royal County Down and Glassdrumman Lodge are approximately three hours north of Dublin Airport. From the airport, drive north on the N1 through Drogheda and Dundalk, cross the border into Northern Ireland, and at Newry turn right onto the A2, which you follow all the way into Annalong and Newcastle. Glassdrumman Lodge is located just up the hill from the highway. Royal County Down is located on the northern edge of the village of Newcastle.

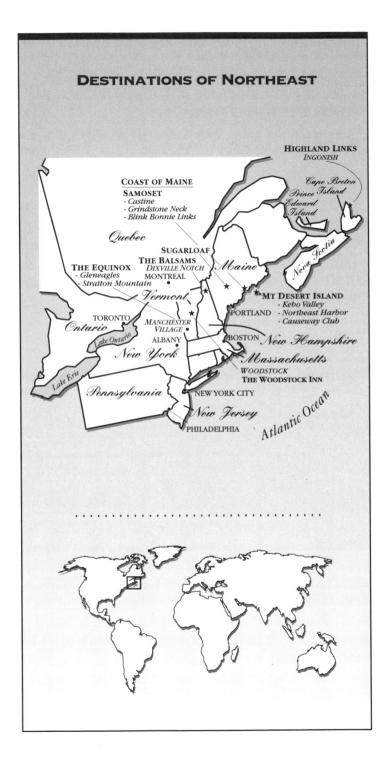

DESTINATIONS OF NORTHEAST

HIGHLAND LINKS
INGONISH

Cape Breton

Prince Edward Island

COAST OF MAINE
SAMOSET
- *Castine*
- *Grindstone Neck*
- *Blink Bonnie Links*

Quebec

Nova Scotia

SUGARLOAF
THE BALSAMS
DIXVILLE NOTCH

THE EQUINOX
- *Gleneagles*
- *Stratton Mountain*

Maine

MONTREAL

Vermont

MT DESERT ISLAND
- *Kebo Valley*
- *Northeast Harbor*
- *Causeway Club*

PORTLAND

TORONTO

Ontario

MANCHESTER VILLAGE

Lake Ontario

ALBANY

BOSTON

New Hampshire

New York

Massachusetts

Lake Erie

WOODSTOCK
THE WOODSTOCK INN

Pennsylvania

NEW YORK CITY

New Jersey

Atlantic Ocean

PHILADELPHIA

NOVA SCOTIA AND THE NORTH-EASTERN UNITED STATES

NOVA SCOTIA AND THE NORTHEASTERN UNITED STATES

It is a country full of evergreen trees, of many silver birches and watery
maples, the grounds dotted with insipid, small red berries, and strewn with
damp and moss-grown rocks—a country diversified with innumerable lakes
and rapid streams, peopled with trout . . . with salmon . . . and other fishes;
the forest resounding at rare intervals with the note of the chickadee, the
blue jay and the woodpecker, the scream of the fish-hawk and the eagle, the
laugh of the loon, and the whistle of ducks along the solitary streams; and at
night with the hooting of owls and howling of wolves. . . . Such is the home of
the moose, the bear, the caribou, the wolf, the beaver, and the Indian.

—Henry David Thoreau, *The Maine Woods*

Maybe it's because Jack Frost nips at your nose a bit harder up here. Maybe it's because people walk and talk faster here. Or maybe it's because Northeasterners work
longer hours and live more closely huddled together than other Americans. But in
no other region of the country is spring—and with it the exhilarating onset of golf
season—so eagerly awaited as in the Northeast. Spring is often short up here, but at
the first hint of warmer weather after the long, confining, gray winter—when the returning birds begin to sing, when tree buds strain to open, and when the morning
sun shimmers off the frosty turf—Northeasterners rush to the attic to dust off the
clubs, tighten up the spikes, put on some bulky clothes, and make a beeline for the
links.

Golf season starts late and ends early in the Northeast, but it is spectacular. The
golfing landscape is at once rocky and rugged—oftentimes the same terrain used by
cross-country skiers—always richly varied, full of vivid colors, and incredibly inviting. These days the region is bursting with golfers. In New England, one out of every
eight persons is a golfer, which is more than enough to strain the limits of most
courses during the summer. For this reason, come autumn, once the children are
back in school and the less hardy have already set off to Florida until springtime,
northeastern courses become especially idyllic. As the setting sun of Indian summer
bathes the northern oaks, maples, and hickories and we realize we have the entire
back nine to ourselves, we wouldn't trade golf in the Northeast for anything in the
world.

So leave the city, the office, and the pager behind, and come with us to another
part of the Northeast. The courses we will take you to are scenic and stately, effortlessly molded into their environment, and refreshingly devoid of real estate development. Our golfing expedition leads us up the magnificent rocky coast of
Maine, where numerous old but exquisitely designed courses offer a wonderfully
unpretentious, idiosyncratic game. Also don't forget to bring your lobster bib!
Cross the border with us and proceed farther north, all the way to the Highlands
Links in Cape Breton Highlands National Park and the Keltic Lodge, whose sublime

cliffside setting gives views of the sea in all directions—this Stanley Thompson course and the view from the lodge are truly worth the journey to this remote Canadian peninsula.

Follow us back to Dixville Notch, New Hampshire (just a two iron from the Canadian border), to the charming Balsams resort course that lies on the pass between two mountains. After meandering through the Maine woods, through birch and pine forests, we reach the tenth and eleventh holes at Sugarloaf, which are two of the most wonderful golf holes in all America. In Vermont wake up to a breakfast of hot buttermilk pancakes and rich maple syrup before beginning your round against the panoramic backdrop of Mount Equinox and the Green Mountains; the redesigned Gleneagles Course is now one of the best mountain courses in New England. Our northeastern adventure also takes us to the quaint, comfortable town of Woodstock, also in Vermont. Looking as if it were straight out of a Currier and Ives print, Woodstock attracts countless antiques hunters every weekend, but it also boasts a lovely, short golf course that is a joy to walk.

The Northeast is the most densely populated region of the United States, yet it offers families innumerable opportunities to escape the cities and crowds and yet still keep busy with fascinating activities. Most of the destinations described below are either seaside or mountain retreats. Nearby you will find superb hiking trails, lovely beaches, old fishing villages, whale watching, lighthouses, covered bridges, Indian burial sites, and Revolutionary War battlegrounds. You can learn how to make maple syrup and apple cider and how to shear the wool off a sheep.

The golf courses in the Northeast are, for the most part, excellent walking courses. Although they will give you a good workout because of their up-and-down terrain, these short-to-moderately-long layouts seldom present unmanageable distances between greens and tees. Even during the height of summer, when the Northeast can get quite steamy, golfers who make their way to mountain or seaside courses will find that it's never too hot to walk. Come mid-September, however, when the Northeast's fall foliage begins to reach its peak, the beauty of the region and the quality of its golf are absolutely sublime.

Nova Scotia

▶THE HIGHLANDS LINKS

	The Golf	Golf Services	Lodging	Restaurants	Non-Golf Activities	Total
Rating	18	15	17	17	17	84

Next June, July, or August—but not in May, when it is still too chilly, nor in September, when the warmest days have decidedly passed—point your compass north, farther north than you habitually do, for a midsummer vacation destination. Just when the heat index in your community has browned the lawn and created ambient air as stifling and heavy as lead, consider Nova Scotia—or, more particularly, Cape Breton

Keltic Lodge

Island, the northernmost tip of Nova Scotia—the perfect tonic to remedy the symptoms of summertime suffocation.

Windblown, sea-tossed Nova Scotia is a region so remarkably quiet, unpopulated, and fresh that it makes the coast of Maine feel like midtown Manhattan. Nova Scotia, in fact, reminds us of a more innocent Maine from decades past, before L. L. Bean brought the masses to Freeport, before Camden sprouted suburban sprawl, and before Bar Harbor suffered its first bout with gridlock. Nova Scotia is brisk and bracing, and its lifestyle is seductively simple. Summer mornings are sweater and windbreaker weather, and the evenings—even in August—are so cool and invigorating that you will crave the hot seafood chowder offered on the menu as the perfect dinner appetizer. Nova Scotia produces yet another valid comparison with the state of Maine: its lobsters, at least those we had the pleasure to sample, were every bit as good.

Canada's Maritime Provinces, jutting northeast into the Atlantic Ocean, are located in their own Atlantic time zone (one hour ahead of Eastern Standard Time) and consist of New Brunswick, Prince Edward Island, Newfoundland (famous for its lovable big black dogs), and Nova Scotia (New Scotland), discovered by the Englishman John Cabot in 1497 but bitterly contested among the English, the Scottish, and the French for over three hundred years. Cape Breton Island, a seven-hour drive from Halifax, the provincial capital of Nova Scotia, was the cultural center of Acadia, the original French colony established in the New World in the early 1600s. A large contingent of French-speaking Cape Breton Acadians were defeated in battle by the English in 1715 and routed from the region. They ultimately established themselves in Louisiana, where their descendants later became known as Cajuns, a famously high-spirited species who immediately began creating their own distinct French culture and cuisine.

Today, Cape Breton Island presents a uniquely Canadian panorama; it is bilingual and bicultural, a delightful mix of Scottish and French traditions. At the wonderful Keltic Lodge, just four hundred yards up the road from the Highlands Links, the young girls behind the reception desk wear tartan kilts, the young waiters in the dining room speak with a Gaelic singsong lilt in their gentle voices, and a bagpiper in full regalia honors a great Scottish custom by performing outside the hotel on the windy hillside every evening before dinner. The dining room, on the other hand, echoes with conversations in French; indeed, just down the road in the town of Cheticamp you'll find French-speaking Acadian arts and crafts communities.

The precipitous decline of the Canadian dollar ($1 Canadian = $0.77 U.S.) means that for Americans, Canada offers one of the best travel bargains in the world today, certainly half the price of a trip to Europe and far less expensive than any comparable experience in the United States. Two examples: a room in the lovely Keltic Lodge, including breakfast and a five-course dinner, cost us just C$265 ($204) per night; the greens fee down the road at the Highlands Links cost just C$48 ($37) for a day ticket in summer and C$38 ($29) in shoulder season, the months between peak and off-season, when fees are comparatively low. In purely financial terms, therefore, Keltic Lodge and the Highlands Links are a steal. So—short of purchasing a summer home along the scenic shores of Nova Scotia or making a currency play by going long with futures on the Canadian dollar—take advantage of the extremely favorable exchange rate by vacationing in Canada and eating more than just one lobster.

The only downside? Getting to Cape Breton Island is an awesome trek. It is a full day's expedition even if you come by plane. We flew into Halifax and then took a commuter flight of one hour's duration to Sydney Airport, only to face a two-hour drive to Ingonish Beach, where Keltic Lodge is situated. We also encountered many considerably more ambitious American travelers, some from as far away as North Carolina and Florida, who drove to Bar Harbor, Maine, took the comfortable overnight ferry to Yarmouth, Nova Scotia, and then drove the entire length of Nova Scotia (ten hours) via the Canso Causeway to Cape Breton Island and Keltic Lodge. Whew! And these folks had small kids in the car.

No matter how you arrive, however, the journey is worth it. Keltic Lodge and Highlands Links are situated within Cape Breton Highlands National Park on Middle Head, a rocky, spruce-and-birch-covered finger of land overlooking the crashing Atlantic surf. The scenery is wild and spectacular, the scent of pine is all-pervasive, and whales, bald eagles, and moose live in and around the area. We did not see any whales, eagles, or moose ourselves, but we could not miss the large red fox trotting nonchalantly up the first fairway of the Highlands Links. This brazen red fox is a well-known local character around the golf course, respected and appreciated by everyone.

THE GOLF

 Do not be misled by the rural and isolated location of the **Highlands Links.** This course—rated four stars by *Golf Digest* and awarded a silver medal by *Golf Magazine*—is one of the thoroughbreds of Canadian golf. Canada's most august golf course architect, Stanley Thompson, the creator of Banff Springs and Jasper Park in Alberta, designed the course in 1937. Thompson was an urbane, literary figure who spoke Gaelic and called the Highlands Links his *Na Beanntan agus a'Mhuir*—his mountains and ocean course. "Nature must always be the architect's model," Thompson said, and the expanse of land he employed on Middle Head is as great a natural golfing ground as exists in North America.

Highlands Links features tight fairways lined with thick forests (a fertile hunting ground for stray golf balls), stupendous views of the mountains and the sea, and deep gullies and swales that produce uneven lies and awkward stances. If you are striking the ball reasonably well, you can get to the beautifully tended greens in fairly good order. Putting is an entirely different matter; putts as short as eight or nine feet can have two or three huge breaks in them.

We hereby offer two special challenges on the Highlands Links for our readers:

1. The owner of this book who simply scores par on the 570-yard, par five seventh hole at Highlands Links (par six for women) will be mailed a sleeve of new Titleists. Drive from the regular tees, play the ball down, and no mulligans, please.

2. The owner of this book who can merely reach the green in two on the 460-yard, par five sixteenth hole will also be sent a sleeve of new Titleists. Just putting the ball on the green in two on a short, 460-yard par five? Piece of cake, right?

All we can say is: wait until you see the place. We wager we won't be giving away too many new golf balls. Full honor system rules prevail, but, just in case, be sure to send your signed scorecard and greens fee receipt to GOLF TRAVEL. Limit: one sleeve of balls per person. Challenge expires July 1, 1998. (The above challenges are made by GOLF TRAVEL, and not the publisher of this book. Broadway

Books will not be responsible for honoring claims made in response to these challenges.)

The Highlands Links is an out-and-back arrangement that measures nearly seven miles from the first tee to the eighteenth green. The actual eighteen holes measure just 6,198 yards from the white tees (6,596 from the blues, which no one appears interested in playing, and 5,664 yards from the reds), but the distances from green to tee are vast, particularly between numbers six and seven, where you traverse the Clyburn River, and between twelve and thirteen, which requires an uphill climb of a quarter mile through the forest and along the riverbed. Elderly golfers, or those attempting to squeeze in a second round of golf in the afternoon, frequently play a ten-hole version of the course: holes one through five, and then, by skipping through the trees, holes fourteen through eighteen. Sadly, the sheer length of the Highlands Links—combined with heavy play and a dire shortage of course rangers—routinely produces six-hour rounds, especially for those who have the misfortune of starting late in the morning or early in the afternoon. By teeing up no later than 8:30 A.M., however, we were able to finish in four and a half hours on the two consecutive days we played.

Playing two (or more) days in a row is a good idea here because the Highlands Links is all about local knowledge, strategy, and touch. Take the fabulous fourth and fifth holes as examples.

The fourth hole—called *Heish O'ʃaʃh* (heap of trouble)—is one of two magical, short par fours at Highlands Links. The hole measures 270 yards uphill to a postage-stamp green guarded in front by two enormous Scottish-style bunkers. Aggressive players, examining this hole from the tee for the first time, will be sorely tempted to go for the green, and almost always the consequences will be dire. The smart idea here is to drive below the green into the right-center of the fairway with a three or four iron and then hit a little half wedge up onto the putting surface. Yet even this plan can seriously backfire if you miss your wedge shot either short or long. This fourth hole is pure genius.

The fifth is a great, quirky, 162-yard downhill par three whose green is protected in front and on the right by one of the Highlands Links's trademark swales. Hitting out of a swale is as bad as hitting out of a deep bunker or a ravine. What you want to do on five is aim your tee shot well left and watch it kick and roll down toward the pin.

The Highlands Links has an extraordinary variety of golf holes: five par fives, five par threes, and two sweet, short par fours: the fourth hole, already noted above, and the 312-yard eighth, which opens with a blind tee shot over the hillside. If you can merely drive it straight on eight and stay out of the trees you are in business, for your second shot is steeply downhill with no more than an eight or nine iron to the green.

This layout also requires muscle. In fact, the very first hole—in front of the modest little clubhouse—is a bear. This tough opener has been likened to the first hole on the King's Course at Gleneagles, Scotland, yet it is longer (408 yards), more challenging, and more precipitously uphill. Even two huge shots can leave you short of the first green.

Notorious number seven provides our special challenge hole on the front side. With forest looming on both sides, this 570-yard monster is the number one handicap hole at Highlands Links. The hole's Gaelic name—*Killiecrankie*—means a "long and narrow pass," precisely the way the golfing landscape appears from the tee. Even if you smash a big drive on this brute and follow it up with an equally big fairway wood, you are still left with an accurate midiron onto the green. When and if you reach the green in regulation with three good shots, you still have to putt—onto a green with more severe undulation than any other on the course. Three putts are reasonable on the seventh green, four a distinct possibility. Good luck!

Highlights on the back side include the eleventh hole, which can be played either as a par four or a par five, depending upon your choice of tee; the wonderful downhill fifteenth, a par five with superb views of the ocean and Ingonish Island out at sea; and our second challenge hole of the round, the 460-yard sixteenth, *Sair Fecht,* or "hard work." The sixteenth is straight uphill. In fact, the second shot on sixteen is almost vertical; from as few as ninety yards out on your approach shot, all you can see is the top of the flagstick. Dear Reader: We profoundly respect your extraordinary strength and golfing ability, but there is no way you can reach this green in two.

Like everyone who has played it, we fell in love with Highlands Links. Admittedly, the first time we played the course in 1995, it suffered from severely dry, hardpan fairways, but such conditions are a thing of the past due to a new sprinkler system installed in 1996. Joe Robinson is a friendly, hardworking, and accommodating head pro who makes a point of learning everyone's name and getting all players on the course. The unusual division of labor at the Highlands Links (it is owned and operated by the Canadian Park System) leaves Mr. Robinson with little actual control over the pace of play or the condition of the course. The bunkers, especially, could benefit enormously from the least little attention. When we played, virtually every bunker was either unraked, filled with dozens of deep footprints, or nearly empty of sand. Highlands Links deserves better.

Highlands Links. Cape Breton Highlands National Park, Box 171, Ingonish Beach, Nova Scotia BOC 1LO. Tel: 902-285-2600. Fax: 902-285-2866. Credit cards accepted.

• 1937. Designer: Stanley Thompson. Par 72. 6,596 yards. 72.3 par rating. 139 slope rating. Greens fees: C$48 ($37) from July-August and weekends in September, C$38 ($29) during shoulder season, the months between peak and off-season, when fees are comparatively low. Walking permitted. Caddies available if prebooked. Carts cost C$32 ($25). Season: May–October.

GOLF SERVICES

Golf services are limited at the Highlands Links. For example, there is no practice range, but locals have devised a unique way of warming up—they hit a couple of drives over the road into the ocean. Caddies (teenage boys from the village) are available if booked in advance, and pull carts are always on hand. The new clubhouse is very modest and stocked with only the bare necessities. During peak season you can get a hot dog at a stand on the tenth tee.

LODGING

The **Keltic Lodge** is the best hotel in Nova Scotia. It commands an unforgettable cliffside setting with views of the sea in all directions. Beyond the rocks looms the sea's wide expanse, and beyond the sea—Europe. Golfers we know have hit balls into the water from this remarkable spot and watched them soar and hang before dropping far below into the ocean. No hotel anywhere is built on more memorable land.

Keltic Lodge offers three types of accommodation: rooms in the original lodge (recommended); rooms in the White Birch Inn, a very bland and uninspiring modern motel that is just one hundred yards down the road from the lodge; and tidy, red-log cottages hidden in clusters among the birch groves. These two- and four-bedroom cottages are ideal for families traveling with children.

The lodge suggests the style and flavor of a Scottish country-house hotel, with its large entry hall, open fires, and rambling ground-floor lounge where pianist Barbara Alcorn performs in the evenings. We stayed in room 210, which, although not opulent, was a comfortable and unadorned room with a view of the sea, a large bath, and a television. The Keltic Lodge opens for the season on the first of June and closes in mid-October. The hotel staff will gladly book your tee times.

Keltic Lodge. Middle Head Peninsula, Ingonish Beach, Nova Scotia, Canada B0C 1L0. Tel: 800-565-0444 or 902-285-2880. Fax: 902-285-2859. 101 rooms and cottages. In high season, doubles range from C$265 to C$285 ($204 to $219) and include breakfast and a four-course dinner. A golf package is available. Credit cards accepted.

RESTAURANTS

The large and attractive dining room at the **Keltic Lodge** features fabulously fresh seafood—mussels, scallops, seafood chowder, absolutely sublime oysters, and lobsters that are slightly more sweet to the palate than those plucked from the waters of Maine. We found the decent Nova Scotia wines from the local Jost Vineyard worth a try if only because the Keltic Lodge wine list is so limited—the only other wines available by the glass are Gallo. Because the Keltic Lodge serves as a stopover for many tour groups traveling through the region, the dining room is often crowded and the service, while friendly and sincere, can be slow. The dress code for men calls for jackets or "smart casual." A four-course, prix-fixe menu costs C$40 ($31).

Dining room at the Keltic Lodge. Middle Head Peninsula, Ingonish Beach, Nova Scotia, Canada B0C 1L0. Tel: 800-565-0444 or 902-285-2880. Fax: 902-285-2859. Credit cards accepted.

NON-GOLF ACTIVITIES

Nova Scotia attracts a hearty breed of active hikers and bicyclists who find the region heaven on earth. An extraordinary (1.2 miles) trail begins just behind the hotel and leads to the rocky tip of Middle Head. The wealth of activities on the hotel property or in the immediate area include tennis and swimming in the hotel's heated outdoor pool, exploring Cape Breton Highlands National Park via the world-famous Cabot Trail (considered one of the most beautiful drives in North America), visiting the Alexander Graham Bell historic site in Baddeck, and whale-watching cruises.

GETTING THERE: From Halifax Airport, take the TransCanada Highway toward Cape Breton/Truro/New Glasgow/Antigonish. Take the Englishtown Ferry exit (exit 11), which will be on your left. You will come to a short ferry ride (cost: C$1.75, $1.35). Following the ferry, you simply stay on the same road (Cabot Trail) all the way into Ingonish and the Keltic Lodge. The drive should take roughly five hours.

Maine

▶THE COAST

OFF THE BEATEN TRACK

	The Golf	Golf Services	Lodging	Restaurants	Non-Golf Activities	Total
Rating	18	14	17	17	17	83

Picture the dramatic scenery along the sharply etched rocky coast of Maine and we will wager that golf is not the first— nor even the second or third—image that springs to mind. The Maine coastline is justifiably ranked among the most magnificent in the world, yet the Maine golf scene has not yet earned a prominent place in our collective consciousness. We all think of heavenly lobster dinners, homemade blueberry pie, roaring wood

Asticou Inn, Northeast Harbor

fires on August evenings, L. L. Bean, George Bush flying along in his cigarette boat, and ruddy-looking East Coast—establishment types in Top Siders fussing with sailing paraphernalia. But golf? For the uninitiated, for whom Phoenix or Florida may be the center of the universe, golf on the Arctic Circle may seem about as likely.

But during that enchanting, all-too-brief season from June through August when Maine truly becomes "Vacationland" (the official state motto), the Pine Tree State (its official nickname) provides the adventurous golfer with a host of experiences unlike any other. At its best, the Maine game combines elements of antiquity, eccentricity, and downright nostalgia. The pure simplicity of it all—the rudimentary facilities ("clubhouse" may be far too grand a word) and the very low greens fees—may well remind you of your early childhood and the course where you first learned the game and fell in love with it. Those were the days before "resort golf," days when locker rooms were just that and not luxury digs swathed in sheets of Italian marble.

The most intriguing golf in Maine is also a step back in time. Several courses noted below date from the late nineteenth and early twentieth centuries and are virtually unchanged since then, museum pieces from the hickory-shaft era designed by the likes of Willie Park, Jr., the British Open champ of 1887 and 1889, and Donald Ross of Pinehurst Number 2 fame. And as far as eccentricity goes, well, some layouts are nine holes with double greens and shared fairways, while another course had, until very recently, just fifteen playable holes. At the peculiar Blink Bonnie Links in Sorrento, we saw a man on the course playing in knee-high rubber boots, as if he had just come off a lobster boat.

This section does not focus on George Bush country in southern Maine but on the far more scenic central coast region near Acadia National Park and Mount Desert Island. All of the courses are within easy driving distance of Acadia. If you have a week to spare for your holiday in Maine, consider splitting your time between Acadia and Samoset (reviewed separately), with five nights at the historic Asticou Inn on Mount Desert Island and a couple of nights farther down the coast at the Samoset Resort in Rockport.

Acadia is one of the most glorious and popular national parks in the United States, attracting more than three million visitors every year. The largest part of Acadia occupies approximately half the total area of horseshoe-shaped Mount Desert Island, hence, the two names—Acadia National Park and Mount Desert Island—are more or less used interchangeably. The island's commercial center is Bar Harbor, the fashionable nineteenth-century summer enclave of Rockefellers and Vanderbilts, now somewhat blighted by the seasonal tourist trade and its unquenchable thirst for T-shirts, ice cream, and inexpensive trinkets to appease Junior. Rockefeller and du Pont heirs still come to Mount Desert Island, but they can be found in the shingled cottages of Northeast Harbor and Southwest Harbor, villages that far better exemplify the traditional flavor and elegance of downeast Maine. Northeast Harbor, in particular, can feel like a country extension of Madison Avenue on a sleepy Sunday, with its coffee bars, antique shops, and chic restaurants filled with well-dressed guests poring over *The New York Times.*

THE GOLF

There are six unforgettable courses worth your attention in the immediate vicinity, three on Mount Desert Island itself and another three off the island yet within an hour's drive of Northeast Harbor. The on-island courses include the Kebo Valley Golf Club in the hills above Bar Harbor, the Northeast Harbor Golf Club, just minutes from the Asticou Inn, and the Causeway Club at Southwest Harbor. The mainland courses include stunning Grindstone Neck in Winter Harbor, eccentric Blink Bonnie Links in Sorrento, and the historic Castine Golf Club in the simply exquisite coastal village of Castine. All have spectacular ocean views, with the exception of the course at Kebo Valley, which plays in the shadow of Cadillac Mountain, and the course at Northeast Harbor Club, which wends its way through an enchanted forest. Traffic is wonderfully light everywhere, save again for Kebo Valley, which likely sees more action in a week than the others do during the entire season. Each of these eminently walkable courses is open to the public with delightfully low greens fees ranging from $15 to $25 and, in the case of Kebo Valley, $25 to $50, depending upon when you visit.

Kebo Valley Golf Club was established in 1884 at the height of the Gilded Age when Bar Harbor was the last word in American resorts. It remains the only truly tournament-quality course in the area. In addition, it is the most popular on Mount Desert Island and provides the fullest services: electric carts, a well-staffed clubhouse with food and bar service, and rental clubs (if nearly as antique as the course itself). As elsewhere in Maine, its historic architectural features have been preserved with care. There are lovely vistas of mountains and forest all around. The magic at Kebo begins on the fifth, a 500-yard par five with three blind shots to a shaded green hidden beyond a tranquil stream. The fifteenth is a beautiful, little par three that plays through the trees to a level green, and the seventeenth has to be seen to be believed. The elevated green is guarded by a monster bunker that looks like a mistake—it's a hundred yards across. President Taft reportedly took a twenty-seven on the seventeenth in 1911!

The aristocratic **Northeast Harbor Golf Club,** with its posh clientele, paneled clubhouse, and distinguished lineage, reflects the utter gentility of its community. We played the 5,430-yard, par sixty-nine layout with representative members: a couple from Newport who sail up the coast every summer to their island home. The Northeast Harbor Club has been compared—with reason—to Pine Valley and the Country Club in Brookline, Massachusetts. One writer has called it the best course in Maine, while another singled out its fifth hole as the best short par four in all New England. The first nine was laid out by J. G. Thorpe in 1895. Donald Ross added a second nine in 1920 that fell into disuse during World War II. Geoffrey Cornish, New England's premier architect, restored holes ten through fifteen in 1974. Three new holes have been built to bring the total up to eighteen, but, as we went to press, golfers using carts are required to park (to prevent driving through "reserved" land) after hole fifteen and walk the next two holes with whatever clubs they need. Carts, lessons, and rental clubs are available at this exquisite hidden gem.

The **Causeway Club** at Southwest Harbor is a short, nine-hole layout dating from 1930 that plays just 2,302 yards with five par fours and four par threes. The ocean views are not as dramatic as at the courses discussed below, but this is a lovely little course with two holes playing directly over the water.

Grindstone Neck in exclusive Winter Harbor is one of the few courses we have visited anywhere in the world with an ocean view on every hole, and the views—of Frenchman's Bay and the mountains of Acadia—are breathtaking. Given this spectacular setting, Grindstone Neck is as undiscovered as they come. We played on a Sunday morning at the height of the season and saw a total of perhaps seven or eight other golfers. Established in 1891, Grindstone measures 3,095 yards with one par five, one par three, and a collection of par fours ranging from 317 to over 400 yards in length. The third hole is its crown jewel: a sharp dogleg-left from an oceanside tee to an oceanside green. This beautiful course is well worth the drive from Mount Desert Island.

Blink Bonnie Golf Links in Sorrento makes Grindstone Neck appear positively up-to-date. No carts, no balls for sale, and no telephone until just recently (and the phone number we have might be different next year because the club cancels phone service in winter), but you are certain to be mesmerized the moment you see the place. The haunting mood music of Sorrento is linked to the dramatic terrain. The golf course was cut in 1919 from a deeply wooded ravine leading down to the ocean, midway between Hancock Point and Winter Harbor, exposing a romantic landscape of enormous oaks, granite beaches, and ocean waves. The magic helps you accept the quirkiness of the course: its uneven conditioning; the slow, soft, feather-bed greens; and the rather dangerous double fairways. Every hole is a beauty, particularly the second with its waterside green, and the seventh, a challenging, downhill, 170-yard par three. Blink Bonnie, by the way, means "beautiful view."

The **Castine Golf Club** also has thoroughbred bloodlines. It was founded in 1887 by wealthy summer residents who got seriously ambitious in 1921 by inviting Willie Park, Jr., the two-time British Open champ, to design a permanent nine-hole layout. Park's own description of Castine still fits: "The course laid out by me will equal the best in this country. The location is ideal. The views are exceptionally fine, and the air is bracing and clear." The course does not actually abut the water; it occupies a hillside above the immaculate village and its storybook harbor. Founded by French traders in 1613 and fought over by the British and Americans during both the Revolution and the War of 1812, Castine boasts an incredible inventory of perfectly preserved eighteenth-century homes. Budget time before or after your game to explore its nooks and crannies, especially the lighthouse and park at Dyces Head. One can only fantasize about an entire summer in Castine, enjoying its sailing and village life and strolling up the hill to the Willie Park course in the afternoons.

Kebo Valley Golf Club. Eagle Lake Road, Bar Harbor, ME 04609. Tel: 207-288-3000. Fax: 207-288-3378. Credit cards accepted.

• 1884. Designer: H. C. Leeds. Par 70. 5,925 yards. 69.0 par rating. 129 slope rating. Greens fees: $25 to $50. Walking permitted. No caddies. Carts cost an additional $30. Season: May 15–October 31.

Northeast Harbor Golf Club. Sargeant Drive, Northeast Harbor, ME 04662. Tel: 207-276-5335. Credit cards accepted.

• 1895/1920/1974. Designers: J. G. Thorpe/Donald Ross/Geoffrey Cornish. Par 69. 5,430 yards. 67.8 par rating. Greens fees: $25 to $40. Walking encouraged. Caddies available if arranged in advance. Carts cost an additional $30. Season: May 15–October 15.

Causeway Club. Fernald Point Road, Southwest Harbor, ME 04679. Tel: 207-244-3780. Credit cards accepted.

• 1930. Designer: Alonzo Yates. Par 32. 2,302 yards. 30.4 par rating. 95 slope rating. Greens fees: $15 to $24. No caddies. No carts. Season: May 1–November 1.

Grindstone Neck Golf Course. Grindstone Avenue, Winter Harbor, ME 04693. Tel: 207-963-7760. Credit cards accepted.

• 1891. Designers: Alex Findlay, Charles Clarke. Par 36. 3,095 yards. Greens fees: weekday: $22, weekend: $25. Walking permitted. Carts available. Season: April 1–November 1.

Blink Bonnie Golf Links. Box 363, Sorrento, ME 04677. Tel: 207-422-3930. No credit cards.

• 1916. Designer: unknown. Greens fees: weekday, $15; weekend, $20. No caddies. No carts. Season: May 15–October 15. 9 holes.

Castine Golf Club. Battle Avenue, Castine, ME 04421. Tel: 207-326-8844. Credit cards accepted.

• 1887. Designer: Willie Park, Jr. Par 35. 2,977 yards. 68.1 par rating. 116 slope rating. Greens fees: $22 (and only $12 after 4 P.M.). Walking permitted. No caddies. Carts cost an additional $25. Season: May 15–October 15.

GOLF SERVICES

Golf services are uneven, to say the least, among the various courses we visited. A couple of the courses—Kebo Valley and Northeast Harbor Club—offer rental clubs, lessons, carts, and a distinguished clubhouse, while another course—the charming and eccentric Blink Bonnie Links— does not even offer golf balls for sale. Our advice is to bring along all the equipment you might need so that nothing prohibits you from enjoying this marvelous combination of spectacular scenery and truly unique and unspoiled golf.

LODGING

The best place to stay on Mount Desert Island is the **Asticou Inn** at Northeast Harbor, a 115-year-old inn that is several degrees more elegant than any other hotel in the region. It has a beautiful hillside setting overlooking yachts in the harbor, a handsome interior with Persian carpets and antique furnishings, and the island's prettiest dining room, with bright Oriental wallpaper, Windsor chairs, and, again, that spectacular view of the water. The best guest rooms are oriented toward the views, but all are spacious, uncluttered, and finely appointed. The suites feature sitting rooms and private balconies. Service throughout the hotel and restaurant is excellent. The Asticou Inn is open from May 16 to October 15 and operates on the modified American plan with full breakfast and dinner included in the room rate. It is recommended that men wear jacket and tie at dinner.

Asticou Inn. P.O. Box 408, Northeast Harbor, Maine 04662. Tel: 800-258-3373 or 207-276-3344. Fax: 207-276-3373. 45 rooms and suites ranging in price from $264 to $349 in July and August and $184 to $259 from May through June and from September until the end of the golf season. Rates are based on double occupancy and include full breakfast and dinner. Open from early May to mid-October. Credit cards accepted.

R E S T A U R A N T S

You need step no further than the dining room of the **Asticou Inn** for a great dinner. Specialties include filet mignon and lobster in a *beurre blanc* sauce over angelhair pasta, and most entrées range in price between $16 and $25. The lovely formal dining room overlooking the water is entirely inviting. Whether you stay at the inn or not, do stop by for dinner. Reservations required.

And, of course, no travel story about Maine is worth the paper it's printed on without recommending a special spot to dine on fresh lobster. That place is the **Tidal Falls Lobster Pound** just outside Hancock and about ten minutes from Blink Bonnie Golf Links, where the view of fast-flowing, saltwater rapids is as fine as the food. Bring your own wine, salad, and dessert, and grab a picnic table overlooking the reversing falls while your lobster is being prepared. Open only from 5 P.M. until 9 or 10 P.M. A lovely setting and wonderful, fresh seafood!

Another day, plan to spend the day in Acadia Park and make sure to have lunch at **Jordan Pond House.** After your tour of Acadia, the restaurant provides a lovely spot to sit, relax, and have an excellent meal in an absolutely gorgeous setting. Famous for its homemade popovers, Jordan Pond House also serves excellent salads and sandwiches at lunch (when it can be quite crowded, as it is the only place to get a bite to eat in the park). Others love to come to Jordan Pond House for tea later in the afternoon. Regardless of whether you stop in for lunch, afternoon tea, or an early dinner, make sure afterward to take the time to wander up the wide carriage roads heading into the nearby woods. This is a glorious place to enjoy the whole afternoon.

Asticou Inn. PO Box 408, Northeast Harbor, Maine 04662. Tel: 800-258-3373 or 207-276-3344. Fax: 207-276-3373. Credit cards accepted.

Tidal Falls Lobster Pound. Tidal Falls Road, East Hancock, ME 04640. Tel: 207-422-6818. No credit cards.

Jordan Pond House. Park Loop Road, Acadia National Park, ME 04675. Tel: 207-276-3316. Fax: 207-288-2420. Credit cards accepted.

NON-GOLF ACTIVITIES (17)

You could spend a big chunk—if not all—of your free time in Acadia Park, driving the loop, stopping in at some of the beaches, and strolling or biking on its fifty-seven-mile network of gravel carriage roads constructed by John D. Rockefeller in 1915 (and conveniently accessible right behind Jordan Pond House). Acadia Park is a mecca for hikers, and you can pick up a detailed map of various hikes at the visitors' center; there are more than two dozen trails, of varying degrees of difficulty, within the park. Another day, learn to kayak with one of the local kayaking tour companies—no previous paddling experience required!

GETTING THERE: To get to the Asticou Inn from Bangor Airport, turn right onto Union Street after exiting the airport. Take I-95 South, exiting to I-395 East toward Bar Harbor. Then get onto Route 1A South, again, toward Bar Harbor. Proceed south on 1A through Ellsworth, where Route 1A becomes Route 3, following signs for Bar Harbor. As you come onto Mount Desert Island, bear to the right at the fork and onto Route 102. Proceed on 102 until you come to a traffic light. Turn left onto Route 3/198 and proceed. The Sound will be on your right. Continue straight on Route 3/198 toward Northeast Harbor. When nearing Northeast Harbor, you will be at the top of a hill overlooking the harbor and the outer island (a large stone-walled home will be on the left). At the bottom of this hill, take a left onto Route 3 toward Bar Harbor. The inn sits at the head of the harbor approximately five hundred yards on the right.

►SAMOSET

ROCKPORT

	The Golf	Golf Services	Lodging	Restaurants	Non-Golf Activities	Total
Rating	17	16	16	17	16	**82**

Samoset Resort

The very pleasant Samoset Resort is located just outside Rockport, Maine, on a rocky, 230-acre peninsula that juts out into the waters of Penobscot Bay. The golf course at Samoset—rated by *Golf Digest* second in the state of Maine (after Sugarloaf) and twenty-sixth among America's seventy-five best resort courses—was completely rerouted in 1995, when the course's two weak holes (numbers ten and eleven) were eliminated altogether and replaced by two very good golf holes. The fresh Maine lobster served in Marcel's, the resort's showcase dining room, makes Samoset all the more worthy of a return visit. We were not disappointed on any score; Samoset exudes an appealing, low-key, family-resort flavor, while its golf course has been admirably improved.

THE GOLF

The terrific holes at **Samoset** that trace the rocky edges of Penobscot Bay have not been altered. Number three is a 239-yard par three to an uphill double green shared with the sixth hole. Four is the great 485-yard dogleg-left around the rocky bay. And five is an excellent, short, 324-yard par four that plays much longer because the hole is entirely uphill. Water comes into play on the new holes, ten and eleven. The tenth requires a tee shot to a landing area just short of the lake, and eleven is all carry, 143 yards across the water. Fourteen and fifteen, however, both par fours, remain Samoset's two best holes. Fourteen features a blind tee shot over a hill and down to the water's edge, and fifteen plays along the entire length of the bay. Samoset has three sets of tees. From the blues, the course measures 6,515 yards (slope 128), from the whites 6,021 yards (slope 122), and from the reds 5,432 yards (slope 122).

Samoset Resort. 220 Warrenton Street, Rockport, Maine 04856. Tel: 800-341-1650 or 207-594-2511. Fax: 207-594-0722. Credit cards accepted.

• 1974. Designer: Bob Elder. Par 70. 6,515 yards. 70.3 par rating. 128 slope rating. Greens fees: $75 (resort guests), $95 (public), cart included. Walking permitted. No caddies. Season: Mid-April–early November.

GOLF SERVICES

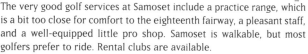

The very good golf services at Samoset include a practice range, which is a bit too close for comfort to the eighteenth fairway, a pleasant staff, and a well-equipped little pro shop. Samoset is walkable, but most golfers prefer to ride. Rental clubs are available.

LODGING

The three concrete, motel-like block buildings where guests stay at **Samoset** look rather stark from the exterior, while room interiors are by no means the height of luxury. All rooms, however, are spacious, comfortable, clean, and well furnished. The best rooms provide nice views of the bay. During high season rates range from $230 to $305 for a double. Condominiums and town houses are also available.

Samoset Resort. 220 Warrenton Street, Rockport, Maine 04856. Tel: 800-341-1650 or 207-594-2511. Fax: 207-594-0722. 150 rooms and suites, 72 condominiums, and 34 town houses. Doubles cost $230 to $255 and suites are $305. Credit cards accepted.

RESTAURANTS

Marcel's is one of the most attractive restaurants on the central Maine coast. It features excellent lobster and other seafood, fine service, and a very good selection of wines. Jackets are required. Dinner for two with wine and tip at Marcel's costs approximately $100. The casual restaurant at Samoset is the **Breakwater Café,** ideal for breakfast or lunch. A small grill is located in the golf shop.

The restaurants at Samoset Resort. 220 Warrenton Street, Rockport, Maine 04856. Tel: 800-341-1650 or 207-594-2511. Fax: 207-594-0722. Credit cards accepted.

NON-GOLF ACTIVITIES

Other activities at Samoset include tennis, swimming, and an outstanding indoor fitness center with indoor pool, Nautilus equipment, aerobic classes, and massage. Many fine shops may be found in the picturesque town of Camden, which is just a ten-minute drive away.

GETTING THERE: From the Portland Airport, take 295 North, which becomes 95 North, to exit 22 (Brunswick exit). Head north on Route 1 for about an hour and fifteen minutes. In Rockland (not Rockport!) take a right at the light at Waldo Avenue (you will see a VIP Auto Center). The Samoset Resort is about a half mile down Waldo Avenue.

▶SUGARLOAF
PURE GOLF IN THE MAINE WOODS

	The Golf	Golf Services	Lodging	Restaurants	Non-Golf Activities	Total
Rating	19	17	15	13	16	80

We include the Sugarloaf USA resort in the Carrabassett Valley of central Maine in this book for one reason: those of you who truly love the game of golf will want to enjoy a tryst with the gorgeous golf course here again and again. For us, it was love at first sight. Sugarloaf's Robert Trent Jones, Jr., golf course is so dramatic and so stunningly beautiful that it ranks among the best tracks that we at GOLF TRAVEL have ever played.

Sugarloaf Golf Club

Sugarloaf's fame as a resort rests in its ski operations, among the most awesome in the East. If you come up to Sugarloaf (two and a half hours north of Portland) for a day or two of golf, however, be advised that the roads up the ski mountain are rough and dusty. (Take the Jeep and leave the Mercedes at home!) Be advised also that while the entire Sugarloaf summertime operation is run in a very friendly and professional manner, the resort itself does not nearly match the splendor of its wonderful mountain setting. Golf travelers who head in this direction should prepare for average accommodations in dull ski condos and forgettable food in a handful of unremarkable resort restaurants.

There is some talk among the movers and shakers at Sugarloaf of adding a second golf course on an adjacent piece of property. This is a great idea. But before carrying it through, let's hope the resort owners come to a fuller appreciation of what an exceptional, year-round property they have and upgrade the resort's lodging and dining facilities.

THE GOLF 19

Sugarloaf's tenth and eleventh holes are two of the greatest golf holes in America. Both are included in the course's String of Pearls, a famous sequence of six holes on the back nine that runs alongside the rock-strewn Carrabassett River. These holes are the highlights of the Sugarloaf golf experience, but rest assured that this entire course is a thing of exceptional beauty. The condition of the fairways and greens is utterly immaculate, the mountain and river views are exceptional, and the hardworking golf staff could not be more accommodating. The Sugarloaf golf course—a vision of white birch, towering pine, and the occasional 1,400-pound moose trotting across the fairway—is honestly so good that it makes you forgive and forget, at least temporarily, the resort's lackluster food and lodging. Honestly, every hole offers an unusual challenge. If pure golf is your passion, you will have no complaints at all with Sugarloaf. But try to hit it straight, for balls hit into the deep woods are ancient history.

Ten and eleven alone are worth the greens fee. The tenth is a short (278 yards), downhill par four that is actually reachable from the mountaintop tee for big hitters. Be careful not to hit it too far, however, because the Carrabassett River is hidden behind the green. After you putt out on this hole, you then ascend another summit to number eleven, Sugarloaf's signature hole, a 190-yard par three straight down to a large green protected on the left by the boulder-strewn river.

Number fourteen, a 370-yard par four that doglegs to the left, is yet another beauty. Drive the ball on fourteen with a long iron, and hit your second shot over the rocky riverbed onto the green. Seventeen and eighteen are two tough finishing holes—both are long, uphill par fours.

Sugarloaf Golf Club. RR 1, Box 5000, Kingfield, ME 04947. Tel: 207-237-6812 or 207-237-2000. Fax: 207-237-6985. Credit cards accepted.

• 1986. Designer: Robert Trent Jones, Jr. Par 72. 6,451 yards. 70.8 par rating. 137 slope rating. Greens fees: $69 in high season ($45 through June 30 and for part of October). Carts cost an additional $16 per person. Walking permitted. Caddies available upon request. Season: mid-May to mid-October.

GOLF SERVICES 17

Golf services are excellent, with a good practice area and a golf school that offers two-day to five-day programs. Because of the length and steepness of the course, Sugarloaf strongly recommends that all golfers take a cart. The clubhouse is not an elaborate facility.

LODGING 15

There are two types of accommodations at Sugarloaf: the hotel rooms in the **Sugarloaf Inn,** which is badly in need of refurbishment, and the condominium units that are spread out in several rambling buildings at the foot of Sugarloaf Mountain. We stayed in unit 388, which features a kitchen, sitting room, bedroom, and bath on the ground floor and a second bedroom in the loft area. This unit is functional and well equipped but not particularly attractive.

Sugarloaf USA. RR 1, Box 5000, Kingfield, ME 04947. Tel: 800-843-5623 or 207-237-2000. Fax: 207-237-3052. 42 rooms in the Sugarloaf Inn; 205 suites and condominiums. In summertime, doubles rooms range from $100 to $122. Make sure to ask about golf packages. Credit cards accepted.

RESTAURANTS (13)

There are a variety of dining options at Sugarloaf or nearby. Two restaurants open during the summer—the Sugarloaf Brewing Company and Gepetto's—are managed independently of the resort, and offer some of the better fare available. Although its menu, consisting of nachos, burgers, and pastas, is somewhat unambitious, we enjoyed the **Sugarloaf Brewing Company** best of all. Dinner for two with beer will run approximately $50. Another casual spot, **Gepetto's** serves select beef cuts, a variety of pastas, stir-frys, and seafood entrées ranging in price from $10 to $17.

Although the view of the mountain from the dining room is inspiring, the food served in **Seasons,** the restaurant located in the Sugarloaf Inn, was disappointing. Dinner entrées, ranging in price from $15 to $25, include duck, seafood, and Maine lobster. Every night but Saturday, Seasons offers a special entrée priced at $10. **Strokes** in the modest golf clubhouse serves sandwiches and drinks.

The restaurants at Sugarloaf USA. RR 1, Box 5000, Kingfield, ME 04947. Tel: 207-237-2000 (Seasons and Strokes); 207-237-2211 (Sugarloaf Brewing Company); 207-237-2192 (Gepetto's). Fax: 207-237-3052 (for Seasons and Strokes only). Credit cards accepted.

NON-GOLF ACTIVITIES (16)

During the summer, non-golf activities include biking, hiking, fishing, and working out in a small indoor fitness club. The ski season remains Sugarloaf's busiest time of year.

GETTING THERE: Take the Maine Turnpike from Portland to the Auburn exit and follow Route 4 North through Farmington, then pick up Route 27 and proceed through Kingfield to Sugarloaf.

New Hampshire

►THE BALSAMS

A DONALD ROSS GEM IN THE MOUNTAINS

	The Golf	Golf Services	Lodging	Restaurants	Non-Golf Activities	Total
Rating	18	16	14	18	17	83

One of the true highlights of any golf tour of New England should be the fun and fanciful Panorama golf course at the charming Balsams resort in beautiful, but very remote, Dixville Notch, New Hampshire. Located four hours due north of Boston and just thirteen miles south of the Canadian border, Dixville Notch, as followers of political campaigns know, is the first voting precinct in the United States to report in presidential elections. Among the first to cast their ballots are employees of the Balsams, which occupies a stunning site in Dixville overlooking the "notch," or pass, between two large mountains.

The scenery is spectacular—truly New England at its best—but we quickly grew to love the Balsams because of the wonderful golf, the absolutely superb food, and the outgoing

The Balsams

family spirit that prevail here among guests (many of whom return year after year), employees, and management. The Balsams is owned by four working partners (one caddied at the Balsams when he was a kid), who are very visible in the resort's everyday routines. Obvious friendships develop between returning guests and management, so a summer holiday at the Balsams can feel like a reunion.

When we first entered the hotel, we weren't quite sure what to expect. The main hotel building represents an odd marriage of architectural styles—half Italian, half New England. The entry area looked a tad dreary, the corridor leading to our room was dark and dimly lit, and the room we stayed in, number 9, was small and spartan. Our concerns later gave way to pleasure, however, once we got our bearings on the golf course and warmed up to the Balsams' charms.

THE GOLF

The aptly named **Panorama Course** is a Donald Ross masterpiece dating from 1912 that we rate among the best resort and public-access courses in all New England. It is on a par with the famous Taconic Golf Club in Williamstown, Massachusetts, but it is better, in our estimation, than the newly reconfigured Gleneagles Course at the Equinox in Vermont, the course at the Woodstock Inn Country Club in Woodstock, Vermont, and the course overlooking Penobscot Bay at the Samoset Resort in Maine.

The Panorama Course is located 2,100 feet above sea level on the slopes of Mount Keyser, about two and a half miles from the hotel on a road that winds its way up through the woods. Once you arrive at the clearing at the top, you will find the historic stone clubhouse with its huge fireplace and great mountain views that look out in every direction. Canada is just to the north and Vermont only a few miles to the west. This is an inspiring site for a golf course. There's not a home or condo anywhere within miles, just rolling hills, majestic mountain scenery, and all those diabolical Donald Ross greens in the shape of inverted saucers.

The historic golf courses of New England, much like those in Scotland, are a joy to play because they conform so nicely to the existing terrain. They bear little resemblance to the name-brand, look-alike courses that have gobbled up much of our nation's countryside. Along with its great charm and personality, the Panorama Course is long (6,804 yards from the blues) and offers the highest slope rating of any course in New Hampshire (136). Low handicappers owe it to themselves to play it from the tips at least once. Thanks to the American plan at the Balsams—where you pay one fixed daily charge for room, meals, and all resort activities—you can play the course as often as you like without worrying about the greens fees. Carts are not mandatory, but we preferred to ride given the layout's very steep terrain. The green on the eighteenth hole, for example, is 142 feet above the tee.

One of the most memorable holes on the front nine is number three, a 403-yard par four with a blind second shot over a massive bunker down to a sunken green. The fourth hole (432 yards) features a blind tee shot over the hill; look through the periscope on the tee to make sure the fairway is clear. Number six is a long, uphill par five, while the ninth is short and tricky, just 316 yards from the white tees, with water to the left and thick woods to the right. Great holes on the back side include eleven, which provides a superb view from its elevated tee; the dramatic twelfth, where a gully lies between the elevated tee and green; thirteen, which requires another blind drive into the wind; and the finishing hole, a long, 560-yard march straight uphill. Weather and wind can be factors as well. We played during mid-August and contended with low temperatures (54 degrees), a cold breeze, and intermittent showers.

Golfers who are not staying at the Balsams can play the Panorama Course for $80 from July to September and $65 the rest of the golf season. The Balsams also operates an executive course, the **Coashaukee Course,** adjacent to the main hotel building; the day ticket rate for public play on this nine-hole track is $25.

The Balsams. Route 26, Dixville Notch, NH 03576. Tel: 603-255-4961. Fax: 603-255-4221. Credit cards accepted.

• *Panorama Course.* 1912. Designer: Donald Ross. Par 72. 6,804 yards. 73.9 par rating. 136 slope rating. Greens fees: included in resort rates; public: $80 (July–September), $65 (low season). No caddies. Walking permitted, but carts strongly recommended. Season: late May to mid-October.

• *Coashaukee Course.* 1965. Designer: James Smith. Par 32. 1,917 yards. Greens fee: included in resort rates; public: $25 (day ticket). No caddies. Walking permitted. Season: late May to mid-October.

GOLF SERVICES

Golf services at the Balsams are very good. Head pro Bill Hambelin could not be friendlier or more easygoing. There is a nice practice range, a fleet of golf carts, a decent pro shop, a historic clubhouse for lunch, and a fine staff of baggage boys.

LODGING

Our disappointment with our room at the **Balsams** never did diminish with time. Tiny room number 9 was barely large enough to accommodate our suitcases. Once we got settled we found the room reasonably comfortable with a nice bath, but, like all of the other rooms at the Balsams, it had no television. The walls were so thin that we clearly overheard conversations coming from the room next door. In high season, rates range from $175 to $205 per person per night and include room, three meals a day, and all resort activities. The very best rooms at the Balsams are the extremely large Tower Suites ($625 per couple). Given the remote location of the Balsams, guests generally stay a while, frequently for a full week.

The Balsams

The Balsams. Route 26, Dixville Notch, NH 03576. Tel: 800-255-0600 (in New Hampshire: 800-255-0800) or 603-255-3400. Fax: 603-255-4221. 219 rooms and suites. High-season rates range from $175 to $205 per person per night and include room, three meals, and all golf and resort activities. Other times of the year, rates range from $124 to $156 per person. Credit cards accepted.

R E S T A U R A N T S

The culinary scene at the **Balsams**—like the golf—is one of the best reasons for going there. Among the New England golf resorts that we have reviewed, the Balsams wins the Best Food award hands down. When you arrive at the Balsams, you are assigned a specific table in the elegant dining room, and it remains your table for all meals (except lunches taken at the golf club) for the duration of your stay. Hence, you have regular waiters and waitresses and the same neighbors at adjoining tables, all of whom you can get to know quite well.

The dining room, especially at dinner, is a very pleasant scene. All the items from the extensive menu are displayed on a table in the center of the room. Your waiter or waitress will urge you to try more than one appetizer and dessert, yet be assured that such encouragement springs not from a desire to run up your tab, but rather from a genuine hope that you thoroughly enjoy your meal. Only beverages—and discretionary tipping during the busy months of July and August—will cost you extra. Men must wear jackets in the evening.

If you plan to have lunch at the golf house, don't forget to pick up a lunch chit in the dining room the morning before you play.

The restaurants at the Balsams. Route 26, Dixville Notch, NH 03576. Tel: 800-255-0600 (in New Hampshire: 800-255-0800) or 603-255-3400. Fax: 603-255-4221. Credit cards accepted.

N O N - G O L F   A C T I V I T I E S

The wonderful non-golf activities at the Balsams include hiking, fly fishing for rainbow trout in Lake Gloriette just in front of the hotel, cycling, swimming in a nice, heated outdoor pool, tennis on six courts, nightly movies, dancing, and evening entertainment. Loafing is a popular enterprise at the Balsams, too. During the winter the Balsams attracts downhill and cross-country skiers.

GETTING THERE: The closest airport to the Balsams is in Portland, Maine, some 130 miles away. Take the Maine Turnpike for about thirty miles to exit 11 (Route 26). Follow Route 26 the rest of the way to Dixville Notch and the resort.

Vermont

▶THE EQUINOX
MANCHESTER VILLAGE

	The Golf	Golf Services	Lodging	Restaurants	Non-Golf Activities	Total
Rating	17	15	17	15	18	82

Those with a taste for fine golf, outstanding shopping, the pristine beauty of Vermont, and the pure Americana of historic New England—covered bridges, period homes, and white church steeples rising through the tree-tops—will find that Manchester Village has it all. It is the only town in America with marble sidewalks. Manchester Village is home to the sparkling Equinox Hotel and Resort, a national landmark that began operating as a country inn in 1769. The venerable inn, which is owned in part by the Guinness Corporation (the owner of the Equinox's younger-sibling re-

The Equinox

sort, the fabulous Gleneagles in Scotland), closed for three months in 1992 for a lavish $9 million overhaul. When we visited some time after the renovation, we found the hotel quite enchanting, save for a few disappointing glitches in service and cuisine noted below. During our stay the place was filled to capacity with guests from Boston (a three-and-a-half-hour drive) and the New York metropolitan area (about a four-and-a-half-hour drive). The elegance of the renovated Equinox, its wonderful golf course, the multiple attractions of Manchester Village, and the resort's proximity to large urban populations should guarantee a bright future. We only hope that the hotel staff learns to be more attentive and that the food improves.

THE GOLF ⒘

The Equinox golfing pedigree also goes back a long way. New England is loaded with old, unrestored golf courses from the late nineteenth and early twentieth centuries—casual walk-on nines and eighteens with low overhead and low greens fees. The handsome new **Gleneagles Course** at the Equinox is not one of these.

Originally designed by British and U.S. Amateur champ Walter Travis in 1926 at the behest of Mrs. Franklin Orvis (the widow of the fly-fishing king and a previous owner of the Equinox) and thoughtfully improved (but not rerouted) by Rees Jones in 1991, the Gleneagles layout is now one of the best mountain courses in all New England. Although a grand, championship affair (6,423 yards), the course is nonetheless extremely forgiving from side to side, hence eminently playable for the average golfer, who is more likely to meander along the rough rather than follow the direct route to the green. Only the most errant shots are out of bounds or severely penalized here. Almost every hole on the course presents a pleasing panorama of Mount Equinox (3,816 feet). The thirteenth is the course's signature hole. Known as the *Snake Pit,* the elevated green on this 421-yard dogleg-right is flanked by a very large, seldom mowed pit located just short and right of the green. Problem is, most people hit short because they neglect to take into consideration just how elevated (forty feet above the fairway) the green is, and so end up in the unforgiving clutches of the hazard.

Another outstanding golf option in the vicinity is the **Stratton Mountain Country Club** with its twenty-seven holes and acclaimed Stratton Golf School. In years past Stratton Mountain hosted an LPGA Tour event. The best of the three nines at Stratton Mountain is the Mountain Nine.

Gleneagles Golf Course. Historic Route 7A, Manchester Village, VT 05254. Tel: 802-362-3223. Fax: 802-362-4861. Credit cards accepted.

• 1926/improved 1991. Designers: Walter Travis/Rees Jones. Par 71. 6,423 yards. 71.3 par rating. 129 slope rating. Greens fees: guests $65 weekday, $75 weekend; public: $85 weekday, $95 weekend. Walking permitted on weekdays. No caddies. Carts cost $36. Season: May 1–October 31.

Stratton Mountain Country Club. Stratton Mountain Road, Stratton Mountain, VT 05155. Tel: 800-787-2886 or 802-297-4114. Fax: 802-297-2939. Credit cards accepted.

• *Mountain Nine.* 1969. Designers: Geoffrey Cornish, William G. Robinson. Par 36. 3,277 yards. 126 slope rating.
• *Lake Nine.* 1969. Designers: Geoffrey Cornish, William G. Robinson. Par 36. 3,325 yards. 125 slope rating.
• *Forest Nine.* 1986. Designers: Geoffrey Cornish, Brian Silva. Par 36. 3,201 yards. 125 slope rating.
• Greens fees for all play: $75 weekdays, $85 weekend, cart included. Walking permitted on weekdays only. No caddies. Season: May 10–October 30.

GOLF SERVICES 15

Although there is no practice range (a net behind the first tee is all the practice you will get), golf services at the Equinox are fairly good. The counter staff in the nice pro shop is accommodating, the Grill (as previously noted) is pleasant, and the locker facilities are adequate.

LODGING 17

The handsomely renovated white-columned **Equinox Hotel** is very New England but with a Scottish twist. Public rooms and lounges sport that warm, rich Gleneagles look with much brocade, tapestry-backed sofas grouped around fireplaces, and bookcases full of old volumes. The guest rooms are not as elegant as the public areas, and indeed they are far more spartan than their Scottish counterparts at Gleneagles, yet they are comfortable, attractive, and bright. We stayed in one of the larger rooms at the Equinox, number 230, which featured pine accents, cable television, and brand-new furnish-

The Equinox Hotel

ings and fabrics. The room, however, was a bit noisy at night, and when we took a shower before dinner the water temperature ran hot-cold, hot-cold, as if the system was strained by other guests in adjacent rooms attempting to bathe at the same time. We also have to say that the hotel's new floor plan is a little odd; for example, why aren't the elevators more conveniently located?

The association with Gleneagles in Scotland means a great deal here—one waitress told us that the Equinox staff had been shown an instructional videotape about the Gleneagles' traditions—but with few exceptions, the Gleneagles gentility in service has not yet trickled down. Many of the younger staff members struck us as inadequately trained.

The Equinox Hotel and Resort. Historic Route 7A, Manchester Village, VT 05254. Tel: 800-362-4747 or 802-362-4700. Fax: 802-362-4861. 183 rooms and suites. Doubles from $180 to $320. Two-night golf packages are available. Credit cards accepted.

RESTAURANTS

The two principal restaurants at the Equinox, the **Colonnade Room** and the historic **Marsh Tavern,** are very attractive. Sadly, however, the cuisine in both establishments (especially at dinner) falls short of the setting. Dinner entrées in the Colonnade Room, the more casual of the two, include salmon, red snapper, veal medallions, and filet mignon starting at around $20. We thoroughly enjoyed our casual lunch overlooking the ninth green at the **Dormy Grill** after our golf game (good salads and sandwiches). Every Wednesday through Saturday evening during the summer, the Dormy Grill is the site of the Equinox's new and hugely successful lobster-fest dinner. If you don't like lobster, you can also order chicken or steak. Another exciting addition to the Equinox's lunch fare is just a short drive away at the **Artist's Palette,** the restaurant at the Southern Vermont Arts Center where the view from the patio is spectacular. Finally, the buffet breakfast in the Colonnade Room was also good. Although some of the more ambitious fare served at the Equinox still seems lackluster, we are encouraged by the clear signal that the resort intends to improve its kitchen.

The restaurants at the Equinox Hotel and Resort. Historic Route 7A, Manchester Village, VT 05254. Tel: 800-362-4747 or 802-362-4700. Fax: 802-362-4861. Credit cards accepted.

NON-GOLF ACTIVITIES

The non-golfer will find plenty to fill the day. All visitors to the Equinox are likely to spend considerable time bargain hunting for new wardrobes, as Manchester Village is renowned throughout New England as a center for factory outlet stores. The stores, mostly located in a busy outlet complex about a mile from the hotel, include Polo/Ralph Lauren, Anne Klein, Cole-Haan, Burberrys, Coach, Orvis, Hickey-Freeman, Calvin Klein, Donna Karan, Movado, Benetton, Brooks Brothers, Pendleton, J. Crew, Jones New York, Polly Flinders, and many others. Retail prices are frequently marked down as much as 70 percent. Outlet shopping has its rewards but is not without its frustrations, like finding the perfect $600 Ralph Lauren jacket (marked down to $165) that is not quite the right size. There are also many fine antiques shops, art galleries, and interesting secondhand bookshops in the area.

Activities at the hotel include the nice fitness and spa facility (weight room, exercise classes, massage, sauna and steamrooms, and heated indoor pool), three tennis courts, outdoor pool, and mountain bikes available for rent. Orvis operates a fly-fishing school in Manchester Village and offers fishing packages in conjunction with the Equinox. The American Museum of Fly Fishing is located next to the hotel. Orvis also directs a shooting school here. The most important historic site in Manchester Village is Hildene, the splendid summer home of Abraham Lincoln's son, Robert Todd Lincoln.

GETTING THERE: The closest major airport to the Equinox is in Albany, New York, about sixty-two miles away. From Albany, take Route 87 North, get off at exit 7 (Troy, Route 7 East). Follow 7 East to the Vermont border, where it turns into Route 9 East. Continue to Bennington, Vermont, make a left onto 7 North, and proceed to exit 4 (Manchester Center). At the exit ramp, make a left onto Route 11 West, follow one mile to Manchester Center and a blinking light. At the light turn left onto Route 7A South. The Equinox is 1.5 miles ahead.

►THE WOODSTOCK INN

GOLF AND THE GREEN MOUNTAINS

	The Golf	Golf Services	Lodging	Restaurants	Non-Golf Activities	Total
Rating	17	16	15	15	16	79

The Woodstock Inn

Surrounded by the thick pine forests and gothic peaks and valleys of the Green Mountains, the historic and unmistakably prosperous town of Woodstock, Vermont, is one of the most beautiful villages in all New England. For fifty years, the local chamber of commerce described storybook Woodstock as "the village which, probably more than any other in Vermont, has reverently preserved both the physical setting and spiritual flavor of an earlier day."

With its manicured village green, enchanting Currier and Ives architecture, and pricey art galleries that cater only to the wealthiest of travelers, Woodstock (population 3,500) is still the picture-perfect—if quite image-conscious—New England village. When the heat and humidity of midsummer begin blasting destinations to the south, many travelers—and not just history buffs and antiques dealers—will look to Woodstock for an appealing holiday getaway.

For golfers and all sorts of visitors, Woodstock's center point is the renowned Woodstock Inn and Resort, delightfully located square in the middle of town just fifty paces from the village green. The Woodstock Inn was built in 1967 by Laurance Rockefeller, who still owns the property, still loves golf, and who became forever linked to this community long ago by marrying a local girl.

On our previous visits to the Woodstock Inn, quite frankly, we found the food, the accommodations, and the service to be less than inspiring. After a major expansion and renovation program had been completed, we recently returned and found matters considerably improved on nearly every front. Today, service in the informal restaurant just across from the lobby may remain uneven, but the Woodstock Inn is now a far more attractive and dependable place than it was six or seven years ago.

THE GOLF

First laid out in 1895 and redesigned by Robert Trent Jones, Sr., in 1967, the golf course is located at the **Woodstock Country Club,** one mile south of the inn. Set on the floor of a long and narrow mountain valley with dramatic scenery all around, this picturesque course is a joy to walk. The club's short layout (6,001 yards from the back tees) may not be a match for the longer championship course at the renovated Equinox resort in Manchester Village, Vermont, just forty-five minutes south of Woodstock, but it is historic, nicely updated, and well maintained. Golfers of every handicap will find it lovely and challenging and full of idiosyncratic appeal. Characteristics of the course include small greens, tight, parallel fairways, and so many creeks and little lakes that ball retrievers are standard issue among local members.

The course's best holes are numbers three, four, and twelve. The 346-yard third hole requires a layup drive to a landing area bordered by a stream and a very big second shot to the elevated green. Both four and twelve are gentle doglegs-left that demand two water crossings. All six par threes on this par sixty-nine course are nifty, especially number seven (162 yards) with its elevated tee and pond guarding the green.

The Woodstock Inn

The Woodstock Country Club. South Street, Woodstock, VT 05091. Tel: 802-457-6674. Fax: 802-457-6699. Credit cards accepted.

• 1895. Designer: Robert Trent Jones Sr. (1967). Par 69. 6,001 yards. 69.0 par rating. 121 slope rating. Greens fees: hotel guests: $36 (weekdays), $45 (weekends); nonguests: $55. Walking permitted. No caddies. Carts cost $32. Season: May 1–October 31.

GOLF SERVICES

Golf services at the country club are very good. The clubhouse features a nice pro shop, locker facility, and a pleasant restaurant/bar upstairs. There is a small but adequate practice area. Electric carts, hand carts, rental clubs, and lessons are available.

LODGINGS

The best and most luxurious rooms at the **Woodstock Inn,** which come with refrigerators, VCRs, and working fireplaces, are located in the new Tavern Wing and are priced from $295. We stayed in a standard room (number 247, $195), which we found comfortable and adequate but certainly not as large or luxurious as the Tavern Wing rooms. The Woodstock Inn's concierge, Meredith, was extremely pleasant and helpful to us during our stay.

The Woodstock Inn and Resort. 14 The Village Green, Woodstock, VT 05091. Tel: 800-448-7900 or 802-457-1100. Fax: 802-457-6699. 140 rooms from $155 to $295. Golf packages are available. Credit cards accepted.

RESTAURANTS 15

The cuisine has also improved since our last visit. Our dinner in the handsome and dressy **Dining Room** (jackets are strongly encouraged) included fine smoked salmon, good grilled swordfish, wonderful desserts, and a good selection of wine. A complete dinner for two in the Dining Room with wine and tip costs approximately $125. The **Eagle Café** serves breakfast, lunch, and dinner in a more casual atmosphere. Breakfast and dinner meal plans at the inn are available for $53 per day per person. Golf packages are available.

If you tire of the resort restaurants, try **Bentley's** in Woodstock, a popular and informal place that is particularly good at lunch. The most expensive item on the dinner menu here is the Jack Daniel's steak at $20. Reservations are not required.

The restaurants at the Woodstock Inn and Resort. 14 The Village Green, Woodstock, VT 05091. Tel: 800-448-7900 or 802-457-1100. Fax: 802-457-6699. Credit cards accepted.

Bentley's. 3 Elm Street, Woodstock, VT 05091. Tel: 802-457-3232. Fax: 802-457-3238. Credit cards accepted.

NON-GOLF ACTIVITIES 16

Other activities at the inn include the Sports Center, which has indoor pool, tennis, squash, racquetball, and exercise rooms. There is fine shopping in Woodstock, plus tours of Billings Farm, one of the premier agricultural museums in the United States.

GETTING THERE: Woodstock is 148 miles from Boston. Take 93 North to Manchester, New Hampshire, where you pick up Route 89 North. Take 89 North into Vermont. Get off at exit 1 onto Route 4, make a left heading west. Go ten miles, into the village of Woodstock. The village green will be on your left, and the Woodstock Inn will be on your right.

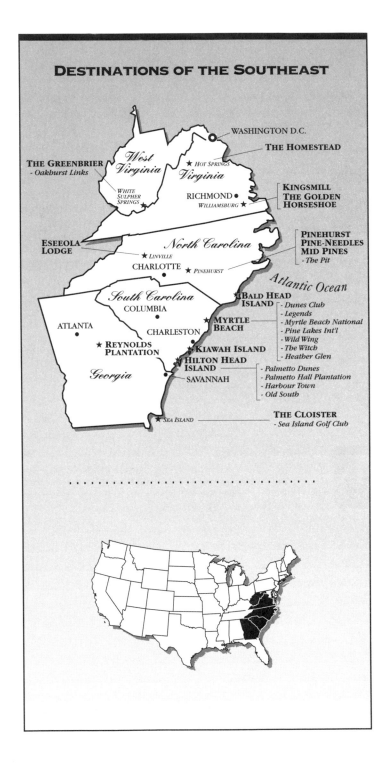

DESTINATIONS OF THE SOUTHEAST

WASHINGTON D.C.

THE HOMESTEAD

West Virginia

★ *HOT SPRINGS*

Virginia

THE GREENBRIER
- *Oakhurst Links*

WHITE SULPHER SPRINGS

RICHMOND ●

WILLIAMSBURG ★

KINGSMILL
THE GOLDEN
HORSESHOE

ESEEOLA LODGE

North Carolina

★ *LINVILLE*

CHARLOTTE

★ *PINEHURST*

PINEHURST
PINE-NEEDLES
MID PINES
- *The Pit*

Atlantic Ocean

South Carolina

COLUMBIA

★**BALD HEAD**
ISLAND

- *Dunes Club*
- *Legends*
- *Myrtle Beach National*
- *Pine Lakes Int'l*
- *Wild Wing*
- *The Witch*
- *Heather Glen*

ATLANTA ●

★**MYRTLE**
BEACH

CHARLESTON

★ **REYNOLDS PLANTATION**

★**KIAWAH ISLAND**

★**HILTON HEAD**
ISLAND

SAVANNAH

- *Palmetto Dunes*
- *Palmetto Hall Plantation*
- *Harbour Town*
- *Old South*

Georgia

★ *SEA ISLAND*

THE CLOISTER
- *Sea Island Golf Club*

THE SOUTH-EASTERN UNITED STATES

THE SOUTHEASTERN UNITED STATES

Well, they're Southern people, and if they know you are only working at home they think nothing of walking right in for coffee. But they wouldn't dream of interrupting you at golf.

—**Harper Lee**

Southerners harbor an abiding love for their region and its landscape. And who can blame them? Each April we watch the Masters on television and wish just once to walk in step at Augusta amid the dogwoods and the perfectly manicured greenery. Could there possibly be a more perfect place on the planet? How the South blooms in springtime—with its daffodils and forsythia, hyacinth and honeysuckle, jasmine and jonquils, redbuds and Bradford pear trees! Indeed, is it any wonder that each hole at Augusta is named for a different flower?

A vast plain hugs the Southern coast from Virginia to Florida and westward around the Gulf of Mexico to Texas. This marshy low country, or tidewater region, nourished by slow rivers and tall pines, gives way to the gentle rolling hills of the Piedmont Plateau. The rivers quicken as they rush downward from the upcountry mountains, known alternately as the Blue Ridge, the Cumberlands, the Smokies, and, further west, in Arkansas, as the Ozarks. At the far western reaches of the Southern frontier, the landscape leads out into the Western prairies.

When a breeze blows in the South, it stirs up history and character. The love of landscape in the South is inextricably tied to the past. Across this diverse geographical tableau were fought the battles of the Civil War, still the outstanding event in America's historical consciousness. From Manassas to Fredericksburg, from Shiloh to Vicksburg, from Fort Sumter to Chickamauga, the bloody battlefields on Southern soil afford the region's inhabitants a special connection with their past. Anyone who has ever stepped foot on such hallowed turf can feel the power of these unforgettable places. In an instant you are walking over the very fields of battle where so many were wounded and killed, keenly aware of where the artillery was positioned, where the charges were made, and which ridges offered protection.

Golf courses resemble these preserved fields of battle in one important way: they allow players of all abilities to tread upon the same turf where historic action—albeit the history of golf—has occurred. Whether it is the first tee of Hilton Head's Harbour Town Links, site of the PGA Tour's Heritage Classic, or the final green of Pete Dye's Ocean Course on Kiawah, where the Ryder Cup was decided in 1991, the weekend hackers among us come face-to-face with the same testing shots and difficult-to-read putts that the pros have to tackle. All golfers play in the shadows of those who came before them. Like the sacred Southern battlefields, golf's fields of battle provide a rich connection to the character and history of the landscape.

The great golfing destinations in the South are as varied as the region's geography. Some of the loveliest mountain golf courses in the world are located in this part of the United States, courses you should not miss—the Linville Golf Club, the courses at the venerable Homestead resort, and, saving the best for last, the incomparable courses at the Greenbrier in West Virginia.

Prefer islands? Outstanding resort courses welcome you on Hilton Head, Kiawah, Bald Head Island, and the Cloister at Sea Island, Georgia. Or, for the ultimate, casual coastal destination, you can comb the sandy coastline of South Carolina's Myrtle Beach area and examine the amazing variety of golf courses there. Back in Virginia, at Colonial Williamsburg on the James River, you can divide your time between playing the excellent assortment of golf courses available in the area and touring the carefully and painstakingly restored Colonial town of Williamsburg. We can think of few other golfing destinations where, while playing golf, there is a good chance of hearing a fife and drum corps in the distance, punctuated by occasional cannon fire.

Should business or pleasure draw you inland, we'll introduce you to the Sandhills of North Carolina, where you will find the eight courses of Pinehurst Country Club. The sheer volume of golf holes at Pinehurst makes this classic resort a true golfing mecca. Just down the road a few miles in Southern Pines, you will revel in two lovely and heavily forested courses: Mid Pines and Pine Needles, host of the 1996 U.S. Women's Open. Farther south, Reynold's Plantation sits on a wooded peninsula on Georgia's second largest lake and presents, as do all the other courses in this section, Southern hospitality at its finest.

Aside from the mountain layouts, Southern golf courses generally stay open throughout the year. Below the fall line in South Carolina, the climate turns semitropical, meaning winters are mild and golf can be played comfortably practically year-round. Summers, however, are hot and humid and considered off-season by many resorts. Spring and fall are really the best times to visit.

Yet regardless of when you play, Southern history echoes throughout the landscape. A trip to the South presents wonderful opportunities to introduce your family to the region's rich cultural heritage. Civil War battlefields make for memorable family outings. You can also explore the region's myriad historic homes, plantations, and outdoor museum villages. So whether you are on the golf course or touring an historic attraction with your family, you are sure to be inspired by the Southeast's storied soil.

Virginia

▶THE GOLDEN HORSESHOE AND THE WILLIAMSBURG INN

GOLF IN COLONIAL WILLIAMSBURG

	The Golf	Golf Services	Lodging	Restaurants	Non-Golf Activities	Total
Rating	17	16	17	16	19	85

Williamsburg, Virginia, is simply one of the finest and most complete family vacation destinations anywhere in America or, for that matter, anywhere in the world. At the heart of the sights and myriad activities around Williamsburg is the fascinating Colonial capital of Virginia—restored in the 1920s by John D. Rockefeller—a vast, intriguing, and spectacularly beautiful collection of eighteenth-century American buildings tended by

Williamsburg Inn

hundreds of "colonists" dressed in vintage apparel. The view down Duke of Gloucester Street—from the Wren building at William and Mary College all the way down to the Capitol, where Patrick Henry made his passionate plea for independence—is something no American child should miss.

Yet Colonial Williamsburg is just the beginning. Beyond the thickly wooded, 3,000-acre buffer zone that surrounds the historic city and protects it from the crush of modern civilization, you will find the carefully preserved settlements of nearby Jamestown and Yorktown, old Virginia plantations such as Carter's Grove, huge amusement parks like Busch Gardens and Water Country USA (the largest waterslide park on the East Coast), and, of course, many other smaller attractions and shopping galore.

Golf, we are happy to report, plays a very central role in the overall Williamsburg experience. So central, in fact, that the first tee of the renowned Gold Course is within a four- or five-minute stroll of the historic attractions of Duke of Gloucester Street. While golfing, you can sometimes hear a fife and drum corps in the distance, hardly typical background music for a game of golf!

The Golden Horseshoe golf resort in Colonial Williamsburg consists of the Williamsburg Inn, clearly the best and most elegant hotel in the entire region, and three excellent golf courses: the Gold Course, designed by Robert Trent Jones in 1963; the Green Course, designed by his son Rees Jones in 1991; and the beguiling and quite tricky little nine-hole layout called the Spotswood Course, which is a replica in miniature of the Robert Trent Jones layout. This entire resort complex has been awarded *Golf Magazine*'s gold medal.

THE GOLF ⑰

Despite the beauty of the new Green Course, the **Gold Course** remains Williamsburg's premier track. Both courses, however, have much in common. Both layouts sensitively follow the natural contours of the land—hillsides, gullies, ravines, and little dales—and both are cut through canyons of mature oak, cedar, and pine without a single homesite to mar the view. The forest on both sides of the fairways can be so thick with tall trees that a quiet hush is produced on the course. Thanks to this impenetrable wall of trees, you can be heard by your partner from a considerable distance without raising your voice. And when you strike the ball especially well off the tee, it sounds like Mickey Mantle cracking one out of Yankee Stadium. This is the sound track of golf in Williamsburg.

The true heart of the Gold Course is the serpentine lake that comes into play on four different holes—the second, seventh, twelfth, and sixteenth—perhaps the course's four best holes. Seven, twelve, and sixteen are the par three holes that have made the Gold Course famous, and, truly, they are all fabulous beauties. All three are quite similar in appearance: the tees are perched up high on grassy overlooks and present a vast expanse of water certain to unnerve all but the most steady of golfers. (Note: The Gold Course will be closed for renovation when this book is first published. Plans call for the renovation, which includes the installation of a new irrigation system and a reworking of all the greens and tee boxes, to be completed by late June of 1998.)

The **Green Course** plays from 6,200 to 7,100 yards and is somewhat less majestic in appearance than the Gold, but it is a bit more manageable for the average golfer. Water is a factor on six holes. The charming **Spotswood Course** is an executive-length nine (1,880 yards, par thirty-one), but it is also one of the most challenging short courses we have ever seen. Holes range in length from 100 to 470 yards. Walking is permitted on all of the Golden Horseshoe golf courses, although the greens fees for the Gold and Green courses include a cart.

The best seasons for golf in Williamsburg are spring, when the dogwood and azaleas are in bloom, and fall, when the colorful leaves are at their autumn peak. If you visit in midsummer, try to play early in the morning, for Tidewater Virginia can be hot, muggy, and buggy. The Golden Horseshoe bills itself as a year-round golf club, but snow, sleet, or freezing temperatures can and will occasionally curtail play during the winter.

Golden Horseshoe Golf Club. 401 South England Street, Williamsburg, VA 23185. Tel: 757-220-7696. Fax: 757-565-8841. Credit cards accepted.

• *Gold Course* (closed until June 1998). 1963. Designer: Robert Trent Jones, Sr. Par 71. 6,700 yards. 73.1 par rating. 137 slope rating. Greens fees: Colonial Williamsburg hotel guests: $95; public: $125, cart included. Walking permitted. No caddies. Season: year-round.

• *Green Course.* 1991. Designer: Rees Jones. Par 72. 7,100 yards. 73.4 par rating. 134 slope rating. Greens fees: Colonial Williamsburg hotel guests: $95, public, $115, cart included. Walking permitted. No caddies. Season: year-round.

• *Spotswood Course.* 1963. Designer: Robert Trent Jones, Sr. Par 31. 1,880 yards. 105 slope rating. Greens fees: Colonial Williamsburg hotel guests: $30, public: $40 ($20 and $25 in the off season). Walking permitted. No caddies. A cart for eighteen holes costs an additional $25. Season: year-round.

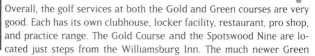

GOLF SERVICES   16

Overall, the golf services at both the Gold and Green courses are very good. Each has its own clubhouse, locker facility, restaurant, pro shop, and practice range. The Gold Course and the Spotswood Nine are located just steps from the Williamsburg Inn. The much newer Green Course facility is about a mile away.

The only weaknesses here are the practice ranges, which have too few stations to meet demand. Many golfers stand around the practice area waiting for a spot to become available. Also, the pace of play, especially on the Gold Course, can be very slow—nearly five and a half hours in our case. It would have been nice to have seen a ranger on the course speeding up play.

LODGING   17

The **Williamsburg Inn** enjoys a perfect location midway between the historic district and the Gold Course. It is also right next door to the Craft House, which sells exquisitely made (and quite expensive) Williamsburg furniture and other accessories for the home.

Built in 1937, the Williamsburg Inn is far and away the best of several hotels owned and run by Colonial Williamsburg. Service is extremely pleasant all around, from the porters who greet you at the entrance to the very accommodating staff behind the front desk. Public areas include large lounges, a handsome outdoor terrace, a gift shop, an informal restaurant, and the elegant Regency Room, the inn's formal dining room. The guest rooms are all very comfortable and attractive, both in the main inn and the annex. We stayed in room 3156, furnished with lovely Williamsburg reproduction furniture, a television, and a big marble bath.

Williamsburg Inn. PO Box B, 136 East Francis Street, Williamsburg, VA 23187. Tel: 800-231-4201 or 757-220-7978. Fax: 757-565-8797. 135 rooms. Doubles from $250 to $365. Golf packages including room, breakfast, dinner, unlimited golf with cart, yardage book, and range balls begin at $550 per couple, per night. Credit cards accepted.

RESTAURANTS   16

Many of the restaurants in Colonial Williamsburg are full of history—particularly the handful of eighteenth-century taverns along Duke of Gloucester Street—but the cooking in most of these establishments is without real distinction.

Our best meal during our recent visit was dinner in the lovely **Regency Room** at the Williamsburg Inn—good crab cakes, a rather average sirloin with bland vegetables, a very good selection of desserts, a fine assortment of wines, and nice service. A complete dinner for two in the Regency Room with wine and tip costs approximately $135. Men must wear a jacket and tie and women either a dress or pants suit. Be sure to make reservations.

Of the four historic taverns operated by Colonial Williamsburg, we recommend the **King's Arms Tavern,** where waitresses and entertainers in period costumes serve peanut soup, Virginia ham, a Colonial version of chicken potpie, and Sally Lunn bread. Dinner reservations are essential. About $90 for two, wine and tip included.

Finally, a third restaurant we can recommend with confidence is the ever-popular **Trellis,** located in Merchant Square, just a ten-minute walk from the Williamsburg Inn down Duke of Gloucester Street. This bistro-style restaurant with outdoor terrace features an upbeat decor and an agreeable selection of grilled fish, good salads, and steak. About $80 for two at dinner, wine and tip included.

Regency Room. Williamsburg Inn, 136 East Francis Street, Williamsburg, VA 23187. Tel: 800-231-4201 or 757-220-7978. Fax: 757-220-7096. Credit cards accepted.

King's Arms Tavern. 409 East Duke of Gloucester Street, Williamsburg, VA 23185. Tel: 800-231-4201 or 757-229-1000. Fax: 757-220-7729. Credit cards accepted.

Trellis. 403 Duke of Gloucester Street, Williamsburg, VA 23185. Tel: 757-229-8610. Fax: 757-221-0450. Credit cards accepted.

NON-GOLF ACTIVITIES   19

As previously noted, the non-golf activities around Williamsburg are outstanding. Beyond a tour of Colonial Williamsburg, they include the aforementioned Water Country USA and Busch Gardens; other historic sights such as Carter's Grove on the James River, Yorktown, and Jamestown; and wonderful shopping at the Craft Shop or the area's many outlet stores. Other options include two fine museums, the Abby Aldrich Rockefeller Folk Art Center and the DeWitt Wallace Decorative Arts Gallery, plus tennis, swimming, walking trails, bicycle rentals, and the fitness center and indoor pool at the Williamsburg Lodge (to which guests of the inn have access).

GETTING THERE: From the Newport News Airport take a left onto Jefferson Road. Take Jefferson to 64 West until exit 242 A (Highway 199). Take the second exit off Highway 199 onto Route 60 West. Take a left at the first light (York Street) and continue until it turns into Francis Street. The Williamsburg Inn is approximately five hundred yards down Francis Street on the left.

▶KINGSMILL

HOME OF THE ANHEUSER-BUSCH GOLF CLASSIC

	The Golf	Golf Services	Lodging	Restaurants	Non-Golf Activities	Total
Rating	18	16	17	16	18	85

Williamsburg, Virginia, like Disney World in Orlando, Florida, is not known first and foremost as a golf destination. Disney is known for its theme parks, just as historic Williamsburg is celebrated for the extraordinary preservation of its magnificent Colonial architecture. Peek behind the facade of either resort, however, and you will find hole after hole of wonderful golf. Indeed, Williamsburg offers golf travelers two highly regarded golf resorts situated virtually side-by-side.

Kingsmill Resort

In addition to the splendid golf at the Williamsburg Inn (reviewed separately), there is also the attractive Kingsmill Resort, which is owned and operated by Anheuser-Busch, one of America's premier corporations, and home to the Anheuser-Busch Golf Classic. Represented on the PGA Tour by Williamsburg native Curtis Strange, Kingsmill goes the Williamsburg Inn one better, with four outstanding golf courses: the lovely River Course, designed by Pete Dye; the Plantation Course, designed by Arnold Palmer and Ed Seay; the handsome new Woods Course, opened in 1994 and designed by Tom Clark and Curtis Strange; and a short but magical, nine-hole par three called the Bray Links. The Anheuser-Busch Classic is played each year on the River Course.

So how do you know which of these two fine Williamsburg resorts—the Williamsburg Inn or Kingsmill—is best suited for you? This question is not difficult to answer because the establishments are as different as night and day. Wisely, Busch Properties did not attempt to replicate the Early American atmosphere of Colonial Williamsburg and aimed Kingsmill, stylistically at least, in a much more contemporary direction. Kingsmill and the Williamsburg Inn, therefore, are complementary, not competitive.

Located on the edge of Colonial Williamsburg, the inn is a historic experience from beginning to end, perfectly suited for first-time visitors to Williamsburg or couples traveling with small children. Kingsmill, occupying a dramatic site on the mile-wide James River and set within its own carefully manicured, 2,900-acre plantation compound, is much more low-key and relaxed.

The inn will suit those who love history and golf, while Kingsmill, with its wonderful indoor athletic complex (pool, squash courts, exercise facilities, and much more), in addition to its four golf courses, will appeal to the sports-minded traveler or to couples who just want to get away from it all. Kingsmill is also a large, upscale residential community whose resident homeowners share the sports facilities with guests of the resort. At the Williamsburg Inn, you stay in the hotel; at Kingsmill, you stay in fully equipped one-, two-, or three-bedroom villas within walking distance of all resort facilities.

The overall Kingsmill experience can be an extremely good value. Packages that include golf and accommodations start at just $290 per couple from April through November—about half the price of golf and accommodations at the Williamsburg Inn.

 THE GOLF

The **River Course** at Kingsmill, the resort's premier track, is one of Pete Dye's most understated masterpieces, not one of his diabolical, PGA West–style, sadomasochistic nightmares. Dye at his best (Teeth of the Dog, the Ocean Course, La Romana Country Club) is simply one of the most amazing architects in golf—appreciative of the natural contours of the land, sensitive to golfers of every ability, while always throwing down the gauntlet to low handicaps.

The River Course, which measures 6,797 yards (slope 137), is best known for its four superb finishing holes, largely because these four beauties receive the most television coverage at tournament time. Yet from start to finish, this is an appealing and mellow layout, not terribly long, very strategic in nature, and extremely beautiful and well maintained.

Crossed by deeply wooded gullies and ravines, the River Course moves away from the James River on the front nine and then turns around and plays back to the river's edge on the final nine. The course's strategic nature is evident from the first tee. A straight drive will land you in a big fairway bunker; instead, try to hit it left. Perhaps the most beautiful hole on the front side is number five, a 151-yard par three with a rocky stream and a large, receptive green.

The River Course, however, truly comes alive on the back side. The fifteenth, a short, 506-yard par five (and the course's number two handicap hole) requires a big drive over a substantial waste area and features a deep, unplayable gully down the hole's entire right side. The sixteenth, a long, 427-yard par four, features an unusual and beautiful double-tiered fairway. From the sixteenth tee you gaze upon the entire length of the fairway to the James, which looks as mighty as an ocean. The seventeenth is the River Course's most famous hole. This 138-yard par three (177 yards for the pros) plays alongside the river and is exposed to gusting winds. In windy conditions, the pros frequently do not even attempt to land the ball squarely on the seventeenth green. Instead, they try to hit it into the bank left of the amphitheater green with the hope that it will roll back toward the pin. And eighteen, a 435-yard par four, is a great finale. Your drive on eighteen is slightly uphill and over a large lake, and the second shot demands another big hit to the elevated green.

The **Plantation Course** is a very enjoyable but less testing 6,092-yard layout (6,602 yards from the gold tees) that features steep hills, wooded fairways, and water on eight holes. The Plantation Course, like the River Course, is dotted with interesting historic artifacts from Williamsburg's eighteenth-century heyday, but it is also marred in spots by homes built too close to the fairways. Par for the Plantation Course is seventy-two.

The new **Woods Course,** located within Kingsmill but approximately two miles from the River Course clubhouse, looks extremely mature for a newborn golf course. This 6,784-yard layout (just over the fence from the Busch Gardens theme park) is flatter than either the River or Plantation courses and features generous fairways lined with tall pines, perilous ravines, and a dozen water hazards. Par is seventy-two.

The charming **Bray Links,** a nine-hole pitch-and-putt located next to the River Course clubhouse, is also worth playing. At Bray Links you can polish your wedge work while introducing the game of golf to a beginner.

Kingsmill Resort. 1010 Kingsmill Road, Williamsburg, VA 23185. Tel: 800-832-5665 (if you have reservations at the resort), 757-253-1703, or 757-253-3906 (golf). Fax: 757-253-8237. Credit cards accepted.

• *River Course.* 1975. Designer: Pete Dye. Par 71. 6,797 yards. 73.3 par rating. 137 slope rating. Greens fees: guests: $125 (spring and October)/$90 (summer), public: $150/$100, cart included. No walking. No caddies. Season: year-round.

• *Plantation Course.* 1986. Designers: Arnold Palmer, Ed Seay. Par 72. 6,092 yards. 72.1 par rating. 126 slope rating.

• *Woods Course.* 1994. Designers: Tom Clark, Curtis Strange. Par 72. 6,784 yards. 72.5 par rating. 126 slope rating.

• Greens fees: Plantation and Woods courses: guests: $110 (spring and October)/$80 (summer), public $125/$90, cart included. No walking. No caddies. Season: year-round.

• *Bray Links.* 1987. Designer: Tom Clark. Par 27. 715 yards. Greens fee: no charge for guests, $10 for nonguests. No carts. No caddies. Season: year-round.

  GOLF SERVICES

The River Course, the Plantation Course, and the Bray Links are served by one large, handsome clubhouse with a big pro shop and restaurant. There is a large practice green and range just outside. Walking is permitted on Bray Links, but carts are required on Kingsmill's other courses. The Woods Course has its own clubhouse with a far smaller shop and grill. Staff members are friendly and welcoming at each venue.

LODGING

The best and most expensive guest accommodations at **Kingsmill** are located in the newer villas of Richmond's Ordinary, behind the Sports Club and over-looking the James. We stayed in one of the less expensive villas in Pelham's Ordinary, number 1201, which we found extremely spacious, well maintained, and very comfortable. This unit, with a back porch over-looking the ninth fairway of the River Course, is typical of Kingsmill. It has a fully equipped kitchen with a welcome bottle of wine from the excellent Williamsburg Winery, a large living room with fireplace and television, and a large bedroom (with a second television) and bath. Service throughout the Kingsmill resort could not be more friendly and outgoing.

Kingsmill Resort

Kingsmill Resort. 1010 Kingsmill Road, Williamsburg, Virginia 23185. Tel: 800-832-5665 or 757-253-1703. Fax: 757-253-8237. 375 rooms and suites. Doubles range from $162 to $225 between March and November; one-bedroom suites are $225 to $288. Golf packages start at $290 per couple from April to November. Credit cards accepted.

 RESTAURANTS

There are four restaurants in Kingsmill: the handsome **Bray Dining Room** (which was closed during our visit), the casual **Peyton Grille** in the Sports Club, the **Kingsmill Café** in the River Course clubhouse, and **Moody's Tavern** in the Conference Center. All four restaurants have views of the James. Specialties include the excellent Michelob shrimp, blue crab and corn chowder, Chesapeake Bay backfin crab cakes, fresh fish, and steaks. **Peyton Grille** offers a good selection of wines, but the beers are especially recommended. Given Kingsmill's proximity to Anheuser-Busch's Williamsburg brewery, the beers served at Kingsmill are particularly fresh and delicious.

The restaurants at Kingsmill Resort. 1010 Kingsmill Road, Williamsburg, VA 23185. Tel: 800-832-5665 or 757-253-1703. Fax: 757-253-8237. Credit cards accepted.

NON-GOLF ACTIVITIES

There is a plethora of non-golf activities nearby, from Yorktown, Jamestown, and the historic plantations along the James River to theme parks like Busch Gardens and Water Country USA, plus excellent shopping. The attractions and museums of Colonial Williamsburg are just five minutes away via the Kingsmill shuttle bus. Within the Kingsmill resort you will find fourteen tennis courts and the superb Sports Club with an indoor/outdoor swimming pool, game room for children of all ages, Nautilus-equipped weight room, even half-court indoor basketball.

GETTING THERE: Coming from Washington or points north, take I-95 South and pick up I-295 South to bypass Richmond. Get onto 64 East, take exit 242A, and follow Route 199 West. At the first traffic light you'll see Kingsmill on the right.

▶THE HOMESTEAD IN HOT SPRINGS
REGAINING ITS POSITION AS ONE OF THE SOUTH'S PREMIER RESORTS

	The Golf	Golf Services	Lodging	Restaurants	Non-Golf Activities	Total
Rating	**18**	**18**	**17**	**15**	**17**	**85**

The Homestead

GOLF TRAVEL has carefully monitored developments at the Homestead in recent years, not only because we honestly love this grand old resort in the spectacular mountains of western Virginia but also because the 1993 acquisition of the Homestead by Robert Dedman of Club Resorts, the owner of Pinehurst and Barton Creek, promised a future worthy of the Homestead's brilliant past as one of the grandes dames of Southern resort hospitality.

Just prior to this acquisition, when the Homestead was still owned by the Ingalls family, our assessment of the resort was almost completely negative. Despite a wondrous natural setting and outstanding golf, the Homestead was badly marred by rude service, mediocre cuisine, and a dilapidated interior. At that time, the Homestead earned a total score of just seventy-five points in GOLF TRAVEL's five-part rating system. We considered the resort's gold medal rating from *Golf Magazine* a joke.

We next returned to Hot Springs in March 1995, fifteen months after the Club Resorts acquisition, and were staggered by the volume of long-overdue improvements. Hotel employees were bustling and smiling at guests, substantial renovations to the vast 15,000-acre resort complex had been completed in a first-class way, and the Homestead's total score jumped to a much improved 83. The Homestead was well on the road to recovery, despite the fact that much work—for example, renovation of its terrible old spa building—still remained on the horizon.

The rapid pace of improvements at the Homestead in the first two years of new ownership led us to hope that we would find the transformation nearly complete when we returned in 1996. Instead, the sense of exhilaration and promise, so palpable last time, now seems tempered, replaced by an air of vague frustration. The Homestead, indeed, continues to improve, but the pace of these improvements has slowed. The spirit of some hotel employees now seems less upbeat as well. Genuine goodwill is less ubiquitous. When we arrived, no one came outside to greet us; we emptied the car ourselves and carried our bags to the room. The same on departure: we toted our bags downstairs and loaded our car while the baggage man stood idly by. Service in two of the restaurants—Café Albert and the Grille—struck us as indifferent and lackluster.

Now, we must add that management has our sympathy and understanding. Renovating the enormous Homestead property must be as costly and complicated as renovating the Eiffel Tower or the Golden Gate Bridge. The Homestead had fallen so hard under the previous management that complete improvements could easily exceed the bankroll of even an individual such as Mr. Dedman. But we express our wish that the Homestead build on the big improvements it has already made with renewed commitment. This family-oriented resort, always full of happy children running and laughing, can be one of the greatest showplaces in the entire world of golf.

THE GOLF   18

The golf picture has seen a marked change for the better. We have enjoyed many glorious days of golf on the fabulous Cascades Course and the fine Lower Cascades Course, but on this visit we returned especially to play the **Old Course** (formerly the Homestead Course), an 1892 Donald Ross design now incredibly improved thanks to its brand-new Rees Jones face-lift. Club Resort's renovation of the Old Course has converted a historic and very pretty little golf course into a far more majestic and challenging track while still retaining its charming, antique flavor. This is no surprise, of course, because Rees Jones is perhaps our most sensitive architect when it comes to historic renovation. In the past, the Old Course was generally considered the weakest of the resort's three layouts. Now it has moved into second place, ahead of the occasionally ho-hum Lower Cascades Course, designed in 1963 by Robert Trent Jones, Sr., and just behind the truly magical William Flynn–designed Cascades Course, built in 1924 and the site of many major championships.

The Old Course has been lengthened from 5,957 yards to 6,211 yards, the slope rating has increased from 115 to a respectable 120, and the par rating has been bumped up a couple of shots to 69.7. Several of the original par fours have been extended to par fives—there are now six par fives on the course to match the six par threes—the most spectacular of which is the newly reconfigured thirteenth hole. Thirteen is the new, number one handicap hole on the course, a downhill-uphill, 581-yard par five with its newly elevated tee set up high and way back in the woods. The panoramic view of the surrounding mountains from the thirteenth tee is simply glorious. The only totally new hole on the course is the eighteenth, a lovely, 171-yard par three surrounded by mature hardwoods. The Old Course is as pretty as ever, but now it is a real test as well.

The **Cascades** and the **Lower Cascades** courses have likewise undergone some renovation with new tees and bunkers on certain holes, but the scale of improvements has been far more modest. The Cascades, open from April through mid-November, remains the Homestead's true gem. One of the most enchanting courses in America, the Cascades hosted the 1994 U.S. Women's Amateur, the 1988 U.S. Men's Amateur, and the 1980 U.S. Senior Amateur. The Cascades measures 6,566 yards from the tips, carries a slope rating of 136, and a par rating of 72.9. The Lower Cascades, also open from April through mid-November, is 6,619 yards long from the back tees (par rating 72.2/slope rating 127).

The Homestead. Hot Springs, VA 24445. Tel: 800-838-1766 or 540-839-1766. Fax: 540-839-7670. Credit cards accepted.

• *The Old Course* (formerly the Homestead Course). 1892/1995. Designer: Donald Ross/Rees Jones. Par 72. 6,211 yards. 69.7 par rating. 120 slope rating. Greens fees: $95 (guests), $110 (public), cart included. Walking with caddie only. Caddies available. Season: year-round.

• *Cascades Course.* 1924. Designer: William Flynn. Par 70. 6,566 yards. 72.9 par rating. 136 slope rating. Greens fees: $125 (guests), $160 (public), cart included. Walking with caddie only. Caddies available. Season: April–mid-November.

• *Lower Cascades Course.* 1963. Designer: Robert Trent Jones, Sr. Par 72. 6,619 yards. 72.2 par rating. 127 slope rating. Greens fees: $95 (guests), $110 (public), cart included. Walking with caddie only. Caddies available. Season: April–mid-November.

GOLF SERVICES 18

Club Resorts knows how to create a world-class golf operation. Golf services at the Homestead are now outstanding. If service elsewhere in the hotel is slightly dour, the same cannot be said of the golf personnel, who are eager and outgoing. Wayne Nooe, the director of golf, is hands-on and hardworking; Don Ryder, the Old Course's pro, and Barry Carpenter, the Cascades' pro, bend over backward to accommodate any request. The Golf Advantage School, so successful at Pinehurst, is now in operation at the Homestead, too. Three-day instructional programs are offered April through October. The new practice range and teaching facility located adjacent to the Old Course are excellent.

LODGING 17

Of the 521 rooms at the Homestead, nearly half had been beautifully renovated and upgraded by the time of our visit. Further renovations are continuing, but some rooms will not be in tiptop shape until all the renovations are completed at the end of 1998. It is essential, therefore, that you request a recently remodeled room when you book, like the pleasant standard room we occupied, number 1228, with a spacious bedroom, large closet, and bath. The very best rooms at the Homestead are the Tower rooms; a choice example is number 2102, a lovely one-bedroom junior suite on the twenty-first floor with a spectacular view of the valley. Golf packages at the Homestead start at $246 per person per day, including room, breakfast, dinner, unlimited golf on the Homestead and Lower Cascades courses (there's a $30 surcharge to play the Cascades Course), and cart for one round.

The Homestead. Hot Springs, VA 24445. Tel: 800-838-1766 or 540-839-1766. Fax: 540-839-7670. 521 rooms and suites. Doubles range from $375 to $425, including breakfast and dinner. Golf and other discount packages available. Credit cards accepted.

RESTAURANTS

GOLF TRAVEL has always found the food at the Homestead acceptable but not exceptional or truly distinguished. Yet most recently, we found the dining somewhat improved. Despite its rather dreary decor, our dinner in the somewhat formal **Grille** (men must wear jackets) was very tasty. Dinner in the handsome, formal main **Dining Room,** where jackets and ties are required, is a grand event, with attentive service, live music, and fathers dancing with their tiny daughters on the dance floor. We ordered a good shrimp and crabmeat salad, trout with vegetables and mashed potatoes, and a fine dessert from a tempting selection. The wine list is good. The Dining Room also serves as the site of the resort's excellent breakfast buffet.

Lunch can be less satisfactory. **Café Albert** is charming, but its cooking is only passable. **Sam Snead's Tavern** and the **Casino Grill** in the Homestead golf clubhouse give you a couple of other informal options. Although the resort is open year-round, these two restaurants, as well as the Grille, close during the off season.

The restaurants at the Homestead. Hot Springs, VA 24445. Tel: 800-838-1766, 540-839-1766 (general), or 540-839-7989 (dining reservations). Fax: 540-839-7670. Credit cards accepted.

NON-GOLF ACTIVITIES

There is a wide array of appealing non-golf activities at the Homestead—skiing and ice skating during winter months, hiking along Cascades Gorge, fully supervised programs for children, horseback riding, carriage rides, shooting, fishing, tennis, or simply relaxing with a good book in a rocking chair on the Homestead's gracious front porch. The wonderful Warm Springs pools, located five miles from the hotel, are one of the Homestead's greatest attractions. The two natural warm springs, one for men and one for women, were discovered in the eighteenth century and once enjoyed by Thomas Jefferson. Today, lucky resort guests can soak in the pools to their hearts' content.

The $4 million renovation of the Homestead's spa building is proceeding floor by floor toward completion, but inconvenience is kept to a minimum because all normal services and activities are still offered.

GETTING THERE: From Washington, take 66 West to 81 South. From 81 South take 257 West into Bridgewater. In the town pick up 42 South to 39 West. Take 39 West to Route 220 South. The Homestead will be five miles ahead.

West Virginia

▶THE GREENBRIER

THE WORLD'S BEST GOLF DESTINATION

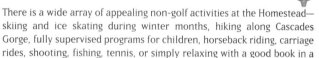

	The Golf	Golf Services	Lodging	Restaurants	Non-Golf Activities	Total
Rating	19	20	18	17	20	94

An instantly recognizable figure—indeed, a living legend of American golf—was giving an informal lesson out on the practice range the morning we arrived at the spec-

The Greenbrier

tacular Greenbrier in beautiful White Sulphur Springs, West Virginia. A small cluster of resort guests, casually leaning on their wedges, stood quietly behind this twosome at a respectful distance, thoroughly transfixed by the proceedings.

"Slow, slow, slow," the teacher-legend was telling his student. "Go straight back. Stay in your shirt. Now smack it. Hit it square in the back. Just pop it. Good! You ought to bottle that one."

Then the legend began to strike balls himself—automatic seven irons all fired to the same little patch of turf 140 yards down the range. His swing is as sweet as ever and as slow and easy coming down to the ball as it is going up. His attire is as famous as that flawless swing—the bright pink shirt, the crisply pressed trousers, the high-gloss black shoes, and the trademark straw hat with its colorful hatband—a style so original and distinctive that it may, one day, land him in the Smithsonian Institution.

Sam Snead, now eighty-five years old, is the Greenbrier's "golf professional emeritus," the resident ambassador of the resort's big, booming, and absolutely impeccable golf operation. Snead was visible everywhere during our recent visit to the Greenbrier—having drinks and dinner early one evening in the Casino, puttering around the golf courses with his faithful golden retriever, and shaking hands with strangers friendly and bold enough to come over and say hello. A glimpse of Sam Snead hitting balls on the practice range can inspire you to play better golf as little else can.

With a total score of 94 out of 100 possible points, the Greenbrier reigns supreme among the world's greatest golf resorts—better than the Lodge at Pebble Beach (90), better than the Inn at Spanish Bay (92), better than the American Club in Kohler, Wisconsin (92), and superior to other glorious properties like Gleneagles in Scotland (90), Mauna Kea in Hawaii (92), and the Four Seasons on Nevis (90).

There are three chief reasons why this is so. First, the three exquisitely maintained golf courses at the Greenbrier—perhaps the best conditioned of any resort links that we have played—are the most complementary set of courses possessed by any resort in the world. That this stunning valley in the mountains of West Virginia could contain three such different courses is nothing short of miraculous. The gorgeous Greenbrier Course, designed by Jack Nicklaus in 1978, is long and difficult; the Lakeside Course, designed by Dick Wilson in 1963, is lovely, serene, and some would say—mistakenly, in our opinion—easy; and the Old White Course, designed by Charles Blair Macdonald, is pure golf at its best—a classic masterpiece dating from 1913.

Second, the "golf culture" at the Greenbrier, more so than any other resort we have visited, welcomes and inspires the expert and beginning player alike. The high handicapper feels comfortable and unintimidated in this unique atmosphere, while the low handicapper believes this might just be his or her chance to shoot a career-low round.

And third, the golf services at the Greenbrier are virtually unparalleled. Robert Harris, who perhaps better than anyone embodies what a director of golf should be, holds his enormous staff to the highest standards. It is, in a word, superlative. We played on two extremely busy days, yet employees never looked frazzled and never said "no." Every wish was accommodated in stellar style.

On top of all this, the Greenbrier has the finest and widest assortment of non-golf activities of any resort in the world—from its renowned spa to its riding and tennis facilities, from croquet to falconry. And then there is the overall Greenbrier experience itself, including the vast scale of its interior spaces vividly decorated by Dorothy Draper and preserved by Carlton Varney, the impeccable gardens, the arcade of elegant shops, the famous medical clinic, the army of attentive and smiling employees who always extend a friendly word, and the traditional, well-dressed clientele (jackets and ties are required in the evenings, but suits and long dresses are common). In fact, our mixed foursome on the Greenbrier Course late one afternoon included the CEOs of two Fortune 500 companies, while the next morning a former United States senator was seen teeing off on the Old White Course with his wife. The airport in the nearby town of Lewisburg is always filled with private and corporate jets. If you have never been to the Greenbrier, take our advice and go. It simply does not get any better than this.

THE GOLF   19

The **Greenbrier Course,** which has hosted the Solheim Cup as well as the 1979 Ryder Cup, opens with six extremely tough golf holes and is ideally suited for the low-to-mid-handicap player. This 6,681-yard layout (par rating 73.7/slope rating 136) features a slew of forced carries, tight fairways lined with pines and oaks, very quick double- and triple-tiered greens, and five long and difficult par threes. The Greenbrier resort's great golf pedigree is capped by this gorgeous course, but oh those first six holes!

The opening hole on the Greenbrier Course—an uphill, 423-yard par four—sets the challenging tone. Your approach shot to the green on the first hole must ascend a hill and clear a pair of yawning bunkers. The second hole, a 403-yard par four, features a lake that guards the green and swallows up every ball hit short and to the right. The beautiful third hole is a short, 475-yard par five with a fairway that becomes progressively more narrow; the small green is tucked away among the towering trees. The fourth hole, the first par three on the course, is 177 yards long but more or less straight uphill. The fifth is a monster par five, 551 yards long but mercifully downhill all the way. Then you come to number six, the most intimidating hole on the course and rated the single toughest hole of golf in the state of West Virginia. Par is an exceptionally good score on this brutal hole, which measures 456 long yards uphill to a plateau green. In fact, if you manage to shoot your handicap on the Greenbrier Course, consider it a significant accomplishment.

The **Old White Course,** the resort's most esteemed layout and popular among golfers of all handicaps, is as different from the Greenbrier Course as night is from day. The Scottish-style Old White follows the interesting natural contours of the valley floor and has no big artificial mounds or forced carries created by a pack of bulldozers. The greens on Old White can be attacked either with lofted shots or bump-and-runs, and the subtle putting surfaces, unlike the deep undulations of the multitiered greens on the Greenbrier Course, can yield birdies from almost any distance. In other words, shooting your handicap on Old White is a distinct possibility.

The first tee on Old White, elevated high above Howard's Creek, enjoys as dramatic a setting for an opening drive as exists in American golf. Although it does not compare with the incredible adrenaline rush and huge public spectacle of the first tee at St. Andrews in Scotland, we know of no other course in the United States where your first shot of the day can be inspected by so many casual witnesses. If you begin play early in the morning, no one will be around to analyze your backswing. Yet if you tee off around noon, expect to be scrutinized by the seventy-five or so resort guests enjoying lunch on the Casino terrace, playing tennis, or strolling down to the golf shop.

Outstanding holes on Old White include number twelve, a long and tough 549-yard par five that doglegs gently to the right and plays to a steeply elevated green, and the four great finishing holes that cross Howard's Creek time after time. Fifteen is a 220-yard par three; sixteen, perhaps the most exquisite hole on Old White, demands two creek crossings and actually features two greens (a sign on the tee indicates which green is in play that day); seventeen is a 514-yard par five with the creek on the right threatening errant tee shots; and eighteen is a very pretty, 160-yard par three that plays considerably longer than the posted yardage.

Lakeside Course

Idyllic **Lakeside,** the shortest course at the Greenbrier, is perfectly suited for the mid-to-high handicapper. The course can produce delightfully low scores and, consequently, a wonderful sense of euphoria and accomplishment. In addition, with its parklike setting and panoramic views of Kate's Mountain, Lakeside is the resort's prettiest and most charming layout. At the same time, it still offers plenty of challenge for even the most accomplished golfer and has the single longest hole at the Greenbrier, number four, a 579-yard par five.

Lakeside's first hole is also a terrific opener; a drive hit far right on this short 353-yard par four will splash into the waters of the creek.

The greens fees at each of the Greenbrier's three courses are $95 for resort guests and $200 for the general public. Carts cost an additional $18. Walking is permitted with a caddie.

A fascinating golf experience just two miles from the Greenbrier is **Oakhurst Links.** Founded in 1884, Oakhurst was the first organized golf club in the United States. Today, a visitor to Oakhurst pays $45 to play the enchanting nine-hole course with vintage, hickory-shafted clubs and new gutta-percha balls supplied by Oakhurst's owner, Lewis Keller. The course measures 2,035 yards, but there is no par—golfers play the old rule that the first ball holed in the fewest strikes wins the hole. Beautiful little Oakhurst is well worth a special outing, especially for those already in the vicinity of White Sulphur Springs. The season runs from April through October.

The Greenbrier. White Sulphur Springs, WV 24986. Tel: 800-624-6070 or 304-536-1110. Fax: 304-536-7854. Credit cards accepted.

• *Greenbrier Course.* 1978. Designer: Jack Nicklaus. Par 72. 6,681 yards. 73.7 par rating. 136 slope rating. Season: March–November.
• *Old White Course.* 1913. Designer: Charles Blair Macdonald. Par 70. 6,640 yards. 72.7 par rating. 128 slope rating. Season: April 1–November.
• *Lakeside Course.* 1963. Designer: Dick Wilson. Par 70. 6,336 yards. 70.4 par rating. 121 slope rating. Season: year-round.
• Greens fees for all courses: Day ticket: $95 (resort guests), $200 (public). Carts cost an additional $18. Walking permitted with caddies. Caddies available.

Oakhurst Links. PO Box 639, White Sulphur Springs, WV 24986. Tel: 304-536-1884. Fax: 304-536-1884. Credit cards accepted.

• 1884/1994. Designers: Russell Montague, Lionel Torrin/Bob Cupp. No par. 2,035 yards. No par or slope ratings. Greens fee of $45 includes period equipment. No carts. No caddies. Season: April–October.

GOLF SERVICES 20

The Greenbrier is one of the few remaining golf resorts in the United States—along with Pebble Beach, the Cloister on Sea Island, Georgia, and Bay Hill in Orlando—with a thriving caddie program. We played two days with a terrific older caddie named Harrison whose advice and local knowledge cut at least a half-dozen shots from our score. Caddies get $30 per bag plus tip.

Golf services are honestly so good at the Greenbrier that it is hard to know where to begin. Perhaps the most unique feature on the courses are the elaborate halfway houses. These pillared mini-Greenbriers are no doubt the best-stocked halfway houses in golf, with fine cigars, exotic beers, and other delicacies. Head pro Hill Herrick is a gifted teacher; the range features buckets of complimentary balls; the pro shop and locker facilities are handsome and staffed with friendly personnel; and, most important, no one gets lost in the shuffle. The Greenbrier attracts large business groups, yet the single golfer is never shunted aside. Two new developments include a lightning warning system and the move to "soft" spikes. The shoe attendants will replace your spikes at no charge.

LODGING  18

Dorothy Draper's "Return to Tara" decor lends a vibrant color scheme not only to the Greenbrier's palatial public spaces but also to its large and gracious bedrooms, with wallpaper of yellow roses, pink tulips, or flowering white azaleas, along with bright-green carpeting, vivid blue drapery, scarlet club chairs, quilts on the beds, and white-painted furniture with big hardware. The standard, amenity-filled room we occupied, number 3199, with its high ceiling, luxurious bathroom, and thoughtful appointments, was delightfully decorated and extremely comfortable. Our only complaint? The main elevators are slow and a bit rickety, while the corridors leading to the guest rooms are somewhat dreary and in need of a face-lift. The best and most costly accommodations at the Greenbrier are the "cottages" on Spring Row and Paradise Row.

Obviously, the Greenbrier is not inexpensive. During our thirty-six hours at the resort, playing two days of golf and staying one night in the hotel as a single, the bill totaled $679. At checkout, a pleasant young clerk quickly examined the invoice and mentioned in a friendly way: "You were a good boy." Her meaning? We did not spend a lot of money on the premises. The price for a couple on a getaway spree enjoying spa treatments, fine wines with dinner, and other diversions easily approaches—and in many cases exceeds—$1,000 per day. Golfers headed to the Greenbrier should opt, as we did, for one of the golf packages, which include room, unlimited golf, breakfast, and dinner.

The Greenbrier. White Sulphur Springs, WV 24986. Tel: 800-624-6070 or 304-536-1110. Fax: 304-536-7854. 672 rooms, suites, and cottages. Doubles from $440 to $540, breakfast and dinner included. Golf packages from $528 to $600 per couple. Credit cards accepted.

RESTAURANTS 17

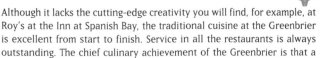

Although it lacks the cutting-edge creativity you will find, for example, at Roy's at the Inn at Spanish Bay, the traditional cuisine at the Greenbrier is excellent from start to finish. Service in all the restaurants is always outstanding. The chief culinary achievement of the Greenbrier is that a resort so vast (nearly seven hundred rooms, suites, and cottages) produces food so universally good. Dinner in the **Main Dining Room** is a grand event (carpaccio of beef, green salad, roast beef, an excellent wine list) accompanied by a violin and piano duo performing on a central stage. The **Ryder Cup Grill** is ideal for lunch after a morning round of golf. **Draper's Café** serves good breakfasts and light lunches, while the **Tavern Room,** downstairs from the Old White Club, serves fine American cuisine and rotisserie specialties.

The restaurants at the Greenbrier. White Sulphur Springs, WV 24986. Tel: 800-624-6070 or 304-536-1110. Fax: 304-536-7854. Credit cards accepted.

NON-GOLF ACTIVITIES 20

The wealth of activities at the Greenbrier includes gourmet cooking classes; hiking, riding, and bicycling on miles of tranquil mountain trails; indoor and outdoor tennis; carriage rides; white-water rafting trips; fishing; a gun club and shooting preserve; indoor and outdoor swimming pools; a magnificent, 29,000-square-foot spa featuring mineral baths, massage, and exercise facilities; the art colony on Cottage Row; the acclaimed medical clinic, where many guests go for their annual checkups; and world-class croquet and bowling.

GETTING THERE: From Washington, take I-66 West to 81 South to Lexington, Virginia. Pick up I-64 West to Exit 181 (White Sulphur Springs). At the bottom of the exit ramp, turn right and drive 1.5 miles to the Greenbrier.

North Carolina

▶PINEHURST

NUMBER 8, THE PIT, AND PINEHURST VILLAGE

	The Golf	Golf Services	Lodging	Restaurants	Non-Golf Activities	Total
Rating	19	18	16	16	17	86

Pinehurst, the golf mecca of the Sandhills, continues to grow at an explosive rate thanks to both the incredible boom enjoyed by the sport of golf worldwide and the aggressive management style of ClubCorp, which has owned the Pinehurst Resort and Country Club since 1984. The extraordinary growth of Pinehurst, however, has both positive and negative ramifications that the discriminating visitor will quickly detect. Overall, Pinehurst remains unique, but aspects of the Pinehurst experience now feel mass-produced.

Pinehurst Resort and Country Club

On the positive side, the Pinehurst Resort has just opened course Number 8, the Centennial, designed by one of America's most esteemed architects, Tom Fazio. Number 8 was constructed on the site of the old Pinehurst Gun Club, once run by Annie Oakley and located about a mile and a half from the historic Pinehurst Hotel, with its copper roof glistening in the North Carolina sunshine and the neat rows of rocking chairs lining its deep porches.

With the addition of Number 8, Pinehurst now has 144 holes of golf, making it the single largest golf resort in the known universe. Number 8 is pure Pinehurst, a traditional, classic beauty. When we visited in the fall of 1996 we overlooked its inevitable new-course scars—drainage trenches cutting across some fairways, mud and dust around the new clubhouse that will be among the most handsome in America once its construction is complete, and brand-new fairways and greens that were not yet exactly thick with grass. In truth, Number 8 needs another year of TLC before its physical condition can be accurately described as optimum. This new Fazio layout may be a bit torn up and raw right now, but it promises great sport in the near future.

A second new Pinehurst plus, prosperity—in the form of golf-tourism dollars and increasing numbers of retirees settling in Pinehurst and Southern Pines—has brought vitality and sophistication to the Sandhills without disrupting its slower pace of life, its genuine Southern charm, and the wholesome values that lie at the foundation of this community. One of the great, if rather low-key, delights of staying at the Pinehurst Hotel is strolling every evening after dinner in Pinehurst Village, originally laid out in 1895 by Frederick Law Olmsted, the codesigner of New York's Central Park. The shady streets that encircle Pinehurst Village are lined with lovely "cottages" from the 1920s and 1930s, architectural jewels that could have been purchased for as little as $100,000 four or five years ago. Now fully restored, some are selling in the neighborhood of $750,000. The smart shops in Pinehurst Village make it a Southern version of Carmel, the golf mecca of the Monterey Peninsula.

Since the essence of Pinehurst Village is its wonderful human scale, we find it mystifying that many of the new "golf communities" that surround Pinehurst are so sterile and unattractive, indeed, blights upon the landscape. And why—can anyone out there please tell us—do nearly all such golf communities built in America in the past ten years look so much alike? You are already familiar with the formula—massive, built-to-impress, 8,000-square-foot "McMansions" in gated communities constructed on postage-stamp lots with at least a dozen pillars and Palladian windows—houses that look like *Gone With the Wind* movie sets from the front and brick-veneer trailers from the rear.

Several fine old golf courses in Pinehurst have been badly disfigured by poor real estate planning, which has placed homes and condominiums virtually on top of the fairways. And now a few of the newer golf courses have been equally victimized by bad taste and a rapacious profit motive. When we visited Pinehurst years ago, for example, we were very impressed with the Rees Jones–designed Number 7, brand-new at the time, and the real estate development that surrounded the course, called Fairwoods on 7. Now, years later, we must report that the big, look-alike homes on Number 7 detract from the golfing experience. When Fairwoods on 7 broke ground, like any number of new golf course developments elsewhere in the country, it occasioned excitement and heavy sales. Years later, it just looks dreary and poorly planned, however expensive and prestigious the homes and lots might be.

No one, perhaps, knows this better than ClubCorp itself. The new Number 8, for example, is advertised as having "no real estate interferences or distractions." Indeed, there are only a handful of homes on the distant periphery on Number 8, and for this reason alone both ClubCorp and Number 8 are to be applauded. Golf *without* a real estate angle—we hope this is the beginning of a trend.

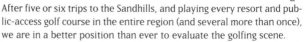

THE GOLF

After five or six trips to the Sandhills, and playing every resort and public-access golf course in the entire region (and several more than once), we are in a better position than ever to evaluate the golfing scene.

The four best area courses, in order, are Number 2 (home of the 1999 U.S. Open), Pine Needles (site of the 1996 U.S. Women's Open), the Pit, and Number 8. Any dream trip to Pinehurst will include rounds on each of these four superb, and very different, layouts.

Mid Pines, Number 7, Number 1, Number 4, and Number 6 (listed here in descending order of excellence) are all very good, but not great. Number 7 was not in particularly good condition when we played it recently. The courses to avoid at Pinehurst are Numbers 3 and 5.

Pine Needles and Mid Pines are reviewed below. The new revelation for us was the **Pit Golf Links,** which, we admit, has a regrettable name. Located five miles from the Pinehurst Hotel on Route 5 toward Aberdeen, the Pit was designed by Dan Maples, a true Pinehurst blueblood whose grandfather, Frank, was Donald Ross's longtime construction superintendent, and whose dad, Ellis, designed Pinehurst Number 5, now sadly hemmed in by condominiums.

The Pit, built on the site of an old sandpit, is a pure golf experience (no real estate here either), as well as one of the best values in the region with greens fees ranging from $42 to $86 throughout the year, cart included, and just $35 after 2 P.M. in summer. Rated among America's Top 50 public-access courses by *Golf Digest*, the Pit is outstanding from start to finish, with a terrific back nine, including three holes (eleven, twelve, and thirteen) that play around a lake. Number twelve, a 167-yard par three, features an island green. From the blues, the course measures 6,600 yards (par rating 72.3/slope rating 139). The forward tees shorten the course to 4,759 yards (par rating 68.4/slope rating 121). Walking is permitted. For tee times call 800-574-4653.

Profoundly respected for his sensitivity to the environment, Tom Fazio carefully situated the front nine of lovely **Number 8** within towering pine forests and the back nine within beautiful, natural wetlands. Vast sand waste areas, typical of Pinehurst, can be found all over the course. The front nine resembles a contemporary interpretation of Number 2, while the back side combines traditional Pinehurst characteristics with marshland treatment reminiscent of Fazio's work in Florida and South Carolina. Great individual holes include the third, an uphill par four that plays far longer than its 386 yards; the sixth, a 604-yard par five that requires a tee shot to an uphill landing area across the lake; the thirteenth, a 209-yard par three to an elevated green; and fourteen, a fabulous 402-yard par four that doglegs to the left and demands another mighty water crossing with the drive.

Number 8 is much tougher than its par and slope ratings indicate. From the gold tees it measures 7,092 yards (par rating 74.0/slope rating 135), from the blues the course is 6,698 yards long (par rating 71.7/slope rating 125), and from the whites it measures 6,302 yards (par rating 69.8/slope rating 121). From the red tees Number 8 is 5,177 yards long (par rating 68.9/slope rating 112). At Number 8 and all the other courses at the Pinehurst Country Club, the courses are restricted to members and resort guests. On a strictly space-available basis, golfers who are not staying at the resort may be able to play Pinehurst's courses by calling first thing on the day they want to play.

Pinehurst Resort. PO Box 4000, Pinehurst, NC 28374. Tel: 800-487-4653 or 910-295-8141. Fax: 910-295-8466. Credit cards accepted.

• *Pinehurst Number 2.* 1907. Designer: Donald Ross. Par 72. 7,020 yards. 74.1 par rating. 131 slope rating. Greens fees: resort guest: $150, public: $200, includes cart. Walking permitted. Caddies available. Season: year-round.

• *Pinehurst Number 8.* 1996. Designer: Tom Fazio. Par 72. 7,092 yards. 74 par rating. 135 slope rating. Greens fees: resort guests: $120, public: $180, includes cart. Walking permitted. Caddies available. Season: year-round.

The Pit Golf Links. PO Box 5789, Highway 5, Pinehurst, NC 28374. Tel: 800-574-4653 or 910-944-1600. Fax: 910-944-7069. Credit cards accepted.

• 1985. Designer: Dan Maples. Par 71. 6,600 yards. 72.3 par rating. 139 slope rating. Greens fees: $42–$86, includes cart. Walking permitted. Caddies available. Season: year-round.

GOLF SERVICES

Golf services at Pinehurst, in terms of its physical facilities, are unsurpassed. Pinehurst caddies can read the greens in their sleep; Maniac Hill is perhaps the best practice range in golf; the main clubhouse is spectacular; and the new clubhouse serving Number 8 will be marvelous on completion. Personnel, however, can sometimes be hardened, especially the young gentlemen working at the tee-time booking desk inside the pro shop. Hundreds of thousands of rounds are played at Pinehurst every year. The sheer volume of activity seems to have taken its toll on the spirit of these critical employees, who frequently appear to care not a whit if you get out on the golf course.

LODGING

Staying at the **Pinehurst Hotel** is still a deeply satisfying experience despite the bigger and bigger crowds that descend upon the place year after year and the hectic atmosphere that can prevail at the front desk and elsewhere within the resort. Large groups checking in and out, arriving at the bars and restaurants en masse, and quickly filling up the hotel shuttle buses mean that service—especially during the height of the spring season—can frequently be slow. But the vast majority of resort employees retain their pleasant Southern humor. The baggage boys out front, the superb bartender in the Ryder Cup Bar, and the staffs in both the main Carolina Dining Room and the Donald Ross Grill in the Clubhouse all deserve special praise.

The Pinehurst Hotel

Our standard room on the hotel's third floor was comfortable and more than satisfactory in every regard. All rooms are equipped with stocked minibars and cable television, and the baths are clean and modern.

Avid golfers should take advantage of one of the two available golf packages. The Donald Ross Package includes room, breakfast, dinner, and one round of golf per day with cart and costs $691 per person, double occupancy in high season. The Putterboy Package includes all of the above but allows you to play thirty-six holes a day. The Putterboy is priced at $843 per person, double occupancy. Surcharges are added for rounds on Numbers 2, 7, and 8.

Pinehurst Resort. PO Box 4000, Pinehurst, NC 28374. Tel: 800-487-4653 or 910-295-6811. Fax: 910-295-8466. 220 rooms. Doubles start at $174 per person, including room, breakfast, and dinner. Golf packages available. Credit cards accepted.

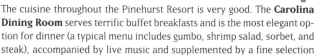

RESTAURANTS

The cuisine throughout the Pinehurst Resort is very good. The **Carolina Dining Room** serves terrific buffet breakfasts and is the most elegant option for dinner (a typical menu includes gumbo, shrimp salad, sorbet, and steak), accompanied by live music and supplemented by a fine selection of wines. Jackets, but not neckties, are required in the evening. The **Donald Ross Grill** in the clubhouse is the best spot for a casual lunch between rounds of golf.

The restaurants at Pinehurst Resort. PO Box 4000, Pinehurst, NC 28374. Tel: 910-295-8434 (dining reservations), 910-295-8139 (Donald Ross Grill). Fax: 910-295-8402 (dining reservations). Credit cards accepted.

NON-GOLF ACTIVITIES

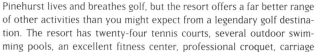

Pinehurst lives and breathes golf, but the resort offers a far better range of other activities than you might expect from a legendary golf destination. The resort has twenty-four tennis courts, several outdoor swimming pools, an excellent fitness center, professional croquet, carriage rides, bicycle rentals, and supervised children's programs. Pinehurst Village, as already noted, is another worthwhile diversion.

GETTING THERE: From the Raleigh Airport take 40 East to US 1 South. Follow 1 South into Sanford, where you will pick up Highway 15 and 501 South. Continue until you enter a traffic circle, and get on Route 2 West. Follow 1.5 miles; the resort is on the right.

►PINE NEEDLES AND MID PINES
THE TRUE ESSENCE OF PINEHURST

	The Golf	Golf Services	Lodging	Restaurants	Non-Golf Activities	Total
Rating	**18**	**17**	**16**	**14**	**14**	**79**

At the very pinnacle of the Pinehurst pyramid sits the grand Pinehurst Hotel along with the region's premier golf course, Donald Ross's majestic Number 2. Yet the unique Sandhills of North Carolina offer the visiting golfer a great deal more to choose from than its most expensive resort. Hidden away among the towering, aromatic pines you will find more than forty other golf courses, clubs, residential communities, and fine golf resorts that are less universally well known.

The two best and most interesting golf resorts among this "second tier" of Pinehurst facilities are Pine Needles Golf Resort and Mid Pines Inn and Golf Club, two properties as historic as any in Pinehurst. Pine Needles and Mid Pines are now both owned by the famous golfing family led by the highly regarded Peggy Kirk Bell, an influential force in women's golf and one of the greatest teachers in the game. The Bells have owned Pine Needles since the 1950s and acquired Mid Pines in 1994; the two are located just across the street from one another on Midland Road between Pinehurst and the community of Southern Pines, about four miles from Pinehurst Village.

Genuine Pinehurst insiders would strenuously insist that there is nothing second tier or second fiddle at all about Pine Needles and Mid Pines. In fact, many frequent visitors to the region believe that Pine Needles and Mid Pines may represent the authentic spirit of traditional Pinehurst far better, in many respects, than the present-day Pinehurst Hotel.

It cannot be denied that both Pine Needles and Mid Pines have serious shortcomings as resorts (see below), but each has its own beautiful and captivating Donald Ross golf course and an atmosphere that is relaxed, homey, and engaging. Make no mistake: neither Pine Needles nor Mid Pines is in the same overall class as the posh Pinehurst Hotel. Yet if you want a low-key experience that combines pure golf with reasonable prices—and if you wish to capture some of the true flavor of Pinehurst in the process—then these two mellow old properties are worth your consideration.

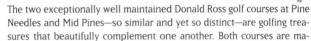

THE GOLF   18

The two exceptionally well maintained Donald Ross golf courses at Pine Needles and Mid Pines—so similar and yet so distinct—are golfing treasures that beautifully complement one another. Both courses are mature, magical tracks built in the 1920s with towering pines lining the fairways, pinecones the size of small footballs lying in clusters at the base of trees, and thick blankets of soft pine needles that crunch underfoot in the rough areas. Both courses wend their way through attractive, rolling countryside, yet there are real differences between them that make this particular combination of courses especially compelling.

Mid Pines is easily three or four strokes tougher than Pine Needles. The fairways are tighter at Mid Pines, the greens are smaller and more undulating, the woods are denser, and the bunkers guarding the greens are more menacing and numerous. Mid Pines is also slightly longer, measuring 6,515 yards from the blue tees (slope 127) versus 6,318 yards (slope 126) at Pine Needles. Of the two, Pine Needles, host of the 1996 U.S. Women's Open won by Annika Sorrenstam, may be the more elegant layout. Mid Pines is clearly the more intimidating. There is a wonderful almost yin and yang chemistry between the two: Pine Needles representing the feminine and Mid Pines the masculine. Resort guests at Pine Needles and Mid Pines have unlimited access to both layouts.

The front nine wins the beauty prize at **Pine Needles,** although the most dramatic holes are located on the back. There are interesting relics to be discovered along the course as well, like the Elizabethan-style St. Joseph's of the Pines behind the second tee, now a nursing home but once the original Pine Needles Inn.

The par threes at Pine Needles are especially good. In fact, the fifth (207 yards) and the thirteenth (189 yards) may be two of the more difficult holes on which to score par. The tenth hole, however, is probably the most unique at Pine Needles. A 485-yard par five, number ten is a dogleg-left from an elevated tee over a lake. A big drive cutting the corner over the pines, however, will put you in exquisite position to make birdie, or even eagle. The seventeenth hole repeats the pattern of ten. A courageous drive over the dogleg shortens the seventeenth by thirty to forty yards. And eighteen, a 426-yard par four, is a great finishing hole. You drive the ball over the hill and bring your approach shot down to the green. It is an inspiring sensation.

Both nines are equally lovely at Mid Pines. Outstanding holes include beautiful number two, a 178-yard par three; the third, a fabulous 414-yard par four that demands a drive over a lake; the sixteenth, a downhill, 400-yard par four; and the eighteenth, a long par four that finishes in front of the clubhouse. Mid Pines is less forgiving from side-to-side than Pine Needles and places a *big* premium on accuracy.

Walking is permitted on both courses, but given conditions that are at times steep (particularly on Mid Pines), carts are advised. Since the courses are just two or three minutes apart, it is a breeze to play one in the morning and the other after lunch.

Mid Pines Inn and Golf Club. 1010 Midland Road, Southern Pines, NC 28387. Tel: 800-323-2114 or 910-692-2114. Fax: 910-692-4615. Credit cards accepted.

• 1921. Designer: Donald Ross. Par 72. 6,515 yards. 71.4 rating. 127 slope rating. Greens fees: resort guests: $85 (high season)/$45 (low season), public: $99 (high season)/$59 (low season), cart included. Walking permitted. No caddies. Season: year-round.

Pine Needles Golf Resort. PO Box 88, Southern Pines, NC 28388. Tel: 800-747-7272 or 910-692-7111. Fax: 910-692-5349. Credit cards accepted.

• 1927. Designer: Donald Ross. Par 71. 6,318 yards. 70.2 par rating. 126 slope rating. Greens fees: resort guests: $90 (high season), public: $109 (high season), cart included. Walking permitted. No caddies. Season: year-round.

GOLF SERVICES

Golf services are excellent at both Pine Needles and Mid Pines. Peggy Kirk Bell created one of the first golf schools in the country and her women-only Golfaris are extremely popular. There are a variety of five-day Golfari instruction packages (for both women and men) that include lodging, meals, golf, and instruction and start at $925. The practice range at Pine Needles, as well as the instruction area adjacent to the first green, are outstanding. The range at Mid Pines is adequate. Range policies are inconsistent: at Pine Needles, range balls are free; at Mid Pines you pay about $2 for a bucket. The pro shops at both resorts are attractive and well stocked. The shop at Pine Needles—appropriately, since this is Peggy Kirk Bell's establishment—has a good inventory of women's golf apparel.

LODGING

For your most satisfying accommodations, we strongly recommend that you stay in one of the handsome, newly renovated rooms at **Mid Pines,** like lovely number 207, with its fresh white paint, fine new fabrics and furnishings, and its wonderful view of Mid Pines's eighteenth green. When making your reservation at Mid Pines be certain to request a renovated room that faces the golf course.

The opportunity to host the 1996 U.S. Women's Open brought big benefits to the **Pine Needles Golf Resort.**

Mid Pines Inn

One of the biggest was the remodeling of all the resort's rooms that are located in the chalet-style cottages. Deluxe doubles feature two double beds and a small sitting area and are priced at $135 per person (including three meals a day) during the spring and fall.

Costs at both hotels are extremely reasonable. Almost everyone who golfs and stays at either resort comes on a golf package. At Mid Pines the Donald Ross Package, which includes your room, breakfast, lunch, dinner, and two guaranteed tee times each day at Mid Pines and Pine Needles, is priced at just $562 per person for a stay of three days and two nights in a superior room in the spring and fall. A similar package at Pine Needles costs $542 per person. Service at both hotels is friendly and welcoming.

Mid Pines Inn and Golf Club. 1010 Midland Road, Southern Pines, NC 28387. Tel: 800-323-2114 or 910-692-2114. Fax: 910-692-4615. 112 rooms. Doubles range from $120 to $180. Credit cards accepted.

Pine Needles Golf Resort. PO Box 88, Southern Pines, NC 28388. Tel: 800-747-7272 or 910-692-7111. Fax: 910-692-5349. 75 rooms. Doubles range from $180 to $270 and include three meals daily for two people. Credit cards accepted.

RESTAURANTS 14

The terrace dining area and the formal dining room at **Mid Pines** are attractive and put us in the mood for a fine meal. Our lunch on the terrace after a morning round at Mid Pines was quite pleasant, but, in all candor, the cooking at Mid Pines is not truly distinguished. Men must wear jackets during dinner in the main dining room at each hotel.

We found the cuisine at **Pine Needles** also only fair. The buffet breakfast, with a chef preparing waffles and eggs, was very good, and the luncheon buffet was also agreeable, but our dinners were uninspired. The shrimp cocktail consisted of four rather tiny shrimp, and the prime rib served with rather bland vegetables proved forgettable. Pine Needles does, however, have a nice selection of wines.

The dining room at Mid Pines Inn and Golf Club. 1010 Midland Road, Southern Pines, NC 28387. Tel: 800-323-2114 or 910-692-2114. Fax: 910-692-4615. Credit cards accepted.

The dining room at Pine Needles Golf Resort. PO Box 88, Southern Pines, NC 28388. Tel: 910-692-7111. Fax: 910-692-5349. Credit cards accepted.

NON-GOLF ACTIVITIES 14

Pine Needles and Mid Pines are recommended strictly for golf purists. Non-golfers—unless satisfied with tennis and swimming—could well be bored to tears. Pine Needles has two beautiful grass tennis courts, an outdoor swimming pool, and a decades-old game room with pinball machines, but that is basically the extent of its activities. Come for the golf only.

GETTING THERE: From Washington, take I-95 South to the Benson exit (Route 27 West). Take Route 27 West to US 1. Proceed on US 1 South to Southern Pines. Take the Midland Road exit and proceed to either resort.

►BALD HEAD ISLAND

BEACH MUSIC

	The Golf	Golf Services	Lodging	Restaurants	Non-Golf Activities	Total
Rating	17	17	17	15	18	84

Bald Head Island

At the southernmost tip of coastal North Carolina, where the Cape Fear River empties into the Atlantic, you will find Bald Head Island, one of the most attractive, successful, and fashionable of the new resorts to have been developed along the coast of the Carolinas in recent years.

To be frank, Bald Head Island initially captured our imagination with its persistent marketing blitz in *The Wall Street Journal*. The airbrushed photos of stylish couples dressed in white linen gazing wistfully into the sunset while strolling down the beach, along with images of immaculately attired golfers with perfect backswings hitting from emerald greens, presented just the sort of advertising campaign that always hits us right in the gut.

Bald Head Island, originally settled by a lighthouse brigade that warned ships at sea not to pass too closely to the dangerous shoals and sandbars of Cape Fear, is a fragile but quite sizable barrier island typical of the exquisite Carolina Low Country. The island is laced with salt marshes and populated by seabirds and a handful of large, inscrutable alligators that dwell in the tidal creeks and—from time to time—crawl from the lagoons to doze in the sunshine on the golf course. Gnarled live oaks hung with webbed tendrils of Spanish moss are the dominant form of local vegetation. In other words, Bald Head and its environs—Southport and historic Wilmington, North Carolina—present a landscape familiar to anyone acquainted with the novels of Pat Conroy, the true laureate of these tides and Southern beaches.

Especially appealing is the unusual mode of island transportation. Cars, very wisely, are prohibited on Bald Head. You leave your vehicle in the secured parking lot at Southport and ride one of the resort's large ferries to the island, a delightful twenty-minute channel crossing. All accommodations on Bald Head come equipped with a golf cart for use over the paved lanes that lead to the wonderful beaches, restaurants, pool, shops, nature trails, and lovely golf club. In our estimation, the East Beach on Bald Head is one of the most wonderful beaches in all America—wide, sandy, perfect for swimming, and spectacularly beautiful at low tide.

We have, however, real concerns about Bald Head's future. With six hundred homes already constructed, services and facilities on the island feel stretched to their extreme limit. With more than 2,000 homes planned—and extraordinary construction taking place at this very moment—Bald Head could well be ruined or turned into, as Conroy himself might worry, the next Hilton Head. Indeed, during our visit, Bald Head's accommodations were filled to the brim with vacationers from across the nation. Finally, however, Bald Head Island may not necessarily lose all of its idyllic tranquillity, for, of the island's 12,000 acres, roughly 10,000 are maintained as an ecological preserve.

THE GOLF   17

Seagulls catching dragonflies in midair, Bermuda greens so thick they actually crunch underfoot, the swirling, ever-changing sea winds, frequent water crossings, and the occasional alligator sighting—after three days of golf at Bald Head Island, we became more and more delighted with the special characteristics of the island's extremely lovely, George Cobb–designed golf course. Not only is the Bald Head Island course genuinely pretty—with beautifully conditioned fairways and wonderful views of the forest and the sea—it is also friendly enough to yield birdies when the wind is down. The extremely slow greens, which have virtually no break in them, help keep your score intriguingly low. And while Bald Head Island itself may be in some danger of becoming overbuilt, to date the homes do not obtrude in any way upon this idyllic golf course. Indeed, there are plenty of homes hidden behind the tropical foliage, yet the golf course feels like a private, green sanctuary.

The Bald Head course measures 6,855 yards from the blue tees, where it carries a lofty 143 slope rating; most golfers, however, opt to play from the whites, which measure 6,239 yards, with a slope of 136. From the red tees, Bald Head is 5,536 yards long, with a slope of 132, but do not be scared by all the big slope numbers because, in our opinion, the course, overall, is not as intimidating as its ratings suggest.

The best holes on the course at Bald Head Island are nine through eleven, number fourteen, and sixteen through eighteen. The ninth hole, a 410-yard par four, features a creek (with floating alligators) along the entire left side and a fairway in the shape of an hourglass with more water threatening play from the right. Par is an outstanding score on Bald Head's ninth. The tenth hole demands a long, uphill drive over a lagoon; the eleventh hole is a very tough, 510-yard dogleg-left that requires two water crossings; and the fourteenth hole, a deceptive, 385-yard, dogleg-right, can ruin your scorecard. Fourteen demands a straight tee shot that is long enough to open up a view of the green tucked away in a forest on the right.

The stretch of three final holes is enormous fun. Sixteen is an exhilarating par three with a wonderful view of the sea, while seventeen and eighteen are two long marches back to the clubhouse—and into the wind.

Walking is permitted, although the summertime heat means that the overwhelming majority of golfers ride. The greens fee, including cart, is $60 for resort guests. If you want to make a day trip of Bald Head Island, a package that includes your round-trip on the ferry and a round of golf runs about $95 per person in season.

Bald Head Island Club. PO Box 3070, Bald Head Island, NC 28461. Tel: 800-234-1666 or 910-457-7310. Fax: 910-457-7395. Credit cards accepted.

• 1975. Designer: George Cobb. Par 72. 6,855 yards. 74.2 par rating. 143 slope rating. Greens fees: island guests: $60 ($50 off season) including cart, day visitors: $95, includes ferry and cart. Walking permitted in season after noon. No caddies. Open year-round.

GOLF SERVICES 17

Golf services are excellent. The pro shop is well stocked, the golf staff is friendly and professional, and there is a nice practice range and putting green. Two warnings: breakfast should be, but is not, available for early morning golfers, and do not arrive without your bug spray—the mosquitoes can be overwhelming.

 LODGING ⑰

The lovely homes and villas on Bald Head Island rent weekly during the summer season (June to mid-September) at prices ranging from $1,300 for a villa near the golf club to $4,400 for a large home with five bedrooms overlooking the ocean. The resort publishes an attractive, annually updated *Armchair Guide* with photos and prices for every home available for rent on Bald Head. To receive a copy call 800-234-1666.

Cottage on Bald Head Island

We stayed in Lighthouse Landing 9, a bright, spacious, fully equipped, beautifully maintained, and attractively furnished unit that costs $1,350 for the week. The **Lighthouse Landing** complex overlooks the marsh and is conveniently located near the marina (with its small grocery store and restaurants), about a mile from the golf club and two miles from dazzling East Beach. The homes located in the Flora's Bluff and Killegay Ridge neighborhoods are also some of the most attractive—and expensive—on Bald Head Island.

There are two lodging options for those who wish to visit Bald Head Island for less than a full week. **Theodosia's** is a bed-and-breakfast with ten guest rooms on the harbor with nightly rates ranging from $145 to $190. For reservations call 800-656-1812. The **Marsh Harbor Inn** offers fifteen rooms with pinewood floors with doubles ranging from $215 to $240 from spring through fall. For reservations call 800-432-7368.

Bald Head Island (Information Center). 5079 Southport Supply Highway, Southport, NC 28461. Tel: 800-234-1666. Reservations: 800-432-7368. Fax: 910-457-7524. Credit cards accepted.

Theodosia's. 2 Keelson Row, PO Box 3130, Bald Head Island, NC 28461. Tel: 800-656-1812 or 910-457-6563. Fax: 910-457-6055. 10 rooms ranging in price from $145 to $190. Credit cards accepted.

Marsh Harbor Inn. Keelson Row, Bald Head Island, NC 28461. Tel: 800-432-7368 or 910-457-5002. Fax: 910-457-7218. 15 rooms ranging from $215 to $240. Credit cards accepted.

 RESTAURANTS ⑮

Restaurants are in short supply on Bald Head Island. During the crush of the summer season, the three restaurants on the island are bursting at the seams.

The most elegant place to dine is the dining room at the **Bald Head Island Club.** On Saturdays the clubhouse sets up a gala buffet costing $20 per person (wine and tip not included). The **River Pilot Cafe** is an informal restaurant that is open for breakfast, lunch, and dinner. Our favorite dinner spot, however, was **Eb & Flo's Marina Steam Bar,** a casual outdoor restaurant and bar overlooking the harbor and specializing in steamed shrimp, softshell crab, and other good seafood dishes. Eb & Flo's is inexpensive, about $18 a person.

The **Lounge** in the clubhouse serves lunch, and **Peli Poolside** serves sandwiches and drinks to golfers making the turn between the ninth and tenth holes.

The restaurants at the Bald Head Island Club. PO Box 3070, Bald Head Island, NC 28461. Tel: 800-234-1666 or 910-457-7320. Fax: 910-457-7395. Credit cards accepted.

River Pilot Cafe. PO Box 3069, The Chandler Building at the Marina, Bald Head Island, NC 28461. Tel: 910-457-7390. Fax: 910-457-7220. Credit cards accepted.

Eb & Flo's Marina Steam Bar. At the Marina, Bald Head Island, NC 28461. Tel: 910-457-7509. Fax: 910-457-7220. Credit cards accepted.

NON-GOLF ACTIVITIES

Bald Head Island excels at non-golf activities. For those who crave a beach vacation, there is no better destination on the East Coast. There are also four tennis courts, two championship croquet greenswards, where all-white dress is required, and a large outdoor pool that, unfortunately, was filled with brown-colored water during our visit. Other possible activities include sailing, canoeing, fishing, crabbing, cycling, and jogging.

GETTING THERE: The closest airport to Bald Head Island is forty-five miles away in Wilmington, North Carolina. Keep in mind that no cars are allowed on the island, so renting a car for an extended stay is not wise. Faith Services (800-406-4949) or Oak Island Cab (910-278-6373) will take you from the airport to the ferry landing. If you are driving from Wilmington, take Route 17 South. Once you cross the Cape Fear Bridge, proceed approximately ten miles before making a left onto Route 87 heading to Southport. Make a left onto Howe Street (Route 211), which runs down the middle of Southport. Turn left onto West 9th Street and continue to the ferry landing to unload your car. The ferry leaves every hour on the hour, except for twelve noon, and takes twenty-five minutes. Ferry reservations and tram service to your rental unit on the island should be made in advance by calling 800-234-1666.

▶THE ESEEOLA LODGE AND THE LINVILLE GOLF CLUB

THE HIGH COUNTRY

	The Golf	Golf Services	Lodging	Restaurants	Non-Golf Activities	Total
Rating	18	16	17	17	17	85

Anyone who makes the effort to get to Linville, North Carolina, is certain to become infatuated with the place. The Eseeola Lodge and the Linville Golf Club are among the best-kept travel secrets in America. Linville is relatively unknown, off the beaten track, exquisitely beautiful, and extremely underrated. The golf, accommodations, food, setting, and value all set Linville in a category of its own. Its flavor is the complete antithesis of the modern, highly standardized golf resorts that now dot the entire United States from Florida to California.

Eseeola Lodge

Pat Conroy, the author of *The Prince of Tides* and *Beach Music*, celebrated the now famous Low Country of South Carolina, the lush, marshy, river-cut lowlands to the north and south of Charleston, a region, incidentally, that is liberally sprinkled with great golf courses from Kiawah to Hilton Head.

But far less well known than the exquisite South Carolina coast is the dramatic High Country of western North Carolina, a vast, mountainous region with the highest elevations east of the Mississippi (well over 6,000 feet), spectacular scenery and wildlife, and summer temperatures fifteen degrees cooler than what you would find on the flatland. Located south of the Virginia-Tennessee border and north of the city of Asheville (where you will find the nearest airport), the High Country is known for its traditional folk art, fishing, hiking, hunting, skiing during the winter, the Blue Ridge Parkway, and historic associations with Daniel Boone, Davy Crockett, and Annie Oakley. In addition, the High Country has always lured a gracious—if somewhat homogeneous—Southern clientele, consisting mainly of families from Charlotte and Atlanta. The spectacular homes built around Linville during the 1920s and the fanciful cottages lining the first and second fairways of the Linville Golf Club are articulate symbols of the standard of living enjoyed by Linville residents for seventy-five years. During the twenties and thirties life was so sweet that residents believed that idyllic Linville was a reincarnation of Camelot, and, after our recent visit, we are not about to disagree.

Due to its isolated setting (Linville *is* hard to get to), its completely Southern flavor, which scares off some Northerners, and its entire lack of publicity (save for a silver medal in *Golf Magazine*), Linville has not changed very much over the years. The town itself is no more than a crossroads at the foot of Grandfather Mountain, with a gas station and convenience store. The Eseeola Lodge, built in 1926, is on the National Register of Historic Places. One hundred yards down the road from the lodge you will find the welcoming Linville Golf Club, where lodge guests enjoy playing privileges. Its course is a Donald Ross design from 1926 and, along with the William Flynn–designed Cascades Course at the Homestead in Virginia and the Ross-designed Panorama Course at the Balsams in New Hampshire, one of the three best mountain courses on the East Coast. The Eseeola Lodge and the Linville Golf Club make the perfect formula for a true, one-of-a-kind golfing holiday.

THE GOLF   18

The golf course at the historic **Linville Golf Club**, established in 1892, is crossed time and again by the crystal-clear waters of trout-filled Grandmother's Creek, a deep, rocky, serpentine stream that winds its way picturesquely all over the course on its way to Lake Kawana. The course is situated 3,800 feet above sea level on the floor of a mountain valley, and in places it is quite steep. This is a beautifully conditioned and incredibly scenic layout with massive rhododendron, mountain laurel, pine forests, panoramic mountain views, and the kind of deep quiet that is all-pervasive.

The Linville course can play at either a very difficult 6,780 yards (slope 135) or a more manageable 6,286 yards (slope 126), but either way it is a joy. Like most Ross courses, you will score better by running the ball with a low shot rather than lobbing it up onto the green.

The third hole, a 449-yard par four and Linville's number one handicap, requires two water carries, the second to an uphill green. The fourth hole is a 565-yard par five with a fairway that narrows sharply as it approaches the green, which backs up to Lake Kawana. The seventh and eighth holes are a nifty pair of doglegs. The second shot on seven is to a green perched well above the fairway. The tee shot on eight (no more than a three wood) is to a landing area in front of the creek. Nine is a dramatic, downhill par three; number ten is a short (331 yards), uphill par four; and number eleven may be the prettiest hole on the course: from the dramatically elevated tee you drive down shy of the creek about 260 yards out. Seventeen and eighteen are two good final par fours. The handsome Tudor-style clubhouse overlooks the final green.

Like the accommodations and meals at the Eseeola Lodge, golf at the Linville Golf Club is an extraordinary bargain given the course's high quality. The first round of eighteen holes, including cart, costs $55, and a second round on the same day is just $35 more. A weekly rate of unlimited golf for $325 (excluding cart) is also available.

The Linville Golf Club, like the Eseeola Lodge, has a very short season—from mid-May to late October. We visited and played on the last weekend of the season and had the course virtually to ourselves—but not the lodge, which was filled to capacity. During July and August both the hotel and golf course are in high demand, so make reservations and tee times well in advance.

Linville Golf Club. PO Box 99, Linville, NC 28646. Tel: 704-733-4363. Fax: 704-733-3227. Credit cards accepted.

• 1926. Designer: Donald Ross. Par 72. 6,780 yards. 72.7 par rating. 135 slope rating. Greens fee: $55, cart included. Walking permitted only later in the afternoon. No caddies. Restrictions: guests must make reservations through Eseeola Lodge. Season: mid-May to late October.

GOLF SERVICES

Services at the Linville Golf Club are very good. The clubhouse itself is quite handsome; the pro shop staff and the starters are friendly and pleasant; the shop is well stocked with all the necessities; the locker rooms are large, comfortable, and modern; and there is a good practice range just fifty yards across the road.

LODGING

The **Eseeola Lodge** is a national landmark dating from the 1920s, not a brand-new resort built to the latest specifications of opulent luxury. This means that the rooms—while very comfortable, tastefully decorated and furnished, and beautifully maintained—are not nearly as spacious or lavish as those at famous golf hotels such as Turnberry in Scotland or the Lodge at Pebble Beach. Like many buildings around Linville, the Eseeola Lodge features bark-clad exterior walls,

Eseeola Lodge

which lend it a rustic, informal atmosphere. Dogs and cats wander around the mature gardens, and large brown trout swim along in the creek, which actually runs beneath the hotel. The lodge may be rustic from the outside, but it is quite elegant within. The public areas, which are especially lovely when wood fires are blazing in the big stone fireplaces, are furnished with antiques and decorated in an understated manner.

The Eseeola Lodge has just twenty-eight guest rooms. The best rooms have private, outdoor porches; be sure to request one when booking. We stayed in number 208, which, although without a porch, was attractive and pleasant, with cable television and a well-equipped bath.

Room rates that include both a wonderful buffet breakfast and an excellent five-course dinner are extremely reasonable. In fact, at just $240 to $300 per couple per night, the Eseeola Lodge ranks as one of the best buys in the United States. The lodge is managed with obvious care by Linville native John Blackburn. The staff will be happy to book your tee times at the Linville Golf Club.

Eseeola Lodge. Linville, NC 28646. Tel: 800-742-6717 or 703-733-4311. Fax: 704-733-3227. 28 rooms and 1 cottage. Doubles are $240 to $300 per couple, including breakfast and dinner. Open May 15 to late October. Credit cards accepted.

 ## RESTAURANTS

The dining room in the **Eseeola Lodge** exhibits a country elegance; jackets and ties are required. The young waiters and waitresses, students from nearby Appalachian State University, are professional, well trained, and more polite than their counterparts up north. A typical five-course dinner at the lodge might include carpaccio of duck, white bean soup, green salad, steak with mixed vegetables, and strawberry shortcake. The wine list, though limited, has been carefully selected. In addition, the pleasant bar adjacent to the dining room opens at five o'clock every afternoon. Along with dinner, the fabulous breakfasts—eggs Benedict, blueberry pancakes, sausage, fresh fruit, and homemade breads—are included in the room rate. Excellent lunches are served daily upstairs in the Linville Golf Club overlooking the eighteenth hole.

The restaurants at Eseeola Lodge. PO Box 99, Linville, NC 28646. Tel: 800-742-6717 or 704-733-4311. Fax: 704-733-3227. Credit cards accepted.

 ## NON-GOLF ACTIVITIES

Despite the Eseeola Lodge's diminutive size, guests can participate in a wide range of non-golfing activities. Aside from hiking, bicycling, and the wonderful sightseeing in the High Country, popular activities include excellent trout fishing, shopping for antiques and local crafts, swimming in the hotel's heated pool, and simply unwinding on your private porch or in the garden with a good book. During the height of the summer season the Eseeola Lodge plans and supervises recreational programs for small children.

GETTING THERE: From Winston-Salem, come up I-40 to Morganton, exit 105, which puts you on 18 North. Continue straight through the town of Morganton. The route turns into 181 North and runs to Linville. Follow the Eseeola Lodge signs.

South Carolina

▶MYRTLE BEACH

	The Golf	Golf Services	Lodging	Restaurants	Non-Golf Activities	Total
Rating	19	18	15	15	17	**84**

Upscale Myrtle Beach may strike some readers as an oxymoron. This particular combination of adjective and place is especially intriguing because readers may reasonably inquire whether Myrtle Beach, that most democratic of golf destinations, has an upscale aspect at all. Myrtle Beach—bluest of blue collar, paradise for the public links player, haven of the value-conscious—is the Everyman's Riviera. The variety and quality of its golf is simply astounding, everyone knows that. But what about the balance of the travel experience, the atmosphere of Myrtle Beach, and the character of its hotels and restaurants? Beyond the extraordinary golf, is Myrtle Beach tacky from top to bottom, or are there truly outstanding places hidden away where one may stay and dine in style?

It must be said that the long and narrow Myrtle Beach region is now so vast that any attempt to sum it up with two or three general flourishes will badly miss the mark. When you discuss Myrtle Beach today you are talking about a magnificent fifty-mile swath of sandy beach from Pawley's Island in South Carolina all the way up to Calabash and Southport, North Carolina, with almost ninety golf courses and hundreds of hotels in between. New golf courses open as quickly in Myrtle Beach as new restaurants do elsewhere. And everything in Myrtle Beach is big: big billboards along the road, big seafood emporiums seating hundreds of diners, big beach shops selling thousands of bathing suits, the world's largest golf discount shops, big golf clubhouses, and huge golf complexes with not just one or two eighteen-hole layouts but frequently three or four.

We must report, however, that Myrtle Beach frequently conforms to its redneck reputation. We checked into what is universally regarded as the best hotel in the area (the Radisson at Kingston Plantation, see below) and were told by the bellhop that all we needed to wear into any Myrtle Beach restaurant was a tank top and flip-flops (he was wrong). And, the next morning at breakfast the waitress asked us in a matter-of-fact way if we wanted ketchup for our scrambled eggs.

Occasionally, we have encountered a group of golfing chums trying to figure out whether to take their next junket to Pinehurst or Myrtle Beach. "We ended up going to Myrtle Beach last year because two of the guys like the nightlife." That is an insider's joke. Whereas highbrow Pinehurst has golf and no nightlife, nightlife in earthy Myrtle Beach—a twenty-four-hour-a-day affair—includes a raucous, raunchy element. Enormous strip joints along the highway promote their wares to visiting foursomes with catchy titles like *Golfer's Fantasy, Golfer's Delight,* and so forth. In the end, Hooters might be the most representative restaurant in town: lots of golfers smoking, drinking, and flirting with the trim waitresses in their tiny T-shirts and shorts.

Face it: unlike most of the resorts reviewed by *Golf Travel,* Myrtle Beach is not a "smart" destination. It has no cachet, no snob appeal. We once heard someone say that a vacation in Myrtle Beach is about as sophisticated as having a couple of Twinkies for dessert. Yet you are going to play an endless succession of absolutely fabulous golf courses in Myrtle Beach, and, unless you are a snob yourself, you will have a lot of fun in the process.

THE GOLF

Myrtle Beach is a smorgasbord: it is the rare bird who discovers one golf course he or she especially loves and plays it day in and day out. The Myrtle Beach custom is to move from one golf course to another and, in the process, sample as many as possible.

The two gentlemen we played with on the Heathland Course at Legends were typical golf visitors to Myrtle Beach. They had already stayed in the area a month and were playing their sixteenth different layout. At that pace it would take them six months to play every course in the area. After a while, the names begin to blur. These nice fellows could not recall the courses they had played two or three weeks earlier. "Harry, was that Wild Wing, Tidewater, or Caledonia?" Much argument ensues as the confusion builds. A degree of amnesia regarding the names of golf courses is a symptom manifested by nearly every golfer afflicted with Myrtle Beach's green bounty.

A handful of general comments: despite very unreliable weather in January and February, Myrtle Beach is fast becoming a year-round destination for golfers. This means that its courses can be very crowded even in the dead of winter and that advanced tee times are always mandatory. During the high season (spring and fall), Myrtle Beach, legendary for its low prices, actually becomes quite costly. Golfers intent on playing thirty-six holes a day should pay careful attention to the location of their morning and afternoon layouts; poor planning can leave you with an hour's drive between golf games. The megaclubs like Myrtle Beach National, Wild Wing, and Legends must be visited if only so you can be awestruck by the sheer size of these incredible operations, which extend as far as the eye can see. The heavy volume of traffic means that the attitudes of staff members at certain clubs (see below) can be very hardened and unpleasant to visitors. Finally, a John Daly signature course called Wicked Stick has joined the parade of Myrtle Beach courses. Wicked Stick was actually designed by Clyde Johnston; Daly merely furnished his name and received a fee. The advance notices have been decidedly mixed.

The nearly unanimous choice among insiders for the number one golf course in the entire Myrtle Beach region is the elegant **Dunes Club,** a Robert Trent Jones, Sr., design from 1948 and the site of dozens of tournaments from the Senior Open to the Senior Tour Championship. A private club open to guests of certain hotels or to members of private clubs who have their local pro call and make an introduction, the prestigious Dunes Club is a mature, tree-lined layout that features the best four-hole golf sequence in the area. Alligator Alley, the tenth, eleventh, twelfth, and thirteenth holes that weave their way through lakes and marshland, has been likened to Augusta's Amen Corner. The thirteenth, a 595-yard par five, is the toughest hole on the course, a severe dogleg-right around Singleton Lake. The Dunes Club is within sight of the sea but has no holes along the ocean. The course measures 7,165 yards (slope 141) from the gold tees, 6,565 yards from the blues (slope 132), and 5,390 yards from the reds (slope 132).

As part of your overall Myrtle Beach orientation, play another older course, **Pine Lakes International,** during the first few days of your stay. Also known as the Granddaddy, Pine Lakes is the oldest course in Myrtle Beach, designed in 1927 by Robert White, a Scotsman from St. Andrews and the first president of the PGA. Located in downtown Myrtle Beach and abutting busy Route 17, this course has a unique atmosphere. The elegant, Southern Colonial–style clubhouse is all moonlight-and-magnolia, but the entire staff, from the baggage boys to the pro shop personnel, is clad in Scottish kilts, kneesocks, and dress jackets to honor the founder's heritage. The course itself—a traditional parkland layout with undulating tree-lined fairways—is beautifully conditioned and stresses accuracy and clear thinking over distance and brute strength. Pine Lakes measures 6,609 yards from the back tees (slope 125) and 5,376 yards from the front tees (slope 118).

With the Dunes Club and Pines Lakes tucked away, you are now prepared for the megacomplexes with their multiple courses and monumental clubhouse facilities. Legends, Wild Wing, and Myrtle Beach National are our favorites in this genre. Plan to arrive early and spend the entire day, including lunch between rounds, in a lavish setting. All three clubs are located on Route 501 about five miles west of Myrtle Beach.

Legends is a Scottish-style concept that really is reminiscent of Scotland. It has three eighteen-hole courses (Heathland, Moorland, and Parkland) and a brooding, baronial, 50,000-square-foot clubhouse surveying the treeless panorama. The **Heathland Course** is the premier draw at Legends, a par seventy-one links designed by Tom Doak, who modeled certain holes (with limited success) after holes at Cruden Bay, Royal St. George's, Royal Lytham & St. Anne's, and St. Andrews. For example, the Heathland version of the Road Hole does not have a road behind the green. But never mind; Heathland is still an authentic links re-creation with the look, feel, and windswept conditions of Scotland with its uneven lies and stark terrain. The **Moorland Course** (par seventy-two) was designed by P. B. Dye in 1990, and the **Parkland Course** (par seventy-two), designed by Legends's in-house staff, was completed in 1992. Moorland is the toughest track at Legends.

Wild Wing is two miles west of Legends and has four eighteen-hole tracks, **Hummingbird** and **Wood Stork,** both designed by Willard Byrd; the **Falcon,** designed by Rees Jones; and the stunning and difficult **Avocet,** designed by Larry Nelson. Wild Wing is the most impressive and well-run golf complex in the area. The courses are superbly conditioned, the staff hustles to get you on the course, and the contemporary-style, 35,000-square-foot clubhouse is lovely.

Myrtle Beach National has three courses—the very popular **King's North** (designed by Arnold Palmer), the **West,** and the **South Creek** courses—and a clubhouse as grand as the Lincoln Memorial. The Myrtle Beach National Company will also book your tee times for its other courses sprinkled around the Myrtle Beach area, including the Long Bay Club, a Jack Nicklaus design that is particularly beautiful.

After the Dunes Club, our two favorite courses in the region are the Witch and Heather Glen. The **Witch** is off the beaten track and qualifies as the "hidden links" of Myrtle Beach. Located on Route 544 in North Conway about fifteen minutes west of Myrtle Beach, the Witch is an enchanting, 6,702-yard Dan Maples design that has four miles of wooden bridgework that spans hundreds of acres of scenic wetlands. Tight and beautifully conditioned, the Witch is much more welcoming and low-key than other Myrtle Beach clubs. In fact, the Witch has the friendliest staff in the area. Highly recommended.

The Witch

Heather Glen is located on Route 17 just two miles south of the North Carolina border and features twenty-seven challenging holes created by Willard Byrd and Clyde Johnston. There is some good-natured Scottish nonsense going on at Heather Glen: creeks are called burns, some male staffers wear kilts, and holes have pseudo-Scottish names like Auld Hoos, Wunz Moor, and Piney-Ho. Despite the marketing ploy, Heather Glen is a great place to play golf. The second nine is the best of Heather Glen's three loops; its ninth hole is a stunning par five that plays along a lake and demands a heroic approach shot over the water.

Dunes Club. 9000 North Ocean Blvd., Myrtle Beach, SC 29572. Tel: 803-449-5914. Fax: 803-497-5326. Credit cards accepted.

• 1948. Designer: Robert Trent Jones, Sr. Par 72. 6,565 yards. 72.1 par rating. 132 slope rating. Greens fees: $108 (guest), $130 (reciprocal club member), cart included. No walking. No caddies. Restrictions: club open to members of private clubs by prior arrangement and guests of the following hotels: Breakers, Caravelle, Caribbean, Driftwood, Dunes Village, and Southwind. Season: Year-round.

Pine Lakes International. PO Box 7099, 506 Woodside Drive, Myrtle Beach, SC 29577. Tel: 800-446-6817 or 803-449-6459. Fax: 803-497-0078. Credit cards accepted.

• 1927. Designer: Robert White. Par 71. 6,609 yards. 71.5 par rating. 125 slope rating. Greens fees: peak season: $90, low season: $45 to $75, cart included. No walking. No caddies. Season: Year-round.

Legends. 1500 Legends Drive, Myrtle Beach, SC 29577. Tel: 800-552-2660 or 803-236-9318. Fax: 803-236-0516. Credit cards accepted.

• *Heathland.* 1990. Designer: Tom Doak. Par 71. 6,785 yards. 72.3 par rating. 127 slope rating.
• *Moorland.* 1990. Designer: P. B. Dye. Par 72. 6,799. 73.1 par rating. 128 slope rating.
• *Parkland.* 1992. Designer: Legends staff. Par 72. 7,170 yards. 74.3 par rating. 131 slope rating.
• Greens fees: peak season: $75, off season: $40 to $55, cart included. No walking. No caddies. Season: year-round.

Wild Wing. Highway 501 North Myrtle Beach, SC 29578. Tel: 800-736-9464 or 803-347-9464. Fax: 803-347-5732. Credit cards accepted.

• *Hummingbird.* 1992. Designer: Willard Byrd. Par 72. 6,853 yards. 73.6 par rating. 135 slope rating.
• *Wood Stork.* 1991. Designer: William Byrd. Par 72. 7,044 yards. 74.1 par rating. 130 slope rating.
• *Avocet.* 1993. Designer: Larry Nelson. Par 72. 7,127 yards. 74.2 par rating. 128 slope rating.
• *Falcon.* 1994. Designer: Rees Jones. Par 72. 7,082 yards. 74.4 par rating. 134 slope rating.
• Greens fees: Falcon and Avocet: $115 (high season), $55 to $90 (off season). Wood Stork and Hummingbird: $100 (high season), $45 to $82 (off season), cart included. No walking. No caddies. Season: year-round.

Myrtle Beach National. PO Box 1936, Myrtle Beach, SC 29578. Tel: 800-344-5590 or 803-347-4653. Fax: 803-347-2696. Credit cards accepted.

• *King's North Course.* 1972/1995. Designer: Arnold Palmer. Par 72. 6,827 yards. 72.6 par rating. 136 slope rating.
• *West Course.* 1972. Designers: Arnold Palmer, Frances Duane. Par 72. 6,866 yards. 73.0 par rating. 119 slope rating.
• *South Creek Course.* 1972/1993. Designer: Arnold Palmer/Frances Duane. Par 72. 6,416 yards. 70.5 par rating. 125 slope rating.
• Greens fees: North Course: $118, West and South Creek: $71 (high season), $39

to $56 (off season), cart included. No walking on North Course; walking permitted on West and South Creek courses after 1 P.M. No caddies. Season: year-round.

The Witch. 1900 Highway 544, Conway, SC 29526. Tel: 803-448-1300. Fax: 803-347-5328. Credit cards accepted.

• 1989. Designer: Dan Maples. Par 71. 6,702 yards. 71.2 par rating. 133 slope rating. Greens fees: $90 (high season), $39 to $65 (off season), cart included. No walking. No caddies. Season: year-round.

Heather Glen. PO Box 297, North Myrtle Beach, SC 29597. Tel: 800-868-4536 or 803-249-9000. Fax: 803-249-4968. Credit cards accepted.

• 1987/1990. Designers: Willard Byrd (18 holes)/Clyde Johnston (9 holes). Par 72. 6,850 yards. 72.0 par rating. 130 slope rating. Greens fees: $86 (high season), $38 to $75 (off season), cart included. No walking. No caddies. Season: year-round.

GOLF SERVICES

The golf services from the physical standpoint are unmatched anywhere in the world. There are no better practice ranges, no larger putting greens, and no more lavish clubhouses to be found. Golf services from the human standpoint, however, can frequently leave much to be desired. Staff members at certain clubs can sometimes treat visitors with outright contempt. A few examples: the starter at the prestigious Dunes Club was extremely unpleasant and unfriendly; the pro shop employee at Pine Lakes International cross-examined us about where we were staying and how long we had been in town when we attempted to pay for our greens fees with a credit card. And the atmosphere at a few of the megaclubs feels like a cattle call, with everybody putting out a hand for a tip. The only club with universally friendly service is The Witch.

LODGING

The **Radisson at Kingston Plantation,** a modern, twenty-story high-rise on the ocean, is the best hotel in Myrtle Beach. It has a central, midbeach location, a wonderful health club just a short stroll from the hotel, an outdoor pool, a fine concierge (Joanne Eckelman), a good golf staff that will arrange your tee times, a decent restaurant, and spacious, comfortable, well-equipped, and reasonably priced rooms. We stayed in room 1015, a very pleasant oceanfront suite with bedroom, large bath, and living room with a fully equipped kitchen. During high season this room is priced at $239 per night.

The Radisson at Kingston Plantation. 9800 Lake Drive, Myrtle Beach, SC 29572. Tel: 800-333-3333 or 803-449-0006. Fax: 803-497-1017. 300 rooms. Doubles from $149. Credit cards accepted.

RESTAURANTS

Three pleasant restaurants that we recommend with confidence are Chestnut Hill, Marker 350, and Rossi's. Chestnut Hill and Rossi's are located on Route 17 within ten minutes of the Radisson. Marker 350 overlooks the Intercoastal Waterway west of Cherry Grove, about twenty minutes from the Radisson.

Based on our experience, **Chestnut Hill** is the best restaurant in Myrtle Beach. It has a gracious, subdued atmosphere with ladderback chairs, black-tie service, and a wide-ranging menu that includes fine seafood (oysters, tuna, grilled dolphin, crab, and shrimp) plus a variety of beef dishes. The wine list is outstanding. About $130 for two at dinner, wine and tip included.

Marker 350 is an attractive all-seafood restaurant overlooking the marina with specialties like Cajun-fried squid, seafood creole, grilled black grouper, and pecan-crusted snapper. Marker 350 has an excellent selection of wines. About $110 for two at dinner, wine and tip included.

Rossi's is a popular, centrally located Italian restaurant in the Galleria shopping center that serves good pasta dishes, fish, softshell crabs, and steaks. About $90 for two at dinner, wine and tip included.

Each of the golf clubs serves lunch. **The Grill** at the Dunes Club provides an especially good lunch in a refined setting.

Chestnut Hill. 9922 North Kings Highway, Myrtle Beach, SC 29572. Tel: 803-449-3984. Fax: 803-449-7308. Credit cards accepted.

Marker 350. 4 Harbor Place, North Myrtle Beach, SC 29582. Tel: 803-249-3888. No fax. Credit cards accepted.

Rossi's. 9636 North Kings Highway, Myrtle Beach, SC 29572. Tel: 803-449-0481. Fax: 803-626-4578. Credit cards accepted.

The Grill. Dunes Club. 9000 North Ocean Blvd., Myrtle Beach, SC 29572. Tel: 803-449-5236, ext. 230. Fax: 803-499-8696. Credit cards accepted.

NON-GOLF ACTIVITIES ⑰

When it comes to other activities, Myrtle Beach has it all, from the beautiful beach and water slide parks for kids, to shopping at Barefoot Landing, to and swimming, tennis, and workout facilities at the Radisson's health club. The traditional nightlife smacks of Southern culture: the Gatlin Brothers Theater and Dixie Stampede (where Dolly Parton performs) are two Myrtle Beach favorites.

GETTING THERE: The Radisson is located in the north section of Myrtle Beach. A half mile north of the Business 17 and 17 Bypass merge, turn right at the first light onto Lake Arrowhead Road. Then turn left at the first left onto Kings Road. The hotel is ahead on the right.

►HILTON HEAD

HARBOUR TOWN AND BEYOND

	The Golf	Golf Services	Lodging	Restaurants	Non-Golf Activities	Total
Rating	17	16	16	16	17	**82**

Hilton Head is no sleepy South Carolina island. Despite its well-nurtured image as a haven for privacy and tranquil island life, the island has become so popular that it frequently suffers from overcrowding. Luckily, Hilton Head has been saved from all-out disaster by enlightened planning. The island's carefully conceived formula has worked well for both residents and the visitors who come from all over the world largely to unplug amid the palmetto trees or, just as often, to play golf. The resort developments have been set back from the island's main drag, busy Route 278, and are hidden in "plantations" (i.e., condominium developments) behind thick groves of mature pines. Behind the shroud of pines you will find thousands of hotel rooms and

Harbour Town, Hilton Head

rental villas, at least 150 restaurants, dozens of factory outlet stores, and every imaginable service ever created for a resort of this magnitude. Hilton Head was initially conceived as an exclusive destination, but the resort community has changed focus. More and more, the direction today appears aimed toward the mass market. During our recent visit to Hilton Head, for example, we stayed in the best hotel on the island, the nice Hyatt Regency at Palmetto Dunes, but its atmosphere was dominated by conventioneers. After the American Society of Travel Agents had left the premises, the chlorine bleach delegates arrived, and we found it hard to believe how many people make their living in the chlorine bleach business.

Hilton Head, however, still has its upscale side and charms galore: nice beaches, fine restaurants and accommodations, twenty-three public access golf courses, and a wealth of non-golf activities.

THE GOLF

Hilton Head is a wonderful place to golf, even if the weather is unpredictable during the winter months and can be frigid in January. In fact, visitors cannot absolutely bank on the weather until April, even though early March will find Hilton Head filled to capacity with foursomes trying to pack as much golf in in as short a time as possible. The brand-name consumer will find courses designed by Nicklaus, Player, Dye, Hills, Zoeller, the Fazios, and all the Joneses. So where should one start? Which are the private, member-only affairs, and, of the resort courses, which are the very best?

The private-private courses—where you must be introduced by a member in order to play—include Long Cove on Hilton Head Island, Haig Point on nearby Daufuskie Island, the Fazio course on Dataw Island, and the new, highly acclaimed Nicklaus course at Colleton River Plantation. These courses are open only to those nonmembers who might be seriously considering acquiring property within the developments and who are willing to endure listening to a sales pitch from the marketing department. Some folks, we have heard, feign interest in order to get on Long Cove and Colleton River, the most desirable of the private layouts.

The best resort courses are Harbour Town (despite its precipitous fall in the *Golf Digest* ratings), all three courses at Palmetto Dunes (the Arthur Hills Course, the Robert Trent Jones Course, and the George Fazio Course), the Arthur Hills Course at Palmetto Hall, the controversial Robert Cupp Course, also at Palmetto Hall, and the very lovely Old South Golf Links located on the mainland just before the Hilton Head bridge. These seven challenging layouts should be sufficient for anyone's two-week holiday. There are inferior courses on Hilton Head as well. Do not, for example, waste your precious time on the other Sea Pines courses aside from Harbour Town.

Harbour Town, designed by Pete Dye, gets a bad rap because of its condition, which can be uneven, and its price ($175 from March to November), which is high.

However, long after your Hilton Head holiday is a distant memory, you will still recall Harbour Town's seventeenth and eighteenth holes. The seventeenth is a superb par three into the wind, and the eighteenth is a dramatic finishing hole to the striped lighthouse familiar to anyone who has seen the MCI Classic on television. Harbour Town is a tough course with tight fairways compressed by towering pine trees.

Clubhouse, Harbour Town

If Harbour Town is the most intimidating track on Hilton Head, the **Arthur Hills Course** at **Palmetto Dunes** wins the popularity contest. If you asked Hilton Head homeowners to name their favorite local course, this congenial layout would stand atop every insider's list. The Hills Course has great natural beauty and is challenging, but not punishing. In high season, the greens fee is $110, cart included.

The handsome **Robert Trent Jones Course,** also at Palmetto Dunes, opens with a series of holes along noisy Route 278, but then heads toward the ocean on the back nine. The signature hole is number ten with its greenside view of the Atlantic. The **George Fazio Course** is the toughest and longest of the three at Palmetto Dunes. The greens fee at both courses (for Palmetto Dunes guests) is $81, cart included.

The two courses at **Palmetto Hall** by Arthur Hills and Robert Cupp are quite new and still have that raw new course look, yet both are pleasing and will get better with time. The **Cupp Course**—which was created on a computer and features sharp, geometrical shapes like square greens and triangular sand traps—will entice the curious. The **Hills Course** is much more traditional. The greens fee at both is $81.

The **Old South Golf Links** is worth the trip off-island, just twenty minutes from the Hyatt Regency. This interesting new course has a number of showcase holes looking back across the sound to Hilton Head. The greens fee is $77 during the peak spring and fall seasons.

Harbour Town Golf Links. Sea Pines Plantation, 11 Lighthouse Lane, Hilton Head Island, SC 29928. Tel: 800-845-6131 or 803-842-8484. Credit cards accepted.

• 1969. Designer: Pete Dye. Par 71. 6,897 yards. 74.0 par rating. 136 slope rating. Greens fees: $175 spring and fall, $140 winter and summer, cart included. No walking in spring and fall. Walking permitted after 1 P.M. in summer and winter. No caddies. Season: year-round.

Palmetto Dunes Golf. 7 Trent Jones Lane, Hilton Head Island, SC 29936. Tel: 800-827-3006 or 803-785-1138. Fax: 803-785-1135. Credit cards accepted.

• *Arthur Hills Course* (1986). Par 72. 6,651 yards. 71.4 par rating. 127 slope rating. Greens fee: $110; $80–$90 (off season), cart included. Walking permitted. Season: year-round.
• *Robert Trent Jones Course* (1967). Par 72. 6,710 yards. 72.2 par rating. 123 slope rating.
• *George Fazio Course* (1969). Par 70. 6,873 yards. 72.6 par rating. 132 slope rating.
• Greens fees for the Jones and Fazio courses: $81 and $60 to $70 (off season), cart included. Walking permitted. No caddies. Season: year-round.

Palmetto Hall Plantation. 108 Fort Howell Drive, Hilton Head, SC 29926. Tel: 800-827-3006 or 803-689-4100. Fax: 803-689-5891. Credit cards accepted.

* *Arthur Hills Course* (1990). Par 72. 6,918 yards. 72.2 par rating. 132 slope rating.
* *Robert Cupp Course* (1993). Par 72. 7,079 yards. 74.8 par rating. 141 slope rating.
* Greens fees: $81 and $60 to $70 (off season), cart included. Walking permitted. No caddies. Season: year-round.

Old South Golf Links. 50 Buckingham Plantation Drive, Bluffton, SC 29910. Tel: 803-785-5353. Fax: 803-837-7169. Credit cards accepted.

* 1991. Designer: Clyde Johnston. Par 72. 6,700 yards. 72.4 par rating. 129 slope rating. Greens fees: spring and fall: $77, winter and summer: $49 to $58, cart included. Walking permitted after 2 P.M., but no pull carts are allowed on the course. No caddies. Season: year-round.

GOLF SERVICES

Golf services throughout Hilton Head are very good. We found the staff especially cordial at Harbour Town, but we experienced good service everywhere with the exception of the Robert Trent Jones course at Palmetto Dunes. There the staff appeared a bit hardened by the heavy traffic. The clubhouse at Harbour Town is also probably the most handsome and best equipped on the island, although all three setups at Palmetto Dunes are first-rate—good pro shops, comfortable changing facilities, and agreeable places to eat before and after your game. Walking is discouraged on these Hilton Head courses, though policies vary; greens fees almost always include your cart. Rental bags are available at each location.

LODGING

The three best hotels on Hilton Head are the **Hyatt Regency at Palmetto Dunes,** the **Westin at Port Royal,** and the newly refurbished **Crown Plaza** (formerly a Marriott but now a Holiday Inn). Every discount motel chain has a representative on Hilton Head. Of the upscale hotels, the Hyatt Regency wins first prize for several reasons: its proximity (walking distance) to the three outstanding Palmetto Dunes golf courses, the fact that Hyatt guests get preferred tee times and reduced greens fees on the Palmetto Dunes courses, and the hotel services and the quality of its rooms are the very best on the island. This very large hotel has a nice beach, swimming pools (including indoor), exercise room, three restaurants, and a nightclub. Be sure to request a "Regency Club" room, which includes complimentary breakfast, a nice evening buffet between 5 and 7 P.M., and free beverages around the clock, all just $10 per night more than a standard room.

Hyatt Regency at Palmetto Dunes. Hilton Head, SC 29938. Tel: 800-233-1234 or 803-785-1234. Fax: 803-842-4695. 505 rooms and suites. Doubles from $270 to $285. Credit cards accepted.

The Westin at Port Royal. Port Royal Resort, Hilton Head, SC 29928. Tel: 800-228-3000 or 803-681-4000. Fax: 803-681-1087. 412 rooms. Doubles range from $250 to $350. Credit cards accepted.

Crown Plaza. 130 Shipyard Drive, Hilton Head, SC 29928. Tel: 800-334-1881 or 803-842-2400. Fax: 803-785-8463. 340 rooms and suites. Doubles from $190 to $260. Credit cards accepted.

RESTAURANTS

The four must restaurants on Hilton Head are as follows:

Primo is one of the most distinguished restaurants on the island from a culinary viewpoint. Contemporary Italian cuisine (fresh pasta made daily, grilled salmon, grouper, and tuna) and excellent wines are served in a sophisticated setting. It runs about $95 for a complete dinner for two, wine and tip included. Open only in the evening.

Charlie's L'Etoile Verte is Hilton Head's most beautiful and fashionable restaurant. This cozy, elegant place, filled with fresh flowers, is just around the corner from the Hyatt Regency. The decor is colorful, eclectic, and tasteful, with Pierre Deux tablecloths and a brick floor. The food is good, but not at the level of Primo. Specialties include softshell crab, blackened amberjack, dolphin, and rack of lamb. Dinner for two will be about $100, wine and tip included.

Le Bistro is a very informal, very busy Mediterranean-style bistro located in the Pineland Mall shopping center. This dark, candlelit, and friendly place features good salads, veal, cod, salmon, steak, shrimp, and pasta. Dinner for two is about $70 with wine and tip.

Reilley's, a friendly Irish pub and a favorite of Hilton Head locals, is the perfect place for lunch after a morning round of golf. Located in the Gallery of Shops just past the Sea Island traffic circle, Reilley's features good burgers, salads, and an assortment of Irish brew. Reservations are not necessary.

Primo. New Orleans Plaza, Hilton Head, SC 29928. Tel: 803-785-2343. Fax: 803-785-5738. Credit cards accepted.

Charlie's L'Etoile Verte. 1000 Plantation Center, Hilton Head, SC 29928. Tel: 803-785-9277. No fax. Credit cards accepted.

Le Bistro. 301 Pineland Mill, Hilton Head, SC 29926. Tel: 803-681-8425. No fax. Credit cards accepted.

Reilley's. 7-D Hilton Head Plaza, Greenwood Drive, Hilton Head, SC 29938. Tel: 803-842-4414. Fax: 803-842-6121. Credit cards accepted.

NON-GOLF ACTIVITIES

The excellent non-golf activities on Hilton Head include tennis, bicycle rentals, beachcombing, deep-sea fishing, nature walks, exploring the nearby islands, excursions to historic Savannah, Georgia (one hour away), and shopping the island's boutiques and shops, the factory outlets, or the large mall at Shelter Cove.

GETTING THERE: From Charleston, head south on Route 17 to I-95 South. From I-95 South take exit 5 (Route 46). Go east on Route 46 and follow the signs to Highway 278, which leads directly to Hilton Head Island.

▶KIAWAH ISLAND

	The Golf	Golf Services	Lodging	Restaurants	Non-Golf Activities	Total
Rating	18	17	15	17	18	85

South Carolina's Kiawah Island is one of the most mesmerizing landscapes/seascapes under the sun and one of this nation's most intriguing golf destinations.

It features great planning, stunning scenery, and a breathtaking variety of golf. The island has ten miles of spectacular private beach and a resolutely uncommercial-looking development that is hidden among the marshes and sea grass. Indeed, this development is so artfully done that it appears to be in perfect harmony with the natural environment. Exotic birds and flowers abound; alligators measuring six feet inhabit the lagoons and roam the

Ocean Course

golf courses more or less at will, and, indeed, we saw four such alligators during our visit, three on the Turtle Point golf course and one in the small lake outside our condo.

As a resort destination, however, Kiawah is not without its shortcomings. The food served in its handful of restaurants can be mediocre at best, and some of the older condominium units available for rent are a little run-down and scruffy-looking. Regrettably, we occupied one such unit ourselves. Yet the island's positive attributes far outweigh its negative ones; Kiawah *is* a place we would gladly return to again and again, either solely for the outstanding golf or as a memorable vacation destination for the entire family, one where we could all enjoy a lovely beach near the infinitely fascinating city of Charleston.

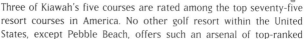

THE GOLF
18

Three of Kiawah's five courses are rated among the top seventy-five resort courses in America. No other golf resort within the United States, except Pebble Beach, offers such an arsenal of top-ranked courses. The awesome Ocean Course, designed by Pete Dye and the site of the tearful 1991 Ryder Cup, is Kiawah's world-famous track, and it is the course that we will devote most of our attention to in this review. Other courses include Turtle Point, a very handsome and fair Jack Nicklaus layout; the lovely Osprey Point, a Tom Fazio creation and far and away the most popular course among Kiawah residents; and Cougar Point, a brand-new redesign by the Gary Player Company of the old Marsh Point Course that Player built in 1976. The new design is a dramatic step up from the old course, which was the easiest, the least interesting, and had the most typical resort-course feel of the Kiawah courses. The new River Course is restricted to Kiawah homeowners. All five golf courses are located on different parts of the 10,000-acre island, and all have their own clubhouse facilities.

Locals have long since given up trying to master the **Ocean Course** and leave it almost entirely to the tourists. One resident golfer with an eleven handicap reported that his scores here, after repeated efforts, had merely escalated upward from 103 to 108 and beyond. Kiawah members, by the way, also avoid the Ocean Course because they have to pay a surcharge to play it.

We left the Ocean Course feeling as if we should pack up our clubs and put them away for a long, long time. After the match-play Ryder Cup was concluded, Ray Floyd described the Ocean Course by saying: "It's so hard it's unbelievable. If you had to play this course with a scorecard, I don't see how you could finish."

Even if you tee off from the whites, the Ocean Course demands long, straight drives to narrow—at times barely visible—landing zones. Dye said that he was sick and tired of pros playing tournament courses with a driver and wedge and that one of the things he wanted to accomplish with the Ocean Course was "to reinstitute long-iron play." As a result, your second shot on the Ocean Course is generally tougher than the first, requiring another massive carry over water or hip-high sea oats to slivers of green that are backed by ball-eating white dunes or even more water.

The Ocean Course is tough enough as it is, but the wind—and it is always very windy here, even in the depths of midsummer—really complicates matters. It is a factor on every hole, from front, back, or side to side. It is our opinion that the seventeenth hole—the par three over water and into the wind that destroyed Colin Montgomerie and Mark Calcavecchia—simply does not work as a golf hole. You might as well play from a shrimp boat onto the beach. Gorgeous? Definitely. Fun? Hardly.

Yet golf inspires strange ambitions. So strange, in fact, that the Ocean Course would be our first stop on any return visit to Kiawah. The Ocean Course occupies three miles of coastline on the most beautiful part of Kiawah Island. Moreover, the routing is spectacular: ten holes run directly along the sea, yet all eighteen offer ocean views. The Ocean Course clubhouse is one of the most exquisite in America, and the practice range—also fronting the sea—is the loveliest practice area we have seen anywhere in the world. The golf course itself has been constructed so unobtrusively that it remains a virtual nature sanctuary combining exquisite wetlands with beautiful birds and wildlife. Next time we would also be smarter and play from the white tees rather than the blues.

Part of the great appeal of **Turtle Point** and **Osprey Point** might be explained by the fact that we found them both—after our trials and tribulations on the windswept Ocean Course—so playable, so welcoming, and, well, so normal. It was great just to be playing golf again. Osprey Point illustrates once more why Tom Fazio is so highly acclaimed by environmentalists, developers, and golfers of every ability. This extremely scenic 6,678-yard course is typical Fazio: it meshes with the surrounding salt marshes and is plenty challenging while allowing you to retain a good measure of self-esteem. While Osprey Point gets the most play on Kiawah, we preferred Turtle Point, which is long (6,925 yards from the tips), has tremendous variety, and is plenty generous with fat fairways and flat, puttable greens. The first thirteen holes on Turtle Point play among forests, lakes, and alligators. Then at fourteen you get a taste of the Ocean Course with three holes, two par threes and a 412-yard par four, that run directly along the beach. They are definitely eye-poppers.

Despite foul weather during our visit, all of the courses at Kiawah were in excellent condition.

Kiawah Island. 12 Kiawah Beach Drive, Kiawah Island, SC 29455. Tel: 800-654-2924 or 803-768-2121 for Cougar Point, Osprey Point, and Turtle Point; 800-845-2471 for Ocean Course. Fax: 803-768-2726 (Cougar Point), 803-768-6079 (Osprey Point), 803-768-6093 (Turtle Point), and 803-768-0412 (Ocean Course). Credit cards accepted.

• *Ocean Course.* 1991. Designer: Pete Dye. Par 72. 7,395 yards. 78.0 par rating. 152 slope rating. Greens fees: spring and fall: $119 (resort guest)/$155 (public), summer: $101/$125. No walking. No caddies. Season: Year-round.
• *Cougar Point* (formerly Marsh Point). 1976/1996. Designer: Gary Player/Gary Player Company. Par 72. 6,523 yards. 70.9 par rating. 130 slope rating.
• *Osprey Point.* 1988. Designer: Tom Fazio. Par 72. 6,678 yards. 72.4 par rating. 128 slope rating.
• *Turtle Point.* 1981. Designer: Jack Nicklaus. Par 72. 6,925 yards. 74.0 par rating. 142 slope rating.
• Greens fees for Turtle Point, Osprey Point, and Cougar Point: spring and fall: $95 (resort guests)/$119 (public), summer: $75/$99, cart included. Walking permitted on Cougar Course. No walking on Osprey Point and Turtle Point. No caddies. Season: Year-round.

GOLF SERVICES 17

Golf services at Kiawah's courses range from good to outstanding. The Ocean Course facility is one of the finest in the United States. Golf course employees are friendly and helpful.

LODGING 15

You have two lodging options on Kiawah—a hotel room in the **Kiawah Island Inn** or a larger condominium unit rented on behalf of private owners—and, as we have said, the accommodations at Kiawah that we saw require updating. Rooms in the inn look as if they have not been painted or decorated in some time, and our condo, while it was spacious, fairly comfortable, and had an attractive floor plan, was banged-up-looking. We stayed in number 4380 in the Windswept complex. This two-story unit had a kitchen, half bath, and living room with television on the first floor and two bedrooms and two baths upstairs. The best inn rooms have ocean views.

Important note: it is possible to book your Kiawah holiday through any number of independent realtors. But golfers absolutely must make their reservations directly through the Kiawah resort itself. Only then are you guaranteed advanced tee times on the golf courses.

Kiawah Island Resort and **Kiawah Island Inn.** 12 Kiawah Beach Drive, Kiawah Island, SC 29455. Tel: 800-654-2924 or 803-768-2121 (the inn). Fax: 803-768-6099. 150 rooms and 300 condominium units. Doubles in the Kiawah Island Inn range from $155 to $205 in summer season. A golf package (requiring a two-night minimum stay) includes one round of golf per guest per day, daily breakfast buffet, cart, and range balls for $280 to $396 per couple. There is a $30 surcharge per person to play the Ocean Course. Credit cards accepted.

RESTAURANTS 17

Sadly, you will have to drive into Charleston for a decent meal. We were being polite above when we called the food at Kiawah "mediocre at best." Overcooked potatoes, bland vegetables, and dry roast beef are the bane of many golf resorts, but Kiawah might just win the bad food award. The prettiest, most costly, and most gastronomically ambitious restaurant within the resort is **Jasmine Porch,** but the she-crab soup and "surf 'n' turf" main course we sampled proved quite disappointing. The casual **Heron Park Grill,** likewise, cannot be recommended with any real enthusiasm, though with entrées ranging in price from $9.95 to $19.95, this well-lit, cathedral-ceilinged restaurant does offer an ample variety of steaks, fresh seafood, and pastas. The best restaurant in the area is the **Privateer,** a seafood establishment located at Bohicket Marina just outside the Kiawah gates. Open only for dinner, the Privateer serves a wide selection of entrées—seafood, steaks, chicken, pastas—ranging from $11.99 to $35.99.

Fortunately, Charleston is loaded with fine places to dine. Three of our favorite Charleston restaurants include **Million,** a fine French restaurant offering an ever-changing prix fixe menu at $45 and à la carte selections from $23 to $27; **Carolina's,** an American-style bistro where we enjoyed a heavenly, almond-encrusted grouper topped with crabmeat; and **Magnolias,** whose Down-South egg rolls (with collard greens, chicken, and Cajun sausage), sautéed crabcakes, and pan-fried softshell crabs make us return again and again.

Jasmine Porch. Kiawah Island Inn. 12 Kiawah Beach Drive, Kiawah Island, SC 29455. Tel: 803-768-2121 (the inn) or 803-768-2701 (restaurant). Fax: 803-768-6099. Credit cards accepted.

Heron Park Grill. 4000 Sea Forest Drive, Kiawah Island, SC 29455. Tel: 803-768-6440. Fax: 803-768-1342. Credit cards accepted.

Privateer. 1882 Andell Bluff, Seabrook, SC 29455. Tel: 803-768-1290. Fax: 803-768-9567. Credit cards accepted.

Restaurant Million. 2 Unity Alley, Charleston, SC 29401. Tel: 803-577-3141. Fax: 803-577-3681. Credit cards accepted.

Carolina's. 10 Exchange Street, Charleston, SC 29401. Tel: 803-724-3800. Fax: 803-722-9493. Credit cards accepted.

Magnolias. 185 East Bay, Charleston, SC 29401. Tel: 803-577-7771. Fax: 803-722-0035. Credit cards accepted.

 N O N - G O L F   A C T I V I T I E S

Kiawah shines in this category. There's the beach, tennis, bicycles for rent, walking trails within the resort, and the glories of Charleston just up the road. For shopping—especially for fine antiques and elegant clothing—Charleston's King Street is impossible to beat. The historic district south of Broad is fascinating.

GETTING THERE: From Charleston Airport take a left onto International Boulevard. Stay in the right lane and turn right onto Highway 526 West. Exit at Route 7, turning right at the exit ramp, and proceed until you take another right onto 17 South. Take 17 South approximately five miles before turning left onto Main Road. Follow Main Road approximately seventeen miles to the Kiawah Resort.

Georgia

▶REYNOLDS PLANTATION

A GREAT TIME AT GREAT WATERS

	The Golf	Golf Services	Lodging	Restaurants	Non-Golf Activities	Total
Rating	19	18	18	13	17	**85**

The site-selection committee for the Andersen Consulting match-play tournaments obviously has an eye for the dramatic. This thrice-annual television spectacle is contested on three of the most beautiful public-access golf courses in America—Black-wolf Run at the American Club in Kohler, Wisconsin; Grayhawk in Scottsdale, Arizona; and the Great Waters Course at Reynolds Plantation, a 4,000-acre residential community on the shores of lovely Lake Oconee, located midway between Atlanta and Augusta, Georgia, and just ten minutes south of Interstate 20. Great

Waters hosts this event on the weekend following the Masters, when the Georgia dogwoods and azaleas are ablaze with color.

Grayhawk is a masterpiece of architectural design, and the American Club rates as one of the best golf destinations that we at GOLF TRAVEL have ever visited, yet the Great Waters Course at Reynolds Plantation, built in 1993 and ranked number two in the state of Georgia (behind only Augusta National), is equally sensational.

Easily one of Jack Nicklaus's finest architectural creations, Great Waters is the glamour eighteen at Reynolds Plantation, although its second track, the Plantation Course, a 1991 Bob Cupp design, is also very good. *Golfweek*, in fact, called

Great Waters Course

Reynolds Plantation "possibly the best thirty-six-hole complex in the country." Were this not enough, a new Tom Fazio course, the National Course, is scheduled to open at this very attractive and fast-growing development late in 1997. But make no mistake: serious golfers come to Reynolds Plantation with their appetites whetted for a taste of Great Waters.

The complete Reynolds Plantation experience, enhanced by the extraordinary Southern hospitality of its genuinely friendly employees (are Georgians simply the nicest people in America?) is remarkable from beginning to end. Overnight guests are accommodated in new, extremely comfortable golf cottages, and the array of activities for the non-golfer—swimming, tennis, boating, and fishing on Lake Oconee—is also extremely good. The only category that requires substantial improvement is the food, which is basic at best and lackluster at worst. Even so, a trip to Reynolds Plantation is recommended with enthusiasm.

THE GOLF   19

The **Great Waters Course** is the stuff dreams are made of. It is situated on a heavily wooded peninsula with so many tentacles of land jutting out into the waters of Lake Oconee that it resembles an octopus. Every hole on this golf course—not just the glorious final holes that appear on television—is a challenge and visual thrill. The breathtaking views of Lake Oconee alone are worth the greens fee. The condition of Great Waters is also truly spectacular. We played during a cold snap in early March (Great Waters is open year-round), yet even then the fairways were unblemished blankets of vivid green and the putting surfaces flawless and true. Holes one through eight are tight and wind their way through forests of towering pine, while the grand finale of Great Waters, holes ten through eighteen, are staggeringly beautiful as they trace the edges of Lake Oconee. Despite the rows of new homes that line some of the fairways and are at times a little too close to the action, Great Waters is an idyllic, peaceful, unforgettable experience. We had the pleasure of playing Great Waters in the company of two young professionals from Michigan's Upper Peninsula who had played Great Waters before and knew it well. "Greatest course I have ever played," one of them mentioned casually before our game began. "By far," echoed the second.

If you play to a low-handicap amateur, you will want to tackle Great Waters from the gold tees, which stretch the course to its maximum limit, 7,048 yards. From the tips, the course carries a big slope rating of 135 and a par rating of 73.8. If you play from the golds, however, expect to hit plenty of fairway woods, even on the par fours, and do not count on reaching many greens in regulation. For most players, the blue tees offer plenty of golf course: 6,545 yards (slope 130/par 71.2). From its shortest tees, Great Waters measures 5,082 yards (slope 117/par 70.9).

Isolating the best holes from the simply outstanding at Great Waters is no easy task. On the front side, five and nine may be the two most memorable holes. Number five, an uphill, 422-yard par four and the number one handicap hole at Great Waters, is a right-to-left dogleg that requires a drive to a tight landing area across a creek and then a second shot over another creek up to the green. Five, in fact, is a good score on the par four fifth. The ninth hole, a 392-yard par four, features a generous landing area for your tee shot, but then presents you with a long, heroic carry over a finger of Lake Oconee that protects the green. This beautiful ninth hole, however, is just a taste of greater things to come.

On the back nine Great Waters becomes sensational. Six of these final holes have greens backed up against the shore of Lake Oconee. The glorious eleventh hole demands an uphill tee shot, then a downhill second shot to a green perched on the water's edge. Twelve is a long, uphill, 549-yard par five that doglegs to the left and requires a long drive to carry over a portion of the lake. But number thirteen may win the beauty prize. This 434-yard par four features an uphill tee shot, then a blind second shot down to the green. Fourteen and seventeen are two exquisite par threes. Although it looks much longer through the lens of a television camera, seventeen measures just 159 yards, while fourteen is 178 yards long. Both holes are all-carry over the lake. The final hole is another knockout, a 540-yard par five with an approach shot to the green into the wind and over the lake.

The Cupp-designed **Plantation Course** at Reynolds Plantation was named "one of the ten best new courses in America" by *Golf Digest* when it opened. While shorter, easier, and less dramatic than Great Waters, this excellent "second" loop is just as idyllic and well maintained. The Plantation Course has three sets of tees: from the blues it measures 6,656 yards (slope rating 122/par rating 71.3), from the white tees it is 6,017 yards long (slope rating 119/par rating 68.5), and from the red tees it measures 5,152 yards (slope rating 117/par rating 69.1).

The rolling-to-hilly terrain and the distances from green to tee make these courses ideally suited for carts. Walking is permitted on the Plantation Course only after 2 P.M. and on the Great Waters Course only when the course is not busy. Both golf courses are open on a daily-fee basis to overnight guests at Reynolds Plantation. Each course is closed one day a week.

Reynolds Plantation. 100 Linger Longer Road, Greensboro, GA 30642. Tel: 800-800-5250 or 706-467-3151 (general), 706-485-0235 (Great Waters pro shop), 706-467-3159 (Plantation Course pro shop). Fax: 706-467-3071. Credit cards accepted.

• *Great Waters Course.* 1993. Designer: Jack Nicklaus. Par 72. 7,048 yards. 73.8 par rating. 135 slope rating. Greens fees: Monday, Wednesday, Thursday: $93, Friday–Sunday: $103. Cart included. Walking permitted only when the course is not busy (at the discretion of the golf shop). No caddies. Restrictions: access restricted to members and Reynolds Plantation guests. Season: year-round. Closed Tuesdays.

• *Plantation Course.* 1991. Designer: Bob Cupp. Par 71. 6,656 yards. 71.3 par rating. 122 slope rating. Greens fee: Tuesday–Thursday: $83, Friday–Sunday: $93. Cart included. Walking permitted after 2 P.M. No caddies. Restrictions: access restricted to members and Reynolds Plantation guests. Season: year-round. Closed Mondays.

GOLF SERVICES

Golf services are outstanding. The good professional shops at both golf courses are run by eager staff members who are clearly in love with the Reynolds Plantation courses. Bag attendants unload your car in the parking lot and clean your clubs after your round. The practice ranges are very good, and there are drink carts that traverse the courses. Rental clubs and lessons are also available.

LODGING

We stayed overnight in golf cottage 230, overlooking the eighth hole of the Great Waters Course. This extremely attractive, well-appointed, spacious, and obviously brand-new unit includes two bedrooms, two baths, a spotless and fully equipped kitchen, a handsome living room with television, and an outdoor deck with a golf course view. Of all the town house and condominium units we have occupied at golf resorts over the years, from Sugarloaf in Maine to PGA National in Florida, this lovely cottage at **Reynolds Plantation** was by far the best. Rates begin at $245 per night based on two people per bedroom in high season from March to July

Guest Cottage, Reynolds Plantation

5. Attractive golf packages are also available. Reynolds Plantation cottages are ideal for a family, for couples traveling together, or for a golf getaway among a group of friends. In the entire complex there is only one one-bedroom unit.

Reynolds Plantation. 100 Linger Longer Road, Greensboro, GA 30642. Tel: 800-800-5250 or 706-467-3151. Fax: 706-467-3071. 65 two- and three-bedroom golf cottages. Two-bedroom condominiums from $245 to $271 based on two people per bedroom in high season. Three-day/two-night golf packages start at $425 per person, including daily round of golf, club cottage accommodations, and breakfast. Credit cards accepted.

RESTAURANTS

Sadly, the culinary offerings of Reynolds Plantation do not begin to match the standards set by its golf courses and accommodations. The cuisine, in fact, is a big disappointment—plenty of carbohydrates but little or no dash or sophistication. The clubhouse dining rooms are pleasant-looking and comfortable, and the friendly young waiters and waitresses provide excellent service, but our overcooked steak tasted like shoe leather, while the bland, microwaved French fries that emerged from the kitchen were so hot they scalded.

The restaurants at Reynolds Plantation. 100 Linger Longer Road, Greensboro, GA 30642. Tel: 800-800-5250 or 706-467-3151 (general), 706-467-3159 (dining reservations). Fax: 706-467-3071. Credit cards accepted.

NON-GOLF ACTIVITIES

Activities for the non-golfer at Reynolds Plantation include walking on the pedestrian trail, swimming in the club's two pools, tennis on six outdoor courts, and fishing and boating on Lake Oconee, Georgia's second largest lake. Fishing equipment, fishing guides, and powerboats are available for rent at the marina.

GETTING THERE: From Atlanta, take I-20 East. After you cross Lake Oconee, take exit 53 (Greensboro—Georgia Highway 44). At the exit ramp turn right (south). Go 7.2 miles. At the Texaco station, turn left and drive to Reynolds Plantation.

►THE CLOISTER, SEA ISLAND

OLD-FASHIONED HOSPITALITY DOWN SOUTH

	The Golf	Golf Services	Lodging	Restaurants	Non-Golf Activities	Total
Rating	**18**	**19**	**16**	**17**	**18**	**88**

The Cloister

No golf resort in America has a stronger sense of place than the Cloister on Sea Island, Georgia. Some of the newer golf resorts in Florida or Southern California, however elaborate they may be, get lost in the caverns of your memory. Yet every facet of the Cloister is distinct and unforgettable: its four great nine-hole layouts on the site of an antebellum cotton plantation; its spectacular teaching facility, the famous Golf Learning Center; its historic hotel built in 1928 and located on a wonderful beach; the absolutely extraordinary hospitality of its staff members; and its very Southern, very traditional clientele. If you have not come here, say, in thirty years or so, have no fear. Despite subtle updating, the Cloister is precisely as you remember it.

There is a charmingly baroque quality about the elaborate rituals that are enacted daily at this very Southern resort. A few examples follow:

Southerners like to dress for dinner. Shortly after our arrival and just as we were getting settled in our nice room, a bellman delivered an engraved invitation from the social director for a hotel-wide cocktail party, black tie optional, where many of the older ladies in attendance wore the same red satin or sequined gown that they have worn at the Cloister since they first started coming here in the 1950s. Or at least that's the way it appeared. We also golfed one morning with a pair of courtly, loquacious lawyers from Atlanta. Whenever one of these fellows topped a shot—an event that took place at least once or twice every hole—the very worst obscenity they could muster was "Lord, have mercy!" And at breakfast, when Hall of Famer and Sea Island golf instructor Louise Suggs entered the dining room to take her meal, she was greeted all around by the restaurant staff with a phrase right out of Margaret Mitchell, "Good morning, Miss Louise!"

Our visit occurred in the off season during the first week of January. The cry of "Happy New Year, y'all" echoed throughout the hotel corridors. Indeed, non-Southerners may feel themselves "y'alled" to death down here, yet even the most stony-faced New Englander will be charmed by the warmth of the Cloister's staff. The tradition of service is simply better and more deeply entrenched in the South than in any other region of the United States. At times, the social whirl at the Cloister harkens back to a bygone era with ballroom dancing at the Beach Club and rumba lessons in the club rooms, but there is truly something for everyone here.

Serious golfers will perhaps love the Cloister most because it is a great place to improve one's game. The Golf Learning Center (owned jointly with *Golf Digest)* is a superb instructional facility. In Jack Lumpkin, Scott Davenport, and Louise Suggs, it also has one of the best teams of golf instructors in the nation. We had a lesson from one of Sea Island's younger professionals. When you come to Sea Island, be sure to book your private lessons at the Golf Learning Center well in advance. The telephone number is 912-638-5119.

By the way, the names "Sea Island" and the "Cloister" are used interchangeably because the hotel is located on Sea Island, which it shares with only a limited number of beautiful private homes. The Golf Learning Center and the resort's thirty-six holes are a ten-minute drive from the hotel on St. Simons Island.

Important note: The Cloister does not accept credit cards. You may settle your account only with cash, traveler's check, or personal check. This antiquated policy was the only inconvenience we experienced there.

THE GOLF ⑱

The wind and the rain (it was January, after all) did not keep hordes of golfers away from the Cloister during our visit. Yet despite the crowds and the elements, the Cloister is as friendly and unhurried a place to play golf as any you will find. Since most of us hurry into our golf games—and thereby destroy them—these words of praise for the ambience at the Cloister are about the highest we can give. The starter sensed our concern about the conditions, assured us that we would indeed be able to finish, and checked with us at the end of the day to be certain that we had enjoyed ourselves. When we came around the next morning, he greeted us by name. We were equally impressed with the considerate attitude of almost every golf course employee we encountered.

The relaxed atmosphere is further enhanced by the long *allée* of live oaks hung with Spanish moss that leads to the golf complex. Historic markers abound on the property, along with the picturesque ruins of a slave hospital from Retreat Plantation.

The four nines are **Seaside** (designed by the English masters H. S. Colt and C. S. Alison in 1929), **Retreat** (Dick Wilson, 1960), **Marshside** (Joe Lee, 1973), and **Plantation** (created by Walter Travis in 1927, altered by Colt and Alison in 1929, and altered again by Rees Jones in 1992). Retreat is the longest (3,390 yards) and Marshside is the shortest (3,192 yards), but all four have great charm and carry a par of thirty-six.

Seaside was singled out by Bobby Jones as "one of the very best nines I have ever seen." In truth, it is the most magical of the resort's collection of courses. Seaside is a great, wide-open links with wonderful views, sea breezes, gigantic bunkers designed to gobble up tee shots, and small, elevated, level, and very puttable greens. The two most stunning holes at Sea Island are located on the Seaside nine: number four, with its tee shot over the marsh (but shy of the huge fairway bunkers), and famous number seven, a tough, 424-yard par four that requires another big and accurate drive. In addition, during our visit Seaside was in better condition than the other courses.

Retreat opens along the ocean but becomes tighter and more difficult as it enters the oak forest. Marshside winds through scenic and challenging natural wetland hazards on every hole. And Plantation shares the bunkering characteristics and sweeping fairways of Seaside but lacks its ocean views.

The Cloister operates one additional eighteen-hole layout, the St. Simons Island Club, located across the street from the main golf complex. It is surrounded by an upscale residential subdivision, and we rate this course by far the least interesting in the area.

The sole discordant element that might mar your golf experience on Sea Island is the bitter paper-mill scent from the Union Camp smokestacks across the water at Brunswick, Georgia. The prevailing winds blow inland, however, so the chances are good that you will be unaffected.

Daily golf fees of $90 for hotel guests ($125 nonguests) are very reasonable. For families staying at the hotel, the Cloister generously allows juniors to play for free. Walking with a caddie is permitted at any time of day, and walkers who tote their own bags are welcome after 3:00 P.M.

Sea Island Golf Club, Sea Island, GA 31561. Tel: 800-732-4752, or 912-638-5118, or 912-638-5110 (starter). Fax: 912-638-5806. No credit cards.

• *Seaside Nine.* 1929. Designers: H. S. Colt, C. H. Alison. Par 36. 3,288 yards.
• *Retreat Nine.* 1960. Designer: Dick Wilson. Par 36. 3,390 yards.
• *Marshside Nine.* 1973. Designer: Joe Lee. Par 36. 3,192 yards.
• *Plantation Nine.* 1927. Designers: W. Travis/H. S. Colt and C. H. Alison (1929)/Rees Jones (1992). Par 36. 3,516 yards.
• Greens fees for all courses: $90 (hotel guest), $125 (public), cart included. Juniors staying at hotel play free. Walking permitted with caddie anytime; permitted without caddie after 3 P.M. Season: year-round.

GOLF SERVICES

When you consider—in addition to the incomparable Golf Learning Center—the Cloister's magnificent practice range, cordial employees, custom-club-fitting division, and excellent caddie program, golf services at the Cloister must be ranked among the best in the country.

LODGING

The best rooms at the Cloister are located right on the beach at **Harrington House** (where George and Barbara Bush stayed on their "second honeymoon" in 1991). We stayed in room 463 in Harrington House and were more than comfortable there. The color scheme—lime green, pink, and yellow—seemed lifted from the palette of Lily Pulitzer or Pappagallo, but the room was very spacious, luxurious, spotlessly clean, and well equipped. We did not care for the older guest rooms we were shown in the main building as they appeared small and drab.

The Cloister

The Cloister. Sea Island, GA 31561. Tel: 800-732-4752 or 912-638-3611. Fax: 912-638-5159. 263 rooms. Doubles range from $274 to $452 per night, including all meals and service. Three-night golf packages include unlimited golf, cart, and three meals daily. With accommodations in Harrington House, this golf package ranges from $170 to $280 per night per person, double occupancy. No credit cards.

RESTAURANTS

All meals at the Cloister are fully included in your room rate. Your restaurant options include the good six-course dinner in the formal dining room, including oyster bisque, crabmeat, green salad, prime rib, and great pecan pie with ice cream; the spectacular seafood buffet in the **Beach Club** (mussels, several shrimp dishes, crab, smoked salmon, caviar, and much more); or more casual dining at the **Golf Club** or **St. Simons Island Club.** Portions are generous, and the service is always superb. There is also a huge breakfast buffet in the dining room every morning. A 15 percent service charge is added to your bill; hence, tipping is unnecessary anywhere in the resort.

Restaurants at the Cloister. Sea Island, GA 31561. Tel: 800-732-4752 or 912-638-3611. Fax: 912-638-5159. No credit cards.

NON-GOLF ACTIVITIES

The Cloister is busy throughout the year, but it is principally a summer resort, and during the summer it takes on its true family flavor. The resort's complete range of supervised programs for children (offered at no extra charge) frees parents to follow their own pursuits, which may include horseback riding on the beach, exercise classes, massage, personal training in the fine health spa complex, tennis (there are seventeen courts), swimming, skeet shooting at the gun club, fishing, boat cruises, bicycling, and shopping in nearby boutiques. There is also nightly entertainment. Ballroom dancing is a signature Cloister activity, and lessons are available. The Cloister is a traditional destination for honeymooners. Romantic young couples are in evidence everywhere.

GETTING THERE: From Jacksonville Airport in Florida, get onto I-95 North, and follow it into Georgia. Get off at exit 6. Turn right onto Highway 17 North. Follow it into Brunswick, Georgia. Look for signs to St. Simons Island and Sea Island. Go across the causeway, which will put you on St. Simons Island. Take a left at the first light, onto Sea Island Road. Go over another little causeway, which will put you on Sea Island. Once on Sea Island proper, take the first left and the Cloister will be right there on your right. Sea Island is roughly seventy miles away from the airport.

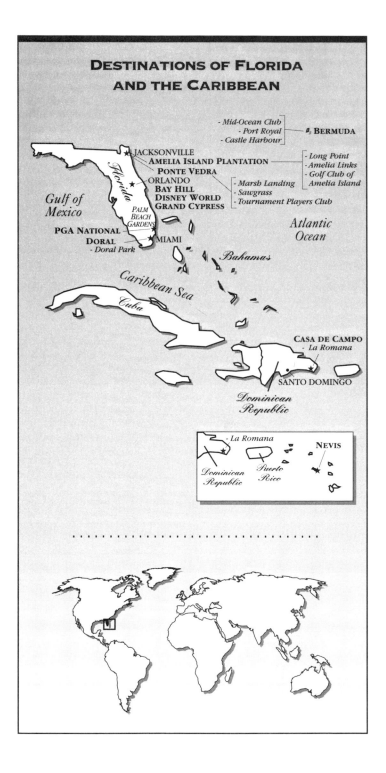

DESTINATIONS OF FLORIDA AND THE CARIBBEAN

- Mid-Ocean Club
- Port Royal
- Castle Harbour

B **BERMUDA**

JACKSONVILLE
AMELIA ISLAND PLANTATION
PONTE VEDRA

- Long Point
- Amelia Links
- Golf Club of Amelia Island

ORLANDO
BAY HILL
DISNEY WORLD
GRAND CYPRESS

- Marsh Landing
- Sawgrass
- Tournament Players Club

Florida

Gulf of Mexico

PALM BEACH GARDENS

PGA NATIONAL
DORAL
- Doral Park

MIAMI

Atlantic Ocean

Bahamas

Caribbean Sea

Cuba

CASA DE CAMPO
- La Romana

SANTO DOMINGO

Dominican Republic

- La Romana

Dominican Republic

Puerto Rico

NEVIS

FLORIDA AND THE CARIBBEAN

FLORIDA AND THE CARIBBEAN

Oh, take me again to the clime of my birth,

The dearest, the fairest, to me on earth,

The clime where the roses are sweetest that bloom,

And nature is bathed in the rarest perfume!

When the hills of the North are shrouded in snow,

When the winds of Winter their fiercest do blow—

then take me again to the clime of my birth

Dear Florida—dearest to me on the earth.

—"Dreams of Life," Timothy Thomas Fortune

Florida and the Caribbean—the stuff of our dreams. Columbus sailed off the ends of the known universe to discover a New World in this region. Ponce de León came in search of fantastic gold and a magic fountain that would restore youth. In more modern times the dream still burns, rekindled with the arrival of every postcard that reminds us that we are not there. These are the lands of our vacations, our retirement, our winter getaways. Florida and the Caribbean are blue skies and sleepy, warm sunshine, soothing breezes and white sand beaches, sailboats drifting by and salty margaritas, bright colors and bronzed bodies, spring break and unrepentant leisure, a procrastinator's delight where one need not do much of anything and yet never seem bored.

Florida and the Caribbean offer us more than just the opportunity to luxuriate in the sun; they also give us golf, even sublime golf. Who among us does not harbor a not-so-secret desire to flee the kids at Disney World and take to the tee at one of the ninety-nine world-class golf holes of Disney's Magic Linkdom? Find us a golfer who hasn't yearned to play at one of the big Florida golf resorts—the best being Grand Cypress—and we will wager that he or she isn't *that* serious about the game. Each year more than 55 million rounds of golf are played on Florida's more than one thousand golf courses. Florida is the home of great courses such as memorable Doral, Arnie's Bay Hill, and Long Point on Amelia Island. The PGA nurses its empire in Palm Beach Gardens at PGA National, and the tour players hold their own tournament at the TPC in Ponte Vedra. The seventeenth hole at the TPC's Stadium Course lingers in all our dreams—how many times have we closed our eyes and imagined taking a shot at that famous island green? Take away Florida and our golf dreams lose their luster.

And we now have a new and growing romantic vision: golf in the Caribbean. These beautiful islands, a hedonistic archipelago for sun and fun, are suddenly teeming with golf. The Dominican Republic alone has sixteen golf courses with several others under construction or in the planning stage. The great resorts on Nevis and the Dominican Republic—oh, and we mustn't forget Bermuda farther north in the Atlantic—boast brilliant golf courses designed by many of the world's best course architects. Pete Dye's creations at Casa de Campo and La Romana in the Dominican Republic rank among the most spectacular anywhere in the world. Nevis is consistently rated among the top two or three resorts in the world, a perfect cure for the wintertime blahs.

Golf is a year-round proposition in Florida and the Caribbean, but the region's balmy winter weather is what gives substance to our dreams and lures the big crowds. You can usually count on Caribbean temperatures to be in the eighties throughout the dead of winter, and spring is a delightful season to visit any and all of these memorable golf destinations. The crowds—and the greens fees—drop precipitously in summertime, when the weather is hot and humid, although the waters of the Atlantic Ocean and Gulf of Mexico act as a moderating influence on Florida, while the Caribbean islands can usually count on comforting breezes. Still, there's a good reason why golf courses in Florida and the Caribbean are far less crowded in summer—conditions are often very uncomfortable. Do stay alert, also, to the weather forecasts during the hurricane season, which lasts from June through November.

But no matter whether it's spring, summer, winter, or fall, come to Florida and the Caribbean and make real your dreams.

Florida

▶GRAND CYPRESS

THE BEST OF FLORIDA

	The Golf	Golf Services	Lodging	Restaurants	Non-Golf Activities	Total
Rating	18	18	17	17	20	90

Over the years, GOLF TRAVEL has reviewed a substantial number of golf resorts in the Sunshine State, some very well known and high-profile, others little known and off the beaten track, from Amelia Island in the north all the way down south to Key West. It has been a challenge to discover a single golf destination in the entire state of Florida that satisfies us in every regard. Up until now, our trips to Florida have always ended on a bittersweet note.

Hyatt Regency, Grand Cypress

Every golf resort we have visited, while frequently outstanding in one or two departments, has had one or two equally troubling flaws. Doral in Miami and Sawgrass in Ponte Vedra, for example, feature a great collection of scintillating golf courses; both resorts, however, are sadly undistinguished in other important categories such as food and lodging. At the Breakers in Palm Beach and Turnberry Isle in Aventura, we discovered that the imbalance was reversed: both offered marvelous accommodations, refined service, and elegant restaurants, but their golf courses can only be described (charitably, at that) as less than truly exceptional.

Grand Cypress in Orlando is not only well rounded and wonderful in every facet of its operation, but it is indeed the premier golf resort in the entire state of Florida. This 1,500-acre complex, a *Golf Magazine* gold medalist, is situated just twenty minutes west of the Orlando Airport, ten minutes from the Magic Kingdom and Epcot Center, and five minutes from Disney Village and Pleasure Island, Disney's nightlife complex. Grand Cypress consists of an immaculate, eighteen-story, 750-room Hyatt Regency in the shape of an Inca pyramid with a dramatic, tropical atrium; the elegant Villas of Grand Cypress; forty-five holes of golf designed by Jack Nicklaus; leisure activities that include swimming in a stone grotto, horseback riding, sailing on a twenty-one acre lake; and a plethora of fine dining options within the resort. You will have to look very hard around Grand Cypress to find a single detail amiss. We looked, and came up nearly empty. We noted only one trivial problem; unless you prefer to drive yourself, riding the shuttle bus to either the hotel restaurants or to the golf courses is a fact of life at Grand Cypress. But, as we said, this is only a minor irritant: the shuttles are prompt and comfortable.

THE GOLF   (18)

The golf complex at **Grand Cypress** consists of a large, lovely clubhouse with a pro shop, locker rooms, and restaurants; a lavish teaching facility called the Grand Cypress Academy of Golf; and forty-five exquisitely maintained holes of golf, including the New Course—an absolutely stunning replica of the Old Course at St. Andrews—and the outstanding North, South, and East nines, which hosted the LPGA Tournament of Champions through 1996.

During our visit, Grand Cypress was a busy place. On the morning we were there we noted PGA Tour stars Paul Azinger signing copies of his biography, *Zinger*, in the locker room, Jeff Maggert shooting a television ad for a golf clothing manufacturer under the direction of a sizable film crew, and Loren Roberts having lunch with friends in the bar. As it turned out, all three of these Orlando residents were relaxing at Grand Cypress before heading out to their next tournament stop.

One of Grand Cypress's best qualities is that it offers a great variety of golf. Its two chief tracks—the North-South and the New courses—bear absolutely no similarity to each other. In a comparison of the two tracks, the North-South combination gets our vote as the resort's premier eighteen-hole loop and its best test of golf, while the delightful New Course clearly wins as the resort's most *joyous* layout.

The **New Course** is anything but a contrived experience, even for those who have played St. Andrews time and again. Of course, the huge differences in climate and culture between Florida and Scotland are much in evidence. There are no orange groves adjacent to the links in St. Andrews, no exotic tropical birds on its fairways, and no carts gliding along paths that have been scored and grooved to resemble flagstone rather than poured concrete. There is no huge crowd of tourists and bystanders watching your first tee shot of the day at Grand Cypress, no imposing Royal & Ancient clubhouse, and no venerable Rusacks Hotel looming on the eighteenth fairway.

But *like* St. Andrews, there is a small starter's shed adjacent to the first tee, a vast fairway shared by the first and eighteenth holes, a burn and a stone bridge, seven double greens, over 150 bunkers, and a precise replica of the Road Hole, complete with road and stone wall behind the green. There is even a Valley of Sin on the New Course's eighteenth green. Unlike the North-South Course, which is target golf, the New Course often invites you to play the Scottish-style bump-and-run shot onto the open greens. A high-tech detail we could do without, however, are the little messages on the cart's computer range finder—"The New Course pays tribute to St. Andrews. Notice the similarities?"—as if you are supposed to carry on some sort of inane conversation with it.

From the white tees, the New Course plays short (6,181 yards) and relatively easy (par rating 69.4/slope rating 117). Most good golfers, therefore, should consider playing from the blue tees, which lengthen the New Course to a still not overly difficult 6,773 yards (par rating 72.1/slope rating 126). From its shortest tees, the New Course measures 5,314 yards, with a par rating of 69.8 and a slope rating of 117.

Good holes on the New Course are those that bring St. Andrews most vividly to life. Thanks to the great width of the fairway, your drive on the first hole can call forth a flood of Old Course associations, even with no crowd and no Royal & Ancient clubhouse. Your second shot on number one is a stiff challenge; a winding and surprisingly deep burn (stream) lurks unseen from the fairway before the first green, so be certain to take at least one or two extra clubs in order to carry the water. This winding, deep-faced, Scottish-style burn also threatens play on numbers eight and ten, two very good par fours. Number eight is 440 yards long and the number one handicap hole on the New Course. A big drive down the left side on eight will open up the green, but don't be short with your second shot, or you will end up at the bottom of the burn. Ten is a short (330-yard), downwind par four. If you hit a good drive on ten, all you are left with is a touch shot, a flip wedge that must carry the burn onto the sizable green. And eighteen is a great finisher. You drive into the big double fairway, cross the burn for the last time via a stone bridge, and putt on an enormous green surrounded by a knee-high white picket fence.

The **North-South Course**— completed in 1986, two years prior to the opening of the New Course—was the original eighteen at Grand Cypress and is still the resort's most popular track, despite the fact that it is easily four or five shots more difficult than the New Course. The North-South nines are laden with Nicklaus-designed hazards: high, fescue-covered mounds lining both sides of the fairways and ample water coming into play on thirteen of its eighteen holes. This tough, 6,993-yard golf course (75.1 par rating) requires lengthy tee shots and precise iron play all day long.

The South Course

Outstanding holes include the ninth holes on both the North and South nines, which finish at the same double green. The ninth hole on the North is a 435-yard par four that plays with a lake down its entire left-hand side. The ninth hole on the South is a 463-yard par four that plays along the opposite side of the same lake. Number two on the South is another beautiful golf hole. This 553-yard par five doglegs to the right and requires a big drive over the water and an approach shot to a green guarded with more water.

The **East** nine at Grand Cypress stands alone because it shares neither the windswept Florida flavor of the North-South Course nor the Scottish ambience of the New Course. The East nine is as pretty and well maintained as the others at Grand Cypress, but its atmosphere is more reminiscent of the Carolina Low Country than of either Florida or Scotland. The signature hole on the East is number five, a 152-yard par three to an island green.

Grand Cypress Golf Club. 1 North Jacaranda, Orlando, FL 32836. Tel: 800-835-7377 or 407-239-4700 or 407-239-1909. Fax: 407-239-1969. Restrictions: play limited to resort guests only. Credit cards accepted.

• *North-South Course.* 1986. Designer: Jack Nicklaus. Par 72. 6,993 yards. 75.1

par rating. 137 slope rating. Greens fee: $130, cart included. Walking permitted. Caddies available if booked in advance. Season: year-round.
  • *New Course.* 1988. Designer: Jack Nicklaus. Par 72. 6,773 yards. 72.1 par rating. 126 slope rating. Greens fee: $130, cart included. Walking permitted. Caddies available if booked in advance. Season: year-round.
  • *East Course.* 1988. Designer: Jack Nicklaus. Par 36. 3,434 yards. Greens fee (with either the North or South nines): $130, cart included. Walking permitted. Caddies available if booked in advance. Season: year-round.

GOLF SERVICES

Golf services at Grand Cypress are outstanding. The Grand Cypress Academy of Golf, although not headed by a famous teaching professional, ranks as one of the top instructional facilities in the country. Some of the academy's most successful programs include three-day instructional regimens; specialty schools for women, seniors, and novices; a special three-hole practice course for students; and an indoor clinic in which your swing will be taken apart and put back together again with the assistance of sophisticated video equipment. Golf clubs are available for rent in the very welcoming pro shop. The New Course is easy to walk and best enjoyed on foot; caddies are available, too, if booked in advance. Walking is now also permitted on the considerably more hilly North-South Course.

LODGING

The one hundred forty-four **Villas at Grand Cypress**—the resort's best accommodations—are Mediterranean-style stucco cottages with tiled roofs and private patios overlooking the fairways and lakes of the North nine. All the villas are attractively decorated and well furnished with fully equipped kitchens. The larger two-, three-, and four-bedroom units are ideally suited for families or two couples traveling together. A villa at Grand Cypress costs roughly $400 per bedroom.

The Villas at Grand Cypress

We stayed in a standard room in the handsome **Hyatt Regency,** number 639, which we found extremely comfortable. In fact, we actually preferred the Hyatt over the Villas because the energized and extremely well run Hyatt is the hub of activity at Grand Cypress. The Villas are located in a more isolated and quieter setting adjacent to the golf club. The recently remodeled room we stayed in had a nice view of the lake and was well furnished and well equipped. Room rates at the Hyatt Regency range from $255 to $380.

The elegant ground-floor public areas of the Hyatt Regency include an attractive piano bar called Trellises and an arcade of shops; there is also easy access to the wonderful outdoor pool and the hotel's four fine restaurants. Service at Grand Cypress—from top to bottom—is especially outstanding. From the front desk of the Hyatt Regency to the staff in the pro shop, every employee of the resort we encountered was friendly and hardworking.

Hyatt Regency, Grand Cypress. 1 Grand Cypress Boulevard, Orlando, FL 32836. Tel: 800-233-1234 or 407-239-1234. Fax: 407-239-3800. 750 rooms. Doubles from $255 to $380. Credit cards accepted.

Villas at Grand Cypress. 1 North Jacaranda, Orlando, FL 32836. Tel: 800-835-7377 or 407-239-4700. Fax: 407-239-7219. 144 condominiums. One-bedroom condos start at $400. Credit cards accepted.

 R E S T A U R A N T S   ⑰

We dined at least once in every restaurant operated by Grand Cypress. Based on our experience, the resort's culinary efforts earn excellent marks but don't approach the stellar level of top restaurants found at true "gourmet golf" destinations like Seattle or the Monterey Peninsula. Nonetheless, we thoroughly enjoyed every meal we ate at Grand Cypress.

The fine dining restaurant at the Villas at Grand Cypress is the **Black Swan.** This rather small, one-room restaurant serves American cuisine in an elegant setting overlooking the golf course. We especially enjoyed the peppercorn- and herb-marinated venison. Men are requested to wear jackets. Dinner for two with wine and tip will cost about $150.

La Coquina, one of the best French restaurants in all Orlando and open only at dinner, is the Hyatt's most elegant dining room. Jackets are required. Specialties at La Coquina include foie gras, seared tuna, and grilled swordfish. The restaurant features a fine selection of wines, refined service, and a guitarist who performs from the marble stage in the center of the room. Dinner for two with wine and tip costs approximately $150.

Hemingway's, also at the Hyatt, is a charming restaurant specializing in steak and delicious, fresh seafood. Decorated in colorful Key West style and built atop the stone grotto near the outdoor swimming pool, Hemingway's is open for lunch and dinner. Approximately $120 for two at dinner, wine and tip included.

The **White Horse Saloon** is the Hyatt's delightful Western bar and grill that features just three entrée choices: prime rib, the excellent barbecued beef, and grilled free-range chicken. Dinner for two in the White Horse Saloon, including drinks and tip, costs approximately $80.

Cascades is the Hyatt's main, casual dining room. With its trademark, a thirty-foot indoor cascade, it overlooks the pool and the lake. Cascades offers soups, salads, pizzas, and *cuisine naturelle,* a tasty, low-fat addition to the menu. The wonderful breakfast choices here include fresh fruit, omelettes, and eggs Benedict. **Fairways,** the restaurant at the golf clubhouse, is an ideal spot for lunch between rounds of golf.

The restaurants at the Villas at Grand Cypress. 1 North Jacaranda, Orlando, FL 32836. Tel: 800-835-7377 or 407-239-4700 or 407-239-1999 (Black Swan). Fax: 407-239-7219. Credit cards accepted.

The restaurants at the Hyatt Regency. Grand Cypress, 1 Grand Cypress Boulevard, Orlando, FL 32836. Tel: 800-233-1234 or 407-239-1234. Fax: 407-239-3800. Credit cards accepted.

NON-GOLF ACTIVITIES 20

The non-golf activities at Grand Cypress, both within the resort and just minutes down the road in Orlando, are unparalleled. On the Grand Cypress property you can pamper yourself at the spa, work out at the well-equipped health club, play tennis on one of the racquet club's eight clay and four hard-surface tennis courts, put a horse through its paces at an equestrian center that features an outdoor jumping ring or ride along miles of riding trails, and rent a sailboat on Lake Windsong. Orlando, of course, is the home of Disney MGM Studios, the Magic Kingdom, Epcot Center (all ten minutes from Grand Cypress), Sea World, and Universal Studios (about fifteen minutes away), to name only a few attractions.

GETTING THERE: From Orlando Airport take the Beeline Expressway (528 West) to the I-4 heading west toward Tampa, then take exit 27 (Lake Buena Vista). Turn right onto 535-North. After about a half mile you will make a left and stay on 535-North. Almost immediately you will see the Hyatt Regency on the left, and the entranceway to the Villas is about 1.5 miles later.

▶DISNEY WORLD

NEW GOLF, NEW HOTELS, AND NEW ATTRACTIONS

	The Golf	Golf Services	Lodging	Restaurants	Non-Golf Activities	Total
Rating	17	18	17	16	20	**88**

Disney's Osprey Ridge

On each successive visit to Disney World in Orlando we were always astounded by three never-changing elements: the massive crowds, the massive costs associated with a Disney vacation, and the massive transformations to the Disney landscape since our previous holiday.

Back in 1991, for example, we stayed at the Grand Floridian (still Disney's premier resort hotel by a very wide margin), visited the Epcot Center, and played golf on the excellent Palm and Magnolia courses. A few years later, the area provided a wealth of new destinations to explore: we stayed at the brand-new Yacht Club resort (designed by Robert Stern, one of America's most celebrated architects), played golf at the new Eagle Pines Course (Pete Dye) and at the new Osprey Ridge Course (Tom Fazio), and toured Disney's most delightful theme park, Disney–MGM Studios.

Of course, Disney's progress continues unabated. Now we can book accommodations at the Disney Institute, an adults-only New Age retreat for personal and creative growth that has been modeled after the Esalen Institute in California. The Disney Institute features daily classes in wellness, gardening, and cartoon animation, as well as a couple of different golf instruction programs.

Indeed, perhaps the biggest change of all that we noted is the great number of adults coming to Disney World without kids and with no intention of shaking hands with Mickey Mouse. This new wave of adult travelers comes for conventions, business meetings, and, of course, golf getaways. And make no mistake: as a golf resort, Disney World has outstanding qualifications, as it now boasts five fine eighteen-hole courses and one nine-hole layout. Disney World is not only great for kids, it is also a *Golf Magazine* gold medalist.

THE GOLF

The enormous Disney World complex encompasses three principal golf venues. The Shades of Green resort (formerly the Disney Inn) near the Magic Kingdom and just a minute or two from the Grand Floridian serves the Palm and Magnolia courses. The beautiful new Bonnet Creek Golf Club serves Osprey Ridge and Eagle Pines, and the Lake Buena Vista Course is located near the Disney Village resort. Of Disney's five eighteen-hole layouts, **Lake Buena Vista** is the least highly regarded and is in the worst overall condition. Disney also operates a par thirty-six, nine-hole course called Oak Trail, described by the company as "perfect for those just learning the game." These six courses constitute the ninety-nine holes of the "Magic Linkdom."

Disney's two best layouts are the new Osprey Ridge, which displays Tom Fazio's true genius and environmental sensitivity, and the **Palm,** a classic Joe Lee design that rates as one of the top courses in Florida. The Palm, in fact, hosts the final round of the Disney-Oldsmobile Classic and receives *Golf Digest's* highest rating among all the courses at the resort. If you have time for just two golf games during your visit to Disney World, therefore, we suggest you schedule tee times for these two beauties.

The Palm, which measures 6,957 yards from the back tees, is a tight course that demands straight shooting, particularly on the fantastic back nine. The front nine, visible from the busy road, offers good resort golf, but the back nine is where the Palm truly comes to life, with water playing a crucial role on just about every hole.

The contemporary Osprey Ridge layout complements the handsome, traditional appeal of the Palm. **Osprey Ridge** is a lovely course that plays through natural wetlands and provides a wonderful feeling of isolation despite a location five minutes from the Epcot Center. The four sets of tees correspond to handicaps and measure 7,101 yards (135 slope), 6,680 yards (128 slope), 6,103 yards (121 slope), and 5,402 yards (122 slope). Memorable holes include the difficult fourth, a punitive 439-yard par four with sand down the entire left-hand side; the ninth, a 510-yard par five with water on the right; and the spectacular sequence of its final three holes, sixteen through eighteen. The sixteenth is a majestic par five with a lake in play on the approach shot; seventeen is a heroic, downhill, 216-yard par three with water guarding the left side of the green; and eighteen is a beautiful, 454-yard dogleg-right with bunkers and more water awaiting slices and fades.

If you have additional time, we recommend that you play, in order, Eagle Pines, Magnolia, and Lake Buena Vista. **Eagle Pines,** which shares the fanciful Bonnet Creek clubhouse with Osprey Ridge, is flatter and shorter than Osprey Ridge, but its greens are much more undulating and difficult to read. **Magnolia** is

Disney's Eagle Pines

quite long from the back tees (7,190 yards), but it is a more forgiving, if less interesting, layout than the others. Provided you are staying at a Disney resort, you can ride a shuttle bus to any of the courses from your hotel.

Walt Disney World Golf Complex. PO Box 10000, Lake Buena Vista, FL 32830. Tel: 407-WDW-GOLF (939-4653) or 407-824-2270. Fax: 407-354-1866. Credit cards accepted.

• *Lake Buena Vista.* 1972. Designer: Joe Lee. Par 72. 6,829 yards. 72.7 par rating. 128 slope rating. Greens fees: $90 to $115, mandatory cart included. No walking. No caddies. Season: year-round.

• *Palm.* 1971. Designer: Joe Lee. Par 72. 6,957 yards. 73.0 par rating. 133 slope rating. Greens fees: $90 to $115, mandatory cart included. No walking. No caddies. Season: year-round.

• *Osprey Ridge.* 1991. Designer: Tom Fazio. Par 72. 7,101 yards. 73.9 par rating. 135 slope rating. Greens fees: $100 to $135, mandatory cart included. No walking. No caddies. Season: year-round.

• *Eagle Pines.* 1991. Designer: Pete Dye. Par 72. 6,772 yards. 72.3 par rating. 131 slope rating. Greens fees: $100 to $135, cart included. No walking. No caddies. Season: year-round.

• *Magnolia.* 1971. Designer: Joe Lee. Par 72. 7,190 yards. 73.9 par rating. 133 slope rating. Greens fees: $90 to $115, cart included. No walking. No caddies. Season: year-round.

GOLF SERVICES 18

Golf services are excellent—from that famous Disney employee smile to crowd control, another Disney hallmark. Rental clubs, shoes, lessons, range balls, and merchandise are available at all golf locations. The Bonnet Creek clubhouse that serves Osprey Ridge and Eagle Pines is a delightful Disney environment with a pleasant restaurant and locker rooms. Carts are mandatory at all courses except the nine-hole Oak Trail. In high season, greens fees for resort guests are $100 at Palm and Magnolia and $120 for Osprey Ridge and Eagle Pines, cart included. If you are not staying at a Disney hotel the fees rise $15. Summer and twilight specials reduce the fees by more than half.

LODGING 17

If you want the best, look no further than Disney World's hotel extravaganza, the **Grand Floridian,** which is always filled to capacity despite its lofty room rates. The Grand Floridian is elegant, stylish, spacious, extremely well run, and conveniently located on the Disney monorail.

Disney World's imposing new hotels—the so-called Epcot resorts—built on Stormalong Bay (a man-made lake) and within walking distance of Epcot, do not hold a candle to the Grand Floridian, although their room rates are nearly as high, up to $400 per night. These four very large hotels include the Yacht Club, the Beach Club, the Swan, and the Dolphin. Located virtually side by side, they have an urban, high-density feeling about them, with an atmosphere that can be oppressive and congested.

The Yacht Club and Beach Club are actually linked and share facilities such as restaurants and swimming pools. Both hotels were designed by Robert Stern and are obvious imitations of the Grand Floridian theme, but they fail to capture the generous spirit and style of the Grand Floridian. Our room in the **Yacht Club,** number

5177, was brightly decorated and nicely furnished, but the public areas of the hotel feel cramped and dark. The Swan and the Dolphin were both designed by the acclaimed Michael Graves. While intriguing as pieces of statuary, as hotels the Swan and Dolphin are simply too massive for us.

Disney World. PO Box 10100, Lake Buena Vista, FL 32830. Tel: 407-934-7639. Fax: 407-354-1866.

• **Grand Floridian.** 900 rooms. Doubles range from $284 to $530. Credit cards accepted.

• **Yacht Club.** 630 rooms. Doubles from $230 to $430. Credit cards accepted.

R E S T A U R A N T S   16

The best restaurants from among the more than one hundred dining establishments operated by Disney World include **Victoria and Albert's** at the Grand Floridian (the only restaurant in Disney World that requires jackets at dinner) and **Bistro de Paris** at Epcot. The seven-course "premium meal" with wine at Victoria and Albert's costs $110, while entrées at the Bistro de Paris range between $21 and $27. Skip Ariel's, an overpriced disappointment, as well as the ambitious restaurants in the Yacht Club/Beach Club complex. The **Sci-Fi Dine-In Theater** restaurant at Disney–MGM Studios is a treat for lunch. Outside Disney World—but located at Pleasure Island, Disney's late-night complex—you will find **Planet Hollywood,** an entertaining choice for dinner. Hundreds of diners line up outside Planet Hollywood every night and wait more than an hour to get in. To bypass this line, get a VIP pass to the restaurant from your Disney resort concierge, who will also be happy to book your reservation.

The restaurants at Disney World. PO Box 10100, Lake Buena Vista, FL 32830. For reservations, Tel: 407-934-7639. Fax: 407-354-1866. Credit cards accepted.

N O N - G O L F   A C T I V I T I E S   20

In addition to the theme parks, enjoy the beaches, sailing and windsurfing, fishing, swimming, tennis, horseback riding, water parks, and exercise facilities. Smart travelers get to the theme parks at 8 A.M., when parts of the park open exclusively for resort guests. Otherwise, the parks open at 9 A.M. More can be accomplished between 8 and 9:30 A.M. than in the rest of the day, so take our advice: come early in the morning and beat the notoriously long lines.

Our choice for Disney World's best ride is the Tower of Terror at Disney–MGM Studios. Based on an installment of "The Twilight Zone" from the 1960s, the Tower of Terror is an amusing re-creation of an old Hollywood hotel with a rickety elevator that suddenly drops into a harrowing ten-story free fall.

GETTING THERE: Disney World is twenty minutes from the Orlando Airport. Take the South exit upon leaving the airport, putting you on Highway 417 South to the Osceola Parkway West, and take exit 3 to Disney World. Once you are on the resort property, you will see big signs for the hotels and golf courses.

▶BAY HILL

ARNIE'S WORLD

	The Golf	Golf Services	Lodging	Restaurants	Non-Golf Activities	Total
Rating	18	18	14	16	20	86

Bay Hill

Bay Hill—owned by Arnold Palmer and his wife, Winnie, who tours the grounds in a golf cart accompanied by her golden retriever—is located thirty minutes west of the Orlando Airport and fifteen minutes north of Disney World in a pleasant, rather unpretentious, residential subdivision. Bay Hill is legendary in the world of golf, but one's first impression of the place is hardly overwhelming. It is dowdy in a classic, old-fashioned style; think of Arnold Palmer back in his heyday in the 1960s. Arnie's Orlando winter retreat—which looks and feels more like a high-traffic, private country club than a resort—has not changed much physically since that period.

Actually, Bay Hill is not a full-scale resort at all. It is a pure golf experience. Indeed, despite its relaxed and low-key aura, Bay Hill is an intense golf venue where you can work on your game and enjoy the golf. The golf course, an annual stop on the PGA Tour and rated high among America's seventy-five Best Resort Courses by *Golf Digest*, is a masterpiece; Bay Hill's teaching staff is first-rate; and its corps of fabulous caddies adds a wonderful extra dimension. If you don't like golf, however, you will wonder why you came here.

If Bay Hill's 1960s-vintage buildings—the modest stone lodge and the clubhouse—look frumpy and old-shoe from the exterior, that first impression is only reinforced once you step inside. The guest rooms, equipped with older furnishings, can only be described as drab.

Yet we appreciate Bay Hill for these very reasons. Glitziness and high gloss are in no short supply elsewhere in Orlando, but Bay Hill has personality. It stands in stunning contrast to Grand Cypress and Disney World. Bay Hill is also good value relative to the other Orlando-area golf destinations; a single guest can enjoy lodging, a round of golf, a bucket of range balls, club storage, and breakfast for only $239 ($378 for two) a day in high season, whereas you can expect to spend nearly double that amount elsewhere in Orlando.

THE GOLF   ⑱

For PGA players, **Bay Hill** holds three distinctions: it features the PGA Tour's toughest opening hole, its toughest finishing hole, and its easiest par five—the sixteenth. For the rest of us, Bay Hill is eminently fair, straightforward, without gimmicks, and an absolute joy to walk, especially in the company of one of Bay Hill's fine caddies. Bay Hill's fairways are generous, the bunkers are fairly positioned, and the greens are excellent. If you are playing well, you will be rewarded with a low score. If you do not quite have it together, there is plenty of water to catch errant shots.

In addition to its memorable eighteenth hole, the hallmarks of Bay Hill are its long par fours and fine collection of par threes. The first hole is a bruising initiation, a 441-yard, uphill dogleg to the left that demands a long drive and a long second shot with a fairway wood. The third hole is another dogleg to the left, this time along a sizable lake. The third, however, is a mere warm-up for the sixth, a 543-yard par five that double doglegs to the left and demands a tee shot that must fly the lake, a carry of some 215 yards. Eight is a pretty, tree-lined, downhill dogleg-right with a second shot to an elevated green, and nine is long (467 yards), straight, and formidable. The eleventh is rated the second-toughest hole on the back side. Eleven has water on the left that threatens both your drive and second shot, which is inevitably a wood. The last three holes at Bay Hill are gems. Sixteen is a short and easy 481-yard par five with a lake guarding the entrance to the green. Seventeen is a long, 219-yard par three over the same lake to an elevated green, and eighteen is Bay Hill's signature hole, a 441-yard par four. It is nearly impossible to reach eighteen in two unless you can strike a massive fade around the lake with your fairway wood. A plaque on the eighteenth fairway marks the spot from which Robert Gamez holed a seven iron for the eagle that sunk Greg Norman in the 1990 Bay Hill Invitational. Drop a ball there and see if you can replicate his heroics.

Bay Hill offers another set of tees even more challenging than the championship tees. The Palmer tees stretch the course to its absolute limit of 7,207 yards (par rating 75.1/slope 139). We watched several mid-to-high handicappers play from the Palmer tees and scratched our heads in wonder. Only solid, low single-digit players should even consider the Palmer tees. Our caddie, the remarkably helpful Billy, suggested that Bay Hill offers plenty of golf course from the championship markers, which shortens the course to a more manageable 6,638 yards (par rating 72.4/slope 130). From the forward tees Bay Hill measures 5,235 yards (par rating 72.7/slope 130). Whichever tees you select, walk the course with a caddie. Bay Hill's principal loop consists of the *Challenger* and *Champion* nines. The Charger nine is Bay Hill's shorter "third" nine.

Bay Hill Club. 9000 Bay Hill Boulevard, Orlando, FL 32819. Tel: 800-523-5999 or 407-876-2429. Fax: 407-876-1035. Credit cards accepted.

- *Champion-Challenger Course.* 1961/1980. Designer: Dick Wilson/Arnold Palmer. Par 72. 6,638 yards. 72.4 par rating. 130 slope rating.
- *Charger nine.* 1986. Designer: Arnold Palmer. Par 36. 3,409 yards.
- Greens fees: daily round included in lodging rates; additional round, $35; additional nine, $21. Walking permitted. Caddies available. Carts. Restrictions: play limited to guests of Bay Hill. Season: year-round.

 ## GOLF SERVICES 18

Golf services at Bay Hill are superb, from the caddies to the terrific practice range and putting green to the fine attitude of staff members. We enjoyed meeting the engaging starter, who sets the cordial tone at Bay Hill. Electric carts, rental clubs, and shoes are available. Bay Hill also runs its own golf school; call for details.

 ## LODGING 14

Bay Hill offers fifty-six guest rooms, each with bath and private patio or balcony. We stayed in a room overlooking the practice range, number 107, which looked quite forlorn. It was plainly decorated and poorly equipped; the television with cable channels was virtually the room's only amenity, and we especially missed having a clock in the room.

Bay Hill Club. 9000 Bay Hill Boulevard, Orlando, FL 32819. Tel: 800-523-5999 or 407-876-2429. Fax: 407-876-1035. 56 rooms. In high season, a golf package including lodging, a round of golf, range balls, club storage, and breakfast costs $239 for a single and $378 per couple per day. Credit cards accepted.

RESTAURANTS

Bay Hill has two restaurants, the casual Grill, which is ideal for breakfast and lunch, and the much more elegant Bay Window Room, where we enjoyed excellent service. The **Grill** serves soups and sandwiches at lunch. Dinner entrées range between $11 and $20. The **Bay Window Room**'s sophisticated menu includes a warm salad of wild mushrooms, fresh snapper, and a good rack of lamb. Dinners start at about $40 before wine and tip. The Bay Window offers a fair selection of wines by the bottle and glass. Jackets and tie are required here, and the dining room is open only to Bay Hill guests.

The restaurants at the Bay Hill Club. 9000 Bay Hill Boulevard, Orlando, FL 32819. Tel: 800-523-5999 or 407-876-2429. Fax: 407-876-1035. Credit cards accepted.

NON-GOLF ACTIVITIES 20

Any resort this close to Disney World and other Orlando attractions is going to receive our highest mark in this category—twenty. Bay Hill really offers little else besides golf, although there is a small swimming pool on the property. Yet just fifteen minutes down the road some of the world's best entertainment can be found.

GETTING THERE: The drive to Bay Hill from the Orlando Airport takes about twenty-five minutes. Go west on the Beeline Expressway to the I-4 exit. Stay on the I-4 East only a short time to exit 29 (Sand Lake Road). Take a left onto Sand Lake Road, and follow it to Apopka-Vineland Road, where you will take a right. About a half mile up this road, take a left onto Bay Hill Boulevard. The resort will be on the right.

▶DORAL

SLAYING THE BLUE MONSTER

	The Golf	Golf Services	Lodging	Restaurants	Non-Golf Activities	Total
Rating	18	18	15	16	18	85

Doral Golf Resort and Spa in Miami is one of the largest, most impressive, and best-run golf resorts in America. Indeed, Doral is a perennial winner of *Golf Magazine*'s gold medal. Unfortunately, Doral is hardly located in an idyllic part of Florida. We drove to Doral from the island fortress of the Breakers in Palm Beach, about ninety minutes south on I-95, extremely aware that the neighborhoods were deteriorating the closer we got to Doral, that there was far more construction, destruction, graffiti, high-rises, and urban blight amid the palms.

Doral

"Driving to Doral?" someone at the well-buffered Breakers asked us skeptically. "Well, just be sure you get off at the correct exit."

Doral truly stands out as a 2,400-acre oasis with ninety-nine holes of golf, including the awesome Blue Monster, amid the industrial parks and office blocks of west Miami. The resort is located just minutes down the street from the always busy Miami Airport. Doral, in fact, lies directly under the flight path of arriving and departing planes, which can roar overhead at low altitudes every two or three minutes. Until they learn to ignore the incessant activity in the skies overhead, some Doral golfers might feel a little bit like Saddam Hussein in his bunker at the height of the air war over Baghdad.

Easy proximity to the airport has another unfortunate consequence for the individual traveler who may be seeking peace and quiet along with great golf. The conveniently located airport means that Doral is a favored site among business meeting planners, and the resort can be filled to capacity with conventions and large groups. Such conventions affect Doral in two ways: the bar is always overflowing with guys having too much fun on a Tuesday night, and the courses can be bumper to bumper with inexperienced, once-a-year golfers who seriously slow down play. A note about the weather: during our visit it was rainy, windy, and fifty-two degrees—sweater and turtleneck conditions—more like Scotland than the tropics. Winter weather in south Florida can be fantastic but unpredictable. It is no wonder that the Doral Ryder Open is held in March, when the weather is more dependable.

Doral's positives, however, far outweigh its negatives.

The first thing you will notice about Doral is that it is shaped like a nautilus shell—and that this plan works extremely well. At the center of the resort complex, you will find the clubhouse with the hotel registration desk, four restaurants, and the large pro shop. Just outside, in a circle ringing the clubhouse, are all the golf courses, the practice area, the wonderful Doral Saturnia Spa, which is one of the best spas in the country, and the Golf Learning Center run by the remarkable Jim McLean (see Golf Services, below). With this arrangement everything is immediately accessible.

The Doral staff also gets high marks for crowd control, even if the golf courses can suffer from slow play. It seems that nearly everyone who comes to Doral plays golf, but we had no trouble securing choice starting times during our visit. In fact, service throughout the resort—from the starters and caddies to the waiters in the restaurants—struck us as prompt and always courteous.

But it is the sheer scale of the golf operation here that will astound you—four eighteen-hole courses and one nine-hole layout serving guests staying in nearly seven hundred rooms, nineteen miles of fairways, one hundred acres of lakes, three hundred and fifty sand bunkers, and one of the largest fleets of golf carts (304, to be precise) operated by any resort in the world.

On the surface, Doral may appear to emphasize quantity at the expense of quality. Management, for example, certainly could do a better job separating individual travelers from the junket attendees. Yet Doral has a great deal to offer.

THE GOLF ⑱

Doral's **Blue Course**—the Blue Monster—designed by Dick Wilson and his assistant Robert von Hagge in 1961 and toughened up most recently by Raymond Floyd, is the resort's best track by a wide margin. This is the course that won Doral its prestigious golfing reputation. The resort's secondary courses, while good to very good, are not truly exceptional. We rate the Gold as Doral's second-best course, followed by the Red Course, then the White Course. We did not play the nine-hole Green Course, a 1,085-yard, par three layout. Von Hagge, working at times in conjunction with Bruce Devlin, originally designed all the other Doral courses.

All by itself, the Blue Monster makes a trip to the resort more than worthwhile for the skilled golfer. The Blue Monster gets the "blue" because it has a lot of water and the "monster" because it is very, very long (7,100 yards). This deadly combination of aqua, featured on nearly every hole, and great length means that high handicappers ought to be realistic and confine themselves to the Gold, Red, or White courses, which are shorter and far more manageable. But even from the regular tees the Blue Monster still weighs in at a hefty 6,597 yards. This course is also very heavily bunkered on those few holes where there is no water. Many holes on the Blue Monster have so much sand they resemble Pinehurst Number Two or the Links at Spanish Bay. The par threes can be real brutes, and a couple of the par fives (especially the 591-yard twelfth) are absolutely interminable. It's a tough course any day, but particularly if you play it in a driving rainstorm as we did. Greg Norman's record sixty-two in 1993 here strikes us as nothing short of a miracle.

The Blue Course turns into a monster on the fourth hole, a 237-yard par three into the wind and over water to an elevated green. There is a bailout area to the left, but anything hit right is in the drink. This is one challenging golf shot. On windy days anything short of a perfectly struck driver is simply not going to make it. Eight and nine—which head back toward the clubhouse—may be the most fun holes on the Blue. Eight, the 528-yard par five, requires a water carry on both your drive and approach shot. Unless you have hit a career tee shot, a layup second shot, rather than going for the green, is the wise play on this hole. Number nine is all carry, 163 yards over water. Since the green is slightly uphill, you will need an extra club (or two) off the tee.

Holes ten through thirteen, however, clearly comprise the toughest sequence of golf holes on the course. Ten is 563 yards long and doglegs left around a lake; eleven is a short but sneaky par four (348 yards) that is bunkered nearly from tee to green; twelve is a long, straight march of 591 yards (which Norman reached in two); and thirteen is a very tough 246-yard par three that will play as a par four for most golfers because of its length and substantial greenside bunkers. Eighteen is Doral's scenic finishing hole, a 425-yard par four (par five for mere mortals) with two more tests of courage over water. We bet the Blue Monster rips your handicap card to shreds.

The **Gold Course** (5,700 yards from the regular tees, 6,600 from the tips) combines a tough golfing challenge with striking scenery. Water, in the form of lakes or lagoons, comes into play on every hole. Raymond Floyd's redesign has brought the greens down to the level of the fairways, thereby making the course more enjoyable for the average player. The eighth is a memorable hole, as are number twelve, a par three over water, and eighteen with its island green. Sometimes the striking scenic characteristics are far from aesthetically pleasing. Number eleven has been marred by condominiums built too close to the left side of the fairway. A few other unsightly things along the way on the Gold—like large warehouses and parking lots along the fifth and sixth holes—somewhat spoil the golfing spell.

The **Red Course** (6,120 yards) has recently been renovated by von Hagge. The fairways, originally flat, are now rolling and mounded. The **White Course,** which opened in 1965, measures 6,208 yards.

Walking is permitted on all the courses at the Doral Golf Resort and Spa, and caddies are available. Almost everyone who plays the Blue Monster opts for a caddie. Nonresort guests may make tee times at Doral up to one month in advance.

The **Silver Course** at **Doral Park Golf and Country Club,** located in an upscale subdivision called Doral Park, is just a five-minute drive from the Doral Golf Resort and Spa complex. The Silver Course, a mini–Blue Monster, was part of the Doral resort property until 1993. Surrounded by a new residential development, the Doral Park Silver Course is extremely tight, unforgiving, highly contoured with large mounds, and—like every other Doral layout—rife with water hazards. Hit it straight or a watery grave awaits you on this course. Thirteen is the toughest hole—437 yards with water all the way down the right side. The fourteenth hole, a 155-yard par three, features an island green. The yardages from the Silver's tees range from 4,661 to 6,614 yards. Greens fees in high season top out at $73. The twilight rate of $33 after 2 P.M. is very inviting.

Doral Golf Resort and Spa. 4400 NW 87th Street, Miami, FL 33178. Tel: 800-713-6725 or 305-592-2000. Fax: 305-591-6413. Credit cards accepted.

• *Blue Course.* 1961. Designers: Dick Wilson, Robert von Hagge. Par 72. 7,100. 74.5 par rating. 130 slope rating. Greens fees: $175 (guest), $220 (public), cart included. Walking permitted. Caddies available. Season: year-round.

• *Gold Course.* 1969/1995. Designers: Robert von Hagge/Raymond Floyd. Par 70. 6,600 yards. 70.5 par rating. 129 slope rating. Greens fees: $150 (guest), $185 (public), cart included. Walking permitted. Caddies available. Season: year-round.

• *Red Course.* 1962. Designers: Robert von Hagge, Bruce Devlin. Par 71. 6,120 yards. 68.5 par rating. 118 slope rating. Greens fees: $125 (guest), $160 (public), cart included. Walking permitted. Caddies available. Season: year-round.

• *White Course.* 1965. Designer: Robert von Hagge. Par 72. 6,208 yards. 69.1 par rating. 117 slope rating. Greens fees: $90 (guest), $110 (public), cart included. Walking permitted. Caddies available. Season: year-round.

Doral Park Golf and Country Club. 5001 NW 104 Avenue, Miami, FL 33178. Tel: 305-594-0954. Fax: 305-594-9627. Credit cards accepted.

• *Silver Course.* 1984. Designer: Robert von Hagge. Par 72. 6,614 yards. 72.5 par rating. 131 slope rating. Greens fees: $63 (weekday), $73 (weekend). After 2 P.M.: $33, cart included. No walking. No caddies. Season: year-round.

GOLF SERVICES ⓲

Golf services at Doral are outstanding, particularly the Golf Learning Center directed by Jim McLean, the acclaimed teacher and *Golf Digest* author. The essence of McLean's teaching system is to keep the lower body quiet and the left foot firmly planted as the upper body fully coils on the backswing. We took a lesson from one of McLean's "master instructors," which was one of the best and most helpful lessons we have ever had. This hour of instruction made us wish we had signed on for the two-, three-, or five-day golf schools McLean and his staff offered.

The only shortcoming we noted in the golf services is the practice range, which, because it is so popular, does not have enough stations for all the golfers who wish to practice before their rounds. The practice range is open daily from 6:30 A.M. to 7 P.M.

LODGING 15

After purchasing Doral for $100 million in 1994, the owners pledged to devote substantial funds to renovate the resort's 694 guest rooms. It's a good thing, too, for while our room (number 145) was comfortable and spacious enough, it looked as if it had not been refurbished in some time. There is nothing particularly shabby about this room, but it certainly needs freshening up. In-room bars and cable television are standard features. We enjoyed the golf instruction on one of the cable channels by resident pro Jim McLean.

For serious golfers, Doral's best package is the Championship Golf Package, which includes your room, a round on the Blue Monster with cart, a golf clinic, and full breakfast. The cost is $265 per person based on double occupancy Sunday through Thursday ($285 Friday and Saturday).

Doral Golf Resort and Spa. 4400 NW 87th Street, Miami, FL 33178. Tel: 800-713-6725 or 305-592-2000. Fax: 305-591-6480. 694 rooms. Doubles range from $250 to $400. Golf packages are available. Credit cards accepted.

RESTAURANTS 16

The restaurants at Doral are quite good. By far the best and most interesting restaurant in the resort complex is the elegant dining room in the Doral Saturnia Spa, just a two-minute walk from the clubhouse. Although many Doral guests have access to the spa (via a golf package, for example), we found it amazing how many guests neglect to take advantage of this wonderful facility. Amid the crush of people at Doral, the spa can be a welcome haven. The spa's **Atrium** restaurant features wonderfully prepared, delicious, low-calorie dishes like lemon consommé (30 calories) and a superb red snapper with steamed vegetables (230 calories). Dining-room service is the best of any in Doral, and dinner runs about $75 for two people including wine and tip.

The Doral Golf Resort and Spa also offers two other fine dining options. **La Terraza** is a casual, attractive, Italian restaurant overlooking the fountain in the lake on the Blue Monster, with a nice menu of seafood, beef, pasta, and pizza. Diners here may eat indoors or out. The most formal restaurant at Doral is **Windows,** where men are requested to wear a jacket. The cost of dinner from the primarily steak-and-seafood menu is approximately $65 with wine and tip. On weekdays Windows features a fine lunchtime buffet for $20.

Should you wish to leave the resort for dinner, we recommend heading to Miami's ultra-hip, brilliantly revived South Beach section. The cosmopolitan clientele at the streetside cafés and chic restaurants consists of fashion models, celebrities, and a young crowd that is recolonizing the vibrant South Beach area.

The restaurants at Doral Golf Resort and Spa. 4400 NW 87th Street, Miami, FL 33178. Tel: 800-713-6725 or 305-592-2000 or 305-591-4749 (Atrium). Fax: 305-591-6480. Credit cards accepted.

NON-GOLF ACTIVITIES 18

Non-golf activities at Doral are outstanding. The chief diversion from the links is provided by the Doral Saturnia Spa, wonderful in itself and a real plus for the golfer whose spouse may refuse to go to most die-hard golf destinations. Spa activities begin at 7 A.M. and include aqua aerobics, assorted yoga and aerobics classes, massage, beauty salon, and more.

Other activities within the resort include fifteen tennis courts and an outdoor pool. A shuttle bus runs to Doral's sister resort, the Doral Ocean Beach, on Miami Beach, for beach activities at the Aqua Club. Touring the revitalized Art Deco district of Miami Beach is also a real treat.

GETTING THERE: From Miami Airport, take 836 West to 826 North. From 826 North take NW 36th Street heading west. Make a right onto 87th Avenue. The entranceway to the Doral Golf Resort and Spa will be the next left.

▶PGA NATIONAL RESORT & SPA

PALM BEACH GARDENS

Rating	The Golf	Golf Services	Lodging	Restaurants	Non-Golf Activities	Total
Rating	17	19	14	13	16	**79**

PGA National Resort & Spa in Palm Beach Gardens is one of the largest and most impressive golf resorts not just in Florida but in the entire United States. In a nutshell, PGA National, home and headquarters of the PGA of America, offers five courses that range in quality from good to excellent, one of the largest and best golf teaching facilities in the world with an enormous staff of talented instructors, a nice health club, a lovely spa, and a pro shop so large that it is a virtual golf department store stocking merchandise from every club and clothing manufacturer in the game. PGA National is an extraordinary facility, a golf resort of immense scale.

PGA National Resort

On the negative side, PGA National has undistinguished (though expensive) accommodations, disappointing restaurants, and a "golf-factory" atmosphere created by the hordes of visitors and members. The members are residents, either year-round or seasonal, who maintain one of the thousand or more villas, condominiums, and detached homes within the vast, 2,400-acre PGA National complex. PGA National manages to control the crowds quite well, but this resort—which has won a *Golf Magazine* silver medal—will never qualify as a quiet and romantic golf getaway.

THE GOLF

The five courses at **PGA National** include four on the immediate hotel property—the Champion Course, the General Course, the Haig Course, and the Squire Course—plus a fifth layout, the Estate Course, which is located six miles from the resort. The **Champion Course,** with greens fees from $86 to $154 depending upon the time of year, is the resort's premier layout, reconfigured by Jack Nicklaus in 1989 and rated among America's Top 75 Resort

Courses by *Golf Digest.* Tom Fazio designed the Haig and Squire courses and Arnold Palmer laid out the General. Karl Litten was the architect behind the more wide-open Estate Course. The greens fees on the Haig, General, Squire, and Estate courses range from $56 to $100. Each layout is very well maintained.

The Champion Course hosted the 1983 Ryder Cup and the 1987 PGA Championship and is the regular site of the PGA Seniors' Championship. This is a long course made all the more difficult by persistent, swirling winds and water that comes into play on seventeen holes. The back nine, the best loop at the resort, features two exquisite, and nearly identical, par threes, the fifteenth and seventeenth, 179 yards and 166 yards respectively, with semi-island greens guarded by daunting water hazards. The Champion Course has five sets of tees: 7,022 yards (142 slope), 6,742 yards (134 slope), 6,373 yards (129 slope), 6,023 yards (124 slope), and 5,377 yards from the red tees (123 slope).

The **Haig Course** is second in popularity at PGA National, followed, in order, by the **General,** the **Squire,** and the **Estate.**

PGA National Resort & Spa. 400 Avenue of the Champions, Palm Beach Gardens, FL 33418. Tel: 800-633-9150 or 561 627-1800. Fax: 561 627-0155. Credit cards accepted.

   • *Champion Course.* 1981/1989. Tom Fazio/Jack Nicklaus. Par 72. 7,022 yards. 74.7 par rating. 142 slope rating. Greens fees: $154 (December—April)/$132 (April—May)/$86 (June—August)/$145 (September—December). No walking. No caddies. Season: year-round.

   • *General Course.* 1984. Designer: Arnold Palmer. Par 72. 6,768 yards. 73.0 par rating. 130 slope rating.

   • *Squire Course.* 1981. Designer: Tom Fazio. Par 72. 6,478 yards. 71.3 par rating. 127 slope rating.

   • *Haig Course.* 1980. Designer: Tom Fazio. Par 72. 6,806 yards. 73.0 par rating. 130 slope rating.

   • *Estate Course.* 1984. Designer: Karl Litten. Par 72. 6784 yards. 73.4 par rating. 131 slope rating.

   • Greens fees: $99 (December—April)/$80 (April—May)/$56 (June—August)/$89 (September—December). No walking. No caddies. Season: year-round.

GOLF SERVICES   19

Golf services at PGA National are superb, clearly the resort's strongest suit. Mike Adams runs the Academy of Golf at PGA National, one of the best teaching operations we have ever seen. With fifteen instructors— and frequently fifteen lessons taking place simultaneously on the range—PGA National is an incredibly high-powered operation. The resort offers three-day golf schools, two-day minischools, junior programs, and daily clinics. We took one of those quick-fix, thirty-minute lessons from a young professional who was one of the most delightful, helpful, and enthusiastic teachers we have ever encountered. With pros as helpful as he, the golf school must be very fine indeed. Practice facilities include three large ranges and a huge putting green. The resort also operates it own club repair shop.

LODGING   14

PGA National is an impressive resort for its golf courses, but its rooms are undistinguished. There are over four hundred rooms at PGA National: 339 rooms in the main hotel plus 75 cottages, like the one we occupied—Golf Cottage 515. The cottages are spacious two-bedroom, two-bathroom condominiums and come equipped with full kitchen facilities and washer and dryer, but they are decorated in a rather spartan, nondescript fashion. The resort's hotel rooms are also quite large, and each room has its own balcony. Room and cottage rates range from $295 to $380 per night in high season. The weekly rate for a cottage is $2,280.

Most people staying at PGA National come on a golf package. During the high season, a package for two, including accommodations in a double room, unlimited golf and cart, advance tee time bookings, access to the Champion Course with no surcharge, and a daily golf clinic runs just shy of $800 per night. The same package in a cottage costs $865 per night for two or $1,375 per night based on four-person occupancy.

PGA National Resort & Spa. 400 Avenue of the Champions, Palm Beach Gardens, FL 33418. Tel: 800-633-9150 or 561 627-2000. Fax: 561-691-9133. 413 rooms, suites, and cottages. Double rooms range from $295 to $325 in high season from December through April. Two-bedroom, two-bath cottages are $380 in high season. Golf packages are available. Credit cards accepted.

RESTAURANTS ⑬

PGA National operates five good-looking restaurants, but the cuisine served at the resort is probably its weakest link. The service we encountered in the restaurants struck us as especially unprofessional. For example, the hostess in **Arezzo,** the Northern Italian restaurant, suggested we have a sandwich in the bar for dinner because her restaurant was "too busy"— this despite a half-dozen or so obviously empty tables. Expect to pay about $40 to $50 per person with wine and tip. Another evening, in the **Crab Catcher** seafood restaurant, the waiter instructed us, ludicrously we thought, not to order the crab because "it's a two-hour deal—all the meat is in the shell, and you have to dig to get it out." We felt pressed by this same fellow to finish dinner quickly, despite the large number of empty tables also in this room. Finally, the actual cuisine we sampled was no better than average. Entrées at Crab Catcher range between $13 and $32.

The restaurants at PGA National Resort & Spa. 400 Avenue of the Champions, Palm Beach Gardens, FL 33418. Tel: 800-633-9150 or 561-627-2000. Fax: 561-691-9133. Credit cards accepted.

NON-GOLF ACTIVITIES ⑯

Activities at PGA National include the Health and Racquet club, a 27,000-square-foot fitness facility with cardiovascular equipment, free weights, saunas, whirlpools, and racquetball courts. The only hitch? Hotel guests paying as much as $380 per night to stay at the resort must ante up another $12 just to enter the health club. Tennis, world-class croquet, swimming, and lakeside activities like windsurfing are also available. Spa treatments include massage, facials, mineral pools, salon services, and personal training.

GETTING THERE: From the Palm Beach Airport, take I-95 North for about two miles until you reach exit 57B (PGA West Boulevard). Head west about 1.5 miles on PGA West Boulevard. The entrance to the resort is on the left. Follow signs to the hotel.

▶PONTE VEDRA

THE STADIUM COURSE AT SAWGRASS AND OTHER WONDERS

	The Golf	Golf Services	Lodging	Restaurants	Non-Golf Activities	Total
Rating	18	18	15	14	14	**79**

The sunny, sleepy Ponte Vedra/Sawgrass community—the upscale golf resort and bedroom appendage of Jacksonville, Florida—has more quality holes of golf than you can shake a stick at. *Golf Digest*'s Dan Jenkins has even called Ponte Vedra "the Pebble Beach of the East Coast." We cannot argue with the fact that Ponte Vedra has great golf (and outstanding tennis, too, for that matter), but bear in mind that it does not offer the discerning traveler a great deal more. If you are hunting for a well-balanced, multidimensional family destination that combines golf with plenty of activities and diversions for the non-golfer, plus amenities like sophisticated restaurants and truly elegant accommodations, then you can scratch Ponte Vedra from your list. Yet if it is just golf you want, the real purists among you—those who go to bed early and squeeze in as many courses as possible within the shortest period of time—will be babes in toyland at Ponte Vedra.

The first thing every visitor should know about Ponte Vedra is that where you stay determines where you play and that three hotels rule the roost in this particular golf domain: the Marriott at Sawgrass, the Lodge and Beach Club at Ponte Vedra, and the traditional Ponte Vedra Inn and Club.

Easily the winner of the beauty contest, the Lodge and Beach Club is the best hotel of the three, but Lodge guests have no golfing access to lovely Sawgrass Country Club. The large and quite new Marriott is a typical example of what the Marriott chain is known for—one writer has called it "a golfer's barracks"—but guests of the Marriott have one enormous advantage: they can get on all the great courses around Ponte Vedra, including the fine Marsh Landing. The older Ponte Vedra Inn has two rather nice eighteen-hole layouts of its own, but individuals who choose to stay here have only limited access to the Tournament Players Club courses (tee times can be arranged only twenty-four hours in advance) and have no chance of playing either Marsh Landing or Sawgrass. Again, those purists who come to Ponte Vedra exclusively to play golf are apt to feel most secure in one of the fairly nice boxes at the Marriott because only then will they have guaranteed access to every name course in the region.

Another point that may need clarification for the first-time visitor: Sawgrass, home of the two TPC courses, is actually a massive subcommunity within Ponte Vedra proper. Although it is twenty-three miles to the southeast of booming Jacksonville, Ponte Vedra is itself little more than a somewhat barren and nondescript stretch of Atlantic coastline. Sawgrass is set a mile or two inland from the beach and consists of the Tournament Players Club, the PGA Tour headquarters, the Marriott, the small shopping center called Sawgrass Shopping Village, and several fancy residential subdivisions hidden behind their own gateposts.

THE GOLF ⑱

The best courses in Ponte Vedra in order of excellence are the TPC Stadium Course, Marsh Landing Country Club, the three nines at Sawgrass Country Club, and the TPC Valley course.

The **Tournament Players Club**—with its huge clubhouse in the shape of an Aztec pyramid, a pro shop so well stocked with apparel that it would not be out of place on Madison Avenue, its posh and paneled locker facilities, its stunning practice area, and its grassy "stands" built into the hillside behind the first tee and eigh-teenth green—is worth the whole trip on its own. This is the birthplace of stadium golf and remains the best of the breed.

Yet for the rest of us it can be an incredible ordeal. The best advice we can give you here is gastronomic. Have a big breakfast before playing the **Stadium Course** because you will need all the carbohydrates you can put away. As difficult as it is, the Stadium Course could only have been designed by one man—the infernal Pete Dye, the only architect we know who builds golf courses without fairways, or at least fairways that can barely be seen from the tee. After the first two holes there is not another wide-open tee shot on the course. For the remainder of the day you are dri-ving over a serious expanse of water or waste area to a narrow landing area that is generally bounded by more water on both sides. Many of the greens are protected by idyllic little lakes and creeks, so the second shots are just as formidable as the drives. If you let this setup intimidate you, and if you consequently begin to swing extra hard, you will lose nearly as many balls here as you would on Dye's Ocean Course at Kiawah—at least we did.

There are many spectacular holes on both sides of the Stadium Course (four, five, and nine are the highlights on the front nine), but the holes that have made this course famous are seventeen and eighteen. With its island green, number seventeen is probably the world's most photographed par three. The local rule requires you to proceed to the drop area after plunking two in the lake. Our foursome played the Stadium Course on a cold and extremely windy afternoon. Of the eight drives lofted by our foursome, only one ball safely reached the green on seventeen. Dan Jenkins had it at least partially correct, for the eighteenth on the Stadium Course is an ob-vious replica of Pebble's final hole with a large lake extending down the entire left-hand side. If you cannot get onto the Stadium Course, consider playing the **Valley Course,** another Pete Dye design. It is slightly longer, a bit more forgiving, yet still full of challenge and interest.

The greens fee for the Stadium Course is a whopping $160 (plus a $23 cart fee) in high season from mid-February to mid-May. A more attractive option may be to be-come an associate member of the TPC. For $165 you can become a nonresident asso-ciate member, which allows you to play any day of the week and, more important, to bring up to three guests with you each time you play and make tee times up to two weeks in advance. The more guests you bring, the less you wind up paying for greens fees. If you plan to play the course repeatedly, the resident associate membership, which costs $300, provides even greater fee reductions. By becoming an associate member you are also freed up from staying at the Marriott. Memberships are good for one year. Contact TPC Membership Secretary Debbie Weber at 904 273-3233 for details.

Marsh Landing Country Club, designed by Ed Seay, is an easier, less dramatic layout with an especially pretty front side that plays over beautiful marshes and wetlands and a somewhat less appealing back nine that winds its way through an upscale residential development. Owned by Paul and Jerome Fletcher, who also run the Lodge at Ponte Vedra, Marsh Landing has a very happy local membership and a wide following. The Marsh Landing staff—the starters, bag handlers, and the em-ployees in the handsome clubhouse—are good people who treat you well.

Sawgrass Country Club was the site of the Players Championship for five years before the tournament was moved over to the Stadium Course. Also designed by Ed Seay, the twenty-seven holes at Sawgrass have a links flavor combined with trees and considerable water.

Tournament Players Club. 110 TPC Boulevard, Ponte Vedra Beach, FL 32082. Tel: 904-273-3235. Fax: 904-285-7970. Credit cards accepted.

• *Stadium Course*. 1980. Designer: Pete Dye. Par 72. 6,857 yards. 74.0 par rating. 135 slope rating. Greens fees: guests: $160 (mid-February–mid-May)/$120 (May–June, September–November), off season: $90 to $100. Carts cost an additional $23. No walking. No caddies. Restrictions: closed Tuesdays. Access restricted to members, associate members, or guests of certain Ponte Vedra hotels. Season: year-round. Course closes for one month prior to the TPC Tournament.

• *Valley Course*. 1987. Designer: Pete Dye. Par 72. 6,864 yards. 72.6 par rating. 129 slope rating. Greens fees: $95 (February–May)/$80 (May–June, September–November), $60 to 70 (off season). Carts cost an additional $23. No walking. No caddies. Season: year-round.

Marsh Landing Country Club. 25655 Marsh Landing Parkway, Ponte Vedra, FL 32082. Tel: 904-285-6459. Fax: 904-273-9759. Credit cards accepted.

• 1986. Designer: Ed Seay. Par 72. 6,840 yards. 72.7 par rating. 131 slope rating. Greens fees: $90 to $150. Carts cost an additional $22. Walking permitted late afternoon only. No caddies. Restrictions: nonmember play restricted to guests of the Marriott and limited to Tuesday through Friday. Season: year-round.

Sawgrass Country Club. 10034 Golf Club Drive, Ponte Vedra, FL 32082. Tel: 904-273-3700. Fax: 904-273-3729. Credit cards accepted.

• 1972/1984. Designer: Ed Seay.
• *East nine*. 1972. Par 36. 3,476 yards.
• *West nine*. 1972. Par 36. 3,424 yards.
• *South nine*. 1984. Par 36. 3,440 yards.
• Greens fee: $80 to $120. Carts cost an additional $23. Walking permitted after 4 P.M. No caddies. Restrictions: nonmember play restricted to Marriott guests. Season: year-round.

GOLF SERVICES

Golf services are outstanding at all the courses noted above, particularly the TPC, which has one of the most elaborate setups we have ever seen. All the courses have fine pro shops, restaurants and bars for a bite to eat or a drink after your game, good practice ranges, teaching professionals to fine-tune your swing, and accommodating employees who are accustomed to greeting out-of-towners. You are made to feel welcome wherever you play.

LODGING

Our itinerary placed us first at the Lodge and Beach Club because of the great reports we had read about it, but we then moved on to inspect the Marriott and the Ponte Vedra Inn. We have already mentioned that the Marriott is your best choice—not because of its guest rooms, which are adequate, modern, and comfortable, but because it provides nearly unlimited access to the courses noted above, save for Marsh Landing, which Marriott guests may play only Tuesday through Friday.

In our estimation, however, the **Lodge and Beach Club,** a member of the prestigious Preferred Hotel group, is quite overrated. The beachfront location is nice, and our room (number 231) was better by far than anything available at the Marriott, but the service was lackadaisical (particularly at the front desk), the food was very disappointing, and the hotel was clogged with private business parties in the evenings. The Lodge and Beach Club has a fine bath club across the street from the hotel with sauna, whirlpool, steambaths, and exercise classes.

The **Ponte Vedra Inn and Club** runs a distant third to the Marriott and the Lodge. Access to the top courses is a real problem, and the rooms we were shown looked quite woebegone. The service here, however, is very friendly. As we went to press, rumor had it that the Ponte Vedra Inn was about to acquire the Lodge and Beach Club, which will no doubt bring large changes to both establishments.

The Marriott at Sawgrass. 1000 TPC Boulevard, Ponte Vedra, FL 32082. Tel: 800-457-4653 or 904-285-7777. Fax: 904-285-0906. 515 rooms. Doubles range from $150 to $250. Golf packages are available. Credit cards accepted.

The Lodge and Beach Club. 607 Ponte Vedra Boulevard, Ponte Vedra Beach, FL 32082. Tel: 800-243-4304 or 904-273-9500. Fax: 904-273-0210. 66 rooms and suites. Double rooms range from $194 to $284 in high season from March until the end of July. Credit cards accepted.

Ponte Vedra Inn and Club. 200 Ponte Vedra Boulevard, Ponte Vedra Beach, FL 32082. Tel: 800-234-7842 or 904-285-1111. Fax: 904-285-2111. 222 rooms. Doubles range from $170 to $240 between March and July. Credit cards accepted.

R E S T A U R A N T S

The Lodge and Beach Club offers three restaurants. We preferred the casual **Lounge** and the **Oasis** by the water much more than the **Mediterranean Room,** which comes up short of its gourmet aspirations. Even less can be said of the formal restaurant at the Marriott, the **Augustine Grill.** A better place to dine at the Marriott is the casual **Café on the Green,** where steak, shrimp, and pasta dishes start at about $20. The Sunday champagne brunch here is a nice option. The Ponte Vedra Inn and Club features the fine dining **Seafoam Room,** which overlooks the ocean, and the casual **Florida Room.** Jackets are required for dinner at the Seafoam Room, where entrées cost about $30. In the Sawgrass Village Shopping Center, the menu at **Gio's Café** features good pasta, veal, seafood, and steaks. Expect to pay about $75 for two, wine and tip included.

The restaurants at the Marriott at Sawgrass. 1000 TPC Boulevard, Ponte Vedra, FL 32082. Tel: 800-457-4653 or 904-285-7777. Fax: 904-285-0906. Credit cards accepted.

The restaurants at the Lodge and Beach Club. 607 Ponte Vedra Boulevard, Ponte Vedra Beach, FL 32082. Tel: 800-243-4304 or 904-273-9500. Fax: 904-273-0210. Credit cards accepted.

The restaurants at the Ponte Vedra Inn and Club. 200 Ponte Vedra Boulevard. Ponte Vedra Beach, FL 32082. Tel: 800-234-7842 or 904-285-1111. Fax: 904-285-2111. Credit cards accepted.

Gio's Café. 900 Sawgrass Village, Sawgrass, FL 32082. Tel: 904-273-0101. Fax: 904-273-6486. Credit cards accepted.

NON-GOLF ACTIVITIES

Ponte Vedra is home of the Association of Tennis Professionals, and all varieties of court surfaces are available for play. The three principal hotels have swimming pools and exercise facilities. There is no shopping in the area except the small handful of nice shops in Sawgrass Village. The golf, however, is truly the main reason for visiting this part of Florida.

GETTING THERE: From Jacksonville Airport, take I-95 South to exit 101 (Butler Boulevard). Take Butler east toward the beaches—it dead-ends at A1A. Make a right onto A1A, and follow it until you reach the eighth stoplight (TPC Boulevard). Take a right on TPC Boulevard and the Marriott at Sawgrass will be on the left.

►AMELIA ISLAND

THE AMELIA ISLAND PLANTATION AND THE RITZ-CARLTON

	The Golf	Golf Services	Lodging	Restaurants	Non-Golf Activities	Total
Rating	17	17	16	15	17	82

Amelia Island Plantation

Two hotel heavyweights are punching it out for their share of the market on lovely Amelia Island, Florida. The contenders are the long-established Amelia Island Plantation and a formidable newcomer, just three or four miles up the beach, the enormous and elegant Ritz-Carlton, which opened in 1991. Between them, they have more than one thousand guest rooms. The Amelia Island Plantation is better known among golfers. In the past it has won *Golf Magazine*'s gold medal for golf resorts (a distinction it does not fully deserve in our opinion), and *Family Circle* has named it one of the top family holiday destinations in America. This second accolade is on target: the Plantation is great for kids.

Amelia Island is located in the extreme northeast corner of Florida, thirty miles from Jacksonville Airport and just a three or four iron across the inlet from Georgia. Hence, the atmosphere here is really much more Georgian than Floridian—a bonus, in our view. Of course, in midwinter the weather is less dependable here than in south Florida, but the natives are mannerly and hospitable. When you think of Amelia Island, picture Sea Island or Kiawah with their live oaks and Spanish moss rather than south Florida with its high-rises and palm trees. In any case, you know you are in golf country when you arrive at Jacksonville Airport as there is a big golf shop in the main terminal.

During our four nights on Amelia Island in the quiet period between Thanksgiving and Christmas, we split our time evenly between the Plantation and the Ritz-

Carlton and discovered that they are two very different kinds of operations. We also played all the golf courses affiliated with both resorts.

Our findings, in a nutshell, are as follows: the golf and the non-golf activities are far better at the Plantation, while the rooms and the food are superior at the Ritz-Carlton. Consequently, the happiest visitor to Amelia Island is that fortunate individual who can combine the two by staying at the Ritz-Carlton and playing the Plantation's golf courses. This perfect scenario, sadly, is not likely to materialize during large parts of the year. Its success, like much else in golf, depends upon your timing. Ritz-Carlton guests are indeed permitted to play the Plantation's courses, but only if space is available, and space will not be available on most weekends and from mid-January through May. The courses at the Plantation are reserved for its own guests first. If golf is your highest priority and you plan to come here in high season, play it safe and stay at the Plantation, even though it leaves a lot to be desired.

 THE GOLF

The main golf attraction on Amelia Island is Long Point, the stunning Tom Fazio creation built in 1988 and currently rated among the top sixty resort courses in America. Long Point is owned by the Amelia Island Plantation, as is the Amelia Links, twenty-seven exquisite holes of golf designed by Pete Dye. The entire operation clearly looks as if it had been inspired by the incomparable setup at the Cloister on Sea Island, Georgia, just a two-hour drive up the coast. Guests of the Ritz-Carlton have access to the **Golf Club of Amelia Island,** located immediately adjacent to the hotel property and designed by Mark McCumber and Gene Littler. This McCumber-Littler layout is pleasant and easy (it is six or seven strokes easier than Long Point), but it is the least interesting golf course in the area, it is in the poorest condition, and it is the only course we would not care to play again.

Long Point—with emphasis on the *Long*—holds your attention from beginning to end. "Long Point was an easy course to build," Fazio has said. "There is so much variety there. Ocean, marsh, woods, water, and natural dune ridges make for a good golf course. The location is so great that when the course opened it looked as if it had been there for several years." The broader back side is generally regarded as Long Point's prettiest—on seventeen you hit your second shot over a nest of long-billed white herons—but Fazio's best holes are encountered early, like number two, with its narrow bunkers and dramatic setting along Nassau

Long Point

Sound, and the famous back-to-back par threes along the ocean shore, numbers six (166 yards) and seven (158 yards). Long Point's natural beauty is dazzling. You will remember it long after your day of play.

The **Amelia Links** consists of three nine-hole layouts. **Oakmarsh** is the toughest nine, but **Oysterbay** and **Oceanside** are more beautiful and dramatic.

Golf Club of Amelia Island. 4700 Amelia Island Parkway, Amelia Island, FL 32034. Tel: 904-277-8015. Fax: 904-277-7093. Credit cards accepted.

• 1987. Designers: Mark McCumber, Gene Littler. Par 72. 6,681 yards. Par rating 71.7. Slope rating 127. Greens fees: $96, includes cart. No walking. No caddies. Restrictions: public access only to guests of Summer Beach Resort and Ritz-Carlton. Season: year-round.

Long Point. Amelia Island Plantation, 6000 1st Coastal Highway, Amelia Island, FL 32034. Tel: 800-874-6878 or 904-261-6166, ext. 5500, or 904-277-5907 (tee times). Fax: 904-277-5989. Credit cards accepted.

• 1988. Designer: Tom Fazio. Par 72. 6,775 yards. 72.9 par rating, 129 slope rating. Greens fees: resort guests: $105 (high season), $85 (low season); public: $130 (on a strictly space-available basis with one-day advance reservations). Cart included. No walking. No caddies. Restrictions: tee times are reserved for members until 12:30 P.M. every day. Season: year-round.

Amelia Links. Amelia Island Plantation, 6000 1st Coastal Highway, Amelia Island, FL 32034. Tel: 800-874-6878 or 904-261-6166, ext. 5381, or 904-277-5907 (tee times). Fax: 904-277-5990. Credit cards accepted.

• 1972. Designer: Pete Dye.
• *Oakmarsh.* Par 36. 3,308 yards.
• *Oysterbay.* Par 36. 3,194 yards.
• *Oceanside.* Par 35. 2,819 yards.
• Greens fees: resort guests: $87 (high season), $67 (low season); public: $112 (on a strictly space-available basis with one-day advance reservations). Cart included. No walking. No caddies. Season: year-round.

GOLF SERVICES (17)

Golf services and facilities are especially outstanding at Long Point, with its fine clubhouse, pro shop, and tidy little grill. The Amelia Links complex is also very attractive and well run. Services at the Golf Club of Amelia are merely good. Long Point's Golf Academy runs two- and three-day golf schools.

LODGING (16)

Unlike the Ritz-Carlton, the **Amelia Island Plantation** is not a hotel. It is an enormous residential and condominium community spread out over 1,250 acres of prime oceanfront property. When you stay here you are actually renting someone's personal condominium unit. The Plantation provides management and owns the golf courses, the restaurants, and other facilities, but the homes and apartments are private property.

Although Amelia Island Plantation has about two hundred hotel-type bedrooms, the majority of the units are "villas" (suites or condominiums) decorated and equipped to a very high standard, with full kitchens, laundry facilities, vacuum cleaner, and cable television—everything you have at home. It is easy to imagine a family on holiday here saving a little money by doing their own cooking. We stayed in the somewhat remote Sea Dunes building in a beautiful one-bedroom villa with a view of the ocean that rented for $248 a night based on a five-night stay.

The entire resort is a bit too decentralized for our tastes, however. Because none of the residential buildings have restaurants, anytime you elect not to cook for yourself you may have to get in your car or ride the shuttle bus (called the "tram") to a Plantation restaurant. The restaurant and bar scene at the Plantation can also be less than ideal. There were several irritating groups of businessmen on the premises during our visit. Drunk and loud, these guys did little to enhance the atmosphere.

The very worst you can say of the **Ritz-Carlton** is, once you have seen one Ritz-Carlton, you have seen them all. These hotels, as comfortable and luxurious as they are, have no sense of place. They are virtually interchangeable from Rancho Mirage, California, to Amelia Island, Florida. They all look like London during the Edwardian period. But all Ritz-Carltons are undeniably comfortable and attractive. We stayed in a standard-size room, number 625, decorated with chintz fabrics and Audubon prints and equipped with a marble bath, three phones, minibar, and private balcony overlooking the beach—you name it. The public rooms at the Ritz-Carlton are particularly handsome, and the service is excellent—better and more attentive than at the Plantation.

The Amelia Island Plantation. Highway A1A South, Amelia Island, FL 32034. Tel: 800-874-6878 or 904-261-6166. Fax: 904-277-5945. 500 rooms, suites, and condominiums. Hotel-type double rooms range in price from $127 to $239. One-bedroom villas are $148 to $312. Several golf, weekend, and holiday packages are available. Credit cards accepted.

The Ritz-Carlton. 4750 Amelia Island Parkway, Amelia Island, FL 32034. Tel: 800-241-3333 or 904-277-1100. Fax: 904-261-9064. 449 rooms and suites. Doubles priced from $129 to $299 depending on the time of year. Credit cards accepted.

 RESTAURANTS (15)

The finest restaurant on Amelia Island is the **Grill** in the Ritz-Carlton, an opulent, oak-paneled room with crystal chandeliers, bronze statues, Regency-style furnishings, and big windows with ocean views. We had an outstanding dinner here: a wonderful goat cheese ravioli and a sublime grilled pompano with red peppers, artichoke hearts, and capers. The wine list is exhaustive and the service first-rate. Dinner for two with wine and tip at this highly rated restaurant costs approximately $120. Jackets are required, and ties are recommended. The **Café,** which offers American cuisine, and the **Ocean Bar and Grill** by the pool are two less formal restaurants at the Ritz.

The showcase restaurant on Amelia Island Plantation is the **Amelia Island Inn Restaurant and Lounge,** which features excellent seafood but is closed for renovations until late 1998. While these renovations take place, the **Verandah** will serve as the Plantation's premier restaurant; entrées here range between $20 and $34. The **Beach Club Sports Bar,** the **Coop,** the **Golf Shop Restaurant,** and the **Long Point Putter Club** round out the resort's more casual dining options. All restaurants on the Amelia Island Plantation property are open only to residents and guests of the Plantation.

The restaurants at the Ritz-Carlton. 4750 Amelia Island Parkway, Amelia Island, FL 32034. Tel: 800-241-3333 or 904-277-1100. Fax: 904-261-9064. Credit cards accepted.

The restaurants at Amelia Island Plantation. Highway A1A South, Amelia Island, FL 32034. Tel: 800-874-6878 or 904-261-6166. Fax: 904-277-5945. Credit cards accepted.

NON-GOLF ACTIVITIES 17

The Plantation wins this category hands-down. Non-golf activities here include tennis (two major tennis tournaments are held here every year), fishing and sailing, supervised programs for children, horseback riding along the beach, swimming, paddleboat and bicycle rental, and the health and fitness center with saunas, steam rooms, whirlpools, and more.

The Ritz-Carlton has two swimming pools (one indoor, one outdoor) and a beautifully equipped spa.

GETTING THERE: Fly into Jacksonville Airport and take I-95 North to exit 129. Proceed on A1A South thirteen miles to the island. Once across the Intecoastal Waterway Bridge, go a half mile and take a right onto Amelia Island Parkway. Amelia Island Plantation is six miles ahead on the left.

Bermuda

▶GREAT GOLF IN THE GULF STREAM

	The Golf	Golf Services	Lodging	Restaurants	Non-Golf Activities	Total
Rating	19	16	17	16	18	86

Bermuda

For the uninitiated, Bermuda, so close and yet so far away, may require a few brief words of introduction.

The current of warm ocean water that is the Gulf Stream kindly and effectively insulates Bermuda from the endless succession of winter storms that buffet the American continent. When great ice storms paralyze much of the East Coast in January and February, the temperature in Bermuda still holds fast at sixty-eight degrees. Bermudans who cater to tourists—and that is at least half the population—are so confident that the thermometer will hit at least sixty-eight degrees every winter afternoon that certain hotels routinely advertise free rooms if this magic number is not attained. Those of us freezing on the American mainland find this phenomenon amazing, chiefly because Bermuda is just 640 miles off the North Carolina coast, on the same latitude as Cape Hatteras, and actually much closer to New York, Baltimore, and Washington than to the islands of the Caribbean, which are one thousand miles south of Bermuda. Bermudans are right when they say they have two seasons, spring and summer. July and August in Bermuda can be quite muggy.

Another point: despite the island's romantic coves and pristine beaches filled with honeymooners strolling hand in hand, its idyllic pastel-tinted "cottage colonies," its tropical vegetation, the island-concocted rum, and great duty-free shopping, Bermuda probably has more in common with financial centers like Wall Street and London than it does with Jamaica, Haiti, the Dominican Republic, or any number of the sleepy Caribbean islands. Hamilton, Bermuda's capital, is as sophisticated a little city as you will find and home to over 1,200 banks and insurance companies. Do not be deceived by the golden tans and quaint attire of Hamilton's bankers and insurance men (Bermuda shorts, knee socks, and blue blazers with or without neckties), for these hardworking citizens mean business. In fact, everybody in Bermuda marches in happy lockstep to the business beat. Some time ago Bermudans decided they preferred affluence over poverty, and everyone works in harmony to polish Bermuda's already high-gloss image. The results are impressive. Bermuda has a lot of satisfied return visitors, and the resident population is well educated, well traveled, and affluent indeed.

In the shape of a fish hook, Bermuda Island's eighteen square miles are densely populated with people (65,000) and golf courses (eight). Although rental cars are prohibited, traffic still moves at a snail's pace. The only glitch to golf here is figuring out how to get to the course. Either you take a long and expensive taxi ride from one end of the island to another or learn how to ride a scooter while balancing your golf bag behind you. We tried, and it's not easy.

Finally, those who think Bermuda will be too tame, too formal, or too much like home simply have not gone and seen for themselves. Bermuda is civilized, traditional, quite British, and thoroughly international, but there is just enough mellowness and island desuetude to assure you that you are not in Greenwich, Connecticut, or Palm Beach.

Important note: Bermuda is an internally governed crown colony of the United Kingdom. In order to enter you must have a current or recently expired United States passport or your birth certificate with a photo ID.

THE GOLF

Only three of Bermuda's eight golf courses are truly worth your time, but these three are so memorable that they alone make a wonderful golf holiday. Without question, the preeminent course on Bermuda—and one of the great golf courses on a tropical island anywhere in the world—is the dazzling **Mid-Ocean Club** with its historic, fanciful, and incredibly seductive course designed in 1924 by the illustrious Charles Blair Macdonald with Charles Banks.

The other two "must" courses on Bermuda are the government-owned **Port Royal,** designed in 1971 by Robert Trent Jones, Sr., and the very intriguing 1932 Charles Banks layout at **Castle Harbour.** The five remaining courses on Bermuda have some appealing and very scenic characteristics, but Riddell's Bay, Belmont, and St. George's are too short (all well under 6,000 yards), and the Ocean View and Southampton Princess courses each has only nine holes.

Play on the Mid-Ocean Club is open to nonmembers on Mondays, Wednesdays, and Fridays provided they meet the following conditions: tee times may be secured only twenty-four hours in advance; you must stay at a hotel recognized by the Mid-Ocean Club in order to secure a time (see Lodging, below), and your hotel must make your tee time for you. You are not permitted to call the club and book the tee time yourself. A game at Mid-Ocean is by far the most expensive in Bermuda. The greens fee is $140 and caddies (who are excellent) are $25 plus tip.

Yet Mid-Ocean, which is always in immaculate condition, is worth every penny.

This is a great golf course because of its tremendous natural variety—undulating terrain, ocean views, fragrant salt air, exotic birds, colorful foliage, and multimillion-dollar homes—and because of the unusual array of shots—blind shots, uphill shots, big drives over massive lakes, and several interesting shots over public-access roads that happen to be bumper to bumper with car and truck traffic. Our caddie told us that cars do, indeed, get beaned by golf balls, but miraculously no more often than "once every five or ten years."

Mid-Ocean's aesthetic splendor does not let up from start to finish. The course simply serves up one gorgeous golf hole after another. The first three holes play alongside the Atlantic, and seventeen and eighteen finally return again to the ocean shore, but the heart of the course is located amid lakes, marshes, and mature woodland. The very tough, number one handicap is the 433-yard fifth, where, from a tee perched on a towering hillside over Mangrove Lake, you drive to a small target area. After landing safely in the fairway, you must attempt a dangerous second shot to a green protected by the same large lake and three deep bunkers. Par is four, but five is a good score on the fifth. The seventh is one of the most unusual holes at Mid-Ocean. Your avenue to the putting surface on this 164-yard par three is a narrow grass walkway that actually bisects the lake in front of the green.

The back nine at Mid-Ocean gets somewhat easier but is just as spectacular looking as the front. The twelfth hole, a 437-yard par four called Hillside, requires a blind tee shot over the hill down to the fairway and a very big second shot up to an elevated green. It is sixteen, however, that gets our vote as Mid-Ocean's most fascinating hole. Sixteen is called Lookout because its green is the highest point on the course. To get there, you must smash a very long and straight drive directly uphill over an access road. Once you climb to the top, you will be rewarded with a spectacular ocean view. The Mid-Ocean Club measures 6,547 from the back tees. Par is seventy-one.

The courses at Port Royal and Castle Harbour are also great beauties, but because both are true public-access facilities they get a great deal of play and their condition can suffer, especially in comparison with Mid-Ocean. The fees, however, are a bit lower: Port Royal costs $60 weekdays and $65 weekends, while Castle Harbour charges $130 (cart included) in high season and $86 during the low winter season. Crowds and spotty conditioning aside, these are two absolutely wonderful places to play.

Undoubtedly the most famous hole in all Bermuda is the sixteenth at Port Royal, the 162-yard par three over a rocky cove and Atlantic waves that will remind some golfers of the little seventh hole at Pebble Beach. Port Royal's fifteenth—where an old stone fortress is very much in play on the left—is another knockout. Port Royal measures 6,565 yards from the back tees. Par is seventy-two. Walking is permitted.

Castle Harbour, located across the bay from the airport and actually abutting Mid-Ocean's sixteenth tee at one point, is full of fun and curious constructions. Its first hole, for example, is billed as "the most scenic opening hole in the world." The tee on number one is situated high above the fairway—some 175 feet—so the ball sails dramatically before finally touching down. There are celebrity residences along the way, such as Ross Perot's home, which overlooks the second green. We particularly fell in love with the wild back nine at Castle Harbour: number ten, the 305-yard, downhill par four; number thirteen, the stunning, uphill, 190-yard par three across a deep gully; and the grueling sequence of finishing holes. Castle Harbour is 6,440 yards from the tips. Par is seventy-one. Carts are mandatory on this very hilly layout.

Mid-Ocean Club. 1 Mid-Ocean Drive, Tuckerstown, Hamilton HS-02, Bermuda. Tel: 441-293-0330. Fax: 441-293-8837. Credit cards accepted.

• 1924. Designers: Charles Blair Macdonald, Charles Banks. Par 71. 6,547 yards. 72.0 par rating. 138 slope rating. Greens fee: $140. Walking permitted. Carts and caddies available. Restrictions: approved hotels must make your tee times up to twenty-four hours in advance for play on Mondays, Wednesdays, and Fridays only. Season: year-round.

Port Royal. Middle Road, Southampton SN-BX, Bermuda. Tel: 441-295-6500 or 441-234-0974. Fax: 441-234-3562. Credit cards accepted.

• 1971. Designer: Robert Trent Jones, Sr. Par 72. 6,565 yards. 72.0 par rating. 134 slope rating. Greens fees: $65 (weekdays), $70 (weekends); carts cost an additional $17. Walking permitted (no walking prior to 3 P.M. on weekends). No caddies. Season: year-round.

Castle Harbour. 2 South Road, Saint George HS-02, Bermuda. Tel: 441-293-2040. Fax: 441-293-1051. Credit cards accepted.

• 1932. Designer: Charles Banks. Par 71. 6,440 yards. 71.3 par rating. 128 slope rating. Greens fees: $130 (high season), $86 (December–February), cart included. No walking. No caddies. Season: year-round.

 GOLF SERVICES 16

Not surprisingly, golf services are outstanding at the very well run Mid-Ocean Club. There is a very elegant clubhouse, handsome and well-maintained locker rooms, a good practice range with free range balls, excellent caddies, a very friendly starter, and a pleasant staff that works hard to make you feel welcome. Mid-Ocean is everything a great club ought to be.

Services, however, are merely adequate at the sometimes haphazard Port Royal complex and decidedly poor at Castle Harbour. Port Royal has a decent clubhouse, locker facility, and a nice restaurant/bar, but the practice range is in very poor condition and the range balls have been virtually hacked to pieces. Castle Harbour, on the other hand, has no practice area at all. An old net with a large hole in it adjacent to the first tee is all the practice you are going to get.

A reminder: golf balls are costly in Bermuda, nearly $6 each. Be sure to pack at least a dozen of your own.

 LODGING 17

There are two very distinct brands of hotels in Bermuda—large, modern, and somewhat anonymous ones like the Southampton Princess, the Marriott, and the Sonesta Beach—and the small, traditional hotels on the island known as "cottage colonies." Quality-conscious travelers who wish to experience the real charm and essence of Bermuda always opt to stay in one of the choice cottage colonies or smaller beach clubs, such as the very special Reefs Beach Club or the exclusive and revered **Coral Beach and Tennis Club.** We have now stayed at the Coral Beach on several different occasions and always found it to be exceptional; it is ideally located and especially appealing to tennis lovers.

There are literally dozens of cottage colonies from which to choose in Bermuda, but the cream of the crop belongs to an association called "the Bermuda Collection." On our most recent trip we stayed at one of the best member-hotels in the Bermuda Collection, the quiet and elegant hideaway called Cambridge Beaches.

Cambridge Beaches suffers only to one extent: it is located in the far western corner of the island in Sandy's Parish on a private (and gorgeous) twenty-five-acre peninsula, but it is a considerable distance, about a forty-minute drive, from the Mid-Ocean Club and Castle Harbour courses. We found, however, that the beauty, charm, and fine facilities of Cambridge Beaches more than compensate for the inconvenience. This hotel maintains strong connections with all the golf courses and can always secure tee times for guests.

Cambridge Beaches

Cambridge Beaches has subtle tone and patina; it is not a glamorous new resort like the Four Seasons in Nevis. We stayed in a very spacious, newly remodeled room called Skeeters and loved its private terrace overlooking the ocean, handsome mahogany furniture, and large marble bath, but it had no television or minibar. The hotel provides wonderful activities for the non-golfer. Facilities include several lovely private beaches on the ocean and bay sides, hidden rocky coves ideal for picnics, a complete marina with sailboats, powerboats, and snorkeling equipment, three tennis courts, a heated pool, a small spa and exercise room, a putting green, and a croquet lawn. There is also a good—and quite dressy—dining room, and rum swizzles are served nightly in the pleasant Port o' Call bar. Please note that credit cards are not accepted, an unfortunate policy at many Bermuda hotels.

Other recommended addresses include the **Coral Beach and Tennis Club** (introduction by a member is required at certain times of the year), **Lantana, Pink Beach Club, Horizons** (a member of Relais & Château), and the **Reefs Beach Club.**

Coral Beach and Tennis Club. PO Box PG 200, Paget PG-BX, Bermuda. Tel: 441-236-2233. Fax: 441-236-1876. 50 rooms and suites from $248 to $540 in high season, including breakfast. No credit cards.

Cambridge Beaches. 30 Kings Point Road, Somerset MA-02 Bermuda. Tel: 800-468-7300 or 441-234-0331. Fax: 441-234-3352. 80 rooms, suites, and cottages. Doubles from $350 to $490 (high season), including breakfast, afternoon tea, and dinner. No credit cards.

Lantana. PO Box SB 90, Somerset SB-BX, Bermuda. Tel: 800-468-3733 or 441-234-0141. Fax: 441-234-2562. 58 rooms and suites. Doubles from $155 to $230, breakfast and dinner included. Call for golf packages. Credit cards accepted.

Pink Beach Club. PO Box 1017, Hamilton HM-DX, Bermuda. Tel: 800-355-6161 or 441-293-1666. Fax: 441-293-8935. 93 cottages from $370 to $395 (for two people) in high season, including breakfast and dinner. Credit cards accepted.

Horizons. 33 South Shore, Paget PG-BX, Bermuda. Tel: 800-468-0022 or 441-236-0048. Fax: 441-236-1981. 42 rooms, suites, and villas. Double rooms from $310 to $400 (high season), breakfast and dinner included. Villas begin at $700. No credit cards.

Reefs Beach Club. 56 South Shore Road, Southampton SN-02, Bermuda. Tel: 800-742-2008 or 441-238-0222. Fax: 441-238-8372. 67 rooms and cottages. Double rooms from $348 to $418 (high season), breakfast and dinner included. Credit cards accepted.

RESTAURANTS 16

The style of dining in Bermuda, particularly at dinner, is always quite formal—candlelight, multiple courses, and waiters in black tie. Yet the actual cuisine served on the island, even in its finest restaurants, can sometimes be disappointing.

The smartest restaurant in Bermuda is **Fourways Inn,** which is fun, quite elegant, and always bustling. A beamed ceiling, stone arches, Windsor armchairs, and lots of well-dressed guests create an upbeat atmosphere. The food at Fourways is not exceptional, but it is reasonably good, especially the tasty local seafood. The à la carte menu, however, struck us as decidedly overpriced. A small serving of plain steamed rice cost $5.95. We were charged $1 for each glass of mineral water poured into our glasses, even though we had neither ordered mineral water nor requested refills. A complete dinner for two here with an inexpensive bottle of wine plus gratuity will cost approximately $210.

One advantage of staying at a "Bermuda Collection" hotel is participating in its "dine-around" program. Every night of the week the same number of guests at participating cottage colonies may trade places in the main dining room with the guests of another participating property. We particularly enjoyed our dine-around dinners at the **Lantana** and **Reefs Beach Club.** The five-course prix fixe menu costs about $45. Jackets are required in the evening.

The dining room at **Cambridge Beaches** is large, barnlike, and not particularly attractive, but the service is extremely cordial and the cuisine is some of the best in Bermuda. Breakfast at Cambridge Beaches is served on the lovely outdoor terrace beside the swimming pool and overlooking one of the beaches.

For late-night dining and entertainment we suggest the **Henry VIII** restaurant. And finally, if you are looking for a casual place for lunch while shopping in Hamilton, we recommend the fine **Fourways Pastry Shop** on Reid Street for good sandwiches and salads.

Fourways Inn. 1 Middle Road, Paget PG-BX, Bermuda. Tel: 441-236-6517. Fax: 441-236-5528. Credit cards accepted.

The restaurants at Lantana. PO Box SB 90, Somerset SB-BX, Bermuda. Tel: 800-468-3733 or 441-234-0141. Fax: 441-234-2562. Credit cards accepted.

The restaurants at Reefs Beach Club. 56 South Shore Road, Southampton SN-02, Bermuda. Tel: 800-742-2008 or 441-238-0222. Fax: 441-238-8372. Credit cards accepted.

Cambridge Beaches. 30 Kings Point Road, Somerset MA-02, Bermuda. Tel: 800-468-7300 or 441-234-0331. Fax: 441-234-3352. No credit cards.

Henry VIII. PO Box 5N 5S Southampton SN-BX, Bermuda. Tel: 441-238-1977. Fax: 441-238-8096. Credit cards accepted.

Fourways Pastry Shop. Washington Mall, Hamilton, Bermuda. Tel: 411-236-6517. No fax. Credit cards accepted.

NON-GOLF ACTIVITIES 18

The non-golf activities in Bermuda are almost without limit. Shopping heads the list. In bustling Hamilton you will find incredible duty-free shopping for, among other things, Rolex watches, Irish linens, Scottish woolens, Wedgwood, Waterford crystal, Penhaligon's perfumes, and much more. All the principal stores—like Smith's, Crisson, A. S. Cooper, and Bluck's—

are cheek by jowl on Front Street. The smaller designer boutiques are located behind Front Street on Reid and Church streets.

The most popular non-golf activities include sailing, boating, windsurfing, snorkeling and scuba diving over the colorful coral reefs that surround Bermuda, motor scooter touring, picnicking, tennis, and visiting the historic sights on the island like the beautiful town of St. George's.

GETTING THERE: Several airlines fly directly into Bermuda from the eastern United States. There are no car rentals in Bermuda. Once you confirm your reservations with a Bermuda hotel and know your flight arrangements, the hotel will arrange for a taxi to pick you up at the airport. To Cambridge Beaches the one-way taxi fare is $45, payable to the driver. The ride takes about an hour.

The Dominican Republic

▶CASA DE CAMPO

GOLFING PARADISE IN THE CARIBBEAN

	The Golf	Golf Services	Lodging	Restaurants	Non-Golf Activities	Total
Rating	19	18	16	14	16	83

Casa de Campo

Golf in the Caribbean may have been late in developing, but it has certainly been worth the wait. Until the early 1990s, only Jamaica, Puerto Rico, Guadeloupe, Martinique, and the Dominican Republic offered topflight courses. Yet no spot in the Caribbean then or now provides a more exhilarating golf destination than Casa de Campo in the Dominican Republic. Casa de Campo is one of the greatest pure golf resorts we have visited anywhere in the world, bar none. Its three stupendous golf courses—the breathtaking Teeth of the Dog, the even better La Romana Country Club, and the magnificent Links—are three of the most exquisitely conditioned, spectacular-looking, and inspirationally designed golf courses we have ever seen or played. The caddies at Casa de Campo are the best and hardest-working we have ever had the pleasure to go around with, including, heaven help us for we know this is sacrilege, the caddies of St. Andrews. And the stunning pro shop and locker room at Casa de Campo, lined in teak and mahogany, is a wonderfully distinct place perfectly matched to its exotic tropical setting.

THE GOLF

19

All of you golf addicts out there who follow in our footsteps are destined to have a remarkable experience, one you will likely never forget, for the Casa de Campo golf courses are not only the best in the Caribbean, they are among the finest offered by any resort in the world. To our utter amazement, when we visited in the off season all three courses were dead empty. We started early, had the courses virtually to ourselves, finished every round in less than three hours, and easily completed thirty-six holes a day. At Casa de Campo, both Teeth of the Dog and the Links start out from the main clubhouse; this convenient arrangement means you will lose no time moving from one course to the next. If not for the intense heat and brilliant sunshine, fifty-four holes daily would be a distinct possibility. We amused ourselves at Casa de Campo with memories of crowds and five-hour rounds routinely encountered at Pinehurst Number Two, Torrey Pines, Harbour Town, and other world-class layouts.

The first thing you should do at Casa de Campo is get acquainted with the club's pro and the golf staff. Each day Casa de Campo can arrange to send eight people to play at the otherwise private La Romana Country Club, which has its own equally elegant facility five minutes away. Undoubtedly, seasoned golfers are surprised to learn that La Romana Country Club course is even better than the legendary Teeth of the Dog. Well, we were also surprised. Indeed, prior to arriving here we did not even know that La Romana Country Club existed. The pro at Casa de Campo urged us to play it and said that, although it is an inland course without the scenic seaside holes of Teeth of the Dog, it is longer, tougher, somehow more beautiful, and a more perfect layout. Having just finished Teeth of the Dog and being in a state of golfing bliss, we found his comments extremely hard to believe.

Casa de Campo

All three courses were designed by Pete Dye, and we now retract every terrible word we have ever said about the infamous architect. The Casa de Campo courses are Dye's most subtle creations, full of gentle understatement rather than the exaggeration to which Dye is prone. Dye himself has a beautiful home with a thatched roof on the seventh fairway of Teeth of the Dog.

What is less well known about **Teeth of the Dog** is that the course is actually bisected by the long commercial runway that serves the La Romana Airport. This runway, astonishingly, is an integral part of the golf course. Your tee shot on twelve, as well as your drive at eighteen, requires that you hit your ball over the runway. You then get in your cart, pass the armed security guard who blocks the runway, drive over the concrete airstrip, and find your ball somewhere in the fairway on the other side. This feature is so ingenious we laughed out loud. La Romana Airport, by the way, is not busy, so you are not apt to be run over by a plane. There are just two scheduled flights per day.

Unlike Dye's celebrated courses in the United States (such as PGA West and the Ocean Course at Kiawah), the fairways on Teeth of the Dog are big and wide open. Almost anybody can play this course, score well, and fall in love with it. The greens, however, are more in character. They are elevated, heavily bunkered, and hard to hold. Teeth of the Dog's signature hole is number sixteen, called *Diente del Perro*. Aerial photographs reveal that this 185-yard hole over a rocky bay resembles an open mouth full of teeth. As we sank our teeth into Teeth of the Dog, the only problem we had was determining which tees to play. From the back tees (6,888 yards) this course is a monster, but from the middle tees (6,057 yards) it can feel short.

The second course at the Casa de Campo resort, the **Links,** is a short (6,461 yards) inland course, but it is just as beautiful and well manicured as its older and more famous sister. The shot qualities are different here as well. You will chip and pitch from the fairways rather than lob, and you may find yourself playing from Scottish-style pot bunkers.

La Romana Country Club is a very long 7,191 yards, beautifully contoured, incredibly well groomed, and, like Teeth of the Dog, huge from side to side. The course is well inland; you will see the ocean in the distance only from the elevated tees and greens, which are protected by sand, grassy pits, water, and unusually shaped grass trenches. La Romana is the harshest test at Casa de Campo and possibly the most memorable.

All three of these golf courses, by the way, were created by hand thanks to the work of more than three hundred Dominican laborers who sliced the underbrush with machetes and planted the fairways one sprig of grass at a time. The results are impressive. While La Romana Country Club is only a few years old, it has the thick turf of far more established courses.

Casa de Campo. PO Box 140, La Romana, Dominican Republic. Tel: 800-877-3643 or 011-809-523-3333. Fax: 809-523-8800. Credit cards accepted.

· *Teeth of the Dog.* 1970. Designer: Pete Dye. Par 72. 6,888 yards. 74.1 par rating. 140 slope rating. Greens fees: $125, includes half cart; three-day ticket: $165; seven-day ticket: $330. Carts are extra on three- and seven-day tickets. No walking. Caddies available. Season: year-round.

· *Links.* 1976. Designer: Pete Dye. Par 71. 6,461 yards. Par rating 70.0. Slope rating 124. Greens fee: $85, includes half cart. No walking. Caddies available. Season: year-round.

La Romana Country Club. La Romana, Dominican Republic. Tel: 809-523-3333, ext. 2480. Credit cards accepted.

· 1990. Designer: Pete Dye. Par 72. 7,191 yards. 74.5 par rating. 144 slope rating. Greens fee: $125, includes mandatory cart. No walking. Caddies available. Restrictions: Nonmember access arranged by Casa de Campo. Limit of eight players per day. Season: year-round.

 GOLF SERVICES

Upon arrival at the clubhouse you will find a dozen or more caddies milling around. Casa de Campo offers three categories of caddies. The fee for a topflight caddie with tip is about $20. Every one of the caddies we encountered spoke English and was impeccably polite; most are also very fine golfers. All golfers are required to ride even if they take a caddie, and your bags ride with you on the back of the cart. There is a lovely range and practice green at the main clubhouse.

 LODGING

Accommodations at **Casa de Campo** consist of hotel rooms set amid the gardens and within walking distance of the front desk, the main restaurants, and the golf clubhouse, as well as separate villas spread out among the resort's 11,000 acres. All villas come equipped with a golf cart, so you are able to drive almost anywhere. Longer trips to the resort's lovely private beach and to interesting Altos de Chavón, a medieval-style crafts community owned by Casa de Campo, must be made by shuttle bus.

The hotel rooms are located in two-story stuccoed buildings with red tin roofs. We stayed in two rooms, number 419 and the room immediately downstairs. Both were virtually identical. They certainly are not the pinnacle of luxury like the Four Seasons resort on Nevis. The bathrooms, although basic, are spacious and well maintained. Everything works. Cable television and minibars are standard features. The central complex of buildings is undeniably elegant. Fellow travelers here during our visit included many Europeans and several big American business groups.

Casa de Campo. PO Box 140, La Romana, Dominican Republic. Tel: 800-877-3643 or 011-809-523-3333. Fax: 809-523-8394. 430 rooms and villas. Double rooms range from $180 to $225 in high season. Two-bedroom villas cost $445 per night in high season. Golf, meals, and 23 percent tax are extra. Credit cards accepted.

RESTAURANTS

Casa de Campo operates nine restaurants, three near the central complex, one at the beach, one at the golf clubhouse, and four at Altos de Chavón. **Casa del Rio,** a French restaurant with gourmet specialties, is the resort's most elegant place to dine; the view overlooking the Chavón River is inspiring, much more so than the food. The most expensive entrée on the menu, the marinated salmon, costs about $12. We enjoyed the pre-golf breakfasts at **Lago Grill,** which includes freshly squeezed juices of every type, fresh fruit, and omelettes made to order. Lago Grill is also good for lunch. It has a friendly staff and a fine view of Teeth of the Dog. You will want to spend a morning or afternoon at Minitas Beach. Casa de Campo operates a very agreeable outdoor seafood restaurant there called **El Pescador,** a delightful spot for lunch. Our dinner in the **La Tropicana** dining room was not nearly as satisfying. **La Piazzetta** is an Italian restaurant that features homemade pasta and a large antipasto bar. The dress code for men at Casa de Campo's most elegant restaurants is a collared shirt and long pants.

The restaurants at Casa de Campo. PO Box 140, La Romana, Dominican Republic. Tel: 800-877-3643 or 809-523-3333. Fax: 809-523-8394. Credit cards accepted.

NON-GOLF ACTIVITIES

Horseback riding is a major activity at Casa de Campo, which is one of the only resorts we know where novices can take polo lessons and actually play in a polo match especially designed for beginners. Half and full-day snorkeling and scuba-diving trips are available, as is deep-sea fishing, tennis on thirteen clay courts, a range of shooting and hunting options, and a fitness center.

GETTING THERE: This one is easy. The plane to La Romana and Casa de Campo comes in on a runway that bisects a fairway on the resort's Teeth of the Dog golf course. When you know your flight details, inform the hotel, which will arrange for a van to transport you from the airport to your room.

Nevis

▶THE FOUR SEASONS RESORT

GOLF AND THE VOLCANO

	The Golf	Golf Services	Lodging	Restaurants	Non-Golf Activities	Total
Rating	17	17	20	17	19	90

The small, dreamlike, and nearly perfectly round island of Nevis—in brilliantly clear Caribbean waters an hour's flight from San Juan, Puerto Rico—measures a mere fifty square miles. Most of Nevis is taken up by a massive, cone-shaped volcano called Mount Nevis, which reaches 3,596 feet in elevation. Technically speaking, Mount Nevis is an active volcano, but its extremely sporadic activity is hardly menacing. It periodically puffs out a few

Nevis

whiffs of smoke and produces just enough heat to warm the supposedly medicinal waters in the municipal baths of Charlestown, Nevis's capital city, which has a population of 4,000. This particular volcano, in fact, is somehow so benign and friendly that the super-luxury Four Seasons group chose Nevis as the site for its stunning resort hotel, one of the most spectacular resort complexes in the entire Caribbean. The Four Seasons resort on Nevis has something for hedonists and sportsmen alike. For golfers, it comes equipped with a Robert Trent Jones, Jr., golf course—a dazzling championship affair, not your standard Caribbean resort course—that begins near the beach, ascends the vivid green of the volcano, and finishes back at the sandy shoreline. Nevis sounded so good that we had to go and see it for ourselves. In retrospect, our only regret is that we did not stay longer.

Nevis's dreamlike attributes are its two most memorable physical features: its flat beach that rises so precipitously to the volcano peak and the huge white cloud that perpetually hangs over the top of Mount Nevis. It is always sunny on the beach and always cloudy in the rain forest atop Mount Nevis. Sometimes, when the wind is blowing, a fine mist of rain from the mountaintop will blow down on you—much like the Evian spritzers administered to beachcombers by the Four Seasons staff. When Christopher Columbus discovered Nevis and its sister island, St. Kitts, on his second journey to the New World, he was struck, as you will be today, by this very strange white cloud. Columbus named the island Nuestra Señora de las Nieves (Our Lady of the Snows), shortened over the centuries to Nevis.

Nevis and St. Kitts broke from Britain in 1983 to form an independent nation. The combined population of both islands is 44,000, and the British influence endures. Princess Diana is a regular December visitor, everyone speaks English, the customs officials in St. Kitts Airport dress like British master sergeants, and the inhabitants of the island are apt to bear English colonial names like Alistair, Nigel, and Philip. Neither crime nor racism seems to be a problem here, and there is not a shred of anti-American sentiment. Nevis is about as close to paradise as one can get.

But it takes a full day of travel to get to Nevis. We left Washington, D.C., on an 8 A.M. flight and finally arrived in our room at five o'clock in the afternoon. You fly to San Juan and from there on dependable American Eagle (in a comfortable ATR–44) to Golden Rock Airport in St. Kitts, where you clear customs. Customs can be arduous; all of our bags were carefully searched. *And remember: a current passport is required.* Then the journey becomes an adventure. The Four Seasons staff greets you at the St. Kitts Airport, takes charge of your reassembled luggage, and transfers you by van to its luxurious private launch for a forty-five-minute ride across the water to Nevis. Room assignments and payment details are attended to during this boat crossing. The delicious rum punch served on board softens the blow of the high prices. You dock at the Four Seasons private pier and walk across the hot white sand to your beautiful room. It's a stunning way to arrive.

THE GOLF 17

The breathtaking views from the upper reaches of the golf course—of the island, the beach, cruise ships out at sea, and neighboring St. Kitts—are so amazing that a non-golf-ing spouse might just want to come along for the ride. A number of other interesting sights help lend Nevis its unique character-istics: packs of goats, island boys selling balls they have retrieved from the under-brush, jungle ravines, exotic foliage, and, most of all, Mount Nevis. Half the time you strike your ball directly at the volcano. This is a great, uphill-downhill layout that encompasses radical changes in scenery, terrain, and even microclimate, but you al-

The Four Seasons Resort

ways know you are at a Four Seasons. The drinks trolley that roams the course, for ex-ample, also dispenses sanitized cold towels to the perspiring golfers.

Competent golfers are urged to play this course from the back tees (6,766 yards). The middle tees (6,199 yards) shorten the course too much and diminish the grandeur of certain holes, especially numbers ten and fifteen. The prettiest hole on the front side—and simultaneously the toughest hole on the entire course—is number eight, a long, uphill par five with an incredible view of the Caribbean. How-ever, the signature hole—and the highest point on the course—is fifteen, the 663-yard, downhill par five. There are no gimmes among the par threes, every green is a challenge, and you have a real sense of satisfaction at the end of the day.

The golf course—thanks to a freak rainstorm the day before—was not in peak condition during our recent visit. Sand had washed away from some of the bunkers, and the eighteenth fairway looked awful. The gracious head pro told us that the French firm that constructed the course had never built a golf course before, and, consequently, there were serious erosion problems with the bunkers almost every time it rained hard. The Four Seasons has worked diligently to rectify this deficiency and is committed to maintaining the course in the best possible manner.

Nevis. Four Seasons Resort Nevis, PO Box 565, Pinney's Beach, Charlestown, Nevis, West Indies. Tel: 800-332-3442 or 869-469-1111. Fax: 869-469-1112. Credit cards accepted.

• 1991. Designer: Robert Trent Jones, Jr. Par 71. 6,766 yards. Greens fees: $110 (guest), $135 (public). Cart included. No walking. Caddies available. Season: year-round.

GOLF SERVICES

Golf services are very good, there is a lovely practice area and a nice pro shop. The pro sponsors frequent golf clinics and is available for lessons. Walking is not permitted on this steep course except when torrential rains keep carts from the course. Regrettably, the golf clubhouse lacks a restaurant.

LODGING

Year in and year out the readers of *Condé Nast Traveler* magazine rate the **Four Seasons Resort Nevis** at or near the top of the list for the best resort destinations in the world. All we can say is: with good reason! The twelve individual hotel buildings grouped around the elegant, plantation-style Great House are designed in a simple island idiom, but on the inside the spacious and very romantic guest rooms are purest luxury: colonial-style furnishings in handsome mahogany and wicker, a huge marble bathroom with a large shower and Jacuzzi tub, and private patios overlooking the beach. CNN and HBO are available on cable television, and the fax edition of *The New York Times* is delivered to your room with breakfast every morning. We stayed in room 713 and loved it.

In the Great House you will find the reception desk, sports activities desk, the resort's two exquisite restaurants (the beautifully decorated Dining Room and the less formal Grill Room), two or three lovely shops, the children's center, and two very stylish bars. The staff is so willing to please, so naturally cordial, and obviously very proud of its Four Seasons affiliation. Friendliness reigns.

The Four Seasons is not inexpensive. A seven-day golfer's package—called the "Caribbean Golf Vacation"—costs $6,650 per room and includes accommodations in a deluxe oceanfront room, unlimited golf, cart, breakfast, and dinner for two. All transfers, taxes, and service charges are fully included. The only extras you pay for are lunch each day, motorized water sports, and your beverage tab. During the off season from May 1 to November 14 the cost of this golf package drops to between $3,600 and $5,100.

Four Seasons Resort Nevis. PO Box 565, Pinney's Beach, Charlestown, Nevis, West Indies. Tel: 800-332-3442 or 869-469-1111. Fax: 869-469-1112. 196 rooms and suites. Doubles range from $575 to $625, but most guests come on five- to seven-night packages. Credit cards accepted.

RESTAURANTS

The cuisine at the Four Seasons is excellent. Both the Dining Room and the Grill Room are located in the Great House. Dinners in the **Dining Room** are absolutely delectable: spicy Caribbean lobster, monkfish, swordfish, perch, duck, beef, fine salads, and a great selection of French and American wines. The buffet breakfast served in the **Grill Room** is a dream: hot apple beignets, fresh pastries, eggs, and a cornucopia of exotic fruit. Dinner in the Grill Room features lighter fare from an à la carte menu. In addition, a couple of times each week there is a lavish poolside dinner buffet. Service throughout the resort can only be described as sublime. The dress code is casual for dinner, but men must wear shirts with a collar. When we asked what to wear to dinner in the Dining Room we were told: "a smile." On Nevis, smiling comes easily.

The restaurants at the Four Seasons Resort Nevis. PO Box 565, Pinney's Beach, Charlestown, Nevis, West Indies. Tel: 800-332-3442 or 869-469-1111. Fax: 869-469-1112. Credit cards accepted.

NON-GOLF ACTIVITIES   19

Even the most addicted golfer will be lured from the course to participate in other activities at the Four Seasons. There are ten all-weather and clay tennis courts (three are lighted for night play), a fully equipped health club with a complete range of equipment and services, guided tours of Charlestown and the rain forest, deep-sea fishing, and stupendous snorkeling and scuba diving on the extensive coral reefs off St. Kitts. Novices ourselves, we went on a thrilling, two-hour snorkeling trip across the narrows to the clear waters of St. Kitts in

The Four Seasons Resort

the company of Ken, a New Jersey native who spends six months a year on Nevis. Be sure to ask for Ken if you plan to snorkel. He is a superb guide. Other beach activities at the Four Seasons include windsurfers, motorized inner tubes, and easy-to-handle catamarans, all available for rent.

When night falls, Nevis becomes even more intoxicating. The steel-drum band is playing, the torch lamps are burning, the frogs and crickets are singing in the trees, a half moon is shining in the sky, and the wind is blowing up from the sea. You may find yourself dancing.

GETTING THERE: Most arriving guests fly first to San Juan and take an American Eagle flight to St. Kitts. When you know your flight itinerary, call the resort with the details. Four Seasons Nevis will meet you at St. Kitts and transport you by boat to the resort. The cost of this transfer is included in resort packages.

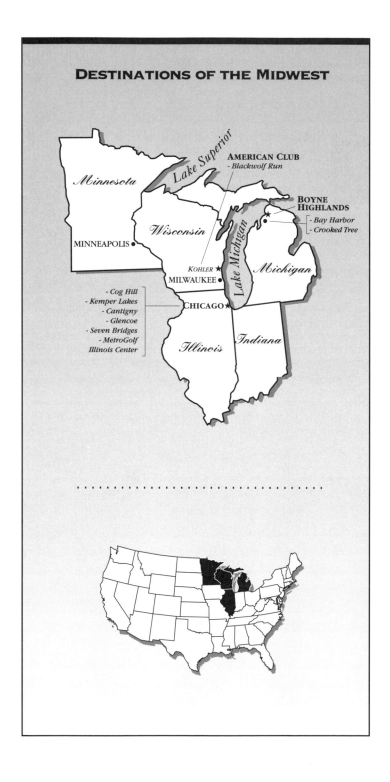

DESTINATIONS OF THE MIDWEST

Lake Superior

Minnesota

Wisconsin

MINNEAPOLIS •

AMERICAN CLUB
- Blackwolf Run

BOYNE HIGHLANDS
- Bay Harbor
- Crooked Tree

KOHLER ★

MILWAUKEE •

Lake Michigan

Michigan

- Cog Hill
- Kemper Lakes
- Cantigny
- Glencoe
- Seven Bridges
- MetroGolf
Illinois Center

CHICAGO ★

Illinois

Indiana

THE MIDWESTERN UNITED STATES

THE MIDWESTERN UNITED STATES

The cities of the East, and of the long Pacific slope are important, but they are not the heart of the country. They talk more, and mean less. They travel the world and broaden their minds but when the ill winds begin to blow it is not the East and West that stand unshakable. It is that valley in the middle that cannot be conquered.

—**A. D. Macdonnell,** *A Visit to America,* **1935**

Since 1992 the central Midwest (Michigan, Indiana, Ohio, and Illinois) has led the nation in new golf course starts, and many of the courses—old and new—throughout the entire Midwest merit your consideration for a golf getaway. The area from the central Great Lakes to the western plains remains vastly underrated as a golf destination, in part because of the persistence of a couple of erroneous assumptions. We at GOLF TRAVEL want to put to bed the myth that the Midwest is boring. Whoever said that the region is flat and its inhabitants even flatter obviously has never been to the upper Great Lakes. Could Minnesota—the "Land of 10,000 Lakes" and the state that inspired the characters of Lake Wobegon—really be boring? The resurgence of the Green Bay Packers has rekindled the nation's love affair with the honest folks up in Wisconsin, while Chicago remains one of the most friendly and fascinating cities in America. And, just a short drive from the automobile assembly lines, Michigan proves to be one vast and varied playground—if you time it right.

There's another element about Chicago and Wisconsin and the upper Great Lakes that we, as golfers, are reminded of during football season, when officials are often busy shoveling snow and ice off the playing field in order just to see the yardage markers. While watching the Packers we caught a bone-shivering glimpse of the *frozen tundra* . . . need we say more?

Yes, the Midwest can be the nation's ice bucket. Every year we track the region's winters with blind wonder and awesome respect for those who bear them, and we also thank our lucky stars not to be buried under a blizzard of snow the way they are. Anyone who lives near the upper Great Lakes will tell you, however, that the summers are divine. This is a true vacationland—all the better appreciated because of those long, harsh winters—that, come summertime, lures hundreds of thousands of families to its friendly cities, lakes, parks, resorts, and, increasingly, its golf courses.

Admittedly, the golf season is frustratingly short in the upper Midwest. But golf travelers who come here to play from late spring to early autumn will discover an unforgettable golfing experience. The combination of abundant land, the stark beauty of the Great Lakes setting, and the work of some of the best golf course architects makes you wish you had discovered the Midwest long ago.

Rustic northern Michigan is home to Boyne USA, a high-powered resort operation that includes the Bay Harbor Golf Club and Boyne Highlands. The new courses at Bay Harbor, situated right on a spectacular, rocky section of Lake Michigan, are reminiscent of Pebble Beach and the Links at Spanish Bay. The best two courses at Boyne Highlands are the Heather Course, designed by Robert Trent Jones, Sr., and the Donald Ross Memorial Course, which features a painstakingly accurate, computer-enhanced re-creation of Ross's greatest signature holes.

Golf travelers who journey to Wisconsin are also in for a real treat; the American Club rates as one of the two or three best golf resort destinations not only in the United States but in the world. That's right, better than more famous meccas

216

such as Pebble Beach and the Boulders in the United States and Gleneagles in Scotland. The two Pete Dye championship courses at the American Club's Blackwolf Run golf operation annually host the Andersen Consulting Million Dollar Match Play Tournament, and in 1998 they will host the U.S. Women's Open. Also in 1998, a new Dye course, situated on a peerless, windswept Lake Michigan site, will be unveiled at the resort. Called Whistling Straits, the course will closely resemble a traditional Scottish links, with absolutely no carts allowed!

The American Club is just two and a half hours by car from Chicago's O'Hare Airport, but don't speed away from Chicago too hastily. The Chicago metropolitan area boasts eight of the top hundred courses in the country, which is reason alone for residents to walk a bit haughtily even before we mention the fabulous museums, the skyscrapers and wonderful architecture known worldwide as the Chicago School, the Magnificent Mile on Michigan Avenue, one of the world's great bastions of learning—the University of Chicago—and, of course, Michael Jordan and the Bulls. And yet, where denizens of other cities would have developed a veneer of arrogance, Chicago residents remain delightfully unpretentious, as befits the entire Midwest. Chicago is, at heart, a working-class city, and its golf is likewise, at heart, public.

Whether you are in the city for business or pleasure, we urge you to explore the myriad, outstanding, public-access courses in the Windy City. Cog Hill, Kemper Lakes, Glencoe Golf Club, Cantigny, and Seven Bridges are the best in the area, but do not miss the nine-hole layout at MetroGolf Illinois Center, which sits in the midst of the city's skyscrapers and bills itself as "the ultimate urban golf experience."

So do yourself a favor and follow us to the Midwest. Along the way, take in a major- or minor-league baseball game (the Chicago Cubs still play most of their games in glorious sunlight), tour a maritime museum, and go fishing. To get the most out of your trip, do yourself another favor and take your upper Midwest golfing vacation no earlier than late spring and no later than early autumn.

Michigan

▶BAY HARBOR AND BOYNE HIGHLANDS

NORTHERN MICHIGAN AT ITS BEST

	The Golf	Golf Services	Lodging	Restaurants	Non-Golf Activities	Total
Rating	18	18	15	15	16	82

Boyne USA, the extremely well run northern Michigan resort company that caters to skiers during the winter months, turns its attention to golfers from May through September with three distinctive properties, including the highly regarded and ever-improving Boyne Highlands, the just slightly less appealing Boyne Mountain, and the brand-new and utterly spectacular Bay Harbor. Located just ninety minutes north of the Traverse City Airport, Boyne Highlands is unquestionably the premier, full-service golf resort in the brisk, windswept landscape of northern Michigan, a region long known to golf insiders and vacationers as a hotbed of great golf.

Boyne Highlands

Northern Michigan has always enjoyed popularity as a simple summer retreat, an escape getaway to a rustic cabin in the woods, and the remote setting for some of Ernest Hemingway's fabulous fishing fables. High-powered Bay Harbor—with its $3 million homes and yacht club on Lake Michigan, its equestrian center and twenty-seven knockout holes of golf designed by Arthur Hills—is in the process of transforming that rustic reputation. Bay Harbor intends to become the ultimate residential-golfing-yachting-riding community in otherwise low-key northern Michigan.

The advertising copywriters trying to come up with a sensational slogan for the extraordinary golf course at the Bay Harbor development laud it as the "Pebble Beach of the Midwest." The ad campaign conveys (albeit a bit unimaginatively) the majesty of the new course and its gorgeous lakeside setting. Bay Harbor is built on high, grassy, windy bluffs overlooking Lake Michigan, just south of Petoskey, on the site of the former Penn-Dixie cement plant. Only the first nine holes (the Links) are currently open for play, but seven of the nine offer sensational views of Lake Michigan, hence the inevitable comparisons with Pebble.

Indeed, you will discover—after processing all the hype—that super-upscale Bay Harbor offers the best holes of golf in all northern Michigan. The Links is a glorious track and already one of the top golf courses in the Midwest. The Quarry nine is scheduled to open in mid-1997, and the final nine, the Preserve, will open in late 1997. Jack Berry, secretary of the Golf Writers Association of America, has said of Bay Harbor: "There is nothing like it in the Midwest." But you had better get there within the next couple of years. Bay Harbor will remain public access only until it sells out its private memberships, at which point the course will be closed to the public, or at least that is the plan currently in circulation.

So here is the ideal northern Michigan scenario. Fly to Traverse City, pick up a rental car, and head north. Check into Boyne Highlands, and play first at Bay Harbor. Then play the outstanding Donald Ross Memorial Course, the idyllic Heather Course, and the nice Moor Course at Boyne Highlands. Once Bay Harbor finishes construction on its Victorian-style inn, which should be sometime in late 1998, you should certainly consider staying there. In between rounds, explore the countryside and the antique and craft shops that line the streets of the villages.

 THE GOLF

The **Links at Bay Harbor,** on bluffs high above the waters of Lake Michigan, actually reminds us more of Spanish Bay. The course features exposed sand hills, hip-high grass beyond the fairways, and forced carries over gorges and ravines. Even the harshest critic must concede two important points: the developer utilized prime, lakefront property for the golf course, and architect Hills has created a delightful and imaginative layout. During our visit in September, when we were met with bracing, sunny, typically northern Michigan weather, the massive new golf clubhouse at Bay Harbor was nearing completion and nearly all the cart paths had been installed.

To date, only a handful of new homes have been built on the course, but we found one hole, the fourth—Bay Harbor's signature hole, a fabulous, downhill par three on the shores of Lake Michigan—disfigured by an enormous, new mansion built beyond the gully that lurks just behind the undulating green. From the dramatically elevated tee, this house is dangerously within range. It certainly throws off the golfer standing high on the tee trying to figure out the distance and select the right club. We wager that the owner of this impressive new mansion can look forward to several broken windows every summer. It is a shame for golfer and homeowner alike and the only unfortunate ingredient we noted at Bay Harbor.

Numbers three, four (despite the mansion), five, seven, and eight are outstanding golf holes. Three is a great, downhill par four that requires a laser-straight drive and a short iron down to a postage-stamp green. Five is a strategic par four. Drive the ball over the huge sand hill, and play the second shot onto the green from about 125 yards, or lay up off the tee in front of the sand hill, which leaves you with a blind second shot of 165 yards. Seven is an eye-popping par five that demands a drive over a grassy waste and features a green perched on the edge of a cliff above Lake Michigan. Eight is another long (225 yards), dramatic, downhill par three. The course was in beautiful condition when we played it.

With its steep slopes, long distances between green and tee, and large waste areas between tee and fairway, the Links at Bay Harbor is not a walking course, and tee selection is critical. This course will devour mid- to high-handicappers who ill-advisedly choose to play from the back tees. From the tips, the Links measures 3,432 yards; from the middle tees, it is 3,023 yards long; and from the forward tees it measures 2,661 yards. The forthcoming **Quarry** and **Preserve** nines will each measure approximately 3,400 yards from the tips.

Additionally, Boyne USA now manages the **Crooked Tree Golf Club,** which is located right across the street from the Bay Harbor Golf Club. This picturesque Harry Bowers–designed course overlooks the water. Guests of Boyne Highlands are entitled to discount greens fees at both Bay Harbor and Crooked Tree, and the Boyne Highlands golf staff will gladly book your tee times at these clubs.

Boyne Highlands has five courses. The **Heather Course,** designed by Robert Trent Jones Sr., is located immediately adjacent to the hotel at Boyne Highlands. The Bill Newcomb–designed **Moor Course,** the **Donald Ross Memorial Course,** and the new **Arthur Hills Course,** which is now just nine holes but soon to be expanded to eighteen, are all situated at the country club, about a mile from the hotel. Boyne Highlands also has a par three **Executive Course** and an excellent practice facility. Noted golf instructor Jim Flick, who has a summer home here, runs a Nicklaus-Flick Golf School at Boyne Highlands.

By far the two best layouts at Boyne Highlands are the Donald Ross Memorial Course and the Heather Course. The Moor Course is considered the easiest of the lot.

The **Donald Ross Memorial Course,** named the best new U.S. resort course in 1990 by *Golf Digest,* is a composite of eighteen classic golf holes designed by Ross. Armed with grids and blueprints, engineers traveled to Ross's most renowned courses in order to re-create the distances, bunkers, hazards, and green complexes that were Ross trademarks.

These holes—based on holes at Seminole, Pinehurst Number 2, Oakland Hills, Inverness, Royal Dornoch, and Bob O'Link, among others—are obviously not exact copies of the originals, but they are very convincing facsimiles. The Seminole replicas are the least successful because Boyne is located in northern Michigan, not tropical Florida, yet, as a whole, the Donald Ross Course captures the flavor and philosophy of many of the Ross courses we have played around America and provides a taste of the famous private courses Ross designed that the passionate golfer may never get the chance to experience firsthand. It is equally important to add that this is an excellent and exquisitely maintained course even without the Ross association.

The best holes include number ten, a copy of *Foxy* (the fourteenth at Royal Dornoch); the sixteenth, taken from Pinehurst Number 2; and the difficult home hole, number eighteen, a copy of the sixteenth hole at Oakland Hills.

The Ross Memorial Course is 6,840 yards (par rating 73.4/slope rating 132) from the back tees, 6,308 yards from the middle tees (par rating 70.9/slope rating 128), and 4,977 yards from the forward tees (par rating 68.5/slope rating 119).

The pretty **Heather Course,** the top-rated resort course in all of Michigan according to *Golf Digest,* features wide fairways lined with thick forests and water hazards in play on ten of its eighteen holes. Like the Ross Course, a round on the Heather is a peaceful and idyllic outing, although overcrowding and slow play can plague all the Boyne Highlands courses during the height of summer. The best holes on the Heather Course include the fifth, a long par five that doglegs left around a lake; the ninth, a wonderful, uphill par five that finishes in front of the Tudor-style clubhouse; and the absolutely tantalizing eighteenth, a long downhill par four. Try to hit your tee shot on eighteen into the neck of the fairway left of the lake, a position offering a far easier approach to the green. Taking this lake out of play for your approach is critical: over 40,000 balls were hit into it last year.

The Heather is 7,210 yards long from the tips (par rating 74.0/slope rating 131), 6,527 yards from the middle tees (par rating 71.2/slope rating 126), and 5,245 yards from the forward tees (par rating 67.8/slope rating 111).

Bay Harbor Golf Club. 850 Vista Drive, Bay Harbor, MI 49770. Tel: 800-462-6963, 616-439-4028, or 616-549-6026. Fax: 616-439-2020 or 616-549-6094. Credit cards accepted.

• *The Links at Bay Harbor.* 1996. Designer: Arthur Hills. Par 36. 3,432 yards. Greens fees: guests: $67 (early May and October), $83 (mid-May and September), $110 (June–August), cart included. Public: $84 (early May and October), $105 (mid-May and September), $140 (June–August), cart included. No walking. No caddies. Season: May 1 to October 31.

Crooked Tree Golf Club. 600 Crooked Tree Drive, Petoskey, MI 49770. Tel: 800-462-6963 or 616-348-7000. Fax: 616-439-2020.

• 1995. Designer: Harry Bowers. Par 71. 6,584 yards. Par rating 72.8. Slope rating 140. Greens fees: Boyne resort guests $39 (early May and October), $56 (mid-May and September), $65 (June–August), cart included. Public $45 (early May and October), $56 (mid-May and September), $75 (June–August), cart included. Walking permitted after 5 p.m. No caddies. Carts available. Season: May 1 to October 31.

Boyne Highlands. 600 Highlands Drive, Harbor Springs, MI 49740. Tel: 800-462-6963 or 616-549-6026. Fax: 616-526-3095 or 616-549-6094. Credit cards accepted.

• *Donald Ross Memorial Course.* 1989. Designer: Boyne Highlands, from replicas of historic Donald Ross holes. Par 72. 6,840 yards. 73.4 par rating. 132 slope rating. Greens fees: guests: $48 (early May, October)/$60 (mid-May and September)/$80 (June–August), cart included. Public: $60 (early May and October), $75 (mid-May and September), $99 (June–August), cart included. No walking. No caddies. Season: May 1–October 31.

• *Heather Course.* 1990. Designer: Robert Trent Jones, Sr. Par 72. 7,210 yards. 74.0 par rating. 131 slope rating. Greens fees: guests $51 (early May and October), $64 (mid-May and September), $85 (June–August), cart included. Public: $66 (early May and October), $83 (mid-May and September), $110 (June–August), cart included. Walking permitted after 5 p.m. No caddies. Season: May 1–October 31.

• *Moor Course.* 1975. Designer: William Newcomb. Par 72. 6,973 yards. Par rating 74.0. Slope rating 131. Greens fees: guests $36 (early May and October), $45 (mid-May and September), $60 (June–August), cart included. Public $42 (early May and October), $53 (mid-May and September), $70 (June–August), cart included. Walking permitted after 5 p.m. No caddies. Carts available. Season: May 1 to October 31.

GOLF SERVICES

Golf services are outstanding at Boyne Highlands. Both of its golf complexes—at the Heather Course and the country club—have terrific pro shops stocked with fine merchandise, friendly personnel, fine practice ranges, and smiling bag attendants who hustle to get you out on the course. Golf staff members are glad to see you. Even the groundskeepers wave as they drive by on their mowers. Instruction is a big part of the Boyne Highlands golf scene. Boyne is the site of a Woman's Week of Golf, the Nicklaus-Flick school, and a Junior Golf Academy for juniors between the ages of ten and eighteen. Not a detail has been left out. Roving bar and restaurant carts offer food and drink, and we loved the computerized "Yardmark" range finders installed on all the carts, the best computer range finders we have seen. Although practice facilities will not be ready at the Bay Harbor Golf Club this season, the upscale clubhouse offers a fine restaurant, lounge, and locker room.

LODGING

Once it opens in late 1998 or early 1999, the new Inn at Bay Harbor will easily surpass the quality of the quite standard guest accommodations at **Boyne Highlands.** Our somewhat dull-looking room at Boyne Highlands (number 322) was really no better than average. Television was the only amenity—no minibar and no room service. On the positive side, the hotel at Boyne Highlands is surrounded by attractive gardens and is within walking distance of the Heather Course. Room rates range from $140 to $310 in peak season. Full golf packages that include room, golf with cart, breakfast, and dinner are $135 per person per day.

Boyne Highlands. 600 Highlands Drive, Harbor Springs, MI 49740. Tel: 800-462-6963 or 616-526-3000. Fax: 616-526-3095. Over 400 rooms and condos. Doubles cost $95 to $155 from June through August and $57 to $93 the rest of the year. Credit cards accepted.

RESTAURANTS

The dining options at Boyne Highlands are not especially distinguished. By far the best restaurant in the resort complex is the elegant golf **Clubhouse Dining Room,** where the dinner menu includes local whitefish from Lake Michigan, veal, beef, lamb, salmon, and lobster, accompanied by a reasonably good selection of wines. The comfortable **bar and grill** in the clubhouse is the ideal spot for lunch after a round on the Ross Course. **Bartley House** features a mostly Italian menu. The **main hotel restaurant** at **Boyne Highlands,** however, is a disappointment. The room itself is somewhat dreary and unattractive, the service is poor, and the food only fair. Dinner entrées range between $17 and $21, except for the shrimp platter and rack of lamb, which cost $26.

The restaurants at Boyne Highlands. 600 Highlands Drive, Harbor Springs, MI 49740. Tel: 800-462-6963 or 616-526-3000. Fax: 616-526-3095. Credit cards accepted.

NON-GOLF ACTIVITIES

Other activities at Boyne Highlands take a distant backseat to golf, but tennis, croquet, swimming, and supervised children's programs are available. In July and August, the Young Americans, a music and dance ensemble, present a popular dinner theater at the resort. The Gaslight District in nearby Petoskey has over a hundred specialty shops.

GETTING THERE: Boyne Highlands is about a four-and-a-half-hour drive from Detroit. Go north on I-75, get off at exit 282 (Gaylord), turn left, take 32 West, and follow this to the junction of Route 32 and US 131. Go north on US 131, through Petoskey and Bay View. Turn left onto M-119, proceed four miles to Pleasant View Road, then turn right, go another four miles, and follow signs to Boyne Highlands. The closest airport to the resort is Pellston Regional Airport, about ten miles away. Take Route 31 into Pellston, turn right onto Robinson Road, then take a left onto Pleasant View Road, and Boyne will be ahead a bit on the right.

Illinois

▶CHICAGO

WINDY CITY GOLF

	The Golf	Golf Services	Lodging	Restaurants	Non-Golf Activities	Total
Rating	18	18	19	18	17	**90**

Chicago—in our estimation—is the greatest city for golf in the United States.

Think we're exaggerating? Then ask Mickey Powell, former honorary president of the PGA of America. "Chicago is a hotbed of golf. There isn't anywhere in the country where you will find so many fine golf courses within a fifty-mile radius," Powell said.

According to *Golf Digest*, eight of the nation's top hundred golf courses are within an hour's drive of the city. "Eight percent of the hundred best golf courses in America are in the Chicago metro area. That's incredible," Powell continued. "Florida—the whole state—has more courses ranked in the top hundred [ten], but they're not in one small cluster as they are in metropolitan Chicago."

Chicago boasts a distinguished golfing pedigree. The great golfer and influential golf course architect Charles Blair Macdonald was a Chicago native. By 1899 nineteen golf clubs had been established in Chicago. Prior to 1934, the city's courses had hosted the U.S. Open nine times. Today, Chicago is the home of superb private clubs like Skokie, Bob O'Link, Medinah, Chicago Golf Club, Onwentsia, North Shore, and Northmoor.

Yet Chicago, at bottom, is a great public links town. In fact, the true spirit of Chicago, golf-wise at least, is public links. Chicago is the least snobbish, most down-to-earth, and friendliest of our major cities. Only a city with the populist texture and immigrant history of Chicago, for example, could give rise to a character like Studs Terkel, the celebrated author, raconteur, and working-class hero.

Chicago, not coincidentally, also produced Joe Jemsek, who might be called the Studs Terkel of American golf. Jemsek, owner of Cog Hill, has been dubbed "the father of public golf." In 1995 Jemsek was honored with the William D. Richardson Award by the Golf Writers' Association of America for his contributions to golf. Since acquiring Cog Hill in 1951, Jemsek has always set the tone in Chicago. The unique atmosphere at Cog Hill, a friendly and low-key flavor combined with remarkable golf, ought to be experienced at least once by every passionate golf pilgrim.

Chicago's plethora of fine links might seem the perfect balm for the strains of the workaday world, and so they would be, but for one fly in the ointment: the city's absolutely abysmal climate. The sole element that plagues Chicago golf is the frequently dreary weather: dark, overcast, cold, and windy conditions that prevent golfers from playing in earnest until mid-May.

From June through October, however, the play at Chicago's wonderful public-access golf courses to the west, north, and northwest of the city—all within an hour's drive of the Magnificent Mile of North Michigan Avenue—is comfortable and thoroughly enjoyable. Chicago boasts two truly fantastic city hotels—the new Four Seasons, located in a stunning Art Deco skyscraper, and the Ritz-Carlton, recently voted the premier city hotel in all America. No matter where you stay, you will find a superb collection of restaurants, outstanding shopping, a spectacular city skyline, and an airport that never sleeps. You can also enjoy one of the most amusing and amazing city golf experiences anywhere on earth in the shadow of the ninety-story Standard Oil building at MetroGolf Illinois Center (see below). But if you come in the spring or fall, just pretend it is Scotland, and don't forget to bring your rain suit and long johns.

For the record, the eight golf courses in the Chicago metropolitan area in the top hundred are Kemper Lakes (public), Butler National (private), Medinah Country Club (private), Olympia Fields (private), Chicago Golf Club (private), Bob O'Link (private), North Shore (private), and Cog Hill Number Four (public). A spectacular public facility in Wheaton, Cantigny Golf, was named the best new public course in America by *Golf Digest* in 1989. Cantigny (along with Kemper Lakes and Cog Hill) is also listed among *Golf Digest*'s top twenty-five public courses in America.

As always, our ratings, recommendations, and candid commentary are based on a recent, anonymous visit to each establishment.

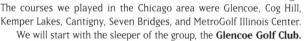

THE GOLF 18

The courses we played in the Chicago area were Glencoe, Cog Hill, Kemper Lakes, Cantigny, Seven Bridges, and MetroGolf Illinois Center. We will start with the sleeper of the group, the **Glencoe Golf Club.** Since over 40,000 rounds are played here each year, Glencoe is hardly an unknown entity in the Chicago area. With its elegant older layout nestled in a beautiful setting, Glencoe has obvious charms, yet it is not in the same world-class category as the other trophy courses on our list. However, its greens fee is a very reasonable $33, which is less than half of what you pay elsewhere, making it one of the great Chicago golf bargains.

Located twenty miles north of Chicago on the wonderful North Shore, the village of Glencoe is one of Chicago's prettiest and most affluent suburbs. The old Glencoe Golf Club was created in 1921, but its exact ancestry remains unclear. Donald Ross, of Dornoch, Scotland, created the Skokie Country Club (also in Glencoe) and the course at Northmoor Country Club (in nearby Highland Park). The staff at Glencoe likes to claim that Ross—or one of his protégés—had a hand in the design of their course. Indeed, Glencoe fits the typical Ross profile, with natural contours and simple bunkering that allow you to play a bump-and-run onto almost every green. Little seems to have changed at Glencoe. Family continuity is a tradition here: the club's management has rested in the Poletti family for three generations. Waddy Poletti was the longtime manager, and today his pleasant grandson manages the operation. The tidy collection of three little half-timbered buildings at the Glencoe Golf Club—the pro shop, the restaurant/locker rooms, and the bag storage shed in the shade of towering trees—has also remained unchanged for nearly seventy-five years. These buildings constitute a charming Tudor "village" in their own right.

For a championship layout, Glencoe is on the short side. Good golfers can score well here and feel marvelous about golf and life after their round is complete. The course measures 6,517 yards from the tips (70.9 par rating/121 slope rating), 6,233 yards from the regular tees (68.9 par rating/118 slope rating), and 5,713 yards from the front (71.8 par rating/117 slope rating), with not a single weak hole on the course. Memorable holes include both the first and the second. Your first drive of the day from the grassy terrace in front of the pro shop will soar toward a green that is perched atop a modest hill four hundred yards away. Your drive on number two, a 527-yard par five, sends you careening back down the hill along a narrowing fairway that features deep woods along the entire right side. Five is a good score on the second, Glencoe's number one handicap hole. Number six is another fine hole on the front side, a short 359-yard par four bordering the beautiful Botanical Gardens that has a small lake guarding the right side of the green. The final two holes at Glencoe, numbers seventeen and eighteen (two par fives), present challenges aplenty: seventeen is a long 508-yard dogleg that makes a ninety-degree turn to the left, and eighteen measures 536 yards straight into powerful prevailing winds.

Cog Hill

Cog Hill Number Four in Lemont, Illinois, about an hour west of downtown Chicago, rates five stars in *Golf Digest's Places to Play*, which puts it in the same league as Pebble Beach, Pinehurst Number Two, and the astounding River Course at Blackwolf Run in Kohler, Wisconsin. Heady company indeed, particularly for a golf complex that makes such a bizarre first impression. When you drive into Cog Hill all you see at first is the vast asphalt parking lot that separates the two clubhouses: the main clubhouse, which serves courses One and Three, and a smaller, entirely nondescript building that serves courses Two and Four. On the surface, Cog Hill is as simple, wholesome, and midwestern as they come, and the atmosphere is wonderfully unpretentious. "Golf for the people" could be Cog Hill's motto. But step inside and any initial uncertainty will vanish. The Cog Hill staff is friendly, welcoming, and competent. You are made to feel at home immediately.

Cog Hill Number Four, a.k.a. Dubsdread, is the annual site of the Western Open, which is contested in the second week of July. Each May, Joe Jemsek sets up Dubsdread with the same pin positions and tee placements used during the final round of the Western Open, so public players are given the opportunity to play a championship course as it is set up for the PGA Tour. This thoughtful gesture is typical of Jemsek's love of the game. Dubsdread, however, is already difficult enough without playing the Western Open pins. In fact, only low single-digit handicaps should contemplate playing Cog Hill from the blue tees. From the white tees, Cog Hill Number Four already measures a hefty 6,354 yards (71.8/138); from the tips it measures 6,976 yards (with a par rating of 75.6 and a 142 slope). Dubsdread is long and relentless and features over a hundred massive, strategically placed sand bunkers. "Manly" is probably the best adjective to describe it. Cog Hill Number Four represents the finest work of architects Dick Wilson and Joe Lee. It is a grand collaboration between

Mother Nature (who says the Midwest is just boring and flat?), Wilson, and Jemsek's huge grounds crew, which keeps Cog Hill in peak condition.

The heart of Dubsdread is its group of extremely difficult par threes. Probably the toughest (and most picturesque) sequence of holes at Cog Hill are twelve, thirteen, and fourteen. Numbers twelve and fourteen, both par threes, are Dubsdread's fourteenth- and eighteenth-rated handicap holes, but we challenge the first-time player at Cog Hill to make par on either. Number twelve is 206 yards long, downhill, and backed by a deep ravine; hit one club too much off the tee and you are a goner. Thirteen is a gorgeous 446-yard par four with an undulating green perched on a natural ledge above the fairway. Miss the thirteenth green to the right and you are finished. Fourteen is just 190 yards long, but by now you have become so conservative in your club selection that you are bound to hit it short. The thirteenth hole is reminiscent of Royal Birkdale in England. The resemblance would be even keener were there not a massive factory across the road belching out a chemical stench. But hey, this is Chicago, City of the Big Shoulders. The number one handicap hole at Cog Hill is the ninth, an overpowering 565-yard par five that plays through an intimidating chute of mature oaks. Despite this, the back nine at Cog Hill Number Four is tougher—and steeper walking—than the front.

Cog Hill's three other courses are also worth playing, especially **Number Two,** which measures 6,268 yards from the tips (69.4 par rating/120 slope). Numbers One and Three are flatter and less interesting than Dubsdread and Number Two.

Kemper Lakes, site of the 1989 PGA Championship, the 1992 U.S. Women's Amateur, and several LPGA events, is located in Long Grove, about thirty-five miles northwest of Chicago. Kemper Lakes has a prettier, more rural setting than Cog Hill (there are no factories in Long Grove); if Cog Hill prides itself on its democratic flavor, then Kemper Lakes much more resembles an exclusive private club with its impressive contemporary clubhouse, bag-drop area, and hustling bag boys and polite cart attendants. And if Cog Hill can be described as

Kemper Lakes

manly, then Kemper Lakes's gender, like many courses favored by the LPGA, is decidedly feminine. Kemper Lakes was designed by Ken Killian and Dick Nugent, and developed in 1975 by the Kemper Insurance Company, whose modern corporate offices overlook the golf course.

As its name implies, Kemper Lakes is defined by water, particularly on its very difficult three final holes. A game at Kemper Lakes entails a beautiful rhythm. Kemper Lakes actually allows you to warm up with three fairly simple opening holes: two par fours of moderate length and a par three to a semi-island green. But after that you are on your own. The par five fourth swings dramatically from left to right around a large lake, and on the difficult seventh, a par-five 557 yards long, water is in play down the entire left-hand side. The two most beautiful holes at Kemper Lakes may be eleven and twelve. Eleven is a long, 534-yard par five that doglegs to the right, with mature oaks on both sides of a tight fairway and a creek guarding the green. Twelve is a short, uphill par four with a blind tee shot to a fairway lined with more massive old oaks. But the homestretch—sixteen, seventeen, and eighteen—will make or break your round. Sixteen is a very long (469 yards) par four with water menacing on the right; seventeen is a 203-yard par three to another semi-island green; and eighteen demands two water crossings—one on your drive, and another, more difficult, on your approach shot. If your second shot on eighteen is not both long and straight, then you are in the drink.

Despite its lovely, feminine appearance, Kemper Lakes is a haul—7,217 yards from the gold tees (75.7/140), 6,680 yards from the blues (73.2/138), 6,265 yards from the whites (71.2/132), and 5,638 from the reds (67.9/125). The greens fee (cart included) is $110 per person.

If the overall Kemper Lakes experience is a notch or two more luxurious than Cog Hill, then **Cantigny Golf,** perhaps the single most opulent public golf facility in Chicago, raises the stakes even further. Located in suburban Wheaton, thirty miles west of Chicago, Cantigny (pronounced Canteeny) is situated on the estate of Robert R. Mc-Cormick, former publisher of the *Chicago Tribune,* and is owned and operated by a foundation that was instructed by McCormick's will to create an enterprise that would serve as a source of recreation and welfare for the people of Illinois. Cantigny gets its name from the French village that was the site of the first U.S. army offensive in World War I. Mr. McCormick was an artillery commander in that battle. Cantigny today consists of three outstanding nine-hole layouts—Woodside, Lakeside, and Hillside—plus an interesting museum of World War I artifacts adjoining the golf club. Cantigny is upscale all the way—from its tree-lined entrance drive to the friendly bag attendants in knickers and knee socks to the elegant clubhouse overlooking the courses.

Woodside-Lakeside is the preferred routing at Cantigny, but all three nines are exquisitely maintained and more or less equally difficult. **Lakeside** plays the toughest of the three nines because water is in play on five of its holes. And the ninth at Lakeside is Cantigny's signature hole—certainly the most dramatic in the twenty-seven-hole complex. Lakeside, however, is popular and can be hard to get on. **Woodside's** best holes are numbers two, six, eight, and nine. Two is a very tight, 539-yard par five that requires two crossings of a creek that winds its way about the fairway. Six is a great driving hole, a handsome 440-yard par four; eight is a 165-yard par three to a semi-island green; and nine is a wonderful 420-yard par four that demands a razor-sharp second shot into a green guarded on the left by one of Cantigny's serpentine lakes. **Hillside,** which is almost as pretty as Woodside, features less water and fewer bunkers. Its most memorable hole is number six, with its large double green shared with number eight of Woodside. The greens fee at Cantigny is $65 for walkers and $80 if you use a cart.

When we first saw **MetroGolf Illinois Center** we laughed out loud—with absolute amazement and delight. Dubbed "the ultimate urban golf experience," Metro-Golf Illinois Center is a nine-hole, par-three, executive golf course designed by Dye Designs International (complete with an island-green water hole!), an enormous practice range with ninety-two hitting stations, a golf learning facility, and a 7,000-square-foot clubhouse—all located amid the skyscrapers of downtown Chicago two blocks east of Michigan Avenue. Optical illusions bring on an exhilarating sense of danger—that you can put out a window in the Standard Oil building or crack a good tee shot into the traffic on Wacker Drive. This utterly imaginative facility was created for downtown denizens taking a golf break from the office. During our visit we saw plenty of guys losing their jackets and ties for a quick nine-hole loop. The course measures 969 yards; five holes are over one hundred yards in length, four are less than one hundred yards. The ninth hole (and number one handicap) is a for-real, 142-yard shot over a lake to an island green. Illinois Center is a terrific outing, beneficial for your short game, and one of those not-to-be-missed golf experiences. The greens fee is just $12 on weekdays and $15 on weekends. The course stays open year-round, and play is possible even in the dead of winter. From April through September the facility stays open for play until 11 P.M.

Seven Bridges, a Dick Nugent—designed course in suburban Woodridge, is ranked among the top five of Chicago's public courses. This eighteen-hole course

(7,100 yards from the back tees, 74.4 par rating/132 slope) features a lovely—and rather easy—front nine and a much tougher back nine that has lots of water and some golfers describe as unnecessarily harsh. Seven Bridges takes a backseat to the other Chicago area courses noted above, but it still makes for a pleasant outing.

Glencoe Golf Club. 621 Westley Avenue, Glencoe, IL 60022. Tel: 847-835-0250. Fax: 847-837-3715. Credit cards accepted.

• 1921. Designers: original members. Par 72. 6,517 yards. 70.9 par rating. 121 slope rating. Greens fees: $33 weekdays, $35 weekends. Walking permitted. No caddies. Carts available. Season: March 15–November 15.

Cog Hill Golf and Country Club. 12294 Archer Avenue, Lemont, IL 60439. Tel: 630-257-5872. Fax: 630-257-3665. Credit cards accepted.

• *Number Four (Dubsdread).* 1964. Designers: Dick Wilson, Joe Lee. Par 72. 6,976 yards. 75.6 par rating. 142 slope rating. Greens fee: $95, includes cart. Walking permitted. Caddies available. Season: April 12–mid-October.
• *Number Two.* 1930. Designer: Burt Coghill (revised by Dick Wilson and Joe Lee). Par 71. 6,268 yards. 69.4 par rating. 120 slope rating. Greens fee: $41. Walking permitted. Caddies available. Carts cost $26. Season: mid-April–mid-October.

Kemper Lakes Golf Club. Old McHenry Road, Long Grove, IL 60049. Tel: 847-320-3450. Fax: 847-320-4315. Credit cards accepted.

• 1975. Designers: Ken Killian, Dick Nugent. Par 72. 7,217 yards. 75.7 par rating. 140 slope rating. Greens fee: $110, including cart. Walking permitted. No caddies. Carts available. Season: April 1–mid-November.

Cantigny Golf. 27 West 270 Mack Road, Wheaton, IL 60187. Tel: 630-668-8463 or 630-668-3323. Fax: 630-668-8682. Credit cards accepted.

• 1989. Designer: Roger Packard.
• *Woodside-Lakeside.* Par 72. 6,709 yards. 71.4 par rating. 130 slope rating.
• *Hillside-Woodside.* Par 72. 6,760 yards. 72.2 par rating. 125 slope rating.
• *Lakeside-Hillside.* Par 72. 6,625 yards. 71.1 par rating. 126 slope rating.
• Greens fee (all courses): $65. Walking permitted. Caddies available. Carts cost $15 per person. Season: April 15–October 31.

MetroGolf Illinois Center. 221 North Columbus (lower level), Chicago, IL 60601. Tel: 312-616-1234. Fax: 312-856-9467. Credit cards accepted.

• 1994. Designer: P. B. Dye. Par 27. 969 yards. Greens fees: $12 weekdays, $15 weekends. No caddies. No carts. Season: year-round.

Seven Bridges Golf Club. 6300 South Route 53, Woodridge, IL 60517. Tel: 630-964-7777. Fax: 630-964-7975. Credit cards accepted.

• 1991. Designer: Dick Nugent. Par 72. 7,100 yards. 74.4 par rating. 132 slope rating. Greens fee: $85, includes cart. Walking permitted. Caddies available. Season: April 1–October 15.

 GOLF SERVICES

Golf services are outstanding and the golf personnel are attentive and welcoming at all the golf courses noted above. We did not experience one service glitch during our entire golf odyssey in Chicagoland. Glencoe, of course, is the most rudimentary operation, but Cog Hill,

Cantigny, Kemper Lakes, Seven Bridges, and MetroGolf Illinois Center all have state-of-the-game facilities with top practice ranges, good sets of rental clubs, full-service pro shops, instructors on hand to iron out your swing, and locker rooms that are as well maintained as the courses. Caddies, however, are no longer a fixture on the Chicago scene, not even at Glencoe, where packs of boys used to gather by the first tee in the hope of picking up a few bucks on bright Saturday and Sunday mornings.

Cantigny and Kemper Lakes have very elegant dining rooms in their clubhouses, ideal for breakfast, lunch, a drink, or even dinner after your round. The dining facilities at Cog Hill and Seven Bridges are very good but not up to the lofty standard of Cantigny and Kemper Lakes. The Glencoe Golf Club's simple grill serves sandwiches, hot dogs, and drinks.

LODGING

We stayed in four different hotels during our Chicago sojourn: the Ritz-Carlton and the Four Seasons, both downtown on North Michigan Avenue, the Oak Brook Hills Resort in suburban Oak Brook, and an elegant historic hotel in beautiful Lake Forest: the Deer Path Inn.

Let's begin with the **Deer Path Inn,** the dark horse in this elite crowd of costly hotels. At just $130 per night for a double room (breakfast included), the Deer Path Inn is one-third the price of the Ritz-Carlton and the Four Seasons and is truly one of the best hotel bargains in the region. Lake Forest itself is a wonderful place to stay; the Deer Path Inn is located on the edge of this stunning suburban community within a minute's walk of the cafés, galleries, and fine boutiques in Market Square. Built in 1929 and modeled after a Tudor manor house in Chiddingstone, England, the Deer Path Inn has fifty-four rooms and is decorated with English antique reproductions. The Anglophile atmosphere is authentic, even down to the English pub, called the White Hart, in the basement. Rooms are comfortable, clean, and well equipped but not lavish. The Deer Path Inn is recommended for anyone looking for a charming hotel in a wonderful quiet setting off the beaten track in the Chicago area.

Our experience at the **Ritz-Carlton,** located a block behind North Michigan Avenue in Water Tower Place (one of Chicago's landmark buildings) and recently voted the single best hotel in the United States, was truly exceptional. When they are at their best, hotels in urban areas serve as sanctuaries from the madness and chaos beyond. In this role the Ritz-Carlton excels. We were more than happy with the Ritz's elegance and physical appointments—from its grand twelfth-floor lobby overlooking the striking Hancock Building to the decor of the guest rooms. Yet we were especially impressed with the service at the Ritz. The attitude and work ethic of the entire staff—from the hustling doormen to the accommodating staff in the hotel's health club—is remarkable. The ever-smiling concierge made several restaurant reservations for us on the spot. Another asset is the spectacular location: Chicago's best shops and many of its finest restaurants are just steps away on the Magnificent Mile. Our standard room, number 2616, featured a large marble bath, fine furnishings, and every imaginable amenity. The Ritz-Carlton is expensive. Room rates start at $315 for a single and $355 for a double. Highly recommended.

Located just three blocks away from one another, the **Four Seasons** and the Ritz-Carlton have much in common. Both are operated by the same management company, and both are situated on the upper floors of beautiful buildings above elegant, multistory shopping atriums. Yet there are differences in atmosphere: the Four Seasons is more hushed and buffered; the Ritz is busier and more bustling. Room rates are comparable; at the Four Seasons, double rooms start at $380.

The **Oak Brook Hills Resort** was the only hotel disappointment we experienced in Chicago. This new golf resort in suburban Oak Brook had been recommended to us because of its relative proximity to Cog Hill and Cantigny. But its proximity (really no more than ten or fifteen minutes closer to the courses than the other hotels on our list) could not make up for its sterile atmosphere. The Ritz and Four Seasons offer the vibrancy of downtown Chicago; the Deer Path Inn enjoys a quaint village setting; but the Oak Brook Hills Resort felt as if it were in the middle of nowhere. While comfortable, modern, and well run (and certainly convenient to O'Hare Airport and the Oak Brook shopping malls), the Oak Brook Hills Resort lacks character. We did not play the resort's eighteen-hole golf course, which looked treeless and barren in comparison with the others reviewed above. Assets of the resort include a fine health club, three restaurants, and a sports bar.

Deer Path Inn. 255 East Illinois Road, Lake Forest, IL 60045. Tel: 800-788-9480 or 847-234-2280. Fax: 847-234-3352. 53 rooms with singles from $120 and doubles from $130 (breakfast included). Credit cards accepted.

The Ritz-Carlton. 160 East Pearson Street, Chicago, IL 60611. Tel: 800-621-6906 or 312-266-1000. Fax: 312-266-1194. 429 rooms and suites. Doubles from $355 to $395. Credit cards accepted.

The Four Seasons Chicago. 120 East Delaware Place, Chicago, IL 60611. Tel: 800-332-3442 or 312-280-8800. Fax: 312-280-1748. 343 rooms and suites. Doubles range between $380 and $450 during May through October. Credit cards accepted.

Oak Brook Hills Resort. 3500 Midwest Road, Oak Brook, IL 60522. Tel: 800-445-3315 or 630-850-5555. Fax: 630-850-5556. 383 rooms and suites. Doubles range from $119 to $179. Credit cards accepted.

RESTAURANTS   ⑱

A few of the very best restaurants in Chicago that we had the distinct pleasure to visit recently include the extraordinary Charlie Trotter's, the finest restaurant in Chicago for several years and one of the best restaurants in America; Ambria, a subdued, Art Deco establishment that tops the popularity charts in Chicago; and Phil Smidt's, a Chicago area dining legend since 1910.

Golfers should not be misled at **Charlie Trotter's** by the chef's casual usage of his informal name, "Charlie." With its atmosphere, service, and cuisine, Charlie Trotter's is the most refined, seriously haute cuisine restaurant in the Midwest. Young chef Trotter is an inveterate traveler, particularly to the great restaurants of France, and his cuisine has only gotten finer since he first opened on West Armitage Avenue in 1987. Charlie Trotter's is best suited for diners who have a true appreciation of ambitious cuisine and extraordinary wine. The $85 six-course dinner menu can include skate wing with razor clams, Olympia oysters and herb sauce, delicious Sonoma foie gras in a white asparagus soup, Maine halibut, California pigeon breast with a ragout of fresh vegetables, Iowa lamb loin with sweetbreads in a white truffle oil, and a medley of five spectacular desserts. This great dinner is amply complemented by an exceptional selection of wines, available by the bottle and by the glass. There are three separate dining areas at Charlie Trotter's: the understated front room, a cozy room upstairs, and a special dining area in the center of the hectic kitchen that consists of just one table. The restaurant is closed Sundays and Mondays.

Chicago is a muscular, hard-driving business town, which accounts for the long-standing popularity of **Ambria,** owned by Chicago restaurant impresario Richard Melman. Soft, dimly lit, and paneled in dark woods, Ambria is the restaurant equivalent of a well-coifed Parisian woman in a classic Chanel suit. Specialties include smoked salmon, crab, veal, duck, snapper, and steak, but even these great dishes must take a backseat to the heavenly foie gras and rack of lamb. The wine list is excellent. About $175 for two, wine and tip included. Ambria is open for dinner only; the restaurant is located in the Belden Hotel, across the hall from another interesting Melman eatery, Un Grand Café.

Phil Smidt & Son stands in an unlikely location amid the smokestacks, steel girders, and oil tankers of Hammond, Indiana, about a forty-five-minute drive south from downtown Chicago. But as *Gourmet* magazine recently attested, "Regular patrons drive hundreds of miles to relish its unique Great Lakes feast, which has remained unchanged for decades." Surrounded by a decorative motif of pink roses emblazoned on the walls, on the glassware, and on the waitress's aprons, diners begin with a series of relishes (marinated kidney beans, pickled beets, crunchy coleslaw, mustard-flavored potato salad) and move on to the perch or, even better, the tender sautéed frog legs, a local passion. "At Phil Smidt's, the frog legs are ravishing," says *Gourmet*. We concur. About $70 for two at lunch, $90 at dinner, including wine and tip.

Charlie Trotter's. 816 West Armitage Avenue, Chicago, IL 60614 Tel: 773-248-6228. Fax: 773-248-6088. Dinner only. Open daily. Credit cards accepted.

Ambria. 2300 North Lincoln Park West, Chicago, IL 60614 Tel: 773-472-5959. Fax: 773-472-9077. Credit cards accepted.

Phil Smidt & Son. 1205 North Calumet Avenue, Hammond, IN 46320 Tel: 800-376-4534 or 219-659-0025. Fax: 219-659-6955. Open daily for lunch and dinner. Credit cards accepted.

NON-GOLF ACTIVITIES

After you have completed your round of golf, head back to the Chicago metropolitan area, where your non-golfing options are virtually boundless. One of our favorite things to do is walk from the Chicago Art Institute at one end of Michigan Avenue to the Oak Street beach at the other. In between, you will find Saks, Henri Bendel, Neiman Marcus, and every other boutique, clothier, and upmarket retailer known to man. Even if you make no purchases, strolling along North Michigan Avenue is the quintessential Chicago experience. You will also find fabulous blues and jazz clubs in the city, along with good theater, and don't forget da Bulls, da Cubs, and da Bears.

GETTING THERE: The ride from Chicago's O'Hare Airport to downtown Chicago can take anywhere from thirty minutes to an hour, depending on traffic. Taxi fare to the city center is about $35. If you are renting a car at the airport, take the Kennedy Expressway (I-90) eastbound, which will merge with I-94. Exit at Ohio Street, go about five blocks, and turn left onto Michigan Avenue. The Ritz (on East Pearson Street) and the Four Seasons (on East Delaware Place) are just off Michigan. Ask your hotel concierge for directions to the various golf courses in the Chicago area.

Wisconsin

▶ THE AMERICAN CLUB

IS AMERICA'S GREATEST GOLF RESORT IN WISCONSIN?

	The Golf	Golf Services	Lodging	Restaurants	Non-Golf Activities	Total
Rating	19	19	18	18	18	92

The American Club

The rhetorical question posed above can only be answered with the following statement: the American Club in Kohler, Wisconsin, is one of the best golf destinations that we at GOLF TRAVEL have ever visited—not just in the United States but throughout the entire world.

The American Club's sum total of 92 points in GOLF TRAVEL's five-part rating system—based on our recent anonymous visit—places it above more famous gems such as the Boulders (91), Pebble Beach (90), Gleneagles in Scotland (90), and the Four Seasons on Nevis in the Caribbean (90). Other golf destinations equaling the American Club with 92 points are the glorious Mauna Kea on Hawaii's big island, Spanish Bay, and the overall experience offered by Paris, London, Hong Kong, and the legendary city of St. Andrews, Scotland. Only the Greenbrier in West Virginia (with 94 total points) surpasses it.

The American Club excels in every department. It is one of the few golf destinations visited in our five years of publication that consistently merits superlative marks in every one of GOLF TRAVEL's five discriminating categories. It is especially sweet, we will note, to make such a discovery not on some distant shore but in the wholesome breadbasket of our own nation. The American Club is also extremely good value: upward of 25 percent less expensive than any of the other golf resorts mentioned above.

So how in the world did these happy events happen to converge in such an improbable location—in a company town on the shores of Lake Michigan, across the street from a large factory and an hour north of Milwaukee? The American Club is a unique story that involves the Ice Age, the Great Depression, an extraordinary company that manufactures plumbing fixtures, and a magician of golf course architecture named Pete Dye.

During the Ice Age, receding glaciers created strange and beautiful landforms in the Kohler area called kettles (deep holes) and moraines (steep hills) that architect Dye ingeniously incorporated into his design of the American Club's two great courses at Blackwolf Run, the River Course and the Meadow Valleys Course. The area around Kohler is full of dramatic natural beauty, from idyllic farmland to the rushing, trout-filled waters of the Sheboygan River.

The American Club did not become a hotel until 1981. This handsome, red-brick structure with slate roof was built in 1918 to house European immigrants, mostly Germans, Dutch, and Polish, who came to work at the Kohler plumbing factory located directly across the street. Now a National Historic Landmark, this residence was meant to aid in the Americanization of these immigrant employees, hence its name—the American Club.

The American Club, as well as the vast and extremely clean Kohler Company factory and the tidy, utterly charming town of Kohler (designed by the Olmsted Brothers landscape architecture firm in the tradition of their father, Frederick Law Olmsted, the designer of New York's Central Park and Pinehurst Village in North Carolina), have been and continue to be the province of the Kohler family. The Kohler Corporation is one of the largest privately held companies in the world. Heading the family today is Herb Kohler, respected as a passionate golfer, a compassionate boss, and, apparently, a very nice guy.

The American Club is well known in Wisconsin and Illinois, but the Japanese and Germans are discovering it—and so should you. Any avid golfer with a taste for unusual travel, especially those who regularly come through Chicago on business trips, should consider taking a two-and-a-half-hour detour due north from O'Hare Airport and staying in lovely Kohler, Wisconsin, for a couple of days of spectacular scenery and sport. You will not be disappointed.

THE GOLF

The American Club's spectacular golf complex at **Blackwolf Run,** accessible by hotel shuttle bus, is located one mile from the hotel. The centerpiece of Blackwolf Run is a sprawling and delightful log clubhouse, decorated with Indian artifacts, that exudes a wonderful pioneer spirit and the flavor of the remote North Woods. Built on a hillside above the river, this unique clubhouse commands views of both courses. The inspirational setting of Blackwolf Run derives in part from its feeling of absolute isolation. The golf courses are surrounded by an eight-hundred-acre nature sanctuary called River Wildlife, which is part of the American Club resort. There are no homes, condos, apartments, or other human habitations within sight. Wildlife, however, is in abundance: enormous turtles make slow progress across the fairways, trout dance in the river, herds of deer can be seen.

The two courses at Blackwolf Run are beyond question two of Pete Dye's greatest all-time hits. The River Course is the resort's marquee course, home of the Andersen Consulting $1 million match-play competition in July, but the Meadow Valleys track is also sublime. The rushing Sheboygan River winds its way through both courses, although water comes into play on nearly every hole on the more startlingly dramatic River Course. The River and Meadow Valleys courses are tough but ultimately playable; they are not ridiculously brutal Dye creations like PGA West and the Ocean Course at Kiawah. The entire world will see for itself in 1998 when holes from both the River and Meadow Valleys courses will be configured to host the 1998 U.S. Women's Open.

Schedule at least three rounds of golf at Blackwolf Run. Play the River Course twice, as it will take two rounds to get the hang of it, but do not neglect the less-heralded Meadow Valleys. This is as great a two-course combination as is offered by any golf resort in the world. The River Course enjoys a five-star rating in *Golf Digest's Places to Play*, which puts it on a par with Pebble Beach, Cog Hill Number Four, and Pinehurst Number Two. The River Course plays to a 151 slope rating from the black tees (that's right folks, 151); the slope for Meadow Valleys from the tips is 143. Resort golf simply does not get any better than this.

And yet, there's more. Blackwolf Run, not about to rest on its laurels, is planning to open a third course for play sometime in 1998. Also designed by Pete Dye, the **Whistling Straits** course will be a walkers- and caddies-only links course or, as Dye himself says, the closest thing to a traditional Scottish links course as is possible in the United States. The course is located on a spectacular site on Lake Michigan at the old Camp Haven military grounds. We await it with eager anticipation.

Let's start our review of Blackwolf Run with the supposedly easier **Meadow Valleys,** a great championship layout in its own right with panoramic views, majestic fairways, and perhaps the greatest three-hole sequence of golf at the entire Blackwolf Run complex—holes thirteen, fourteen, and fifteen.

Meadow Valleys was built on open farmland. Unlike the River Course, the fairways are broad and forgiving—at least on the front side. For the first few holes you can spray your shots a bit without terrible retribution, a statement that cannot be made about Meadow Valleys' sister course. The best holes on the front side are four and nine. The fourth hole is a 565-yard par five that doglegs to the right past seven large bunkers, including one massive bunker on the right side of the fairway that will capture long tee shots. The ninth hole, 462 yards, features an equally generous driving area but demands a tighter second shot into a green surrounded by water on three sides.

It is the back nine, however, that you will not forget, particularly thirteen through fifteen. Thirteen is a great short par four of 351 yards with a blind drive over a hillside and then a partially blind second shot from the fairway floor up to an elevated pedestal green. The 423-yard fourteenth is a downhill dogleg-right; you have to stop your tee shot before the waste area and then lob down a little eight or nine iron to the green below. Everybody knows about Dye's railroad ties; on the fourteenth at Meadow Valleys you actually walk through a railroad car employed (with humor, we believe) as a bridge over the river. The thrilling fifteenth, *Mercy,* is the signature hole at Meadow Valleys, a gorgeous 227-yard par three with a huge green perched above the precipice. All in all, Meadow Valleys reminds us of another Dye masterpiece, La Romana Country Club in the Dominican Republic. The course measures 7,142 yards (par rating 74.7/slope 143) from the back tees.

The **River Course,** which measures 6,991 yards from the back tees (rating 74.9/slope 151), is an exhilarating roller-coaster ride uphill and down, past thick forests, over kettles and moraines, and across the crystal-clear Sheboygan River time and again. It is easily six to eight strokes more difficult than Meadow Valleys and many times more dramatic. Two of the most spellbinding holes in American golf may be found on the River Course, the fifth, *Made in Heaven,* and the eighth, *Hell's Gate,* and these are not even Kohler's signature holes.

The staff at Blackwolf Run sensibly pairs its tees with handicaps: zero to five handicaps play from the blacks; six to fourteen play from the blues; fifteen to twenty-three play from the whites; and those twenty-four and over play from the red tees. But the views and shot values are so breathtaking from the blue tees that even inconsistent golfers will want to consider at least playing from these. Only a Davis Love or a Corey Pavin should play the River Course from the black tees.

Made in Heaven and *Hell's Gate* present amazing tee shots. On the fifth hole, you stand on a wooded ledge and drive the ball over the river and down to the fairway far below. On the eighth hole, you stand on even higher ground and hit your drive through a narrow chute of trees where "hell" awaits anyone who does not make it through the "gate." A well-struck drive will hang and sail for an eternity before descending to the fairway floor far below. The ninth hole, *Cathedral Spires,* a short, 337-yard par four and the River Course's signature hole, offers three different approaches to the green. Here's a hint: the shortest route to the green, to the right over the Sheboygan River, is a sucker play.

The back nine of the River Course is more Dye-esque with its huge, submerged bunkers along the fairways of the fifteenth and sixteenth holes. The eleventh hole is a great, 560-yard par five that doglegs to the right around a big bend in the river and that will sorely test the longest of hitters; the twelfth hole is a long, majestic par four;

and thirteen is one of the toughest par threes in golf. In fact, thirteen, 205 yards long, with the wide river on the right and massive oaks blocking the green, is probably unfair. In two days of golf we did not see one ball even come close to the thirteenth green. Of course, every Dye layout has to have at least one hole like thirteen.

Walking is permitted on both Meadow Valleys and the River Course, but both have been designed for carts. The distances between green and tee—particularly on the very steep River Course—can frequently be as long as four hundred yards. We saw plenty of walkers, but all looked uncomfortable or exhausted by the ninth hole. The sheer length of these courses, combined with the distance from green to the next tee, means that a typical round at Blackwolf Run takes a minimum of four and a half to five hours.

Advance tee times can be made when reserving your room at the American Club hotel. Club guests receive a break on greens fees, while those golfers who do not stay at a Kohler property, in addition to paying more, can only reserve tee times within two weeks of when they wish to play. Two-night golf packages, which include your room, breakfast, and two rounds of golf per person with cart, are available.

Blackwolf Run Golf Club. 1111 West Riverside Drive, Kohler, WI 53044. Tel: 800-344-2838 or 414-457-4446. Fax: 414-457-1684. Credit cards accepted.

• *Meadow Valley Course.* 1988. Designer: Pete Dye. Par 72. 7,142 yards. 74.7 par rating. 143 slope rating. Greens fees: $80 (guests), $100 (public). Walking permitted. Carts ($32) and "Cart-Caddies" are available. Season: April 1–November.

• *River Course.* 1990. Designer: Pete Dye. Par 72. 6,991 yards. 74.9 par rating. 151 slope rating. Greens fees: $114 (guests), $134 (public). Walking permitted. Carts ($32) and "Cart-Caddies" are available. Season: April 20–late October.

 ## GOLF SERVICES

Golf services are among the best in the world. The superb staff at Blackwolf Run (dressed in knickers and kneesocks) comprise a veritable army of starters, rangers, bag boys, pro shop personnel, and men patrolling the courses in carts dispensing food, drink, and encouragement. There is a fine practice range, a large putting green, and a well-stocked pro shop. Lessons and rental clubs are available. "Cart-caddies," who drive your cart and do everything a caddie would do except carry your clubs, are available on a first-come, first-served basis for about $25 per bag plus tip.

 ## LODGING

Guest rooms in the magnificently renovated **American Club** are handsome, comfortable, and extremely well equipped. We stayed in room number 144 ($236), one of the smallest and least expensive rooms in the hotel, but we found it cozy, warmly decorated with natural wood finishes, and very much to our liking. All the guest bathrooms in the American Club are lavish productions showcasing the latest Kohler products. Even the smallest rooms, for instance, have whirlpool baths. The more costly rooms and suites have separate showers and whirlpool baths for two. During the high season (May 1 through October 31) room rates range from $200 for a small, standard double room to $425 per night for the most luxurious double. The two-night golf package starts at $915 for two people in high season.

The historic public rooms inside the American Club, as well as the courtyard gardens with their slate and brick walkways and lovely wildflowers, are elegant and perfectly maintained.

All the service personnel we encountered throughout the resort—from the

American Club's front desk to the Blackwolf Run pro shop and virtually everyone else in between—were earnest, helpful, and sincere. Professional yet genuinely friendly service is one of the American Club's strongest assets.

The Kohler Corporation opened a second, lower-priced hotel in the summer of 1994 in the Village of Kohler shopping center. The sixty-room **Inn On Woodlake** does not have the rich allure of the American Club, but it is modern, attractive, and good value with double room rates from $125 to $200 from May through October. Guests at the inn also receive a break on the greens fees.

The American Club. Highland Drive, Kohler, WI 53044. Tel: 800-344-2838 or 414-457-8000. Fax: 414-457-0299. 236 rooms and suites. Doubles cost $200 to $425 from May 1 to October 31. Credit cards accepted.

Inn On Woodlake. Tel: 800-919-3600 or 414-452-7800. 60 rooms. Doubles from $125 to $200 from May through October. Credit cards accepted.

RESTAURANTS

The American Club offers a slew of delightful dining possibilities—from the informality of the enchanting bar in the golf clubhouse, perfect for lunch after your round on the River Course (try the Sheboygan bratwurst), to the elegant Immigrant Restaurant, a gourmet dining room located downstairs in the American Club. Other dining options include the attractive **Wisconsin Room** (perfect for breakfast), a busy pub called the **Horse & Plow,** the **Greenhouse** for snacks and sandwiches, and the restaurant in the **River Wildlife Lodge.** The **golf clubhouse** has a separate dining room where lunch and dinner are served, but the unique **clubhouse bar** must not be missed.

The **Immigrant Restaurant,** the best dining spot in the resort, has an excellent wine list and features imaginative, heartland cuisine and the "pure lean" (virtually fat-free) beef raised at Kohler Farms. A complete dinner for two with wine and tip in the Immigrant costs approximately $125. Jackets are required.

The restaurants at the American Club. Highland Drive, Kohler, WI 53044. Tel: 800-344-2838 or 414-457-8000. Fax: 414-457-0299. Credit cards accepted.

NON-GOLF ACTIVITIES

You will discover a plethora of outstanding non-golf activities at the American Club. We saw nearly as many fly fishermen standing hip-deep and casting into the Sheboygan River as golfers driving along the courses in electric carts. In addition to fishing, the River Wildlife Preserve offers trap shooting, hunting, horseback riding, canoeing and kayaking, hiking, and cross-country skiing.

The Sports Core is Kohler's outstanding indoor sports facility and includes six indoor tennis courts, a full-service spa, an indoor pool, fully equipped weight rooms, and fitness classes.

The spectacular Kohler Design Center, located next door to the American Club, is a fascinating exhibition hall equipped with twenty-five designer kitchens and bathrooms displaying the complete range of Kohler products.

If shopping is your pleasure, head for the attractive mall called Woodlake Market.

GETTING THERE: From Milwaukee, travel about fifty-five miles north on I-43 North to exit 126 (Highway 23). Go west on Highway 23 about two thirds of a mile to County Road Y (Highland Drive) and turn right. At the yield, bear right and you will come to the entrance of the American Club.

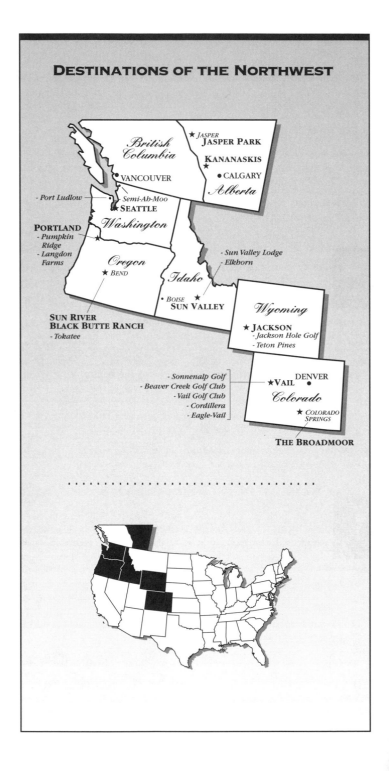

DESTINATIONS OF THE NORTHWEST

British Columbia

★ *JASPER*
JASPER PARK

KANANASKIS
★

● VANCOUVER

● CALGARY

Alberta

- Port Ludlow —
● *Semi-Ah-Moo*
★ **SEATTLE**

PORTLAND
- Pumpkin
  Ridge
- Langdon
  Farms

Washington

Oregon
★ *Bend*

Idaho

- Sun Valley Lodge
- Elkhorn

● *BOISE*
★
SUN VALLEY

SUN RIVER
BLACK BUTTE RANCH
- Tokatee

Wyoming

★ **JACKSON**
- Jackson Hole Golf
- Teton Pines

- Sonnenalp Golf
- Beaver Creek Golf Club
- Vail Golf Club
- Cordillera
- Eagle-Vail

★**VAIL**
DENVER
●

Colorado

★ *COLORADO*
  SPRINGS

THE BROADMOOR

THE
PACIFIC
NORTHWEST

THE PACIFIC NORTHWEST

[It] awakens those grandest and subtlest elements in the human soul.

—**Walt Whitman**

Scenery to bankrupt the English language.

—**Theodore Roosevelt**

The Pacific Northwest. Even before Lewis and Clark reached the Pacific Ocean on their 1804–1806 overland journey, the region lured English, Spanish, French, Russian, Native American, and American explorers and adventurers. Today this region of awesome snowcapped mountains, idyllic mountain passes, tall waterfalls, rushing rivers teeming with salmon and trout, thick evergreen forests, and an abundance of bear, wolves, elk, and eagles continues to attract a diverse array of international vacationers. Now they come not in search of the mythic Northwest Passage but for great hunting and fishing, hiking, boating, world-class downhill skiing, and, increasingly, outstanding golf.

GOLF TRAVEL's exploration of the great golf courses in the Pacific Northwest extends from Colorado westward to the Pacific Ocean and northward to the Canadian Rockies. Colorado alone boasts fifty-four eternally snowcapped peaks of over 14,000 feet. The venerable Broadmoor resort—with its three outstanding courses designed by Donald Ross, Robert Trent Jones, Sr., and Arnold Palmer/Ed Seay—is situated on the eastern edge of the mountains near Pikes Peak, while Vail lies in the heart of the mountains amid some of the nation's finest ski country and trendiest resorts. Because the Rockies act as a giant shield against many weather systems, golfers can count on brilliant sunshine and comfortable conditions throughout much of the year.

To the northwest, Jackson, Wyoming, first earned its reputation among travelers as a dude-ranch destination. Now two superb golf courses—Jackson Hole Golf & Tennis and Teton Pines—lure golfers to this character-filled, Western mountain town. Idaho's Sun Valley is consistently rated one of the top ski-resort destinations in the country, yet anyone who has experienced a summer day on the links here will swear that heaven couldn't be much more pleasant. At these altitudes, you will think your golf ball is receiving a little heavenly assistance, for shots fly at least 10 percent farther. Your toughest adjustment will be catching your breath.

As we leave the Rockies' lofty peaks for the more gentle summits in Oregon's Willamette and Deschutes national forests, we begin to see why nineteenth-century pioneers on the overland trail often chose to settle in the Pacific Northwest instead of California. The area surrounding the town of Bend, Oregon, is a perfect evergreen playground for anyone who loves the outdoors. In addition to outstanding hiking, camping, and fishing, there are more than twenty golf courses to whet your appetite. Our favorites include Tokatee, one of the nation's top public links courses, and the tracks at the Sun River and Black Butte resorts.

Portland and Seattle are oftentimes maligned for their rainy climates, but people who live there can attest that the surveys ranking these cities as America's most livable have got it right. The cultural and dining offerings are outstanding, and the mild weather makes for an outdoor paradise; fanatical fisherman will find five varieties of salmon in the Puget Sound region alone. Portland and Seattle each hold waterfront festivals at the slightest excuse, and street life is vibrant. These are lovely cities for strolling, jogging, rollerblading, or bicycling on countless bicycle paths. As you explore the cities, you will find interesting architecture, museums, zoos, and arboretums.

Golf travelers will especially admire Portland's Pumpkin Ridge Golf Club, the site of the 1997 U.S. Women's Open, and the unforgettable Semi-Ah-Moo and Port Ludlow courses within two hours of Seattle.

From Seattle, we head into Alberta, to two of its most famed vacation destinations. Canadian resort owners have learned a thing or two about running world-class golf operations from their years of winter vacationing in Florida and Arizona. Jasper Park Lodge and the Hotel and Lodge at Kananaskis are both big resorts that offer great golf courses and unmatched mountain scenery and activities. The Stanley Thompson—designed course at Jasper Park ranks as our favorite course in Canada.

In the Pacific Northwest, temperatures turn progressively colder the further north in latitude and the higher in elevation you climb. The climate is wettest along the coast and becomes drier as you move inland. At all these courses, you will likely start out wearing a warm sweater and windbreaker as you begin your early-morning round. Once the sun heats up, however, your cold-weather gear will quickly find its way back into your golf bag. Peak season here lasts only from July through August, but the region is so enchanting during this time that the resorts—or at least their more reasonably priced rooms—get booked up nearly a year in advance. To avoid being shut out, plan ahead and book early. South of the Canadian Rockies the season extends from spring to early autumn. You will love the Pacific Northwest and its stunning beauty—so don't forget your camera!

Colorado

▶THE BROADMOOR

GOLF AT ITS BEST IN THE ROCKIES

	The Golf	Golf Services	Lodging	Restaurants	Non-Golf Activities	Total
Rating	19	19	17	17	19	91

Nestled snugly against the foothills of the Rockies in the southwestern part of Colorado Springs, the Broadmoor has proudly reigned supreme for nearly a century as *the* resort of the whole Rocky Mountain region. Much of this roughly hundred-year reign was deserved, but there have also been sporadic periods when the Broadmoor has rested complacently on its laurels. We visited the Broadmoor often in the late 1970s and early 1980s, a time when service had slipped badly, paint was chipping, fabrics were worn, and the cuisine throughout was wretched. Now, under new ownership and boosted by an infusion of tens of millions of dollars, service is bright and courteous, the cuisine at

The Broadmoor

the multitude of restaurants is very good indeed, the physical plant glistens, and the grounds are lush and manicured. These days, when any facet of the "Riviera of the Rockies" needs renovation or even complete reconstruction, management gets the job done promptly. For example, the outmoded white building that used to house the golf pro shop, lockers, and grill has been leveled, thankfully, and replaced by a $12 million edifice that houses a lovely new pro shop and impressive spa facility.

The Broadmoor is one of America's four or five finest destination resorts. It provides a diversity of activities for its pampered guests that is virtually unparalleled anywhere in the world. At the core of this Broadmoor activity is golf. There are three dazzling eighteens here—each with its own distinct character and feel and all beautifully maintained.

After staying several days at the Broadmoor, we respectfully tip our hat to the management for what it has achieved in its level of service. From the front desk to the waiters and golf course staff, service at the Broadmoor is virtually flawless. Never once—that's right, never once—did we pass a Broadmoor employee without receiving a friendly "hello," "good morning," or "good night." Before continuing to extol the Broadmoor's virtues, it is important to point something out. The Broadmoor, a giant resort of 700 rooms and 1,600 employees, is sustained, like all big resort hotels now, by meetings and convention dollars. In today's world, without this major source of revenue, all of our great resort hotels would have to fold up in short order. Thus, during most of the year, the Broadmoor is dominated by guests attending meetings. Therefore, although the hotel is in no way shabby and the service is infinitely friendly, some of the guests are both shabby and rude, displaying at times disgraceful etiquette on the golf course. On occasion, five or six or ten conventioneers will get in one of those unpleasant frenzies that make us feel like fleeing to our rooms or fetching a high-powered water hose. Fortunately, these episodes are rare, and, whatever the circumstance, we marveled at the courtesy and patience of the Broadmoor staff.

A note regarding Colorado Springs weather: The climate in Colorado Springs, which has more than three hundred days of sunshine, is nearly perfect. Neither the heat nor the humidity is oppressive here; rather, day after day the skies are blue, even in the winter. Golfing weather remains ideal from April through October, although you will need sweaters and warmer clothing for April, May, September, and October. Evenings, even in the summer, become refreshingly cool. The best, most predictable golfing weather is in June, July, August, and September.

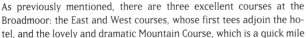

THE GOLF 19

As previously mentioned, there are three excellent courses at the Broadmoor: the East and West courses, whose first tees adjoin the hotel, and the lovely and dramatic Mountain Course, which is a quick mile and a half south of the resort. The **East Course,** perhaps the best known, was designed by Donald Ross in 1918, the same year the hotel was built. Like the other courses at the Broadmoor, the East is in excellent condition—fairways are lush and greens perfect and notoriously fast. Of the three courses, the East is the flattest, as only three of its holes climb into the foothills. The East's visual beauty lies in the verdant, carpeted fairways lined by pines and scrub oaks and dotted with ponds scattered across the course. You also play with the Rockies looming to the west and the pale pink buildings of the Broadmoor usually in view. Although listed at 7,091 yards from the blue tees, the East plays significantly shorter because of the altitude, but it plays tough with a par rating of 73.0, slope 129, and par 72. Fairways are fairly wide, but water and sand traps put a premium on good shot making. The fast greens, if you are not used to them, can lead to three-putts from ten feet. Holes five, six, and seven climb into the foothills, and the par three fifth is one of the most dramatic holes on the East. Like all truly fine courses, the East has an aura about it; its history, the many tournaments played here, the challenge, and the absolute majesty of the setting combine to form a truly first-rate golf course.

The **West Course,** which also begins at the hotel and Broadmoor Lake, is a Robert Trent Jones, Sr., course that was built in two stages—the first nine in 1950 and the second in 1965. Teeing off at number one on the West, you begin to wonder why the East Course gets everyone's praise; this hole seems an endless and alluring invitation into the Rockies looming in front of you. If you duff your drive here, you can be excused because the view is a breathtaking distraction. As you approach the first green, the magic from the tee begins to fade quickly; the immediate surroundings overwhelm the more distant beauty of the Rockies. Busy, noisy, and unattractive El Pomar Road runs just beyond the green—certainly not the serenity of the Rocky Mountain foothills here. Number two, a boring, 477-yard par five, plays parallel to El Pomar Road, and at this point you are yearning for either the East Course or the Mountain Course. Despite this unfortunate first impression, tranquil beauty reigns from holes three through eighteen.

As the West Course climbs higher and higher into the foothills, it creates more and more memorable and inspiring views of the Broadmoor resort and of Colorado Springs, seemingly spread out at your feet. The views culminate on the green at ten and the tee of eleven, the two highest points on Jones's masterpiece. Devilishly surrounded by water and sand, the green at the 214-yard, downhill, par three eleventh seems to be saying "Hey! It's time to get back down to earth, and here's where the descent starts!" Number eleven is a remarkable challenge and an even more remarkably scenic golf hole. Twelve, a 460-yard par four, continues your descent down to the resort's elevation and the concluding six holes of this fine course. From the blue tees the West measures 6,937 yards and has a 73.4 par rating and a slope of 134.

The **Mountain Course** (formerly the South Course), designed by Arnold Palmer and Ed Seay in 1976, is the newest of the three Broadmoor courses. Just a five-minute shuttle from the main hotel, the Mountain Course should not be missed. Separated as it is from the rest of the resort, this course provides a whole new golf environment. It will remind you of a high desert course; it sports much more of an open feel than the East and West. But do not be deceived—an errant shot into the high desert is just as hard to find as a hook or slice into the trees. Very high-priced, stylish homes are interspersed along the course to take advantage of the Rockies' wondrous views. Course maintenance, as on the East and West, is flawless; lush fairways, perfect and fast greens, and plenty of bunkers along the fairways and protecting the greens make this a delightful course with a challenging layout. In fact, the eighty-nine bunkers on the North Course average out to five sand traps per hole. Be sure to bring your sand wedge!

The Mountain Course is served by a very sleek clubhouse containing a well-stocked pro shop and Spencer's, the perfect restaurant for lunch. This par seventy-two course measures 6,781 yards from the back tees with a course rating of 72.1 and slope rating of 135. The fine putting green and driving range afford you an ideal opportunity to warm up before your round.

The Broadmoor. 1 Lake Avenue, Colorado Springs, CO 80906. Tel: 800-634-7711, 719-634-7711, or 719-634-5150 (golf reservations); 719-577-5790 (main pro shop). Fax: 719-471-6111. Credit cards accepted.

• *East Course.* 1918. Designer: Donald Ross. Par 72. 7,091 yards. 73.0 par rating. 129 slope rating.
• *West Course.* 1950/1965. Designer: Robert Trent Jones, Sr. Par 72. 6,937 yards. 73.4 par rating. 134 slope rating.

• *Mountain Course* (formerly South). 1976. Designers: Arnold Palmer/Ed Seay. Par 72. 6,781 yards. 72.1 par rating. 135 slope rating.

• Greens fees for all courses: $125 (May–October), $80 (November–April). Walking permitted May through September after 3 P.M. and at all times throughout the rest of the year. Caddies available June–August. Carts available unless conditions preclude their use. Restrictions: public access limited to the Broadmoor guests. Season: year-round.

GOLF SERVICES 19

The Broadmoor is always a very busy place, but the resort and golf service staff could not be more accommodating. Under tough circumstances they are friendly, patient, and remarkably efficient. The same is true of the boys who handle the clubs and carts, the caddies, the starters, and the men on the driving range. Be sure to hone your putting stroke on the superb putting green.

LODGING 17

Four different buildings house the hotel's seven hundred rooms: Broadmoor Main, the original hotel structure, the less attractive and much newer South and West buildings, and the nearly brand new West Tower, which was built in 1995. The rooms in the West Tower are the resort's most luxurious. Of the other buildings, the South and West buildings are rather nondescript from the exterior, although the rooms in both are lovely and spacious. Broadmoor Main and Broadmoor South are the only buildings with rooms offering views of both the mountain and the lake together. Some of the rooms in Broadmoor Main are a bit dated, but they are still pleasant and offer plenty of space and comfort.

The Broadmoor. 1 Lake Avenue, Colorado Springs, CO 80906. Tel: 800-634-7711 or 719-634-7711. Fax: 719-577-5700. 700 rooms. Doubles range from $265 to $355 (May–October) and $165 to $255 (November–April). Credit cards accepted.

RESTAURANTS 17

The Broadmoor offers a great variety of choices for dining, from the casual pub service at the **Tavern** to the more formal dining in the **Penrose Room** (jacket and tie required), with its amazing view of Colorado Springs and Cheyenne Mountain. There are, in fact, nine different places where you can eat at the Broadmoor, and all have excellent service and good food. The Penrose Room serves quite good Continental cuisine, with à la carte entrées ranging in price from $24 to $38.50. The Penrose is also quite famous for its desert soufflés. Our favorite dining experiences at the Broadmoor, however, were the Sunday brunch ($21 per person) in the elegant **Lake Terrace** dining room and dinner at the **Charles Court.** Serving contemporary American cuisine, the Charles Court offers a wide variety of selections, including lots of fresh seafood, game, and prime beef. Here you can also enjoy a fine wine list and lovely view toward the lake and the regal Broadmoor Main. Entrées cost between $21 and $36.50.

The restaurants at the Broadmoor. 1 Lake Avenue, Colorado Springs, CO 80906. Tel: 800-634-7711 or 719-577-5733 (central dining reservations). Fax: 719-577-5779. Credit cards accepted.

The diversity of non-golfing activities at and near the Broadmoor for both adults and children is almost mind-boggling. First, you have a wide range of sightseeing, all within an hour and a half of the resort. The Rockies, dominated by Pikes Peak, rise right from your front yard. One fun way to make the Pikes Peak ascent is by the Pikes Peak Cog Railway, which takes you all the way to the summit, making it the highest cog railway in the world. The delightful Cheyenne Mountain Zoo is just five minutes from the resort. Hop in your car and you can make the easy drive to the U.S. Air Force Academy, Royal Gorge (which features the world's highest suspension bridge), the Manitou Cliff Dwellings Museum, the U.S. Figure Skating Hall of Fame, the Garden of the Gods with its amazing rock formations, Cripple Creek and the old mining town, the U.S. Olympic Training Center, the fantastic Pro Rodeo Hall of Champions and Museum of the American Cowboy, and on and on. There are also a number of good, although not spectacular, shops right at the Broadmoor, where you can buy everything from men's and women's clothing to fly-fishing equipment. There are excellent tennis courts, two of which are available from November through April. Shooting enthusiasts will be impressed with the outstanding shooting facilities on the resort grounds, which include skeet, trap, and fabulous sporting clays. First-rate shotguns and shells are available at the shooting grounds. If you are in the mood to fish, you can borrow one of the Broadmoor's top fly-fishing guides and head out for a full or half day to excellent trout rivers and streams in the mountains. For your own tour of the grounds there are top-quality bicycles for rent. You can also ice skate, take a paddleboat out on the resort lake, cross-country ski on the golf course in winter, play croquet, swim in one of the three pools, play squash, work out in the exercise room, and take cooking classes.

GETTING THERE: From Colorado Springs Airport, take Drennan Road to Academy Boulevard, from which you turn left onto I-25 North. Get off at exit 138 (Circle Drive). Take a left off the exit and proceed straight to the Broadmoor.

▶VAIL AND BEAVER CREEK

GOLF ON TOP OF THE WORLD

	The Golf	Golf Services	Lodging	Restaurants	Non-Golf Activities	Total
Rating	18	17	17	17	18	87

Up here at well over 8,200 feet above sea level, the ball just flies forever. Whether playing on the stunning Sonnenalp course, the beautiful course at Beaver Creek, the handsome layout at Vail Golf Club, or one of a number of other excellent courses in the Vail area, you'll strike your drive, admire the ball in flight silhouetted against the mountains, bend down to retrieve your tee, exchange a few pleasantries with your companions about the quality of the shot or the weather, and then turn to see the ball still climbing. Mega-hitters or Schwarzenegger-types who can belt a golf ball 280 yards in the humidity of South Carolina may hit 330 yards off the tee all day long in the glorious Colorado Rockies. For the muscle-bound, holes of 420 yards in length can play as a driver and a three-quarters wedge. In addition to the incomparable scenery (and, perhaps, some discomforting shortness of breath), astonishing distance and hang time are what you may remember most about golf in the dramatic, hedonistic, and ultra-glamorous Vail Valley.

As skiers, we know Vail well. Yet prior to our visit here in late September, we had serious reservations about the resort as a golf destination. These doubts, we discovered, were completely unfounded. There are currently ten courses in the Vail Valley, and the number is rising. The three we played, listed above in order of excellence, rate at the top of the list, although two new courses—the Hale Irwin–designed Mountain Course and Tom Fazio's just-opened Valley Course, both at Cordillera—are also extremely impressive. The golf season is short (generally, late May through mid-October, give or take a couple of weeks), but visitors and residents make the most of it. The courses are packed, and enthusiasm for the game is universal. Just about everyone skis, and just about everyone plays golf.

In the summer, when room rates can be reduced by as much as half, Vail remains as sports-oriented and fitness-obsessed as ever—and as style-conscious as any resort in Europe or America. If you have a potbelly and are generally comfortable with it elsewhere, Vail will make you feel suddenly self-conscious. The tanned and taut population that frequents Vail exhibits the disciplined contours of its tummies and tushes in uniquely fitting jeans and other eye-riveting apparel. There are no square people in Vail, no poverty, no recession, and no litter. Carefully regulated Vail is the ideal holiday getaway from Bad Taste. The entire community is zoned for active sports, major-league consumption, and stylish preening. Even the city police look cool in their dashing Saabs. The same goes for the street performers, who are so well dressed that they must have been granted permits from the town council. At its worst—and this is the only downside we can think of—Vail might strike you as a bit narcissistic. The Church of Self-Love has the biggest congregation in town.

Other pluses include brilliant summertime weather, the fantasy-Tyrolean architecture of Vail Village, fine hotels, extraordinary shops and galleries, and outstanding restaurants. Aside from the obvious Swiss Alpine influence with fondues and goulashes at Pepi's and the Swiss Chalet, there is a wonderful assortment of California- and French-inspired restaurants with innovative cooking, hip, polished service, and urbane interiors. But you won't see a single necktie within—save for the odd maître d' or two. Mountain biking is another passionate pursuit in Vail. People here are as wild about their high-tech bikes as folks in Los Angeles are about their automobiles. Rollerblades are ubiquitous as well. Vail, at bottom, is all about fun.

Beaver Creek, developed by Vail Associates (whose investment in Beaver Creek now exceeds $1 billion), is trying hard, though still with questionable success, to create an even more exclusive and upscale image than Vail itself. Vail remains considerably more chic than Beaver Creek, even though first impressions of Beaver Creek can make Vail *seem* positively democratic. You will not even be allowed to enter Beaver Creek—the security gatehouse at the base of the mountain screens all visitors—unless you are a homeowner or guest in one of Beaver Creek's two hotels (the fabulous Hyatt Regency in Beaver Creek gets our nod as the best hotel in the Vail/Beaver Creek area). In addition to its step up in exclusivity and privacy, another distinct Beaver Creek feature is its natural setting, which is more Alpine than Vail's. Vail sits in a narrow valley with steep mountains on either side. The mountains are overwhelming and the views are basically straight up, whereas Beaver Creek's little valley, nestled partway up the mountain, is quieter and several miles from the intrusive traffic noise of I-70, the highway to Denver (two hours). Beaver Creek is smaller than Vail and has far fewer shops and diversions. It is also Jerry Ford's place. His annual Pro-Am Tournament is held at the Vail Golf Club, but the ex-president lives happily in the hills high above Beaver Creek.

THE GOLF

Whatever courses you intend to play, a number of general statements apply to the game in the Vail Valley. For one, the winds and weather are highly variable. On a summer morning you may begin your round wearing a short-sleeved shirt, a cotton turtleneck, wool sweater, and windbreaker. By the third or fourth hole the jacket, sweater, and turtleneck will probably be stashed in the back of the cart. However, by the fifteenth or sixteenth hole, you may put everything back on again. The thermometer drops suddenly when the cold wind whips up. Second, the golf here is as wonderfully relaxed as life in Vail generally is. If you are playing as a single or as a twosome, the other partners you may be paired with will exhibit on the golf course that famous, mellow Vail demeanor. It might have been plain good luck, but the amiable local residents we went around with were always easygoing, friendly, and completely free of the obscene utterances routinely, and sadly, encountered at many other resort courses. Our games here were enhanced by the good manners of our fellow golfers. And third, the courses' steep terrain means that even the most physically fit ride rather than walk.

Sonnenalp and Beaver Creek are the two courses you must not miss. Of the two, Sonnenalp has the most devoted following. Sonnenalp, in fact, is far better than Eagle-Vail, more appealing than Vail Golf Club, and, in our estimation, a simpler and fairer test of golf than Beaver Creek.

Sonnenalp Golf Club

Located in Edwards, nine miles west of Vail, the golf course at **Sonnenalp Golf Club** was designed by Jay Morrish and Bob Cupp. The club (formerly known as Singletree) is owned by the fine Sonnenalp Hotel in Vail, and its course has been rated among the top sixty resort courses in the nation by *Golf Digest*. With its generous fairways, fast greens, and panoramic vistas, this 7,059-yard layout provides a wonderful outing for golfers of every ability. The back nine, which climbs the mountains and returns to the valley floor, is particularly beautiful. At Sonnenalp you will experience that Rocky Mountain hang time with drives from elevated tees to fairways far below. The prettiest hole on the course might be number seventeen, a 193-yard par three guarded at the front and rear by five massive bunkers. Sonnenalp has a good practice area, a very handsome clubhouse with restaurant and well-stocked pro shop, and an obliging staff. The Sonnenalp's "country-club" facilities are located adjacent to the golf course: tennis courts and two swimming pools. Greens fees for guests of the Sonnenalp in the high season are $82 for guests and $125 for nonguests, cart included. Although open to the public on a space-available basis, guests of the Sonnenalp Resort enjoy preferred tee times.

The mountain panoramas offered on the Robert Trent Jones, Jr.–designed course at **Beaver Creek Golf Club** are even more breathtaking than Sonnenalp's, while the fanciful, multimillion-dollar homes along the fairways, some with massive turrets and extraordinary stone chimneys, add to the course's appeal. However, this visually stunning and carefully manicured course is a tricky, finesse-oriented layout that portends many lost balls for players who do not know it well. "If only I could have gotten past the first three holes" is the steady lament from any golfer who has experienced the course. The first hole is a long and narrow 546-yard downhill par five that requires a layup off the tee. The second hole, 193 yards, has such a steep slope that it actually plays as a short iron shot. The third is a 567-yard par five that requires an iron off the tee in order to hit the bend in the dogleg-left. The course finally widens and flattens out at the fifth hole, where you will use a driver off the tee for the first time despite already having played two par fives. At 8,500 feet, Beaver Creek has the highest elevation of any course in the area. The course is available to guests of the Beaver Creek Resort (which includes the Hyatt Regency) during a block of tee times from 10:30 A.M. until 12:30 P.M., as well as in the afternoons as space permits. Between June 15 and September 15, the club allows *only* members and guests of Beaver Creek Resort. During the remainder of the season, Sonnenalp guests can also reserve tee times on a limited, space-available basis. The greens fee of $110 includes your cart.

After Sonnenalp and Beaver Creek, we played at the lovely **Vail Golf Club** (7,024 yards from the back tees). The course is located in East Vail; you pass it on the left as you drive into town from Denver on I-70. The Vail Golf Club is a flat, out-and-back affair laced by Gore Creek, which runs along the valley floor. The facilities—an outstanding practice range and an elegant clubhouse—are excellent. Greens fees for this public-access golf course cost either $70 without a cart or $85 with a cart. Tee times can be made two days out, or, if you want to reserve a tee time more in advance (for tee times even months away), there is an additional $10 advance reservation fee. The club does enjoy a reciprocal relationship with most, if not all, of the major hotels in town, so as a guest at any of them, you can book an advance tee time through your hotel without the additional fee. Because this public course is so popular, we recommend making an advance tee time through your hotel as soon as you know when you will be in Vail.

Two extraordinary courses we must mention, although we have not yet had the opportunity to play them, are the Mountain and Valley courses at **Cordillera.** Located five miles apart, the **Valley Course,** which opened in July 1997, has a longer season because it faces the south and is situated 1,000 feet lower than the **Mountain Course.** Word has it that both courses are spectacular.

One course in the area that did disappoint us is **Eagle-Vail.** Great views of the mountains have been marred on certain holes by unattractive homes built far too close to the golf course. A big hook off the first tee, for instance, will send you careening through someone's kitchen window. Greens fees range from $80 to $90.

Sonnenalp Golf Club (formerly Singletree). 1265 Berry Creek Road, Edwards, CO 81632. Tel: 970-926-3533. Fax: 970-926-3572. Credit cards accepted.

• 1980. Designers: Jay Morrish, Bob Cupp. Par 71. 7,059 yards. 72.3 par rating. 138 slope rating. Greens fees: hotel guests: $82 (mid-June to mid-September), $67 (off season); public: $125 (mid-June to mid-September), $77 (off season). No walking. Restrictions: public is allowed only on a space-available basis. Season: April–early November.

Beaver Creek Golf Course. 103 Offerson Road, Beaver Creek, CO 81620. Tel: 970-949-7123. Fax: 970-845-6223. Credit cards accepted.

• 1980. Designer: Robert Trent Jones, Jr. Par 70. 6,400 yards. 69.2 par rating. 133 slope rating. Greens fee: $110, includes cart. No walking. Restrictions: public access limited to guests of Beaver Creek Resort from June 15 to September 15. Season: May–October.

Vail Golf Club. 1778 East Vail Valley Drive, Vail, CO 81657. Tel: 970-479-2260. Fax: 970-479-2355. Credit cards accepted.

• 1968. Designer: Ben Krueger. Par 71. 7,024 yards. 70.8 par rating. 121 slope rating. Greens fee: $70. Walking permitted. No caddies. Carts cost an additional $15 per person. Season: May–November.

Cordillera. PO Box 988, Edwards, CO 81632. Tel: 970-926-5100 (Mountain Course), 970-926-5900 (Valley Course). Fax: 970-926-5101 (Mountain Course), 970-926-5901 (Valley Course). Credit cards accepted.

• *Mountain Course.* 1994. Designer: Hale Irwin. Par 72. 6,789 yards. 70.8 par rating. 137 slope. Season: late May–October 15.
• *Valley Course.* 1997. Designer: Tom Fazio. Par 71. Less than 7,600 yards. Exact yardage, par and slope ratings as yet undetermined. Season: April 1–October 31.
• Greens fee for both courses: $195 per golfer, cart and complimentary forecaddie (per foursome) included. Restrictions: Limited outside tee times (only after 1:30 P.M.) available one day before on a space-available basis.

Eagle-Vail Golf Club. 0431 Eagle Drive, Avon, CO 81620. Tel: 800-341-8051 or 970-949-5267. Fax: 970-949-4160. Credit cards accepted.

• 1975. Designers: Bruce Devlin, Robert von Hagge. Par 72. 6,819 yards. 71.3 par rating. 131 slope. Greens fee: $80, cart included. Season: May 1–October 31.

GOLF SERVICES

Services and facilities are excellent at all the golf courses in the area. All have large, modern clubhouses, good practice ranges, cordial employees, and thoughtful amenities. Sonnenalp's operation is probably the best among this very upscale group.

LODGING

Two of the best hotels in the Vail/Beaver Creek area are the Sonnenalp in Vail and the Hyatt Regency in Beaver Creek. For golfers who wish to play the two best courses in the region—Sonnenalp and Beaver Creek—we would have to lean toward the Hyatt, simply because Hyatt guests do have—albeit limited—access to the Sonnenalp course, while outside play at Beaver Creek Golf Club is limited to Beaver Creek Resort guests from June 15 to September 15. One non-golf advantage in Sonnenalp's favor is that it is conveniently located in the heart of Vail Village, within easy walking distance of Vail's fine restaurants and shops. Hyatt guests will spend more time in the car driving the ten miles to and from Vail. Having stayed at both hotels, here is our report:

Beaver Creek is a magnificently planned community with an extraordinary collection of outdoor statuary (enormous bronze bears, Native American figures, and Wild West frontiersmen), spectacular private homes, and elaborate condominium complexes. In a town of important and unique edifices that vie for your attention, the **Hyatt Regency—Beaver Creek,** built in 1989, stands out. It has a stately stone and stucco exterior and an interior that is redolent with the romance of the Old West. It is staffed by a very eager, friendly, and well-groomed group of young people who, like their counterparts in Vail, seem extremely delighted to be living and working in idyllic Beaver Creek and very happy to be of service. The hotel stands at the foot of the Beaver Creek chairlifts. Its lovely restaurant, Patina (serving Southwest and Pacific Rim cuisine), has an outdoor dining terrace that is the village's *après-ski* meeting spot and that is equally wonderful during the summer. Every imaginable service is provided, like free shuttle buses that take you down the hill to the golf club, or to any destination in Beaver Creek, and in and out of Vail. Beaver Creek has fewer shops than Vail, but the stores that are there—like the large Gorsuch shop—are outstanding. The Hyatt has several retail shops of its own (including a great carryout bakery), plus the most stunning health spa of any hotel in the region, with exercise classes, a newly equipped weight room, swimming pools, and massage therapists. It is quite a setup.

We stayed in a standard room, number 4070, which was larger, better, and more comfortable than our standard room at the Sonnenalp. It had a gas fireplace with stone mantel, a separate sitting area with sofas and armchairs, a small private balcony with wonderful mountain views, a service bar, cable television, and a well-equipped bath with fine toiletries, heated towel bar, and bathroom scale.

Sonnenalp Resort

When you first arrive at the **Sonnenalp Resort of Vail** with its Hansel and Gretel architecture and unfailingly polite staff dressed in traditional Bavarian costume, you might think you should be speaking German. Owned by the Fässler family, the Sonnenalp, one of the very best hotels in Vail, occupies three separate buildings in the village: the Swiss Chalet (which houses the lobby, the Swiss Chalet Restaurant, a gift shop, one of the hotel's two health spas, and an array of standard rooms), the elegant Bavaria Haus (a gorgeous, recently rebuilt, and entirely renovated facility that houses the hotel's luxury suites, a European-style spa, two restaurants, an après-ski lounge, and a cozy, inviting library with a big fireplace), and the more modest Austria Haus (which is also slated to be entirely rebuilt and renovated in 1997, yet which for now houses another restaurant and more standard rooms). If you stay at the Sonnenalp, be sure to request the Bavaria Haus, with its renovated suites and lovely, overall ambience. The breakfast buffet in the Swiss Chalet, however, is spectacular, particularly the homemade pastries. Don't miss it, even if you do not stay there.

Hyatt Regency—Beaver Creek. PO Box 1595, Avon, CO 81620. Tel: 800-233-1234 or 970-949-1234. Fax: 970-949-4164. 295 rooms and suites. Rates for double rooms range from $120 to $160 in spring and fall and $235 to $280 during summer. Credit cards accepted.

Sonnenalp Resort of Vail. 20 Vail Road, Vail, CO 81657. Tel: 800-654-8312 or 970-476-5656. Fax: 970-476-1639. 133 rooms and suites from $170 to $500 for two, including a buffet breakfast. Golf packages available. Note: when you call the hotel to reserve your room, let the hotel reservation clerk book your tee times. In many cases, hotel guests get discounts (as much as $25 per round) and preferred times as well. Credit cards accepted.

RESTAURANTS (17)

Our favorite restaurants in Vail/Beaver Creek are briefly noted below.

Sweet Basil has been our favorite restaurant in Vail for more than a decade. Under the able, demanding, and discriminating direction of owner Kevin Clair, it has shown the highest level of consistency in Vail year after year. A contemporary-style restaurant with large windows overlooking Gore Creek, Sweet Basil features an imaginative American cuisine and utilizes the finest ingredients. Specialties include the wonderful ravioli with goat cheese, the grilled swordfish with whipped fennel potatoes, the fillet of sea bass with peppers and onions, the excellent breads, and homemade sorbets. The wine selection is one of the best in Colorado. Service is attentive, friendly, and professional. Even during the slower summer months, Sweet Basil can be filled to capacity with Vail's smartest set, so advance reservations are always necessary. About $100 for two, wine and tip included.

Vail's major hotels have showcase restaurants. The Left Bank restaurant at the Sitzmark Lodge can be terribly pretentious. Ludwig's at the Sonnenalp features somewhat heavy game and seafood. But the best and most beautiful hotel restaurant in Vail is in the Lodge. The **Wildflower Inn** is a colorful, bright, and lavishly decorated room with huge floral arrangements (mostly artificial, but nonetheless attractive), a superb wine list, a friendly staff, and an appealing menu with a choice of at least six appetizers and even more entrées, as well as a nice selection of desserts. We thoroughly enjoyed the roasted cod with garlic mashed potatoes, the sautéed medallions of monkfish, and the grilled Texas antelope. About $125 for two, wine and tip included. In addition to the Wildflower Inn, the Lodge at Vail now boasts a second distinctive restaurant, **Cucina Rustica.** After closing and undergoing a $2.5 million renovation, Cucina Rustica now offers a lovely new setting that beautifully complements the sophisticated Italian cuisine it serves. The Lodge at Vail clearly has a way with restaurants. Entrées in the Cucina range from $13 to $30.

Beano's Cabin is an exceptional restaurant located *on* the mountain at Beaver Creek and accessible only by horseback, horse-drawn wagon ride, or four-wheel-drive shuttle van. A prix-fixe menu costing $76 for adults and $46 for kids includes a six-course gourmet meal as well as transportation up and down the mountain, whether it be the hour-long horseback ride, the equally long wagon ride, or the fifteen-minute shuttle van. This handsome log cabin—a dramatic mixture of wood, stone, and glass—is the perfect spot for a romantic evening with fine food and wine. When we visited, the prix-fixe menu included no less than ten dinner entrées and seven dessert selections to choose from. Both the service and the Rocky Mountain/Continental cuisine are superb. In addition, there is live entertainment. A magical experience. Be sure to book *far* in advance.

Sweet Basil. 193 East Gore Creek Drive, Vail, CO 81657. Tel: 970-476-0125. Fax: 970-476-0125. Credit cards accepted.

The Wildflower Inn and Cucina Rustica. The Lodge at Vail, 174 East Gore Creek Drive, Vail, CO 81657. Tel: 970-476-5011 (general) or 970-476-8111 (Wildflower Inn). Fax: 970-476-7425. Credit cards accepted.

Beano's Cabin. PO Box 915, Avon, CO 81620. Tel: 970-949-9090. Fax: 970-845-5232. Credit cards accepted.

NON-GOLF ACTIVITIES

Vail has something for everyone, particularly active travelers. Rollerblades and mountain bikes may be rented at numerous locations. Hiking, horseback riding, fly fishing (local guides are available), swimming, tennis, jeep tours, white-water rafting on the Colorado River, chairlift rides—all this and more can be arranged by your concierge. Nighttime activities during the summer include a wide range of music and theater. We probably don't have to tell you that Vail also offers shopping. Wonderful art galleries, jewelry stores, and antique shops stretch from one end of Vail to the other.

GETTING THERE: From Eagle Airport, take I-70 East toward Denver. After approximately thirty-five miles, take exit 167 (Avon exit) and turn right (south) into town. At the third stoplight, you should see the entrance to the Hyatt Regency.

Wyoming

▶JACKSON HOLE

GOLFING IN THE SHADOW OF THE SPECTACULAR TETONS

	The Golf	Golf Services	Lodging	Restaurants	Non-Golf Activities	Total
Rating	17	18	18	16	19	88

Teton Pines

Unlike Vail, Aspen, and Sun Valley, Jackson Hole first earned its reputation as a summer dude-ranch resort. Skiing only came to Jackson Hole in the mid-1960s, and, in spite of its incredible downhill terrain and its 4,000-foot vertical, the skiing operation has always played second fiddle to the region's summertime attractions.

Anyone who has ever enjoyed a typical summer day at Jackson Hole—with its deep-blue skies and dry, clean, fresh air—understands why it is one of the most heavenly summer destinations on earth. Although known more for its river runners, mountain climbers, and wranglers, Jackson Hole now attracts golfers to two of the finest resort golf courses in the country—Jackson Hole Golf & Tennis, rated number ten by *Golf Digest*, and Teton Pines, which has been rated forty-ninth in the United States. Just several miles apart as the golden eagle flies, these two courses are distinctly different in personality. Playing both over the course of a week or ten days would keep even the most die-hard golfer content, amused, and challenged. For those of us who knew Jackson in its pre-golf days back in the sixties, we still have this nagging notion that perhaps golf, golf carts, and manicured greens are a contradiction to this region's Western spirit. In Jackson Hole, shouldn't we wear Tony Lamas rather than Foot-Joys, and shouldn't we travel from point A to point B on a Buckeye rather than on an electrically powered golf cart?

Despite these feelings, we cannot help but be comforted and exhilarated when playing these two wondrous courses in the shadow of the majestic Teton mountains. With the mountains as a glorious backdrop, the Jackson Hole Golf & Tennis and Teton Pines golf courses give visitors yet another choice among a dazzling array of outdoor recreational options. Jackson Hole offers some of the finest hiking and mountain climbing in the world, excellent fly fishing, river rafting, horseback riding, ballooning, and mountain biking.

Be forewarned that Jackson Hole has, indeed, been discovered. During July and August, the famous Jackson Square teems with gawking tourists from every country, auto traffic at times backs up on the roads in the valley, and tee times at the two courses should be made days, if not weeks, in advance. People love Jackson Hole, and consequently real estate prices have skyrocketed. In spite of its popularity, Jackson Hole has miraculously maintained an engaging friendliness, casualness, and lack of pretense. Vail embodies a vapid, slick, somewhat *Town & Country* social scene; Aspen exudes the glitz of Rodeo Drive; meanwhile, Jackson ambles along with its authenticity and connection to the past intact. Jack Nicholson is Aspen. Harrison Ford is Jackson. In Jackson Hole, no one seems impressed by who or what you are but rather by your personal character—a refreshing switch from our fame-driven media world.

A note of clarification may be needed here. Jackson Hole refers to the whole valley, and Jackson is the name of the town. Naturally, Jackson Hole's popularity stems from its breathtaking beauty; it is truly one of the most spectacular places on earth. When first entering the valley, especially from the north or the east, one cannot help but be awestruck by the deep-blue Jackson Lake to the north, the sparkling Snake River running the north-south length of the valley, and the magnificent Teton Range rising abruptly over 6,000 feet from the valley floor and showcased by the craggy, looming presence of the 13,766-foot Grand Teton.

THE GOLF

Both golf courses in Jackson Hole are a curious but successful blend of public course and private country club. Private members get a preferential nod on tee times, but any nonmember can get on if he or she calls early and is willing to take a later tee time. In its infinite lack of snobbism, the county leadership granted Teton Pines the necessary zoning approval only after the stipulation was agreed upon that the golf facilities would always remain public-access.

Jackson Hole Golf & Tennis lies on the east side of the Snake River, eight miles north of the town of Jackson and just south of the airport. Built in the mid-sixties and originally designed by Bob Baldock, Jackson Hole Golf & Tennis is certainly the more mature of the two valley courses. In fact, as you play many of the holes bordered by cottonwood trees over a hundred feet tall, you feel as if you were playing a course fifty or sixty years old rather than just over thirty. People who have played this course from its inception credit Robert Trent Jones, Jr., who redesigned the course in 1967, for creating the masterpiece layout that it is today. Other than being fairly flat, the Jackson Hole Golf Course has everything—top on the list being the spectacular view of the Tetons from every hole as well as some of the best views of Sleeping Indian, the rocky configuration of a sleeping chief in the Gros Ventre mountains to the east. Water comes into play on eleven of the eighteen holes here, thanks to the crisscrossing of gurgling streams and the Gros Ventre River. One of the most memorable holes on the course is number eleven, a 527-yard par five from the whites, where you need nearly a two-hundred-yard carry (from the back tees) to get across the river.

Where Teton Pines can bring you to your knees with errant shots into the water, Jackson Hole Golf plays long and fair at 7,148 yards from the blues and 6,036 yards from the reds. Most par fours are more than 375 yards, and even with the added distance you get from the altitude, you will find long approach shots to the greens even after good drives. Because it is located on the eastern side of the Snake River, which gets considerably more wind than the protected western side, wind is often a factor, especially in the afternoon. The course's condition is nearly flawless: excellent tee boxes, lush fairways, and beautifully maintained, medium-speed greens. Jackson Hole Golf & Tennis, like most courses, is the raison d'être of a real estate play, but other than the hideous condos lining the second hole, the homes on the course are set well back, liberally spaced, attractive, and in no way a distraction from the aesthetics of this lovely course. The greens fee in high season is $100, cart included.

Teton Pines, which lies on the western side of the Snake River on the road to the ski area, is a high-powered, well-run resort. Real estate development was inau-

Teton Pines

gurated here in the early 1980s but really only hit high gear when the Arnold Palmer and Ed Seay course was completed in 1987. Less than twenty years ago these several hundred acres were hay fields; now they are a breathtaking golf resort with a magnificent golf course sprinkled with numerous ponds and streams creating endless water hazards, a stunning two-story clubhouse, many $500,000 to $700,000 town houses, and $2- to $3-million homes on the course. Homes that go on the market are typically sold in a matter of days. After playing the course on two consecutive days, we found it easy to see why—the views of the Tetons and Gros Ventre are inspirational from almost any vantage point. What Palmer and Seay did with this course is masterful, and though still only a decade old, it is an intriguing layout that will get even better as it matures fully.

The course is especially interesting because water comes into play on all but three of the eighteen holes. For the real macho low handicappers, Teton Pines offers two championship alternatives—the gold tees at 7,412 yards and the blues at 7,168. It is very important to realize that both Jackson Hole golf courses, although they have some contour, are very flat; the Tetons as a background create the panoramic mountain views. The ever-present water on both courses is complemented by well-placed bunkers. The 560-yard par five number ten at Teton Pines is a perfect example. You hit over water off the tee, dogleg right, hope to hit a great second shot, and dogleg left to the green over more water. Greens are fast, fairways nearly perfect, and the course is reasonably bunkered.

Jackson Hole Golf & Tennis. 5000 North Spring Gulch Road, Jackson, WY 83001. Tel: 307-733-3111. Fax: 307-733-0642. Credit cards accepted.

• 1965/1967. Designers: Bob Baldock/Robert Trent Jones, Jr. Par 72. 7,148 yards. 72.3 par rating. 133 slope rating. Greens fees: $100 (July–August) and $50 to $80 (off season), cart included. Walking permitted. No caddies. Season: early May–late October.

Teton Pines Resort and Country Club. 3450 North Clubhouse Drive, Jackson, WY 83001. Tel: 800-238-2223 or 307-733-1005. Fax: 307-733-2860. Credit cards accepted.

• 1987. Designers: Arnold Palmer, Ed Seay. Par 72. 7,412 yards. 74.2 par rating. 137 slope rating. Greens fees: guests: $45 to $95 (depending on the season), cart included; public: $50 to $140 (depending on the season), cart included. Walking permitted. Caddies available. Season: May–mid-October.

GOLF SERVICES

The Jackson Hole Golf establishment is not the high-powered golf operation that Teton Pines is—the clubhouse here is a single, one-story structure with a pleasant restaurant, clean and attractive men's and women's locker rooms, and a small, friendly pro shop. Golf services are adequate, and all employees are friendly, casual, and laid-back. There are also tennis courts and a swimming pool. The club is owned by CSX, the owner of the Greenbrier Resort in West Virginia. There is a putting green and a driving range that hits straight at the Grand Teton. Range balls are included with your greens fee.

The maintenance of Teton Pines meets or exceeds what the golfer will find anywhere. While Jackson Hole Golf is a bit casual when it comes to services, Teton Pines runs like a well-oiled machine. As you pull up to the front of the clubhouse, a young man greets you, grabs your golf bags, and has them strapped to the cart before you have checked through the pro shop. Pro shop personnel could not be more helpful and engaging, and the merchandise selection is phenomenal, especially the clothes. There is a putting green, chipping green, and superb driving range with top-condition balls that are included in your greens fee. Teton Pines is a truly first-rate course, which makes the overzealous and intrusive real estate presence all the more lamentable.

LODGING

Naturally, a place with as many winter and summer tourists as Jackson Hole will have loads of bed-and-breakfasts, motels, and hotels. Of the many, three places stand out as being particularly fine.

Teton Pines Resort and Country Club, from top to bottom, is a class act. This assessment certainly includes the club's very fine lodging. There are three choices for accommodations: master bedrooms, master bedroom suites with living room, and two-master-bedroom suites with living room. High season (mid-June to late September) rates start at $325 per night and go up to $425. All suites are very spacious and beautifully decorated and feature wonderful views, private decks, and two bathrooms for every bedroom. Service is first-rate. The Teton Pines location is one of the best in the valley. Situated between the ski resort and the town of Jackson, it is only minutes from either.

Just a few hundred yards north of Teton Pines on Teton Village Road, the **Wildflower Inn,** with five guest rooms, is an idyllic log home nestled among cottonwoods and aspens with glorious views of the Tetons. All guest rooms have private baths, and four of the five have private decks. Shooting Star, an upstairs room, is quite dramatic with its private balcony and a view of the Grand Teton. Guests are encouraged to use the rest of the house, as well as the outdoor terrace and yard. Vegetable gardens, flowers, and pets abound. Breakfasts are terrific and mountain-size—the hearty type that keep you going for a full day on the course, ski slopes, or river. Room rates range from $150 to $160 (with one additional suite at $225), including breakfast.

The Rusty Parrot in the heart of Jackson, just a few minutes' walk from the main square, is a statement of good taste and Rocky Mountain elegance. There are thirty-two comfortable rooms, a lobby, and living room that are right out of the pages of a Ralph Lauren catalog. Gourmet breakfasts, with your choice of omelettes, excellent granola, fruits, juices, and pancakes, are included. A hot tub is located on the second-floor deck. The Rusty Parrot is a very well run inn with friendly and efficient service. Rates for a double room range from $190 to $225 (and one super-suite at $450) in high season. Although situated right in the town, North Jackson is a quiet street in this block, and the Rusty Parrot is peaceful and relaxing.

Teton Pines Resort and Country Club. 3450 North Clubhouse Drive, Jackson, WY 83001. Tel: 800-238-2223 or 307-733-1005. Fax: 307-733-2860. 16 rooms and 8 suites. Doubles go from $160 to $195 from May to mid-June, $325 to $425 from mid-June through August, and $195 to $215 in September and October. Credit cards accepted.

The Wildflower Inn. Teton Village Road, PO Box 3724, Jackson, WY 83001. Tel: 307-

733-4710. Fax: 307-739-0914. 5 rooms from $150 to $160 (and 1 suite at $225). Credit cards accepted.

The Rusty Parrot. 175 North Jackson, Jackson, WY 83001. Tel: 800-458-2004 or 307-733-2000. Fax: 307-733-5566. 32 rooms from $190 to $225. Credit cards accepted.

RESTAURANTS

At the outset we must say that Jackson Hole is not the culinary epicenter of the Rocky Mountain resorts. Dining in Vail, Aspen, and Sun Valley leaves Teton Valley cuisine in the dust, but the food here is getting much better. We have been visiting Jackson for well over twenty years, and as recently as ten years ago, in our opinion, there was not a fine restaurant in Jackson. Happily, there are now several.

Snake River Grill, on the main square in Jackson, is a very handsome restaurant with straightforward, very good food. Service is professional and friendly, and almost from its opening in 1993, Snake River Grill established itself as the best place in town, as well as the most popular. Reservations should be made days in advance. Choices include delicious filet mignon, fresh seafood specials, pizza (especially the margerita pizza), and game dishes, including elk sausage. Located at Crabtree Corner on the Town Square.

The Grille at the Pines, located in the clubhouse of Teton Pines, is our second most favorite restaurant in the valley. The dining room, with its Western art and expanse of windows facing the mountains and golf course, is stunning. Service is prompt and infinitely friendly. Outstanding seafood specials are featured every night, like king salmon, Alaskan halibut, and ahi tuna. The Grille also has a better-than-average wine list.

Steiglers, which is located at the Jackson Hole Racquet Club on Teton Village Road, is owned and operated by the brother of Olympic Gold Medalist Pepi Steigler and has been a local favorite for years. The restaurant is good but overpriced and rather self-impressed. The cuisine has a slight but not overpowering Austrian influence.

The **Alpenhof,** located at the base of the ski area, offers "fancy" dining that we found remarkably forgettable.

Shades Cafe, just off the main square, is the perfect spot for a casual, quick sandwich and a latte. Its relaxed feel creates a winning charm; enjoy the small patio for outdoor lunch.

Nora's Fishcreek Inn, just a few miles northwest of Jackson, is the place for breakfast in the valley. Fantastic *huevos rancheros* and pancakes. High cholesterol, but an engaging Jackson Hole institution that is enormously popular with local residents.

Jenny Lake Lodge, about a half hour north of Jackson, is a must for its Sunday-night buffet. For most restaurants, the weekly buffet presents an opportunity to clean out the refrigerators and freezers, but not so at Jenny Lake Lodge. Here it is the culinary highlight of the week. Make reservations weeks in advance. As you drive up the western part of the valley in early evening to Jenny Lake, you'll see groups of noble elk in the fields. Closed October through May.

Billy's Burgers, which is right next door to and under the same ownership as the Cadillac Grill on the main town square, is the place to get a burger in Jackson. The mood is trendy and lively, and the burgers are a bargain—a half-pound Billy burger costs just $4.95 ($5.25 with cheese) while the Betty burger, weighing in at a trim one-third of a pound, costs just $3.95.

The **Blue Lion** in the town of Jackson is one of our new favorites. With a cuisine variously described as eclectic, New American, and Continental, the Blue Lion serves an excellent rack of lamb and grilled elk. The restaurant is also known for its fresh seafood selections. Dinner for two including wine and tip will run around $75.

As for bars, the **Stagecoach Bar** in Wilson has plenty of Western flair and is a favorite of many locals of all ages; a great watering hole, the Stagecoach also serves a terrific burger. This is also the place to go on Sunday evening, although all bars close at 10 P.M. on Sundays. The **Mangy Moose,** located at the mountain base in Teton Village, is a colorful bar and restaurant for all seasons, although the food was terrible the last time we were there. Featuring live music, the Mangy Moose really wakes up around the time the clock strikes ten or eleven.

Snake River Grill. 84 East Broadway, Jackson, WY 83001. Tel: 307-733-0557. Fax: 307-733-5767. Credit cards accepted.

The Grille at the Pines. 3450 North Clubhouse Drive, Jackson, WY 83001. Tel: 800-238-2223 or 307-733-1005. Fax: 307-733-2860. Credit cards accepted.

Steiglers. Teton Village Road (Highway 390), Teton Village, WY 83025. Tel: 307-733-1071. No fax. Credit cards accepted.

Alpenhof. 3255 West McCollister Drive, Teton Village, WY 83025. Tel: 307-733-3242. Fax: 307-739-1516. Credit cards accepted.

Shades Cafe. 75 South King Street, Jackson, WY 83001. Tel: 307-733-2015. Fax: 307-733-8033. No credit cards.

Nora's Fishcreek Inn. 5600 West on Highway 22, Wilson, WY 83014. Tel: 307-733-8288. Fax: 307-739-2233. Credit cards accepted.

Jenny Lake Lodge. Inn Park Road, Grand Teton National Park, WY 83013. Tel: 307-733-4647. Fax: 307-733-0324. Credit cards accepted.

Billy's Burgers. 55 North Cash Street, Jackson, WY 83001. Tel: 307-733-3279. Fax: 307-739-0110. Credit cards accepted.

Blue Lion. 160 North Millward, Jackson, WY 83001. Tel: 307-733-3912. Fax: 307-733-3915. Credit cards accepted.

Stagecoach Bar. 5755 Highway 22, Wilson, WY 83014. Tel: 307-733-4407. Fax: 307-733-4405. Credit cards accepted.

Mangy Moose. South end of Teton Village, WY 83025. Tel: 307-733-9779. Fax: 307-739-1827. Credit cards accepted.

NON-GOLF ACTIVITIES ⑲

As mentioned earlier, the diversity of activities in Jackson, mostly outdoor, is endless. If your interest is mountain climbing or rock climbing, the Grand Tetons are world-renowned and inviting to climbers of all levels. The Exum School of Mountaineering is the premier company for climbing lessons and for booking guides (tel: 307-739-3300). Because of the scenery, hiking in the Jackson Hole area is a joy, and all you need is the *Grand Teton Official Map and Guide,* which shows countless trails. For Grand Teton National Park information, call 307-543-2851. Fly fishing around Jackson is excellent—the Snake, a great cutthroat fishery, runs the entire length of the valley. The Fall River and Henry's Fork are just west of Jackson in Idaho, the South Fork is less than an hour away, and all the fishing of Yellowstone National Park is just two hours north. For further information on fishing and excellent guide service, contact the Jack Dennis Outdoor Shop (tel: 307-733-3270). River rafting in the area is superb—the two most available opportunities are the Snake from Jackson Lake down to Moose and the good white-water section of the Snake south of town. The list goes on and on— wildlife viewing, ballooning, mountain biking and, in winter, downhill skiing, cross-country skiing, and snowmobiling. In town, the fascinating National Wildlife Art Museum features a very fine permanent collection and fabulous rotating exhibitions. Although you will find an extremely nice Ralph Lauren outlet store on the main square, Jackson does not offer high-fashion shopping. It does, however, offer unparalleled outdoor clothing and equipment shopping. The town is also loaded with galleries specializing in Western art and Indian jewelry. No question that Jackson is touristy, especially the square, but despite that it is great fun to stroll the streets and slip into the shops and galleries.

GETTING THERE: To get to Teton Pines Resort and Country Club from Jackson Airport, take a right onto Highway 89 South and follow it into the center of town. At the town square, turn right at the light onto Broadway and continue for roughly two or three miles until you reach a Y intersection. Turn right onto Highway 22 (to Wilson and Teton Village) and at the first stoplight again turn right, onto Teton Village Road. Drive for an additional 2.5 miles, and you will see the resort on your left.

Idaho

▶SUN VALLEY

GLORIOUS GOLF IN CENTRAL IDAHO

	The Golf	Golf Services	Lodging	Restaurants	Non-Golf Activities	Total
Rating	17	17	18	18	18	88

Sun Valley, Idaho

Sun Valley, Idaho, just a mile up the hill from the stylish and seductive little town of Ketchum, was the first destination ski resort ever built in the United States. Founded in 1936 by W. Averell Harriman, then head of the Union Pacific Railroad, Sun Valley was patronized by stars and other notables whose portraits now line the corridors of the elegant Sun Valley Lodge: Clark Gable, Mary Pickford, Darryl Zanuck, Gary Cooper, Marilyn Monroe, the Shah of Iran, and Ernest Hemingway, who lived in Ketchum for much of his life and died there in 1961. In 1996, after sixty years of operation, Sun Valley again ranked number one (ahead of Vail and Aspen) on *Ski* magazine's list of the best ski resorts in the United States.

We at GOLF TRAVEL have reviewed many resorts that, although they originated as ski destinations, now enjoy a thriving summer season by offering great golfing facilities—outstanding places like Jackson Hole, Vail, and Sugarloaf in Maine. All these resorts have their individual strengths, but after all the pluses and minuses are computed, we believe that the complete package at Sun Valley is about as good as it gets.

Why is Sun Valley the best ski-cum-golf destination in America? Simply because, in addition to its other attractions, Sun Valley is home to the lovely town of Ketchum, which gives Sun Valley character, class, and, as we heard time and again from residents during our visit, "a sense of place and community." If you love to ski *and* love to play golf, and if you equally appreciate fine food, stunning surroundings, great shopping, and genuine charm, then consider Sun Valley, one of the most intoxicating places to live or visit in the world.

Ketchum—a town of 3,200—boasts twelve espresso bars, eighteen bicycle shops, and more than twenty massage therapists. Despite its swank galleries, java joints, fishing and hunting outfitters, and fine restaurants, Ketchum retains its wonderful Old West flavor with such carefully preserved architectural details as wood-plank sidewalks right out of old installments of *Gunsmoke*, albeit with one important difference: most of the cowboys here are from Beverly Hills.

Half the working population, it seems, sells real estate. Realty offices populate almost every block and with good reason: even the most humble cottages on the distant periphery of Ketchum sell for $650,000. Choice residential lots in Sun Valley proper fetch over a million dollars per acre. Real estate mania may have quieted in other corners of America, but in Sun Valley it remains intense. A couple of high-profile realtors drive their clients around in red Hummers, the prestige vehicle of the moment. Everyone else gets by in the latest Jeep, Range Rover, or Suburban. We played golf with an off-duty Sun Valley realtor who, after learning we were from out of town, vowed—on the first tee no less—that he would sell us a property "before the round is over."

The Ketchum/Sun Valley area, set in the southern Sawtooth Mountains, is not only incredibly scenic, it is also glamorous. Local celebrities include Bruce Willis and Demi Moore, Arnold Schwarzenegger and Maria Shriver, Mariel Hemingway, and winter sports stars like Picabo Street, Katarina Witt, and Peggy Fleming. Sun Valley is a bit tough to get to—you must fly to Salt Lake City and take a one-hour commuter flight from there—yet your efforts will be rewarded: the summer weather is sunny, dry, and sublime. For golfers, the optimum time to visit is from May to the first week of October.

THE GOLF

There are two outstanding, eighteen-hole, Robert Trent Jones, Jr., golf courses in Sun Valley: the Sun Valley and Elkhorn courses. The Sun Valley Course is by far the better, more exciting, and more memorable.

Both layouts are extremely different in appearance. Sun Valley is wooded and tight, while Elkhorn is wide open and windswept, yet both share the same elevation of 6,000 feet above sea level. Tee shots soar, and approaches to the green must be hit with one or two clubs less than routinely played from the same distance back home.

The par seventy-two **Sun Valley Course** should be played from the blue tees (6,674 yards/slope 126) even by high handicappers because the views and shot values from the blues are simply sensational. The white tees (6,057 yards/slope 122) shorten the course too much and diminish its charm. When playing from the blues, you will hit drives from steep tees perched far above the fairways. Good

Sun Valley Course

drives here produce a sense of exhilaration as you watch your towering tee shots sail high and hang in the mountain air before settling on the perfectly groomed fairway floor. The Sun Valley course is a natural paradise complemented by material splendor; it not only features groves of birch and aspen, clear rushing streams, it also provides an informal tour of the most spectacular and fanciful private mansions in the Sun Valley area. Our realtor friend ticked off the prices, anywhere from $3 to $6 million.

The first great hole on Sun Valley's front side is number two, an extremely challenging, 428-yard par four. The elevated tee requires that you drive the ball far enough beyond the trees on the left to open up a second shot over a creek to the green. Number seven confirms that beautiful things come in small packages. A creek bisects the landing area and lurks on the left side of the green on this short (278-yard) par four.

Highlights of Sun Valley's back nine include number eleven, another hole whose tee is perched high above the fairway; twelve, an uphill par four that presents perhaps the toughest second shot on the golf course—one that demands a lofted approach over two mammoth bunkers; and thirteen, a downhill par four that frequently produces drives of well over three hundred yards, thanks to prevailing winds from the rear. But clearly the most dramatic hole at Sun Valley is number fifteen, a 244-yard par three that plays through the trees from an elevated tee to the green far below.

The greens fee at Sun Valley is $90 for resort guests and $100 for nonguests, cart included. Walking is permitted before June 15 and after September 12. The course is walkable for the very energetic, but given the altitude and steep tees, most golfers prefer to ride. The length from the red tees is 5,241 yards (slope 125).

The **Elkhorn Course,** about one mile from Sun Valley, features great views of the brown Sawtooth Mountains, broad fairways that are mounded on the sides to keep balls in play, and two very disappointing holes—numbers eight and nine—where rows of expensive condominiums have been built far too close to the course. A large net has been installed on the right side of the ninth fairway to protect guests in the resort's outdoor swimming pool from sliced golf balls. Put the eighth and ninth holes aside, however, and Elkhorn makes for an excellent day of golf.

Elkhorn features a handful of fine holes, including the fifth, a very long 644-yard par five; the seventh, a terrific, uphill par four; the tenth, which requires a strategic drive over the first waste area that will fall short of the second; number thirteen, a dogleg-left where big hitters can cut the corner; seventeen, another good dogleg to the left; and eighteen, a 544-yard par five to an uphill green.

Elkhorn measures 7,101 yards from the back tees (slope 133), 6,524 yards from the white tees (slope 128), and 5,424 yards from the red tees (slope 120). Par is seventy-two. Walking is permitted after 4 P.M. and also before 9 A.M. for those golfers who play just nine holes off the back nine. Greens fees are $75 for resort guests and $95 for nonguests, cart included.

In addition to the resort courses at Sun Valley and Elkhorn, there are two other golf courses in the Sun Valley region: a nine-hole municipal course at Bigwood and the beautiful, new Valley Club, a private golf club designed by Hale Irwin, which opened in 1995.

Elkhorn Resort and Golf Club. 100 Elkhorn Road, Sun Valley, ID 83354. Tel: 800-355-4676 or 208-622-3300 (golf reservations). Fax: 208-622-3261. Credit cards accepted.

• 1973. Designer: Robert Trent Jones, Jr. Par 72. 7,101 yards. 72.4 par rating. 133 slope rating. Greens fees: $75 (guests), $95 (nonguests), cart included. Walking permitted after 4 P.M. No caddies. Season: May 1–October 20.

Sun Valley Lodge. 1 Sun Valley Road, Sun Valley, ID 83353. Tel: 208-622-2250 or 2251. Fax: 208-622-2030. Credit cards accepted.

• 1938. Designer: Robert Trent Jones, Jr. Par 72. 6,674 yards. 71.4 par rating. 126 slope rating. Greens fees: $90 (guests), $100 (nonguests, depending on availability forty-eight hours prior to play), cart included. Walking permitted before June 15 and after September 12. No caddies. Season: mid-April—end of October.

GOLF SERVICES

Golf services at both Sun Valley and Elkhorn are excellent, although, again, Sun Valley's facilities edge out those at Elkhorn. Sun Valley and Elkhorn have practice ranges, but Sun Valley's range is the larger of the two. Sun Valley even provides an alternate hole that can be played when one of its regular eighteen is closed for repair. Neither pro shop is exceptionally large, yet the staffs at both courses are cordial and welcoming. Rental clubs, rental golf shoes, and lessons are also available at both courses.

LODGING

Just as the Sun Valley golf course is better than the Elkhorn course, so, too, the Sun Valley Lodge is a far better place to stay than the rather dreary, motel-type units in the Buena Vista–run Elkhorn Resort. We stayed at both the Sun Valley Lodge and the Elkhorn Resort and found that there was no contest.

The **Elkhorn Resort** is an impressive, well-planned, and well-maintained complex, with its large hotel, tennis courts, swimming pool, indoor gymnasium, outdoor plaza with several shops and restaurants, and hundreds of nearby condominiums. Yet during our visit, the large, somewhat characterless hotel was virtually empty, and the hotel staff, such as it was—just one desk clerk and a handful of housekeepers—appeared completely dispirited. Our room at Elkhorn (number 242) was clean and decent, but certainly not special or luxurious in any way. The chief advantage of staying at Elkhorn is its low prices. We paid just $134 per night.

The mood and atmosphere could not be in greater contrast just a mile up the road at the **Sun Valley Lodge.** Where Elkhorn is lackluster and unimaginative, the Sun Valley Lodge is abuzz with stylish guests and energized by a large and friendly staff dressed in Tyrolean outfits. Full of fanciful design flourishes in both its guest rooms and public areas, the Sun Valley Lodge is a local scene and social hub.

Special features of the recently remodeled Sun Valley Lodge include the Duchin Lounge, an intimate bar where the popular and talented pianist Joe Fos performs on Friday and Saturday nights, a wonderful skating rink at the rear of the hotel, where future Olympic stars learn to jump and spin, a fine assortment of shops in Sun Valley Village, and an excellent dining room.

Sun Valley Lodge

We stayed in a standard room at the back of Sun Valley Lodge overlooking the ice rink, number 365 ($159), which we found spacious, comfortable, and attractively decorated.

The only other hotel option worth considering in the Sun Valley area is the **Knob**

Hill Inn, a very pretty, Alpine-style, twenty-four-room hotel located on Main Street just north of Ketchum. The more expensive doubles come with fireplaces, while the suites have fireplaces and living rooms. Two "penthouses" offer yet more space. The Knob Hill Inn is also the home of Felix's, one of the best restaurants in the region.

Elkhorn Resort and Golf Club. 100 Elkhorn Road, Sun Valley, ID 83354. Tel: 800-355-4676 or 208-622-4511. Fax: 208-622-3261. 200 rooms and suites from $114 to $285. Credit cards accepted.

Sun Valley Lodge. 1 Sun Valley Road, Sun Valley, ID 83353. Tel: 800-786-8259 or 208-622-2151 (reservations), 208-622-4111 (general). Fax: 208-622-2030. 254 rooms and suites from $135 to $340. Credit cards accepted.

Knob Hill Inn. 960 North Main Street, Ketchum, ID 83340. Tel: 800-526-8010 or 208-726-8010. Fax: 208-726-2712. 24 rooms and suites ranging from $160 to $300. Credit cards accepted.

R E S T A U R A N T S

Ketchum has a fine collection of restaurants, particularly for a town of just 3,200. A short list of the best restaurants in the region follows.

Elegant, sophisticated **Evergreen** is the best restaurant in the entire Ketchum–Sun Valley region. Evergreen features outstanding contemporary American cuisine, a noteworthy wine list that has earned praise from the *Wine Spectator*, utterly professional, friendly service, and a comfortable interior with stone fireplaces and attractive artwork. Our dinner at Evergreen included a sublime ahi tuna and a good rack of New Zealand lamb. About $125 for two at dinner, wine and tip included. Reservations required. Highly recommended for that special evening.

Madrid-born Chef Felix at **Felix's** serves the Spanish/Mediterranean cuisine of his homeland with real skill. The paella ($19.85)—full of Mexican shrimp, clams, mussels, calamari, chicken, and spicy sausage—was truly memorable, as was the rack of lamb ($25.95), the chef's signature dish.

The ultimate lunch spot in always fashionable Ketchum, **Cristina's** is an elegant bakery with an attached dining area filled with good-looking patrons sampling the crusty Italian breads, fresh pasta, summer salads, and grilled vegetables. Lots of Mercedes and Range Rovers are parked out front. The dining area is open for breakfast, lunch, and Sunday brunch; the bakery itself is open until 5:30 P.M.

Another outstanding place for breakfast or lunch, **The Kneadery** is far more low-key than Cristina's. This Ketchum institution features inexpensive soups, salads, omelets, and burgers.

Other recommended Ketchum-area restaurants include the fine **Lodge Dining Room** at the Sun Valley Lodge, serving French and Continental cuisine with entrées ranging in price from $17 to $24; **Java on Fourth,** the best coffeehouse in town; and **Michel's,** a classic French restaurant on Sun Valley Road where a delicious dinner for two will run about $80.

Evergreen. 171 First Avenue, Ketchum, ID 83340. Tel. 208-726-3888. Fax: 208-726-2448. Credit cards accepted.

Felix's. 960 North Main Street, Ketchum, ID 83340. Tel: 208-726-2712. Fax: 208-726-2712 (Attn: Felix's). Credit cards accepted.

Cristina's. 520 Second Street East, Ketchum, ID 83340. Tel. 208-726-4499. Fax: 208-725-0751. Credit cards accepted.

The Kneadery. 260 Leadville Avenue, Ketchum, ID 83340. Tel. 208-726-9462. No fax. Credit cards accepted.

Lodge Dining Room. Sun Valley Lodge. 1 Sun Valley Road, Sun Valley, ID 83353. Tel: 208-622-2151 (general), 208-622-2150 (restaurant), 208-622-2097 (concierge for reservations called in before 5:30 P.M.). Fax: 208-622-2030. Credit cards accepted.

Java on Fourth. 191 4th Street East, Ketchum, ID 83340. Tel. 208-726-2882. Fax: 208-726-1771. No credit cards.

Michel's. Corner of Walnut Avenue and Sun Valley Road, Ketchum, ID 83340. Tel: 208-726-3388. Fax: 208-726-9727. Credit cards accepted.

NON-GOLF ACTIVITIES

Activities include fly fishing in Silver Creek, tennis, biking, rafting the Salmon River, picnics in the mountains, browsing for real estate, and shopping in Ketchum and Sun Valley Village. One of the most exceptional shops in Ketchum is the Silver Creek Outfitters on North Main Street, which sells fine clothing for men and women along with hunting and fishing equipment. The Sun Valley Symphony performs throughout the summer.

GETTING THERE: From Sun Valley Airport take 75 North approximately twelve miles into Ketchum. Turn right on Sun Valley road (second stoplight) and follow approximately 1.3 miles. Entrance to the Sun Valley Lodge is on the right.

Oregon

▶PORTLAND

	The Golf	Golf Services	Lodging	Restaurants	Non-Golf Activities	Total
Rating	18	17	18	17	17	87

Virtually every "best" list published in the national magazines these days ranks Portland, Oregon, at or near the top of its popularity charts. Despite a reputation for bleak weather that was dramatically substantiated by the horrific winter of 1996 that brought rainstorms of biblical proportions, historic floods to the Willamette River, snow, and sheets of ice to city streets, Portland still emerged in *Money* magazine as "the best place to live," in *Entrepreneur*

Ghost Creek at Pumpkin Ridge

Magazine as "the best place to start a small business," and in *Barron's* as (along with Atlanta) "the hottest real estate market in the United States."

Portland boasts a spectacular natural setting near the mountains and the sea, a youthful population with an environmentally correct mind-set, the largest urban forest in America, a healthy economy (software, Nike shoes, fine wines, and top microbreweries), a population growth fueled by arriving numbers of disgruntled Californians, and an image—which the locals shrug off, to their credit—as the most fashionable city in the country.

The irony, of course, is that Portland, while fashionable today, has always emphasized comfort over style. Portland itself did not actively seek such trendy acclaim; instead, it has benefited from the shifting tastes and more simple values that now prevail in America. Armani suits, Maseratis, and other icons of the 1980s never quite made an impression on the residents of the Rose City. Portland's true fabric has always been 100 percent cotton. It is clean-scrubbed, casually styled, clear-complexioned, wholesome, and all-American. Sometime during the early 1990s, the rest of America decided it liked that look, too.

The visitor to Portland will discover great golf, a handful of outstanding and innovative restaurants, one sublime hotel among several very interesting hotel options in Portland's vital downtown, and a wide range of sightseeing and non-golf activities. Any city nicknamed the "Rose City" is not going to have the climate of Phoenix or El Paso. Roses thrive under generally overcast conditions, like those in England. But the sun does shine in Portland, and when it does, it is magical. The best time to visit Oregon for a golfing holiday is September, when you optimize your chances for sunny weather.

THE GOLF

Two golf complexes in the Portland area that we recommend with pleasure are Pumpkin Ridge, rated the number one golf facility in the state, and the brand-new Langdon Farms, an interesting, self-styled "public resort" layout that is immature now but will only get better with time.

Pumpkin Ridge, which hosted the 1996 U.S. Amateur Championship and the 1997 U.S. Women's Open, is one of the finest public golf facilities in America. This thirty-six-hole complex is set in quiet, rolling farmland twenty-one miles west of Portland, in Cornelius.

Pumpkin Ridge is actually a hybrid: half the club is public and half is private. **Ghost Creek** is the acclaimed public course at Pumpkin Ridge. When it opened in 1992, Ghost Creek was named the Best New Public Course in America by *Golf Digest*. **Witch Hollow** is the complex's gorgeous private track, yet members of other private golf clubs occasionally can play it on a reciprocity basis if tee times are available. If you wish to play Witch Hollow—and in our opinion, you most certainly do—ask your golf professional to call and make inquiries on your behalf. Each of the two eighteens at Pumpkin Ridge is served by its own lavish clubhouse. Bob Cupp, one of the premier architects in the Pacific Northwest, and John Fought designed both courses at Pumpkin Ridge.

Do not make the mistake of assuming that Witch Hollow is the better of the two courses at Pumpkin Ridge simply because it is private. The general consensus among members is that Ghost Creek's front nine is the toughest of the four nines at Pumpkin Ridge, followed by the back nine on Witch Hollow. All thirty-six holes, however, are tranquil, beautifully maintained, and unmarred by roads, real estate, traffic noise, or other man-made intrusions. We suggest spending an entire day at Pumpkin Ridge, playing rounds on both courses if you can arrange it; in between rounds, make sure to enjoy lunch in one of the two handsome clubhouses.

Ghost Creek has four sets of tees. From the tips, it measures 6,839 yards and carries a big slope rating of 140 and a par rating of 73.8. From the blue tees, it is 6,451 yards long (par 71.9/slope 135), and from the white tees, it measures just 5,956 yards (par 69.0/slope 130). From the red tees, Ghost Creek is 5,206 yards long (par 70.4/slope 117). Outstanding holes on Ghost Creek include the fourth, a 533-yard par five and the course's number one handicap hole, and the ninth, a 469-yard par four that completes the very difficult front side. Generally speaking, Ghost Creek is a bit more generous from side to side than Witch Hollow.

Langdon Farms, located twenty miles south of Portland, in Aurora, opened for play in May 1995. It will take some time for the newly planted trees, greens, and fairways to mature fully. Nonetheless, the course's layout is thoughtful and fun, and it is clear that Langdon Farms will improve with time. One department that will *not* improve is its location. Sadly, several holes are situated just off Interstate 5, one of the busiest highways in Oregon. Traffic whooshing by at high speeds on the opposite side of a chain-link fence does little to enhance your concentration as you stand over your next shot.

Langdon Farms features heavy mounding on both sides of the fairway, intended to keep balls in play. It also has big, undulating greens and—its most unique design element—large aprons, or collection areas, that are contiguous with the greens and appear on almost every hole. These aprons appear in front of the greens as well as behind them and are cut nearly as short as the green itself. You may either chip or putt from the aprons, but some of these putts can be sixty to seventy feet long. No matter what you decide, you face a challenging little touch shot from the aprons on Langdon Farms.

Outstanding holes on this course include the seventh, a 558-yard par five with dramatic mounding down the entire right side. A creek protects the front of the green, which means the second shot on seven is typically a layup. The eighth hole, the number one handicap, is a long, 464-yard par four that doglegs right and features a large red barn that is actually in play on the left side of the fairway. One of the best holes on the back nine is number seventeen, a 224-yard par three guarded by multiple bunkers.

Langdon Farms measures 6,935 yards from the back tees (par 73.3/slope 125), 6,525 yards from the champion tees (par 71.2/slope 121), 6,057 yards from the resort tees (par 68.9/slope 116), and 5,249 yards from the forward tees (par 64.8/slope 108).

Pumpkin Ridge Golf Club. 12930 Old Pumpkin Ridge Road, Cornelius, OR 97113. Tel: 503-647-9977 (general) or 503-647-9977 (golf reservations). Fax: 503-647-2002. Credit cards accepted.

- *Ghost Creek.* 1992. Designers: Bob Cupp, John Fought. Par 71. 6,839 yards. 73.8 par rating. 140 slope rating. Greens fees: $75 Monday–Thursday, $90 Friday–Sunday and holidays. Walking permitted. Caddies available if requested in advance. Carts ($25) available. Season: year-round.

- *Witch Hollow.* 1992. Designers: Bob Cupp, John Fought. Par 72. 6,572 yards. 72.3 par rating. 138 slope rating. Greens fee: $100. Walking permitted. Caddies available if requested in advance. Carts ($25) available. Season: year-round.

Langdon Farms. 24377 NE Airport Road, Aurora, OR 97002. Tel: 503-678-4653. Fax: 503-678-3263. Credit cards accepted.

• 1995. Designers: Bob Cupp, John Fought. Par 71. 6,935 yards. 73.3 par rating. 125 slope rating. Greens fees: March–May and October–November: $45 (Monday–Thursday), $55 (Friday–Sunday); June: $50–$60; July–September: $52 (Monday–Thursday), $65 (Friday–Sunday), cart included. Walking permitted. No caddies. Season: year-round.

GOLF SERVICES (17)

Golf services are outstanding at both courses. The two clubhouses at Pumpkin Ridge feature well-equipped pro shops, friendly and attentive personnel, excellent locker facilities, and very pleasant restaurants and bars. The practice facilities at Pumpkin Ridge are also exceptionally good.

Services at Langdon Farms do not attempt to replicate the private-club atmosphere of Pumpkin Ridge, but Langdon Farms is still a very well run operation, with a large new clubhouse, pro shop, informal restaurant, and friendly service. The range at Langdon Farms is very good, but when we visited there were more golfers waiting to hit shots than there were available stations.

LODGING (18)

The Vintage Plaza, the Governor, and the Benson are three excellent hotels in downtown Portland, but the **Heathman** is the city's premier hotel address by a considerable margin. Indeed, the Heathman is the best hotel we have seen in the entire state. Located in the midst of Portland's charming and eminently walkable downtown, the Heathman scores high marks in every category—service, comfort, and style. It also has a highly regarded restaurant (see below) that is, arguably, Portland's finest.

The Heathman is the hub of business and social life in Portland; its urbane Marble Bar is a favored meeting place and watering hole for professionals who work downtown. The public areas include attractive lounges with eucalyptus paneling, an upstairs bar patronized by Portland's cigar aficionados, a small gift shop, and a front desk whose staff is genuinely nice and extremely hardworking. In addition to its refined ground-floor restaurant, the Heathman also operates a casual bakery and pub just a few steps down the street.

Guest rooms at the Heathman are spacious and very pleasant, yet not opulent in the fashion of a Four Seasons or Ritz-Carlton. This is Portland, after all, and the decor of the Heathman rooms reflects the agreeable and comfortable Oregon style. We stayed in a standard room, number 911, and found it very much to our liking. Strongly recommended.

Heathman Hotel. 1001 SW Broadway at Salmon, Portland, OR 97205. Tel: 800-551-0011 or 503-241-4100. Fax: 503-790-7110. 151 rooms and suites from $180 to $375. Credit cards accepted.

RESTAURANTS (17)

A great place to go for a drink before dinner in Portland is the bar at **Atwater's,** located on the thirtieth floor of the U.S. Bancorp Tower; the bar offers dazzling views of the city as well as of Mount Hood and Mount Saint Helens in the distance. While at Atwater's, try a pint or two of the wonderful Widmer hefe weizen, one of Portland's best microbrews.

Three of the best restaurants in Portland—in descending order of excellence—include the dining room at the Heathman Hotel; Zefiro, which has garnered the praise of Bryan Miller in *The New York Times;* and L'Auberge, a long-standing favorite.

The bustling **Heathman** restaurant gets busy early every evening. The very handsome dining room, with its smoked-glass windows, was filled to capacity when we took our seats just after 7 P.M. A smart, casually dressed Portland crowd was there to enjoy chef Philippe Boulot's innovative cooking and the city's finest selection of outstanding Oregon pinot noirs and chardonnays. Our party sampled a variety of utterly superb dishes including fresh oysters, sweetbreads, a sublime warm chanterelle soup, smoked salmon, grilled ahi tuna, crab cakes, fresh halibut, and free-range veal. A complete dinner for two with wine and tip costs approximately $110. The Heathman restaurant is highly recommended.

Stylish, contemporary, and energized **Zefiro** leans toward Italy in terms of its bright and vivid decor yet serves a wonderful "world cuisine" with strong influences from the Pacific Rim, Europe, and even Africa. We particularly enjoyed the Asian ravioli filled with shrimp, scallions, and ginger; the heavenly Kumamoto oysters on the half shell; and the Moroccan chicken tagine with couscous, black Kalamata olives, lemon, and saffron. A reasonable selection of wines is available by the bottle and by the glass, although surprisingly—and lamentably—few Oregon wines are offered. Expect to spend $85 for a complete dinner for two at Zefiro, wine and service included.

The elegantly rustic **L'Auberge,** with its casual dining room and smart bar, has been a favorite of informed Portland residents for many years. Simple French country dishes are featured on the menu, as well as excellent salads and pastas. In addition to à la carte selections, the restaurant offers a creative prix fixe menu (generally priced at around $37) that is shaped around the various specialties of a particular region of France. For example, in the last year the restaurant has offered a Basque menu, a Normandy menu (where the chef hails from), and an extraordinary Parisian menu, among others. If only we lived in the vicinity of this restaurant year-round!

Atwater's. 111 SW 5th Avenue, Portland, OR 97204. Tel: 503-275-3600. Fax: 503-275-8587. Credit cards accepted.

Heathman Restaurant. Heathman Hotel, 1001 SW Broadway at Salmon, Portland, OR 97205. Tel: 800-551-0011 or 503-241-4100 (hotel), 503-790-7163 (restaurant). Fax: 503-790-7110. Credit cards accepted.

Zefiro. 500 NW 21st Avenue, Portland, OR 97209. Tel: 503-226-3394. Fax: 503-226-4744. Credit cards accepted.

L'Auberge. 2601 NW Vaughn Street, Portland, OR 97210. Tel: 503-223-3302. No fax. Credit cards accepted.

NON-GOLF ACTIVITIES

A few of the many non-golf activities in the Portland area include driving via the magnificent Columbia River gorge to Mount Hood for lunch at Timberline Lodge, heading west an hour and a half to the Pacific coast and the gorgeous beaches between Manzanita and Cannon Beach, and shopping in Portland's lovely, tree-shaded downtown—try Powell's, one of the best and largest bookstores in America.

GETTING THERE: From the Portland Airport, take I-205 South for five to six miles; then take I-84 West to I-5 South. After crossing a bridge, get into the left lane and take I-405 North. Take the Salmon Street exit (2A), and turn right onto Salmon. Go five blocks and you will find the Heathman Hotel on the corner of Salmon and Broadway. The hotel provides valet parking at the entrance.

▶CENTRAL OREGON

SUNRIVER, BLACK BUTTE, AND SENSATIONAL CROSSWATER

	The Golf	Golf Services	Lodging	Restaurants	Non-Golf Activities	Total
Rating	18	16	15	15	17	81

Bend, Oregon, is a small but growing city in the high desert on the eastern edge of the pine-scented and densely wooded Deschutes National Forest. Bend has gained special notoriety because it serves as the collection point and base camp for ever-increasing numbers of outdoor enthusiasts who rightly consider central Oregon one of the premier meccas in America for active sports. In the sunny, rugged, spectacularly scenic region surrounding Bend, you can snow ski nearly year-round on Mount Bachelor, fish for trout and salmon, go white-water rafting on Class IV rapids, hike, camp, mountain bike, and tee it up on one of twenty-two different golf courses, where the ball sails a little further because these courses are set at 3,200 to 4,200 feet above sea level.

Getting there is pure adventure. Bend is a three-hour drive from Portland through authentic "Twin Peaks" scenery: vertigo-inducing roads, down gorges, up mountainsides flanked with immense fir trees, past ancient lava fields and the great volcanic peaks of the magnificent Cascade Range.

The two best golf resorts in central Oregon—both *Golf Magazine* silver medalists—are low-key residential communities that are strikingly similar in style and appearance. The Sunriver Resort, with its own shops, business park, and runway for homeowners' private aircraft, is about thirty minutes south of Bend, while the somewhat smaller and more tranquil Black Butte Ranch is forty-five minutes to the north.

Sunriver is considerably larger and busier than Black Butte, yet both destinations offer stunning mountain scenery, golf courses we rate good to outstanding, and pleasant accommodations in comfortable—if rather basic and nearly identical looking—condominium units with stone fireplaces. In addition, both resorts provide a wonderful assortment of beers from the excellent local Oregon microbreweries. Sadly, however, both Sunriver Resort and Black Butte Ranch dish up rather mediocre food, with a slight edge in the culinary category going to Sunriver.

The stunning highlight of our trip, by a considerable margin, was our round of golf on Sunriver's windblown Crosswater Course, the spectacular new Bob Cupp design built immediately adjacent to Sunriver and clearly now the single best golf course in the entire Pacific Northwest. Crosswater, named Best New Resort Course in 1995 by *Golf Digest*, is also an upscale real estate play, with just ninety-four homesites and twenty-four cottages planned within a private, gated community that, once finished, is destined to make next-door neighbor Sunriver look decidedly middle class. Although Crosswater and Sunriver are two distinct communities, resort guests at Sunriver have access to the dramatic Cupp layout at Crosswater. As of this writing, Crosswater is still a wonderful wilderness of river marshland with not a single home yet built along this extraordinary golf course, although construction of the handsome, new clubhouse was nearing completion during our visit.

THE GOLF

18

The best resort and public-access courses to play in central Oregon include Crosswater, Sunriver Resort's premier, private track; Big Meadow at Black Butte, and the Sunriver Woodlands Course. The area does offer one additional jewel that the visiting golfer should not miss: Tokatee, a Ted Robinson design rated among America's Top Twenty-five Public Courses. The Sunriver Meadows Course and the Glaze Meadow Course at Black Butte are considered the second tracks at their respective resorts.

If you are driving to Bend from Portland, remote and enchanting **Tokatee** can be visited and played en route, located as it is off Route 126 in Blue River, thirty-nine miles east of Eugene and forty-five minutes west of Black Butte. Tokatee has a relaxed, public links flavor. It is a good walking course set on a flat mountain valley floor surrounded by thick forests and jagged, snow-covered peaks. The course measures 6,843 yards from the blue tees (slope 126), 6,245 yards from the whites (slope 119), and 5,651 yards from the reds (slope 115). Tokatee's storybook setting reflects the pure essence of peaceful Oregon, with lakes, ponds, creeks, pine-scented air, and amazing fir and cedar trees, some five hundred years old. The first four holes at Tokatee are uneventful, treeless, and wide open and must be considered warm-ups for the tougher challenges offered later in the round. By the fifth hole, however, where your approach shot must be hit through a narrow gap of towering pines, Tokatee radically changes its character. From the fifth onward—and especially on the more beautiful back nine—Tokatee becomes a Northwest wonderland of forest and water.

The best holes at Tokatee are twelve, thirteen, and seventeen. Twelve is a 509-yard par five with a collection of tall firs standing in the center of the fairway. The conservative play is to drive into the landing area right of the firs. But a big drive down the left side can set you up for an eagle. Thirteen is a 420-yard par four with a ninety-degree dogleg-right that requires a tee shot through a tight chute of pine, fir, and cedar. Seventeen is a terrific 152-yard par three from a rocky pedestal tee, over a lake, and down to a large green. Par at Tokatee is seventy-two. Finally, with a greens fee of only $32 (carts are an additional $24), the course is a *real* bargain.

Sunriver Resort's Crosswater Course is striking and memorable because it incorporates a visually stunning, environmentally correct design that makes spectacular use of the Deschutes River, its lesser tributaries, and surrounding wetlands. In addition, the course offers enormous challenge and superb shot qualities on every hole, and—like other great golf courses we have played, notably the Ocean Course at Kiawah Island and the River Course at the American Club in Kohler, Wisconsin—it provides the visiting golfer with a splendid sense of profound isolation, of the individual pitted against the elements in all their glory.

It is also important to know that Crosswater is immensely long—a whopping 7,683 yards from the gold tees—with a par rating of 76.9 and a slope rating of 150, which happens to be the second highest slope rating of any resort or public access golf course in the United States. (The River Course at Kohler has a slightly higher 151 slope.)

Crosswater has five sets of tees to suit every level of play, but even from the forward tees Crosswater is not a track for high handicaps or beginners, who, in all likelihood, will only experience frustration with the inherent difficulty of the course, the range of shots required, and the multitude of water carries over the Deschutes River. Indeed, Crosswater gets its name from the fact that you must cross the river again and again—sixteen times, to be exact, during the course of a round, and not just on your drive, but frequently with second and third shots as well. Crosswater has four of the longest and toughest par fives in golf—along lakes, over waste areas with hip-high marsh grass, and into strong winds. We played from the silver tees in windy conditions, and our scores were high. From the gold tees Crosswater measures 7,683 yards (150 slope), from the blues 6,842 yards (134 slope), from the whites 6,286 yards (128 slope), and from the reds 5,389 yards (137 slope).

Golfers of every handicap, however, will admire the course's natural setting, the obvious artistry of its layout, and the gorgeous mountain backdrops. We were especially impressed with Crosswater's outstanding condition, particularly given the fact that it opened for play June of 1995.

Crosswater does not have a single weak hole, but several are especially remarkable creations. On the front side, holes four through eight are incredible beauties. The highlight of the fourth hole, a par four that measures 413 yards from the back tees, is a make-or-break second shot onto an island green guarded left, front, and rear by waste areas marked with signposts that state: "Sensitive Area, Do Not Enter to Retrieve Your Ball." The fifth hole, a 460-yard par four that doglegs left, requires an absolutely massive drive with at least 230 yards of carry in order to get safely across the Little Deschutes River. The sixth hole is one of the most unusual par fives we have seen. This 645-yard monster features a landing area across the Little Deschutes for your drive, then a two-tiered fairway separated by grassy meadows, one on high ground to the left and the other on lower ground to the right, designed to receive your second shot. On eight, your approach to a large, elevated green must carry over the rushing Little Deschutes once again.

Twelve, seventeen, and eighteen are the three best holes on Crosswater's back side. Twelve is a 687-yard par five that bends to the left along a pretty lake. The sheer length of number twelve is compounded by the fact that it plays directly into strong prevailing winds. Twelve requires three full shots in order to reach the green. The seventeenth hole is a long, 244-yard par three with natural wetlands along the left side. And the fine eighteenth hole requires a final, dramatic crossing of the Deschutes River, this time on your second shot to the green on this 456-yard par four. Crosswater is Sunriver Resort's private track, so only members and resort guests are allowed access to the course.

Sunriver's **Woodlands Course,** a 1981 Robert Trent Jones, Jr. design, is the second-best layout in central Oregon after Crosswater. With water in play on seven holes, the Woodlands course measures 6,880 yards (slope 131) from the back tees.

One astute critic—Brian McCallen of *Golf Magazine*—described the **Meadows Course** at Sunriver as "long, flat, and bland." We concur.

Big Meadow—the marquee track at Black Butte designed in 1970 by Robert Muir Graves—is far less awesome and untamed than Crosswater. Although a good and not overly difficult resort course that is easy to walk and has fine mountain views, Big Meadow does not get truly interesting until the back nine. The fairways on the front side are lined with look-alike condominiums and vacation homes hidden among the trees.

Black Butte

Twelve and fourteen, though, are two outstanding holes. The twelfth is a 390-yard par four uphill all the way, and from the fourteenth tee, perched high above the fairway, there are spectacular views of the mountains and the golf course. Par at Big Meadow is seventy-two. The course measures 6,850 yards from the tips (slope 127), 6,456 yards from the middle tees (slope 124), and 5,716 from the reds (slope 115). The greens fee for both Big Meadow and Glaze Meadow is $55 for resort guests; carts cost an additional $28.

Glaze Meadow, the second course at Black Butte, is 276 yards shorter than Big Meadow and places a higher premium on accuracy than distance.

Tokatee. 54947 McKenzie Highway, Blue River, OR 97413. Tel: 541-822-3220 or, in Oregon, 800-452-6376. Fax: 541-822-6094. Credit cards accepted.

• 1967. Designer: Ted Robinson. Par 72. 6,843 yards. 72.0 par rating. 126 slope rating. Greens fee: $32; carts cost an additional $24. Walking permitted. No caddies. Season: February–November.

Sunriver Resort. PO Box 3609, Sunriver, OR 97707. Tel: 800-547-3922 or 541-593-1000 (general); 541-593-8285 (strictly for Crosswater); 800-962-1769 or 541-593-4402 (golf reservations for either the Woodlands or Meadows courses). Fax: 541-593-6501 (Crosswater), 541-593-4285 (Woodlands and Meadows courses). Credit cards accepted.

• *Crosswater Course.* 1995. Designer: Bob Cupp. Par 72. 7,683 yards. 76.9 par rating. 150 slope rating. Greens fees: $115, includes cart ($95 in the spring and fall). Walking allowed only with permission of the head pro. No caddies. Restrictions: available only to members and guests of Sunriver Resort. Season: mid-March–late October.
• *Woodlands Course.* 1981. Designer: Robert Trent Jones, Jr. Par 72. 6,880 yards. 73.0 par rating. 131 slope rating. Greens fees: $50 (resort guest), $65 (public), with reduced rates after 3 P.M. and in the spring and fall. Walking permitted. No caddies. Carts cost an additional $15 per person, or $25 for two riders. Season: mid-March–late October.
• *Meadows Course.* 1968. Designer: Fred Federspiel. Par 72. 6,908 yards. 72.9 par rating. 130 slope rating. Greens fees: $40 (resort guest), $50 (public), with reduced rates after 3 P.M. and in the spring and fall. Walking permitted. No caddies. Carts cost an additional $15 per person, or $25 for two riders. Season: mid-March–late October.

Black Butte Ranch. PO Box 8000, Black Butte Ranch, OR 97759. Tel: 800-452-7455 (general), 800-399-2322 or 541-595-1500 (golf reservations). Fax: 541-595-1293. Credit cards accepted.

• *Big Meadow.* 1970. Designer: Robert Muir Graves. Par 72. 6,850 yards. 72.0 par rating. 127 slope rating.
• *Glaze Meadow.* 1979. Designer: Gene "Bunny" Mason. Par 72. 6,574 yards. 71.5 par rating. 128 slope rating.
• Greens fee for both courses: $55. After 2 P.M. Sunday through Thursday, the rate is reduced to $39. Carts cost an additional $28. Walking permitted. No caddies. Season: mid-March–mid-November, weather permitting.

GOLF SERVICES

Golf services are very good at Sunriver and Black Butte and will be superb at Crosswater once its new clubhouse is completed. The staffs at all three courses are friendly and helpful, the pro shops are well stocked, and practice facilities are very good.

LODGINGS

Although guest accommodations at both **Sunriver Resort** and **Black Butte Ranch** are comfortable and

Sunriver Resort

moderately priced, they certainly lack architectural distinction. Both resorts, in fact, look as though they were built according to an identical formula: an informal central lodge housing the front desk, restaurants, and bar, with guest rooms spread out on the grounds in condominium units sheathed in redwood or cedar siding. The landscape of central Oregon is one of the most majestic in America, yet the developers of these properties have not responded to the inspirational setting with resort buildings of beauty or imagination. The new, upscale Crosswater community promises to improve upon the dull architectural standards set by Sunriver and Black Butte.

Having said this, we believe that Sunriver is the superior resort. It has the advantage of proximity to the great Crosswater golf course, a slightly better restaurant than Black Butte, and a more active and invigorating atmosphere. We stayed in room 154, which was simple and inexpensive ($139) and had a small bath, stone fireplace, television, and patio overlooking the golf course. At Black Butte we stayed in unit 15 ($115), again with fireplace, cable television, and private patio. The best time of year to visit central Oregon is September, when the crowds have gone and the weather can be superb.

Sunriver Resort. PO Box 3609, Sunriver, OR 97707. Tel: 800-547-3922 or 541-593-1000. Fax: 541-593-5458. 211 rooms and suites ranging from $130 to $205. Credit cards accepted.

Black Butte Ranch. PO Box 8000, Black Butte Ranch, OR 97759. Tel: 800-452-7455 or 541-595-6211. Fax: 541-595-2077. Condominium units and houses for rent; doubles range from $95 to $195. Credit cards accepted.

RESTAURANTS 〈15〉

An unpleasant waiter in the dining room at **Black Butte Ranch,** combined with the lackluster food—including a dull salad, poor crab cakes, and an average New York steak—produced an entirely forgettable experience. The pinot noir from the Rex Hill Maresh Vineyard was the high point of our dinner. Entrées range from $14 to $20.

At Sunriver, we found the service friendlier and the menu more sophisticated in the resort's one restaurant, the **Meadows.** A wide variety of entrées—including some appealing Pacific Northwest specialties—are offered from $10.95 to $23.95. Both the Black Butte and Sunriver dining rooms are casual and feature fine mountain views.

A good choice for lunch or dinner in Bend is the **Pine Tavern,** a popular and informal spot with two-hundred-year-old ponderosa pines growing in the center of the Garden Room at the rear of the restaurant, which has been in operation for over sixty years. Famous for its prime rib, the Pine Tavern also serves a wide variety of seafood and pasta dishes. Entrées range in price from $10.95 to $18.95.

Oregon microbreweries are among the best in the country, and the **Deschutes Brewery** in Bend is an excellent place to try some of the local brew. The brewery has on tap anywhere from five to ten beers that are brewed on the premises. The lunch menu offers a nice selection of burgers, sandwiches, and creative vegetarian options. The restaurant also makes its own sausages and soups. Go have lunch there and try the Black Butte porter.

Dining room at Black Butte Ranch. PO Box 8000, Black Butte Ranch, OR 97759. Tel: 800-452-7455 or 541-595-1260. Fax: 541-595-2077. Credit cards accepted.

The Meadows. Sunriver Resort. PO Box 3609, Sunriver, OR 97707. Tel: 800-547-3922 or 541-593-1000 (general); 541-593-4609 (the Meadows). Fax: 541-593-5458. Credit cards accepted.

Pine Tavern. 967 NW Brooks Street, Bend, OR 97701. Tel: 541-382-5581. No fax. Credit cards accepted.

Deschutes Brewery. 1044 NW Bond Street, Bend, OR 97701. Tel: 541-382-9242. Fax: 541-385-8095. Credit cards accepted.

NON-GOLF ACTIVITIES

The High Desert Museum, six miles south of Bend off U.S. Highway 97, features fascinating exhibits of the arid high desert plateau that covers large portions of Oregon and the West. Both Sunriver and Black Butte have tennis, swimming, horseback riding, cross-country skiing, fishing, canoeing, and miles of walking trails.

GETTING THERE: Sunriver Resort is approximately 175 miles southeast of Portland. Take Interstate 26 East until Madras; then take Highway 97 South. Signs will point the rest of the way.

Washington

►SEATTLE

PACIFIC NORTHWEST GOLFING JEWELS

	The Golf	Golf Services	Lodging	Restaurants	Non-Golf Activities	Total
Rating	17	16	18	18	19	88

The Semi-Ah-Moo and Port Ludlow golf courses, both of which are within a two-hour drive of Seattle, are *Golf Digest* silver medalists and fantastic places to play. They are also parts of rather average and somewhat confused resort complexes. For this reason, and because we find Seattle one of the most enchanting cities in the United States, we strongly recommend that for your golfing holiday to the Pacific Northwest, you stay in Seattle, drive out and play these two magnificent courses, and return to Seattle each afternoon. We also advise you to confine your travel to the months of June, July, and August. A lovely May or September day in the Pacific Northwest sounds great in theory, and we have experienced a few, but so often—other than in the summer months—the weather can be bleak, drizzly, and miserable.

Semi-Ah-Moo

GOLF TRAVEL's Guide to the World's Greatest Golf Destinations

Yet when the sun shines in the summer, which is often, there is no place more magical than Seattle, the Puget Sound, and golfing at Semi-Ah-Moo and Port Ludlow, two courses on the Sound. If you follow our advice, we think you'll agree that Seattle is home to the best restaurants and hotels in the West outside San Francisco. Sorry, L.A., we know you are infinitely bigger, but Seattle beats you hands down. So stay in Seattle: walk the streets, buy the best lattes in America from street vendors, duck into fascinating antique shops, visit the Pike Place Market, one of the most vibrant and colorful markets on earth, shop at Eddie Bauer and Nordstrom, and dine on some of the best seafood you'll ever have anywhere.

THE GOLF

When **Semi-Ah-Moo,** an Arnold Palmer/Ed Seay course, was completed in 1987, it was voted the year's top resort course—and for good reason. An easy two-hour drive directly north of Seattle, within a two iron's distance of Canada, Semi-Ah-Moo will delight you with its utterly superb maintenance, fascinating course layout, and scenic beauty. Although the property is right on the Sound, the course is carved out of the dense fir forests, and you get only occasional peeks of the water. Despite the fact that the course is carved through the woods, the fairways are quite wide and present no fear to high handicappers. This is a good, honest course with no tricks or gimmicks, but plenty of white sand traps in the fairways and around the greens put a premium on accurate shot making. Unfortunately, town houses close to the fairways on the back nine distract from the tranquillity of your round. The front nine, which has larger lots and fewer homes, is much more peaceful. Although the fairways are wide, Semi-Ah-Moo is a real challenge, measuring 7,005 yards from the back tees, par seventy-two, with a rating of 73.6 and slope of 130.

Esquire magazine once rated **Port Ludlow** as one of the top six courses in the world, although we at GOLF TRAVEL rank it below Semi-Ah-Moo. Port Ludlow, a half-hour ferry ride and thirty-minute drive from Seattle plus normal delays, will take you approximately two hours from downtown Seattle. On a clear day, the ferry ride from Seattle to the small Puget Sound town of Winslow is a scenic joy. You are surrounded by one of the most breathtaking panoramic views anywhere: the wondrous Seattle skyline, noble Mount Rainier to the southeast, and the Olympic Mountains to the west. Port Ludlow is actually a twenty-seven-hole track with the Tide, Timber, and Trail nines. The Tide and Timber nines were completed in 1975, and Trail was opened in 1993. They were all designed by Robert Muir Graves, who has a very distinctive style. Carved out of the dense Olympic Peninsula forests, the course is brimming with doglegs and blind shots, which, though not without a certain interest, we find tiresome in overuse and, in this case, quite claustrophobic. Like Semi-Ah-Moo, Port Ludlow is certainly a real estate play, but we did not find the handsome homes and town houses on the course an intrusion. In fact, Graves made generous use of the land—every tee is at least fifty yards from the preceding green, and each hole is individually carved out of the woods. Whereas Semi-Ah-Moo lies on relatively flat terrain, Port Ludlow is hilly and has plenty of contour. On every tee shot, one seems to be hitting either up or down a hill, sometimes a very steep grade, like the 404-yard, par four number one on the Tide Course, where you actually need to look through a periscope to see if the fairway is clear. Uphill or downhill lies are the norm, which is one of the reasons why this course is so tough; indeed, the Trail/Tide combination boasts a course rating of 73.1 and slope of 138. Fairways are moderately wide. If you do stray into the woods, the ball is history. Play another.

Semi-Ah-Moo Golf and Country Club. 8720 Semi-Ah-Moo Parkway, Blaine, WA 98230. Tel: 360-371-7005. Fax: 360-371-7012. Credit cards accepted.

• 1987. Designers: Arnold Palmer, Ed Seay. Par 72. 7,005 yards. 73.6 par rating. 130 slope rating. Greens fees: $68 weekdays, $75 weekends. Walking permitted. Caddies can be arranged with advance notice. Carts ($30) available. Season: year-round.

Port Ludlow Golf Course. 751 Highland Drive, Port Ludlow, WA 98365. Tel: 800-455-0272 or 360-437-0272. Fax: 360-437-0637. Credit cards accepted.

• *Trail Nine.* 1993. Par 36. 3,326 yards.
• *Tide Nine.* 1975. Par 36. 3,357 yards.
• *Timber Nine.* 1975. Par 36. 3,430 yards.

Designer: Robert Muir Graves. Greens fees for 18 holes: $29 (November–February), $35 (March–April, October), $39 (May), $55 (June–September). Walking permitted. No caddies. Carts cost an additional $14 per person. Season: year-round.

 ## GOLF SERVICES

The whole Semi-Ah-Moo operation is beautifully run by Nippon Landic, the Japanese company that owns it. The staff could not be more cordial and helpful. The clubhouse is beautiful with its pleasant bar and grill and wonderfully stocked pro shop. During the week the course gets very little play. There is a first-rate driving range with putting and pitching greens. Semi-Ah-Moo is an amazing statement of how a course should be maintained.

The Port Ludlow course is kept in very fine condition, fairways are lush and well bunkered, and greens are excellent, if a tad slow. The clubhouse is quite simple, with a laid-back, somewhat dingy bar and grill. Unfortunately, the clubhouse and course personnel seemed remarkably apathetic and unprofessional.

 ## LODGING

Now we can tell you about Seattle. For this perfect Pacific Northwest golfing holiday we recommend two hotels: the small, intimate, and classy Alexis Hotel and the high-powered, full-service, centrally located Four Seasons Olympic Hotel. We love both.

The **Alexis Hotel,** located just a bit off the beaten track at the corner of First Avenue and Madison, has 109 rooms and suites and is typical of a small, deluxe, and elegant London or Parisian hotel. All the rooms are handsomely decorated, spacious, and well appointed; rates range from $175 to $380 (for the best two-bedroom suite). Some suites actually have wood-burning fireplaces, whirlpool baths, and wet bars. Rates include Continental breakfast, welcome sherry, morning newspaper, and shoeshine service. The lobby, off First Avenue, is intimate and stylish. Service is exceptional, with personable bellmen and superb front desk personnel. A town car or limousine can be made available to guests; the one-way rate to the airport is $40 and from it $50. Breakfast, featuring excellent coffee, breads, croissants, and jams, is served at the Painted Table restaurant downstairs.

The **Four Seasons Olympic Hotel,** at 411 University Street, across the street from Eddie Bauer, enjoys a shopper's dream location in downtown Seattle. From here you can easily walk to all the fine downtown shopping and you are a minute's downhill walk to the remarkable Pike Place Market. This is the old Olympic Hotel, which has been Seattle's leading hotel for decades. From the instant you drive up to the grand, pillared entrance of this 450-room hotel, you will marvel at the extraordinary service that will be part of your stay. Front desk service is very competent, and the large concierge desk is one of the best to be found anywhere, including the finest hotels of Paris. The concierge will make all your dining reservations in Seattle, provide you with maps on how to get there, and arrange your tee times at Semi-Ah-Moo and Port Ludlow. The lobby is stunning and multi-storied. Of special note is the utterly elegant dining room, the Georgian, with its handsome paneling, sparkling chandeliers, and dramatic two-story Palladian windows. Serving breakfast and dinner (except Sunday evening), it is especially wonderful for a leisurely, grand breakfast. Shuckers, specializing in seafood, is also in the hotel and, though quite good, is not in the league of the restaurants reviewed below. All guest rooms are spacious and luxurious, especially the corner ones. Double room rates go from $290 up to $625, with two-bedroom suites climbing from $810 up to $1,250 for the hotel's Presidential Suite.

Of special note at the Olympic is the first-rate health club, with its good-size pool, outstanding facilities, and a helpful staff. The Four Seasons Olympic is a very fine hotel from top to bottom.

Alexis Hotel. 1007 First Avenue at Madison, Seattle, WA 98104. Tel: 800-426-7033 or 206-624-4844. Fax: 206-621-9009. 109 rooms and suites ranging from $175 to $380. Credit cards accepted.

Four Seasons Olympic Hotel. 411 University Street, Seattle, WA 98101. Tel: 800-223-8772 or 206-621-1700. Fax: 206-682-9633. 450 rooms and suites. Double rooms range from $290 to $625. Credit cards accepted.

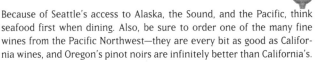

RESTAURANTS ⑱

Because of Seattle's access to Alaska, the Sound, and the Pacific, think seafood first when dining. Also, be sure to order one of the many fine wines from the Pacific Northwest—they are every bit as good as California wines, and Oregon's pinot noirs are infinitely better than California's. In our opinion, here are the best restaurants in Seattle for your dining excitement:

Dining at **Il Terrazzo** is as close as you will come to a fine Florentine trattoria. South of downtown a couple of miles, in the shadow of the Kingdome, Il Terrazzo is a must for lunch or dinner. Don't let the rather nondescript, red-brick office building that houses it throw you off. With its terra-cotta tile floors, blond high-beamed ceiling, floral curtains, and Pavarotti opera in the background, Il Terrazzo will win your hearts. The service is very efficient, and there is a good wine list of Italian and Pacific Northwest wines. The grilled tuna and lightly poached halibut had us swooning. Dinner for two with wine and tip will run about $100.

Elliott's Oyster House, right on the docks, is a bit touristy, but it is the perfect place for a quick lunch of five or six different types of Puget Sound oysters on the half shell, very good seared oysters, fresh salmon, Dungeness crab, and a draft beer. Entrées cost between $6 and $15 at lunch and between $13 and $30 at dinner.

Ray's Boat House, several miles northwest from downtown and right on the water overlooking the Sound, is a yearly pilgrimage for us. Try to get a table as close to the windows as possible, and be sure to get there while it is still light. Watching the sun set over the Sound, with all the sailboats gliding by, is as romantic as it gets. Although it has a slightly franchised feeling (it's not), the service is terribly professional, the wine list extraordinary, and the seafood exquisite. Stay simple at Ray's, for instance, order grilled king salmon or halibut.

A big player on the Seattle restaurant scene, Tom Douglass now operates three outstanding restaurants. Located on 4th Avenue just north of downtown in a bit of a funky block—but sharing the block with Seattle's finest fly shop, Kaufman's—the **Dahlia Lounge** has been a favorite of ours for about five years. The restaurant, in a very uncontrived way, will dazzle you with its hipness and its eclectic decor, highlighted by the giant neon CAFÉ sign in the middle of the downstairs dining room. Dahlia's is a jazzy, Art Deco fashion statement, with mirrored walls, a twenty-foot red ceiling, papier-mâché fish lamps, and a giant stairway in the middle of the room leading to the open upstairs dining room. Our only decor complaint is that it is too dark. The menu is innovative and good, if a bit inconsistent. Our smoked cod with bean pancakes was excellent, as were the Dungeness crab cakes with lemon rice salad, but the grilled Alaska king salmon was sadly overcooked. Dahlia's is a fun, exciting place. The wine list is brief but well selected.

The **Palace Kitchen,** which opened in March of 1996, is Douglass's newest spot. This is the current "happening" place in Seattle and features creative Pacific Northwest specialties like the delicious Hawaiian ono (also known as white mackerel) with celery-root mashed potatoes and wild mushroom butter. The high-ceilinged room showcases a huge tile-and-wood, horseshoe-shaped bar along with over a dozen booths and tables that are set in a rustic Pacific Northwest decor. Although offering a somewhat limited menu, yet with a large selection of appetizers, the Palace Kitchen has an open grill and spit that features a daily roasted special like goose or lamb. Vibrant and noisy with music, conversation, and sounds from the kitchen, we are not alone in loving this special spot where dinner for two before wine will run about $60.

The very latest to hit the Seattle scene is Wolfgang Puck and his new restaurant **Obachine,** which offers a Pan-Asian "fusion" cuisine that is both intriguing in its combination of influences as well as delicious. The ultra-hip decor brings together modern, contemporary, and Asian influences. The first floor is devoted to a large bar and about ten tables offering a variety of satay choices, while the large second floor serves a full menu both at lunch and dinner. Expect to spend about $65 for two before wine.

Etta's Seafood Grill exudes a charming café atmosphere with low ceilings and your choice of bar seating, tables, or booths. It features deliciously prepared fresh seafood such as salmon, halibut, and their noted crab cakes. Bright, colorful, and casual, this is an ideal choice for a leisurely summer lunch.

Last, but far from least, is **Ponti Seafood Grill,** just next to the Fremont Bridge right on the waterway coming off Lake Union. Ponti is one of the most popular restaurants in Seattle and for good reason: its outstanding food, superb wine list, excellent service, and ever-so-vibrant ambience. On balmy summer evenings, bypass the handsome, with-it bar and go out onto the terrace overlooking the water—romantic! If we had but one night to dine in Seattle, it would be here at Ponti. The wine list is an absolute marvel—with all the best of the Pacific Northwest, an exhaustive California selection, and a very fine selection of Bordeaux, Burgundies, Rhônes, and Italian wines. The wine steward is exceptional. The cuisine is very good; be sure to order the pan-fried oysters or the steamed mussels with garlic and wine. Very good entrées were the broiled Canadian halibut with smoked tomato coulis, the ahi tuna "charred blue" with a minted cucumber vinaigrette, and the pan-fried sand crabs with fresh rémoulade sauce. Dinner for two will run about $70 before wine.

Il Terrazzo. 411 1st Avenue South, Seattle, WA 98104. Tel: 206-467-7797. Fax: 206-447-5716. Credit cards accepted.

Elliott's Oyster House. Pier 56, Seattle, WA 98101. Tel: 206-623-4340. Fax: 206-224-0154. Credit cards accepted.

Ray's Boat House. 6049 Seaview Avenue NW, Seattle, WA 98107. Tel: 206-789-3770. Fax: 206-781-1960. Credit cards accepted.

Dahlia Lounge. 1904 4th Avenue, Seattle, WA 98101. Tel: 206-682-4142. Fax: 206-467-0568. Credit cards accepted.

Palace Kitchen. 2030 5th Avenue, Seattle, WA 98121. Tel: 206-448-2001. Fax: 206-448-1979. Credit cards accepted.

Obachine. 1518 6th Avenue, Seattle, WA 98101. Tel: 206-749-9653. Fax: 206-521-0690. Credit cards accepted.

Etta's Seafood Grill. 2020 Western Avenue, Seattle, WA 98121. Tel: 206-443-6000. Fax: 206-443-0648. Credit cards accepted.

Ponti Seafood Grill. 3014 3rd Avenue North, Seattle, WA 98109. Tel: 206-284-3000. Fax: 206-284-4768. Credit cards accepted.

NON-GOLF ACTIVITIES (19)

This is Seattle, queen of the Pacific Northwest, where non-golfing activities abound. You can choose from boating in the San Juan Islands, to climbing Mount Rainier, to outfitting the family at Eddie Bauer, and everything in between. Take the long activity list from the concierge, go get a double hazelnut *latte* from Starbucks, sit on a bench outside in the lovely summer Seattle air, and study your options.

GETTING THERE: To get to the Alexis Hotel from the Seattle/Tacoma Airport, take I-5 South into Seattle; the drive will take approximately forty-five minutes. Take the Madison Street exit. Turn left onto Madison Street. At the corner of Madison and First Avenue, you will see the hotel. Ask the concierge for directions to Semi-Ah-Moo and Port Ludlow.

Alberta, Canada

▶JASPER PARK LODGE
JEWEL OF THE CANADIAN ROCKIES

	The Golf	Golf Services	Lodging	Restaurants	Non-Golf Activities	Total
Rating	19	17	17	16	19	**88**

We at Golf Travel have recently returned from a weeklong expedition to the vast, majestic, and forbidding Canadian Rockies in the western province of Alberta, where we stayed at the region's three most celebrated golf destinations—the outstanding yet highly underrated Kananaskis resort, the slightly disappointing and somewhat over-rated Banff Springs resort, and Jasper Park Lodge with its stupendous Stanley Thompson golf course dating from 1925, simply the finest and most beautiful course that we have played in all Canada. We flew into the conveniently located airport in Calgary, host city of the 1988 Winter Olympics, and drove our rental car west across the high prairie into the Rocky Mountains, which suddenly erupt from the flat prairie floor about an hour out of Calgary. We then crossed the Columbia Icefield Parkway, one of the most spectacular and dramatic highways on earth, and stayed, in turn, at all three resorts. Bottom line? We highly recommend a visit to this marvelous region to play any or all of these world-class courses, all of which are extremely different in character, style, and appearance. After carefully weighing the relative merits and demerits of each, Jasper Park Lodge—with Kananaskis running second and Banff Springs third—easily emerges as the finest and most memorable destination of all, one we ourselves would most happily return to again. (Note that Kananaskis is reviewed separately.)

The entire geographic area—from Kananaskis in the south to Jasper in the north and Banff Springs and Lake Louise in between—offers spectacular mountain and glacier scenery; extraordinary wildlife such as bear, moose, elk, and mountain goats loiter amazingly close to the roadways. Yet, on a much less positive note, enormous numbers of tourists from all over the world occupy big lounge chairs in the hotel lobbies and pour from motor coaches with cameras slung about their necks in ready position to snap photographs of the snow-capped peaks or an idle black bear lolling by the roadside. Information notices on the golf courses are posted in three languages: English and French (the two official tongues of Canada) and Japanese.

Indeed, the single fault the region suffers from is the oppressive hordes of people who descend during the all-too-brief summer season. As snowstorms are not uncommon in both June and September, July and August become the optimal months to visit, although the official season does extend from May into October. The hotels, however enormous (Château Lake Louise, for example, has over eight hundred rooms), are filled to capacity during July and August, and the roads can be clogged, particularly in the afternoons, with snail-paced recreational vehicles. Hotel restaurants—some seating as many as a thousand patrons—are stretched to absolute capacity at peak dining hours, and the golf courses are exceptionally busy places, too, although every round we played in the Canadian Rockies took a reasonable four and a half hours or less. We found that arriving early, especially for golf and meals, saved us a considerable amount of time.

Jasper Park Lodge—set at the foot of Lac Beauvert, a glorious, glacial lake—consists of a large, centrally located, modern, yet architecturally undistinguished stone lodge building with a rambling, comfortable, and handsomely furnished interior. With snowcapped mountains in the distance, the view from the Lodge's outdoor terrace is typical of the ravishing Canadian Rockies. Guest accommodations are located in dozens of log cabins and cedar chalets that dot the peninsula and line the pine-fringed lake. The best guest rooms, like number 396 that we occupied, are in the older and more whimsical log cabins. The newer chalets are more sterile in appearance and have far less charm. The golf course and other resort facilities are within walking distance of the guest rooms. The village of Jasper, about three miles from the Lodge, is attractive and relatively uncommercial, especially when compared to Banff and its Hard Rock Cafe, T-shirt shops, and fast-food emporiums. At an elevation of 3,500 feet, Jasper is lower than Banff and Kananaskis, both of which are approximately 5,500 feet above sea level. Direct driving time to Jasper from the Calgary Airport is a slow and laborious six hours.

Canada, with its heavily devalued dollar, remains a superb travel value for Americans, yet it must be noted that the resorts in the Canadian West are roughly twice the price of Keltic Lodge and the Highlands Links in Nova Scotia (see *Nova*

Scotia). Higher prices are a direct result of limited supply and extraordinary demand. Visitors from across the globe vie for space in the legendary hotels of the Canadian Rockies and book their reservations many months in advance. The resorts in New Brunswick and Nova Scotia, on the other hand, generally cater only to an American and Canadian clientele. Jasper Park Lodge—like the Algonquin (in New Brunswick, Canada), Banff Springs, and the Lodge at Kananaskis—is owned and operated by Canadian Pacific.

THE GOLF

The Stanley Thompson–designed golf course at Jasper Park Lodge is not only the greatest golf experience in the Canadian Rockies, it is also one of the premier courses ever reviewed by Golf Travel, and we issue this proclamation in absolute confidence despite the few unfortunate service glitches we experienced from harried employees in the golf pro shop, where a smile and a pleasant welcome would go far to improve the overall atmosphere. We were taken aback when we learned we would have to pay for range balls, overnight club storage, and even tees. All this seemed a bit much for a resort guest spending C$450 ($340) per night for a room at the Lodge. Nevertheless, the golf is breathtaking.

Stanley Thompson, Canada's greatest native-born golf architect, also designed the incomparable Highlands Links on Cape Breton Island, and any golfer fortunate enough to have played both courses will be immediately struck by their common ancestry. An enormous difference exists, however, between the Highlands Links and the course at Jasper Park Lodge. Despite its grand scenery, Highlands Links can be ill tended, whereas Jasper Park is stunning and virtually as well groomed as Augusta National. This course is as idyllic, peaceful, and beautiful as one is likely to experience, a scenic gem creatively routed over an exquisite piece of property with no distractions except awe-inspiring views of snowcapped peaks in all directions.

Jasper Park is not unduly difficult. Better golfers are urged to tackle this layout from the blue tees, where the course measures 6,663 yards, not overly long at this altitude. The par and slope ratings (70.5; 121 from the blues) indicate that on a good day you can shoot a low score even from the tips. The four par fives are relatively easy. The heart of Jasper Park is its five very testing par threes and the truly spectacular sequence of holes—numbers fourteen, fifteen, and sixteen—on the little peninsula surrounded by the icy waters of Lac Beauvert.

The first hole at Jasper Park is a mirror image of the opening hole at Highlands Links, a gorgeous, uphill, 391-yard par four that plays a club or two longer than the posted yardage. Other great holes on the front side include number three, a downhill 454-yard par four that doglegs to the right and features a blind tee shot over a ridge. By carrying the trees on the right, long hitters can cut the corner and find their balls nestled perfectly in the fairway no more than 150 yards from the uphill green. The fourth hole is a sensational 240-yard par three that plays from a spectacularly elevated tee sixty feet above the fairway floor. As is noted in the course guide, "rarely do we see balls hit over this green." The seventh hole is another tough par three with a long, narrow green 178 yards off the tee. If you miss the green on seven, either to the left or in the gully in front, you are in deep trouble. But number nine, the 231-yard par three, is the real brute of Jasper Park, especially when the wind is blowing. Missing the green right (into the trees) or left (into the bunkers) means disaster. Indeed, seven and nine, two par threes, are the toughest holes at Jasper Park.

The back nine offers its own slew of stunning challenges. The thirteenth, a 603-yard par five, is a true three-shot hole with a blind approach to a green nestled in a grove of spruce. Number fourteen, however, wins the Jasper Park beauty prize, with its tee box perched on the shore of Lac Beauvert. Fifteen is a short 138-yard par three with a postage-stamp green, and sixteen, a 380-yard par four, plays along the lake for its entire length.

From the white tees, Jasper Park measures 6,368 yards (par rating 69.5/slope rating 116). From the forward tees the course is 5,935 yards long (par rating 73.5/slope rating 122). In high season, the greens fee is C$75 ($57), and carts cost C$32 ($24). At twilight (after 5 P.M.), the greens fee drops to C$50 ($38), which includes a cart and even clubs! Many golfers take advantage of the twilight rate since it does not get dark in Jasper in July until 10:30 P.M. Walking is permitted, but there are no caddies.

Jasper Park. PO Box 40, Jasper, Alberta TOE 1EO Canada. Tel: 403-852-3301 (general) or 403-852-6090 (golf reservations). Fax: 403-852-5107. Credit cards accepted.

• 1925. Designer: Stanley Thompson. Par 71. 6,6663 yards. 70.5 par rating. 121 slope rating. Greens fees: May 15–June: C$62 ($47), July–September: C$75 ($57), October: C$40 to C$62 ($30 to $47). Twilight greens fee C$50 ($35), including cart and clubs. Walking permitted. Carts cost C$32 ($24). No caddies. Season: May–October.

GOLF SERVICES

Golf services include a good practice range, a well-stocked pro shop, excellent rental sets consisting of Callaway woods and irons, a terrific little halfway house, and a very good restaurant and bar, the Spike Lounge, with an outdoor terrace overlooking the first tee. As noted above, service is inconsistent. The first day we felt brushed off by the pro shop's curt staff. By the following morning, however, matters had improved; suddenly, range balls were complementary and the pleasant starter did a good job of putting together foursomes.

LODGING

The tranquil and beautifully maintained cabin (number 396, C$620/$465 in high season) that we occupied on the lake is one of the very best of the 499 guest rooms and suites at the Jasper Park Lodge. It features a stone fireplace, private porch, stocked minibar, cable television, a nice bath, and separate sitting room. As previously noted, the older log cabins have more charm and appeal than the newer chalet buildings. *Be certain* to request one when booking. Doubles range from C$400 to C$510 ($300 to $383) during the high summer season.

Jasper Park Lodge. PO Box 40, Jasper, Alberta TOE 1EO Canada. Tel: 800-441-1414 or 403-852-3301. Fax: 403-852-5107. 499 rooms and suites; doubles cost C$400 to C$510 ($300 to $383) during high season. Credit cards accepted.

RESTAURANTS

The cuisine at Jasper Park Lodge is the resort's weakest link, no doubt due in part to the sheer volume of guests served daily. Every meal we sampled at the resort earned at least satisfactory marks, yet not one meal, nor one dish, could be described as truly exceptional. Service, too, was very good in all the resort restaurants, but we found it awkward and silly that comment cards requesting that you grade your waitperson on the spot were passed around after every meal. All the restaurants, save the very good **Spike Lounge** at the golf club, are located in the central Lodge.

The **Edith Cavell** dining room is the resort's top gourmet venue and the only restaurant at Jasper Park that requires a jacket during the summer, while for the other Jasper Park restaurants the summertime dress code is smart casual, no jeans. The Edith Cavell features a superb lake view, an outstanding selection of wines, and a creative menu utilizing local ingredients prepared by chef David MacGillivray, including venison sausage, grilled Alberta lamb, and a unique chowder made with forest mushrooms; entrées generally range from C$16 to C$25 ($12 to $19). The **Beauvert** dining room, seating a thousand diners, is an informal, attractive spot favored both by families with children and the international tour groups that flock to Jasper. Good smoked salmon, a green salad, and tasty prime rib is a typical dinner in this bustling, pleasant restaurant where three meals are served daily. Although a bit less formal than the Edith Cavell dining room, prices at the two restaurants are comparable. The **Moose's Nook,** housed in a rather dark and dreary room, serves Canadian specialties—salmon, mountain trout, blackened Alberta sirloin, and buffalo stew with wild Alberta mushrooms. The **Emerald Lounge**, located just off the lobby, is popular for drinks and afternoon tea. Lunch is also served on the outdoor terrace overlooking the sparkling, outdoor swimming pool. **Meadows Cafe**, the resort's most casual place to dine, serves Italian fare; main entrées cost between C$10 and C$20 ($8 and $15).

The restaurants at Jasper Park Lodge. PO Box 40, Jasper, Alberta, Canada T0E 1E0. Tel: 403-852-3301 (general) or 403-852-6091 (dining reservations). Fax: 403-852-5107. Credit cards accepted.

NON-GOLF ACTIVITIES

The range of non-golf activities in the Jasper area is superb. Some of the activities within the resort include tennis, fishing and boating on Lac Beauvert, hiking, horseback riding, the health spa with sauna, steam, and exercise equipment, and shopping in the arcade of fifteen elegant shops on the ground floor of the Lodge building. The 4,200-square-mile Jasper National Park surrounds the resort in all directions. Sights within the park include the receding glacier at the Columbia Icefield; Maligne Canyon, where the Maligne River plunges into a steep walled gorge; the impressive Athabasca Falls; and Maligne Lake, the largest and deepest lake in the park. Wonderful walks and trails are marked throughout the park system. Guided white-water rafting trips on the Athabasca River and guided canoe trips on Lac Beauvert can be arranged by the concierge.

GETTING THERE: From the Calgary Airport take Highway 1 West to Highway 93 North (Columbia Icefield Parkway) past Banff Springs and Lake Louise. At the Jasper exit, turn right at the first set of lights and follow signs to Jasper Park Lodge. The entire drive takes about six hours.

▶KANANASKIS COUNTRY

	The Golf	Golf Services	Lodging	Restaurants	Non-Golf Activities	Total
Rating	18	18	16	16	18	86

The three best golf resorts in the Canadian Rockies are Jasper Park Lodge, Banff Springs, and Kananaskis, all within two hundred miles of each other in the mountains of Alberta, west of Calgary. Kananaskis, better known as a ski resort than a golf destination, is the most underrated of this famous trio. As a golf resort, it does not

quite measure up to the lofty standards of the sublime Jasper Park Lodge, but it surpasses the overall Banff Springs experience. Golfers touring the forbidding Canadian Rockies are well advised to include Kananaskis in their itinerary.

Kananaskis country, just one hour and thirty minutes by car from Calgary Airport, consists of the Fortress Mountain and Nakiska ski areas, which hosted the downhill ski events at the 1988 Calgary Winter Olympics; two stunning Robert Trent Jones, Sr., golf courses built in 1983–84 and situated at 4,900 feet above sea level; and the Kananaskis Village complex, comprised of three hotels/inns built around an outdoor courtyard, with restaurants, bars, and shops. Like every other great resort in the Canadian Rockies, Kananaskis is filled to capacity during July and August with visitors from around the world.

THE GOLF

Mount Lorette and **Mount Kidd,** the two wonderful courses at Kananaskis, are located down the hill from the cluster of Kananaskis hotels, and both start play from an extremely busy, but also extremely well run central clubhouse area. Indeed, Kananaskis excels—as it must—at crowd control. Service is outstanding. The young valet parkers at the clubhouse greet you with a big smile and hustle to get you on your way. We were very impressed with the attitude and efficiency of the well-trained service staff and with the overall spirit of the entire Kananaskis golf operation.

The golf day here begins early and ends late. The clubhouse restaurant opens at 6 A.M., and golfers are teeing up their first drives of the day by 7. Early afternoon is the slowest time to be on the course. Start play as early in the morning as possible if you wish to avoid a five-hour round. At this latitude, you will find packs of golfers on the course well past 9 P.M. because of the long summer days.

Both golf courses at Kananaskis are routed along the valley floor, which is crossed time and again by the translucent waters of the fast-flowing Kananaskis River. As a result, an abundance of water hazards exist, as well as lots of sand bunkers. In addition, both of these beautifully maintained courses are surrounded on all sides by snow-packed granite peaks that are 8,000 to 9,000 feet high. Like Jasper Park and Banff, this is a dramatic and inspirational setting for golf.

Mount Lorette and Mount Kidd are rated among the top eleven courses in all of Canada and justifiably so. Mount Lorette, however, is the longer, tighter, and slightly more difficult layout of the two; it is also quite walkable, even in the thinner air at 4,900 feet above sea level, where the ball travels easily 10 percent further. The hillier Mount Kidd course is walkable only for the most vigorous golfers.

The best sequence of holes on Mount Lorette are fifteen, sixteen, and seventeen. Fifteen and seventeen are superb par threes. Fifteen is 188 yards long, and seventeen is 185 yards. Both require exhilarating tee shots over the rushing river. Sixteen, an uphill 380-yard par four, demands another river crossing with your drive. Mount Lorette has four sets of tees ranging from 5,429 yards (par rating 69.8/slope rating 123) to 7,102 yards (par rating 74.1/slope rating 137).

The par five eighteenth hole on Mount Kidd is the longest hole at Kananaskis: 642 yards from the back tees. The three longest sets of tees on Mount Kidd range from 6,039 yards (par rating 68.2/slope rating 124) to 7,083 yards (par rating 72.8/slope rating 134). From the forward tees Mount Kidd measures 5,539 yards (par rating 70.1/slope rating 127).

Another real plus about Kananaskis is that it's reasonably priced. In fact, it's a steal. The greens fee for both courses is C$45 ($34); carts cost an additional C$13 ($10) per person. There is a twilight greens fee of C$38 ($29) that includes your cart; twilight generally begins one-half hour after the last booked tee time.

Kananaskis Country Golf Courses. PO Box 1710, Kananaskis, Alberta, T0L 2H0 Canada. Tel: 403-591-7272. Fax: 403-591-7072. Credit cards accepted.

• *Mount Lorette.* 1983. Designer: Robert Trent Jones, Sr. Par 72. 7,102 yards. 74.1 par rating. 137 slope rating.
• *Mount Kidd.* 1984. Designer: Robert Trent Jones, Sr. Par 72. 7,083 yards. 72.8 par rating. 134 slope rating.
• Greens fees for both courses: C$45 ($34); carts cost an additional C$13 ($10) per person. Twilight fee: C$38 ($29), includes cart. Walking permitted. No caddies. Early May—early October.

 GOLF SERVICES 18

Golf services, as already noted, are first-rate, including the excellent staff of starters and course marshals, a good pro shop, and the decent practice range.

LODGING 16

Kananaskis Village basically consists of two hotel properties: the Lodge at Kananaskis and the Kananaskis Inn. The Lodge at Kananaskis is a single property comprised of two separate but interconnected buildings or wings, one of which is called the "Lodge," while the other is called the "Hotel." The Lodge at Kananaskis is more upscale, while the Kananaskis Inn is for the budget-minded.

The **Lodge at Kananaskis** is owned and run in fine fashion by Canadian Pacific and features outstanding service and excellent guest accommodations. The Hotel wing is the completely nonsmoking section of the complex, while many of the amenities—restaurants, indoor pool, health club, indoor/outdoor hot tub, steam room, massage salon—are located in the Lodge proper. The Hotel, however, is where the fine L'Escapade dining room is located, as well as a small "executive spa" with saunas, hot tubs, and some exercise equipment. In a comparison of the Lodge and Hotel wings, the rooms in the Hotel tend to be a bit more luxurious and geared toward couples rather than families. Without question, the Lodge at Kananaskis fills up very early for the brief, yet intensely popular, summer season in the Canadian Rockies.

The **Kananaskis Inn,** although just steps from the Lodge, is a different story. This Best Western—owned property is the budget choice, filled with families with small children and featuring guest rooms that are considerably more basic. Our room at the Inn, number 2316, was actually dirty, with a soiled bedspread on one of the two beds and frayed towels in the bath. Services at the Inn are decidedly more rudimentary that what you will find at the Lodge.

Again, relative to Jasper, Kananaskis is a good value. Summer season rates at the Kananaskis Hotel and the Kananaskis Lodge range from C$260 to C$340 ($198 to $258) for doubles. Double rooms at the Kananaskis Inn range from C$95 to C$125 ($72 to $95) per night.

The Lodge at Kananaskis. Kananaskis Village, Alberta, ToL 2Ho Canada. Tel: 800-441-1414 or 403-591-7711. Fax: 403-591-7770. 251 rooms and suites in the Lodge and 68 nonsmoking rooms and suites in the Hotel range from C$260 to C$340 ($198 to $258). Credit cards accepted.

Kananaskis Inn. Box 10, Kananaskis Village, Alberta, ToL 2Ho Canada. Tel: 800-528-1234 or 403-591-7500. Fax: 403-591-7633. 94 rooms and suites from C$95 to C$125 ($72 to $95). Credit cards accepted.

RESTAURANTS 16

The premier restaurant in Kananaskis Village is the candlelit **L'Escapade** dining room, which is located on the main floor of the Hotel wing of the Lodge at Kananaskis. Smoked salmon, buffalo, and grilled Alberta beef are some of the Canadian specialties served at L'Escapade, which also features excellent service and a fine wine list. Entrées range in price from C$12 to C$18 ($9 to $14).

We also thoroughly enjoyed **Brady's Market,** a delightful restaurant serving innovative Mediterranean cuisine. Brady's offers all sorts of tasty tapas, out of which an entire feast can easily be created. Considered the hip place to dine, Brady's earns our kudos for its ambience and creative cuisine. We loved the marinated tiger prawns with garlic and chilies.

A number of other eating options also exist in the Lodge complex, including **Peaks,** the main—or family-style—dining room at the Lodge, which serves a varied menu including Alberta beef, chicken, salmon, and trout. Entrées generally range between C$10 and C$18 ($8 and $14). There is also **Big Horn Lounge,** with its pub-style fare including club sandwiches, nachos, chili, burgers and other grilled selections. The **Fireside Lounge,** after being completely renovated in early 1997, now offers a fondue menu. None of the restaurants at the Lodge at Kananaskis has an official dress code, as it is a priority that guests are comfortable throughout their stay. Reservations are accepted only for L'Escapade and Peaks.

At the Kananaskis Inn, there is the **Garden Café,** which offers reasonably priced fare for the entire family. The Inn also has **Woody's Bar,** a lively, fun nightspot. Finally, the **golf clubhouse** serves excellent breakfasts and lunches.

The restaurants at the Lodge at Kananaskis. Kananaskis Village, Alberta, ToL 2Ho Canada. Tel: 403-591-7711 (ext. 52 for dining reservations). Fax: 403-591-7770. Credit cards accepted.

Restaurants at the Kananaskis Inn. Box 10, Kananaskis Village, Alberta, ToL 2Ho Canada. Tel: 403-591-7500. Fax: 403-591-7633. Credit cards accepted.

NON-GOLF ACTIVITIES 18

A plethora of non-golf activities exists, from helicopter tours, horseback riding, and hiking, to bird-watching, bicycling, and boating. There is also, of course, touring the spectacular Rockies by car. The Lodge at Kananaskis offers an indoor swimming pool, indoor/outdoor hot tubs, six tennis courts, and use of the health club, including saunas, an aerobics room, exercise equipment, and tanning beds.

GETTING THERE: From Calgary Airport, take Highway 1 West for approximately thirty minutes to Highway 40 South to Kananaskis. Follow 40 South into Kananaskis Village.

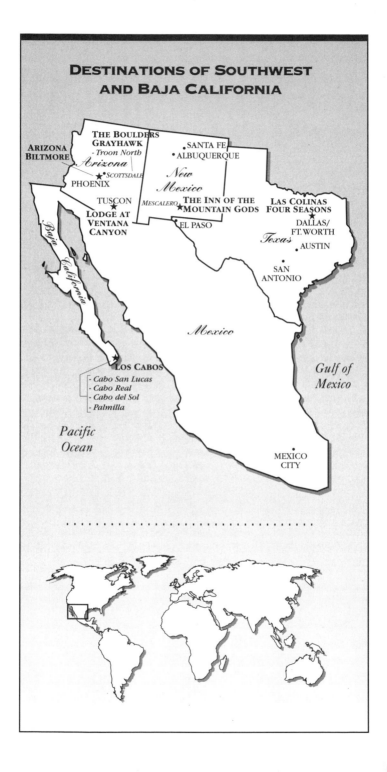

DESTINATIONS OF SOUTHWEST AND BAJA CALIFORNIA

ARIZONA BILTMORE

THE BOULDERS
GRAYHAWK
- Troon North
Arizona
★ •*SCOTTSDALE*
PHOENIX

• SANTA FE
• ALBUQUERQUE

New Mexico

TUSCON
LODGE AT VENTANA CANYON

Mescalero **THE INN OF THE MOUNTAIN GODS**
★
• EL PASO

LAS COLINAS FOUR SEASONS
★
DALLAS/ FT.WORTH

Texas
• AUSTIN

SAN ANTONIO

Baja California

Mexico

Pacific Ocean

LOS CABOS
- Cabo San Lucas
- Cabo Real
- Cabo del Sol
- Palmilla

Gulf of Mexico

MEXICO CITY

THE SOUTHWEST AND BAJA CALIFORNIA

THE SOUTHWEST AND BAJA CALIFORNIA

The Southwest is big, wide land. . . . The stimulation of thin air; the intense blueness of the sky; the towering thunderheads of summer that rumble and flash and produce sheets of rain with a sudden rush of water that soon passes, leaving only a wet arroyo to dry within an hour; the quick change of climate, from burning dry heat that allows no sweat to wet one's clothing to a shivering cold during the rainfall; these are among the attributes of a land that gets into one's blood and bones.

—Eliot Porter, *Eliot Porter's Southwest*

Now it's time to saddle up your clubs and head with us to the Southwest, a massive, dramatic terrain that stretches from the heart of Texas to the very tip of Baja California. The glue that binds this magnificent region together is the desert, a rich and wondrously complex ecosystem with stately cactus, an infinite variety of landscapes, and all sorts of new and strange wildlife. The Western desert is America's most exotic geographical region, and no region has loomed larger in our popular imagination.

For the golfer, the arid Southwest means a whole new type of golf course. Golf courses are often unforgettable places, especially in the desert, where the rich lushness of fairways and greens forms an instant and always striking contrast with the gray-beige desert floor. The early desert resort courses embodied the long-held attitude that the desert is an inhospitable, forbidding wasteland. Virtuoso golf course designs immersed players in an environment that almost completely eradicated the desert landscape. The desert floor, flora, and fauna were boldly and ruthlessly torn up and replaced by luxuriously wide and green fairways, newly installed trees, and man-made water hazards, all nourished by lavish irrigation systems. An outstanding example of this type of course construction is the William P. Bell—designed Adobe Course at the Arizona Biltmore in Phoenix.

More recently, an environmentally sensitive attitude toward the desert, coinciding with the implementation of strict local water ordinances that restrict irrigation, has produced a new type of golf course that reveres the wild, Western landscape. Desert target courses minimize earthmoving and give desert flora and fauna free reign. An imperative exists: stay on the sometimes excruciatingly narrow fairways and greens, or else you're done for. Players are repeatedly forced to carry their shots over canyons, ravines, and all sorts of natural desert hazards. Tom Fazio's Ventana Mountain Course, nestled in the rugged foothills outside Tucson where the desert meets the Santa Clara Mountains, and the two Jay Morrish courses at the Boulders are prime examples and rate at the top of our list of favorite desert tracks. Cactus, mesquite, and arroyos are essential to these courses. The large, multipronged saguaro cactus, which grows to a height of forty to fifty feet and sports an exotic white bloom in May and June, stands sentinel in the desert landscape. The saguaro makes a convenient marker as you plot your line to the green—you will find them just about everywhere, including the middle of sand bunkers. These environmentally correct golf courses teem with wildlife—everything from Gambel's quail and doves to cottontails, roadrunners, rattlesnakes, gila monsters, deer, bobcat, and the occasional coyote.

We invite you to join us now on a fascinating golf journey from Las Colinas, near Dallas, the home course of the legendary Byron Nelson, to a stunning concluding

The Southwest and Baja California

crescendo at Los Cabos, located at the southern extremity of the Baja Peninsula in Mexico, which boasts two of Jack Nicklaus's finest courses. In between, scout a terrific course on an Apache reservation in the mountains of New Mexico; settle into the tranquil world of the Boulders—one of the best small resorts anywhere in the world—in Carefree, Arizona, from which you can explore the legendary courses in the Scottsdale area; revel in the splendor of the Frank Lloyd Wright–inspired Arizona Biltmore Hotel in Phoenix; and admire the views of Tucson and the surrounding mountains from the Ventana Mountain golf courses.

Golf is played year-round in the desert sunshine, although with different levels of comfort. When calling for price quotes at Arizona resorts, you will marvel at how low the rates drop during the summer. Once you have spent a few summer days in Tucson, you will know why. The weather is often impossibly hot. Tucson's average high temperature in summer is ninety-eight degrees. It is quite common for Arizona desert temperatures to soar above 110 degrees and stay there for days. Fortunately, humidity is low, but most people stay out of the heat and sun when it is this hot.

The weather from October through April in southern Arizona is glorious. December through February offers cool evenings and brisk mornings, with daily temperatures averaging seventy degrees in the Phoenix/Scottsdale/Carefree region and sixty-five degrees in Tucson. If traveling to Tucson in the winter, be sure to pack a sweater and a light jacket. The weather in Texas is a bit less predictable. Dallas occasionally experiences severe ice storms in the winter and sometimes debilitating heat and humidity in the summer.

The exotic variety of the desert Southwest makes it an ideal destination for a family vacation. Explore Indian ruins, study the intricacies of pueblo architecture, and visit an Indian reservation and a Spanish mission. This is cowboy country, and you can get a genuine feel for the Wild West by staying at a dude ranch or visiting a restored ghost town. When you tire of sightseeing, there's no shortage of horseback riding, boating, white-water rafting, fishing, and hiking.

Now you know where and when to go. So get the limes ready for the margaritas, leave the errant tee shots for the rattlesnakes, and welcome to the extraordinary world of desert golf!

Texas

▶LAS COLINAS
THE FOUR SEASONS RESORT

	The Golf	Golf Services	Lodging	Restaurants	Non-Golf Activities	Total
Rating	17	19	18	17	19	90

Despite the slightly iridescent glow from its strange and somewhat garish orange-pink brick facade—and a location directly under the noisy flight path of the gigantic and always busy Dallas–Fort Worth Airport—the Four Seasons Resort and Club at Las Colinas is far and away the premier golf resort in the golf-mad state of Texas. We entertained serious misgivings about this resort based upon an initial perusal of photographs and hotel brochures. The stark, orange-pink, high-rise hotel set in a sterile, urban-suburban office-block setting did nothing to whet our

287

The Four Seasons Resort

appetites, yet as events unfolded, our doubts proved completely unfounded. In a word, the Four Seasons is a masterpiece, an assessment that should come as no surprise to those familiar with superb Four Seasons properties elsewhere. Our visit to the Four Seasons was sublime in every department, thanks to the resort's extremely handsome interior, opulent and well-appointed guest accommodations, friendly and utterly professional service staff, and enormous health spa (one of the finest in the world). In addition, the golf operation, located just steps from the hotel, proved to be a model of precision and pleasure.

The Four Seasons at Las Colinas is the site of the GTE Byron Nelson Classic, a major PGA event held at the resort in May. A heroic, nine-foot bronze statue of Byron Nelson stands sentinel immediately adjacent to the first tee of the resort's TPC Course, the tranquil corridors of the lavish golf clubhouse are decorated with interesting Nelson memorabilia, and the famous man himself, now eighty-five but still routinely shooting in the low seventies, was highly visible during our visit, signing autographs and greeting well-wishers. The Four Seasons, given its refined services, facilities, and convenient airport location, is a popular destination for upmarket business groups, yet all travelers to Dallas—coming for business or vacation—are strongly urged to consider a visit.

THE GOLF 17

The Byron Nelson Classic is contested over both of the resort's excellent golf courses—the TPC Course and the shorter and easier (by two or three strokes) Cottonwood Valley Course. Unlike other notoriously difficult TPC, stadium-type layouts that have badly shaken our golfing self-esteem (the courses at Ponte Vedra and PGA West, for example), the TPC Course at Las Colinas is far from punitive. This is no great wonder because both courses at the Four Seasons were designed by the wonderful Jay Morrish, one of our most inventive and user-friendly golf course architects. Courses bearing the name of Jay Morrish—including the North and South courses at the Boulders, Troon North, and the Loch Lomond Club in Scotland—are not only delightful, beautiful to behold, and full of fun, but they are also real tests of golf. We will not say that this is the easiest TPC Course in America, yet, in our experience, it is the fairest and the least "tricked up." In other words, a very good golfer visiting Las Colinas has a good shot at scoring below his or her handicap.

There are two unfortunate and unavoidable glitches to the golf experience at Las Colinas—both a function of the resort's location—that must be noted. The fourteenth hole of the TPC Course is a terrific hole of golf, a challenging downhill and downwind par four with water guarding the front of the green. This hole, however, runs for its entire length parallel to a major highway filled with traffic rushing to and from the airport. The second glitch is what we might call the "La Guardia Airport atmosphere" of the Cottonwood Valley Course. This course is located closer to the airport runways than the TPC Course, with planes flying very low overhead as they take off and prepare to land. The golfer, sadly, can actually smell airplane fuel and exhaust while deciding whether to hit a six or seven iron to the green. At times, you have to raise your voice in order to be heard over the aircraft's thrust. These details aside, all else is virtually perfect. Both courses are routed over attractive, rolling terrain and maintained to exquisite standards.

As a general rule, the TPC Course is intended to accommodate resort guests while Cottonwood Valley is the "private" layout serving local members. Cottonwood Valley is open to resort guests only on the one day a week (generally Monday or Tuesday) when the TPC Course is closed.

Of the two layouts, the **TPC Course** is not only the tougher and better but also the more beautiful. Despite the handsome, modern office buildings that surround it—and our caveat about the fourteenth hole—the TPC Course actually manages to achieve an air of peaceful tranquillity. The course plays to a par of seventy and measures 6,899 yards from the championship tees (par rating 73.5/slope rating 135), 6,500 yards from the blue tees (par rating 71.4/slope rating 129), 6,004 yards from the whites (par rating 68.9/slope rating 122), and 5,340 yards from the reds (par rating 70.6/slope rating 116).

The TPC layout opens gently enough with a short, downhill par four followed by a short and straightforward par three. But the third, the number one handicap hole, is a brute, a 490-yard par four that demands a tee shot over a lake, tempting the player to cut it close to the water's edge. The fifth hole is a good, 176-yard par three with a green protected by a broad canal, and the seventh is a very long, tough, up-hill par five that plays into strong prevailing winds. Indeed, par on number seven is a brilliant score, particularly when the wind is in your face. Outstanding holes on the back nine include number twelve, a 426-yard par four with a green tucked away on a wooded hillside; number thirteen, a difficult, 183-yard par three; and sixteen, a 554-yard par five and a true three-shot hole. The eighteenth hole is a relatively un-eventful par four that finishes in front of the clubhouse.

Cottonwood Valley, on the other hand, provides little time to find your swing. Its opening hole is also the number one handicap, a 448-yard par four that requires a long carry over water if you intend to hit the green in regulation. But the best holes on Cottonwood Valley are found on the back side. Eleven is a downhill, down-wind par five that plays to an elevated green; sixteen, another long, downhill par five with thick rough on both sides of the fairway, plays from an elevated tee, the highest point on the golf course; seventeen is a 204-yard par three into the wind; and eighteen is the uphill, 439-yard finisher.

Cottonwood Valley measures 6,862 yards from the championship tees (par rating 73.4/slope rating 133), 6,367 yards from the blue tees (par rating 70.5/slope rating 126), 5,961 yards from the white tees (par rating 68.4/slope rating 117), and 5,320 yards from the red tees (par rating 70.6/slope rating 116). The greens fee for resort guests on both courses is $125 per round, cart included. For tee times call 214-717-2455.

Four Seasons Resort and Club. 41500 MacArthur Boulevard, Irving, TX 75038. Tel: 972-717-2455 or 972-717-0700. Fax: 214-717-2487. Credit cards accepted.

• *TPC Course.* 1985. Designer: Jay Morrish. Par 70. 6,899 yards. 73.5 par rating. 135 slope rating. Greens fee: $125, cart included. No walking. Caddies available upon request. Restrictions: public play restricted to guests of the Four Seasons Resort. The course is closed one day a week (generally Monday or Tuesday) for mainte-nance. Season: year-round.

• *Cottonwood Valley Course.* 1985. Designer: Jay Morrish. Par 71. 6,862 yards. 73.4 par rating. 133 slope rating. Greens fee: $125, cart included. No walking. Caddies available upon request. Restrictions: open to resort guests only when the TPC Course is closed. Season: year-round.

GOLF SERVICES  (19)

Golf services are superb. The new Byron Nelson Golf School and a large practice facility were recently completed just behind the eighteenth green of the TPC Course. The stylish pro shop is handsome and well stocked, the golf staff is friendly and outgoing (the starters on both courses struck us as especially pleasant), and refreshment carts make their way up and down the golf courses. Rental clubs are available. Walking is not permitted.

LODGING (18)

The more than three hundred guest rooms and suites in the nine-story **Four Seasons Resort and Club** at Las Colinas are spacious, exceptionally well equipped, and beautifully decorated with fine furnishings and fabrics. We stayed in a standard room, number 583, which features a large, luxurious marble bath, a separate sitting area with desk, and every amenity from cable television to a fully stocked, in-room bar. The best guest accommodations at the Four Seasons are the forty-four villa rooms adjacent to the eighteenth green of the TPC Course, each featuring private patios or balconies. Public areas in the hotel include the elegant marble lobby, a fine bar, an efficient concierge desk, and a delightful lounge with vintage billiard tables. An underground walkway links the hotel with its truly spectacular, 176,000-square-foot, indoor sports complex. Service throughout the resort is superb.

For anyone preferring to stay in Dallas proper, we highly recommend the exclusive, gorgeous, and intimate **Mansion on Turtle Creek,** which pampers guests with terribly attentive and friendly service.

Four Seasons Resort and Club. 4150 North MacArthur Boulevard, Irving, TX 75038. Tel: 800-332-3442 or 972-717-0700. Fax: 972-717-2550. 357 rooms and suites. Double rooms range from $245 to $305. Villas start at $500. Golf packages available. Credit cards accepted.

The Mansion on Turtle Creek. 2821 Turtle Creek Boulevard, Dallas, TX 75219. Tel: 800-527-5432 or 214-559-2100. Fax: 214-528-4187. 143 rooms and suites from $270 to $1,490. Credit cards accepted.

RESTAURANTS (17)

The two principal restaurants at the Four Seasons are both excellent. **Café on the Green,** just off the lobby, serves breakfast, lunch, and dinner in a refined setting overlooking the outdoor swimming pool and the TPC Course. At dinner, guests may opt for the tempting buffet or order meat, seafood, pasta, and gourmet vegetarian dishes from the menu. Dinner entrées range from $18 to $26, and the buffet costs $30. **Byron's,** the handsome restaurant located in the golf clubhouse, is the ideal spot for lunch and features another elaborate buffet. Byron's is open for lunch Monday through Friday.

A twenty-minute drive into Dallas opens up a myriad of dining options. **Café Pacific,** located in the Highland Park Village shopping center (don't let this keep you away from this lovely area—in Highland Park the term "shopping center" is a misnomer!), is one of our longtime favorites and features delicious seafood and meats in a classy, stylish decor. Dinner for two, with wine, will run roughly $85 plus tip. Right across the street is a good, though not inspired, Italian spot called **Patrizio,** where pastas and typical Italian specialties abound. Pasta on the patio with a good Barolo under the shade of live oaks can make an afternoon disappear. Dinner for two, with wine, is about $50 plus tip.

A hot spot on the culinary scene is **Star Canyon,** with owner Stephan Pyles at the helm in the kitchen. A fabulously chic, "real Texas" decor showcases his innovative southwestern cuisine and draws all the rich and famous. Expect to pay about $75 for dinner for two, not including wine.

The **Mansion on Turtle Creek** is a long-revered dining spot with very beautiful decor and outstanding southwestern and Continental food. Dinner for two, not including wine, will cost approximately $150.

For some of the best Mediterranean/Continental in Dallas, head to either of two sister restaurants, Riviera and Mediterraneo. The menu at the elegant **Riviera** features a wide selection of entrées from southern France and northern Italy, including sirloin of lamb, veal, duck, salmon, snapper, and other seafood; dinner for two with wine and tip costs about $130. The cuisine at **Mediterraneo** matches Riviera's quality but entrées at this less formal restaurant range from $15 to $26.

Café on the Green and Byron's. Four Seasons Resort and Club. 4150 North MacArthur Boulevard, Irving, TX 75038. Tel: 800-332-3442 or 972-717-0700. Café on the Green (only): 972-717-2420. Fax: 972-717-2550. Credit cards accepted.

Café Pacific. 24 Highland Park Village, Dallas, TX 75205. Tel: 214-526-1170. Fax: 214-526-0332. Credit cards accepted.

Patrizio. 25 Highland Park Village, Dallas, TX 75205. Tel: 214-522-7878. Fax: 214-443-0714. Credit cards accepted.

Star Canyon. 3102 Oak Lawn Avenue, Dallas, TX 75219. Tel: 214-520-7827. Fax: 214-520-2667. Credit cards accepted.

Mansion on Turtle Creek. 2821 Turtle Creek Boulevard, Dallas, TX 75219. Tel: 800-527-5432 or 214-559-2100. Fax: 214-528-4187. Credit cards accepted.

Riviera. 7709 Inwood Road, Dallas, TX 75209. Tel: 214-351-0094. Fax: 214-351-3344. Credit cards accepted.

Mediterraneo. 18111 Preston Road, Dallas, TX 75252. Tel: 972-447-0066. Fax: 972-447-0060. Credit cards accepted.

NON-GOLF ACTIVITIES ⑲

The vast indoor-outdoor sports complex at the Four Seasons is one of the world's finest. Facilities include indoor and outdoor tennis courts, racquetball and squash courts, an indoor jogging track, an aerobics room, a cardiovascular exercise room, free weights, an indoor basketball half court, indoor and outdoor swimming pools, and truly luxurious health spas for men and women with sauna, steam, plunge baths, massage treatments, and beauty salon. Without exception, all are executed and managed with Four Seasons panache.

In addition, Dallas, with its cultural offerings and outstanding shopping, is only about twenty minutes away. Highland Park Village abounds with upscale shops in pleasant surroundings. North Park Center at I-95 and Northwest Highway features stores such as Neiman Marcus and Barney's New York, as well as an Esté Lauder Spa.

GETTING THERE: From the Dallas—Fort Worth Airport, take the north exit to Highway 114 heading east. After a few miles, exit at MacArthur Boulevard and turn right. The Four Seasons is just about a mile or so up the road on the left.

New Mexico

►INN OF THE MOUNTAIN GODS—MESCALERO
APACHE GOLF

	The Golf	Golf Services	Lodging	Restaurants	Non-Golf Activities	Total
Rating	17	17	16	15	17	82

Inn of the Mountain Gods

Situated 7,200 feet above sea level, the unforgettable golf course at the Inn of the Mountain Gods works its way through peaceful, fragrant forests of pine and cedar. Looming above this gorgeous, scrupulously maintained layout is Sierra Blanca, an impressive, 12,003-foot mountain peak upon which, if you use your imagination and carefully examine it, you can see the face of a woman.

According to a deeply held Apache tradition, Sierra Blanca is a sacred place known as the White Painted Woman. Hundreds of years ago, during a cataclysmic thunder and lightning storm, White Painted Woman gave birth to a ferocious son named Killer of Enemies, who always protected the Apaches and slayed the Giant Monsters that threatened the tribe. The Mescalero Apache were once known as the fiercest of warriors. Women of the tribe were resourceful providers, capable of finding water while others died of thirst; these same tribeswomen were also skilled at preparing food using the mescal plant. That is why the Spanish called them *Mescalero*, "the people who eat mescal."

Today, one of the principal businesses of the Mescalero is luring resort guests (primarily from Texas and other southwestern states) to their vast and spectacularly beautiful 463,000-acre reservation in remote south-central New Mexico, 125 miles northeast of the nearest commercial airport in El Paso, Texas.

The Inn of the Mountain Gods occupies only a small corner of the massive Mescalero homeland, yet it boasts several attractions for visitors, including a simply fabulous Ted Robinson—designed championship golf course that hosts amateur and professional events for New Mexico golfers, several busy gambling casinos, a winter ski operation called Ski Apache, and, perhaps most important, a captivating Native American cultural experience set amid breathtaking scenery. The majority of the resort staff—from the hotel front desk and room maids to the golf pro to the managers and owners of the entire operation—are members of the Mescalero Apache tribe.

The Inn of the Mountain Gods is also a very good buy. Room rates average $150 during the high summer season, while the greens fee and cart will cost you about $55. The minimum bet at the blackjack tables is a budget-minded $5 a hand. The two faces of the resort's dichotomous personality—golf resort and gambling casino—do not clash; in fact, they even manage to operate well together. While the casino lures hordes of price-conscious day-trippers who frequently pay restaurant tabs from coupon books, the golf operation attracts a more upscale clientele.

The golf season typically begins in early April and extends through mid-October, although the course stays open when weather permits from March 1 until December 31. During our April visit to Mescalero, we experienced quite chilly mornings and evenings, while the brilliant afternoons were warm, tinder-dry, and very windy, with gusts on the golf course sometimes exceeding thirty-five miles per hour. At this altitude, a golf ball sails 10 percent further than it does at sea level. When the wind is at your back, the ball just seems to fly forever.

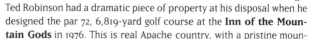

THE GOLF

Ted Robinson had a dramatic piece of property at his disposal when he designed the par 72, 6,819-yard golf course at the **Inn of the Mountain Gods** in 1976. This is real Apache country, with a pristine mountain valley cut by clear, rushing streams and framed by a range of towering mountain peaks that exceed 10,000 feet and remain packed with snow until late spring. As a general rule, Robinson works with the existing, natural terrain rather than against it; he shuns intrusive designs that require pushing the land around into odd shapes with teams of bulldozers. This fine golf course in Mescalero strongly reminds us of another outstanding and all-natural Robinson design—beautiful Tokatee in central Oregon. The only "artificial" element here is the lovely, man-made Lake Mescalero, which comes into play on five holes. The Inn of the Mountain Gods course is rated number eight in New Mexico by *Golf Digest*.

We recommend that most golfers not be intimidated by the posted yardage and tackle this course from the back markers. We have two reasons for this suggestion. First, 6,819 yards from the blue tees is not overly long at this great altitude; second, the shot qualities, particularly on the four fantastic par threes, are simply sensational from the back tees. If you play from the white markers, you will miss much of the fun.

The par threes, in fact, are probably what you will remember most about the golf layout at the Inn of the Mountain Gods. Three of the four are downhill and downwind, yet all four pose an exhilarating challenge.

Take the 230-yard eighth as an example. This delightful hole plays through a narrow chute of pines down to the green from a tee perched fifty feet above the putting surface. One golfer in our foursome, a muscular Apache teenager, employed local knowledge to his best advantage and hit the center of this green with an easy seven iron lofted high and propelled by the wind. The twelfth hole is 214 yards long, also downwind, and mostly carry over the waters of Lake Mescalero. The finishing hole is the best par three of all, 226 yards long from an elevated tee and all carry over the churning waters of the lake. Scary is the best adjective to describe your tee shot on the wonderful eighteenth.

The par threes are fun, but the par fives can be bears. The opening hole at Mescalero—an uphill, 535-yard par five whose fairway becomes progressively more hemmed in by big pine trees as you ascend the hill and approach the green—is the course's number one handicap hole. The 563-yard ninth hole is the longest on the course, a huge, downhill par five that doglegs to the left. The eleventh hole is the shortest of the par fives, measuring just 490 yards, yet it may be the toughest since it plays directly into powerful prevailing winds. Number fourteen, however, is the most exquisite golf hole here. Set far back in the valley amid stunning countryside, the 520-yard fourteenth requires two long, straight woods and a deadly accurate iron shot onto the narrow green.

The signature hole at this course is the par four tenth, which features an island fairway set in the middle of Lake Mescalero. Your tee shot on ten must carry the water but should be hit no more than 190 to 200 yards. Anything longer than that will splash into the lake. Another great par four is the 354-yard sixth, with a blind tee shot over the left half of the hillside. In truth, this entire layout offers nothing resembling a weak hole.

The course managers and groundskeepers take great care of the golf course. Greens, tees, fairways, and sand bunkers were all in excellent condition during our visit. Rangers are effective in moving slow players along, and a refreshment cart makes its rounds on the course. As is frequently the case in the casual Southwest, the dress code on the course is quite relaxed. Walking is not permitted.

The Inn of the Mountain Gods course measures 6,819 yards from the blue tees (par rating 72.1/slope rating 132), 6,478 yards from the white tees (par rating 70.1/slope rating 128), and 5,478 yards from the red tees (par rating 65.5/slope rating 114).

Inn of the Mountain Gods. Carrizo Canyon Road, PO Box 269, Route 4, Mescalero, NM 88340. Tel: 800-446-2963 (golf shop) or 505-257-5141. Fax: 505-257-6173. Credit cards accepted.

• 1976. Designer: Ted Robinson. Par 72. 6,819 yards. 72.1 par rating. 132 slope rating. Greens fee: $35 plus $20 cart fee, per person. No walking. No caddies. Season: March 1–December 31, weather permitting.

GOLF SERVICES

Golf services are excellent at the Inn of the Mountain Gods, despite the fact that its practice range is just 150 yards long, a problem made even worse by the altitude. The large pro shop is well stocked with merchandise, the locker rooms for men and women are more than adequate, rental clubs and golf lessons are available, and service from staff members is friendly and outgoing.

LODGING 16

The 262 guest accommodations at the **Inn of the Mountain Gods** are adequate and reasonably comfortable but by no means luxurious. We stayed in a standard room, number 188 in the Tower building, which struck us as comparable to a typical motel-type unit. The room was spacious enough, with a decent bath, outdoor patio, and cable television, but otherwise it was quite basic and the air conditioning and heating systems needed a little fine tuning. The best rooms at the Inn are the Bizaayi suites and ten parlor rooms, both of which are considerably larger than the standard rooms and priced at just $10 more per night.

Public areas in the main Lodge building include the large bar overlooking the lake, a small gift shop, and an activities desk. Downstairs you will find the pleasant Dan Li Ka dining room and the larger of the two casinos. The golf pro shop and the first tee are located just one hundred yards from the Lodge building. Service throughout the resort is good.

Inn of the Mountain Gods. Carrizo Canyon Road, PO Box 269, Route 4, Mescalero, NM 88340. Tel: 800-545-9011 or 505-257-5141. Fax: 505-257-6173. 262 rooms, suites, and parlors. Doubles from $130 to $160 during high season (June 1 through Labor Day). Credit cards accepted.

RESTAURANTS

The recently remodeled **Dan Li Ka** dining room is very attractive and well run, but the rather unimaginative menu features a predictable assortment of Continental dishes only, including shrimp cocktail and various cuts of beef. We were sorry to discover no tasty Mexican, southwestern, or inventive Native American cooking, although the single best dinner entrée we sampled, the local mountain trout, was excellent. The selection of desserts is also very good. A complete dinner for two with beverage and tip costs approximately $70. Reservations are required.

The casual **Apache Tee** restaurant, located next to the golf shop, serves hearty breakfast buffets and a selection of sandwiches and burgers at lunch. For dinner you can enjoy all-you-can-eat shrimp or a monster T-bone steak at very reasonable prices. Entrées range in price from $6 to $12.

The restaurants at the Inn of the Mountain Gods. Carrizo Canyon Road, PO Box 269, Route 4, Mescalero, NM 88340. Tel: 505-257-5141. Fax: 505-257-6173. Credit cards accepted.

 ## NON-GOLF ACTIVITIES ⑰

Activities for the non-golfer within the resort include tennis, trail rides on horseback, fishing in Lake Mescalero, boating, swimming in the large outdoor pool, and bicycle rentals. Blackjack, poker, and roulette are the most popular games in the very friendly main casino, which is open—and filled to capacity—from 11 A.M. until 1 A.M. A second, equally busy casino with scores of slot machines is open round-the-clock.

South-central New Mexico offers a wealth of fascinating sights for those touring the region by car. The White Sands National Monument, located midway between El Paso and Mescalero, just west of Alamogordo, is the largest gypsum deposit in the world, a sea of shimmering white sand dunes and one of the most spectacular natural sights you will ever see. The first atomic bomb was tested here, at what is now the White Sands Missile Range. The Tularosa Basin Historical Museum features fossils and Indian artifacts. Downtown Ruidoso, home of the richest quarter-horse race in the world at Ruidoso Downs, has attractive art galleries and shops.

GETTING THERE: The Inn of the Mountain Gods is 125 miles northeast of El Paso. From the airport at El Paso, take Highway 54 North past the town of Alamogordo. The road will divide around the town of Tularosa. Turn onto Route 70 East. About 40 miles ahead you will see signs for the resort.

Arizona

▶THE ARIZONA BILTMORE
A STUNNING ARCHITECTURAL OASIS IN THE DESERT

	The Golf	Golf Services	Lodging	Restaurants	Non-Golf Activities	Total
Rating	17	17	19	18	18	89

If the Arizona Biltmore were located in the French countryside, the famous Michelin guidebooks would give the physical structure, the interior, and the grounds of the Biltmore no fewer than three stars. Three Michelin stars for a sight means it is so spectacular or so significant that it deserves a special trip. Ever since it opened it 1929, this architectural marvel—built by Albert Chase McArthur with collaborative contributions from his mentor, Frank Lloyd Wright—has been known as "the Jewel of the Desert." During the Great Depression, the Biltmore was acquired by chewing-gum tycoon William Wrigley, Jr., who owned it for more than forty years and turned it into a world-class getaway oasis that attracted the rich and famous. The exterior and interior design are absolutely stunning, while the immaculate grounds, with their explosion of flowers, mature palms, and fir trees, are magical.

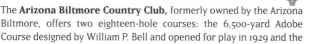

THE GOLF

The **Arizona Biltmore Country Club,** formerly owned by the Arizona Biltmore, offers two eighteen-hole courses: the 6,500-yard Adobe Course designed by William P. Bell and opened for play in 1929 and the 6,000-yard Links Course designed in 1978 by former director of golf Bill Johnston. Although neither of these courses is in the top five in Arizona, both are excellent. Fairways and greens are perfect. Of the two, the **Adobe Course** is certainly the more interesting and challenging. Offering breathtaking views of Squaw Peak and Camelback Mountain, the Adobe is more like a mature parkland or country-club course, with wide fairways abundantly lined with mature palms and pine trees.

The Adobe Course

From the Adobe you will also get a good look at the Wrigley Mansion perched atop a small mountain. Greens are small, undulating, medium speed, and well bunkered, demanding precise approach shots. The Adobe Course, in addition to being in immaculate condition, is a kind course; you can spray your drives a bit and manage to stay out of trouble. Unlike some of the pancake-flat courses around Phoenix, such as the courses at the Wigwam, the Adobe Course stretches out over gently rolling terrain, adding interest to play. The signature hole is the lovely and tough par four third, measuring 433 yards, with a pond in front of the green forcing a hundred-yard carry.

The shorter **Links Course** is much narrower that the Adobe, putting more of a premium on driving accuracy than driving distance. The front nine was created from a greenbelt winding around expensive homes, and it feels a bit like an afterthought. The best hole is the 185-yard, par three fifteenth, with its tee elevated a hundred feet above the green. The view from here of the town of Phoenix and the surrounding mountains is stupendous.

Arizona Biltmore Country Club. 24th Street and Missouri Avenue, Phoenix, AZ 85016. Tel: 602-955-9655. Fax: 602-955-6013. Credit cards accepted.

• *Adobe Course.* 1929. Designer: William P. Bell. Par 72. 6,500 yards. 75.2 par rating. 120 slope rating. Greens fees: $105 (January–May), $68 (May–June), $40 (July–August), $73 (September–December), cart included. No walking. No caddies. Season: year-round.

• *Links Course.* 1978. Designer: Bill Johnston. Par 72. 6,000 yards. 67.7 par rating. 112 slope rating. Greens fees: $105 (January–May), $68 (May–June), $40 (July–August), $73 (September–December), cart included. No walking. No caddies. Season: year-round.

GOLF SERVICES

The driving range and putting green are excellent. The pro shop is well stocked and has a very courteous and attentive staff.

LODGING

Here we must puncture one of the myths about the **Arizona Biltmore.** Although Frank Lloyd Wright had tremendous influence on the Biltmore's ultimate design, Albert Chase McArthur was the architect of record. Present-day Biltmore promotional material does little to dispel the myth because it repeatedly mentions Wright when discussing the resort's design. Because of early confusion and controversy, Wright himself tried to set the record straight in 1930 when he wrote "To Whom It May Concern . . . Albert McArthur is the architect of that building—all attempts to take the credit for that performance from him are gratuitous and beside the mark." The most accurate historical view would be to say that Wright was the visionary of the Biltmore design and McArthur was responsible for the execution of his vision.

Arizona Biltmore

Putting the architectural controversy aside, this resort oasis, just east of Phoenix in the foothills of Squaw Peak, is the most physically dazzling resort complex in the United States. Over seventy years after its construction, the six-hundred-room (including fifty villa suites) resort hotel is still a marvel of modernity. The main building—with its wings built of unique, gray, precast concrete "Biltmore blocks"—has an Aztec or Mayan look, as well as a certain Cambodian or Thai aspect. Whatever the look, the Biltmore blends gracefully into Arizona's desert terrain. The lobby is sleek, marvelously lit, and a perfect beginning to this wondrous place. All the public rooms are tasteful, filled with an eclectic and stunning art collection of sculpture, bas-reliefs, paintings, pottery, and baskets.

Between 1991 and 1994, the Biltmore spent roughly $50 million on renovations—the most noteworthy results being the dramatic pool and cabanas just to the right of the main building and the lovely refurbishment of all the guest rooms. We stayed in room 3409, which faces Squaw Peak to the north and features a balcony overlooking the gardens. The room was beautifully decorated and had a spacious marble bathroom. All rooms come outfitted with stocked minibars, his-and-her terry-cloth robes, and plenty of closet space.

Service throughout the hotel is exceptionally friendly, although the concierge desk is occasionally a bit short with guests. The maids, front desk personnel, and room service could not have been more pleasant.

Arizona Biltmore. 24th Street and Missouri Avenue, Phoenix, AZ 85016. Tel: 800-950-0086 or 602-955-6600. Fax: 602-954-2548. 600 rooms and suites. Doubles from $330 to $475 (suites from $605 to $1,705) in high season (January through May) and $130 to $195 (suites from $310 to $810) out of season (June through August). Credit cards accepted.

RESTAURANTS

There are four viable restaurant options at the Biltmore: **Wright's,** the most formal; the **Biltmore Grill and Patio,** a much more casual venue with a roaring fireplace for cool desert evenings; the **Cabana Club,** featuring casual poolside dining; and the **Adobe Restaurant,** perfect for breakfast and lunch before and after a round of golf.

For a truly special evening, have dinner at Wright's, quite simply one of the finest, most elegant restaurants in the entire Southwest. A jacket is required here, but not a tie. Wright's dining room is quite stunning, with glistening, tiered chandeliers. Chef Joanne Bondy's brilliant and honest cuisine thoroughly lives up to the elegant surroundings. Of special note were the sautéed Hudson Valley foie gras with pan-seared polenta and shitake mushrooms, the smoked breast of squab with porcini mushrooms and chervil vinaigrette, and the roasted loin of venison with golden chanterelles—all dishes to die for. Service was very professional, although we found the very knowledgeable sommelier a tad arrogant. The wine cellar is superb. Dinner for two with wine and tip costs about $125.

The restaurants at the Arizona Biltmore. 24th Street and Missouri Avenue, Phoenix, AZ 85016. Tel: 602-955-6600. Fax: 602-954-2548. Credit cards accepted.

NON-GOLF ACTIVITIES (18)

There is a plethora of non-golf activities both at the hotel and in the immediate vicinity. The hotel offers eight excellent tennis courts, a first-rate exercise room and spa, five swimming pools including the dazzling, new pool right outside the hotel, a "don't-miss" historical tour of the hotel and grounds, and a very good children's program. There are several hotel shops, all of which we found infinitely ordinary. The serious, blue-ribbon, non-golfing activity in the Phoenix area is shopping. Many of the most elegant shops are in a shopping center minutes from the hotel, Saks, Nicole Miller, and Anne Taylor, for instance. Scottsdale, less than twenty minutes away, presents even more shopping opportunities. Bottom line: the Phoenix area is truly one of the shopping meccas of the American West.

GETTING THERE: The Arizona Biltmore is located seven miles from Phoenix Airport. As you exit the airport, take the loop to 24th Street. Turn right onto 24th Street, heading north. After about five miles you will cross the large Camelback Road intersection. The main entrance to the Arizona Biltmore is about a quarter of a mile farther on the right.

▶THE BOULDERS

DESERT ROMANCE

	The Golf	Golf Services	Lodging	Restaurants	Non-Golf Activities	Total
Rating	18	19	18	18	18	91

Golf resorts created in the vast deserts of California and Arizona a generation or more ago were studies in simple contrast: the arid waste of the desert landscape versus the lush greenery of a fully enclosed oasis, an Arabian fantasy with dramatic lakes and waterfalls, transplanted palms to provide the needed shade, and, presumably, Hollywood film stars sunning themselves beside the swimming pool. Far from acting in natural harmony with the existing desert, earlier developers tried to eradicate it. They held the desert as a forbidding, intemperate zone, hospitable to gila monsters, rattlesnakes, and other poisonous life-forms but thoroughly inhospitable to humans.

More recently, our evolving relationship with the desert has changed significantly for the better. Enhanced by an increasing appreciation and understanding of

The Boulders

Native American culture, we now see the desert as full of spectacular natural imagery, colorful life, and ancient folkways that must be honored and preserved. This enlightened attitude has gradually paved the way for enlightened desert development, with no better example to be found than the Boulders, built by Rusty Lyon in 1985 in aptly named Carefree, Arizona, about forty-five minutes north of Phoenix.

The Boulders bears about as much resemblance to a typical 1960s-era golf resort in Palm Springs or nearby Scottsdale as a company like Microsoft does to General Motors. The stark, unforgettable contrast between the brilliant green of the irrigated golf courses and the gray-beige of the dry desert floor still remains at the Boulders, but the entire hotel complex has been carefully integrated into the delicate—and shimmering—desert ecosystem. At the Boulders, the desert is almost the main event. It is elevated as a thing of intrinsic value, beauty, and integrity. This radical departure from the old approach accounts for the Boulders' stunning originality—and universal popularity. Environmentally correct golf tracks like this one have enormous upscale appeal and pay handsome cash dividends as well. When you exchange pleasantries with fellow guests on the practice range, for example, they may answer with strong German or French accents. It has not taken long for the Boulders' reputation to sweep the globe.

Our only tiny twinge of foreboding in this desert oasis concerns the extensive amount of new housing construction going on in Carefree, especially that going up along the golf courses. The sound of pounding hammers, cement mixers, and shouting building crews periodically shattered the desert peacefulness of the golf course, meaning that soon Carefree may come to resemble its southern neighbor, Scottsdale. It appears that lots are marked off all along the golf courses, indicating a course of action that could soon mean a drastic change in the visual effect of the Boulders golf experience. That would be a shame indeed. The Carefree developers have received all sorts of environmental accolades for blending their development into the desert surrounding, but now they seem to be at the threshold of destroying this harmonious marriage with excessive development.

The Boulders is one of the best-run small resorts in America. At the time of our first visit, despite many rave reviews received in advance from discriminating friends, we were still unprepared for the real joy we experienced there: its unusual beauty, the disarming friendliness of its staff, and its simply superb golf. Our recent return visit only confirmed that the Boulders is just about perfect on every score.

THE GOLF   18

The prince—or poet—of the Arizona desert is the gifted golf course architect Jay Morrish, who designed the Boulders' two enchanting eighteen-hole layouts: the very good North Course and the absolutely mesmerizing South Course. Morrish is equally well known locally as the creator (along with Tom Weiskopf) of the acclaimed courses at Troon Country Club (private) and Troon North (open to the public) in Scottsdale, fifteen minutes to the south.

Reached by telephone at home in Tulsa, Oklahoma, Morrish expressed particular pride in the South Course and told us that the most successful golf courses, in his estimation, are "like good novels that just unfold before you; you just can't put them down until the end." But Morrish is not given to grave literary pronouncements like

James Joyce. The "novels" he has written here are more like those in Tolkien's *Lord of the Rings* cycle. The Boulders courses embody a spirit of playfulness and fun, not solemnity. These are not the kind of golf courses where you put your hand over your heart for the national anthem before your first tee shot. "That's right," Morrish agreed. "It's not Augusta."

What you will find out on the golf course—besides Morrish's obvious artistry and the great care of the Boulders grounds crew—are roadrunners poised silently on the fairways like primitive hieroglyphics, rattlesnake tracks in the deep sand bunkers, fat gila monsters (now that they are a protected species) dozing in rocky crevices, families of quail bustling in the rough, and scores of bunny rabbits munching on the grass. If you are lucky, you'll see at least one bobcat, those cuddly little lynx that reside somewhere near the bottom of the desert food chain. We played the South Course with an off-duty ranger who alluded to coyotes; sure enough, we saw one nonchalantly cross the fairway in front of us on the fourteenth hole. You will also find monumental saguaro cactus used frequently, as only golfers are wont to utilize such landmarks, as distant targets for tee shots. "See that saguaro over there?" the ranger would instruct us. "That's your line." There are ingenious details, too. Even the cart paths have been beautifully designed to blend with the color of the desert floor.

The best and most spectacular nine at the Boulders is the front side of the **South Course,** particularly the magical sequence of holes five through eight. The fifth, an uphill, 525-yard par five, requires a 240-yard blast to clear the desert wash. Its green is nestled majestically beneath the mountains. The tee of the sixth hole is perched atop a formation of boulders high above the hotel entrance. You actually drive your ball—it's a pure thrill—over the hotel entrance road! The seventh hole—perhaps the most photographed golf hole in Arizona—plays off Rosie's Rock, a colossal boulder. (Look for that not so adorable gila monster in the shade.) And the eighth is a monster of a different sort, a tough, 461-yard par four that plays from yet another dramatic boulder formation. The Boulders is "target golf" at its most challenging. Prepare in advance by working on that backspin.

When it comes to the weather, the Boulders tops Pebble Beach and St. Andrews. However, the desert sun must be respected—even feared. Take precautions by applying plenty of sunblock and staying hydrated with lots of ice water (available on almost every other hole). We advise spending a minimum of time looking for stray balls for two reasons. First, it goes without saying that rummaging around a large desert for a small, white ball will hold up play, and second, the more time you spend in the desert, the better your chances of running into a rattlesnake. Rough areas must be approached gingerly. Experienced desert golfers hunting for lost balls arm themselves with a club to be used as a weapon against unfriendly wildlife. There is one other distinct attribute of the Arizona game worth noting: the ball just soars in the dry desert air, as if a stiff breeze were behind every shot.

Carts are mandatory, but caddies are available to accompany you. The standard greens fee with cart is $150. Nonguests may make a tee time up to twenty-four hours in advance for $185 a round. The Boulders reseeds its courses every fall but always keeps eighteen holes open for resort guests.

Finally, those of you who are staying several days at the Boulders should take the opportunity to play some of the other great courses in the Scottsdale area. Two that we highly recommend are the Grayhawk Golf Club, which has two world-class courses (see Grayhawk entry) and **Troon North.** Like the Boulders, Troon North is a magical place designed by Jay Morrish, this time in collaboration with Tom Weiskopf. Troon North's original course, now called the **Monument,** opened in 1990 and quickly earned a rating as the number-one course in Arizona, thanks in part to its haunting beauty and the spectacular panoramas visible from its back nine. A second course, the **Pinnacle,** opened in 1996. The greens fee for each course is a steep $160 in high season, yet the memorable Monument Course is worth every penny and should not be missed. For tee-time reservations call 602-585-7700.

The Boulders. 34631 North Tom Darlington Drive, Carefree, AZ 85377. Tel: 800-553-1717 or 602-488-9009. Fax: 602-488-4118. Credit cards accepted.

• *North Course.* 1985. Designer: Jay Morrish. Par 72. 6,950 yards. 73.4 par rating. 144 slope rating.
• *South Course.* 1985. Designer: Jay Morrish. Par 71. 7,007 yards. 73.3 par rating. 146 slope rating.
• For both courses: greens fees: $150 (resort guests), $185 (public), cart included. No walking (except last tee-time of the day). Caddies available. Restrictions: each day either the North or the South Course is open to resort guests. Golfers who are not staying at the resort may make reservations up to twenty-four hours in advance on a space-available basis. Season: year-round. Alternate nines on each course close for reseeding between September and early November.

Troon North. 10320 East Dynamite Boulevard, Scottsdale, AZ 85255. Tel: 602-585-7700 or 602-585-5300. Fax: 602-585-5161. Credit cards accepted.

• *The Monument.* 1990. Designers: Jay Morrish, Tom Weiskopf. Par 72. 7,028 yards. 73.3 par rating. 147 slope rating.
• *The Pinnacle.* 1996. Designers: Jay Morrish, Tom Weiskopf. Par 72. 7,044 yards. 73.4 par rating. 147 slope rating.
• Greens fees: $160 (December–March), $75–$150 (April–November). Walking permitted. Caddies available if requested in advance. Carts available. Season: year-round.

 GOLF SERVICES (19)

The Boulders' guiding philosophy as it pertains to service—the client is king—carries over in unadulterated form to the golf courses. The anxious-to-please team will stop whatever it is doing to serve you with a welcoming smile. The staff's great attitude puts you in the right frame of mind and can actually enhance your golf game. The shuttle bus service between the casitas and the golf courses is always prompt. Club storage and care is provided, and at the range all practice balls are complimentary. The free course guides prove especially useful for those who have not played the Boulders before.

Single players will find they do not have to ask about advanced tee times. "Just come over when you're ready to play and we'll get you out on the course" is the reassuring reply.

 LODGING (18)

It takes the better part of a day to orient yourself fully within this nontraditional resort landscape. The Boulders has been planted so unobtrusively amid the desert flora and the startling rock formations that large sections of the hotel and club complex are barely visible. The entrance, off the main Scottsdale Road, is rather difficult to locate. Yet once you have arrived at the front gate—where a polite attendant issues guest passes to this very private property—you will proceed with relative ease to the magnificent Lodge building, which acts as a reception area and houses the lounge/bar and the hotel's two principal dining rooms.

The actual guest accommodations are located away from the Lodge in 160 stunning adobe-style casitas. You will be driven to your own casita in an oversize golf cart by one of the Boulders' cordial staff members. In addition, the Boulders offers thirty-eight Pueblo Villas, which are fully equipped one-, two-, and three-bedroom homes.

There is nothing plain or rustic about the "adobe-style" casitas at the Boulders. These accommodations offer absolute elegance and tremendous amounts of room. Ours, number 322, was utterly luxurious, spotlessly clean, and decorated in the relaxing color scheme of the

The Boulders

surrounding desert. The huge living/sleeping area features a heavy beamed ceiling, lovely carpeting, a wood-burning fireplace, private bar, a large sitting area with desk and comfortable armchairs, Indian paintings along the walls, television, and an outdoor patio. The bathroom—with terra-cotta tile floors, glassed-in shower, separate tub, illuminated dressing table, double sinks, and great closet space—is nearly as large as the bedroom. All fixtures, fabrics, and furnishings are of the highest quality. There are also many thoughtful little touches, like complimentary sunscreen, coffee machines, even pocket flashlights for walking at night. (The Boulders is laced with footpaths; it's a stroller's paradise.) Needless to say, we were more than comfortable here.

Service is one of the resort's strongest attributes. You will forever remember the Boulders for the incredible artistry of the Morrish golf courses, the spectacular beauty of the private casitas, and the extraordinary civility and pride of every staff member on the property—every waitperson, bartender, baggage attendant, golf employee, and room attendant. Your happiness is their personal mission. The Boulders is a superb golf experience enhanced by great people.

The Boulders. 34631 North Tom Darlington Drive, Carefree, AZ 85377. Tel: 800-553-1717 or 602-488-9009. Fax: 602-488-4118. 160 casitas and 38 Pueblo Villas. Daily room rates range from $180 to $525 for a casita and $325 to $1,100 for a Pueblo Villa. Credit cards accepted.

RESTAURANTS ⑱

The Boulders operates five fine restaurants, affording a wide choice of cuisine and atmosphere: the formal Latilla and Palo Verde restaurants in the Lodge, the fabulous Cantina in the posh El Pedregal shopping mall (about a quarter mile from the casitas), the casual restaurant and bar in the Golf and Tennis Club, and the **Bakery Café,** with its excellent assortment of sandwiches, salads, and pastries, also in El Pedregal.

Latilla, a handsome round room with tree-trunk columns overlooking the resort's spectacular swimming pool, is the most formal of the five restaurants, but dinner here struck us as a bit uninspired. We much preferred Latilla for the wonderful big breakfast buffet. The dishes in the cool and airy **Palo Verde** restaurant have a decidedly southwestern flavor. Try the good field salad with garlic croutons and vinaigrette dressing and the fresh trout with a bacon and corn relish. Good wine lists are offered in both dining rooms.

We enjoyed ourselves most in the delightful and colorfully decorated **Cantina del Pedregal,** which features a menu of traditional and modern Mexican specialties. With its smart clientele and an outdoor terrace that looks out on the horizon to the night lights of Phoenix and Scottsdale, the Cantina is the liveliest restaurant at the Boulders. Dinner for two (including wine and tip) here costs approximately $60, while you can expect to spend $100 for two at Latilla and Palo Verde.

The restaurants at the Boulders. 34631 North Tom Darlington Drive, Carefree, AZ 85377. Tel: 800-553-1717 or 602-488-9009. Fax: 602-488-4118. Credit cards accepted.

NON-GOLF ACTIVITIES

About half of the Boulders' guests come principally to play golf, but the other half find much more to occupy their leisure. Desert walks, exercise classes, water fitness, and personal training are available in the fully equipped Fitness Center. There are six plexi-cushion tennis courts and two swimming pools: the beautiful pool beneath the natural waterfall at the hotel and a lap pool at the Fitness Center. Balloon rides, horseback riding, jeep tours of the desert, and other exotic activities can be arranged by the concierge. Interesting sights nearby include the Frank Lloyd Wright complex at Taliesin and Paolo Soleri's architectural experiments at Cosanti. For shopping aficionados, the marketplace at El Pedregal (only a short walk from the resort) offers a tasteful group of shops and galleries. And, of course, for the power shopper, Scottsdale, one of the West's renowned shopping meccas, is only about twenty-five minutes south of Carefree.

GETTING THERE: The Boulders is thirty-three miles from the Phoenix Sky Harbor Airport. The resort can arrange to have a van pick you up at a cost of $45 (one-way) or $70 (round-trip) per passenger. The trip from the airport to the resort by van generally takes one hour. If you are driving, as you approach Scottsdale, take Scottsdale Road North into the town of Carefree. Just past a four-way stop for the Carefree Highway, you will see the Boulders on the right.

▶VENTANA CANYON

	The Golf	Golf Services	Lodging	Restaurants	Non-Golf Activities	Total
Rating	18	19	17	18	17	89

The highlight of our recent visit to Tucson was the magical round of golf we experienced one brilliant desert morning on the Mountain Course at the Lodge at Ventana Canyon. An evening rain had fallen the night before, making the high desert air even fresher and more fragrant, and we had the amazing good fortune of being the first to tee off that day on this inspired Tom Fazio course. Each hole was fresh, pure, new, virginal—wildlife was everywhere, and knowing that we were the first golfers that day was intoxicating. We shared every tee with quail, doves, and inquisitive cottontails. It was truly what Shivas Irons, the hero of Michael Murphy's *Golf in the Kingdom*, had in mind: the score is important, but it is the sensual experience that counts most.

Tom Fazio's Mountain and Canyon courses at Ventana Canyon are superb layouts. Of the two, the Mountain Course is the more spectacular as it climbs higher into the hills, but both courses provide stunning views of the city of Tucson just to the south and the Santa Catalina Mountains rising majestically to the north. Both courses are an absolute wonder of maintenance. Tees are perfect, fairways are superb, and the greens are in beautiful condition. Although private homes overlook both courses, they in no way resemble the crass real estate developments that dominate many resort courses.

These Fazio courses are harmonious with their desert surroundings, the result of a minimum of intrusive earthmoving. While playing you feel as if

Ventana Canyon

each fairway is an oasis in a beautiful desert environment. Everything was done to save the desert's flora, and the giant, noble saguaro cacti are everywhere, standing sentinel in the desert landscape.

THE GOLF ⑱

On the **Lodge's Mountain Course,** the fairways are relatively narrow, putting a real premium on accuracy and playing within yourself. If you hook or slice a shot into the desert, forget about locating your ball. A particularly stunning hole is number three—a short 107 yards from the back—with its elevated tee facing right into the Santa Catalina Mountains, a barranca between you and the flag, and the green looking very, very small indeed. Number four, a 598-yard par five, is another glorious hole with an elevated tee that offers a lovely view; this slight dogleg-left is guarded by water on the right as you approach the green. The Mountain Course has no gimmicks, hidden hazards, or tricks, and certainly qualifies as one of our favorite desert courses. The course has four sets of tees ranging from 4,709 to 6,948 yards with a par seventy-two and a slope rating from the back tees of 146 and a par rating of 74.2. Our hats are off to Fazio for creating this stunning, high-desert delight!

The **Canyon Course** suffers just a little in comparison to the Mountain Course, but on its own it is a very fine course with plenty of beauty and interest. Several homes are scattered along the course, but we are talking about sleek, Spanish-style structures with red-tile roofs and lovely grounds sporting price tags exceeding $800,000. The Canyon Course, 6,818 yards with a slope rating of 141 and a par rating of 72.7, is beautifully carved out of the desert, with more of a target approach than its neighbor. The par five eighteenth is our favorite hole, playing back toward the stunning hotel framed against the Santa Catalina Mountains.

Both courses are owned, managed, and maintained by the Lodge at Ventana Canyon. Guests of both the Lodge and Loews Ventana Canyon Resort, an elegant, 398-room hotel, are able to play "the resort course of the day" while the other course is reserved for members. On even dates, guests play the Mountain Course, and on odd dates they play the Canyon Course. Guests at either resort can reserve tee times up to thirty days in advance. Golfers who are not staying at the resort can arrange tee times up to seven days in advance.

The Lodge at Ventana Canyon. 6200 North Clubhouse Lane, Tucson AZ 85750. Tel: 800-828-5701 or 520-577-4061 (golf shop). Fax: 520-577-4065. Credit cards accepted.

　• *Ventana Mountain Course.* 1984. Designer: Tom Fazio. Par 72. 6,948 yards. 74.2 par rating. 146 slope rating.

　• *Canyon Course.* 1988. Designer: Tom Fazio. Par 72. 6,818 yards. 72.7 par rating. 141 slope rating.

　• Greens fees for resort guests on both courses: $135 (January–April), $105 (May),

$75 (June–September), $105 (October–December); for public play, rates range from $95 to $150, cart included. No walking. No caddies. Restrictions: each course is open to the public on alternate days. Season: year-round.

GOLF SERVICES

Golf services at both courses could not be more friendly and helpful. This holds true for all the pro shop personnel, the starter, and the maintenance people out on the course. Beverage and snack carts tour the courses, bringing cool supplements to you as the desert sun heats up. Men's and women's locker rooms are well kept, spotless, and staffed with cordial employees. Both a fine driving range and putting green complete the experience.

When you drive up to the Lodge at Ventana Canyon, bellmen will hustle your golf bags off and you will find them in your cart at the appointed hour. Service is excellent, and the pro shop is well stocked with fine golf apparel and a full line of golf equipment.

LODGING

You have your choice: the 398-room Loews Ventana Canyon or the simpler, more intimate forty-nine-suite facility, the Lodge at Ventana Canyon.

Snuggled into the foothills of the Santa Catalina Mountains, in the high Sonoran Desert, **Loews Ventana Canyon** is one of the best-run hotels in the West. It is elegant and comfortable and offers its guests a full range of services and activities. The rooms and suites are all spacious and handsomely decorated, and all look out on the spectacular mountains or the city of Tucson. All but two of the rooms have terraces, the perfect spot to enjoy a drink before dinner as you bask in the fresh, cool desert evening. All rooms have minibars and televisions. The luxurious bathrooms have designer soaps and terry-cloth robes.

The concierge desk at Loews Ventana is superb; its staff will promptly line up auto rentals and tours and make recommendations and reservations at Tucson's best restaurants. The lobby is grand, with lofty windows facing the mountains and a harpist playing every afternoon at tea. This hotel is the pride of the Loews chain—it is a very well run establishment.

The **Lodge at Ventana Canyon** is now a Carefree Resort, owned and operated by the same company that runs the Boulders so spectacularly. Carefree has already completed a $5 million renovation and promises exciting changes in the near future. The entire look of the Lodge has improved thanks to a bold landscaping and rock-facing project. Inside, the public area has been resurfaced with dark wood and trim. Each one of the forty-nine suites has received new furniture and a complete renovation, and the one- and two-bedroom suites come with a fully equipped kitchen and are spacious and attractive. We recommend the suites facing north because of their wonderful mountain views.

Loews Ventana Canyon Resort. 7000 North Resort Drive, Tucson, AZ 85750. Tel: 800-234-5117 or 520-299-2020. Fax: 520-299-6832. 398 rooms. Doubles range from $295 to $395 in high season from January through May and $235 to $325 from October through December. Credit cards accepted.

The Lodge at Ventana Canyon. 6200 North Clubhouse Lane, Tucson AZ 85750. Tel: 800-828-5701 or 520-577-1400. Fax: 520-577-4065. 49 suites. One-bedroom suites from $325 to $375 from January through April, and $290 to $345 from October through December. Credit cards accepted.

RESTAURANTS ⑱

The dining at Ventana Canyon and in nearby Tucson is very good. **The Ventana Room,** the remarkably romantic and splendid restaurant on the second floor of the Loews Ventana Canyon Resort, offers very good food and service, along with an excellent wine list. All tables in this open, two-tiered venue are elegant, with spectacular views of Tucson sparkling below. Especially noteworthy were the fine venison carpaccio and the mesquite-grilled buffalo tenderloin with grilled wild oyster mushrooms in a Burgundy truffle sauce. **Daniel's Restaurant and Trattoria,** located just a ten-minute drive from Ventana Canyon in a very deluxe, stylish shopping center, serves superb Northern Italian cuisine. Specialties of the house include roasted tenderloin of smoked pork with a caramelized apple tarragon relish and charbroiled salmon on a bed of sautéed spinach. Entrées range from $17 to $28. This rather trendy restaurant also has a terrific bar.

The best restaurant in the Tucson area is **Janos,** located in the city's historic section. Trained in France, Janos Wilder is a master chef with a deep respect for the Southwest's influence. Here you can savor a fine bisque of Guaymas shrimp; sliced duckling on a coulis of red pepper; tender, thick, grilled pork chops; or fresh salmon with a delectable lobster sauce. Housed in a series of elegant, smallish rooms with high-beamed ceilings and white adobe walls, Janos is currently one of the more inspired restaurants in America. Entrées range in price from $22 to $33.

The Ventana Room. Loews Ventana Canyon Resort. 7000 North Resort Drive, Tucson, AZ 85750. Tel: 800-234-5117 or 520-299-2020. Credit cards accepted.

Daniel's Restaurant and Trattoria. 4340 North Campbell Avenue, Suite 107, Tucson, AZ 85718. Tel: 520-742-3200. Fax: 520-529-1907. Credit cards accepted.

Janos. 150 North Main Avenue, Tucson, AZ 85701. Tel: 520-884-9426. Fax: 520-623-1472. Credit cards accepted.

NON-GOLF ACTIVITIES ⑰

For shoppers, Loews Ventana offers attractive boutiques in the hotel, especially the fine jewelry shop featuring handsome (and expensive) Indian works. There is also an excellent spa and health club. Ten lighted tennis courts, a croquet court, and a beautiful pool offer other options. Another possibility is to spend a few hours taking a hike along the trails leading into the mountains.

Although not on the grand scale of the neighboring Loews, the Lodge at Ventana Canyon does have twelve lighted tennis courts, a small exercise room, and a twenty-five-meter swimming pool.

There are a myriad of sights around Tucson. We especially recommend the Arizona-Sonoran Desert Museum, a renowned living museum featuring flora and fauna of the Southwest. Other worthwhile sights include the Pima Air Museum, Old Tucson (which has provided the sets for more than one hundred movies), Saguaro National Monument, the Tucson Museum of Art, and Tombstone, an hour and a half distant, the town made famous by the legendary gunfight at the O.K. Corral.

A note on what to wear. As in most of the West, dress is casual everywhere. A sport coat in the evenings is nice, but not necessary. You can leave your ties at home.

GETTING THERE: From the Tucson Airport, take Tucson Boulevard to Valencia Road. Turn right on Valencia, proceed roughly five miles, turn left onto Kolb Road, and follow about seven miles to a right turn onto Tanque Verde Road. Take a left onto Sabino Canyon, go two miles, and turn left onto Kolb Road once again. Continue on Kolb until you see the security gate for the Lodge at Ventana Canyon on the right.

▶GRAYHAWK

DESERT JEWEL

	The Golf	Golf Services	Lodging	Restaurants	Non-Golf Activities	Total
Rating	18	18	18	18	18	90

Talon Course

Californians have always been a restless lot, so it should not come as any surprise to learn that even as our most populous state grows larger, there are those—quite a sizable number actually—who are quitting California. But where are these folks fleeing to? If you have been to Arizona in the last few years, you know at least part of the answer. Hordes of Californians are moving to Arizona, creating there what they left behind in Lotus Land, hundreds of square miles of planned residential communities, gobbling up the Sonoran Desert at a breathtaking rate, and pulling more and more water from an ever-diminishing Western water supply. If there is a bright side to this explosive population increase, it has to be that the cornerstone of each new, upscale residential community in Arizona has a very good golf course. Naturally, the golf course becomes the top salesman for each project—just another example of the "build-it-and-they-will-come" strategy.

One such golf jewel in Scottsdale is Grayhawk, a golf club set in a 1,600-acre residential community that is developing at a hyperaccelerated speed. First, the Talon Course in 1994 and then, a year later, the Raptor Course burst upon the golfing scene. Each course presents the best in desert golf. The club is just up the road from the Boulders resort (*see* the Boulders below for lodging, restaurants, and non-golf activities). If you stay at the Boulders, do not miss the opportunity to play a round or two at Grayhawk's first-class golf facility.

THE GOLF ⑱

Few golf establishments have ever achieved such immediate and universal acclaim as the **Grayhawk Golf Club.** By the end of its first year of operation, the club's very fine David Graham/Gary Panks Talon Course had begun hosting the annual Andersen Consulting World Championship of Golf, and Phil Mickelson was Grayhawk's acting ambassador on the PGA Tour. Then, in late 1995, Grayhawk celebrated the opening of its second track, the more traditional, Tom Fazio—designed Raptor Course, which has proven to be every bit as good as the Talon Course. The Raptor Course is now set to host the World Championship final in 1998. Both courses are kept in absolutely superb condition throughout the year.

The **Talon Course** is a masterpiece of architectural design. Stunningly scenic and infinitely challenging without being unfair or gimmicky, the exquisitely maintained course has great character. Not a dime has been spared on the creation of this memorable golf course. On the Talon Course, as on all great courses, you never feel constricted in the landscape. There are a minimum of doglegs—most holes lie gloriously out in front of you as you stand on the tee box. This target course leaves the desert environment intact (for the time being) wherever possible. Errant shots are costly here, often putting your ball in the desert among the thorny flora and the reptiles. The two most dramatic holes are eleven, a 175-yard par three called Swinging Bridge that, in fact, features a swinging bridge to get to the back tees as well as a perilous carry across a canyon, and number seventeen, called Devil's Drink, a 125-yard par three featuring an island green.

Tom Fazio's 7,108-yard **Raptor Course** incorporates more than three hundred saguaro cacti and one thousand paloverde, ironwood, and mesquite trees into an environmentally friendly track. The gentle, rolling fairways on this target course are guarded by vast bunkers and mounding. Man-made streams and ponds, linked by a water-circulation system, add to the challenge on many holes. The course's majesty first becomes evident on the long and winding 562-yard, par five fourth hole, which has Pinnacle Peak as a backdrop. The par three eighth hole is devilishly difficult thanks to the huge mound and bunker fronting the green. The signature hole on the Raptor Course, however, is number eighteen, a 521-yard par five that features a sky-line view, a stream running down the length of a narrow fairway, and the clubhouse sitting on the water near the green. The greens fee in high season at both courses is $165, cart and range balls are included.

Grayhawk Golf Club. 8620 East Thompson Peak Parkway, Scottsdale, AZ 83255. Tel: 602-502-1800. Fax: 602-502-3164. Credit cards accepted.

• *Talon Course.* 1994. Designers: David Graham, Gary Panks. Par 72. 6,973 yards. 74.3 par rating. 141 slope rating. Greens fees: $150–$165 (December–April), $120–$150 (April–May). Includes cart. Walking permitted. No caddies. Season: year-round.

• *Raptor Course.* 1995. Designer: Tom Fazio. Par 72. 7,108 yards. 74.0 par rating. 136 slope rating. Greens fees: $150–$165 (December–April), $120–$150 (April–May). Includes cart. Walking permitted. Season: year-round.

GOLF SERVICES 18

Everything has been done first-class thus far at Grayhawk. Practice facilities—putting greens, chipping greens, and driving ranges—are excellent. In addition, Grayhawk is home to the esteemed Kostis/McCord Learning Center, run by the two CBS golf analysts. A single clubhouse serves the two courses, and golf services are as good as they get. The pro shop is well stocked, and the golf staff provides impeccable support throughout the entire operation. As you pull up to the bag-drop area, courteous young men instantly approach your car, open your doors, greet you, and take your clubs—in short, they make you feel like a king with a large retinue. Each golfer even receives a keepsake copy of a golf book. Offerings have included *The Legend of Bagger Vance* by Steven Pressfield, *Follow the Wind* by Bo Links, and Michael Murphy's classic, *Golf in the Kingdom.* Someone here really knows how to do it right when it comes to exceeding customer expectations.

GETTING THERE: We recommend that you sample the Grayhawk Golf Club during your stay at the Boulders. As you exit the Boulders, get onto Scottsdale Road and head south. Take a left onto Thompson Peak Parkway, and the clubhouse is about a mile and a half straight ahead. If coming from the Phoenix Sky Harbor Airport, take 51 North until it ends at Shea. Head east on Shea, and take a left heading north on Scottsdale Road. Turn onto Thompson Peak Parkway and proceed to the clubhouse.

Baja California

▶LOS CABOS

A NEW GOLFING MECCA

	The Golf	Golf Services	Lodging	Restaurants	Non-Golf Activities	Total
Rating	19	18	19	16	18	90

Back in the 1950s and 1960s, Bing Crosby, Desi Arnaz, John Wayne, and other Hollywood stars used the Hotel Pamilla on the southernmost tip of the Baja peninsula in Cabo San Lucas, Mexico, as their fishing lodge. These celebrities—and many other travelers who followed in their footsteps—relished the seclusion, the unspoiled charm, the superb fishing, and the authentic Mexican feeling of the Cabo San Lucas (or, Los Cabos, as it is also called) area.

Palmilla Golf Club

Today, the ghosts of Bing, Desi, and the Duke would be dismayed at the changes along the twenty-one-mile stretch of beachfront from San José del Cabo to Cabo San Lucas. The developers who own the majority of the property are deeply committed to creating a Mexican Riviera, complete with thousands of homes, condominiums, town houses, and expanded resort facilities. What is being created here is a pretty, charming, hedonistic, and rather inane extension of Southern California—one more place, along with Montana, Idaho, and Wyoming, to which Californians can escape. Los Cabos will always remain remarkably beautiful, but as more buildings (admittedly with stucco walls and red-tile roofs to replicate their surroundings) go up, its days as an old Mexican hideaway destination are gone forever, even if the fishing remains quite fine.

This having been said, if you travel to Los Cabos with a realistic expectation of what will greet you, and take your golf clubs in addition to your fishing rods, you will have a great time. Granted, room rates have skyrocketed (expect to pay approximately $300 per room at the Hotel Palmilla and more at Las Ventanas), but the service is still very Mexican—engagingly friendly, polite, and gracious. You will be charmed by the wait staff, room attendants, bartenders, gardeners, and front desk personnel.

One of the two classiest resorts in the Los Cabos area is the luxurious Hotel Palmilla, built nearly forty years ago by Abelado Rodríguez, son of Mexico's provisional president from 1932 to 1934. Nestled unobtrusively on a rocky promontory midway between San José de Cabo and Cabo San Lucas, the Palmilla is a lovely, red-tile, white-stucco group of structures with many open terraces, fountains, loads of arches, and beautifully mature, well-maintained grounds. It is a resort with an aura and history.

The property and its nine hundred acres were purchased in 1984 by Dan Koll, a high-powered, international developer from Newport Beach, California. In the ensuing decade, Koll purchased another nine hundred acres and completely refurbished and renovated the Hotel Palmilla—the public rooms, the guest rooms, and the pool and grounds. Palmilla is now one of the most luxurious and well managed hotels in Mexico.

Today, the Koll company owns over 1,800 acres of prime real estate in Los Cabos, including more than two miles of beachfront and hillside property with incredible views of the ocean—where the fresh, cool Pacific meets the more temperate waters of the Sea of Cortez. To a real estate developer, this translates into building sites—hundreds of which are currently being developed. In these times, where is an upscale real estate development without a golf course? Enter Jack Nicklaus.

THE GOLF

19

In the world of golf course design, Jack Nicklaus currently ranks with Tom Fazio and Pete Dye as the craft's leading practitioners. No one place more clearly displays Nicklaus's mastery of the art than the two magnificent courses he designed for the owners of the Hotel Palmilla—the Palmilla Course, which opened in 1992, and the Cabo del Sol Course (also known as the Ocean Course) completed in 1994. Here we see how far Nicklaus has come in working harmoniously with the natural environment.

Set up in the hills high above the resort and the ocean, the **Palmilla Course** at **Palmilla Golf Club** enjoys one of the most magical settings of any of the courses Nicklaus has designed. Although Nicklaus-designed courses are sometimes gimmicky and brutally unfair, after having played Palmilla, we bow to the master in awe. In short, Palmilla is fair, challenging, infinitely interesting, and breathtakingly beautiful.

At Palmilla, Nicklaus abandoned an inclination to line the fairways with mounds. Elsewhere, he often engaged in massive earthmoving, which serves to separate his tracks from their environment; here he opted for a design that brings the golf course and its lovely desert surroundings into harmony. This course glorifies the stunning desert landscape instead of screaming "Don't you dare hit your drive into that godforsaken land of cactus, arroyos, lizards, and snakes."

As you play the Palmilla Course, you will gawk at the overwhelming views of the ocean and the mountains. For now, though not for much longer we sadly believe, the course is pristine; few dwellings line the fairways. And desert wildlife abounds—rabbits hop across the tees, quail and roadrunners scurry across the fairways, and mourning and white-wing doves coo peacefully as hawks glide overhead in the brilliant blue sky.

Unlike those Nicklaus tracks that bring you to your knees in tears, Palmilla is a joy to play. Memorable holes abound, like our favorite, number fourteen, a 401-yard dogleg right requiring a carry over a formidable arroyo to a relatively narrow fairway, then a return carry across the same arroyo down to the green. Jack, you did yourself proud here. We also loved the seventh, a 560-yard par five, where from the tee you seem to be driving straight down to the Palmilla resort and the azure ocean, although in between you must contend with a wasteland of cactus and mesquite. The next hole, also hitting toward the Sea of Cortez, is a downhill, 243-yard par three from the back tees to the green, some eighty feet below. We found all the holes on the course inspirational, with the notable exception of number four, which is almost consumed by an ugly desert "sand trap" the size of a football field that flanks the right side of the fairway. Yet we are being picky. Nicklaus has designed one hell of a golf course here.

Although not a punishing course, do not expect Palmilla to be a cakewalk. This course was Jack's first Latin American signature design, a design he likens to his Desert Mountain Course, a private track, in Carefree, Arizona. The slope rating for Palmilla is 144 from the back, with a par rating of 74.3 and a distance of 6,939. There are five sets of tees, so the course is playable for all types of hitters.

The Palmilla Golf Club's other track, the 7,037-yard **Cabo del Sol Golf Course** (i.e., the Ocean Course) is one of the best golf courses you will ever play in your life—period. The comparisons to Pebble Beach are inevitable because of its magnificent setting along two miles of rugged coastline where the Sea of Cortez meets the Pacific Ocean. Nicklaus himself has said this is the finest piece of golf property he has ever seen and that designing the Ocean Course gave him his chance to design Pebble Beach. Seven of the holes play along the water's edge, and Nicklaus is so proud of the finishing hole that he rather giddily calls it one of the finest finishing holes in all of golf. Course maintenance on this Bermuda grass layout is flawless; although just several years old, the fairways are lush, and the gently undulat-

Palmilla Golf Club

ing greens are in perfect condition. Cabo del Sol has been featured on "Shell's Wonderful World of Golf" and, like the Palmilla Course, has hosted the annual Seniors Slam Tournament for the winners of the majors on the Seniors Tour. Both the Palmilla and Cabo del Sol courses are classics.

There are two other fine, though not sublime, golf courses, in the Los Cabos area. **Cabo Real Golf Club,** a Robert Trent Jones, Jr., course, was completed in 1993. It is in excellent condition and helps round out the links montage that is making Los Cabos a major golf mecca. The other eighteen in the area is the **Cabo San Lucas Country Club,** a Roy Dye design situated right on the Pacific, close to the town of Cabo San Lucas. This fine Dye course completes the bouquet of Los Cabos/Cabo San Lucas golf courses. At 7,220 yards, the longest of the four courses in the area, it is also the most forgiving. Current plans call for the construction of four more golf courses in the next few years at Los Cabos. Frankly, this seems like overkill—each new course will mean one more megaresort and eighteen more holes of golf to be lined with casitas, condos, town houses, and, of course, many more people.

In just four years, Los Cabos/Cabo San Lucas has become one of the premier golf destinations in the world. Those of us who harbor nostalgic yearnings for Cabo San Lucas's halcyon days as a sleepy little fishing mecca take some solace that Nicklaus, Jones, and Dye have brought glorious golf to the tip of Baja California. And, unlike the desert golf of Palm Springs and Arizona, where the months of May through September are usually beastly hot months, the weather in Los Cabos is nearly perfect year-round. Los Cabos boasts of 350 days of sunshine a year!

Palmilla Golf Club. KM 27 Carretera Transpeninsular, San José del Cabo, Baja California Sur, Mexico 23400. Tel: 800-386-2465. Palmilla Course: Tel: 011-52-114-80525. Caba del Sol Course: Tel: 011-52-114-58200. Fax: 714-476-1648. Credit cards accepted.

• *Palmilla Course.* 1992. Designer: Jack Nicklaus. Par 72. 6,939 yards. 74.3 par rating. 144 slope rating. Greens fees: hotel guests: $115–$135 (October–June), $100 (July–October). Includes cart, bottled water, and use of practice facilities. Public: $152–160/$112. No walking. No caddies. Season: year-round.

• *Cabo del Sol Course* (also known as the Ocean Course.) 1994. Designer: Jack Nicklaus. Par 72. 7,037 yards. 74.1 par rating. 137 slope rating. Greens fees: hotel guests: $132–$155 (October–June), $100–$110 (July–October). Includes cart, bottled water, and use of range facilities. Public: $165–$176/$127–$135. No walking. No caddies. Season: year-round.

Cabo Real Golf Club. KM 19.5 Carretera Transpeninsular, Baja California Sur, Mexico 23410. Tel: 800-393-0400 or 011-52-114-400-40. Fax: 011-52-114-40-231. Credit cards accepted.

• 1993. Designer: Robert Trent Jones, Jr. Par 72. 7,100 yards. 73.8 par rating. 135 slope rating. Greens fee: $143, includes cart. No walking. No caddies. Season: year-round.

Cabo San Lucas Country Club. KM 3.7 Carretera Transpeninsular, Cabo San Lucas, Baja California Sur, Mexico 23410. Tel: 011-52-114-34653. Fax: 011-52-114-34653. Credit cards accepted.

  • 1995. Designer: Roy Dye. Par 72. 7,220 yards. 75.4 par rating. 138 slope rating. Greens fees: $125 (October–June), $105 (June–September). Includes cart. No walking. No caddies. Season: year-round.

GOLF SERVICES

Golf services at all the Los Cabos golfing venues are superb—all have excellent practice facilities, well-stocked pro shops, first-rate carts, and, without exception, very friendly, hospitable staffs.

LODGING

We urge you to stay in one of the oceanfront rooms at the **Hotel Palmilla;** they are infinitely romantic. All the rooms have been renovated and are spacious, with plenty of closet space and ample, deluxe bathrooms. Most rooms have terraces—the perfect spot for a breakfast of *huevos rancheros* and *chorizo,* as well as for a margarita before walking up to dinner. The oceanfront rooms, as one would expect, feature stunning views of the beach and sea. All rooms are outfitted with well-stocked minibars, double basin sinks, large windows, and telephones.

  Las Ventanas al Paraiso is the newest entrant on the Los Cabos resort scene, having opened early in 1997. Operated by Rosewood Hotels and Resorts of Dallas—which also runs the Mansion on Turtle Creek and the Crescent in Dallas—Las Ventanas is certainly the most luxurious and most expensive of the Los Cabos resorts. Situated right on the ocean alongside a portion of the Cabo Real Golf Club, Las Ventanas is every bit as stunning and romantic as the heavenly hotels in tropical paradises such as Phuket and Bali. There are sixty-one suites at Las Ventanas, all of which are extraordinarily elegant and spacious. Spacious here means really spacious—the minimum suite size is 960 square feet. Nice touches such as wood-burning fireplaces, individual telescopes for stargazing (some of the best in the hemisphere), his-and-her terry-cloth robes, and terraces add to the romantic aura of these suites. Las Ventanas has a fine spa and fitness center, sport fishing, two ninety-foot sporting yachts, and all the water sports available in the Los Cabos area.

Hotel Palmilla. KM 27 Carretera Transpeninsular, San José del Cabo, Baja California Sur, Mexico 23400. Tel: 800-637-2226 or 011-52-114-45000. Fax: 714-851-2498. 114 rooms and suites. Double rooms range from $290 to $490 from October through May and $180 to $350 from June to October. Credit cards accepted.

Las Ventanas al Paraiso. KM 19.5 Carretera Transpeninsular, Cabo San Lucas–San José del Cabo, Baja California Sur, Mexico 23400. Tel: 888-525-0483. Fax: 214-871-5440. 61 suites. One-bedroom suites range from $325 to $1,650. Credit cards accepted.

RESTAURANTS

The setting for dining at **La Paloma** in the Hotel Palmilla, on the upstairs verandah above the front desk, is idyllic. Service is friendly but at times a bit confused. We recommend the fresh grilled seafood, such as sea bass, red snapper, yellowtail, yellowfin, or dolphin. Dinner for two will cost about $100. One other suggestion: the Mexican fiesta around the pool on Friday night is a must, a diverse sampling of superb Mexican food and colorful, live mariachi music. The bar on the same floor as the dining terrace is handsome, the perfect spot for one of the best margaritas in Los Cabos. The elegant dining room at Las Ventanas had not yet opened when we visited.

Los Cabos abounds in fine dining. The best restaurant in the area may be **Peacocks** in Cabo San Lucas, which offers a menu with a mixed Asian, Mexican, and European influence. Chef Bernard Voll's specialties include shrimp with spinach fettuccine and linguini with grilled chicken. The famous desserts at Peacocks are worth a visit even if you choose not to eat dinner here.

The restaurants at the Hotel Palmilla. KM 27 Carretera Transpeninsular, San José del Cabo, Baja California Sur, Mexico 23400. Tel: 800-637-2226 or 011-52-114-45000. Fax: 714-851-2498. Credit cards accepted.

Peacocks. Paseo Pescador near Playa Medano. Tel: 011-52-114-31858. Credit cards accepted.

NON-GOLF ACTIVITIES

The sports facilities at the Hotel Palmilla include two tennis courts and two paddleboard courts, as well as shuffleboard, croquet, volleyball, and horseback riding. The eternal attraction of Los Cabos, however, is the sea. Sport fishing—for dorado, marlin, sailfish, roosterfish, yellowtail, and yellowfin tuna—is world-class here. Since the ocean bottom drops so precipitously and so close to the shore (within a mile), it is not surprising to hook a three-hundred-pound blue marlin within sight of the hotel. The Hotel Palmilla has its own excellent fleet of thirty-one-foot fishing boats and twenty-five-foot parangas available to guests. This is first-class equipment and has expert skippers. The larger boats run $395 per day, accommodating up to four anglers; the parangas run $150 per day, including captain. The resort also has a dive shop for both scuba and snorkeling. Again, the equipment is first-rate, the dive personnel excellent, and the dive sights—all within forty-five minutes—superb. There are two excellent massage therapists available at the resort to help you relax after a full day on the course or on the boat.

Las Ventanas also offers a plethora of non-golf activities. You can play tennis, go horseback riding, and explore the desert by jeep. But our favorite activities led us back to the sea. From the resort property you can go deep-sea fishing, windsurfing, sea kayaking, snorkeling, and scuba diving. The waters of Los Cabos are a diver's paradise, as they are filled with large schools of many kinds of fish, including hammerhead sharks, and giant sea turtles.

GETTING THERE: The Hotel Palmilla is very close to the San José del Cabo Airport. Take either the airport shuttle ($7 per person) or a taxi ($20) to the hotel. The ride will take fifteen to twenty minutes.

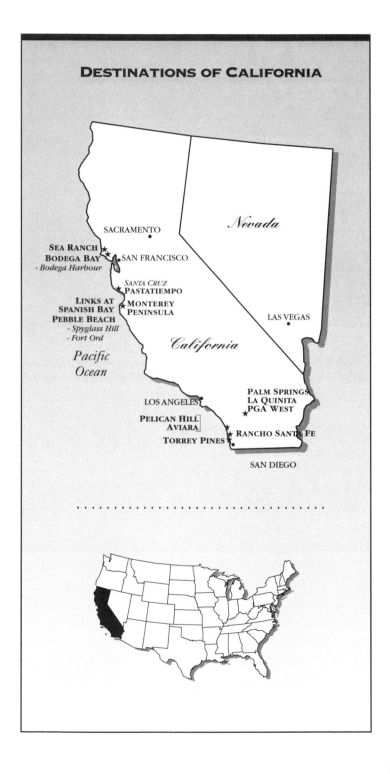

DESTINATIONS OF CALIFORNIA

Nevada

SACRAMENTO

SEA RANCH
BODEGA BAY ⭐⭐
- Bodega Harbour   SAN FRANCISCO

SANTA CRUZ
PASTATIEMPO ⭐

LAS VEGAS

LINKS AT
SPANISH BAY ⭐ **MONTEREY**
PEBBLE BEACH **PENINSULA**
- Spyglass Hill
- Fort Ord

California

Pacific
Ocean

PALM SPRINGS
LA QUINITA
PGA WEST ⭐

LOS ANGELES

PELICAN HILL
AVIARA ⭐
TORREY PINES ⭐ **RANCHO SANTA FE**

SAN DIEGO

CALIFORNIA

CALIFORNIA

*California, the most spectacular and most diversified state. California so
ripe, golden, yeasty, churning in a flux, is a world of its own. . . . There are
several Californias, and the state is at once deserted and very sane,
adolescent and mature, depending on the point of view.*

—**John Gunther**

*The attraction and superiority of California are in its days. It has better days,
and more of them, than any other country.*

—**Ralph Waldo Emerson, 1871**

The glories of California are best explored from a convertible with the wind in your
face and the sun in your eyes. Thankfully, many of the state's most memorable golf
courses are located along Highway 1, the two-lane coastal road whose hairpin turns
hug the seaside cliffs, wind around mountains, and pass through deep canyons, all
just a lob wedge from the pounding surf below. From north of San Francisco, at
Bodega Bay, we'll head south through peerless scenery and spectacular sunsets to
the excellent courses, best hotels, and finest restaurants in and around Santa Cruz,
the Monterey Peninsula, Carlsbad, and San Diego with an added stop at California's
best desert resort golf courses thrown in for good measure.

Although California's Pacific shore stretches some 1,200 miles, the state's geography is incredibly varied. Northern California is the land of redwood forests, rapid
rivers, and venerated vineyards. Gorges, canyons, and the thick-banded Sierra
Nevada mountains extend throughout the upper two thirds of the state. The glaciers that formed the Sierras have also carved deep valleys—the most beautiful of
which is Yosemite—through the mountains. To the south, the mountains eventually
give way to the Great Basin and its low-lying desert. Back along the Pacific, Northern California ends and Southern California begins when the coast turns right and
faces south instead of west. This Southern exposure accounts for the region's wonderfully sunny and balmy conditions.

The one constant amidst all this splendid geographical diversity is California's
celebrated climate—the best in the contiguous forty-eight states—which permits
ready access to its superb courses twelve months a year. Certainly, San Diego and
Palm Springs are much more popular destinations in January and February than Sea
Ranch and Bodega Bay, yet even these northern venues can be blessed with brilliant
days during the unhurried winter season. Coastal currents and fog moderate the
temperature throughout much of coastal California and ensure that average winter
and summer temperatures vary by no more than ten to fifteen degrees. In truth, California has only two seasons, a rainy season and a dry season. The so-called rainy
season in fall and winter typically yields only twenty-five to thirty-five days of rain
even in the wettest areas. To the south, heed the words of the song that says it never
rains in Southern California—they're not far off the mark.

But back to Highway 1. First stop: Bodega Harbour and Sea Ranch, two Sonoma
Coast layouts usually overlooked by golf travelers who fly into San Francisco and
head south in their haste to reach the famed courses on the Monterey Peninsula.
The tortoise-paced play and bottleneck conditions on California's most popular
courses are a distant memory up here. Both courses present a Scottish-links flavor

amid classic Northern California scenery of crashing waves, tidal inlets, and golden hills. Low-key Sonoma County offers an exceptional package: a great stretch of Highway 1, excellent golf, fresh, succulent seafood just off the boat, and spectacular local wines, all at about one-third the cost of the overall Monterey Peninsula experience.

We won't tarry too long up here, however, because now that we have gotten our feet wet in Northern California, we are ready for Alister Mackenzie's superbly designed Pasatiempo golf course in the hills above Santa Cruz. Pasatiempo is a souvenir from the golden age of golf course architecture. Anyone who has played this intriguing and deceptively long course will immediately see why Mackenzie is credited with inventing camouflage!

Pasatiempo is really only a way station on our pilgrimage to the best course in California, and, arguably, America and the world—Pebble Beach. Pebble, along with Spanish Bay and Spyglass Hill, its majestic neighbors on the Monterey Peninsula, is a must-play for every serious golfer. At a cost of nearly $300 per round, compounded with frequently windy and foggy playing conditions and chronically slow play that extends ordinary rounds to nearly six hours, Pebble Beach is not without its frustrations. But when you finally take to the tee and glance out toward Carmel Bay, your legs will wobble and you will feel the absolute awe of your surroundings. No matter what the cost, it's worth it—every hole is an event at Pebble Beach.

After sampling the glorious variety of golf in the vicinity of Monterey's Seventeen Mile Drive, we head further south. Moving from Northern to Southern California, the craggy shoreline and steep cliffs increasingly give way to the gentler beaches of the south. Down the coast, between Los Angeles and San Diego, we enter a region affectionately dubbed the Cavity-Back Coast because it is home to so many high-tech golf club manufacturers. The new Pelican Hill and Aviara golf courses offer a glimpse of golf's future; their formidable layouts seem designed to test the limits of the added distance and accuracy made possible by today's state-of-the-art equipment.

Before heading inland, our coastal-road excursion makes its way to Torrey Pines, the site of the PGA Tour's San Diego Open in La Jolla. The two Torrey Pines courses are managed by the city of San Diego. City residents can play these storied courses for just $20, and everyone seems to take advantage of the opportunity. Visitors, however, can arrange tee times well in advance through the unique Golf Playing Package, in which groups start their rounds by playing three holes with a Torrey Pines pro. As we leave the moderate temperatures of the coast for the inland desert, we pass many humdrum, overhyped hotels and look-alike golf courses. But amid the desert's tall grass and mountain peaks, La Quinta stands head and shoulders above the other golf resorts, as it has for almost eighty years. Now La Quinta is bolstered by PGA West, which features a truly outrageous course by golf's most sadomasochistic designer, Pete Dye.

In truth, California's excellent golf courses are too numerous to explore in any one trip. Besides, you and your family will be busy sampling California's other delights. You can take your sun lazily on the beach, or you can turn into a California adventurer, perhaps by going white-water rafting or hot-air ballooning. California's state and national park system is truly magnificent—there are eight national parks alone. The famed redwoods will amaze you with their height and girth, and, for bird lovers, the state offers an incredible variety of species. Don't neglect California's signature cities, either. San Francisco, Los Angeles, and San Diego are three very different meccas for popular culture. After a day of window-shopping and people watching, you will know what we mean.

Each year California entertains more and more tourists. Highway 1 becomes anything but idyllic in July and August, when bumper-to-bumper traffic and exhaust fumes take the joy out of the route. You are better off making your tour of California in spring or fall. But if you follow our Pacific Coast Highway tour, you will be assured of playing the top resort and public-access courses in the state. Just remember a couple of things when you get repeatedly distracted by California's staggering scenery. On the golf course, keep your head down and your eyes on the ball. And, on the hair-raising curves of Highway 1, make sure to keep *at least* one eye on the road.

▶BODEGA BAY AND SEA RANCH

GREAT GOLF IN NORTHERN CALIFORNIA

	The Golf	Golf Services	Lodging	Restaurants	Non-Golf Activities	Total
Rating	17	17	16	17	18	85

Bodega Harbour Golf Links

The overwhelming majority of avid golfers arriving at San Francisco Airport step off the plane, quickly collect their rental cars, and then head about 125 miles south to the Monterey Peninsula, the land of legendary golf and honey-hued chardonnay. A few make a stop en route at Alister Mackenzie's glorious Pasatiempo course in the hills above Santa Cruz, but most are too impatient for any detour, even for one of such great stature. Further south they press, exceeding the speed limit no doubt, to Pebble Beach, Spanish Bay, Spyglass Hill, Cypress Point, the Monterey Peninsula Club, Quail Lodge, and Carmel Valley Ranch, among others. They make their way to glorious hotels like the Lodge at Pebble Beach and the Inn at Spanish Bay, to the glamorous restaurants, and to a total tariff that can easily approach $1,000 per person per day if you toss in food, lodging, golf, caddies, wine, and the occasional spa treatment. Even at such a cost, all serious golfers consider a trip to the Monterey Peninsula—Robert Louis Stevenson called it "the most beautiful meeting of land and water that nature has produced"—as part of their golfing birthright.

Far, far fewer golfers arrive in San Francisco and then drive *north*, not to the equally famous Napa Valley, mind you, but directly up the coast, two hours north of San Francisco to Bodega Bay, then another hour and a half north to Sea Ranch. This is the spectacular Sonoma Coast—known as the Redwood Coast when you drive as far north as Sea Ranch—with its classic Northern California coastal imagery of crashing waves, tidal inlets, sheltered coves with sea lions basking in the sun, and barren hillsides standing starkly above the shore.

The Bodega Bay region possesses a mysterious, almost eerie, quality—particularly when the fog is in—that was made famous by Alfred Hitchcock, who filmed *The Birds* in Bodega Bay, and by the artist Christo, who constructed his famous "Running Fence" on one of Bodega Bay's hillsides. Indeed, Hitchcock's avian horror classic required just a subtle leap of his imagination. The marshes around Bodega Bay are filled with myriad waterfowl, many of which delight in tracking through the plentiful sand bunkers on the Robert Trent Jones, Jr., golf course at Bodega Bay.

Unlike ultracool Monterey, the low-key Sonoma Coast is real country inhabited by real people, despite its proximity to stylish San Francisco. Bodega Bay, in fact, is home to the busiest commercial fishing fleet between San Francisco and Eureka. All this means that you can come to Bodega Bay and Sea Ranch, play a pair of superb golf courses, completely relax between rounds, dine on delicious fresh seafood accompanied by great Sonoma wines, and stay at a pair of excellent lodges, one in Bodega Bay and the other at Sea Ranch, all for less than one-third the cost of the Monterey Peninsula experience. And the time is right. The famous but way-off-the-beaten-track Robert Muir Graves golf course at Sea Ranch—long recognized as one of the top five nine-hole courses in the United States by *Golf Digest*—has just been extended by Robert Muir Graves himself to a complete eighteen.

The best strategy for visiting Bodega Bay and Sea Ranch, which are sixty miles apart via winding, two-lane, coast-hugging Highway 1, is to spend two nights at each destination.

Bodega Bay is a compact seaside village with a handful of restaurants, hotels, and bed-and-breakfasts. Sea Ranch, on the other hand, is a 5,000-acre private community that extends for ten miles on both sides of Highway 1. In Bodega Bay, the hotels of choice are the Bodega Bay Lodge and the Inn at the Tides, while the best place for your accommodations up the road in Sea Ranch is the Sea Ranch Lodge. The Bodega Harbour Golf Links and the Sea Ranch Links can be played year-round. Even during the winter months the weather is mild, as temperatures range from the mid-forties in the early mornings to the low sixties in the afternoons.

THE GOLF 17

The **Bodega Harbour Golf Links** in Bodega Bay has two distinct personalities. The beautiful front side and several holes on the back are misty, windswept, fairly wide open, with a purely Scottish-links appearance as the golf course rolls its way up and down the magnificent, golden Sonoma hills. Yet the back nine—in particular the three fabulous finishing holes—gently carve themselves into the low-lying, bird-filled Bodega marshlands and feel more like the Carolina Low Country than anything that can be found in California. This is a terrific, tough layout on a wonderful piece of property with inspiring views from virtually every hole of both the ocean and the uniquely rounded hillsides.

The only negative we have to report is that a couple of holes are marred by homes and condominiums that have been built too close to the fairways. Although open to the public, the Bodega Harbour Golf Links is part of a private residential community. Most of the homes are quite attractive and line the golf course in an unobtrusive manner, yet a few block the view or seem dangerously close to being in play.

Poorly planned real estate, fortunately, has had no effect at all on Bodega Harbour's three great final holes. The sixteenth hole is a short, 291-yard par four that requires a drive over the marsh to a long and narrow landing zone. If you can place your tee shot properly on sixteen, you should be left with a short iron onto the green.

After hitting your drive on sixteen, a small sign instructs you to leave your golf cart and walk to the fairway over a plank bridge—and *also* to bring clubs with you for the seventeenth hole, which is also located in this environmentally sensitive zone on the far side of the marsh. The seventeenth hole is a 192-yard par three to an island-type green surrounded by marshlands. Depending upon the wind, you will want to carry an assortment of clubs. The eighteenth hole at Bodega Harbour is the best hole on the course, a 467-yard par four that calls for an uphill tee shot and a downhill approach to a green guarded by marshlands on the right. The eighteenth hole will require your two best shots of the day; par is indeed an outstanding score on Bodega Harbour's eighteenth.

Bodega Harbour has four sets of tees. From the blue tees it measures just 6,260 yards but carries a slope rating of 130, hefty for a course so short. From the white tees, Bodega Harbour is just 5,685 yards long (slope 125). The two shorter sets of tees measure 5,630 yards (slope 132) and 4,833 yards (slope 123). Par at Bodega Harbour is seventy. Greens fees range from $50 to $75 (cart included), depending upon the day of play. Starting times are available up to sixty days in advance.

The golf course at **Sea Ranch** has enjoyed a cult following since its construction twenty-three years ago and has remained a well-kept secret thanks to its remote location and the fact that it was a mere nine-hole loop. Most golfers simply do not travel hundreds of miles over bad roads to play nine-hole layouts. All this has changed, however, with the opening of the stunning new back nine here.

The original nine at Sea Ranch has the same links flavor as Bodega Bay. The hillside fairways are wide open and windswept; eight of the nine holes on the front nine have spectacular views of the Pacific. The new back nine features tighter fairways and requires more demanding tee shots that must carry creeks and wetlands. Seven of the nine new holes at Sea Ranch offer outstanding ocean views as well. Although there are homes on the course, they are far less obtrusive than the unfortunate few at Bodega Bay.

Two of the best holes at Sea Ranch are number nine and the gorgeous new thirteenth. The ninth, a 391-yard par four, requires a drive of no more than 185 yards onto the upper fairway; anything longer will find the barranca that divides the fairway in two. The second shot is downhill to a green heavily guarded by trees and a hazard on the left. Thirteen, a 476-yard par five that plays directly into strong, prevailing winds, provides the greatest view of the entire course. A long drive to the Snags—a tree in the middle of the fairway—will help open up your second shot.

The new Sea Ranch has three sets of tees. From the blues, the course measures 6,643 yards; from the whites, 6,287 yards; and from the reds, 5,312 yards. Par is 72. The greens fee is a mere $35 weekdays and $50 weekends (carts cost $12.50 per rider). An especially attractive package at Sea Ranch includes accommodations for two people for two nights, two breakfasts, two dinners, and two days of unlimited golf with cart for just $550 Sunday through Thursday and $650 over the weekend.

Bodega Harbour Golf Links. 21301 Heron Drive, Bodega Bay, CA 94923. Tel: 707-875-3538. Fax: 707-875-3256. Credit cards accepted.

• 1976/1987. Designer: Robert Trent Jones, Jr. Par 70. 6,260 yards. 71.9 par rating. 130 slope rating. Greens fees: $50 (Monday–Thursday), $60 (Friday), $75 (Saturday–Sunday), includes cart. Walking permitted. Caddies available in summer by advance arrangement. Season: year-round.

The Sea Ranch Golf Links. 49300 Highway 1, The Sea Ranch, CA 95497. Tel: 800-SEA-RANCH (800-732-7262) or 707-785-2468. Fax: 707-785-3043. Credit cards accepted.

• 1974/1996. Designer: Robert Muir Graves. Par 72. 6,643 yards. 73.9 par rating. 136 slope rating. Greens fees: $35 (weekdays), $50 (weekends). Twilight: $20 (weekdays) and $35 (weekends). Walking permitted. Carts cost $12.50 per rider. Season: year-round.

GOLF SERVICES (17)

Golf services are excellent at both Bodega Harbour and Sea Ranch. The visiting golfer will receive a warm welcome and friendly service. Both courses feature nice clubhouses with restaurants and bars, good pro shops, and adequate practice facilities. Walking is permitted at both courses, but because of the undulating and hilly terrain most golfers will be happier riding a cart.

LODGING (16)

The best place to stay in Bodega Bay is the **Bodega Bay Lodge,** an attractive, well-run, contemporary hotel with seventy-eight rooms that is just two minutes from the Bodega Harbour golf course. We stayed three minutes farther down the road at the Inn at the Tides, which is pleasant, comfortable, and simple, but of the two hotels, we discovered that the Bodega Bay Lodge is the more desirable. Every room at the Bodega Bay Lodge features a private balcony with views of the bay and ocean. Most rooms have fireplaces; all have stocked minibars. The lobby is well appointed, and the Duck Club restaurant is intimate. Just outside you will find a swimming pool and small exercise room. Room rates range from $160 to $225.

The **Inn at the Tides,** recommended if the Bodega Bay Lodge is fully booked, consists of a series of shingled cottages that climb the hillside and offer fine views of the Pacific. We stayed in unit 1206, which featured a fireplace and a good view but lacked a stocked minibar. The Inn at the Tides offers eighty-six rooms and has a nice outdoor pool, whirlpool spa, and restaurant. Rates range from $114 to $184.

Perched dramatically on the edge of a rocky bluff overlooking the Pacific, the twenty-room **Sea Ranch Lodge** is simple and rustic, with fireplaces, cedar siding, and spectacular views. The Lodge emphasizes peace and solitude; hence, its guest rooms have no phones or televisions. Phones are readily available on the premises, however. Rates range from $125 to $180.

Bodega Bay Lodge. 103 Highway 1, Bodega Bay, CA 94923. Tel: 800-368-2468 or 707-875-3525. Fax: 707-875-2428. 78 rooms. Doubles from $160 to $225. Credit cards accepted.

Inn at the Tides. Highway 1, Bodega Bay, CA 94923. Tel: 800-541-7788 or 707-875-2751. Fax: 707-875-2669. 86 rooms. Doubles range from $114 to $184. Credit cards accepted.

The Sea Ranch Lodge. PO Box 44, The Sea Ranch, CA 95497. Tel: 800-SEA-RANCH (800-732-7262) or 707-785-2371. Fax: 707-785-2917. 20 rooms. Doubles range from $125 to $180. Credit cards accepted.

RESTAURANTS (17)

The utterly superb fresh seafood of Bodega Bay, together with the luscious wines of Sonoma County, culminate in some excellent dining at the region's four best restaurants. The **Duck Club** at the Bodega Bay Lodge serves innovative, California-style cuisine, with entrées—lamb, catch of the day, black-and-white sesame-crusted halibut—ranging in price from $16 to $22. Although it does not serve lunch, the Duck Club offers a delicious breakfast.

The inexpensive and informal **Tides Wharf Restaurant** wins as our low-key, casual favorite. Decorated with black-and-white photographs from *The Birds,* the

Tides Wharf offers wonderfully fresh local seafood; in fact, you can be sure the seafood is about as fresh as fresh gets because the restaurant runs its very own fishery! Specialties include oysters, grilled swordfish, and a good selection of Sonoma and Napa wines. Another bonus: a complete dinner for two at Tides Wharf with wine and tip costs around $50.

The **Bayview Restaurant,** across the street, is more intimate and more formal, with an intriguing menu that changes almost daily. At least twice a month, the Bayview offers special, wine-tasting dinners (but beware, they get booked up weeks in advance), at which a particular local vineyard is highlighted, the winemaker is often present, and, of course, the food is perfectly matched with the wines served.

Then there is the **Sea Ranch Lodge Restaurant,** which, like many of the restaurants highlighted, places great emphasis on local fare—local wines, local produce, local game. Its menu, too, changes almost weekly, with specials such as rack of lamb (raised locally), pan-seared ahi tuna with cilantro aioli and citrus salsa, and, for an appetizer, a wild mushroom sauté with asparagus tips and roasted red peppers. All of it was good! The restaurant offers a reasonably priced prix fixe menu at $30, which includes an appetizer, choice of soup or salad, entrée, and dessert.

Finally, if you're looking for some lunch after your round of golf, we suggest the attractive clubhouses at both Bodega Harbour and Sea Ranch.

The Duck Club. Bodega Bay Lodge, 103 Highway 1, Bodega Bay, CA 94923. Tel: 800-368-2468 or 707-875-3525. Fax: 707-875-2428. Credit cards accepted.

Tides Wharf Restaurant. Highway 1, Bodega Bay, CA 94923. Tel: 707-875-3652. Fax: 707-875-3023. Credit cards accepted.

Bayview Restaurant. Inn at the Tides, Highway 1, Bodega Bay, CA 94923. Tel: 800-541-7788 or 707-875-2751. Fax: 707-875-2669. Credit cards accepted.

Sea Ranch Lodge Restaurant. PO Box 44, The Sea Ranch, CA 95497. Tel: 800-SEA-RANCH (800-732-7262) or 707-785-2371. Fax: 707-785-2917. Credit cards accepted.

N O N - G O L F   A C T I V I T I E S

Bodega Bay and Sea Ranch are places to unwind. Low-key non-golf activities include beachcombing, hiking, whale watching, bicycling, and horseback riding. Sea Ranch has a beautiful ten-mile-long bluff trail with a variety of forest and coastal vistas. Wine lovers may easily drive one hour to Healdsburg and visit great Sonoma wineries like Arrowood, Chalk Hill, and Ferrari-Carano. Napa Valley, with its amazing bounty of sophisticated diversions, is just one hour beyond Healdsburg.

GETTING THERE: From San Francisco Airport take Highway 101 North to the East Washington exit in the town of Petaluma. At the end of the exit ramp, turn left. Stay on this road twenty-eight miles until you reach the Bodega Bay Lodge on the left-hand side of the street.

▶PASATIEMPO

ALISTER MACKENZIE FOR THE COMMON MAN

	The Golf	Golf Services	Lodging	Restaurants	Non-Golf Activities	Total
Rating	18	18	17	17	17	87

Pasatiempo

The current greens fee of $110 ($130 with a cart) hardly qualifies gorgeous Pasatiempo, in Santa Cruz, California, as a golf course for the common man. Yet Pasatiempo is, indeed, the only golf course in the United States designed by Dr. Alister Mackenzie that is open for public play and maintained to strict, private club standards. The two existing Mackenzie-designed municipal layouts in California—Sharp Park near San Francisco and Haggin Oaks in Sacramento—are classic 1930s layouts, yet both suffer the consequences of very heavy, muni-style traffic. Pasatiempo, on the other hand, is always pristine. We played there on a stunning morning the day after a torrential downpour. Despite the three inches of rain dumped on the course the previous afternoon, it was in perfect condition thanks to the efforts of a veritable army of greenskeepers. Although it is Alister Mackenzie's hidden gem, Pasatiempo has gained a measure of long-overdue attention now that *Golf Digest* has ranked it among America's top one hundred golf courses.

In truth, a golf outing on an immaculate Alister Mackenzie layout is like a friend loaning you his vintage Bugatti convertible for your big date on Saturday night or the Metropolitan Museum allowing you to hang one of its Old Master paintings in your living room. Considered the most influential architect from the golden age of golf course design, Mackenzie created Augusta National (with Bobby Jones), super-exclusive Cypress Point, the Jockey Club in Argentina, Royal Melbourne in Australia, Crystal Downs in Michigan, and the elegant Valley Club of Montecito near Santa Barbara, among other masterpieces. Have heart, however, if you cannot wrangle an invitation to any of these courses, for Pasatiempo will always be there for the daily-fee-paying public. It can also be strongly argued that of all these magnificent courses, Pasatiempo, which opened in 1929, was actually dearest to Mackenzie's heart. The good doctor lived in a rather modest house on Hollins Drive, just off Pasatiempo's sixth fairway, until his death in 1934.

Located high in the wooded hills above Santa Cruz, Pasatiempo is about a two-hour drive south of San Francisco and some forty-five minutes north of the Monterey Peninsula. The course sits roughly three miles from the ocean and just off a major highway (Route 17), although you would never know it, so tranquil is the Pasatiempo golf experience. Views of the distant ocean from the elevated golf course through the eucalyptus, cypress, and acacia trees are simply spectacular.

The Pasatiempo golf experience is often understood as a not-too-distant adjunct to the Monterey Peninsula scene or as a golfing excursion for those staying in San Francisco. If you are flying into San Francisco and then driving down to Pebble Beach and Spanish Bay, strongly consider a game at Pasatiempo en route. It is an extremely worthwhile detour.

THE GOLF

Alister Mackenzie was a multifaceted genius. He was an army surgeon who became an expert in the art and science of camouflage when he served in South Africa during the Boer War. Indeed, the camouflage techniques Mackenzie developed in the African bush were credited with saving thousands of lives during World War I. Mackenzie later observed that successful golf course design, like camouflage, depended on utilizing natural features to their fullest extent and creating artificial features that closely imitate nature.

The amazing optical illusions on the golf course are, perhaps, the most delightful facet of a round on **Pasatiempo.** Distances are much farther than they initially appear. The tee shots on numbers six and eleven are good examples. Six is a tight, uphill, 521-yard par five. Eleven is a 384-yard par four, certainly one of the finest and most difficult holes on the course. Drives on both holes look as though they ought to be hit conservatively into tight landing zones, but the fairways are actually much deeper and wider than they appear from the tees.

Clubhouse, Pasatiempo

Although it measures just 6,483 yards, Pasatiempo is a tough, par seventy-one course with slope ratings of 141 from the blue tees, 138 from the white tees, and 135 from the red tees, making it a test for every level of golfer. From start to finish, the course is tight, forest-fringed, and crisscrossed by deep ravines and gullies that frequently require heroic carries for your drive or approach shot to the green.

The superb opening hole, so intimidating from the elevated tee, is a harbinger of things to come. This glorious first tee, just steps from Pasatiempo's vintage clubhouse, gazes down upon the narrowest sliver of green fairway flanked on both sides by towering cypress and eucalyptus trees. On the horizon beyond the fairway, sailboats glide in and out of view on the blue waters of the Pacific Ocean. A rifle, rather than a driver, appears to be the practical weapon of choice on this first shot of the day. But again, this alarming perspective from the first tee is another visual trick pulled off by Dr. Mackenzie. Once you descend the hill and reach your ball on the fairway, you will discover that there is a lot more room out there than originally met the eye. In fact, this first hole, a 504-yard downhill par five, is actually rated the easiest hole at Pasatiempo.

The third hole, a 217-yard par three, is the number two handicap hole on the course, no doubt because it, too, cleverly deceives most golfers. Designed subtly uphill, this third hole plays at least 235 to 240 yards long. Every golfer in our foursome selected the wrong stick and came up well short of the green.

The back nine opens with Pasatiempo's three most beautiful holes. The tenth, a 444-yard par four, demands a heroic drive over a ravine to an elevated landing area and then a long, downhill second shot. The eleventh is a dogleg-left. Your second shot on eleven, which should be struck with at least two clubs more than the yardage may indicate, must carry over a barranca to an uphill green. Number twelve is a glorious hole as well. The drive on this 376-yard par four is downhill and wide open, yet the second shot must be laser straight—anything hit to the right will fall off into a ravine guarding that side of the green. Ten, eleven, and twelve comprise an outstanding sequence of golf holes. The finishing hole is another majestic par three, 173 yards downhill.

In his book *Golf Architecture,* Mackenzie codifies thirteen essential features of an ideal golf course that became standards of golf course architecture after World War II. Among them is his observation that "there should be little walking between greens and tees." In the seventy-seven years since Mackenzie wrote those words, Big Bertha and high-compression balls were invented and have come into common usage. As a result, some homeowners at Pasatiempo have installed high fences around their gardens to deflect errant shots, and a few tees are now shielded with high nets that resemble baseball backstops. These nets and fences are the only aesthetic glitches at Pasatiempo. The other glitch we experienced is one that can universally plague the game of golf—slow play. We teed off at 1 P.M. and finished nearly five and a half hours later. With ample reason, Pasatiempo is an extremely busy and popular golf course. Book an early morning tee time if you wish to play at a brisk pace.

Pasatiempo Golf Club. 18 Clubhouse Road, Santa Cruz, CA 95060. Tel: 408-459-9155. Fax: 408-459-9157. Credit cards accepted.

• 1929. Designer: Dr. Alister Mackenzie. Par 71. 6,483 yards. 72.9 par rating. 141 slope rating. Greens fee: $110. Walking permitted. Caddies can be arranged. Carts available for $20. Season: year-round.

 GOLF SERVICES

Service at the club is excellent. You can count on a bag attendant greeting you with a smile at the entrance. The very pleasant and comfortable clubhouse is decorated with fascinating Mackenzie photographs and memorabilia, and the facilities include a well-stocked pro shop, restaurant and bar, and practice range. Staff members are welcoming and friendly. The $110 greens fee is not inexpensive, yet in the case of Pasatiempo, you get what you pay for—and more.

 LODGING ⓱

The sparkling **Seascape Resort** is located about thirty minutes from Pasatiempo on a bluff overlooking the sea. Guests stay in elegant one- and two-bedroom suites with kitchenettes, fireplaces, television-VCR combination, and private balconies. The resort features its own restaurant and two outdoor pools. Guests may also use the health club across the street. A pathway also leads from the resort to the beach.

For more intimate accommodations, the spectacular **Inn at Depot Hill,** selected one of the "Top 10 Inns in the Country" by *Country Inn* magazine, is about ten minutes from Pasatiempo in Capitola, a quaint seaside village. Each of the twelve rooms in the inn is decorated in the style of a different European city. All rooms come equipped with a fireplace, television, and VCR. Guests are served a gourmet breakfast in their rooms and dessert and complimentary port at night.

Seascape Resort. 1 Seascape Resort Drive, Aptos, CA 95003. Tel: 800-929-7727 or 408-688-6800. Fax: 408-685-0615. 190 suites. One-bedroom suites cost $180 to $235 from May through October; $150 to $205 November through April. Credit cards accepted.

Inn at Depot Hill. 250 Monterey Avenue, Capitola, CA. Tel: 800-572-2632 or 408-462-3376. Fax: 408-458-2490. 12 rooms. Doubles cost $160 to $250. Credit cards accepted.

RESTAURANTS

There are a number of very good restaurants within a short distance of Pasatiempo. **Oswald,** in Santa Cruz, serves the most inspired food in the area. The exquisite, California-French menu changes monthly to incorporate seasonal local produce. Vegetarians will find this an especially appealing place. Open for dinner only, entrées cost $13 to $20.

With its creekside location overlooking the ocean and the town of Capitola, the **Shadowbrook Restaurant** is a glorious dinner spot. Although a little touristy, the food at this upscale steak and seafood house is excellent and the wine list quite good.

Davenport Cash Store Restaurant on Highway 1 headed toward San Francisco, is perfect for brunch, offering a wide variety of omelettes, waffles, and Spanish dishes. The large, Spanish-style dining room is filled with exotic artifacts from all over the world. Lunch specialties at the intimate **Café Sparrow,** a Country-French restaurant, include innovative pasta, fresh fish, and unusual salads. The dinner menu features filet mignon prepared six different ways.

If you are staying in accommodations with a kitchenette, don't miss **Gayle's Bakery and Rosticceria** in Capitola, where you can eat casually in-house or takeout. In addition to its full-service bakery, Gayle's serves hot entrées cooked on its wood-fired spit, great seasonal salads, and meat sandwiches on homemade bread.

Oswald. 1547-E Pacific Avenue, Santa Cruz, CA 95060. Tel: 408-423-7427. No Fax. Credit cards accepted.

Shadowbrook Restaurant. 1750 Wharf Road, Capitola CA 95010. Tel: 408-475-1511. Fax: 408-475-7664. Credit cards accepted.

Davenport Cash Store Restaurant. 1 Davenport Avenue (Highway 1), Davenport, CA 95017. Tel: 800-870-1817 or 408-426-4122. Fax: 408-423-1160. Credit cards accepted.

Café Sparrow. 8042 Soquel Drive, Aptos, CA 95003. Tel: 408-688-6238. No Fax. Credit cards accepted.

Gayle's Bakery and Rosticceria. 504 Bay Avenue, Capitola, CA 95010. Tel: 408-462-1200. Fax: 408-462-6863. Credit cards accepted.

NON-GOLF ACTIVITIES

We suggest your free time be spent exploring the nearby beaches, meandering around the tree-lined downtown area with its unique shops, or visiting the dozen or so family-owned wineries in the area. Other options include taking a walking tour of the town's beautifully restored Victorian homes, heading out of the arboretum at the University of California at Santa Cruz, or making your way to one of the area's three state parks that offer well-maintained walking and biking paths that wind through the magnificent coastal redwoods for which California is famous.

GETTING THERE: From the south, travel beyond Monterey on Highway 1. When you reach Santa Cruz, take Highway 17 North (toward San Jose). After about one mile, get off at Pasatiempo Drive. Take a left at the top of the ramp, pass over the freeway to the first stop sign, turn left again, go one block, and take a right onto Pasatiempo Drive and proceed to the club.

▶PEBBLE BEACH

THE MYSTICISM OF THE MONTEREY PENINSULA

	The Golf	Golf Services	Lodging	Restaurants	Non-Golf Activities	Total
Rating	20	16	19	16	19	90

They started coming at the turn of the century, wave after wave of them more or less in unison, disparate figures bound by passion, a profundity of vision, and a deep intuitive understanding of the power of this place. They came separately but together: Samuel Morse, Robinson Jeffers, Jack Neville, John Steinbeck, Alister Mackenzie, Edward Weston, Henry Miller, Jack Kerouac, and Jack Nicklaus. Mr. Morse, the fa-

Clubhouse, Pebble Beach

ther of Pebble Beach, bought 7,000 acres on the Monterey Peninsula the same year the poet Jeffers moved to the snug village of Carmel. Jack Neville laid out the Pebble Beach links, and Mackenzie designed Cypress Point as Steinbeck of Monterey published his first stories and Weston was thoughtfully combing the beaches and composing his celebrated photographs of Point Lobos. Henry Miller and Jack Kerouac, both of Carmel in those days, published *Tropic of Cancer* and *On the Road,* respectively, just before another Jack, then twenty-one, won the U.S. Amateur Championship up the road at Pebble Beach.

One of the peninsula's very first literary pilgrims here was an anomaly indeed: a Scotsman who didn't golf. We are speaking of Robert Louis Stevenson, the author of *Treasure Island.* Stevenson, who knew a bit of the world, called the Monterey Peninsula "the most beautiful meeting of land and water that nature has produced." Today, Stevenson is honored by the wondrous Spyglass Hill Golf Course, which Robert Trent Jones, Sr., named after *Treasure Island.*

The Monterey Peninsula is the site of such diverse human accomplishment and such unusual natural splendor that it takes a gestalt therapist to figure it out, and gestalt practitioners aplenty reside here, too. Gestalt psychology holds that the whole is more than the sum of its parts, that the whole of anything cannot be fully grasped by simply analyzing its parts in isolation. For Monterey, do not focus on individual details—however lovely or overwhelming—such as the dune land, the curling waves and the crescent beaches, the fog bank slashed with columns of sudden sunshine, the virtually domesticated deer roaming the fairways, and the fat, pregnant seals sunning themselves on the rocks. Strive instead for an awareness of the mystery and mysticism of the whole.

The words "mystery" and "mysticism" are not at all inappropriate in a discussion of America's greatest golf course. After all, the Esalen Institute, a famous California establishment devoted to "the promotion of human potential," is just an hour down the coast road amid the wilds of Big Sur. Esalen's proximity to the golf links is no mere coincidence, for its founder and presiding genius is none other than Michael Murphy, author of the cult classic *Golf in the Kingdom*. It strikes us that all the forces of Monterey—its golf, its artistic and visionary aspects—converge in the person of Michael Murphy. Not one of the peninsula's representative figures, not Steinbeck, Nicklaus, or even Samuel Morse, embodies every element to the same heightened degree.

Golf (or at least the inner facets of the game) remains a mini-industry at Esalen. A colleague of Murphy's, gestalt therapist Steve Cohen, teaches a five-day *Golf in the Kingdom* workshop at Esalen with field trips to the Monterey Peninsula. When asked to describe his workshop, Cohen responded: "That which prevents you from maximizing your potential in golf is that which prevents you from maximizing your potential in life." Now, such methodology happens to agree with us, but if you find it all "too California," Murphy himself would not find fault with you. "It's not for everyone," he readily admits, "but the letters I've received in response to the book are simply amazing, hundreds upon hundreds of them, from guys in alligator shirts at very Republican country clubs writing about their occult experiences on the golf course."

Our interview with Murphy illustrated another point as well: almost any time Pebble Beach is mentioned, St. Andrews follows in the next breath. We asked Murphy to name his favorite course on the Monterey Peninsula. His answer—Pebble Beach, which he rated ahead of St. Andrews on his all-time list—was not a given. There are eighteen other courses in the vicinity, several of which, including Cypress Point, are truly awe-inspiring.

Yet, of all the world's courses, only Pebble Beach and St. Andrews are true peers. According to their publicists, Turnberry is the Pebble Beach of Scotland, Pinehurst is America's St. Andrews, and Samoset (in Maine) is the Pebble Beach of the East, but, in truth, only Pebble and St. Andrews may be naturally compared without exaggeration. The common denominators the two share are wonderful golf, public access, and legions of enthusiastic international golfers. Simultaneously, these two great links perfectly embody the vast differences between Scotland and California: Calvinism versus hedonism, classicism versus cool, the grandeur of a cathedral versus the ravishing glamour of Hollywood. Pebble Beach is also a bit more relaxed. The young California-blond starter on the first tee issued us a friendly admonition: "I'm not going to let you go out there unless you promise to have fun." We could not imagine the starter on the Old Course—in his tweed cap and tartan necktie—saying that.

On the Monterey Peninsula, prepare yourself to experience a material and sensual feast. The pagan god of Carmel, for instance, is shopping. Another obsession of religious proportions is real estate: $2 million buys a modest box; $15 million is required for a real house overlooking the ocean or the thirteenth fairway. Each year Monterey hosts an annual jazz festival, Carmel runs a Bach festival, and Pebble Beach puts on a celebrated antique car show. The region's prevailing color—aside from the color of fog—is the golden hue of chardonnay held to the light in a crystal goblet. Try the heavenly, oak-scented Talbott, produced on the peninsula itself. And if Michael Murphy is the secret soul of Pebble Beach, then Clint Eastwood, the former mayor of Carmel, known to everyone as "Clint," is its most visible public figure. Eastwood references abound, like our caddie's remark about the overall caliber of golf at Pebble: "I've seen the good, the bad, and the ugly."

Now for the sobering reality. Golf in the California kingdom is not without its downside. First and foremost, prices are as lofty as the setting. A trip to the Monterey Peninsula with accommodations at the Lodge at Pebble Beach or the Inn at Spanish Bay—the two hotels owned by the Pebble Beach Company—is every bit as expensive as any luxury holiday in Europe. The $500 million current owner Masatsugu Takabayashi paid for Pebble—and the whopping finance charges associated with debt service—mean that huge costs have been passed along to the consumer. Second, the crowds can be overwhelming. Traffic on the scenic Seventeen Mile Drive, which winds through the peninsula and leads to the golf courses, can be bumper to bumper. Despite strenuous efforts at preservation spearheaded by perhaps the most environmentally conscious population in America, the Monterey Peninsula bears the indelible imprint of mass tourism. Carmel, where the village taxis are Volvo station wagons, still fights to protect its heritage, yet the city of Monterey has succumbed to commerce. Fisherman's Wharf in Monterey is just an outdoor shopping mall, and as for Cannery Row, well, you will just have to close your eyes and imagine what it must have meant to Steinbeck.

THE GOLF 20

Let's eliminate Cypress Point from the picture right away. Unless you know a member who is willing to take you out or write a letter on your behalf, any effort to get on Cypress is a complete waste of time. "There are no variations to that policy," said the weary voice on the phone in the Cypress Point golf shop. The tourists we saw actually peeking through the gates at Cypress neatly summarize the situation: you can look, but you cannot touch—or play. The two courses of the Monterey Peninsula Club, located between Spanish Bay and Cypress Point, are also closed to the public. However, the average visitor to the peninsula need not lament because the courses that do welcome the public are so numerous and stunning. In this chapter, we focus on a couple of the big guns—**Pebble Beach Resort Golf's** Pebble Beach and Spyglass Hill. The equally impressive Links at Spanish Bay we will review separately. Other worthy courses in the area include enchanting Pacific Grove (tel: 408-648-3177), tough Poppy Hills (tel: 408-625-2154), the Del Monte Course (tel: 408-373-2700), the cute Peter Hay par three across the street from Pebble (tel: 408-625-8518), and still many others further afield.

Every hole at **Pebble Beach** is famous, even the ones that are less famous than others. Every hole has been written about, photographed, painted by watercolorists, and weighed and measured by the best brains in the business. For this reason alone we reject the absurd testimony, issued elsewhere by certain snobs, that Pebble has one or two weak links, like the first hole, that gentle dogleg-right. How can anyone—other than the most jaded—feel anything other than pounding drama on the first tee of Pebble Beach and anticipation and exhilaration of that first march down the fairway? The twelfth hole, that longish,

Pebble Beach Golf Links

202-yard par three on the upper corniche, may be the only hole somewhat pedestrian in appearance—and that only if you can succeed in isolating it from the splendor of its setting. But then again, how many golf holes in the world look into Leonard Firestone's backyard and down upon the tenth fairway of Pebble Beach and the Pacific beyond? In truth, every hole is an event; each and every one has some special stimulant that puts the central nervous system on full alert—an unusual challenge, an enchanting natural peculiarity, or an hallucinogenic view. First-time players on the course will try to burn it into their memory in order to relive their round another day. Simultaneously, they will have a sense of déjà vu—of Watson's winning shot and the triumphs of Nicklaus and Tom Kite.

That is, of course, if they can see it. All the courses on the peninsula are at the mercy of the mist and fog, which comes and goes at will. At Pebble Beach, the fog is like the curtain rising and falling on the world's most lavish theatrical set. Thanks to the fog, our foursome, which included an English accountant who lives in Bermuda and an utterly charming Japanese couple, missed some of the magic. We played Pebble's great middle holes—numbers six through ten—wrapped in it. We walked through the fog, shot blindly into it, and nearly fell off the cliff on number eight. On the eleventh green the curtain miraculously lifted, exposing the full glory of that view: the course below, the beaches, and the jagged hills above Carmel. After that, we played Pebble with smiles on our faces. Our impression of Pebble Beach replays like a symphony. Like Beethoven's Ninth, it opens quietly (holes one and two), builds gradually (holes three through five), reaches a thundering crescendo in its middle movements (holes six through ten), subdues itself again (holes eleven through fifteen), and then finishes with the clash of cymbals at the end (sixteen through eighteen).

The blockbuster holes require no further praise here. You will quickly see for yourself why holes six through ten comprise the most acclaimed sequence in golf, why seventeen has broken the hearts of many champions, and why eighteen is the game's ultimate finishing hole. But we think you will be equally beguiled by Pebble's more subtle gems, like the third, which requires a crushing drive to clear the barranca from the blue tees, or the fifth, a magical par three through a chute of trees that demands complete precision, or the fifteenth, where another huge barranca looms threateningly before the tee. Is a day here worth more than three hundred bucks, with another price increase (as yet unspecified) due to take effect in 1998? Folks, that's a rhetorical question. Bring your checkbook, your camera, and your Big Bertha (or the equivalent), for Pebble is a hitter's course.

A short final note from Pebble Beach. After your round, once you've quaffed a celebratory drink in the Tap Room at the Lodge and begun to relax and collect your thoughts, walk up the path and return to the eighteenth tee, especially if the fog has cleared and the view is bright. The first tee presents an undeniable scene with gawking tourists and whirring video cameras, but the eighteenth tee is more than that. Go back to see what you may have missed before: pelicans dive-bombing into the bay at low tide, beachcombers scouring for starfish and mussels, and the wide-eyed golfers leaving seventeen and taking their first incredible look across the water to the final green. Do you see how absorbed they are in their game, the animation and enthusiasm in their open faces? That look—of ecstasy—is Pebble Beach.

Spyglass Hill has a reputation even more intimidating than Pebble Beach's. It is rated as one of the toughest courses in the world from the championship tees (par rating 75.9) and is known as a place where only the longest hitters survive. We were disturbed by the pockmarked condition of the fairways at Spyglass when we played, but even this could not diminish the artistry of the layout with its sweeping variety of ocean and forest holes. Robert Trent Jones, Sr., who created the course in 1966, has said: "The first five holes were designed with Pine Valley in mind, and the remainder are designed like Augusta National with its majestic pines." The first hole at Spyglass provides a quick initiation indeed. It is the best first hole on the peninsula, the longest on the course (six hundred yards), and the only hole that gives you a taste of the forest and ocean at the same time—from an elevated tee shaded by pines down to a green surrounded by duneland. Spyglass plays amid the dunes for five holes. Then, at six, it turns uphill into the forest—where you remain for the balance of the day. The current greens fee at Spyglass for Pebble Beach resort guests is $175 ($225 for nonresort guests).

Pebble Beach Resort Golf. Seventeen Mile Drive, Pebble Beach, CA 93953. Tel: 800-654-9300, 408-624-3811 (for tee times twenty-four hours in advance), pro shop: 408-625-8518. Fax: 408-644-7960. Credit cards accepted.

• *Pebble Beach Golf Links.* 1919. Designers: Jack Neville, Douglas Grant. Par 72. 6,799 yards. 74.4 par rating. 142 slope rating. Greens fees: $240 (resort guests), $320 (public), includes cart. Walking permitted. Caddies available. Season: year-round.

• *Spyglass Hill Golf Course.* 1966. Robert Trent Jones, Sr. Par 72. 6,859 yards. 75.9 par rating. 143 slope rating. Greens fees: $175 (resort guests), $225 (nonresort guests), includes cart. Walking permitted. Caddies available. Season: year-round.

 GOLF SERVICES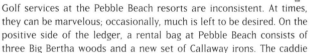

Golf services at the Pebble Beach resorts are inconsistent. At times, they can be marvelous; occasionally, much is left to be desired. On the positive side of the ledger, a rental bag at Pebble Beach consists of three Big Bertha woods and a new set of Callaway irons. The caddie program is also outstanding. Caddies dress in a uniform of beige overalls, and some are tournament-quality golfers. The greens fee includes a cart charge, which is not reimbursed if you elect to hire a caddie. The current caddie fee is $40. A standard tip is $15. Take a caddie for your inaugural round on Pebble Beach; you will enjoy your day much more. Pebble Beach and Spyglass Hill have driving ranges, but they are not in good condition. On the downside, we did not like the fact that there is no club care after your game at any of the courses on the Monterey Peninsula, and we think the resort shuttle bus schedule needs serious revision. If you ride the bus to a course from your hotel, you may find yourself at the end of the day waiting interminably for a lift back home.

LODGING

Hotels on the Monterey Peninsula are in far more limited supply than golf courses. In fact, there are just two hotels on the peninsula proper, the Inn at Spanish Bay, built in 1988 ("The Bounty of Spanish Bay" below) and the traditional Lodge at Pebble Beach, built in 1919. Strong arguments can be made in favor of either establishment. One is busy and glamorous, while the other is more elegant and refined, but both have easy proximity to the links, vast facilities (stunning health spas, swimming pools, and three or four restaurants apiece), plus important perks like preferred tee times and discounts at the golf courses. The tasteful little hotels in and around Carmel are less viable and lure fewer golfers because of their more limited services and relative distance from the action.

The **Lodge at Pebble Beach** is the true center—the eye of the storm—of the

Monterey Peninsula. The buildings at the Lodge form a V shape, with one flank consisting of shops and the other of Lodge guest rooms. Set in the center of that V is the first tee of Pebble Beach. As anyone will tell you, it is a holy place. Think of T. S. Eliot's phrase: "the still point of the turning world." At the Lodge, you feel as if you're on solid ground. The entire staff is wise, polished, and self-assured. The buildings have an air of permanence, and the gardens are beautiful and mature. Fellow guests include movie people, senior management types, and a few guys with name tags. The Lodge is old money, big houses along the golf course, and an established, conservative clientele. Rooms at the Lodge may look like dormitories from the exterior, but they are sheer classic taste within. Negative comments about the Lodge's condition are out-of-date. Our room, number 401, was elegant: large, exquisitely decorated, and equipped with wood-burning fireplace, wet bar, marble dressing area, and huge bath with tub and separate shower. The heated pool and spa at the Lodge are located in the stunning **Beach Club,** adjacent to the seventeenth tee, one of the real scenes at Pebble Beach.

The Lodge at Pebble Beach. Seventeen Mile Drive, Pebble Beach, CA 93953. Tel: 800-654-9300 or 408-624-3811. Fax: 408-625-8598. 161 rooms and suites. Doubles from $350 to $500, suites from $650 to $1,500. Three-day golf packages (exclusive of meals) from $1,150. Credit cards accepted.

RESTAURANTS

The restaurants below are recommended with confidence:

In Big Sur, we recommend stopping by **Sierra Mar,** the restaurant at the Post Ranch Inn. A photograph of the inn adorned a recent cover of *Travel & Leisure;* it is one of the most acclaimed—and unusual—new hotels in America. If you cross Bixby Bridge heading for the redwoods of Big Sur, make a point of stopping here for a light lunch or memorable dinner. The view is unbelievable (airplanes actually fly below you along the coast), and the food is the very best we sampled in the region. In the evening, a prix fixe dinner that includes four wonderful courses is offered at $55. Recent appetizers included pan-seared sea scallops with Thai butter and rice cakes as well as a fire-roasted artichoke with black truffle vinaigrette. A favorite entrée is the pan-seared, coriander-crusted ahi tuna with a potato and lentil hash. A visit here is strongly recommended because the Post Ranch Inn is absolutely unforgettable.

If the Sierra Mar is full, a good backup is right across the road at the well-known Ventana Inn, whose **Ventana Dining Room** we also thoroughly enjoyed. Serving a cuisine labeled California/French, the restaurant offers an appealing assortment of entrées, including a pan-seared, potato-wrapped salmon with whole-grain mustard sauce and a chestnut-crusted ahi tuna. Dinner for two with wine and tip will run around $80.

In 1997, the **Café Fina** was voted by locals as the best seafood restaurant in the Monterey Peninsula, and we agree. Located on Fisherman's Wharf in Monterey, Café Fina offers beautiful views of the bay and an appealing menu full of enticing seafood and pasta dishes. An Italian restaurant with a flair for seafood, Café Fina offers such entrées as blackened snapper salad, fresh Monterey Bay prawns, and mesquite-barbecued halibut. The restaurant proudly makes all of its own pastas. Casual yet not, you will feel equally comfortable here in a suit or shorts. It's a good choice for lunch after touring the interesting Monterey Bay Aquarium. Approximately $35 for two at lunch with wine and tip.

Located at the Lodge, **Club XIX** is the very best restaurant operated by the Pebble Beach Company. Casual bistro-style lunches are served on the sublime outdoor terrace overlooking the eighteenth green. Dinner in the intimate, oak-paneled dining room is a dressier event. We enjoyed the salad of asparagus and endive, the sea bass with black peppercorn crust, and the sautéed medallions of veal with pesto. Most entrées cost $22 to $28. The wine list is outstanding. Open to members, guests, and the general public.

Also at the Lodge, the **Beach Club** has the most fabulous view on the peninsula, overlooking Stillwater Cove and the seventeenth hole at Pebble Beach. The Beach Club restaurant is open only for lunch between noon and 2 P.M. Highly recommended, especially for golfers, who will be mesmerized by the view. Open only to members and guests of the Lodge.

Sierra Mar. The Post Ranch Inn. Highway 1 (41 Mile Post), Big Sur, CA 93920. Tel: 800-527-2200 or 408-667-2200. Fax: 408-667-0485. Credit cards accepted.

Ventana Dining Room. Ventana Inn. Highway 1, Big Sur, CA 93920. Tel: 800-628-6500 or 408-667-2331. Fax: 408-667-2287. Credit cards accepted.

Café Fina. 47 Fisherman's Wharf, Monterey, CA 93940. Tel: 408-372-5200. Fax: 408-372-5209. Credit cards accepted.

Club XIX. The Lodge at Pebble Beach, Seventeen Mile Drive, Pebble Beach, CA 93953. Tel: 408-625-8519. Fax: 408-622-8746. Credit cards accepted.

The Beach Club. The Lodge at Pebble Beach, Seventeen Mile Drive, Pebble Beach, CA 93953. Tel: 408-625-8507. Fax: 408-625-8504. Credit cards accepted.

NON-GOLF ACTIVITIES

Another popular activity on the peninsula—after golf, tennis, and spa treatments—is horseback riding at the Pebble Beach Equestrian Center. Outstanding sights in the area include Seventeen Mile Drive, tours of local wineries like Talbott and Château Julien, the award-winning Monterey Bay Aquarium, and the magnificent redwoods in the beautiful state parks just north of Big Sur. There are nearly three hundred boutiques and galleries in Carmel. Perhaps the most interesting is the Weston Gallery, which sells the photographs of Edward and Brett Weston, Ansel Adams, and others.

GETTING THERE: From San Francisco take Highway 101 South to Highway 156 West, which you take to Highway 1 South. From Highway 1 South go to Highway 68 West. On Highway 68 West you will come to an intersection on the off ramp. Stay in the right-hand lane as you go through the intersection. This puts you onto Seventeen Mile Drive. Stay in the left lane and you will come to the Lodge at Pebble Beach.

▶SPANISH BAY

MAGNIFICENCE ON THE MONTEREY PENINSULA

	The Golf	Golf Services	Lodging	Restaurants	Non-Golf Activities	Total
Rating	19	17	19	18	19	92

The Links at Spanish Bay

"Welcome to the greatest resort in America."

This simple yet inspiring greeting, accompanied by a warm smile and a tip of the cap, was recently uttered to us by a friendly ranger at the entrance to the spectacularly beautiful Seventeen Mile Drive on the Monterey Peninsula. Driving through the mist toward the Inn at Spanish Bay, past the mansions and cypress trees, past the stunning golf courses and the herds of deer grazing startlingly close to the roadway, we relished every moment and anticipated even greater pleasures on the immediate horizon.

As the days passed and our visit happily unfolded, we realized that two or three years can bring enormous change to the aspect and ambience of a resort, even one as gorgeous and glittering as the Inn at Spanish Bay. Indeed, that ranger's gracious greeting was just one of many gestures, both large and small, that confirmed the irrefutable fact that the spirit of Spanish Bay has been radically transformed since our last visit.

Back in 1993, when GOLF TRAVEL made its first visit to the Monterey Peninsula, we were far more impressed with the Lodge at Pebble Beach than the Inn at Spanish Bay. At that time the newer Inn at Spanish Bay (built about 1988) seemed to miss the mark in several important categories. While the lodge was truly impeccable, the inn struck us as inwardly flawed, though outwardly handsome. To be specific, certain members of the service staff were indifferent or rude, and the food, although elaborately presented, was only mediocre at best.

As we said earlier, however, what a difference a couple of years can make. The addition of a new and wonderfully upbeat restaurant—Roy's—has vastly improved the culinary scene at the Inn at Spanish Bay. But equally important, the staff is now one of the best and most outgoing we have encountered anywhere. Rarely will even the most sophisticated traveler stay at a resort of this size (270 rooms) and encounter such pleasant personnel from top to bottom. We are happy to report that the old, rather dismal Dunes restaurant is ancient history and the few sourpusses who used to work at Spanish Bay now ply their trade elsewhere.

During our visit to the Inn at Spanish Bay, we yearned *not once* for Pebble Beach. Indeed, we can think of no greater praise than to be just a couple of miles from Pebble Beach and yet not give it even a moment's consideration. The Inn at Spanish Bay is now, in its own right, one of the greatest golf resort destinations in the world. The entire experience can only be described as scintillating.

THE GOLF ⑲

The **Links at Spanish Bay** was designed in 1988 by an unusual and highly gifted triumvirate: Robert Trent Jones, Jr., five-time British Open champion Tom Watson, and former USGA president Sandy Tatum.

While it is true that the Links at Spanish Bay does not have the flat-out majesty of Pebble Beach, it is nonetheless a gorgeous golf course that, like the hotel, has only improved with time.

Spanish Bay is a true links course. Of obvious Scots-Irish descent, the course features sublime ocean views, superb shot values, six fabulous finishing holes, and now a first-rate staff of friendly people whose good spirits seem limitless. In less than a decade, Spanish Bay has matured rapidly. Today it sits naturally ensconced in the landscape's high, white dunes and sand hills, while the course's physical condition, despite the extraordinarily heavy volume of play, is exquisite year-round. As Spanish Bay continues to season, it is likely to become California's answer to Ballybunion or Lahinch. In fact, both Ballybunion and Lahinch offer less than Spanish Bay in at least one important department: however magical, historic, and enchanting these Irish links are, neither has a staggeringly luxurious hotel located just steps from the first tee.

Like all great golf courses, the Links at Spanish Bay takes on more than one distinct personality. The course presents its ocean visage but also assumes a forest character. You begin play on the ocean shore, move into the forest in the middle of the round, and then return to the glorious Pacific for the grand finale. From the blue tees, Spanish Bay can be tough like Ballybunion, while from the white tees it can be fun like Lahinch. When the wind blows, however, your scorecard can explode no matter which tees you fancy. Spanish Bay also sports a prevailing, two-tone color scheme. Like another utterly superb American links—the Ocean Course on Kiawah Island in South Carolina, a former Ryder Cup venue—the Links at Spanish Bay contrasts the brownish gray and green of its fescue fairways against the brilliant white of its sandy dunes. Tom Watson did not want the fairways of Spanish Bay, built on the site of Samuel Morse's old sand quarry, to have that overwatered shade of deep green. "The color of true links," he has said, thinking of Royal Dornoch, Troon, and Hoylake, "is gray, the color of ocean mist and fog."

One of the toughest opening holes on the Monterey Peninsula, the first hole at Spanish Bay brings you immediately into the heart of the linksland. The landing area for your tee shot on this five-hundred-yard par five (461 yards from the white tees, 434 yards from the red tees) is generous enough, but the distant green is tucked away to the right, guarded by bunkers and sandy dunes with hip-high sea grass and prickly ice plants. Your second shot here should be a very conservative play—a definite layup—because many golfers, heading greedily in the general direction of the green with their second shot, end up with balls lost among the sandy dunes on the right, and a lost ball on the very first hole of any round is no great way to begin your game.

Number three is one of several gems on the front nine. A 405-yard par four (334 yards from the whites, 285 yards from the reds), the third doglegs ninety degrees to the left and features a beautiful fairway naturally nestled between high dunes. You have two options for your tee shot on number three. You can play conservatively and hit it short and straight ahead onto the landing area, or you can cut the left corner and hit a blind drive up over the dune and down safely onto the fairway. This second option, if properly executed, will leave you little more than 130 yards from the flag, easily fifty yards ahead of the golfer who selects the former option. On the other hand, if you miss the shot either short or left, you are doomed. The risk/reward ratio on the tee shot of number three, therefore, is just about perfect.

The seventh hole is a 418-yard par four that runs downhill toward the sea and, again, requires strategic thinking on your drive. The fairway on number seven has been described as "an island fairway." It is bisected by a wasteland approximately 225 yards from the tee. Any drive over 225 yards will likely result in another lost ball and a one-stroke penalty.

Number eight, a terrific par three, is just 163 yards long (148 yards from the whites, 120 yards from the reds), yet it is all carry over a waste area and into strong prevailing winds. When the wind is up, three is an extraordinarily good score here.

The Links at Spanish Bay becomes even more exciting on the back nine, particularly its sequence of six final holes. Tiny number thirteen, just ninety-nine yards long from the white markers, is a copy of the Postage Stamp at Troon and appears at least equally dangerous. But birdie is a distinct possibility on thirteen if you can land the ball softly on the flat plateau green. The fourteenth is an absolutely glorious, 571-yard par five that plunges straight down to the sea; its wide, undulating fairway is surrounded by shaggy, windswept wilderness. Fifteen requires a long and accurate drive over a large waste area directly into the wind, while at sixteen, 200-yard par three, you turn around and play with the mighty wind at your back. Seventeen, which extends along the edge of the Pacific Ocean for its entire length, reverses directions once more. You must play into the wind on this raw and rugged 414-yard par four, where a driver and well-struck fairway wood may still leave you as much as a hundred yards short of the green. Number eighteen is a 571-yard par five that features two more "island fairways," one to receive your tee shot and the other to gather your second shot, inevitably hit with another wood. These fairway collection zones along eighteen are surrounded by impenetrable marshland hazards. This final sequence of holes at Spanish Bay—exposed as they are to the full force of the wild ocean winds—will leave you ruddy-cheeked and invigorated, like a day spent sailing off the coast of Maine.

The Links at Spanish Bay measures 6,820 yards from the back tees (par rating 74.6/slope rating 142), 6,078 yards from the middle tees (par rating 72.1/slope rating 133), and 5,309 yards from the forward tees (par rating 70.6/slope rating 129). Including cart, the greens fee is $160 for resort guests and $190 for public play.

In addition to the Links at Spanish Bay, the Pebble Beach Company owns and operates the Pebble Beach Golf Links ($235 for resort guests, $320 for nonguests), Spyglass Hill ($180 for resort guests, $200 for nonguests), and the venerable Del Monte Course ($85 per round) in Monterey, designed in 1897, making it the oldest course in the United States west of the Mississippi River.

Chances are you wouldn't expect to come across two fine golf courses on an abandoned military base, but that is precisely what we found just twenty minutes north of Spanish Bay at **Fort Ord.** Decommissioned in June 1995, the vast, 25,000-acre Fort Ord army base now has the air of a ghost town, despite the fact that a branch of the California State University system recently took over several large buildings at the base. Ford Ord's Bayonet and Black Horse courses, both of which have always been open to the public even though they were originally established for base personnel, make this a delightful oasis of golf. The Bayonet Course was designed by General Robert McClure, a left-hander whose southpaw bias led to the Bayonet Course being one of the first championship courses ever built for the right-to-left ball striker.

The **Bayonet Course** (par 72, 6,982 yards, par rating 74.2/slope rating 138) dates from 1953 and is the better of the two layouts. It is long and very tight, with forests of pine and oak always threatening from both sides of the fairway. The Bayonet Course has been a favorite of golfing insiders on the Monterey Peninsula for many years. The **Black Horse Course,** built in 1963, is shorter and considerably easier (par 72, 6,396 yards/par rating 71.3/slope rating 128).

When we visited Fort Ord, both the Bayonet and the Black Horse courses were suffering from the signs of neglect occasioned by the uncertain future of this very valuable piece of real estate. The courses were maintained by only a skeleton crew of greenskeepers, conditions were shaggy and overgrown, and the golf club had been without a resident golf professional for three years. All that will change now that the BSL Golf Corporation has taken over the Fort Ord Courses. The new management has already hired a professional, and a thorough renovation of the course and clubhouse are scheduled for completion by late 1997. The greens fee will likely remain at about $50 per round, one of the lowest in the region. For tee times call 408-899-7271.

The Links at Spanish Bay. 2700 Seventeen Mile Drive, Pebble Beach, CA 93953. Tel: 800-654-9300 or 408-647-7500. Fax: 408-644-7956. Credit cards accepted.

• 1987. Designers: Robert Trent Jones, Jr., Tom Watson, Sandy Tatum. Par 72. 6,820 yards. 74.6 par rating. 142 slope rating. Greens fees: $150 (resort guests), $175 (public). Resort guest fee includes cart. Walking permitted. Caddies and carts available. Season: year-round.

Fort Ord Golf Courses. 1 McClure Way, Seaside, CA 93955. Tel: 408-899-7271 or 408-899-2351. Fax: 408-899-7169. Credit cards accepted.

• *Bayonet Course.* 1953. Designer: General Robert McClure, Par 72. 6,982 yards. 74.2 par rating. 138 slope rating. Greens fees: $45 (Monday–Thursday), $50 (Friday), $60 (weekends). Walking permitted. No caddies. Carts available. Season: year-round.

• *Black Horse Course.* 1963. Designers: Fort Ord base personnel. Par 72. 6,396 yards. 71.3 par rating. 128 slope rating. Greens fees: $35 (Monday–Thursday), $40 (Friday), $50 (weekends). Walking permitted. No caddies. Carts available. Season: year-round.

GOLF SERVICES 17

The Links at Spanish Bay has a large, beautiful, well-stocked pro shop and, as noted above, a staff of friendly employees that makes an enormous effort to satisfy its golfing clients on every score. The Pebble Beach Company also operates perhaps the finest caddie program of any golf resort in America. The Links at Spanish Bay, like the Pebble Beach course, is best appreciated on foot rather than from the cart path, while caddies, earning $40 per bag and a $10 to $15 tip, truly enhance your experience. The only caveat? The Links at Spanish Bay does not have a practice range.

LODGING 19

Guest rooms at the **Inn at Spanish Bay** are spacious, well designed, stunningly handsome, and exquisitely appointed with large baths, blond woods, gas-lit fireplaces, and terraces overlooking the ocean or the forest. In an attempt to differentiate the Inn from the Lodge at Pebble Beach, GOLF TRAVEL once reported that "the Lodge at Pebble Beach is for the CEOs, while the Inn at Spanish Bay is for the Senior VPs," yet this statement no longer applies. While it is true that Spanish Bay has a less subdued atmosphere and attracts more business groups wearing name tags than Pebble Beach, we must say that the Inn at Spanish Bay now takes a backseat to no one.

Inn at Spanish Bay. 2700 Seventeen Mile Drive, Pebble Beach, CA 93953. Tel: 800-654-9300 or 408-647-7500. Fax: 408-644-7955. 275 rooms and suites. Doubles from $285 to $400. Credit cards accepted.

R E S T A U R A N T S

On the culinary front, the big story at Spanish Bay is **Roy's,** chef Roy Ya-maguchi's energized, friendly, and bright restaurant with spectacular ocean views and an imaginative cuisine that joyously combines Asian and European influences. Roy's busy pace and vibrant, informal atmosphere (jeans are okay here) is in perfect harmony with the casual grace of the Inn at Spanish Bay. Specialties at Roy's include Pacific yellowtail tuna; Szechuan-style baby back ribs; ravioli of shittake, spinach, and ricotta; crispy calamari salad; and eggplant pizza grilled in a wood-burning oven. Located just off the hotel lobby, Roy's is open for breakfast, lunch, and dinner. Approximately $100 for two at dinner, wine and tip included.

The **Bay Club** is the most elegant dining room (no jeans allowed) at the Inn, and it, too, is much improved since our last visit, with better, more consistent cooking and more attentive and professional service. Our dinner in the handsome Bay Club included an excellent fillet of foie gras followed by a good rack of lamb. The Club has an extensive wine list. Several nights a week a harpist plays during dinner. Dinner for two here can be a very romantic occasion and, with wine and tip, costs approximately $140.

Serving only breakfast and lunch, the **Clubhouse Bar & Grill,** located next to the Spanish Bay pro shop, is ideal for a bite to eat before or after your round of golf. **Traps,** the Inn's comfortable sports bar, offers thirty-eight different single malts, which is excellent news for connoisseurs of Scotch whiskey.

Restaurants at the Inn at Spanish Bay. 2700 Seventeen Mile Drive, Pebble Beach, CA 93953. Tel: 408-647-7500 (general operator), 408-647-7441 (Roy's), 408-647-7433 (Bay Club), or 408-647-7470 (Clubhouse Bar & Grill). Fax: 408-644-7955. Credit cards accepted.

N O N - G O L F   A C T I V I T I E S

The range of activities for the non-golfer in the Monterey Peninsula region is truly exceptional. The Inn at Spanish Bay operates a wonderful spa with heated outdoor swimming pool, weight room, and innovative, low-impact exercise classes. The Pebble Beach Company also has a world-class equestrian center. The *must* sights and activities just beyond the resort complex include the spectacular Monterey Bay Aquarium—one of the finest aquariums in the world—located on Cannery Row in Monterey; shopping and strolling along the charming, gallery-filled streets of Carmel; taking a photograph of the Lone Cypress on Seventeen Mile Drive; and driving fifty minutes south to commune with the towering redwoods in the Julia Pheiffer State Park in Big Sur. The wineries of Monterey County in the Carmel Valley area have earned an outstanding reputation, and many of the best—like Talbott, Chalone, and Château Julien—are open to the public.

GETTING THERE: From San Francisco take 101 S about an hour and a half to 156 West to Monterey Peninsula. 156 West turns into Highway 1. Follow Highway 1 South through Monterey to Highway 68 West. Turn right, follow 68 West to the second streetlight. Turn left onto Samuel Morse Drive, proceed to Pebble Beach Resort gates for instructions.

▶PELICAN HILL AND AVIARA

TWO NEW BEAUTIES IN SOUTHERN CALIFORNIA

	The Golf	Golf Services	Lodging	Restaurants	Non-Golf Activities	Total
Rating	18	17	18	16	16	85

Aviara

If the region between San Francisco and San Jose is known as Silicon Valley, then the region between Los Angeles and San Diego can be called the Cavity-Back Coast, for it is the high-tech golf club center of the universe. Not far from the famous La Costa golf resort, the glistening industrial parks around Carlsbad are home to the always humming manufacturing facilities of Callaway, Taylor-Made, Founder's Cup, and Cobra, all among the most profitable companies in America today. Unlike other golfing venues, a morning round in this area may be complemented with an unusual afternoon activity: a tour of your favorite golf club factory, and, if you happen to be a shareholder, the chance to examine your investment firsthand.

There is a distinct relationship between the newly minted golf equipment and the newly constructed golf courses in this particular stretch of Southern California. The golf courses, in fact, appear to have been built in direct response to the outlandish new technology. Titanium drivers may provide ten or fifteen additional yards off the tee, and Cobra's oversized irons promise greater accuracy, yet you're still going to need every bit of length and accuracy you can muster in order to clear the precipitous canyons and stay in the narrow fairways at Pelican Hill. Aldila, the graphite shaft manufacturer, uses a dramatically foreshortened photograph of an intimidating canyon at Pelican Hill in its advertising campaign. Conventional weaponry, the ad implies, will not suffice at the longer, tighter, more perilous golf courses now making the scene around America.

About forty-five minutes apart by car, Pelican Hill and Aviara represent two sides of the California dream for the 1990s. Both golf courses were designed as the centerpieces for splendid residential communities intended to include luxury hotels and multimillion-dollar homes. Pelican Hill has thrived—it now has two Tom Fazio courses—but parts of the Aviara community got caught in the riptide of California's real estate and construction downturn. The Aviara golf course and its incredibly lavish clubhouse were indeed completed on time, and both are gorgeous; yet residential lots remained unsold and the Four Seasons hotel stood half-complete on a hillside for a full two years, looking like an eerie concrete shell standing sentinel over the golf course. Construction resumed when the California economy rebounded, and now the Four Seasons Aviara is slated to open in the summer of 1997 with 331 rooms. "Aviara," by the way, is one of those only-in-California words. It was the ill-fated developer's original rendering of "aviary." Aviara is located in Carlsbad and is actually within sight of the La Costa resort. Pelican Hill is further up the coast in super-swank Newport Beach.

THE GOLF

The Arnold Palmer/Ed Seay course at **Aviara** is a beauty. Built around an inland waterway called Batiquitos Lagoon, the course measures 7,007 yards from the back tees and carries a slope rating of 137 and an equally intimidating par rating of 74.2. Many of these strokes will pile up on the greens. Aviara is plenty generous from tee to green—the ample fairways do not overly penalize poor shots—but the greens have extraordinary pitch. You will not find a straight putt on this golf course from more than a foot or two out. The back nine is especially pretty. A huge double green serves both the twelfth and fifteenth holes, and the fourteenth is a lovely, 201-yard par three over water from an elevated tee. Other tees shorten the course to 6,591 yards, 6,054 yards, and 5,007 yards. The weekday greens fee, which includes cart, is $110. The Four Seasons clubhouse at Aviara is one of the most elaborate and exquisite we have ever seen. Lined in marble and walnut, the men's locker room even comes equipped with an antique chess set. We can't imagine anyone actually taking the time here for a game of chess, but the set certainly adds to the ambience. The clubhouse also has a very fine restaurant and pro shop.

As good as Aviara is, **Pelican Hill** is even better. With its two Fazio courses—the original Ocean Course (now called Ocean South) and the links-style Ocean North Course—plus a splendid, newly completed, Spanish-style clubhouse, Pelican Hill bills itself as Southern California's answer to Pebble Beach. Both courses at Pelican Hill display Fazio's environmental sensitivity, both showcase views of the Pacific, and both require exhilarating canyon crossings off the tee. This said, of Pelican Hill's two courses, the Ocean Course will doubtless leave you with more indelible memories.

The **Ocean South Course** winds its way through dramatic canyons that Fazio, in characteristic fashion, has utilized as hazards. The course opens uneventfully enough with four fairly straightforward golf holes. However, the fifth and sixth require big drives over deep canyons in order

Ocean Course, Pelican Hill

to reach the fairway. Eleven through fourteen comprise a particularly remarkable sequence of holes. After crossing under the Pacific Coast Highway, the gorgeous eleventh hole runs all the way down to the sea. Then come Pelican Hill's two best-known holes, twelve and thirteen, the back-to-back par threes that overlook the ocean and provide superb views of Catalina Island in the distance. The fourteenth is a handsome, 541-yard par five that heads inland and away from the sea. The sixteenth is another tough and scenic par three (220 yards) that requires a drive over a menacing canyon. Eighteen, however, is the most wonderful and difficult of all at Pelican Hill; a 442-yard dogleg-left, the eighteenth requires two canyon crossings, one from the elevated tee and the second on your approach shot. There are four sets of tees at Pelican Hill. From the tips, Ocean South measures 6,634 yards (72.1 par/130 slope), but it can play as short as 5,240 yards.

The **Ocean North Course,** formerly known as the Links Course, is elevated in a canyon and presents spectacular panoramic views of the ocean on every hole. Without much greenery at all, this course is still a scenic treat. Water comes into play on just two holes, although many holes require forced carries over ravines.

Aviara Golf Club. 7447 Batiquitos Drive, Carlsbad, CA 92009. Tel: 619-929-0077. Fax: 619-438-5372. Credit cards accepted.

• 1991. Designers: Arnold Palmer, Ed Seay. Par 72. 7,007 yards. 74.2 par rating. 137 slope rating. Greens fees: $110 weekday, $130 weekend. After 3 P.M.: $70, cart included. No walking. No caddies. Season: year-round.

Pelican Hill Golf Club. 22651 Pelican Hill Road, Newport Coast, CA 92657. Tel: 714-760-0707. Fax: 714-640-0855. Credit cards accepted.

• *Ocean South Course.* 1991. Designer: Tom Fazio. Par 70. 6,634 yards. 72.1 par rating. 130 slope rating.
• *Ocean North Course.* 1992. Designer: Tom Fazio. Par 71. 6,856 yards. 73.6 par rating. 136 slope rating.
• Greens fees: by advance reservation (seven to fourteen days): $140 (Monday and Tuesday), $160 (Wednesday and Thursday), $175 Friday through Sunday, cart included. Greens fees are $20 less when reservations are made up to six days in advance. No walking. No caddies. Season: year-round.

GOLF SERVICES

Golf services at both Aviara and Pelican Hill are excellent. At both courses you will find outstanding locker rooms, polite employees, and good practice areas. We were delighted with the high-tech—and very accurate—range finders installed on the carts at Pelican Hill. The range finders measure the distance between your ball and the pin and print it out on a small digital display in the cart.

LODGING 18

We recommend with confidence two magnificent hotels within easy driving distance of Aviara and Pelican Hill. Both are far more intriguing hotel options than the frequently inconsistent La Costa resort in Carlsbad. The fabulous Ritz-Carlton at Laguna Niguel is the perfect base for a visit to Aviara, and the stylish Four Seasons Newport Beach is ideally situated for your round of golf at Pelican Hill.

The **Ritz-Carlton at Laguna Niguel** caused a sensation when it opened in 1984. Today, however, it is better run and better looking than ever. Located on a 150-foot bluff above the Pacific, this elegant and bright Mediterranean-style hotel has a stunning view of the California coast, spectacular public rooms looking out to the sea, wonderful service, and beautifully furnished guest rooms. We stayed in number 3518, a spacious ocean-view room with private balcony, furniture covered in fine chintz, and a marble bath. Amenities at the Ritz-Carlton include two heated swimming pools and a fully equipped fitness center. Double room rates range from $275 to $595.

The **Four Seasons Newport Beach** is situated in a twenty-story tower in Fashion Island, one of the most elegant shopping centers in Southern California with a Neiman Marcus, a Hard Rock Cafe, more than two hundred boutiques, and a parking lot filled with Ferraris and Range Rovers. The Four Seasons' guest rooms, decorated in tones of pale beige and rose, are absolutely stunning. We stayed in a standard room, number 1615, which we found spacious and luxurious. There is a lovely swimming pool and fitness center. Pelican Hill golf packages are available. Double rooms range from $295 to $340.

The Ritz-Carlton at Laguna Niguel. One Ritz-Carlton Drive, Dana Point, CA 92629. Tel: 800-241-3333 or 714-240-2000. Fax: 714-240-0829. 393 rooms and suites. Double rooms range from $275 to $595. Credit cards accepted.

Four Seasons Newport Beach. 690 Newport Centre Drive, Newport Beach, CA 92660. Tel: 800-332-3442 or 714-759-0808. Fax: 714-759-0568. 285 rooms and suites. Doubles from $295 to $340. Credit cards accepted.

RESTAURANTS

The remarkably luxurious **clubhouses** at both Aviara and Pelican Hill serve outstanding breakfasts and lunches. Dinner should be taken at the suggested hotels. At the Ritz-Carlton you may choose between the formal and quite expensive **Dining Room** (about $165 for two with wine and tip) and the slightly less formal **Club Grill and Bar** (approximately $140 for two at dinner). Jackets are required in the Dining Room, where, in addition to the à la carte menu, two prix fixe menus are offered at $65 (without wine) and $105 (with wine). Most diners opt for the prix fixe menu because it is a great way to sample the restaurant's innovative French cuisine. Wine connoisseurs especially will also enjoy the Dining Room's wine list, which offers more than 350 different wines. The Club Grill and Bar serves classic American cuisine, with entrées such as prime rib, lobster, and a variety of fish.

At the Four Seasons Newport Beach be certain to have dinner in the **Pavilion,** which presents inventive California cuisine in an elegant setting. Entrées cost $15 to $30. The Pavilion, which requires a coat and a tie, is the hotel's more formal dining option, while the **Gardens Café and Lounge** serves simple salads, pastas, burgers, and pizza.

The restaurants at the Ritz-Carlton Laguna Niguel. One Ritz-Carlton Drive, Dana Point, CA 92629. Tel: 714-240-5008. Fax: 714-240-5054. Credit cards accepted.

The restaurants at the Four Seasons Newport Beach. 690 Newport Centre Drive, Newport Beach, CA 92660. Tel: 714-760-4920 (The Pavilion). Tel: 714-760-4342 (The Gardens Café). Fax: 714-759-0568. Credit cards accepted.

NON-GOLF ACTIVITIES

Eight thousand Great Big Berthas are assembled daily in the busy Callaway plant in Carlsbad, where three shifts of six hundred employees work around the clock in a vain effort to keep up with worldwide demand. The company has grown 150 percent a year, a growth rate that even Eli Callaway says cannot be sustained forever. Tours are offered Monday through Friday. Call Jill Schultz at Callaway for information: 619-931-1771.

Other non-golf activities in the area include tennis, swimming, and spa facilities at the hotels, plus superb shopping at Laguna Beach and Fashion Island in Newport.

GETTING THERE: To get to the Ritz-Carlton from John Wayne Airport take the 405 S, which becomes Highway 5. Exit at Crown Valley, turn right, and proceed eight miles. At the Pacific Coast Highway take a left. Drive one more mile farther to Ritz-Carlton Drive.

►TORREY PINES AND RANCHO SANTA FE

AN INSIDE LOOK

	The Golf	Golf Services	Lodging	Restaurants	Non-Golf Activities	Total
Rating	**18**	**16**	**18**	**17**	**19**	**88**

Golfers who wish to combine fine food, luxurious accommodations, and California hedonism with their golf are certain to find the La Jolla–Rancho Santa Fe area a rewarding destination. Torrey Pines, one of the great municipal golf facilities in the United States and home of the PGA Tour's Buick San Diego Open, is located just outside La Jolla, while Rancho Santa Fe is set in the hills seven miles from the coast in an enormous grove of eucalyptus trees that are always buzzing with hummingbirds.

La Jolla and Rancho Santa Fe have common demographics. Perhaps it is just our imagination—or susceptibility to California glamour—but it seems that everyone in both communities is tanned, good looking, and impeccably dressed and drives a Jaguar. The shops, services, and diversions of La Jolla and Rancho Santa Fe cater to the most elegant and sophisticated of tastes.

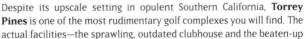

THE GOLF ————————————————— (18)

Despite its upscale setting in opulent Southern California, **Torrey Pines** is one of the most rudimentary golf complexes you will find. The actual facilities—the sprawling, outdated clubhouse and the beaten-up practice range—are among the most basic of any stop on the professional tour. Touring pros, in fact, rank Torrey Pines quite low among the places they visit, but this is due to the humble facilities rather than the courses themselves. Located in La Jolla but owned and run by the city of San Diego, Torrey Pines is a true public-use establishment. Your fellow golfer here is not apt to have a private club affiliation, or dress in the latest Ralph Lauren attire, or unload his or her bag from the back of a new Range Rover. With great ocean holes on both its South and North courses, Torrey Pines has been called "the poor man's Pebble Beach." But it is really a democratic Pebble Beach, where everyone plays because everyone can afford it. Torrey Pines is friendly and extremely likable. American golf may need only a limited number of additional resort courses with $175 greens fees, but it certainly needs more places like Torrey Pines. Getting on the course, however, can be a major problem, particularly if you do not know the ropes. Because Torrey Pines is so good and so inexpensive (city residents pay just $20 per round; nonresidents pay $50), available tee times are few and far between and the crowd outside the starter's shed is always fifteen or twenty players deep.

The real trick at Torrey Pines is knowing about its Golf Playing Package, which includes a preferred starting time, eighteen holes on either course, golf cart, and the assistance of one of the Torrey Pines golf professionals who actually accompanies your group for the first three holes. The cost is a modest $85 ($100 on weekends). Our Torrey Pines pro was an extremely pleasant and easygoing guy who provided course history and instructional tips for every golfer in our foursome, along with advice about yardage, breaks in the greens, and local rules. Playing with a pro is always a great experience, and ours did everything but carry our bag. Plan to take advantage of the golf package on all of your rounds at Torrey Pines because it is the only way to assure yourself of access to the courses. Reservations for the Golf Playing Package can be made up to four to eight weeks in advance by calling 800-985-GOLF (800-985-4653).

The **South Course** is the better course. It is longer, more challenging, and more scenic than the North Course (7,055 yards versus 6,647 yards). The final round of the San Diego Open is always played on the stiffer South, which features enchanting groves of windblown pines, romantic gullies, and panoramic vistas. The one unattractive spot on the course is the left side of the ninth and tenth fairways, where a number of modern office buildings and a large Sheraton hotel predominate.

The third hole on the South Course mirrors famous number seven at Pebble Beach; it is a short par three from an elevated tee down to the green and the sea beyond. The fourth, the course's number-one handicap hole, runs alongside the ocean for its entire length of 453 yards. But the most stunning sequence of holes are numbers eleven through thirteen. The eleventh is a 207-yard par three with wonderful ocean views, the gorgeous twelfth (456 yards) plays slightly uphill from a wide-open fairway to an elevated green, and the thirteenth (535 yards) heads back in the opposite direction and has a deep gully guarding the front of the green. These holes constitute the course's true heart. We played Torrey Pines two weeks before the San Diego Open, and both courses were in excellent condition.

Guests of the Inn at Rancho Santa Fe (reviewed below) have access to the historic, exclusive **Rancho Santa Fe Golf Club** after 12 P.M. Built in 1927 and the host of the Bing Crosby Pro-Am from 1937 to 1941, the Rancho Santa Fe Golf Club is located just two blocks from the center of a charming village. The course was in poor condition during our visit—several fairways were ripped up for drainage and irrigation work—yet this is an elegant older course surrounded by mature eucalyptus trees, magnificent private homes, and trails for horseback riding. The back nine, which ascends the hills, is particularly pretty. Numbers thirteen and sixteen have been called two of the finest golf holes in Southern California. Aside from its affiliation with the inn, the Rancho Santa Fe Golf Club is strictly private. It has an attractive clubhouse and grill (serving breakfast, lunch, and dinner), a nicely equipped pro shop, a decent practice area, and a pleasant staff accustomed to meeting the demands of an upscale membership.

Torrey Pines Municipal Golf Course. 11480 North Torrey Pines Road, La Jolla, CA 92037. Tel: 800-985-GOLF (800-985-4653), 619-570-1234 (golf reservations), or 619-452-3226 (pro shop). Fax: 619-558-1808. Credit cards accepted.

- 1957. Designer: William F. Bell, Jr.
- *South Course.* Par 72. 7,055 yards. 74.6 par rating. 136 slope rating.
- *North Course.* Par 72. 6,647 yards. 72.1 par rating. 129 slope rating.
- Greens fees: $50 (nonresidents). Golf Playing Package: $85 (Monday–Thursday) and $100 (Friday–Sunday). Walking permitted. No caddies. Carts available. Season: year-round.

Rancho Santa Fe Golf Club. 5827 Via de la Cumbre, Rancho Santa Fe, CA 92067. Tel: 619-756-3094. Fax: 619-756-0982. Credit cards accepted.

- 1927. Designer: Max Behr. Par 72. 6,911 yards. 74.3 par rating. 137 slope rating. Greens fees: $100, includes cart. Restrictions: no public play other than for guests of the Inn at Rancho Santa Fe, as arranged by the Inn. No play before noon. Walking permitted. No caddies. Season: year-round.

GOLF SERVICES

16

Golf services at Torrey Pines are inconsistent. On the one hand, it has fine personnel and its innovative Golf Playing Package, but at the same time it makes do with a worn-out clubhouse and barely adequate range. But did these facilities really have a negative impact on our day? Not at all. Torrey Pines has real character, and its quirks simply add to the flavor of the place.

LODGING

18

Visitors to the Rancho Santa Fe/La Jolla area have three distinctive hotel options. The **Inn at Rancho Santa Fe** was built in 1923 by the Santa Fe Railroad, which planted 3 million eucalyptus trees in the area to be used as railway ties. It did not take long to discover that the trees were too soft to support a train's weight, but they were left to flourish and become the symbol of this very refined, low-profile community. Residents of Rancho Santa Fe—like the residents of Malibu—are obsessive about privacy.

Owned by the Royce family since 1958, the inn is located in the center of town and is surrounded by twenty acres of lush gardens, a beautiful croquet lawn, three tennis courts, and a small swimming pool. The actual accommodations consist of a number of small cottages with red-tile roofs that are spread out among the gardens. The Inn maintains a beach house at Del Mar for day use by guests and employs massage therapists.

Although the food at the Inn is quite dull (have no fear, there are two superb restaurants in town), the service is attentive, the decor is classic, and the guest rooms are more than comfortable. We were bumped up from a standard room to cottage number 61-62, which has one bedroom, an enormous living room with wood-burning fireplace, two bathrooms, a fully equipped kitchen, and a screened porch—a very attractive arrangement.

La Valencia Hotel is a romantic and stunningly refurbished historic hotel located on Prospect Street amid La Jolla's finest shops, galleries, and restaurants and overlooks Scripps Park, breathtaking Boomer Beach, and the Pacific Ocean. The lobby, which extends from the street entrance back to the sitting area overlooking the pool and ocean, is very lovely. An ocean-view room here is a must. La Valencia is highly recommended.

The Hyatt Regency has built some remarkable hotels in recent years, but none is more remarkable than the new **Hyatt Regency La Jolla,** designed by acclaimed architect Michael Graves. This stunning (and almost all marble), four-hundred-room hotel looks like a Greek temple on the inside and is linked to a 32,000-square-foot health spa. Rooms on the upper floors provide spectacular views of La Jolla and the Pacific. The Hyatt's only downside is its location in the Aventine complex, about eight minutes from the sights and shops of Prospect Street. Here, unlike at La Valencia or the Inn, you have to get in your car if you want to go anywhere.

The Inn at Rancho Santa Fe. PO Box 869, Rancho Santa Fe, CA 92067. Tel: 800-654-2928 or 619-756-1131. Fax: 619-759-1604. 104 rooms and cottages. Double rooms range from $100 to $200; cottages from $325 to $600. Credit cards accepted.

La Valencia Hotel. 1132 Prospect Street, La Jolla, CA 92037. Tel: 800-451-0772 or 619-454-0771. Fax: 619-456-3921. 100 rooms and suites. Doubles from $180 to $385. Credit cards accepted.

Hyatt Regency La Jolla. 3777 La Jolla Village Drive, La Jolla, CA 92122. Tel: 800-233-1234 or 619-552-1234. Fax: 619-552-6066. 400 rooms and suites. Doubles from $129 to $200. Credit cards accepted.

RESTAURANTS

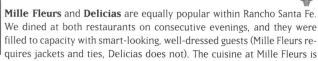

Mille Fleurs and **Delicias** are equally popular within Rancho Santa Fe. We dined at both restaurants on consecutive evenings, and they were filled to capacity with smart-looking, well-dressed guests (Mille Fleurs requires jackets and ties, Delicias does not). The cuisine at Mille Fleurs is classically French: foie gras, smoked salmon, sea bass *en croûte*, venison, squab, rabbit, excellent desserts, and a very good wine list. The chef at Delicias, however, formerly worked for Wolfgang Puck at Spago; hence, the menu here is much more Californian. Our dinner at Delicias included a good green salad, a crispy roasted duck, and an enormous piece of incredibly rich chocolate cake. Although expensive, both restaurants are very handsome and have attentive service. A complete dinner for two with wine and tip at Mille Fleurs or Delicias costs approximately $140. On beautiful Prospect Street in La Jolla, **George's at the Cove** directly overlooks the Pacific. Be certain when booking to request an ocean-view table. A more formal dining room is located on the first floor, while the restaurant's two top levels offer casual, outdoor dining terraces. Head to one of these terraces for lunch after your round at Torrey Pines. The restaurant specializes in seafood, but you can also get great salads, pastas, selections from the grill, and sandwiches. In addition, George's offers excellent wines by the glass, and prompt, friendly service.

Mille Fleurs. 6009 Paseo Delicias, Rancho Santa Fe, CA 92067. Tel: 619-756-3085. Fax: 619-756-9945. Credit cards accepted.

Delicias. 6106 Paseo Delicias, Rancho Santa Fe, CA 92067. Tel: 619-756-8000. Fax: 619-759-1759. Credit cards accepted.

George's at the Cove. 1250 Prospect Street, La Jolla, CA 92037. Tel: 619-454-4244. Fax: 619-454-5458. Credit cards accepted.

NON-GOLF ACTIVITIES

After shopping in La Jolla and Rancho Santa Fe, head into San Diego, where there are a number of wonderful attractions for the entire family. Sea World, the San Diego Zoo, the San Diego Wild Animal Park, boat tours of San Diego harbor, and a visit to Old Town San Diego are the most popular. The best beach for swimming and snorkeling in the area is the La Jolla Cove and Underwater Marine Reserve. The thoroughbred racing season at Del Mar extends from late July through mid-September.

GETTING THERE: To get to the Inn at Rancho Santa Fe from Interstate 5 (San Diego Freeway) take the Lomas Santa Fe Drive exit (S-8). The Inn is four miles to the east on this route.

▶PALM SPRINGS

LA QUINTA AND PGA WEST

	The Golf	Golf Services	Lodging	Restaurants	Non-Golf Activities	Total
Rating	18	17	17	17	17	**86**

PGA West

During America's exuberant post–World War II boom, Miami Beach and Palm Springs emerged as the nation's most popular East and West Coast winter getaways. Yet while Miami's Art Deco South Beach quarter has been revitalized by the young and the stylish, Palm Springs remains a more undiluted retirement community. Retro in their own unique way, notable towns in Palm Springs are filled with streets named after the big icons of another era: Fred Waring, Lawrence Welk, Dinah Shore, Gene Autry, Dwight Eisenhower, Frank Sinatra, and Bob Hope surely have more of the area's roads, boulevards, and cul-de-sacs named after them than probably anyone else. In short, the region is largely influenced by a vast and active senior population, many of whom love to golf and play day after day at the impressive golf venues throughout the area!

In fact, with more than eighty golf courses, Palm Springs has to be considered one of the more important golf destinations in America. GOLF TRAVEL's advice to golfers headed to the region for a top-quality holiday is to bypass the hotels and courses in the central Coachella Valley and head directly for the far superior facilities—better golf courses, better accommodations, and better restaurants—at the La Quinta resort and PGA West. La Quinta and PGA West are just forty-five minutes east of downtown Palm Springs, and their level of excellence is at least a notch or two higher in every significant category than all other golf courses in the Palm Springs area.

First, La Quinta, founded in 1926, is the only hotel in the Palm Springs area that still speaks of old Mexico and retains the true glamour and sophistication of the California desert. Other hotels in the region simply do not have La Quinta's flavor and history. The script for *Lost Horizon* was written in one of La Quinta's casitas, and Errol Flynn, Bette Davis, and Dick Powell were regular visitors in the 1920s and '30s. In addition the golfing options are among the most challenging in America, and, finally, the choices of restaurants and non-golfing activities are excellent.

THE GOLF ⛳ 18

La Quinta and PGA West—ten minutes apart by car—have eight golf courses between them. There are two courses on the **La Quinta** resort property—the public Dunes and Mountain courses; the Citrus Course, now private, stands off by itself. Then there are five more courses at **PGA West:** the Stadium Course, two Jack Nicklaus courses, an Arnold Palmer layout, and a new course by Tom Weiskopf, completed in 1996. Four of the eight existing courses are open to La Quinta hotel guests: the Mountain and Dunes courses at La Quinta and the Stadium Course and the Nicklaus Tournament Course at PGA West.

Although the greens fees are high—ranging up to $165 to play on the Dunes Course and $230 on the Mountain Course at La Quinta and $235 for a round in high season on the Stadium Course—this collection of courses is by far the best in the California desert.

Let's begin with the most difficult: the sadomasochistic **Stadium Course** (Dye is the sadist; you are the masochist). PGA West is almost a mirror image of the enormous TPC complex at Sawgrass. Both have valet parking, a huge and luxurious clubhouse, a couple of playable "normal" golf courses, and a "stadium" course that is fully guaranteed to whip and humiliate you. Three of the toughest golf courses we have ever played in the United States are all Dye designs. They include the Ocean Course at Kiawah, the Stadium Course at PGA West, and the Stadium Course at Sawgrass, in that order.

The Stadium Course at PGA West is visually stunning, with spectacular mountain views and an odd "Dye-scape" of huge mounds, bunkers extending the entire length of the fairway (water frequently borders the other side), and one bunker on the sixteenth hole that is nineteen feet deep. One golfer in our foursome looked as if he were going to finish with a score near his handicap until he landed in that bunker

Stadium Course, PGA West

on sixteen and never got out. Every golfer in our group played over the green from one deep bunker to another at least once. The front side is manageable enough; holes one through four provide a moderate initiation. But then you hit number five, called *Double Trouble,* with a drive and second shot over two lakes. The par three sixth measures 223 yards over water and is almost all carry. Then at seven you have to carry the same lake coming back. It is a great stretch of golf.

If you have not scored well on the front side, you might as well head for the clubhouse bar. Number eleven, *Eternity,* is almost unfair. Your drive on this uphill 593-yarder must carry at least two hundred yards over a wash to a tiny landing area, but there is a big bunker on the left and ball-eating bushes on the right. If you land in the moat bunker guarding the green on twelve, you have our deepest condolences. Like the bunker on sixteen, you need to use the staircase to get to the bottom. And thirteen, which resembles number six, is a 198-yard par three almost entirely over water. Sixteen through eighteen, however, are easily the meanest holes on the course. Sixteen is called *San Andreas Fault* because of its nineteen-foot bunker, seventeen features the famous TPC island green, and eighteen requires a 175-yard water carry with your tee shot, and the water remains a hazard all the way home. Our foursome was too tired even to talk to each other after the game. The best player in our group, a seven handicap, scored 102. From the blue tees the Stadium Course measures 6,753 yards and carries a par rating of 73.0 and a 142 slope. The course measures five hundred yards longer from the tournament tees!

The **Nicklaus Tournament Course**—the second course at PGA West—is a much more straightforward layout, although it still poses plenty of challenge. This attractive 6,546-yard (from the championship tees) test plays over five lakes and has a St. Andrews–style double green serving the ninth and eighteenth holes.

Pete Dye's **Mountain Course** at La Quinta opened for play in 1980, but only recently has it been open to public play. The course is located on the immediate resort property and may be reached by shuttle or, if you've stored your clubs at the course, by a rousing ten-minute walk. Nine of the holes run right up against the mountains, making the Mountain Course an aesthetic treat. The tall grass beyond the fairways will bring your thoughts back to more mundane issues—like finding your ball on all your errant shots.

The **Dunes Course** is the sister course to the Mountain Course, and they share a clubhouse. The Dunes is another Dye design, yet it is one of the easier layouts in the area. The Dunes Course features a variety of sand and grass bunkers, a number of small lakes lined with railroad ties, and slightly elevated greens.

La Quinta Resort and Club. 49-499 Eisenhower Drive, La Quinta, CA 92253. Tel: 800-598-3828 or 800-PGA-WEST (742-9378), 619-564-5729 (golf reservations), 619-564-4111 (general operator). Fax: 619-771-5768. Credit cards accepted.

• *Dunes Course.* 1981. Designer: Pete Dye. Par 72. 6,861 yards. 73.9 par rating. 139 slope rating. Greens fees: resort guest: $110–$120 (October–April), $40–$95 (May–September), cart included. Public: $140–$165 (October–April), $50–$115 (May–September), cart included. No walking. No caddies. Season: year-round. Course closes one month annually for reseeding.

• *Mountain Course.* 1980. Designer: Pete Dye. Par 72. 6,758 yards. 74.1 par rating. 140 slope rating. Greens fees: resort guest: $115–$185 (October–April), $60–$125 (May–September), cart included. Public: $135–$230 (October–April), $70–$130 (May–September), cart included. No walking. No caddies. Season: year-round. Course closes one month annually for reseeding.

PGA West. 56-150 PGA Boulevard, La Quinta, CA 92253. Tel: 800-PGA-WEST or 619-564-5729 (golf reservations), 619-564-4111 (general operator), 619-564-7170 (pro shop). Fax: 619-771-5768. Credit cards accepted.

• *Stadium Course.* 1986. Designer: Pete Dye. Par 72. 6,753 yards. 73.0 yards. 142 slope rating. Greens fees: resort guest: $140–$185 (October–April), $65–$135 (May–September), cart included. Public: $155–$235 (October–April), $75–$140 (May–September), cart included. No walking. No caddies. Season: year-round. Course closes one month annually for reseeding.

• *Nicklaus Tournament Course.* 1987. Designer: Jack Nicklaus. Par 72. 6,546 yards. 71.9 par rating. 131 slope rating. Greens fees: resort guest: $115–$185 (October–April), $60–$125 (May–September), cart included. Public: $135–$235 (October–April), $60–$130 (May–September), cart included. No walking. No caddies. Season: year-round. Course closes one month annually for reseeding.

 GOLF SERVICES

Golf services at PGA West are absolutely outstanding—the clubhouse is as lavish as they come. An extremely pleasant clubhouse on the La Quinta grounds serves the Dunes and Mountain courses. Instruction, practice areas, and good rental bags are available at all three locations.

LODGING

Accommodations in the seductive **La Quinta** hotel are located in Spanish-style casitas (which are built of white stucco and have red-tile roofs) that are spread out among the beautifully manicured gardens and fragrant eucalyptus trees. The casitas themselves are clustered around small, heated swimming pools and outdoor whirlpool baths, perfectly placed for nighttime dips. There is a private pool for every seven or eight casitas. The casitas are spartan and simple yet pleasant, well equipped, and clean. The hotel's public areas are handsome and well maintained, replete with wood-burning fireplaces, elegant antique furnishings, and colorful Mexican tiles.

Casita, La Quinta Resort and Club

La Quinta Resort and Club. 49-499 Eisenhower Drive, La Quinta, CA 92253. Tel: 800-598-3828, 800-PGA-WEST (742-9378), or 619-564-4111. Fax: 619-771-5768. 640 rooms and suites, with doubles ranging between $250 and $320 in high season. Golf packages start at $440 per couple per night during high season for play on the Dunes Course and $595 for play on the Stadium Course. Credit cards accepted.

RESTAURANTS

A fine assortment of dining options await the holiday golfer both within the La Quinta resort itself and just minutes beyond it. The resort's loveliest restaurant is **Montanas,** La Quinta's original 1926 dining room that serves Mediterranean cuisine and is decorated with an attractive collection of modern art. Entrées in Montanas run between $10.95 and $32; we recommend the rack of lamb. Gourmet Mexican cooking is served in the resort's handsome **Adobe Grill.** Were we to judge every Mexican restaurant solely on the merits of its margaritas, the Adobe Grill would earn some of our highest marks! But make no mistake, the food is equally good, with entrées ranging in price between $6.95 and $17.95. **Morgan's,** a vintage, 1920s-style American brasserie, is perfect for breakfast, and there are also restaurants in both the **tennis clubhouse** and the **Dunes clubhouse.**

The best restaurant outside the resort—and well worth the five-minute drive—is **Cunard's.** This elegant and somewhat formal spot (jackets are suggested) features an appealing Continental menu and a fine choice of wines. Approximately $125 for dinner for two, including wine and tip.

The restaurants at La Quinta Resort and Club. 49-499 Eisenhower Drive, La Quinta, CA 92253. Tel: 800-598-3828 or 619-564-4111. Fax: 619-771-5768. Credit cards accepted.

Cunard's. 78034 Calle Barcelona, La Quinta, CA 92253. Tel: 619-564-4443. Fax: 619-777-1132. Credit cards accepted.

NON-GOLF ACTIVITIES

Popular activities for the golfer and non-golfer alike at La Quinta include tennis, shopping in the nice resort boutiques (Sharon's Antiques sells interesting golf memorabilia), swimming, and renting a bicycle. You may also just want to while away the hours reading by the pool and basking in the view of the Santa Rosa Mountains. The resort offers numerous supervised activities for children, twenty-four-hour room service, and a happy hour with complimentary hors d'oeuvres in the La Cantina bar from 5 to 6:30 P.M. daily.

GETTING THERE: To get to La Quinta Resort and Club from the Palm Springs Airport, get onto Interstate 10 East. Drive approximately thirty minutes, past Palm Springs. At the Washington Street exit, turn right. Drive past Highway 111. Take a right onto Eisenhower Drive. Up two blocks, you will see the resort on the right.

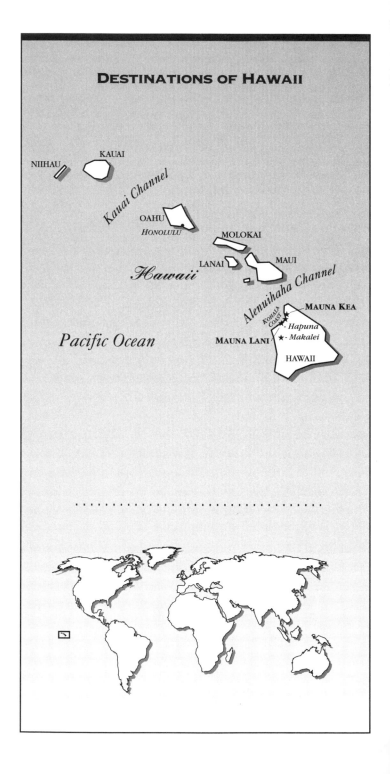

DESTINATIONS OF HAWAII

NIIHAU

KAUAI

Kauai Channel

OAHU
HONOLULU

MOLOKAI

LANAI

MAUI

Hawaii

Alenuihaha Channel

MAUNA KEA

KOHALA
COAST

Hapuna

★ *Makalei*

MAUNA LANI

HAWAII

Pacific Ocean

HAWAII

HAWAII

[No] land in all the world has any deep, strong charm for me but that one, no other land could so longingly and so beseechingly haunt me, sleeping and waking . . . as that one has done.

—**Mark Twain**

According to Hawaiian legend, Wakea, the god of sky, and Papa, the god of earth, gave birth to the Hawaiian Islands. Today, Hawaii is America's tropical paradise, a vacation wonderland perfumed with the scent of exotic flowers and replete with stunning beaches, active volcanoes, magnificent island cuisine, and an ever-evolving multicultural atmosphere that harmonizes Hawaiian, American, and Japanese influences. With the completion of twenty-six new courses since 1993, Hawaii is erupting into a marvelous golf destination as well.

Each year these magical islands attract roughly 8 million tourists from around the world. Oahu and Maui are Hawaii's best-known and most popular destinations, yet our island-hopping vacation took us to Hawaii Island, home of some of the very best golf courses in the Pacific. Called the Orchid Island, the Volcano Island, and more commonly, the Big Island, this landmass, seventy-six miles wide and ninety-three miles long, is twice as large as all the other Hawaiian Islands combined. Whereas large-scale development, excessive traffic, and scads of tourists detract from the idyllic aura of Oahu and Maui, civilization and untamed nature seem to be mixed in just the right proportion on the Big Island, which remains surprisingly off the beaten path. Remarkably, a delightfully relaxed island ambience still prevails even along the resort-dominated Kohala Coast and in Hilo, the Orchid Island's main city. You can find yourself quite effortlessly in step with the slow, soothing rituals of island life.

Golfers and non-golfers alike are won over by the Big Island's cinematic panoramas, brilliant hues, perfect climate, and homespun manner. The beaches at Mauna Kea and Hapuna are annually rated in the top five of all beaches in the United States, while the golf courses enjoy spectacular and dramatic settings. Few other destinations present golfers with the unusual opportunity to play in the shadow of two active, even boisterous, volcanoes—namely, Mauna Loa and Kilauea—which erupt quite frequently.

Volcanoes exert a strong allure, and for those who have a burning curiosity to see them up close, a helicopter sightseeing company will take adventurous visitors right to the boiling mouth of Mount Kilauea. Those who prefer to keep their feet a little closer to the ground can enjoy one of the most scenic—and fragrant—drives in the United States—up Mount Kea, which lays claim to being the world's tallest mountain when measured from its base, located on the ocean floor. You and your family can also snorkel in a marine preserve, hike to spectacularly beautiful, cascading waterfalls, go whale-watching, and take a ride in an observation submarine that gives you a window into the island's teeming, brightly colored undersea world. Hawaii even has a Rain Forest Zoo, where the state bird—the nene, a gooselike creature—is on view.

The Big Island is home to Mauna Kea and Mauna Lani, arguably the two finest and most luxurious resorts in the Hawaiian Islands. Golf at Mauna Kea and Mauna Lani lives up to any fantasy: shots are played on the windy Pacific shore from emerald-green fairways that stand out in strange, sharp contrast to the bordering pitch-black lava flows. The best course on Hawaii may be the beautiful, mature, Robert

Trent Jones, Sr.—designed course at Mauna Kea, or it may be either of the Robin Nelson/Rodney Wright—designed courses at Mauna Lani. Nelson and Wright specialize in Pacific Rim commissions that accentuate the local and regional cultural heritage. Their two Francis H. I'i Brown courses follow the contours of the lava flows and preserve the archaeological resources and petroglyphs, early Hawaiian drawings etched in rock that are found on-site. A novel, conservation-driven course irrigation system utilizes brackish water, wastewater, and freshwater to ensure that the courses remain lush and green despite the aridity of this portion of the Big Island. Two new courses that also should not be missed are the Hapuna Course, designed by Arnold Palmer and Ed Seay, and the Makalei Hawaii Country Club, located in its own amazing ecosystem at nearly 3,000 feet above sea level. Thanks to its high elevation and the fact that it is heavily wooded, the Makalei course remains enticingly cool.

The resorts on the Big Island are most crowded between December and March, i.e., when the weather is bad in other places. The coastal climate is agreeable and sunny year-round, with average highs ranging from eighty-one to eighty-six degrees and lows from sixty-five to seventy. Generally, rain occurs only when an infrequent storm blows in, yet these storms tend to blow away as quickly as they come. Kilauea can produce fog and overcast conditions depending on the severity of its eruptions and the direction of the wind. One final word of advice: if your ball comes to rest in the lava, leave it there. Lava is brittle and very sharp. Don't risk cutting yourself— we want you looking your best at the luau!

▶MAUNA KEA

GOLF ON THE BIG ISLAND

Balls resting or lost in lava may be dropped at point of entry no closer to hole. One stroke penalty.

—**Local Rule**

	The Golf	Golf Services	Lodging	Restaurants	Non-Golf Activities	Total
Rating	19	17	18	18	20	92

The west coast of the Big Island of Hawaii is called the Kohala coast. This arid, sun-drenched, and otherworldly coastline is known for its fields of jet-black lava, its emerald-green golf courses that traverse the lava's blackness, its ancient Hawaiian artifacts called petroglyphs, and aromatic Kona coffee plantations hidden in the rain forest.

For golfers and upscale travelers from the United States and Asia, the Kohala coast today is also known for the very fierce rivalry between its four principal resorts: the legendary Mauna Kea Beach Hotel, along with its larger but less intimate sister hotel, the Hapuna Prince Beach Hotel; the swank Mauna Lani; the Sheraton-managed Orchid at Mauna Lani; and the massive, somewhat tacky, supposedly New Age Hilton at Waikoloa. These five very large hotels are no more than twenty minutes apart by car.

We at Golf Travel recently stayed in all four establishments and played all the golf courses associated with each resort. The very best hotel in this select company is the extraordinary grande dame of the Big Island and the oldest resort of the four, Mauna Kea.

During our visit to Mauna Kea, we met a pleasant woman from San Francisco who, like many of her fellow guests at Mauna Kea, had been coming to the resort year after year since early childhood. She accurately summed up for us the virtues and characteristics of each establishment along the Kohala coast. "The Mauna Kea and the Mauna Lani differ the way San Francisco and Los Angeles do," she said. "Mauna Kea is for old money, Mauna Lani is for new money." "And the Hilton," chimed in her seven-year-old son, thinking of its trains and water slides, "is for kids."

The first-time visitor to the Big Island will be aided by the following background information. The Big Island has two distinct sides, each with its own microclimate. The Kohala coast, where the big resort hotels are located, is hot, sunny, and windswept, with a strange moonscape of black lava that receives less than ten inches of rain a year. The opposite side of the island—the Hilo side—is a jungle of lush greenery with dramatic waterfalls and dense forests of bamboo. Hilo actually receives more rain than any other spot in the United States—120 inches per year. As you ascend the volcano and drive from the Kohala to the Hilo side of the island, you will find that this great transformation takes place at the amazing town of Waimea, location of the famous, 500,000-acre Parker Ranch. Waimea, in fact, actually has a sunny side and a rainy side.

All eight Hawaiian Islands are caught in the pincers of two powerful forces, Japan and California. Hence, real estate values, as well as room rates and meals at the best hotels, remain extremely high. Hawaii is to California what the Caribbean is to the East Coast—the ultimate hedonistic getaway. About 80 percent of the Americans we met on the Big Island were from California. We met plenty of fellow guests from the East Coast, too, but, like us, they had traveled at least fifteen long hours to get there. Regardless of the distances traveled, everyone we met was happy to have made the journey.

Even though the entire Mauna Kea Beach Hotel property was closed in 1995 for a top-to-bottom renovation, rumors persisted that the food and service had badly deteriorated and that the resort had faded far behind Mauna Lani in overall quality. We honestly had to rub our eyes in wonder. Were these folks describing the same resort we had just fallen in love with? The critics of Mauna Kea sound a little like people who have read the bad reviews but have not seen the movie. We at Golf Travel cast stones when the facts merit it. However, in the case of the wrongly accused Mauna Kea, we have an obligation to set the record straight: this remains a truly outstanding resort.

THE GOLF

The Kohala Coast has been likened to Palm Springs thanks to the plethora of spectacular new courses that have been built here in recent years. Despite these stunning additions—most notably the gorgeous North and South courses at Mauna Lani (home of the Senior Skins Game) and Tommy Nakajima's fascinating Makalei Country Club—the original Robert Trent Jones, Sr., course at Mauna Kea, which opened in 1965, is still recognized by real connoisseurs of the game as the single best and most challenging track on all the Hawaiian Islands. The golf scene at the Mauna Kea resort has been further enhanced by the completion of the beautiful Hapuna Golf Course. Designed by Arnold Palmer and Ed Seay, Hapuna is located directly across the highway from the hotel and is accessible by shuttle bus. Guests of the Mauna Kea resort, however, are not strictly limited to the Mauna Kea and Hapuna courses. All the courses along the Kohala coast—including those at Mauna Lani and the Hilton—are open to the public.

The 7,114-yard **Mauna Kea Course** (with its slope rating of 143 from the back tees) is more intimidating and five or six strokes more difficult than any other course on the Big Island. For example, unlike the wide-open courses at Mauna Lani, the Mauna Kea Course is tight and forest-fringed. If you don't hit the ball straight, you can be in for a long day here. Beauty is a highly subjective category, but the Mauna Kea Course probably wins the beauty prize, edging out the South Course at Mauna Lani in a photo finish. Mauna Kea is certainly the most mature golf course on the Big Island, and nearly all golf courses—especially if they are as well maintained as Mauna Kea—improve with

Mauna Kea Course

age. We will also add for anyone who has only seen pictures of Mauna Kea that it is far more spectacular and exquisite-looking than it appears in photographs. Even the most stunning still shots cannot capture the cinematic panoramas, the heavily perfumed scent of flowers in the air, the wind in your face, and the joy of glimpsing a brown mongoose skittering across the fairway. Pictures also cannot reflect the wonderfully relaxed ambience, always so conducive to good golf, which is another happy trademark of the game in Hawaii.

The Mauna Kea Course opens uneventfully enough with a gentle dogleg directly across from the hotel entrance. Number two is more in character: from the elevated tee you gaze out to sea as thick jungle underbrush encloses you on either side. Number three is Mauna Kea's sexy signature hole, the famous, 200-yard par three that is almost all carry over an ocean inlet and lava shore. The green on three, however, is reassuringly enormous. Incidentally, the tee on three is such a spectacular and romantic site that many couples who come to Mauna Kea to get married or reconfirm their marriage vows use it as the spot for their ceremony. Numbers six (344 yards) and nine (372 yards) are the other highlights on the front side of this steep, uphill-downhill layout; these severely downhill and exhilarating golf holes play significantly shorter than their distances on the card. The back nine is tougher, particularly when the wind is up. Eleven is a lovely par three that finishes at the beach, and fourteen is a majestic, 413-yard dogleg-left. It is seventeen and eighteen, however, that will make or demolish your round. Both play straight into the wind. Seventeen, which is already long enough at 555 yards, requires three full shots to reach the green, and eighteen is the perfect concluding hole. Like number nine, eighteen plays downhill over a waste area to a heavily bunkered green.

The lovely **Hapuna Golf Course** itself is beautifully conditioned and full of appeal. It is located on higher ground than Mauna Kea and provides fine elevated views of the ocean. The holes are routed magically among red and black lava fields. The Hapuna Course is steep; the cart paths can at times be hair-raising on the descent, whereas on the ascent you'll doubt that your cart has enough pep to make the climb. The hilly terrain means that the yardages listed on the downhill holes are deceiving. The 406-yard seventeenth hole, for instance, is so steeply downhill that it can play as a three wood off the tee and a wedge to the green. The Hapuna Course measures 6,534 yards from the middle tees and carries a slope rating of 130.

The **Makalei Hawaii Country Club,** which opened in late 1992, is located on the

Hawaii Belt Road seven miles above Kona, about a forty-minute drive from the Mauna Kea hotel. Despite the drive, this memorable course is worth the trip if you want to get away from the resort courses on the Kohala coast and try something completely different. Located in its own amazing ecosystem at an altitude of 2,500 feet and hidden half the time in a fine mist of rain and fog, the Makalei Hawaii Country Club is worlds apart from the sun-blinding and wind-lashing golf experience at the resort hotels. When the sun comes out at Makalei, you are rewarded with spectacular ocean views. Wooded and cool (the lower temperatures come as a nice break), this hilly landscape features romantic ravines, wild peacocks shrieking loudly to each other in the trees, enormous mounds of black and red lava called "cinder cones," and interesting lava-tube caves, which were formed by the lava as it flowed to the sea. Once a cattle ranch, Makalei Country Club is laced with picturesque stone retaining walls. The course itself has been routed via extremely long cart paths so that most of the holes play downhill. The first hole is straight up, a 290-yard par four, but the second hole, for instance, a 222-yard par three, is really no more than a five iron off the tee. The course reaches its highest elevation at 2,900 feet on the tenth, a 598-yard hole, which is downhill all the way. Twelve is an intriguing par three that requires you to play to the green between two tall cinder cones. Designed by Dick Nugent, Makalei is open to the public.

Mauna Kea Golf Course. 62-100 Mauna Kea Beach Drive, Kamuela, Hawaii 96743. Tel: 808-882-5400. Fax: 808-882-7552. Credit cards accepted.

• 1965. Designer: Robert Trent Jones, Sr. Par 72. 7,114 yards. 73.6 par rating. 143 slope rating. Greens fees: $90 (resort guest), $150 (nonguests), cart included. No walking. No caddies. Season: year-round.

Hapuna Golf Course. 62-100 Kauna'oa Drive, Kamuela, Hawaii 96743. Tel: 808-880-3000. Fax: 808-880-3010. Credit cards accepted.

• 1992. Designers: Arnold Palmer, Ed Seay. Par 72. 6,875 yards. 72.5 par rating. 134 slope rating. Greens fees: $80 (resort guests), $130 (nonguests), cart included. No walking. No caddies. Season: year-round.

Makalei Hawaii Country Club. 72-3890 Hawaii Belt Road, Kailua-Kona, Hawaii 96740. Tel: 800-606-9606 or 808-325-6625. Fax: 808-325-6766. Credit cards accepted.

• 1992. Designer: Dick Nugent. Par 72. 7,091 yards. 73.5 par rating. 143 slope rating. Greens fees: $110 ($55 after 1:30 P.M.), cart included. No walking. No caddies. Season: year-round.

GOLF SERVICES (17)

Golf services at the Mauna Kea Course are quite good—the staff is friendly, there is a nice practice range and a good little bar and restaurant, and the locker rooms and pro shop have been renovated. Golf services at the new Hapuna Course are also very good, as the staff goes to great lengths to make you feel welcome. The Makalei Country Club has one of the warmest atmospheres and the nicest staff members we have encountered in golf. It also has a good range and casual restaurant. Excellent sets of rental clubs are available at each of these three golf courses.

LODGING (18)

The **Mauna Kea** was built in 1963 in visionary fashion by Laurance Rockefeller. Like Dorado Beach in Puerto

Rico, the Mauna Kea hotel was one of the original "Rockresorts." Unlike Dorado Beach, however, it is monumental in scale, and its extraordinarily rich architectural detail remains enchanting and perfectly preserved today. In our estimation, the Mauna Kea is the only hotel on the Kohala coast that captures the real spirit of Hawaii. By comparison, the newer hotels fail to grasp the magic.

Mauna Kea's magic arguably begins with its commanding views of the sea—sea views that are, in fact, unmatched. Within

Mauna Kea Beach Hotel

the resort complex, the Hawaiian spirit comes out in the hotel's spectacular, 1,600-piece collection of Oriental art that was hand-selected by Rockefeller himself. A wonderful sense of continuity defines the relationship between hotel guests and staff members. Families return year after year and are served by the same friendly faces. Finally, Mauna Kea offers one extra attraction: every night at around ten o'-clock three or four manta rays appear in the water at "manta point," feeding on plankton, beating their huge wings in the water, moving peacefully to and fro.

It is absolutely imperative that you request an ocean-view room on an upper floor. We occupied one such room ourselves, number 704, and loved it. The views of Mauna Kea's stunning beach and the iridescent sunsets across the water defy description. All ocean-view rooms have beautiful private patios overlooking the sea.

The Mauna Kea Beach Hotel. 62-100 Mauna Kea Beach Drive, Kamuela, Hawaii 96743. Tel: 800-882-6060 or 808-882-7222. Fax: 808-880-3112. 310 rooms priced from $295 to $530 per night. Golf packages that include a round of golf with cart start at $425 per night for two golfers in a double-occupancy room. Credit cards accepted.

R E S T A U R A N T S   19

The **Mauna Kea** receives very high marks for food. The cuisine is outstanding, starting with the fabulous breakfast buffet: rich Kona coffee, homemade pastries, smoked salmon, homemade sausage, the world's best pineapple, eggs any way, French toast, and much more. The breakfast buffet is open from 6:30 until 11:30 A.M., which means that golfers heading out for an early round can grab a pastry at seven and still sit down to a full breakfast at eleven.

At dinner, a refined, Oriental influence permeates the cooking, with countless varieties of sushi and an emphasis on fresh local seafood. Guests enjoy enticing options for dinner: Mediterranean and Pacific Rim cuisine at the **Pavilion** and traditional fare in the **Batik Room.** The Pavilion is Mauna Kea's main dining room and offers indoor and outdoor seating. At the Batik we enjoyed an excellent dinner of fine fish from Hawaiian waters and wonderful wines, but service was slow. Gentlemen are required to wear jackets (but not neckties) in the Batik Room. The Mauna Kea also offers the best luau on the Big Island. Luaus take place every Tuesday—be sure to make reservations in advance.

The restaurants at the Mauna Kea Beach Hotel. 62-100 Mauna Kea Beach Drive, Kamuela, Hawaii 96743. Tel: 808-882-7222 (general) or 808-882-5801 (dining reservations). Fax: 808-880-7552. Credit cards accepted.

NON-GOLF ACTIVITIES ⟨20⟩

Hawaii offers better non-golf activities than any state in the union. *Condé Naste Traveler* recently rated the beach at Mauna Kea the third best in the United States. Hapuna beach, which is located five minutes away, was ranked number one. The truly spectacular Mauna Kea beach is sandy and safe, and just forty yards offshore you'll find great coral reefs loaded with sea turtles, eels, and schools of colorful fish of all sizes. Snorkeling here is absolutely breathtaking. Sailboats, Windsurfers, and scuba equipment (and scuba lessons) are also available at the hotel beach. Deep-sea fishing and whale-watching expeditions can easily be arranged by the front desk, and a fitness center and tennis are available on the hotel property.

Feeling even more adventurous? Hitch up with one of many helicopter tours of the Big Island that take you from the mouth of the active volcano of Kilauea to the thousand-foot waterfalls on the east coast. Another popular attraction is the forty-six passenger *Atlantis* submarine that dives one hundred feet below the ocean surface for a closer look at Hawaii's colorful marine life. Horseback riding and hunting on Parker Ranch, walks through the petroglyph fields, and shopping in Kona are other pleasant activities.

GETTING THERE: Most international flights set down in Honolulu, requiring Big Island guests to switch to a Hawaiian carrier for the short light to Kona Airport. As you leave the Kona Airport, turn left onto the highway and go straight twenty-six miles to the Mauna Kea Beach Hotel. You can also take a shuttle to Mauna Kea for $23 per person.

▶MAUNA LANI
ONE OF HAWAII'S BEST

	The Golf	Golf Services	Lodging	Restaurants	Non-Golf Activities	Total
Rating	18	20	18	15	19	90

Mauna Lani

In 1996, *Condé Nast Traveler* ranked the Mauna Lani Bay Hotel and Bungalows, located on the Big Island of Hawaii, as the second best resort in all the tropics. Truly a marvelous resort, the Mauna Lani more than holds its own ground when compared with its more renowned neighbor, the utterly enchanting Mauna Kea resort (see Mauna Kea, above). We found the quality of the guest rooms and golf services actually superior at Mauna Lani and the snorkeling by the Beach Club without compare. In only one regard does the Mauna Lani fall a bit short. Despite the staff's extraordinary hospitality and wonderful touches, such as the lovely fish ponds that decorate the grounds, the actual hotel building looks as if it could be found anywhere—in Orlando or San Diego, for example. Mauna Kea, on the other hand, is entirely and unmistakably Hawaiian. Perhaps Mauna Lani's only fault, finally, is that it is located next door to one of the most magical resorts *ever* built.

The two establishments also attract a very different sort of clientele. Guests at the more low-key Mauna Kea tend to be families that return year after year (or generation after generation), while the Mauna Lani resort-goers tend to be younger and a bit more flashy. Lounging poolside at Mauna Lani, you are apt to find many more wheeler-dealers from Los Angeles, Tokyo, and Hong Kong temporarily disconnected from their car phones and Rolls-Royces.

THE GOLF ⑱

More than any other Hawaiian resort, **Mauna Lani** lives up to golfers' fantasies. Two truly spectacular Francis H. I'i Brown golf courses bring it all to life—vivid swaths of emerald-green fairway cast against lava fields blacker than midnight, amazing black lava beaches, a translucent sea, and grass so lush that it seems to grow faster than you can replace a divot. Your senses will revel in the warm ocean breezes, the heavily perfumed scent of exotic flowers, and views of volcanic peaks and big white cruise ships plying the Pacific.

Golf at Mauna Lani is also unforgettable because its two courses are capable of yielding low scores. The Mauna Lani courses play plenty long, but their wide-open, generous fairways lie in stark contrast to the tight, forest-fringed fairways up the road at Mauna Kea.

The **South Course** is only slightly more spectacular than the North Course, but it gets a lot more play because of the annual Seniors Skins Game and because its signature hole, number fifteen (with two hundred yards of carry over an ocean inlet), is one of the most awesome and frequently photographed holes in golf. Eleven through fifteen on the South Course may be the best five holes in succession anywhere in the Hawaiian Islands. Eleven is a dogleg-left over a lava flow where big hitters will be tempted to cut the corner, twelve is a tough, 202-yard par three over a lake and into strong winds, thirteen is a wonderful dogleg-right toward the sea (the green is perched above the beach so there is no room for error), and your tee shot on fourteen must carry one lava field but stop short of another. On the front side, four, five, six, and seven (another spectacular par three over a lava beach) comprise another challenging series of incredibly beautiful holes.

The **North Course** is full of beauty, too. Its most famous hole is seventeen, a wonderful par three that requires you to carry a towering lava "cinder cone" set in a sand trap if you wish to reach the green, which is set in an amphitheater of more lava. We also like nine and ten. Nine, a 442-yard par four with the wind at your back, runs down to the beach by the Orchid at Mauna Lani hotel (formerly the Ritz-Carlton hotel), and ten, coming back, runs parallel to a field of petroglyphs (lava drawings made by Hawaiians over one thousand years ago). By the way, the private homes along the sixteenth fairway sell for more than $4 million each.

Francis H. I'i Brown Golf Courses. 68-1310 Mauna Lani Drive, Kohala Coast, Hawaii 96743. Tel: 808-885-6655. Fax: 808-885-9612. Credit cards accepted.

• *South Course.* 1981/1990. Designers: Homer Flint, Raymond Cain. Par 72. 6,938 yards. 72.8 par rating. 133 slope rating. Greens fees: $90 resort guests/$170 public, includes cart. No walking. No caddies. Season: year-round.

• *North Course.* 1981/1990. Designers: Homer Flint, Raymond Cain/Robin Nelson, Rodney Wright. Par 72. 6,913 yards. 73.2 par rating. 136 slope rating. Greens fee: $85 (resort guests), $160 (general public), includes cart. No walking. No caddies. Season: year-round.

GOLF SERVICES

Golf services at Mauna Lani are among the very best in the world. The magnificent pro shop—which sells golf antiques and fine apparel as well as alligator golf shoes at $1,925 a pair—is one of the most beautiful we have seen. More important, perhaps, all of the golf staff members we met, including those in the pro shop and those downstairs who helped us get rolling, were polished, professional, and attentive. Golf carts are equipped with individual coolers stocked with bottles of mineral water. Rental clubs and shoes are available, and you can smooth out your swing on a fine practice range.

LODGING

The rooms at **Mauna Lani** are beautifully furnished and equipped. The height of Hawaiian luxury at the resort consists of five private bungalows (4,000 square feet with three bedrooms, private pool, and twenty-four-hour butler service), which rent for $4,100 to $8,300 per day. But failing that, the oceanfront rooms ($530 per day) and suites ($835) are a very good second best. We stayed in one of the least expensive standard rooms (number 430), which was very much to our liking. Located on a side of the hotel, it offers a partial view of the sea, elegant new furnishings, cable television, VCR, minibar, an elegant and spacious bathroom, and plenty of closet space. An attractive three-night golf package, which includes a round of golf daily (but no meals), starts at about $1,400.

Mauna Lani Beach Hotel and Bungalows. 68-1400 Mauna Lani Drive, Kohala Coast, Island of Hawaii, 96743. Tel: 800-367-2323 or 808-885-6622. Fax: 808-885-1484. 347 rooms and suites. Double rooms from $275 to $530. 5 bungalows from $4,100. Credit cards accepted.

RESTAURANTS

We dined in six of Mauna Lani's seven restaurants and were somewhat disappointed by the resort's culinary aspect. Of these, the very best is the **Canoe House,** a lovely beachfront restaurant that specializes in local seafood and Pacific Rim cuisine and is only open for dinner. Dinner for two with wine and tip averages about $160. We enjoyed an early-morning (6:30 A.M.) golfer's breakfast adjacent to the pro shop at the **Gallery Restaurant and Knickers Bar.** This very scenic dining spot overlooks the golf courses. Dinners here cost about $50 per person before beverages. We also ate good lunches at the **Beach Club** right on the beach and at the **Ocean Grill** beside the pool. However, our Continental dinner at the **Bay Terrace,** Mauna Lani's main dining room, was rather bland and lackluster. Likewise, the buffet breakfast served in the Bay Terrace left much to be desired. This breakfast buffet certainly does not compare well with the one served at Mauna Kea. Dress in the evening is casually elegant. A nice linen jacket and colorful shirt are perfect for gentlemen.

Guests of the Mauna Lani might wish to have dinner at the nearest neighboring hotel, the **Orchid at Mauna Lani,** located within the resort complex and accessible by the hotel's shuttle bus. Innovative Hawaiian cuisine is served in **The Grill** restaurant, where a very fine dinner for two with wine and tip will run about $250.

The restaurants at the Mauna Lani Beach Hotel and Bungalows. 68-1400 Mauna Lani Drive, Kohala Coast, Hawaii, 96743. Tel: 800-367-2323 or 808-885-6622. Fax: 808-885-1478. Credit cards accepted.

The Grill. The Orchid at Mauna Lani, 1 North Kaniku Drive, Kohala Coast, Hawaii 96743. Tel: 808-885-2000. Fax: 808-885-1064. Credit cards accepted.

NON-GOLF ACTIVITIES ⑲

Non-golf activities at Mauna Lani are superb. Recreational offerings include tennis on the resort's ten courts, fully supervised programs for children, workouts in a small exercise facility, swimming in a lovely pool, and a tremendous range of beach and ocean activities. You can opt for world-class snorkeling, sailing on the resort's large catamaran, scuba-diving instruction, whale watching, and deep-sea fishing. There are several fine shops and galleries within the resort complex itself and a wealth of sightseeing beyond.

GETTING THERE: United Airlines is the only carrier with direct flights to the Big Island from the U.S. mainland. All other itineraries require a switch to a Hawaiian commuter airline in Honolulu for the short flight to the Big Island. To get to the resort from the airport, make a left at Queen Kaahumanu Highway, travel north about twenty-five miles, and take a left into the Mauna Lani resort complex. The Mauna Lani also provides shuttle service for $20 per person. Taxi fare is about $38.

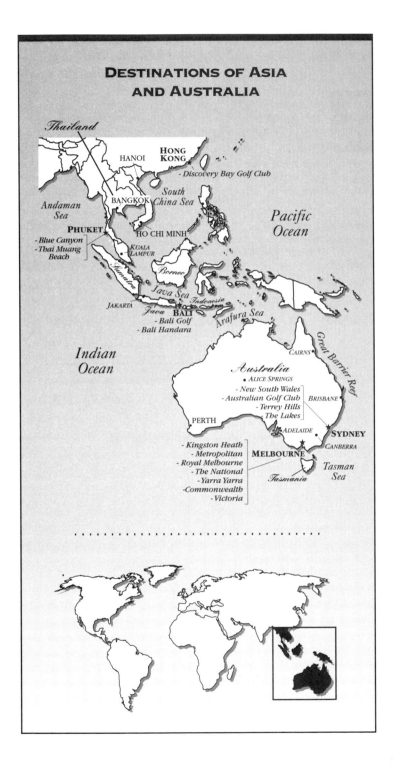

DESTINATIONS OF ASIA AND AUSTRALIA

Thailand

HANOI

HONG KONG
- Discovery Bay Golf Club

South China Sea

Andaman Sea

BANGKOK

Pacific Ocean

PHUKET
- Blue Canyon
- Thai Muang Beach

HO CHI MINH

KUALA LAMPUR

Sumatra

Borneo

Java Sea

Indonesia

JAKARTA

Java **BALI**
- Bali Golf
- Bali Handara

Arafura Sea

Indian Ocean

Australia
• *ALICE SPRINGS*

CAIRNS

Great Barrier Reef

- New South Wales
- Australian Golf Club
- Terrey Hills
- The Lakes

BRISBANE

PERTH

ADELAIDE

SYDNEY

CANBERRA

- Kingston Heath
- Metropolitan
- Royal Melbourne
- The National
- Yarra Yarra
- Commonwealth
- Victoria

MELBOURNE

Tasmania

Tasman Sea

ASIA AND AUSTRALIA

ASIA AND AUSTRALIA

A puff of wind, a puff faint and tepid and laden with strange odours of blossoms, of aromatic wood, comes out the still night—the first sigh of the East on my face. That I can never forget. It was impalpable and enslaving, like a charm, like a whispered promise of mysterious delight. . . . The mysterious East faced me, perfumed like a flower.

—Joseph Conrad

Asia and Australia—the mere mention of these distant continents suggests their beguiling allure. From the first records of travel to the East by Marco Polo, the West has looked upon Asia with excitement and wonder. Today, even the most seasoned travelers find Asia an intriguing and intoxicating mystery. For the golfing enthusiast, it is fast catching up to Australia in great golfing venues and becoming a new paradise destination.

As golf enjoys a boom that has made it the game of the 1990s and beyond, no one in the world has embraced it with as much gusto as Asians. Their appetite for golf, their passion and profound respect for the game, is immediately evident in the sheer number of Asian golfers who make pilgrimages to St. Andrews, Pebble Beach, and other legendary golf grounds. Moreover, in the past ten years golf courses have cropped up throughout Asia itself. Thailand now boasts over two hundred courses, Indonesia and Malaysia each have over a hundred, and tiny Singapore has more than twenty. The rush to play golf is equally frenetic in Asia from Tokyo to Manila to Kuala Lumpur to Hong Kong.

Asia's immense scope and diversity can bewilder the uninitiated traveler. To introduce you to the best of Asian golf, our itinerary includes Hong Kong, the Thai island of Phuket, and Bali in Indonesia. Whether business or pleasure takes you to Hong Kong, this star of the Orient offers a scintillating first taste of golf in Asia. Following a short ferry ride to Lantau Island and a bus ride up the island's volcanic slopes, you arrive at the twenty-seven holes of golf at Discovery Bay Golf Club. You will immediately notice the overhead lights that permit night golf here—a common feature of Asia's most heavily played courses—but the breathtaking panoramic views of the South China Sea are what make this Robert Trent Jones, Jr., course truly memorable. In no time you can find yourself back on Hong Kong Island, atop the Mandarin Hotel, delighting in an exquisitely ethereal dinner at starry Man Wah, which offers an incomparable view of Hong Kong's harbor and skyline. It remains to be seen what impact Hong Kong's reversion to China will have on tourism, but when we visited during the final year of British control, we found the combination of an exotic and ultramodern urban cityscape, luxurious accommodations, mouthwatering cuisine, and tranquil golf to be positively irresistible.

After charting a course to the tiny island of Phuket, you will encounter another Asia, one very remote from the hustle and bustle of Hong Kong. Skyscrapers become a distant memory—on the windy lanes leading to the golf courses you pass water buffalo tethered to clumps of palm. The courses themselves are enveloped by quiet, warm breezes and the Adaman Sea's brilliant turquoise waters. Thai culture lends vivid color to the game here. At many clubs you will still see groups of six or seven players dispensing with the traditional honors etiquette; instead, upon putting out, each player immediately hits his or her tee shot on the next hole and begins walking up the side of the fairway while succeeding players in the group hit their drives. Another Thai custom—much in evidence when we played at both the Blue Canyon

Country Club and the Thai Muang Beach course—is the use of young female caddies and the welcome practice of warding off the intense tropical sun with umbrellas.

From Phuket our destination is Bali, one of the loveliest of the more than 13,000 islands that comprise the Indonesian archipelago. Bali is known as the "Island of the Gods" for good reason: it is a mystical, tropical paradise island, teeming with temples and religious festivals. What could be better than to stop here on the dividing line between the Pacific and Indian Oceans to explore Hindu temples, meander along glistening beaches, hike among rice paddies, and relax by playing golf at both the Bali Handara Country Club and the Bali Golf and Country Club. The Nelson/Wright–designed Bali Golf and Country Club masterfully incorporates Bali's fascinating landscape and cultural traditions. The holes on the front nine climb the terraces of former rice fields; in addition, there is a shrine near the twelfth green, and local wood carvings serve as tee markers. After completing your round, it's time to return to the cool waters of one of Bali's three staggeringly lovely Amanresorts. Amid such pampering luxury, you will swear this entire tropical paradise island is your own private domain.

Like the first explorers who reached Australia in the 1600s, modern-day travelers will feel as if they have reached the ends of the earth by the time they touch land on the continent. Flights from Los Angeles to Sydney take fourteen hours and cross the equator and the international date line, but the effort is worth it. The remoteness of this breakaway continent, once part of a huge southern continent that included Africa, India, South America, and Antarctica, accounts for its extraordinarily unique flora and fauna. In fact, after the explorers' initial reports, European skepticism about kangaroos, wallabies, and other marsupials Down Under persisted for an entire century! Australia's courses appear in rain forests, deserts, mountains, and along shorelines; they wander through forbidding terrain, cross canyons, and scoot by koalas roosting in the ubiquitous eucalyptus trees.

Although Australia is indelibly etched in our golf consciousness as the homeland of Greg Norman ("The Great White Shark"), the game here transcends the fame of its most charismatic figure. Australia is home to some of the world's most renowned courses designed by the likes of Robert von Hagge, Jack Nicklaus, Pete Dye, Robert Trent Jones, Jr., and Alister Mackenzie. Its two preeminent cities—Sydney and Melbourne—have long been rivals in everything from fashion to racehorses, and they duke it out in the golf arena as well. Both offer beautiful courses with interesting layouts and terrain.

Sydney, Australia's gateway city, stakes its claim to great golf on challenging and entertaining courses such as New South Wales, the Australian, Terrey Hills, and the Lakes. Once again, these private courses permit outside play on certain days of the week, so bring along your handicap certificate and a letter of introduction from your home pro. Sydney's exciting restaurant scene is yet another inducement to travel to Australia. The city's most original culinary establishments feature a new Australian cuisine that combines Mediterranean panache with the freshest local produce, meats, and seafood.

Melbourne, a refined and conservative Victorian city, boasts Kingston Heath, Metropolitan, and Royal Melbourne—private clubs that rank as the top three courses in the country and allow overseas visitors to play on weekdays. These tracks, along with several others, earn Melbourne our highest rating for golf.

Whether your itinerary takes you to the boardrooms of Hong Kong or the white sand beaches of Bondi Beach in Australia, you will find a memorable golf course nearby. Even better, the whole family can enjoy a range of exotic activities to make the journey to Asia or Australia truly the trip of a lifetime. Australia's koalas and kangaroos, boat excursions, vintage trains, and amusement parks will fascinate young and old alike. The Aussies love their outdoor sports, and you can try surfing, diving, game fishing, bicycling, and bush walking in the national parks.

Asia, meanwhile, provides a mesmerizing mixture of the old and the new. The rising cityscapes are among the most impressive anywhere in the world. You can shop till you drop for clothing, jewelry, wood carvings, art, and furniture. Asian culture and religion can be often wonderfully expressive. Ask your hotel concierge in Bali or Phuket if there are any religious festivals going on: the temple offerings, parades to the sea, and full-moon ceremonies give you a rare opportunity to immerse yourself in the cultural rituals of these delightful peoples. (Your concierge will also tell you what to wear.)

Because of the size and scope of Australia and Asia, picking the best time to go depends on your ultimate destination. Generally, Southeast Asia is cooler and drier from October to March. In southern Australia, the summer months between December and February are the best months to visit. Expect hot days, but bring along some warmer clothing because temperatures can get quite cool in the evening.

In the pages ahead, GOLF TRAVEL guides you to our favorite Pacific and South Sea destinations—holiday locales that will captivate your curiosity and introduce you to some of the most unique and ancient cultures of the world. The highly refined tourist services in Asia and Australia make traveling throughout these exotic destinations a breeze. Moreover, you will find the peoples of these lands to be wonderfully hospitable and welcoming. So next time you are lazily dreaming of an enchanting, far-flung golf getaway, spin the globe around to the East.

China

►HONG KONG
THE DYNAMIC STAR OF THE ORIENT

	The Golf	Golf Services	Lodging	Restaurants	Non-Golf Activities	Total
Rating	**17**	**16**	**19**	**20**	**20**	**92**

Discovery Bay Golf Club

Hong Kong. A social marvel balanced precariously on the edge of the tumultuous border of the Republic of China. Over a quarter of the world's population inhabits Asia, and Hong Kong, for the moment, holds the financial reins on this market. This tiny haven of capitalism is everything you imagined and much more. But for how long? A brief journey into China points to the assuredly rocky future awaiting this small jewel. On July 1, 1997, as dictated by the Sino-British Joint Declaration signed in 1984, the territory of Hong Kong reverted back to China as a Special Administrative Region, in theory employing the slogan "one country, two systems." Let's hope the optimistic souls are right on this one, for when we played golf here before the reversion, Hong Kong provided a fabulous combination of the best of English civility and the fascination of the Orient.

With Victoria Peak looming in the clouds above, the breathtaking skyline of Hong Kong Island wraps around Victoria Harbour, suggesting you are in a holy temple of the capitalist gods. Not a cent has been spared in the design of the skyscrapers that serve as headquarters to some of the world's most powerful brokerage, commodities, and banking firms. Luxury abounds in everything from shopping to restaurants to accommodations. As one American businessman living in Hong Kong told us, the city's foreign contingent will pay as much as possible for everything, simply because it can. The shopping is reminiscent of Paris's Avenue Montaigne, but tenfold. The dining is unrivaled, and when the hotel sends a chauffeured Daimler to meet you at the airport, enough is said about the accommodations. All in all, in other destinations of Asian travel, luxury comes in spurts, but not in Hong Kong. Revel in it.

Let us not forget the golf, which we found to be one of the true treasures of this intoxicating city.

THE GOLF

Our trip to the **Discovery Bay Golf Club** began with a picturesque thirty-minute ferry ride from Hong Kong Island to Lantau Island, where Discovery Bay buses quickly transported us to the clubhouse in the sky. Taking stock of greens perched high above the South China Sea and fairways that wind through the volcanic peaks of Lantau Island, we thought we might never see a more scenic setting than this twenty-seven-hole golf complex designed by Robert Trent Jones, Jr., in 1983. Of the three nine-hole courses—the Diamond, Ruby, and Jade—the two to play are the original 6,673-yard **Diamond/Ruby** combination. The mountainous Diamond nine is the most difficult of the three, while the Ruby offers the most spectacular views. The less mature and shorter (3,257 yards) **Jade** nine was designed by the club's pros in 1993, but it is the least interesting and scenic; three of its fairways jump back and forth over water-treatment ponds.

Before starting our round, we took the opportunity to warm up at the "practice lake" driving range, where everyone strokes as many of the amazing floating balls (HK$10/US$1 per basket) into the water as he or she desires. There's something profoundly satisfying about being able to unload ball after ball into the water. When we moved from the range to the Ruby's demanding first hole, which dared us to hook one into the practice lake again, we noticed the huge light stands along the fairway that permit night play, just another reflection of how things are done here in Hong Kong. Even so, when we reached the tee on the bunker-lined, par five third, all our thoughts about modern technology vanished as we looked out over the South China Sea and the sheer beauty of the outlying islands in the distance. Play to the right on this hole since any ball hit left will soar off a cliff that drops straight down two hundred feet to the sea.

The Diamond Course provides the most strenuous and demanding test on Discovery Bay's twenty-seven holes. Water comes into play on holes three, five, and eight. The number one handicap third hole is a tough par four with water cutting in before the green, but it is the long, par five sixth that we remember most vividly. The cliff on the right places a premium on an accurate and long drive; the green is protected by a large front bunker. Wind adds an extra hazard on the tricky par three eighth; from the back tees drives must carry a hefty 190 yards over the lake.

The major drawback of the three courses at Discovery Bay is their uneven condition and maintenance: lush, green fairways and greens turned suddenly brittle and burned. Walking is allowed, but there are no caddies, and, when we played, not a soul tackled this hilly terrain on foot. Discovery Bay rents both shoes and clubs. We urge you to request your hotel concierge to book your tee times prior to your arrival in Hong Kong, and, although it was not needed at Discovery Bay, we recommend that you carry a handicap card and letter of introduction from your pro.

Discovery Bay Golf Club. Lantau Island, Hong Kong. Tel. 011-852-2987-3750, 011-852-2987-7271, and 011-852-2987-7273. Fax. 011-852-2980-005900. Credit cards accepted.

  • *Diamond/Ruby Course.* 1983. Designer: Robert Trent Jones, Jr. Par 72. 6,673 yards.
  • *Jade Course.* 1993. Designer: Discovery Bay Club professionals. Par 35. 3,257 yards.
  • Greens fee (eighteen holes): HK$1,050 (US $133). Walking permitted. No caddies. Carts available. Restrictions: open to public only on Mondays, Tuesdays, and Fridays. Season: year-round.

GOLF SERVICES 16

Most of the employees we encountered at Discovery Bay were courteous and willing to answer all of our questions, although we struggled with their accents. The pro shop personnel, although not rude, were indifferent and cool; they were not overly indulgent of our efforts to deal with a new currency and the Chinese language. The driving range is, as previously noted, over water and really a lot of fun, and the putting green is well maintained. The pro shop is stocked with anything you might need, but it is a bit pricey. Locker rooms are modern, spacious, and clean; compared to some of the other Asian courses, these amenities constitute a very welcome change.

After a morning or afternoon round of golf you will probably be ready to sit and relax, as we were, with a Tsing Tao beer and a plate of delicious Chinese noodles and satay. The restaurant/bar is very pleasant and quite a social gathering place; on the day we were there it was somewhat reminiscent of the United Nations. The terrace is quite pleasant when the weather is agreeable.

LODGING 19

Hong Kong's upscale accommodations are exceptional but quite costly, with harbor-view room rates starting at about US$400. Just opposite the Star Ferry on Hong Kong Island, the **Mandarin Oriental,** once *the* place to reside while visiting the Territory, remains one of the island's most luxurious hotels. The lobby is handsome and always bustling with those busily taking care of their business affairs, while others breeze through laden with shopping bags and hotel porters trailing behind them with the overflow. The rooms are indeed luxurious, yet the bathrooms are perhaps a bit small and in need of revamping.

The **Grand Hyatt Hong Kong,** with its grand lobby and spectacular mosaic marble floor, is also an attractive alternative if you are dead-set on staying on the Hong Kong side. Incidentally, after dinner, the bar and nightclub in the Grand Hyatt becomes one of the prime see-and-be-seen places in town.

In our opinion, no hotel in Hong Kong beats the **Regent.** Sitting in the lobby, with the sounds of a string quartet wafting through the air, we looked out upon the glorious nighttime panorama of the Hong Kong skyline and decided that the view alone was worth whatever the hotel charged per night. The Regent is located on the Kowloon Peninsula, but its location is eminently convenient. The Star Ferry terminal is just a five-minute walk from the hotel, and ferries leave every few minutes for Hong Kong Island. The ride itself, which takes about seven minutes, is a very relaxing treat and provides stunning views in all directions.

The Regent, upon request (and you *definitely must),* will send a car and white-gloved chauffeur to meet its guests at the airport. From the moment we entered the confined luxury of our Daimler and were handed an orchid-topped, chilled towel, our stay at the Regent was effortless and thoroughly enjoyable. Our room, although smaller than we had expected, was very comfortable. The posh bathroom was beautifully done in peach Italian marble and had a sunken tub, glass shower, and amenities such as a hair dryer and comfy terry-cloth robes. We reserve our most lavish praise for the room's gorgeous view. We gazed enthralled out the picture window on the myriad sampans, ocean liners, yachts, tugs, and fishing boats that populate Victoria Harbour.

At the Regent, set aside at least an hour after sunset to soothe body and soul in one of the hotels three spa pools, each controlled at a different temperature. The planning of the spa and exercise facilities is unrivaled, but the experience in one of the Jacuzzis will stay with you for quite some time. Perched above the harbor with nothing between you and the bright lights of Hong Kong, you will surely feel you have inherited the world.

Our only concern about a stay at the Regent proved groundless: we were a bit wary of the staff since we had heard they were haughty and even rude, yet during our stay nothing could have been further from the truth. The concierge desk was extremely helpful in setting up our day trips, tee times, and dinner reservations. When we actually confused two dinner reservations, the concierge politely called to correct us, without the slightest hint of annoyance.

Be certain to request a room with a harbor view, for this is the Regent's main attribute, one that many of the other Hong Kong hotels have lost due to the construction of newer and taller buildings.

One can hardly review Hong Kong's lodging options without mentioning the legendary **Peninsula,** a landmark since 1928. The classic charm and Old World feel of this hotel is unrivaled in Hong Kong. The lobby, which stretches from one end of the hotel to the other, is decorated with ornate chandeliers hung far above the palms and regal Victorian furniture. Out of three hundred rooms, over half are in the original building. A new thirty-floor tower has been added to open up some rooms and suites to the harbor view, which the Peninsula lost when the Cultural Center was built across Salisbury Road. Each room is different, but all are equipped with fax machines and laser video players, among other amenities. For guests who wish to make a particularly dramatic entrance, the hotel also offers two rooftop helipads. Finally, everyone visiting Hong Kong ought to visit the Peninsula at least once to savor one of the most civilized breakfasts, afternoon teas, or evening drinks to be found anywhere in the world.

Mandarin Oriental. 5 Connaught Road, Central, Hong Kong. Tel: 800-526-6566 or 011-852-2522-0111. Fax: 011-852-2810-6190. 538 rooms. Doubles from HK$3,375 to $4,500 (US$450 to $600). Credit cards accepted.

Grand Hyatt Hong Kong. 1 Harbour Road, Wanchai, Hong Kong, Hong Kong. Tel: 800-233-1234 or 011-852-2588-1234. Fax: 011-852-2802-0677. 573 rooms. Doubles from HK$2,200 to $4,000 (US$280 to $516). Credit cards accepted.

The Regent. 18 Salisbury Road, Kowloon, Hong Kong. Tel: 011-852-2721-1211. Fax: 011-852-2739-4546. 694 rooms. Doubles from HK$2,423 to $4,020 (US$323 to $536). Credit cards accepted.

The Peninsula. Salisbury Road, Kowloon, Hong Kong. Tel: 011-852-2366-6251. Fax: 011-852-2722-4170. 300 rooms. Doubles range from HK$3,000 to $4,133 (US$400 to $551). Credit cards accepted.

RESTAURANTS 20

Hong Kong is filled with great restaurants. Our two favorites are Lai Ching Heen, the ground-floor restaurant in the Regent, and Man Wah, the restaurant on the twenty-fifth floor of the Mandarin Oriental. **Lai Ching Heen**'s decor is nothing short of boring, although the elaborate jade and ivory table settings, as well as the view, are exquisite. When the food begins to arrive, however, Lai Ching Heen turns into one of the best Oriental restaurants we have ever tried. The chef's specialties on the menu are highly unusual and absolutely tantalizing.

Man Wah makes up for whatever Lai Ching Heen lacks in atmosphere. Although the surrounding buildings have eclipsed much of the view, Man Wah still enjoys a vista of Hong Kong's starry skyline that is absolutely unforgettable. The sensuously dark and romantic decor only makes the lights of Hong Kong and Kowloon sparkle even more brightly. When we took our seat our eyes focused momentarily on the handsome ebony and gold chopsticks—which retail for $270 a pair! The Cantonese cuisine melds beautifully with the splendor of the surroundings. The Peking duck is the best we have ever tasted. For openers, we would suggest the drunken prawns. Our meal got off to a very lively start as we watched the live prawns jump in their glass bowl as they became drunk on the rice wine poured over them. Man Wah's menu is appealing from top to bottom, with such pricey delicacies as shark's fin soup and the curious bird's nest soup made from actual swallows' nests. Be sure to request a window table.

When we began to tire of Hong Kong's Oriental food, we found a plethora of dining options in almost every other cuisine. For French dining, we recommend either **Gaddi's** in the Peninsula or **Plume** in the Regent. When we reached our limit of high-profile dining, we took a much-needed break at **New China Max** in Times Square, which provides an intriguing eclectic atmosphere with superb, very moderately priced, original, orientally inspired Western dishes as well as outstanding Thai and Hunan dishes. Be sure to arrive early if dining on a Thursday, Friday, or Saturday night, for the restaurant transforms itself into a night-club at about ten-thirty. For a quick, simple, Italian lunch, head for **Il Mercato** on Stanley Main Street.

Note: When you take a taxi, have the concierge write out your destination in Chinese for the driver. Although Hong Kong's official languages are English and Chinese, its population of 6 million is 94 percent Chinese and, surprisingly, only a relatively few speak English.

Lai Ching Heen and Plume. The Regent. 18 Salisbury Road, Kowloon, Hong Kong. Tel: 011-852-2721-1211. Fax: 011-852-2739-4546. Credit cards accepted.

Man Wah. Mandarin Oriental. 5 Connaught Road, Central, Hong Kong. Tel: 800-526-6566 or 011-852-2522-0111. Fax: 011-852-2810-6190. Credit cards accepted.

Gaddi's. The Peninsula. Salisbury Road, Kowloon, Hong Kong. Tel: 011-852-2366-6251. Fax: 011-852-2722-4170. Credit cards accepted.

New China Max. 1 Matheson Street, eleventh floor of Lane Crawford Place Building, Hong Kong, Hong Kong. Tel: 011-852-2506-2282. Credit cards accepted.

Il Mercato. 126 Stanley Main Street, Hong Kong, Hong Kong. Tel: 011-852-2868-3068. Credit cards accepted.

NON-GOLF ACTIVITIES

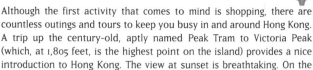

Although the first activity that comes to mind is shopping, there are countless outings and tours to keep you busy in and around Hong Kong. A trip up the century-old, aptly named Peak Tram to Victoria Peak (which, at 1,805 feet, is the highest point on the island) provides a nice introduction to Hong Kong. The view at sunset is breathtaking. On the opposite side of the island, Aberdeen offers sampan rides through its floating population of over 30,000 where traditional life on sampans and junks is framed against twentieth-century skyscrapers. Horse racing at Happy Valley on Hong Kong Island or at Shatin in the New Territories is one of Hong Kong residents' favorite pastimes; of the two tracks, we would suggest Happy Valley. Races take place on Wednesday evenings and weekends from September through May. Our side trip to the outlying islands, reached by ferry, gave us a slightly different view of Hong Kong. Try the forty-five-minute ferry to Lamma Island and select your fish for grilling on the beach, then spend the afternoon touring the sights.

For an all-day trip, especially if you have never been to China, we would strongly suggest a guided, one-day excursion into more typically Chinese territory. In the course of the day we visited three cities—Shenzhen (the first Special Economic Zone in China), Dongguan, and Guangzhou (Canton)—as well as a market, several temples, a traditional village, and even the zoo. At the zoo we caught a quick glimpse of two panda bears and several other indigenous animals that are not on display anywhere else in the world.

From the high-fashion houses of France, Italy, and Japan, to fabulous antiques, to bargain hunting at its best, Hong Kong offers heavenly shopping. At the high end there are countless well-planned arcades that will keep even the most seasoned shopper busy for days. And, of course, at least one trip to the Stanley Market must be on everyone's itinerary. The market is a maze of local crafts, T-shirts, sequined tops, cashmere, linens, running shoes, and everything else, all at incredible prices, and if you ask for a special price, the vendors will go down even lower with very little prompting. Il Mercato serves as a peaceful lunch stop to catch your breath and recharge your batteries. Visits to cricket matches, the Legislative Council building, jewelry manufacturers, custom tailors, and museums comprise a few more of the myriad activities available.

GETTING THERE: All the major Hong Kong hotels offer limousine pickup service for arriving guests. The cost of the forty-five-minute drive from the airport to the hotels is about $40. Check with the concierge at your hotel to make arrangements to get to the Discovery Bay Golf Club.

Thailand

▶PHUKET

GOLF IN AN ASIAN PARADISE

	The Golf	Golf Services	Lodging	Restaurants	Non-Golf Activities	Total
Rating	17	17	20	19	18	91

Phuket, a small Thai island, now appears on virtually everyone's Asian travel itinerary. Sure, a few too many large hotels have sprouted up in recent years, and in some

Phuket

places there are too many tourists, but Phuket still resembles the tropical Asian paradise of our dreams. Step beyond the tourist development and you will discover deserted white sand beaches drifting into the turquoise blue waters of the Andaman Sea, serene rice paddies being tended by women in peaked straw hats, water buffalo tethered near huts along quiet roads, and acres upon acres of rubber tree plantations. Add the colorful, bustling daily life of the local markets, antique and souvenir shops selling stunning artwork and local crafts, and fabulous local festivals such as the bizarre and astounding Vegetarian Festival (featuring fire walking and cheek piercing) in early October, and the combination makes Phuket a fabulous and utterly fascinating holiday destination.

The astronomer Ptolemy first mentioned Phuket in the second century, and since then its popularity has grown steadily. In ancient times, Phuket's population consisted mostly of pirates and fishermen, but the discovery of rich local resources such as tin and later the advent of rubber plantations ensured the island's status as one of Thailand's richest provinces. Despite local wealth, the island's population did not exceed 30,000 until, as is appropriate in this golden age of media coverage, the 1974 James Bond film *The Man with the Golden Gun* was filmed in Phang Nga Bay. Since that time the tourism industry has taken over Phuket and the population has more than quadrupled. Now one of the most popular day cruises is advertised as the "James Bond Island Cruise."

Phuket is located off the southwest coast of Thailand and can be reached via Bangkok on several daily one-hour flights. There are two seasons in Phuket: dry and wet. Most years, little differentiates the two since during the wet season it often only rains for an hour or two each day and the sun emerges again shortly thereafter. The temperature varies from about seventy to ninety degrees year-round with nighttime temperatures always remaining warm and balmy. The wet season lasts from mid-May to mid-October. During the dry season, the hotel rates increase by 20 to 50 percent.

THE GOLF

Even before Tiger Woods's tournament victory in Bangkok, Thailand was already fast becoming "golfland," and Phuket is doing nothing to slow this down. Theoretically, you could stay on Phuket for a week and play a different course each day, although some of them may be a bit rough around the edges. We have sought out for review two courses that are far and away above the others, Blue Canyon and Thai Muang Beach. As both are incredibly different from one another, playing each is a real treat, and we heartily recommend your fitting them into your schedule.

Blue Canyon Country Club, designed by Yoshikazu Kato, was completed in 1993. This is an island course devoid of even a glimpse of the sea's turquoise waters, but its very demanding layout does not lack for natural beauty. Whether winding through old rubber trees from bygone eras or jumping over ravines to elegantly perched greens, this is a decidedly intriguing course that has hosted the Johnny Walker Asian Classic, which Greg Norman has won. The fairways, which are flanked by water in some form on fifteen of the eighteen holes, are in a beautifully lush condition, and the greens are no worse for wear. The club is beautifully planted with neat shrubs, copious flowers, and banana trees lining the walkways. From the moment we teed off at 6 A.M., graciously accompanied by our female caddie, we enjoyed every turn and twist of Blue Canyon.

The excitement really begins on the second hole, where an intimidating marshy area to the left instantly wakes you up. Then you must conquer the green, which is virtually surrounded by bunkers. Obstacles such as these become even more apparent on the third, where a large tree is strategically placed in the middle of the fairway, posing a distinct problem in reaching the bunker-guarded green. Six, which is dotted with palm trees, should be played to the left so that your second shot can carry over the pond. A beautifully situated kiosk located beyond the sixth hole provides a timely stop for a cool drink. The dogleg ninth, with a lake to the left and a marshy area to the right, is made more treacherous by yet more water in the form of a creek before the green; the flag sits directly under the clubhouse with waterfalls surrounding the green. Thirteen again showcases the canyon and is, we think, the prettiest hole on the entire course. The drop zone on the other side may save you from losing a few balls, but then your path to the green is still beyond the canyon to the right and over a slew of bunkers.

As you head down the homestretch, you will find fourteen a breathtaking hole. The tee is high up beside the clubhouse, and the green is perched out on a peninsula in the lake. Fifteen presents a profound psychological challenge with its blind tee shot. One of the only discordant elements about the course becomes evident on sixteen and seventeen, where you can be bombarded by the deafening roar of planes seemingly taking off right above your head. On eighteen, the large lake to the right provides a climactic scenic ending to an enjoyable round of golf. There are four sets of tees, with yardage varying from the lengthy 7,049 yards from the black tees to the 5,964 yards of the reds. Par for the course is seventy-two. Play on the Blue Canyon Country Club course is open to registered guests of the club's golfers' lodge (see below). The club has no riding carts. Also, look for a new Gary Player/Yoshikazu Kato course at Blue Canyon to open in late 1997. It should be lovely!

A forty-five-minute drive from Amanpuri (see Lodging, below), the Pete Dye championship course at **Thai Muang Beach,** which is on the mainland of Thailand but just over the bridge from Phuket Island, came as a wonderful surprise. Opened in December of 1993, this 7,028-yard, par seventy-two course is played by very few Americans, so it often goes unreported. In fact, a large percentage of the relatively few golfers visiting Thai Muang Beach are Thai. On the day we played this challenging course, there were only three other people playing, so we could make detours out onto the beach along the second nine to snap some pictures and stop for cold refreshments. Armed with a caddie and an umbrella for the sun, we found this to be a very pleasant walking course with few inclines.

Thai Muang starts off with an intimidating first tee. The 40-yard sand trap to the right melts away only to be replaced with a medley of mounded bunkers. The steep, wood-ribbed bunkers throughout the course are reminiscent of Thai fans or even large scallop shells. The tee shot at number three plays over water. By the time you reach this double-dogleg, 610-yard monster you see the beginnings of the development that looms ahead for the Thai Muang resort. On seven it is best to stay to the left, playing to the coconut trees that are just beyond the green. Eight provides a break from the forward tees, which do not necessitate playing over the water on this pretty, par three hole. The 517-yard ninth is an especially challenging hole if you tend to pull left since a wide bunker runs almost the length of this crescent-shaped fairway before giving way to water.

The second nine, which we found even more enjoyable than the first, begins with a pleasant par four. The fairway here is long and wide, leading up to a large green, with wood-rimmed bunkers pushing up to its sides. On eleven, the middle and back tees force play over a pond that is itself lined with quite a few sand traps. Twelve was the most poorly maintained hole on the course, but even so it was pleasant to play given the sand-rimmed lake to the right and the deep, rolling bunkers (more than ten feet deep!) to the right of the green. The final hole, the Gem, features a luxuriously wide fairway that runs along the beach and the Andaman Sea. So if you hook left, you could end up on one of the most beautiful, long, white sand beaches on Thailand's mainland, or in the crystal-clear waters of the Andaman Sea. The greens fee is 1,800 baht ($72) and the cost for a caddie 180 baht ($7).

Blue Canyon Country Club. 165 Moo 1, Thepkasattri Road, Maikaw, Thalang, Phuket 83140, Thailand. Tel: 011-66-76-327-440. Fax: 011-66-76-327-449. Credit cards accepted.

• 1993. Designer: Yoshikazu Kato. Par 72. 7,049 yards. Greens fee: 2,300 baht ($92). Caddies (200 baht/$8) available. No carts. Season: year-round.

Thai Muang Beach Golf and Marina. 157/12 Moo 9, Limdul Road, Tambon Thai Muang, Amphoe Thai Muang, Phang-nga 82120, Thailand. Tel: 011-66-76-571-533. Fax: 011-66-76-571-214. Credit cards accepted.

• 1993. Designer: Pete Dye. Par 72. 7,028 yards. Greens fee: 1,800 baht ($72). Walking permitted. Caddies (180 baht/$7) and carts (600 baht/$24) available. Season: year-round.

GOLF SERVICES

In this category, Blue Canyon excels, while Thai Muang Beach is pulling out all the stops to catch up. At Blue Canyon, the clubhouse is in immaculate condition and has a very pleasant, open-air feel about it, even in the enclosed air-conditioned sections. There are two restaurants—the one upstairs is more formal, while its downstairs counterpart proves ideal for either a quick breakfast before heading out to play or a relaxed lunch in the afternoon. On the day we were there the entire clientele was from Japan, and from what we gather this is not unusual. The pro shop, which has panoramic windows looking out onto the course stretched out below, is attractive, and the very helpful salespeople speak English. Clubs are available for rent. While at Blue Canyon, be sure to check out the spa options, which include full Thai massages priced at 300 baht ($13) per hour. Quite a deal.

When we played the course at Thai Muang Beach, the golf facilities included friendly service, pleasant female caddies, and range balls. The caddies and ground crew mill around leisurely and in a good-natured fashion. But make no mistake: Thai Muang Beach is a high-profile resort. The complex includes a marina and a slew of condominiums, restaurants, and sport facilities. A posh, multimillion-dollar clubhouse has relegated the old character-filled wooden clubhouse to the status of a caddie shack. The new establishment is committed to running a first-rate operation, and future plans include the construction of two large resort hotels.

LODGING

The **Blue Canyon Country Club** complex features forty-nine units, which are very clean and quite tastefully furnished. Because management has restricted play at the country club to in-house guests, we would suggest staying the night and rising early to play the course in the very early morning before the sun has a chance to bring the temperature up too high. The country-club setting is quiet and elegant, and there's enough here to keep you satisfied for a few days, but in truth these lodging units do not approach the magnificence of the Amanpuri's.

The **Amanpuri** is the ultimate hide-away to buffer you from everything but the glorious, warm sea breeze drifting in off the Andaman Sea. Opened in 1988 as the first Amanresort, the Amanpuri could be considered one of the jewels of the East. An exaggeration? Frankly, no. From the moment we were met at the airport by one of the hotel's air-conditioned cars, presented with fresh orchids, and given chilled towels to re-fresh ourselves after the flight, the stan-dard of quality never slipped, even in

Amanpuri

the slightest way. The setting is a high knoll rising up over Pansea Beach. Forty private pavilions and villa homes, connected by elevated walkways and cart paths, dot the steep hillside. After arriving at the hotel, we were taken on a brief explanatory tour of the resort and shown the two irresistible gift shops, the black-tiled pool, the beauty salon featuring traditional Thai massage, well-equipped health club facilities, and, finally, a private boulder-protected beach reachable by descending the seventy-eight steep but dramatic steps leading down from the pool.

Each pavilion is set comfortably away from its neighbors and features a large bedroom and sitting area accented with dark wood and beautiful Thai artifacts and art. The bedroom flows into a mammoth bathroom with a sunken tub in the center and a separate cobalt-blue-tiled walk-in shower. Almost every wall slides back to in-vite in the balmy ocean breezes, creating the feeling that you really have found a tropical paradise after all your years of searching. The spaces are accented with lovely orchids and fragrant jasmine. In keeping with Thai tradition, each room's pri-vate, outdoor *sala*—with cushions and sunken table to relax around while reading or enjoying private dining—completes the room's luxurious space. Now, take a mo-ment to sip the complimentary split of chilled champagne that has just arrived with your luggage, and try some of the exotic fruit in the huge fruit bowl, which is re-plenished daily. The mangosteen, if you can figure out how to open it, is the most delicious of the many local fruits.

The pavilions come either with or without ocean views. Although those that face the sea are stunning, the lush palm and treetop surroundings of the others will not be a disappointment. The villa homes offer two-, three-, or four-bedroom accom-modations and are as exquisite as everything else about the resort. Each has a din-ing and living *sala* and can come with your own Thai chef.

If the pool, beach, tennis court, health facilities, and library are not enough to keep you pleasantly relaxed, the Amanpuri also maintains a fleet of luxury yachts with well-trained crews waiting to pamper you beyond your wildest dreams as you sail around the Andaman Sea and explore its many islands. Plan a diving excur-sion on *Plabin*, the thirty-five-foot magnum cigarette-style boat, or take an overnight cruise on *Arral 1*. Or go for a sunset cruise on the converted Chinese sailing junk *Sea Lion*, which has been tastefully outfitted with wicker furniture and lush, cream cushions.

Blue Canyon Country Club. 165 Moo 1, Thepkasattri Road, Maikaw, Thalang, Phuket 83140, Thailand. Tel: 011-66-76-327-440. Fax: 011-66-76-327-449. 49 rooms from 3,500 baht to 6,000 baht ($140 to $240). Credit cards accepted.

Amanpuri Resort. Pansea Beach, PO Box 196, Phuket 83000 Thailand. Tel: 800-447-7462 or 011-66-76-324-333. Fax: 011-66-76-324-100. 40 pavilions ranging in price from $333 to $805. Credit cards accepted.

 ## RESTAURANTS ⑲

Thai food ranks among the most interesting and varied of the ethnic cuisines. If you are adventuresome, the small local restaurants and even the food stalls will keep your palate electrified. For the most part, these are locally owned and operated, assuring a sense of authenticity, but for many Westerners this local food may prove to be a bit much. If you fall into this category, do not be dismayed, for we have managed to find what we believe to be the best restaurant on Phuket, if not all of Thailand—and it is just beyond your room! The Amanpuri's own **Terrace Restaurant** has managed to create some of the most mouthwatering dishes imaginable. With all local Thais in the kitchen, the food that reaches the table is the real thing. Head chef Daniel Lentz, who is actually a California recruit, makes certain that although some of the food is fiery hot, it will keep everyone coming back for more, as we did.

Unless you are completely versed in the ways of Thai cuisine, we suggest asking for a bit of advice. The key is to mix and match appetizers and main dishes, making the final result a kind of smorgasbord of meats, spices, soups, and cooking methods. After eating here several more times and ordering a new myriad of dishes at each sitting, we honestly feel that the entire menu might possibly have been created by the island's food gods. Each item was superb. All the curries were well balanced and smooth, if at times unbelievably hot; the seafood dishes included only the freshest ingredients and some very unusual local fish; the chicken was tender and exquisitely prepared; naturally, the herbs used in the preparation and garnishings were not only fresh but were combined in the most interesting way. Although many of the dishes were traditional and their appearance on the menu unsurprising, their preparation was. Soups such as tom kha gai, which is an herbed soup of chicken and coconut milk, and tom yaam goong, a spiced soup of shrimp, mushroom, and lemongrass, were so far superior to their counterparts we have sampled in other Thai restaurants, it hardly seems fair to call them by the same names. The satays were the best we have ever had, and, consequently, we could not help ordering at least one with every meal. The more unusual dishes, such as the crispy squid salad with green mangos, chili, and cashew nuts and the haw mog ruam, or steamed curried mousse with seafood, were just as invigorating.

In tandem, the superb food and idyllic setting lifted us into a state of Oriental bliss. The open-air restaurant looks out over the black-tiled swimming pool, which is surrounded by sixty-foot palms, each of which is handsomely lit. On the opposite side of the pool, a trio of classical Thai musicians sit cross-legged under an elevated pagoda, emitting delicately ethereal notes from traditional Thai instruments. This setting could not be improved upon. If we were forced to make one suggestion, it would be to do away with the white tablecloths, as they seem out of place and a bit too formal.

Although we would have been infinitely happy to have eaten every meal at the

Thai restaurant, we dutifully sampled the Mediterranean and Italian cuisine at the Amanpuri's other restaurant, blandly named the **Restaurant,** and were very pleasantly surprised. The menu was varied, original, and very enticing, with the likes of pumpkin ravioli with sage butter; local seafood in white wine, tomato, garlic, and saffron; grilled beef with olive paste and asparagus, and tempting pasta dishes. Perched up above the ocean, this slightly more formal option is delightful.

The Terrace is open for lunch, as is the very pleasant open-air bar opposite the Restaurant; lighter lunch fare includes Thai salads and some very interesting sandwiches such as the chicken curry burger. Another attractive option is to dine on the boulder-protected private beach while lounging on a wooden chaise shaded by a Thai umbrella. The dining experience at the Amanpuri is elegant decadence at its best!

The restaurants at the Amanpuri Resort. Pansea Beach, PO Box 196, Phuket 83000 Thailand. Tel: 800-447-7462 or 011-66-76-324-333. Fax: 011-66-76-324-100. Credit cards accepted.

 NON-GOLF ACTIVITIES

One of the joys of staying in accommodations so luxurious is to surrender totally to the carefree environment by availing yourself of all the resort has to offer. Days spent enjoying Thai massages and relaxing on a cushioned, elegant teak chaise, remembering to stroll ten feet to the edge of the crystal-clear water for a snorkel or just a dip, and quietly enjoying the unobtrusive pampering of the beach attendants comprise an island lifestyle to which we could definitely grow accustomed. When you yearn for an activity that expends a bit more energy, tennis is always an option; the hotel will arrange a partner for any expertise level. Scuba diving off Phuket in the Andaman Sea offers many tropical fish in high-visibility waters. Some popular diving locations include Shark Point, famous for leopard sharks, and Koh Dok Mai, where the dive goes through caves and crevices filled with a myriad of brightly colored fish and coral.

Around the island you can partake of many interesting cultural activities from browsing through curios shops to visiting old colonial buildings. The movie *The Killing Fields* used the colonial Government House as a setting. Several museums and an aquarium are worth a visit, as are any of the thirty Buddhist temples and several Islamic mosques on Phuket. Phuket Town offers a vast array of souvenir/antique stores with some beautifully embroidered pillows and tapestries, as well as carvings. Village markets feature a wide array of Indonesian fabrics and fruits and are worth a visit. Check with the hotel to arrange transportion.

GETTING THERE: Most international flights to Phuket land in Bangkok and require a change to a Thai carrier for the final leg to the resort island. Phuket is served by a one-hour flight from Bangkok. The Amanpuri provides complimentary transfers from the airport to the resort.

Bali

▶BALI GOLF AND COUNTRY CLUB
AND BALI HANDARA COUNTRY CLUB
GOLF ON THE MYSTICAL ISLAND OF BALI

	The Golf	Golf Services	Lodging	Restaurants	Non-Golf Activities	Total
Rating	17	15	20	18	19	89

Bali Handara Country Club

"Bali Hai . . ." Perhaps it was Yul Brynner and Deborah Kerr dancing and singing on a land not so distant from this tropical South Pacific island, or perhaps it is the terraced rice fields, the friendly, brightly clad Balinese, the hundreds of enchanting temples, and the beautiful, sandy beaches reaching out to turquoise waters that have created the mystique that shrouds Bali. Dutch sailors certainly found something alluring about the island when, in the sixteenth century, they came ashore and refused to return to their ship for two full years. In more modern times, Bali still has great potential as an island paradise, yet it can also prove to be a vacation nightmare if the uninformed golf traveler is steered in the wrong direction. What you need to remember when visiting Bali is that this small tropical island is akin to Mexico as far as providing an appealing, yet relatively inexpensive vacation destination. Regrettably for those who come seeking to get away from it all, this translates into lots of tourists looking for a dirt-cheap vacation, along with an endless array of restaurants and bars advertising their happy-hour specials on sidewalk chalkboards and countless kids aggressively hawking imitation Rolex watches. Kuta Beach and the village of Legian, in particular, are full of tourists, making them distinct areas to avoid. For the same reason, we also recommend bypassing Denpasar, Bali's capital of over 100,000.

Overpopulation is a very real problem for this small island (fifty by ninety miles), which, at last count, was home to almost 3 million people. The heaviest population concentration lies in the island's eastern half. Here the traffic system that supports the population truly must be seen to be believed! We would suggest hiring a chauffeur-driven car rather than attempting to drive yourself, unless, of course, you are looking for some serious adventure. When we asked our driver, in disbelief, if traffic accidents were common, he turned with an odd smile and said, "Why yes, they are. In fact, just last week my father was hit by a motorcycle and killed." Between the bicycles, mopeds, motorcycles, cars, donkeys, goats, and women carrying hundred-pound bags of rice on their heads, the scene on the roads is nothing short of a circus.

Despite the pandemonium, Bali remains an endearing destination, with an amazing variety of attractions. Unlike the neighboring, larger island of Java, the dominant religion on Bali is Hindu rather than Islam, making the profuse art and music of Bali very unique. Each village on the island is known for a different craft or product; one is famous for its wood carvings, another for its silver, and yet another for its baskets. With all this in mind, Bali promises an intriguing visit.

THE GOLF

Bali's two most famous golf courses—Bali Golf and Country Club and the Bali Handara Country Club—differ in just about every area. Both have their advantages, although we had to look a bit harder to find them at Bali Handara.

Despite arid conditions on most of the island, we found the Robin Nelson/Rodney Wright championship course at **Bali Golf and Country Club** to be a beautifully maintained and lush golf challenge. The course, located in the resort environment of Nusa Dua, combines several different playing conditions: the undulating front nine winds through foliage and flower beds with stone cart paths and is designed in the manner of Bali's terraced rice fields, while the second nine heads down to the lowlands through numerous and massive coconut palms and follows, at times, along the island's white sand beaches.

The course begins with a beautiful uphill par five with the Amanusa resort visible beyond. Lush flowers frame almost every view. The second hole, a par-four dogleg-right, requires a carry over a tree-filled ravine. A rooster wandered onto the green here to inspect our progress and then trotted away, adding a bit of comic relief to our game. Many of the holes at the Bali Golf and Country Club feature exquisite views of the Indian Ocean. The third hole fits this description, as the back tees play over terraced rice paddies. Number seven is a long, 580-yard par five with the ocean beyond and orange, white, and fuchsia bougainvillea lining the fairway. The 394-yard ninth is a testing dogleg to a water encircled green.

When we arrived on the tenth tee, we wondered if we had just entered another course entirely. The extremely flat back nine features an obscene amount of sand. Although there are only ten traps, they are so massive and omnipresent that we seemed unable to steer clear of them. Several stretch for an entire fairway. Although it is virtually the same length as the front nine, the back nine feels much longer. Water comes into play on only two holes (eleven and twelve), until the course leads back across the road to seventeen and eighteen, where a large lagoon looms as a threat. The most difficult hole is the 458-yard, par four sixteenth, which doglegs left as sand guards both sides of the fairway all the way up to the green. This nine will either bring you to your knees or straighten out your attitude toward sand. Bali Golf and Country Club employs three sets of tees: 6,849 yards (slope 125), 6,437 yards (slope 120), and 5,208 yards (slope 113), marked as Crowns, Lions, and Frogs, respectively. Par is seventy-two. The greens fee is $135, mandatory cart included.

Our primary destination on Bali was the **Bali Handara Country Club** near Pancasari, high in the mountains of central Bali, where we expected to play one of the most highly acclaimed courses in all Asia. The anticipation mounted as we made the forty-minute drive from Ubud up into the mountains. Nearing the "crater" in the mountains, we were feeling giddy to find the magical Peter Thomson/John Harris/Ronald Fream–designed course that

Bali Handara Country Club

reputedly puts all others to shame. Sadly, we found no such place.

The funky, rather run-down clubhouse and the condition of the course quickly roused us from our romantic reveries. Our visit was at the end of the dry season when there had not been a drop of rain for eight months, making course conditions brittle, to say the least. Bali Handara has no fairway irrigation system, and although we were told that greens were irrigated, only a few of them had been watered adequately. We also encountered trash on the course, and at one point, while retrieving a ball, we climbed down into a dry riverbed that must have been used for village dumping for some time.

To be fair, though, Bali Handara provides a beautiful setting, and we were not about to let a situation that jarred with our typical experience back home spoil such a far-flung golf odyssey; after all, we were in Bali, not Beverly Hills. As the course makes its way around the base of the mountain, it affords spectacular views of the outlying island. The greens were garnished with what would have been gorgeously lush flower beds and sculpted shrubs had this not been such an abnormally dry season. Bali Handara's elevation also assures considerably cooler temperatures, and, therefore, far more comfortable playing conditions than Bali Golf and Country Club's sea-level location.

When we began our warm-up by hitting a few balls on the driving range, we were flabbergasted to see our caddies chasing down every ball we hit. These young men spoke very good English and kept us amused throughout the day. On the driving range a camaraderie quickly developed as they kindly slapped us on the back after a couple of our better shots and, also, after a couple of our weaker ones. When starting off on the first hole, we were in quite good spirits, thanks in part to such encouragement. Amazingly, one of our caddies pulled out his business card at the conclusion of our round, but his name would be of little help since every family names their children the same name according to their birth order! The caddies remain, arguably, the most endearing feature of a round of golf at Bali Handara.

You are best advised to warm up quickly on Bali Handara because the third hole, a 405-yard par four, is the most difficult hole on the course, with a waste area to the right and a creek cutting across the fairway. Five is a 370-yard par four that brings you straight back up to the mountain base, and the long, par four sixth plays toward the picturesque rice fields.

On the second nine, fifteen, a 483-yard par five, is impressive with its view of Lake Buyan in the distance. Several dangerously placed bunkers must be avoided with both your driver and subsequent shots as the fairway sweeps down the mountain. At sixteen, you will find a small, picturesque drinks hut with carved wooden stools, a village to the right, and the crater out to the left. It plays straight at 432 yards and has only three traps as obstructions.

Bali Handara is 7,024 yards from its back tees and 6,432 yards and 5,781 yards from its forward tee, with a par of seventy-two. The greens fees for Bali Handara are $78 on weekdays and $95 on weekends; the caddie fee is $8. If you have the time after your round, a forty-five-minute massage is only $17.

Bali Golf and Country Club. PO Box 12, Nusa Dua 80361, Bali, Indonesia. Tel: 011-62-361-771495 or 011-62-361-771791 (tee times). Fax: 011-62-361-771797. Credit cards accepted.

• 1991. Designers: Robin Nelson, Rodney Wright. Par 72. 6,849 yards. 72.4 par rating. 125 slope rating. Greens fee: $135, mandatory cart included. No walking. Caddies available. Season: year-round.

Bali Handara Country Club. Pancasari, Bedugul, Bali, Indonesia. Tel: 011-62-361-289431 or -11-62-361-288944. Fax: 011-62-361-287358. Credit cards accepted.

• 1975. Designers: Peter Thomson, John Harris, Ronald Fream. Par 72. 7,024 yards. Greens fees: $78 (weekdays) and $95 (weekends). Walking permitted. Caddies ($8) and carts ($25) are available. Season: year-round.

GOLF SERVICES 15

Golf Services were quite unimpressive at Bali Handara and good but not exceptional at Bali Golf and Country Club. The clubhouse at Bali Handara is run-down and grungy. The carpeting is worn, the paint is chipped, and locker rooms are musty and sparse. The restaurant, which features Japanese dishes, is mediocre. The pro shop did not impress us in the least, and the lodging rooms which we looked at, although some had very nice views, were depressing.

On the other hand, Bali Golf and Country Club sports a very spiffy atmosphere in the clubhouse and in the attractive and well-stocked pro shop. Clubs are available for rent for $25, as are shoes for $7. Carts come equipped with coolers stocked with bottled water. The two open-air restaurants here are quite good for lunch.

LODGING 20

We highly recommend the three Amanresorts on Bali: Amankila, Amanusa, and Amandari. The **Amankila,** on the island's eastern coast, looks out on beautiful views of the Badung Strait. We were warned that the oil tankers anchored in the distance could detract from the tranquil paradise that the Amankila so effortlessly attempts to create, but we barely noticed them. Without question, the beauty of the hillside resort overwhelms everything in the vicinity. The multitiered pool appears to reach right out into the blue beyond. The cushioned, covered enclaves dotted around the pool make an ideal spot to spend the afternoon reading, unless you're staying in one of the seven suites, each of which comes equipped with its own private pool. In a word, from the serenely luxurious suites to the impeccable service to the boutiques brimming with art and local wares, every aspect of the Amankila quietly whispers excellence.

The equally gorgeous **Amanusa,** situated adjacent to the Bali Golf and Country Club on the southern coast of Bali, tops a grassy knoll that affords lovely views of both the Indian Ocean and the golf course. The thirty-seven thatched and airy suites with outdoor living areas are elegantly and luxuriously furnished with canopied poster beds, marble floors, and sunken baths. Eight of the suites have their own private swimming pools.

Five minutes from the art-colony town of Ubud and a forty-five-minute drive from the beach, the **Amandari** is designed in the style of a traditional Balinese village. The twenty-nine suites surrounded by lush, terraced rice fields above the Ayung River showcase their tropical setting with sliding glass walls, outdoor sunken baths, and private gardens. The resort pool is designed in the shape of a rice terrace, and the walkways that connect the suites to the pool, restaurant, and other resort facilities will lead you directly to the villages that dot the rice fields around Amandari.

As different as the three Aman resorts are—the sparkling, glistening, sea-oriented Amankila, the equally luxurious though slightly more sports-oriented Amanusa, and the rural, mountainous Amandari—an ideal stay on Bali would combine both the Amandari and *either* the Amankila or the Amanusa resorts.

One other attractive lodging option on Bali is the **Four Seasons Resort** in Denpasar, just around the beach from the airport. Although the sounds of planes taking off in such an idyllic setting can be awfully disconcerting, the Four Seasons is a stunning hotel equipped with more modern amenities than most comparable hotels stateside. The 147 suites here, all of which have private pools, are arranged along walkways that wind in and about the hillside leading up from the beach. The rooms are absurdly comfortable with an undeniably exotic feel intensified by the mosquito netting draped elegantly over the beds. The marbled rooms also feature indoor and outdoor showers in the private gardens. The luxurious spa at the Four Seasons is an absolute must for a famous Balinese massage. Service at the hotel is impeccable in every aspect. The hotel also organizes beautiful local dancing demonstrations on the beach.

Amankila. Manggis, Bali, Indonesia. Tel: 800-447-7462 or 011-62-363-41333. Fax: 011-62-363-41555. 35 suites from $460 (plus 21 percent tax and services). Credit cards accepted.

Amanusa. Nusa Dua, Bali, Indonesia. Tel: 800-447-7462 or 011-62-361-772333. Fax: 011-62-361-772335. 37 suites from $460 (plus 21 percent tax and services). Credit cards accepted.

Amandari. Kedewathun, Ubud 80571, Bali, Indonesia. Tel: 800-447-7462 or 011-62-361-975333. Fax: 011-62-361-975335. 29 suites ranging from $460 to $715 (plus 21 percent tax and services). Credit cards accepted.

Four Seasons Resort Bali. Jimbaran, Denpasar 80361, Bali, Indonesia. Tel: 800-332-3442 or 011-62-361-701010. Fax: 011-62-361-701020. 147 villas beginning at $475 per night (plus 21 percent tax and services). Credit cards accepted.

RESTAURANTS (18)

Although we chose our repasts conservatively to reduce any chance of coming down with a food-related illness, we found more than enough culinary delights to keep us happy at the resort restaurants. The Four Seasons features three restaurants, all very good. **P.J.'s** beachside seafood restaurant provides a tranquil setting just a few paces from the gentle Indian Ocean and specializes in local seafood prepared in traditional Balinese methods. Other dishes are a bit more "American," such as blackened Cajun-style fish. A casual **poolside restaurant** serves sandwiches, salads, and some very appealing entrées, while **Tan Wantilan** is a more formal, open-air dining room with a tented roof made from pink lavender-toned fabric strips that creates the perfect atmosphere for a warm Balinese evening. On Tuesdays, Thursdays, and Sundays at Tan Wantilan, parties of six or more can make reservations for a Balinese meal served by Balinese girls in traditional dress. Dinner here costs about $45 per person. Service is wonderfully hospitable throughout.

The restaurants at all the Amanresorts are innovative and very stylish. Everything at these resorts is done with impeccable taste, and the restaurants have been wise to emphasize local cuisine and ingredients even while remaining somewhat Western in motif to please a broader spectrum of palates. The fish dishes were among our favorites. Our meals at each of the three Amanresorts were thoroughly enjoyable and definitely worth the visit.

The restaurants at the Four Seasons Resort Bali. Jimbaran, Denpasar 80361, Bali, Indonesia. Tel: 800-332-3442 or 011-62-361-701010. Fax: 011-62-361-701020. Credit cards accepted.

The restaurants at Amankila. Manggis, Bali, Indonesia. Tel: 800-447-7462 or 011-62-363-41333. Fax: 011-62-363-41555. Credit cards accepted.

The restaurants at Amanusa. Nusa Dua, Bali, Indonesia. Tel: 800-447-7462 or 011-62-361-772333. Fax: 011-62-361-772335. Credit cards accepted.

The restaurants at Amandari. Kedewathun, Ubud 80571, Bali, Indonesia. Tel: 800-447-7462 or 011-62-361-975333. Fax: 011-62-361-975335. Credit cards accepted.

NON-GOLF ACTIVITIES

Bali is often referred to as the "Island of the Gods." The Hindu population here has built more temples per person than can probably be found anywhere else in the world. Indeed, there are over 20,000 temples on Bali. Each village follows different traditions, and there are usually several parades or festivals going on somewhere on the island. Remember that while visitors are welcome in any temple, correct dress is requested. Correct dress means long sleeves and no shorts. We suggest bringing a sarong with you to tie around your waist to form a long skirt. This applies to men as well! A sash tied around the waist is imperative to enter a Hindu temple; symbolically, this separates the holy and unholy parts of the body. The Pura Goa Lawah temple is particularly interesting as it is built into a bat cave, and you'll see hundreds of live bats hanging from the cave walls above the worshippers.

Bali has a medley of activities to keep even the most active vacationer busy. We'll never forget our white-water rafting trip down the exotic Ayung River through the rain forests, which culminated in a magnificent Balinese feast. The Amandari makes mountain bikes available to those who want to peddle around the rice paddies, and guides are also available to lead hikes of varying lengths and difficulties. There are literally thousands of shops and galleries to keep the most exhaustive shopper busy. Festivals, dance demonstrations, and concerts are daily occurrences, as are fire walking and other exotic activities.

GETTING THERE: Regular air service to Bali from the United States is provided by Garuda Indonesia and Singapore Air. Once you know your flight schedule, call the resort to arrange transportation from the Denpasar Airport to your suite. The Four Seasons Bali will pick you up in a limousine for $25 per car. The drive takes about twenty minutes.

Australia

▶SYDNEY

NO WORRIES DOWN UNDER

	The Golf	Golf Services	Lodging	Restaurants	Non-Golf Activities	Total
Rating	18	17	18	19	19	91

The journey to Australia from the United States is a daunting trek—fourteen hours in the air from Los Angeles across the equator and the international date line. Your plane departs Los Angeles at noon on February 1, for example, and arrives in Sydney at 11 P.M. February 3. Jet lag is not an issue on this westward leg because, upon arrival in Sydney,

New South Wales

you simply check into your hotel and go to bed. The return trip home, however, is another matter. You depart Sydney at 3 P.M. and, after a fourteen-hour flight, arrive in Los Angeles at 10 A.M. the same day. Your brain is fogged and your legs still feel like spaghetti several days later. By the way, you also change seasons once you arrive in the Southern Hemisphere. Winter in America is summertime Down Under, the ideal time to make your visit. As architect Tom Doak says, "Australia is the best place on earth a golfer can travel."

"No worries, mate"—a cordial phrase uttered universally by every cabdriver and waiter you encounter—expresses an undeniable truth about the Australian travel scene. Indeed, your entire stay in Australia is apt to be hassle-free, given the legendary easygoing dispositions and ready smiles of the Australian people. Truly, virtually everyone we met in Sydney was open, talkative, and delightfully unpretentious. Friendships develop quickly, particularly on the golf courses but also in the hotels and restaurants, where the service personnel at the finer establishments bowled us over with their warmth and friendliness. Our allotted time of two weeks in Australia simply shot past. This is a country experiencing a golden age of innocence not unlike America during the 1950s. Despite its inauspicious origins, Australian society is safe and orderly, with clean streets and little crime.

In addition to its vast harbor, Sydney is a city of bays, beaches, coves, and waterways. Easily one of the most progressive and tolerant cities on earth, Sydney also manages to be both down to earth and stylish—quite a balancing act. Sydney is also ambitious. The residents of more snobbish Melbourne, Australia's second city, disdain Sydney as all too hustling and bustling, particularly now that Sydney is rapidly preparing for the 2000 Olympic Games. Melbourne and Sydney, of course, enjoy a great rivalry. Sydney is larger (nearly 4 million) and the more genuinely sophisticated of the two. Melbourne, equally appealing in its way, is the more traditional and provincial capital, with famous golf courses in the sand belt designed by Alister Mackenzie that are actually superior to those around Sydney.

It also must be noted that the visiting gourmet will discover—to his or her absolute joy—that Sydney is currently experiencing an extraordinary restaurant boom, with local, fresh seafood fueling the explosion and sublime Australian wines making every meal more memorable. Restaurants in Sydney take a backseat to those of no other city.

Golfers should be prepared for a few byzantine eccentricities. For example, men who wish to wear shorts on certain courses are required to wear kneesocks, which may be purchased in the pro shops. Golf maintenance crews in Australia—unlike every other country in the world—have priority on the course. One or two courses (like Royal Sydney) are impossible to get on, while many other courses have strictly limited hours for visitors, hence careful advanced preparation is essential when booking tee times. And *never* wear a hat indoors. If you are detected wearing a hat or visor inside the clubhouse at certain Australian courses, you will be required to buy a round of drinks for everyone on the premises. Trust us: this tradition is taken seriously by several club memberships.

Because of the complexities involved with booking tee times in the rather closed world of Sydney golf, Golf Travel strongly recommends the services of Jeremy Alexander of Northern Beaches Golf Tours, a Sydney-area golf specialist who booked our tee times. Jeremy is delightful, knowledgeable, and so well connected in Sydney that he can secure tee times for clients at the best clubs on weekends and members-only weekdays. He routinely achieves tee-time miracles that the out-of-towner would not be able to pull off alone. To contact Mr. Alexander in Sydney, call 011-612-9975-7755 or fax 011-612-9975-7986.

The top golf clubs in Australia, following the British example, are private-public hybrids that permit outside play on a limited basis only on certain days of the week.

Overseas visitors to Australia who are members of a golf club and have an established handicap will be accommodated on the courses described below during their visitors' hours—provided, of course, that they book early enough in advance. Golfers with no handicap or club affiliation will be relegated to the far less interesting public courses in the area. Be certain to have in your possession a letter of introduction from your head golf pro and current handicap information. Some Australian clubs may request that you fax them this information in advance of your arrival.

Unfortunately, every facet of the game of golf is expensive in Australia. Greens fees for visitors at the best Sydney courses range from a low of $110 AUD ($91) to a high of $230 AUD ($191), and oftentimes credit cards are not accepted. As a result of Australia's having no golf manufacturing facilities, both balls and clubs are imported and subject to enormous duties. Balata balls sell for $70 AUD ($58) a dozen. We could have paid for our entire trip had we brought two golf bags to Australia—the second full of Cobra Titanium drivers, Bubble Burners, and Great Big Berthas, all of which sell for $1,100 AUD, or $912 in U.S. currency.

Other distinct aspects of the Australian game include a brisk pace of play (as in Scotland), walking (rather than riding in a cart, although carts are available at many courses), generally mediocre practice facilities (with hacked-up range balls), distances that are measured in meters rather than yards, and absolutely amazing winds that tear in from the Pacific with awesome power, winds more severe than any we have experienced at any other golf venue in the world.

Be advised: In addition to a valid passport, an Australian tourist visa is required for entry into Australia.

THE GOLF

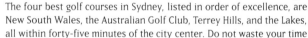

The four best golf courses in Sydney, listed in order of excellence, are New South Wales, the Australian Golf Club, Terrey Hills, and the Lakes, all within forty-five minutes of the city center. Do not waste your time attempting to get on strictly private Royal Sydney. Monash Country Club, St. Michael's, the Coast, Mona Vale, Camden Lakeside, Riverside Oaks, and Long Reef are all very good layouts available for outside play if the top four cannot be worked into your travel schedule.

New South Wales, designed by Alister Mackenzie in 1928 and built on the magnificent exposed headlands overlooking Cape Banks and Botany Bay, is the finest golf course in Sydney by a wide margin. This is the course that President Clinton and Greg Norman played when Clinton visited in November of 1996, and, in fact, the President is now an honorary member of the club. Rated fourth in Australia (after Royal Melbourne, Kingston Heath, and Metropolitan), New South Wales is vastly underrated at number fifty-four in the world. "Magical" and "inspirational" are the two adjectives most commonly used by the membership—which boasts more single-digit golfing handicaps than any other club in Australia—to describe this dramatic and historic site, where Captain James Cook of the Royal Navy first anchored in 1770, claimed Australia for England, and found fresh drinking water for his crew in the pools that still stand below the eighteenth tee.

Unlike the Australian Golf Club and the Lakes, which have suburban settings and abut a major highway on several holes, New South Wales is a spectacularly scenic, oceanside layout that pits the golfer against the elements and features shots from clifftops across pounding surf. The site of New South Wales has to be seen to be believed. Frequently, the course is closed due to dangerously high winds that sweep in from across the ocean. We have never set foot on a windier course than this. Even so, try your best to get here, as New South Wales is truly singular.

The first hole is a short (293 meters/320 yards) and strategic par four; the great third is a blind, uphill, dogleg left, yet it is the fifth and sixth at New South Wales that are arguably the two most memorable holes of golf in all Australia. The fifth is a stunning, 468-meter (512-yard) par five that plays directly into the wind. It is also the point on the course where you get your first real taste of the broad blue Pacific. If you hit your tee shot into the saddle of the hill on five, you will be left with a downhill, 200-meter (218-yard) shot to the green—and a spectacular view of rocky Cape Banks beyond. The sixth hole is pure Cypress Point, a 177-meter (193-yard) par three over the rocks and ocean waves, a terrifying tee shot if there ever was one. The back nine is also packed with ocean-hugging beauties. Number thirteen, a dogleg-left, features a cliffside green perched on the ocean's edge that is fully exposed to fierce winds. New South Wales measures 6,227 meters (6,810 yards) from the members' tees and 5,497 meters (6,011 yards) from the forward tees. Par is seventy-two.

New South Wales has a superb pedigree. It hosted the Australian PGA Championship both in 1994 and 1996, Bruce Crampton was club champ here in 1953, and Steve Elkington makes it his home course today. The handsome and very comfortable clubhouse, built on a hillside overlooking the course, was completely renovated in anticipation of the PGA event. Staff members are very friendly and welcome visitors with a smile, which cannot be said of all Sydney-area courses. New South Wales has just thirteen golf carts, which are reserved for those with a medical condition. All able-bodied golfers walk.

The Australian Golf Club

Clinton wasn't the only American making an important professional appearance in Australia in November of 1996; Tiger Woods was there as well, playing in the Australian Open, held in the Sydney suburbs at the prestigious **Australian Golf Club** (an event won handily by Greg Norman). The Australian is the home club of media mogul Kerry Packer, one of the wealthiest men in Australia.

The Australian Golf Club is rated fifth in Australia (one spot behind New South Wales), and it is an extremely difficult course. The club dates from 1882; the golf course was completed in 1904, when it hosted the very first Australian Open. The course today, however, is a merciless and exquisitely maintained Jack Nicklaus design from 1977. Built within a natural amphitheater, the layout features several very long par fours and undulating greens that are guarded, in characteristic Nicklaus fashion, with strategically placed ponds and multiple bunkers. Those familiar with the better Nicklaus layouts in the United States will feel very much at home here. Critics of the course call it overly Americanized, and, indeed, this is as American a layout as you will find in Australia, a far cry from the all-natural conditions that prevail at New South Wales and quirky St. Michael's, for instance. But Nicklaus did a great job here. We loved the course despite its difficulty.

The Australian's only liability is that this rectangular piece of property is bordered by a major highway on one side and suburban bungalows on the other sides. The Australian offers a far better experience for the visiting golfer than the Lakes, but both courses are marred in areas by highway noise, not exactly the idyllic golf experience we had anticipated in Australia.

Outstanding holes at the Australian include number seven, a 382-meter (417-yard) par four that demands a drive between bunkers on the left side of the fairway and high grassy mounds on the right and a second shot, hit inevitably with a wood or long iron, that must be kept away from the pond protecting the right side of the green. The twelfth, a 367-meter (401-yard) par four, is a spectacular hole that makes you want to air out a long drive from the elevated tee. And the two finishing holes, seventeen and eighteen, feature deadly water hazards. Water threatens the left side of the seventeenth fairway and the right side on number eighteen. The Australian is a monstrously long 6,443 meters (7,046 yards) from the back tees. From the members' tees it measures an only somewhat more reasonable 6,079 meters (6,648 yards). Par is seventy-two.

A day at the Australian is extremely costly. The visitors' greens fee, which includes your cart and a nice, three-course lunch served in the attractive clubhouse, costs $230 AUD ($191), making this one of the world's most expensive golf courses. All major credit cards are accepted. Head professional Ron Luxton's staff in the pro shop is cordial and welcoming, while the clubhouse itself is modern, comfortable, and well run.

Designed by Graham Marsh in 1994, **Terrey Hills** is a lavish, new golf club located forty-five minutes north of Sydney in open countryside very much akin to authentic Australian bush. For such a new course—and, indeed, one that draws instant comparison with any number of big, new American layouts—Terrey Hills exudes an Australian authenticity that will delight the overseas visitor. The club has a well-heeled international membership, a few multimillion-dollar mansions under construction on the periphery of the golf course, a glorious clubhouse with a fine restaurant, bar, and locker facilities, and a very friendly staff manning the pro shop. This is a course clearly created for walking. Carts are not available, but pull carts and remote-control power hand carts are. Terrey Hills is already rated twenty-fourth among Australia courses, a rating certain to improve with time. Craig Parry won the Cannon Challenge here in 1995.

Terrey Hills has a hushed and peaceful forest character on the front nine with its broad, rolling fairways and water hazards in the form of man-made lakes on four of its first nine holes. The back nine is more wide open and windswept, with water hazards on five holes. Terrey Hills does not have a weak link, and the entire eighteen is in immaculate condition. The most outstanding individual holes include the seventh, a tight, downhill par four with water on the right side of the green; the ninth, a long, forest-fringed, 513-meter (561-yard) par five that requires a downhill approach shot to a green guarded by a pond; the eleventh, an uphill par four; and twelve, a dicey, little, 155-meter (170-yard) par three that plays into the wind and features yet more water on the right side of the green.

Flies that swarm around your head are the only problem at Terrey Hills; to combat them we were taught the "Australian salute," a special wave of the hand to swat flies off your face. Insect repellent is available in the clubhouse.

Terrey Hills measures an exhausting 6,418 meters (7,016 yards) from the black tees, 6,070 meters (6,638 yards) from the blue tees, and 5,709 meters (6,243 yards) from the white tees. Par is seventy-two.

Designed by Robert von Hagge and Bruce Devlin in 1970, the **Lakes** is highly regarded in Sydney and rated the number nine course in all Australia. However, except for the excellent holes on the back nine, we found the Lakes extremely disappointing. Our experience here proves yet again that poor

The Lakes

service and mediocre course administration can ruin an otherwise wonderful day of sport. The staff in the pro shop set the lackluster and highly indifferent tone. A gentleman behind the desk took one quick look at our American golf socks, told us they violated the dress code, sold us an interesting pair of pale blue kneesocks to wear instead, relieved us of our greens fee, and sent us out for a five-hour round on a rangerless course behind a cluster of snail-paced foursomes. Of Sydney's name courses, the Lakes is the weakest. Its maintenance is only fair, the clubhouse has a depressing atmosphere, the grounds crew we chatted with was surly, and the course itself is cut in half by a busy highway. Instead of coming here, play a second round at New South Wales.

Having said this, we must also note that the Lakes' back nine offers one stunning challenge after another. Fourteen and seventeen are the showcase holes, but ten, eleven, and fifteen are beauties as well.

Ten is a short par four that requires no more than a long iron off the tee followed by a short iron to the green. But try not to hit it past the pin, as anything hit over the green will disappear into the ravine beyond. Eleven is a gorgeous par five that doglegs around a lake, and thirteen is another testing, short par four. Super-long hitters may be able to drive the green on the downhill thirteenth (303 meters/331 yards) by cutting the corner and hitting the ball over the trees on the right. Fourteen, with complete justification, is the most famous hole at the Lakes. This 488-meter (533-yard) par five requires a lake crossing with an approach shot that is almost always hit into strong prevailing winds. Fifteen is a 190-meter (208-yard) par three across water, and seventeen, another par five, demands a drive across a lake to a generous landing area, followed by another lake crossing with your second shot.

Of the lesser courses in the Sydney area, our favorites include Long Reef and St. Michael's, two historic and very simple seaside links with wonderful ocean views located a half-hour's drive from downtown Sydney, and the Scottish-style Camden Lakeside, a Peter Thomson design from 1993, about an hour from the city center.

New South Wales. Henry Head, La Perouse, NSW 2036, Australia. Tel: 011-612-9661-4455. Fax: 011-612-9311-3792. No credit cards.

• 1928. Designer: Alister Mackenzie. Par 72. 6,227 meters (6,809 yards). Greens fee: $130 AUD ($108). Walking permitted. No caddies. Carts cost an additional $35 AUD ($29). Restrictions: open to the public Monday afternoons, Thursday afternoons, and Friday mornings. Season: year-round.

The Australian Golf Club. 53 Bannerman Crescent, Rosebery, NSW 2018, Australia. Tel: 011-612-9663-2273. Fax: 011-612-9662-6096. Credit cards accepted.

• 1904/1977. Designers: Alister Mackenzie/Jack Nicklaus. Par 72. 6,443 meters (7,046 yards). Greens fee: $230 AUD ($191), cart included. Walking permitted. No caddies. Restrictions: open to overseas visitors on Tuesday and Thursday mornings from 7:30 A.M. to 8:30 A.M., but, again, exceptions may apply. Season: year-round.

Terrey Hills. 116 Booralie Road, Terrey Hills, NSW 2084, Australia. Tel: 011-612-9450-0454. Fax: 011-612-9669-6206. No credit cards.

• 1994. Designer: Graham Marsh. Par 72. 6,418 meters (7,016 yards). Greens fee: $110 AUD ($91). Walking permitted. No caddies. Only pull carts ($4 AUD/$3) and remote-control bag carrier ($10 AUD/$8). Restrictions: open to overseas visitors on weekdays on a limited space-available basis. Season: year-round.

The Lakes. Corner of King Street and Vernon Avenue, Eastlakes, NSW 2018, Australia. Tel: 011-612-9669-1311. Fax: 011-612-9669-6206. Credit cards accepted.

• 1970. Designers: Robert von Hagge, Bruce Devlin. Par 73. 6,315 meters (6,906 yards). Greens fee: $120 AUD ($100); carts cost an additional $40 AUD ($33). Walking permitted. No caddies. Restrictions: Open to overseas visitors on Mondays and Tuesdays on a space-available basis. Season: year-round.

GOLF SERVICES

Due to the exorbitant price of golf accessories Down Under, be certain to bring all the essentials with you, including at least two dozen balls. Golf services in Australia, generally speaking, follow the rudimentary British standard, not the more lavish American model. Services are friendly and comprehensive at New South Wales, the Australian, and Terrey Hills. Each of these courses has an attractive clubhouse with fine restaurants, bars, locker rooms, and pro shops. Caddies are *not* available. Golfers must walk on all courses except New South Wales, the Australian and the Lakes, where carts are available.

LODGING

We stayed at both the Ritz-Carlton on Macquarie Street and the Intercontinental right next door during our own Sydney sojourn. Both establishments are absolutely outstanding, but neither wins top prize in the Sydney hotel sweepstakes. That honor goes to the incomparably located Park Hyatt. Sydney boasts several superb hotels, which are listed in order of excellence below. Book now for the 2000 Olympics.

In America, Hyatt hotels—like Marriotts—are always dependable and excellent, but rarely do they compete at the very pinnacle of the luxury hotel market with the Four Seasons and Ritz-Carlton properties. Across Asia and Australia, however, Hyatt is a dominant player. The gorgeous **Park Hyatt** in Sydney is a good example of this new breed of super-luxurious Hyatts that have become so successful in the Pacific Rim.

The Park Hyatt has a magical location—the very finest of any hotel in Sydney. It is situated under one great Sydney landmark—the Sydney Harbor Bridge—and just across Sydney Cove from another landmark, the spectacular Sydney Opera House. From the hotel, views of the Opera House, the nonstop water traffic in the harbor, and the handsome city skyline are simply incomparable. The immediate neighborhood surrounding the Park Hyatt is called the Rocks; this is Sydney's historic district, and it is packed with the city's most elegant shops, boutiques, galleries, restaurants, and fun-loving pubs. Every conceivable diversion is within ten minutes of the Park Hyatt's front door.

The Park Hyatt has been beautifully designed to optimize the views and water setting. A wall of glass on the ground floor provides views across the harbor, and the long, outdoor dining terrace overlooking the Opera House is the ideal spot for a leisurely lunch. The public areas are beautifully maintained and decorated with fine furnishings and elegant sculptures. The service staff throughout is attentive and personal.

Be certain to request a harbor-view room when booking. All rooms are spacious and extremely comfortable and include luxurious marble baths with separate tub and shower. Other amenities include two restaurants, a lovely bar, a fitness center, and a rooftop terrace with swimming pool. Harbor-view rooms at the Park Hyatt are the most costly double rooms in Sydney, ranging from $440 AUD to $650 AUD ($364 to $539). Suites begin at $700 AUD ($580). The Park Hyatt is small by Hyatt standards, with just 153 rooms and suites. It is essential, therefore, to book far in advance.

Sydney has two Ritz-Carltons: one downtown on Macquarie Street and a second in Double Bay, where Princess Diana stayed during her October 1996 visit to Sydney.

Remote Double Bay—a gentrified neighborhood with trendy boutiques fifteen minutes from downtown—suits camera-shy Di because its location assures a degree of peace and quiet, yet the first-time visitor to Sydney should bypass distant Double Bay in favor of Macquarie Street.

We have stayed in many Ritz-Carltons over the years—from Boston to Chicago to Palm Springs—but the Macquarie Street address has the finest service staff of any Ritz in our experience. And superb service, of course, is a Ritz-Carlton priority.

On a less positive note, we must report that the **Ritz-Carlton**, unlike the Park Hyatt, does not have a strong sense of place. In fact, once you step inside the front door, all Ritz-Carltons look quite similar, with lots of heavy red brocade and antique furnishings from London circa 1890. Ritz-Carltons maintain an excellent standard, yet little distinguishes one from another. In other words, Ritz-Carltons consistently reveal just one, rather unimaginative personality.

However, we stayed in a very beautiful room, number 711, which features a sitting room and bedroom, a lovely view of the Sydney Opera House and the harbor, and a spacious marble bath. Doubles are priced from $269 to $329 AUD ($223 to $273) and suites begin at $419 AUD ($347). Ask about their bed-and-breakfast package starting at $299 AUD ($248). Wonderful breakfast buffets are served in the dining room every morning, and outstanding luncheon buffets are served in the bar each afternoon.

A large and very well run hotel that occupies a historic building on Macquarie Street next door to the Ritz-Carlton, the **Intercontinental** is far more bustling and less personal than the Ritz. Tour groups getting in and out of buses at the front door are not an uncommon sight, yet the guest rooms themselves are handsomely decorated and beautifully appointed. We stayed in a room on the twenty-seventh floor with a wonderful view of the Opera House and Sydney Harbor. Room appointments include fully stocked minibars, luxury bathrooms, and cable television. The Intercontinental has 498 rooms and suites on thirty-one floors. Doubles range from $360 to $425 AUD ($299 to $352).

Although it remains one of Sydney's outstanding hotels, the **Regent** no longer retains the city's number-one rating it held during the 1980s. This very large hotel (594 rooms) offers excellent service and a vast and glorious all-marble lobby, yet some of its guest rooms now require renovation. The Regent has a great location overlooking the harbor and is within easy walking distance of the boutiques and restaurants in the Rocks. Doubles range from $218 to $385 AUD ($181 to $319).

Park Hyatt. 7 Hickson Road, The Rocks, Sydney, NSW 2000, Australia. Tel: 800-233-1234 or 011-612-9241-1234. Fax: 011-612-9256-1555. 153 rooms and suites. Doubles range from $440 to $650 AUD ($364 to $539). Suites begin at $700 AUD ($580). Credit cards accepted.

Ritz-Carlton. 93 Macquarie Street, Sydney, NSW 2000, Australia. Tel: 800-241-3333 or 011-612-9252-4600. Fax: 011-612-9252-4286. 106 rooms. Doubles range from $269 to $329 AUD ($223 to $273). Credit cards accepted.

Intercontinental. 117 Macquarie Street, Sydney, NSW 2000, Australia. Tel: 800-327-0200 or 011-612-9230-0200. Fax: 011-612-9240-1240. 498 rooms and suites. Doubles range from $360 to $425 AUD ($299 to $352). Credit cards accepted.

The Regent. 199 George Street, Sydney, NSW 2000, Australia. Tel: 800-545-4000 or 011-612-9238-0000. Fax: 011-612-9251-2851. 594 rooms. Doubles range from $218 to $385 AUD ($181 to $319). Credit cards accepted.

RESTAURANTS

The golfer who leads a happy double life as a gourmet and wine lover will find Sydney an earthly paradise, for this is truly one of the world's greatest cities for dining out. Australian wines are well known in America, but the best bottles never leave Australian shores. Hence, if you so chose, you may dine and drink to your heart's content night after night. Despite the casual style of Sydney's top restaurants, jackets and ties are advisable at all of the restaurants listed below.

The most famous restaurant in Australia and voted the finest restaurant in Sydney two years in succession, the **Rockpool** more than fulfills its incredible press clippings. Located in the midst of fashionable George Street in the Rocks, Rockpool is polished, stylish, and super-sophisticated in every detail. The handsome, modern interior—a long rectangular room with a bar in front and an intimate dining area in the rear—is packed every night with Sydney's business elite, clusters of well-dressed Australians, Asians, and Americans making deals and discussing the direction of the Japanese stock market. Fresh seafood (Rockpool gets two deliveries every day) is the house specialty. We thoroughly enjoyed the sushi appetizer, the succulent and distinctive Sydney rock oysters, and the wonderful fresh snapper, all accompanied by an excellent 1995 Pipers Brook chardonnay from Tasmania selected from the vast wine list. The service is friendly and outgoing. A complete dinner for two with wine and tip costs approximately $210 AUD ($174).

Hip and happening **Bel Mondo** opened in October 1996 on the top floor of a beautifully renovated historic warehouse at 12 Argyle Street in the Rocks. The elegant Argyle Department Store occupies the lower levels of the warehouse, which can make finding the restaurant a bit difficult; you enter through the department store or, during evening hours when the store is closed, through the Argyle steps off Cumberland Street. Through this wonderful, big, warehouse windows, Bel Mondo offers impressive views of the Sydney Harbor Bridge. Italian dishes dominate the menu, but since this is Sydney, seafood also plays a big role. The harbor prawns and grilled salmon are excellent dishes, and the wine list offers many of Australia's greatest chardonnays, like the Tyrrell's Vat 47 chardonnay (at $113 U.S. per bottle or $12 U.S. per glass), the Petaluma Leeuwin Art Estate Series, and the Lindemans Hunter River Reserve Bin 8080. Dinner for two with wine and tip costs approximately $180 AUD ($149).

The wonderful **Pier** restaurant in Rose Bay is a delightful and beautiful restaurant built on a long and narrow pier and decorated so that it resembles an ocean-going vessel. Dinner guests gaze out at the boats bobbing at anchor and families of ducks paddling along the shore. The setting is inspirational. Australian *Vogue* describes the Pier as "quintessential Sydney dining, the perfect combination of quality food and views." Our dinner included Sydney rock oysters, grilled swordfish, and the wonderful Petaluma house chardonnay. The Pier is highly recommended. Expect to spend $180 AUD ($149) for a complete dinner for two, wine and service included. The Pier is a ten-minute cab ride from the downtown hotels.

A handsome, all-glass restaurant specializing in fresh seafood, **Bilson's** has a wonderful, central location overlooking Sydney Harbor and is within walking distance of the four hotels noted above. We found the cuisine to be extremely good; expect to pay about $180 AUD ($149) for a complete dinner for two.

A traditional Italian restaurant in the Paddington neighborhood, **Buon Ricord** has an unassuming exterior facade and a lovely, cozy interior with a wooden bar at the front, tile floors, a wood-beam ceiling, an exposed kitchen at the rear, and just sixteen tables. Our main course, pasta with fresh scallops, was excellent. A complete dinner for two with wine and tip costs approximately $150 AUD ($125).

Rockpool. 107 George Street, The Rocks, Sydney, 2000 NSW, Australia. Tel: 011-612-9252-1888. Fax: 011-612-9252-2421. Credit cards accepted.

Bel Mondo. Level 3, Argyle Department Store, 12–24 Argyle Street, The Rocks, Sydney, 2000 NSW, Australia. Tel: 011-612-9241-3700. Fax: 011-612-9241-3744. Credit cards accepted.

The Pier. 594 New South Head Road, Rose Bay, Sydney, 2000 NSW, Australia. Tel: 011-612-9327-6561. Fax: 011-612-9363-0927. Credit cards accepted.

Bilson's. Upper Level. International Passenger Terminal. Circular Quay West, Sydney, 2000 NSW, Australia. Tel: 011-612-9251-5600. Fax: 011-612-9251-5609. Credit cards accepted.

Buon Ricord. 108 Boundary Street, Paddington, Sydney, 2021 NSW, Australia. Tel: 011-612-9360-6729. Fax: 011-612-9360-2920. Credit cards accepted.

NON-GOLF ACTIVITIES

It is imperative that you visit one of the fascinating wildlife parks that surround Sydney. After our round of golf at Terrey Hills, we toured the nearby Waratah Wildlife Park, located on the edge of authentic Australian bush country, and were delighted by the experience. At Waratah you may pet koala bears dozing in the gum trees, feed gentle kangaroos, wander through a field with giant emus, and see other amazing Australian marsupials—such as wombats and Tasmanian devils—in their native habitat. Dingo dogs, giant white cockatoos, flocks of colorful parakeets, and sinister saltwater crocodiles can also be seen at Waratah.

While north of Sydney at Terrey Hills and Waratah, do not miss the incredible northern beaches that extend from Mona Vale all the way south to the exquisite village of Manly. With spectacular windsurfing at Long Reef and legendary surfing at Curl Curl, these are among the most spectacular beaches in all the world. Do not miss the extraordinary view of both Sydney Harbor and downtown Sydney from North Point. If you decide to emigrate to Australia, we can think of no better place to live than the lovely town of Manly, which looks like Santa Monica, California, in a state of complete innocence, with no litter or crime, and about one tenth of Santa Monica's current population.

In Sydney, tour the Opera House, walk across Sydney Harbor Bridge, ride a jet-cat from Circular Quay across the harbor to the zoo, tour the Sydney Aquarium, take a walk through safe and spotless Hyde Park, and be sure to have a drink in one of Sydney's top pubs, like the super-friendly Orient on George Street, which is filled to capacity every afternoon and evening. The Rocks neighborhood is Sydney's premier shopping district. David Jones, the city's largest department store, is on Elizabeth Street downtown. Coogi sweaters, made from Aboriginal designs, colorful opals, which are mined in Australia, and traditional "stockman" hats, worn by Australians in the outback, make excellent gifts.

Interesting day trips from Sydney include the Hunter Valley—the great wine region of New South Wales—and the Blue Mountains.

GETTING THERE: To get to the Park Hyatt from the Sydney Airport, there are taxis that cost $20 AUD ($17). If renting a car, from the airport you follow signs pointing you toward Sydney. From Liverpool Street, turn right onto George Street. Continue through the central business district and into the Rocks area. Take a right off George onto Hickson Road, where you will find the hotel.

►MELBOURNE

	The Golf	Golf Services	Lodging	Restaurants	Non-Golf Activities	Total
Rating	**20**	**17**	**17**	**18**	**18**	**90**

The rivalry between Australia's two largest and most important cities, Sydney and Melbourne—a Dallas versus Houston polarity, if you will—generally provokes bemused indifference in Sydney and frustrated gnashing of the teeth in Melbourne.

Sydney figures in the itinerary of every overseas visitor to Down Under because it is Australia's gateway city; Melbourne—a one-hour flight or a ten-hour drive

Commonwealth

from Sydney across the mountains—sometimes gets overlooked because it takes a bit of extra effort and planning to get there. Also working against Melbourne is the fact that it does not have the name recognition of Sydney nor does it possess a powerful and immediately recognizable symbol like Sydney's Opera House or harbor. In addition, Melbourne's lovely setting on Port Phillip Bay and the Yarra River—while handsome and idyllic—cannot compete with the gorgeous natural splendor of Sydney's beaches and waterways.

All that said, however, we still think it is an unpardonable mistake to view Melbourne as Australia's "second city." The two cities are simply very different. Melbourne is more tranquil, traditional, and—some might say—more British than Australian, while Sydney is much more progressive and bustling.

Melbourne is actually Sydney's superior in *at least* one important category: golf. In fact, Melbourne has the most illustrious and unique collection of golf courses of any city in the world, with an amazing cluster of eight vintage layouts in its suburban sand belt dating from the 1920s, many of which were designed by Dr. Alister Mackenzie, the World War I camouflage expert turned golf course architect, the creator of Augusta and Cypress Point, and arguably the most influential course architect of the twentieth century. These breathtaking Melbourne courses from the Mackenzie school—for Mackenzie-trained superintendents spread the gospel throughout the region after Mackenzie's departure from Australia—are all cut from the same cloth. Their rolling fairways are lined with gum and ti trees; the shaggy, overgrown rough areas are comparable to Scottish roughs; the par threes of Melbourne—when examined as a group—are perhaps the most sensational and distinguished par threes that can be found anywhere; and the natural-looking "Melbourne bunkers" are the most beautiful we have ever seen. Local members, as locals are wont to do everywhere, make many hair-splitting distinctions in order to differentiate one sand-belt course from another. In truth, however, these historic and carefully preserved layouts have many more characteristics in common than not.

The three most celebrated sand-belt courses—Royal Melbourne, Kingston Heath, and Metropolitan—are rated one, two, and three in Australia, but three other golf clubs—Victoria (rated number six in the country), Commonwealth (number fourteen), and utterly charming Yarra Yarra (vastly underrated at seventeenth)—are equally sublime. Magazine golf course ratings, of course, are highly political. Victoria, Commonwealth, and Yarra Yarra are all infinitely more interesting layouts than the Australian and the Lakes, which have been rated fifth and ninth in the nation respectively, if only to placate Sydney residents.

Finally, if you throw the National into the Melbourne golfing equation, a spectacular Robert Trent Jones, Jr., design from 1988 on Cape Schanck, with views as great as any course in Australia (including New South Wales), then you have the makings for an utterly superb golfing holiday. Melbourne is an experience no passionate golfer should miss. The Melbourne courses receive GOLF TRAVEL's highest, and distinctly apolitical, rating of 20. Of the lot, only legendary Royal Melbourne disappointed us.

Golf at Melbourne's private clubs is subject to the same idiosyncrasies that prevail in Sydney. All of the top clubs welcome a limited number of overseas visitors, but the actual hours for visitors are not exactly cast in stone; in other words, call well in advance for your tee times, and be prepared to be flexible about the days of the week and hours of the day you can play. Kingston Heath, Royal Melbourne, the National, Victoria, and Yarra Yarra accept credit cards, but your greens fees must be paid in cash at Metropolitan and Commonwealth. Men visiting during the Australian summer (December through March) who wish to wear shorts on the golf course are also required to wear kneesocks. A letter of introduction from your club professional and a handicap card are required at many courses. Brisk walking is the norm (a game of golf rarely lasts more than three and a half hours Down Under), caddies are generally not available, and the only course where carts are a fact of life is the National, with its severe terrain overlooking the ocean. Melbourne's climate is a subject of great conjecture; "four seasons in one day" is the common appraisal. And if you are detected wearing a cap or visor inside the clubhouse, you will be required to buy a round of drinks for everyone on the premises! So take your hat off before stepping inside.

GOLF TRAVEL recommends the services of cordial Jo and Anne Breadmore, owners of Unlimited Golf, a Melbourne tour company that drove us to the courses from our hotel and showed us around the region. Anne is an excellent golfer and former "lady captain" of Kingston Heath; husband Jo is a member of Metropolitan. Both are pleasant company. With their outstanding connections, the Breadmores can simplify the process of getting on the top courses in Melbourne. The Breadmores' telephone number is 011-613-9822-7445. Fax: 011-613-9822-0116.

THE GOLF   20

Membership in certain Melbourne clubs—like Royal Melbourne—is more about social prestige than sport. Kingston Heath has enormous prestige, but it also has the finest, most pure golf atmosphere of all the storied sand-belt clubs. Designed by Alister Mackenzie and Dan Soutar, **Kingston Heath** manages to be elegant and unpretentious at the same time, no mean feat in the rarefied world of Melbourne golf. With its cozy and tasteful clubhouse, friendly staff, and genuinely hospitable membership, Kingston Heath is our personal favorite in Melbourne.

The genius of Kingston Heath lies in its intricate routing pattern over a very compact (just 125 acres) rectangular property, its legendary par threes, its strategic short par fours, and the constant wind factor—in your

Kingston Heath

face, at your back, and blowing from side to side. The most successful approach shots are pitch-and-runs; lofted approaches hit at the pin will bounce hard and skitter off the green. You will also be faced with many long—and generally dead-straight—putts from the apron up to the pin.

The fifteenth hole at Kingston Heath is the most famous par three in Melbourne. Members frequently fortify themselves on the fifteenth tee with a "wee dram" from a hip flask when faced with this daunting shot, hit uphill 142 meters (155 yards) with the wind swirling and the green guarded by a spectacular complex of bunkers. The tenth hole is another little jewel, a 131-meter (142-yard) par three with sinister bunkers left and right. You must hit the green on ten for a reasonable chance to make par. Other great holes include number one, a 419-meter (458-yard) downwind opening hole where you must hit your tee shot to the crest of the hill in order to open up a good view of the green; number three, a deceptive, 271-meter (296-yard) par four that will trick you into trying to drive the green; number eleven, a lovely, 368-meter (402-yard) par four that doglegs right; and number sixteen, another tough dogleg with trees and thick shrubs lining the right side of the fairway. Kingston Heath measures 6,231 meters (6,814 yards) from the back tees. Par is seventy-two.

Metropolitan is a garden spot. Along with Yarra Yarra, it is the most peaceful and idyllic course in Melbourne. Designed by Alister Mackenzie, C. W. Chapman, and J. B. Mackenzie, Metropolitan lost its original back nine in 1959 when the land was requisitioned by the municipal school board. Dick Wilson, the great American architect who renovated Seminole, then created a wonderful new back nine for Metropolitan that now blends seamlessly with the original holes.

We played Metropolitan late one afternoon after a rainstorm and were enchanted by the experience—the mature eucalyptus trees with their strings of hanging, half-shed bark, exotic birds such as golden cockatoos and magpies singing in the trees, and the wonderful, couch-grass fairways underfoot, easily the finest fairways we played on in Melbourne. Couch grass was a revelation to us: it provides exquisite lies, produces effortless walking, and is virtually impossible to cut up with a divot. Metropolitan has hosted the Australian Open numerous times, most recently in 1997.

Metropolitan's four par fives are short and manageable (measuring just 438 meters/479 yards to 476 meters/520 yards long). The heart of the course, however, is its long and difficult par fours. Metropolitan's stunning opening hole is lined with trees on both sides, bends gently to the left, is beautifully bunkered, and measures 380 meters (416 yards) from tee to green. Four is an outstanding score on number one. Ten is a long (427 meter/467 yards) dogleg-left and fifteen, also 427 meters (467 yards) long, is another stiff challenge. Metropolitan measures 6,354 meters (6,948 yards). Par is seventy-two.

Many critics consider **Royal Melbourne** to be *the* premier golf club in the world. Needless to say, we were predisposed to fall in love with the place, despite the frigid tone of voice of the woman who booked our tee time when we called several months in advance from the United States. The great **West Course** at Royal Melbourne was laid out in 1926 by Alister Mackenzie. The considerably less distinguished **East Course** was designed in 1932 by club member Alex Russell, who had worked in collaboration with Mackenzie on the West. For tournaments—like the 1996 Greg

East Course, Royal Melbourne

Norman Challenge, which was played at Royal Melbourne—a composite course is utilized (so that there are no road crossings) consisting of twelve holes from the West and six holes from the East.

So we booked our tee time eleven or twelve weeks in advance by telephone, confirmed via fax the tee time with handicap information and a letter from our club professional, arrived at Royal Melbourne on the appointed morning, paid the $200 AUD ($166) greens fee, and were then instructed, without a word of explanation, to proceed to the number one tee on the East Course.

Traveling 10,000 miles to Royal Melbourne and being told to play the East Course is the equivalent of traveling to St. Andrews and being directed to the Jubilee or the Eden instead of the Old—an enjoyable enough experience in its own right but not at all what we had in mind. Prior to teeing off we inquired in Royal Melbourne's pro shop for the whereabouts of a rest room. An unsmiling attendant—who regarded us like gate-crashers at the spring prom—directed us to a filthy facility located behind the pro shop. The sand bunkers on the East Course were full of unraked footprints. There was a temporary green in place on the twelfth hole, and, while some of the greens had been cut, others remained uncut and shaggy. Without question, the East has several outstanding holes, yet the shabby treatment we met with was certainly not worth $200 in any currency.

On top of this, club protocol at Royal Melbourne must be the most arcane in golf. The toffy-nosed, hyper-Anglo atmosphere—gents strutting about on the putting greens like so many pashas and potentates from Britannia's heyday, what with swirling handlebar mustaches, blazers with the Royal Melbourne crest and gray trousers, brown suede shoes, and ascots—recalled words from *The Fatal Shore*, Robert Hughes's magnificent history of Australia and certainly required reading for anyone headed Down Under. "The colonial gentry," Hughes writes, "with its feudal social pretension, had an obsession with status. It is the provinces that fix on style and correctness." At Royal Melbourne, we felt like explorers from *National Geographic* stumbling upon an enclave of extinct Ubangi tribesmen. The women playing golf in long, flowing tartan skirts reminiscent of the Victorian epoch were, admittedly, quite elegant, yet the stilted and contrived club atmosphere did little to make us feel welcome. Had we known in advance that we would be treated so poorly, we would have bypassed Royal Melbourne altogether in favor of a second round at the more hospitable Kingston Heath, Metropolitan, or Yarra Yarra. If you opt to go to Royal Melbourne, we hope you enjoy it more than we did.

Holes one through four and seventeen and eighteen from the East Course are among the strongest Royal Melbourne holes. The par-three fourth (number sixteen on the tournament composite course) is 184 meters (201 yards) into the wind; anything hit short here will land in one of the brutal bunkers guarding the green. The sixteenth is the course's most beautiful hole, a 153-meter (167-yard) par three to an exquisite green surrounded by bunkers on all sides. And the finishing hole (number eighteen on the composite course) is a very tough, 395-meter (431-yard) par four that plays into prevailing winds. The East Course measures 6,030 meters (6,594 yards) (par seventy-two). The West Course is 6,023 meters (6,586 yards) (par seventy-two).

Located ninety minutes south of Melbourne on the Mornington Peninsula at stunning Cape Schanck, the **National** is a must for golfers touring Melbourne for a slew of reasons. It occupies a spectacular piece of real estate and offers sensational views of the coastline and the Pacific Ocean. The course itself is beautifully laid out and exquisitely maintained, and the club atmosphere is friendly and outgoing. When the wind blows hard you can throw away the scorecard, but make a day of it anyway: have lunch in the luxurious new clubhouse and a tour of the chief sights on the Mornington Peninsula. The National is an American-style club, but its heart and soul are pure Australian; despite severe climbs up and down hills, we were impressed with the large number of members who prefer walking to riding.

Designed by Robert Trent Jones, Jr., in 1988, the National features one magnificent challenge after another. The second hole—a 121-meter (132-yard) par three from an elevated tee to a generous green with ocean waves breaking in the distance—is the course's signature hole and one of the most glorious holes in all Australia. With the wind blowing from left to right, you want to start your shot virtually out at sea and then allow it to be blown back onto the green. The fifth is a 521-meter (570-yard) dogleg-left to a double green shared with the ninth hole. The tenth tee has a great view of the surrounding countryside and demands a dramatic downhill drive into the wind. The twelfth hole, another long par five, has spectacular ocean views. Unlike the generally flat greens of the sand-belt courses, the greens on the National are often multitiered and full of undulation. Fantastic scenery is the consolation if your game deteriorates.

The National has five sets of tees. From the tips it measures an awesome 6,313 meters (6,904 yards). Members generally play from the blue tees, which shortens the course to 5,873 meters (6,428 yards). From the red tees, the National measures 5,332 meters (5,831 yards).

Elegant, utterly charming, and easy-walking **Yarra Yarra** is another classic and compact Alister Mackenzie design in the heart of the Melbourne sand belt, not far from Metropolitan, Kingston Heath, Commonwealth, and Huntingdale. Yarra Yarra and Metropolitan are the two prettiest courses in the region, but Yarra Yarra, host of the 1995 and 1996 Australian Women's Open, is the most feminine. It features

Yarra Yarra

tight couch-grass fairways lined with native gum and ti trees, beautiful pedestal greens, songbirds singing from the trees, and a handsome, historic clubhouse. The course has two par three gems, including the gorgeous, slightly uphill eleventh, which is laden with enormous bunkers and the magical fifteenth, with its two-tiered green and severe bunkers left and right. Do not miss Yarra Yarra. It captures the true magic of Melbourne golf.

Although designed by two of its members, Charles Lane and Sloan Morpeth, **Commonwealth** was actually constructed by Vern Morcom, the Royal Melbourne superintendent who learned his trade from Alister Mackenzie. Commonwealth, therefore, fits neatly in the Mackenzie-inspired sand-belt tradition. Architect Tom Doak considers Commonwealth the best course in Melbourne. Stately trees, water hazards, beautiful bunkers, and a dignified clubhouse are features of this very fine club.

Victoria

Victoria—a beautiful, tree-lined club—is the home course of five-time British Open champion Peter Thomson, the first Australian to win the British Open, and 1954 British Amateur champion Doug Bachli, the only Australian ever to win that title. It has one of the best opening holes in the sand belt: a drivable, 233-meter (255-yard) par four that has been the scene of many eagles in major events. This gentleness, however, yields to genuine difficulty on the next two holes, which are long par fours with heavily bunkered greens. Special note: the Victoria Golf Club has attractive overnight accommodations located above the clubhouse where nonmembers may stay in the heart of the sand belt for generally a very reasonable fee, one to be decided upon application. When we stayed, our room cost a very reasonable $75 AUD ($62), breakfast included.

Kingston Heath. Kingston Road, Cheltenham, 3192 Melbourne, Australia Tel: 011-613-9551-1955. Fax: 011-613-9558-0681. Credit cards accepted.

• 1925. Designers: Alister Mackenzie, Dan Soutar. Par 72. 6,231 meters (6,814 yards). Greens fee: $150 AUD ($124). Walking permitted. No caddies. Carts (for those with a medical condition) cost an additional $25 AUD ($21). Restrictions: open to overseas visitors Monday afternoons and Friday mornings. Season: year-round.

Metropolitan. Golf Road, South Oakleigh, 3167 Victoria, Australia. Tel: 011-613-9579-3122. Fax: 011-613-9570-1703. Credit cards accepted.

• 1898/1961. Designers: Alister Mackenzie, C. W. Chapman, J. B. Mackenzie/Dick Wilson. Par 72. 6,354 meters (6,948 yards). Greens fee: $150 AUD ($124). No caddies. Walking permitted. Carts cost an additional $20 AUD ($17). Restrictions: open to overseas visitors Monday and Thursday mornings and Friday afternoons. Season: year-round.

Royal Melbourne. Cheltenham Road, Suburb of Black Rock, 3193 Melbourne, Australia. Tel: 011-613-9598-6755. Fax: 011-613-9521-0065. Credit cards accepted.

• *West Course.* 1926. Designer: Alister Mackenzie. Par 72. 6,023 meters (6,586 yards).
• *East Course.* 1932. Designer: Alex Russell. Par 72. 6,030 meters (6,594 yards).
• Greens fee for both courses: $200 AUD ($166). No caddies. Walking permitted. Carts costing $30 AUD ($25) available only for members or—possibly—those with a medical condition. Restrictions: open to overseas visitors Mondays, Tuesdays, Thursdays, and Fridays. Season: year-round.

The National. Trent Jones Drive. Cape Schanck. 3939 Victoria, Australia. Tel: 011-613-5988-6777. Fax: 011-613-5988-6744. Credit cards accepted.

• 1988. Designer: Robert Trent Jones, Jr. Par 72. 6,313 meters (6,904 yards). Greens fee: $80 AUD ($66). Walking permitted. No caddies. Carts cost an additional $28 AUD ($23). Restrictions: open to overseas visitors Monday through Friday. Season: year-round.

Yarra Yarra. 567 Warrigal Road, East Bentleigh, 3165 Victoria, Australia. Tel: 011-613-9563-7711. Fax: 011-613-9563-7913. Credit cards accepted.

• 1928. Designer: Alister Mackenzie. Par 72. 6,082 meters (6,651 yards). Greens fee: $125 AUD ($104). Walking permitted. No caddies. Only a few carts costing $20 AUD ($17) are available for those with a medical condition. Restrictions: open to overseas visitors Tuesday mornings, Wednesday afternoons, and Friday from 1–1:30 P.M. Season: year-round.

Commonwealth. Glennie Avenue, South Oakleigh, 3167 Victoria, Australia. Tel: 011-613-5988-6777. Fax: 011-613-5988-6744. No credit cards.

• 1925. Designers: Charles Lane, Sloan Morpeth. Par 72. 5,873 meters (6,423 yards). Greens fee: $100 AUD ($83). Walking permitted. No caddies. Carts costing $20 AUD ($17) are available for those with a medical condition. Restrictions: open to overseas visitors every weekday. Season: year-round.

Victoria. Park Road, Cheltenham, 3192 Victoria, Australia. Tel: 011-613-9584-1733. Fax: 011-613-9583-7557. Credit cards accepted.

• 1927. Designer: overseen by Alister Mackenzie. Par 72. 6,219 meters (6,801 yards). Greens fee: $150 AUD ($124), but it can vary upon application. Walking permitted. No caddies. Pull carts cost $3 AUD ($2), and a few riding carts might be available for those with a medical condition. Restrictions: open to overseas visitors on a limited basis, depending on the time of application. Season: year-round.

GOLF SERVICES

Services are generally excellent at all the clubs noted above with the exception of Royal Melbourne, where we experienced subpar treatment, to say the least. All of the clubs have practice ranges (although range balls in Australia are generally hacked to pieces), good pro shops, and locker facilities that are always satisfactory, with the exception, again, of Royal Melbourne, where we were told to change our shoes in the pro shop.

The National has the most dramatic practice range in the region and the most opulent modern clubhouse. The National is also the only course that operates a fleet of carts. Metropolitan's range is quite short; Kingston Heath's two-part range is eccentric: one part is irons-only and the other is woods-only. Several of the older clubs—Metropolitan, Yarra Yarra, and Kingston Heath—have distinguished interiors and lovely bars, ideal for a drink after your round. The head professionals we happened to meet—especially Henry Cussell at the National, Lindsay Gitsham at Kingston Heath, and Ross Anderson at Metropolitan—struck us as extremely cordial and made us very welcome at their clubs.

Golf equipment in Australia, unfortunately, is monstrously expensive, with balata balls, for instance, selling for $70 AUD ($58) a dozen. Therefore, bring every conceivable item you will require on the course, and, since the weather can be hot, windy, and rainy—"four seasons in one day," as they say in Melbourne—pack for every eventuality. A bungee cord to fix your bag firmly to the hand cart is also a good idea.

LODGING

By far the best hotel in Melbourne is the extremely well run Grand Hyatt, while the Windsor and the Sofitel are very good second choices. The lovely Victoria Golf Club has several pleasant guest rooms where nonmembers may stay at quite low rates ($63 when we were there), breakfast included. If you stay out in the Victoria suburbs, however, you will certainly require a rental car, and you might also find yourself missing the vibrant activity of Melbourne's attractive city center.

In addition to being the city's best hotel, the **Grand Hyatt** is also Melbourne's always busy social hub. This twenty-five-story hotel, with its 547 rooms and suites, boasts a lavish, virtually all-marble interior and wonderful service throughout, especially from the outstanding concierge desk. Dining options include Max's, one of Melbourne's premier restaurants, and an informal food court. You will also enjoy the hotel's location on Collins Street, which puts the city's best shops and boutiques within easy walking distance. We stayed in room 1608 and found it luxurious, spacious, and extremely well equipped. The Regency Club rooms on the top four floors are the Hyatt's best. The Grand Hyatt is highly recommended.

An impeccably maintained hotel dating from 1883, the handsome and historic **Windsor** is far more traditional than the ultramodern **Hotel Sofitel** (formerly the Regent), which occupies the top fifteen floors of a fifty-story Melbourne high-rise. Called the aristocrat of Melbourne's hotels, the Windsor can boast of being the oldest luxury hotel in Australia, evidenced by its distinctive, Victorian facade. An elegant hotel, the Windsor enjoys a convenient location right across from the Victorian Parliament House, which places it near the theaters, parks, and many of Melbourne's finest shops. Where the Windsor exudes Old World charm, the Sofitel is entirely contemporary. Guest rooms in this glossy hotel begin on the thirty-fifth floor of a fifty-story building, and all are organized around a mirrored central atrium. A recent $10 million refurbishment means that the hotel's rooms are some of the very best in town now, and they offer extraordinary views.

Grand Hyatt Melbourne. 123 Collins Street, Melbourne, Victoria 3000, Australia. Tel: 800-233-1234 or 011-613-9657-1234. Fax: 011-613-9650-3491. 547 rooms and suites. Double rooms from $270 AUD to $490 AUD ($224 to $406). Credit cards accepted.

The Windsor. 103 Spring Street, Melbourne, Victoria 3000, Australia. Tel: 800-562-3764 or 011-613-9633-6002. Fax: 011-613-9633-6001. 180 rooms and suites. Double rooms from $225 AUD to $320 AUD ($187 to $265). Credit cards accepted.

Sofitel. 25 Collins Street, Melbourne, Victoria 3000, Australia. Tel: 800-763-4835 or 011-613-9653-0000. Fax: 011-613-9650-4261. 363 rooms and suites. Double rooms from $260 AUD to $350 AUD ($216 to $290). Credit cards accepted.

RESTAURANTS (18)

Melbourne has a truly exceptional array of restaurants, the best of which are noted below. Melbourne's finest restaurant, **Jacques Reymond,** is housed in an elegantly decorated Victorian mansion about fifteen minutes from the city center. Chef Reymond, a gifted Frenchman, produces innovative cuisine that combines the finest Australian ingredients with subtle Asian influences. The *menu dégustation* features six wonderful courses in moderately sized portions: a duck consommé, seafood salad with squid, prawns, and tartare of tuna, a magnificent salmon fillet, perfectly roasted lamb, cheese, and dessert. Service is outstanding. Excellent wines are available by the bottle or by the glass, like the superb Craiglee chardonnay from Victoria and the Vasse Felix cabernet. Jacques Reymond is also Melbourne's most costly restaurant. Expect to spend $225 AUD ($187) for dinner for two, wine and tip included.

Located on Port Phillip Bay in hip and fashionable St. Kilda, about ten minutes from the city center hotels, the **Pavilion—St. Kilda Beach** has a bright white interior decor, a spectacular view of the water, excellent service, and a menu that features utterly sublime fresh seafood. Highly recommended. About $120 AUD ($100) for dinner for two, wine and tip included.

One of the friendliest restaurants in Melbourne, the **Stokehouse** is also possibly the city's most bustling and popular. Located on the water in St. Kilda, the Stokehouse is virtually next door to the Pavilion. Upstairs offers fine dining overlooking the bay, while the ground floor offers a bistro atmosphere with more casual fare. Specialties include succulent fresh Pacific oysters, barbecued John Dory, poached sea bass, and roasted lamb. About $120 AUD ($100) upstairs and $70 AUD ($58) downstairs for a complete dinner for two, wine and service included.

A delightful and cozy Italian restaurant with white walls, pine floors, and just seventeen tables, **Caffé Cento Venti** opened on Collins Street directly across from the Grand Hyatt in August of 1996. The appealing menu includes wonderful oysters, seafood pasta, superb snapper fillets with fresh herbs, and excellent rack of lamb. About $150 AUD ($125) for a complete dinner for two, wine and tip included.

The showcase dining room at the Grand Hyatt, **Max's** is one of Melbourne's most highly regarded restaurants. Our dinner here—tartare of salmon and tuna, steak, and a selection of fine Australian wines offered by the glass—was excellent in every detail. A complete dinner for two with wine and service costs approximately $160 AUD ($133).

Jacques Reymond. 78 Williams Road, Prahran, 3181 Australia. Tel: 011-613-9525-2178. Fax: 011-613-9521-1552. Credit cards accepted.

The Pavilion—St. Kilda Beach. 40 Jacka Boulevard, St. Kilda 3182 Australia. Tel: 011-613-9534-8221. Fax: 011-613-9525-3595. Credit cards accepted.

The Stokehouse. 30 Jacka Boulevard, St. Kilda 3182 Australia. Tel: 011-613-9525-5555. Fax: 011-613-9525-5291. Credit cards accepted.

Cento Venti. 120 Collins Street, Melbourne, Victoria 3001, Australia. Tel: 011-613-9650-5621. Fax: 011-613-9650-5227. Credit cards accepted.

Max's. Grand Hyatt Melbourne. 123 Collins Street, Melbourne, Victoria 3000, Australia. Tel: 011-613-9657-1234. Fax: 011-613-9650-3491. Credit cards accepted.

NON-GOLF ACTIVITIES

Melbourne, which hosted the 1956 Olympics, is a sports-mad city, from the Melbourne Cup (horse racing), to the Australian Grand Prix (auto racing), to the Australian Tennis Open, held in February at Melbourne's National Tennis Center. Melbourne is also home of the Australian Ballet, the Victoria Opera, and the Melbourne Zoo. After golf at the National, visit one or two of the excellent wineries on the up-and-coming Mornington Peninsula: two especially outstanding vineyards are the Red Hill Estate and the Dromana Estate. Melbourne boasts a clean, walkable downtown with wonderful parks and countless elegant shops tucked away in historic arcades. Collins Street, however, is Melbourne's most upscale shopping district. The recently revived Southbank neighborhood along the Yarra River is also worth exploring. Gambling is available in Melbourne in the large Crown Casino.

GETTING THERE: From the Melbourne Airport, take the exit for Tullamarine Freeway. Stay on the freeway until it ends (16 kilometers/9.6 miles). Go left at the traffic light onto Flemington Road. Go 2 kilometers (1.2 miles), until the roundabout. Veer slightly to enter Elizabeth Street. Continue 1.8 kilometers (1.1 miles) to Collins Street. Left onto Collins. Drive 500 meters (545 yards), turn right onto Russell, and the Grand Hyatt Melbourne will be on your left.

DESTINATIONS OF EUROPE

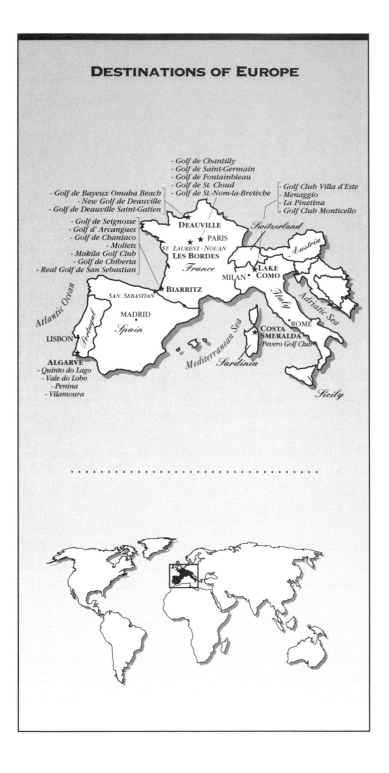

EUROPE

EUROPE

Europe is so well gardened that it resembles a work of art, a scientific theory, a neat metaphysical system. Man has created Europe in his own image.

—Aldous Huxley, *Do What You Will,* 1929

Time passes in America and Asia; in Europe, history occurs.

—John Updike, "Europe, Two Points on a Descending Curve," *Picked-Up Pieces,* 1975

We must excuse Continental Europeans if they have carried their long rivalry with Britain into the realm of golf. Scotland's wind-battered shores gave birth to golf, and the British Isles rightfully claim the game's most storied courses, yet Europe no longer plays the role of humble understudy. Instead, the Continent, which has never taken a cultural backseat to Britain, now offers its own golfing splendor. New golf courses are being built every day—more than two hundred have opened each year since the early 1990s—many of them designed by the biggest names in golf course architecture. Already, Western Europe's $10 billion golf industry is bigger than its winemaking industry. Unlike the United States, where four out of five new courses are modest layouts geared toward attracting the largest number of players, course construction in Europe has leaned toward the high end, with a disproportionate number of elaborate and exquisitely designed courses. These new courses join a short but notable list of older courses long revered by the sport's most discerning critics. By and large, these courses are private, but almost all permit public play during the week. Handicap limits often prevail—be sure to bring your handicap certificate and a letter of introduction from your home pro. The only adjustment you may have to make is that most European courses do not have golf carts. Otherwise, these lovely clubs will go to great lengths to make you feel completely welcome and at ease.

Best of all, Europe's golf courses spread out literally in the shadows of civilization's most magnificent capitals. In Europe, whether you and your family are taking a train through the countryside or strolling through the heart of the old cities, the Continent's beauty, history, art, and architecture never cease to inspire. The chance to combine splendid golf with the paintings of Rembrandt, the châteaux of the Loire, a Mozart opera in Vienna, and a papal mass at the Vatican is absolutely irresistible. Today you can steady yourself over a putt by gazing out on Paris, Madrid, Milan, Avignon, or Rome. From Paris, you can play historic Longères at Chantilly in the morning and coax a smile out of the Mona Lisa in the Louvre that same afternoon when you tell her about your triple bogey on number ten. The incomparable City of Light, home of the world's finest food and wines, offers golf travelers five superb courses for walking off any excess indulgence. France's true golfing capital, however, is Biarritz, a Basque city on the Atlantic Ocean. While staying at the brilliantly refurbished Hôtel du Palais, once known as the "resort of kings," you can immerse yourself in the colorful regional Basque culture, play several rounds with the peaks of the Pyrenees as a backdrop, and even sneak into Spain for a game followed by a sampling of vibrant tapas bars. Back up the coast in Normandy you will be humbled far beyond the foibles of your swing when you play on the shores where the D-Day invasion was launched and feel the presence of the Allied heroes who gave their lives to liberate Europe from the Nazis.

Golf in Europe offers a wonderful mélange of nature retreats and cultural flourishes. A golf expedition to Lake Como high in the Italian countryside north of Milan *must* be combined with a stay at the Villa d'Este Hotel, one of the most luxurious and majestic hotels in the world today, whose magical gardens once hatched the sometimes romantic, sometimes poisonous machinations of the Medicis during the Renaissance. A sojourn to the ruggedly beautiful island of Sardinia yields wonderfully peaceful golf at the Pevero Golf Club. Golfers vacationing in Portugal will imbibe the history and culture of this seafaring nation from the courses of the Algarve, where the weather and beaches are also great. Really, now, can golf in the British Isles top all this?

The best time to visit Europe on a golfing vacation is May or June and early autumn. May is an especially appealing month because the courses are at their lushest and the throngs of summer tourists have not yet arrived. Steer clear of late July and August, when Europeans go on vacation and close down shops and restaurants; the beaches and museums become too crowded, trains are overbooked, traffic frequently comes to a standstill, and you can't get a seat at a café. But at any other time, you will be awed by Europe's historic majesty and great golf.

France

▶PARIS

WONDERFUL COURSES WITHIN FORTY-FIVE MINUTES

	The Golf	Golf Services	Lodging	Restaurants	Non-Golf Activities	Total
Rating	18	15	19	20	20	92

Nothing in our minds is more sublime than spending a full ten days to two weeks in Paris, for us the most captivating, alluring city on earth. Imagine luxuriously lazy days in the City of Light, where your most monumental decision of the day is where to have lunch and dinner. In between dining you leisurely walk the streets of the vibrant Latin Quarter, explore the wonders of Impressionism at the Musée d'Orsay, or dedicate two hours

Golf de St. Germain

just to the Rubens sections of the Louvre. However, after about the fourth full day of museum hopping, bistro lunches with great wines, afternoon naps, and extraordinary dinners in exquisite Parisian restaurants with more fine wine, even the most decadent among us may feel a desperate longing to breathe clean country air, tee up the little white one, and enjoy a good long walk.

We offer here five solutions for golfers who love Paris. Morfontaine is not one of those listed. It is truly one of the best courses in Europe, but it is virtually impossible for a nonmember to play. All the courses we describe below are, in fact, exclusive, private clubs, but they all welcome nonmembers to play during the week—a most hospitable policy. The courses we recommend are Golf de Chantilly, Golf de

Saint-Germain, Golf de Fontainebleau, Golf de Saint-Cloud, and Golf de Saint-Nom-la-Bretèche. All of them are enriched by a colorful history, and all are within forty-five minutes of Paris by train. All of them also rank among the Continent's top hundred courses. Let us play golf first, then we will come back to Paris for some dining and lodging recommendations.

THE GOLF

Take the train to Chantilly from the Gard de Nord train station, a very pleasant forty-five-minute trip straight north of Paris. From the Chantilly train station, **Golf de Chantilly** is less than ten minutes by taxi in the small town of Vineuil. Chantilly is rich in history, having hosted ten French Opens and several European championships. It is also consistently rated among the top five courses of Europe. There are actually two eighteens here, and both are marvelous. Walking both, one cannot help but be struck by the extraordinary layout designed by famed Scottish architect Tom Simpson and by the distant murmur of all the famed golfers who have done battle at Chantilly since it opened in 1909: Faldo, Ballesteros, Langer, Player, Norman, Olazabal, Jacklin, Woosnam, Locke, Strange, de Vicenzo, and so many other greats. Though the clubhouse is a bit tired and scruffy, the overall maintenance of the two courses is quite good. Even the clubhouse and locker rooms, in spite of their threadbare simplicity and somewhat spartan appointments, exert a certain charm with their Tudor design and rich patina.

We all know that the utter joy of playing many old, famed courses lies in their natural and sometimes rugged beauty, their simplicity, their lack of artifice—no great, bulldozed mounding, no island greens, no massive squirting fountains in the middle of man-made lakes, and no cement cart paths with decorative brick borders. Right at the outset, let us make it clear that water does not come into play on any of Chantilly's thirty-six holes. Can you imagine! No greens fronted by water, no gurgling stream crossing the fairway, just the beautifully rolling, forested countryside with which Simpson had to work. In fact, there is barely a dogleg hole or blind hole on either of Chantilly's eighteens. Actually, the lone dogleg—the sixteenth—and the one somewhat blind hole—the eighteenth hole of the Vineuil Course—are two of the least attractive holes on either course. On almost all the other holes at Chantilly you stand on the tee and focus on your glorious destination—the green in the distance. Many new courses are doglegged to death to accommodate not the aesthetics of the golfing experience but the demands of real estate marketers seeking the most spectacular sites for homes and condominiums. You will not find this at Chantilly.

If you think it is water that ups your score during most rounds of golf, play Chantilly with its length (both the Vineuil and Longères courses measure approximately 7,000 yards from the back), its steep, sadistic pot bunkers, and its rough that really is rough! We American golfers have become so accustomed to favorable, even teed-up lies in short-cut rough that it is a shock for us to play a course like Chantilly where the rough is bush-hogged just two times a season. Most of the time a shot from the long rough at Chantilly merits praise if the ball simply gets back into the fairway.

If you have the opportunity, play Chantilly the way it's played during the French Open: fifteen holes on the **Vineuil Course** and three holes on the **Longères Course.** On Vineuil, start with one through eight, skip nine, ten, and eleven, play twelve through eighteen, then complete your eighteen by making ten, eleven, and eighteen of the Longères Course your finishing holes. Ten on Longères is a fabulous, slightly downhill, 202-yard par three fronted by bunkers with fir trees to the right. Number eleven, with three bunkers in the center of the fairway 250 yards out, is a great 418-yard par four with the forest closing in around the green. The eighteenth on Longères makes an inspirational closing hole, a 560-yard par five from the back playing up to an elevated green right in front of the clubhouse. Both Chantilly courses are closed Tuesdays.

Golf de Saint-Germain, an old French course opened in 1922, is carved out of the ancient hunting forests west of Paris. Saint-Germain is only thirty minutes by car or train from Paris. Visitors are welcome Tuesday through Friday. Important to note at the beginning—it is essential to bring your handicap card: men must have a handicap of twenty-four or lower, and women must have a handicap of twenty-eight or below. Saint-Germain, like Chantilly, has also hosted a number of French Opens and is generally regarded as one of the best courses in Europe. The entire club at Saint-Germain, far more than Chantilly, suggests an air of refinement and exclusivity that is evident in the impeccable maintenance of the course, the very pleasant, old-fashioned locker rooms, and the charming clubhouse with its very attractive dining room. Upon your arrival at Saint-Germain, you will immediately notice the aristocratic aspect of the members compared to the more middle-class membership at Chantilly. When you play Saint-Germain, be sure to have lunch there—it is very pleasant indeed and quite reasonable.

The golf course at Saint-Germain resembles Chantilly in that it is set in the middle of a forest and features few doglegs or blind shots; here you'll find neither homes nor condos on the course. Chantilly, although not hilly, has some contour, whereas Saint-Germain is utterly flat. The rugged Chantilly terrain suggests an almost Scottish-like beauty, whereas the Saint-Germain course feels very civilized and refined. The first tee, which is enclosed by a glistening white fence, sets the tone for what follows—a 434-yard par four with woods on either side and the green in the distance. There is not a bad hole at Saint-Germain. We especially like number twelve, where you feel the solitude and tranquillity of a hole surrounded by magical, ancient forests. The seventeenth is an excellent 158-yard par three with an abundance of heather between you and the green. Accuracy is a must here, as it is with most of Saint-Germain. Greens are in excellent condition, fairways are lush, and bunkers are punishing. A very good golf course.

Chantilly and Fontainebleau are our two favorite courses in and around Paris. **Golf de Fontainebleau,** just outside the legendary town of the same name, is a course that will delight and fascinate you. Unlike the other courses around Paris that are primarily carved out of hardwood forests and have dark black soil, Fontainebleau is set in a forest of beautiful specimen pine trees with sandy soil. The clubhouse and locker rooms are luxurious and tasteful, and the practice facilities are some of the best in France. Golf services here are first-rate. The employees, from the caddie master to the engaging bartender, are hospitable and very helpful. The golf course is a scenic, intriguing layout masterpiece. Number two, a 183-yard par three surrounded by towering pines, is an excellent hole. One of the most memorable holes on the whole course follows—the 531-yard par five, which is played from a breathtaking elevated tee to a lush, narrow fairway far below. Number twelve, not a long par five at 465 yards, is a hole you will never forget. Seven large boulders loom ninety yards in front of the green; if your ball falls among them, you could be there for a while. A beautifully conditioned golf course.

Golf de Saint-Cloud is one of the most exclusive, legendary clubs in all Europe, yet its members and staff could not be friendlier to the guests who come to play their course. Saint-Cloud has also hosted many major French and European championships. Of the five courses listed here, it is the closest to downtown Paris, less than ten miles distance. There are two courses here, the Green and the Yellow. Be sure to play the longer, much more interesting **Green Course,** built in 1913 and designed by H. S. Colt. The grounds and clubhouse here are lovely. If you happen to play here in the spring or summer, you will be dazzled by the explosion of flowers everywhere. The Green Course lies in a parkland setting with a great variety of massive hardwood trees. More than half the course is quite flat, although holes six through fourteen play on terrain with rolling contour. The course is beautifully cared for and a real treat to play. Another treat not to miss is an excellent lunch at the clubhouse between nines.

Golf de Saint-Nom-la-Bretèche has the most stunning clubhouse, dining room, and locker room setup in all France. The buildings, which form a courtyard, were converted from nineteenth-century stone farm buildings to house the whole clubhouse complex. The dining room is in a most dramatic, elegant, sunken room and serves very good food. There are two golf courses at Saint-Nom, the Blue and the Red. The **Blue Course** is the more challenging and certainly the better known—it is the course to play. It is the youngest of our five Paris courses, and certainly the least inspired layout on our glorious lineup. The course's condition is quite good but inferior to those at Saint-Cloud, Fontainebleau, and Saint-Germain. Saint-Nom has also hosted major French tournaments, but for an overall great golfing experience, we would rather play Chantilly and Fontainebleau two times apiece before playing Saint-Nom.

Golf de Chantilly. 60500 Vineuil-Saint-Fermin, France. Tel: 011-33-3-44-57-04-43. Fax: 011-33-3-44-57-26-54. Credit cards accepted.

- *Vineuil.* Par 71. 7,035 yards.
- *Longères.* Par 72. 6,972 yards.
- 1909. Designer: Tom Simpson. Greens fee: 350F ($70). Caddies available. No carts. Restrictions: public play weekdays only except in July and August; closed Tuesdays. Season: year-round.

Golf de Saint-Germain. Route de Poissy, 78100 Saint-Germain-en-Laye, France. Tel: 011-33-1-39-10-30-31. Fax: 011-33-1-34-51-23-42. Credit cards accepted.

- 1922. Designer: H. S. Colt. Par 72. 6,728 yards. Greens fee: 350F ($70). Caddies available (200F/$40). Pull carts only. Restrictions: public play Tuesday–Friday only; handicap limits: men under twenty-four, women under twenty-eight; be sure to bring your handicap card. Season: year-round.

Golf de Fontainebleau. Route d'Orléans, 77300 Fontainebleau, France. Tel: 011-33-1-64-22-22-95. Fax: 011-33-1-64-22-63-76. Credit cards accepted.

- 1909. Designer: Tom Simpson. Par 72. 6,681 yards. Greens fee: 350F ($70). Walking permitted. Caddies available. Few carts. Restrictions: closed Tuesdays. Season: year-round.

Golf de Saint-Cloud. 60 rue du 19 Janvier, 92380 Garches, France. Tel: 011-33-1-47-01-01-85. Fax: 011-33-1-47-01-09-57. No credit cards.

- *Green Course.* 1913. Designer: H. S. Colt. Par 71. 6,572 yards. Greens fees: 400F ($80) weekday, 500F ($100) weekend. Walking required. Caddies available. Carts with medical letter only. Restrictions: closed Mondays. Season: year-round.

Golf de Saint-Nom-la-Bretèche. 78860 Saint-Nom-la-Bretèche, France. Tel: 011-33-1-30-80-04-40. Fax: 011-33-1-34-62-60-44. No credit cards.

- *Blue Course.* 1959. Designer: W. Hawtree. Par 72. 6,743 yards. Greens fees: 400F ($80) weekday, 500F ($100) weekend. Walking required. Caddies available. Carts with medical letter only. Restrictions: closed Tuesdays. Season: year-round.

GOLF SERVICES

Other than the fine putting green, golf services are pretty rudimentary at Chantilly. The driving range is mediocre, and the clubhouse and lockers are a bit shabby. There are just a few carts, and caddies, though listed as available, are nearly impossible to find. You can enjoy a good lunch at Chantilly, although the service is apt to be apathetic. In addition to your golf outing to Chantilly, be sure to visit the extraordinary Château de Chantilly and its famous Grandes Écuries, an amazing marble stable overlooking the renowned turf racetrack, certainly one of the most famous racetracks in the world.

There are plenty of caddies and pull carts at Saint-Germain, and, like Chantilly, it is a joy to walk. In fact, at Saint-Germain you have no choice since there are no electric carts. The pro shop is quite adequate, the putting green excellent, and the driving range fair.

Fontainebleau rates as one of our favorite courses around Paris due in part to its excellent golf services. In addition to opulent locker rooms and practice facilities, the staff is disarmingly friendly. Golf services are less impressive at Golf de Saint-Cloud and Golf de Saint-Nom-la-Bretèche, although we urge you to grab a bite to eat at each course, as the food is quite fine and the clubhouse setting dramatic, especially at Saint-Nom-la-Bretèche.

LODGING

Several of the world's most stunning and stylish (and expensive) hotels are located in Paris. The legendary luxury hotels of Paris stand proudly on the famous streets and boulevards on the Right Bank of the Seine, and the city's smaller, more intimate hotels—which in the minds of many sophisticated travelers define the real essence of Paris—are situated on the Left Bank. Because these hotels are in great demand throughout the year, it would be unfair of us to suggest just one. Therefore, four of our current favorite Parisian hotels—two on the Right Bank and two on the Left—are briefly described below.

Although we detected a faint note of smugness among the staff during our most recent visit to the elegant **Hôtel Montalembert,** we have found this hotel, since its exquisite renovation five years ago, the single most appealing hotel on the entire Left Bank. The Montalembert features spacious (for the Left Bank), comfortable, handsomely decorated guest rooms and a superb location on rue Montalembert, within easy walking distance of the Musée d'Orsay, unparalleled shopping, great cafés like Les Deux Magots and Flore, and Brasserie Lipp on boulevard Saint-Germain. Since on previous visits to Montalembert the service has struck us as nothing short of sublime, we highly recommend this hotel.

The **Relais Christine** occupies a seventeenth-century convent located on tiny rue Christine in the heart of the Left Bank's sixth arrondissement and just minutes from the Seine, wonderful cafés like La Palette, nightlife, and shopping. We have been visiting the Relais Christine for more than a decade and because of its recent renovation are happy to recommend it once more. The rooms are spacious and lovely, there is an attractive courtyard and a pleasant breakfast room below the stairs on the lower level, and the service is excellent.

With its exalted location on the Place Vendôme (which it shares with France's most prestigious jewelers), its history of celebrated guests (Hemingway, Proust, and F. Scott Fitzgerald), and its remarkable rooms, services, and superb restaurant, the **Ritz**—notwithstanding its fallen place in rankings of hotels cited in mass-market magazines like *Condé Nast Traveler*—is still the best hotel in France. However, with room rates starting at 3,200F ($640) a night, a stay at the Ritz is like flying the Concorde—everyone loves it, but few can afford the tariff. For that once-in-a-lifetime experience, however, the Ritz is it.

With its glistening marble interior, its sublime two-star restaurant, its completely professional service, and arguably the finest location of any hotel in all of Paris—the Place de la Concorde, next to the American Embassy and within a five-minute walk of the finest boutiques in Paris—the **Crillon** is a perennial favorite of the most discerning travelers to Paris.

Hôtel Montalembert. 3 rue Montalembert, 75007 Paris. Tel: 011-33-1-45-49-68-68. Fax: 011-33-1-45-49-69-49. 51 rooms and 5 suites. Room rates from 1,625F ($325). Credit cards accepted.

Relais Christine. 3 rue Christine, 75006 Paris. Tel: 011-33-1-43-26-71-80. Fax: 011-33-1-43-26-89-38. 38 rooms and 13 suites. Room rates from 1,625F ($325). Credit cards accepted.

The Ritz. 15 place Vendôme, 75001 Paris. Tel. 011-33-1-43-16-30-30. Fax: 011-33-1-43-16-31-78. 142 rooms and 42 suites. Room rates from 3,200F ($640). Credit cards accepted.

The Crillon. 10 place de la Concorde, 75008 Paris. Tel: 011-33-1-44-71-15-00. Fax: 011-33-1-44-71-15-02. 163 rooms and 45 suites. Room rates from 3,200F ($640). Credit cards accepted.

RESTAURANTS

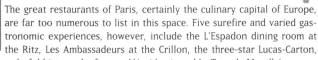

The great restaurants of Paris, certainly the culinary capital of Europe, are far too numerous to list in this space. Five surefire and varied gastronomic experiences, however, include the L'Espadon dining room at the Ritz, Les Ambassadeurs at the Crillon, the three-star Lucas-Carton, and two wonderful bistros: the famous L'Ami Louis and La Tour de Montlhéry.

No longer heavy and dated but now one of the most stunningly decorated restaurants in Paris, the new **L'Espadon** dining room in the Hôtel Ritz is sensational from every perspective, from the exceptional cuisine of chef Guy Legay to the animated and professional service and the extraordinary selection of wines. Dinner for two with wine and tip costs approximately 1,250F ($250). Open daily.

The restaurant at the Crillon hotel, **Les Ambassadeurs,** is one of the great hotel restaurants in France. This scintillating dining room features spectacular views overlooking the place de la Concorde, remarkable service, and a standard of cuisine that has remained consistent year after year. Dinner for two with wine and tip costs about 1,250F ($250). Open daily.

Chef Alain Senderens, the owner of **Lucas-Carton,** is one of the revered intellectuals of French cuisine, and the products of his artistry are put on display every afternoon and evening in his enchanting, landmark restaurant on the Place de la Madeleine. Specialties include *foie gras au chou, homard à la vanille,* and *canard Apicius.* Lucas-Carton is also one of the most expensive restaurants in France. Dinner for two with wine and service costs approximately 1,750F ($350). A prix fixe lunch menu of 375F ($75) is highly recommended. Despite the prices, Lucas-Carton is always filled to capacity; be sure to book far in advance. Closed Sundays and from July 31 to August 25.

Perhaps the most famous, eccentric, and beloved bistro in Paris, **L'Ami Louis** is still thriving under new owners (but with the same waiters and kitchen staff) after the 1987 death of chef/founder Antoine Magnin. Known for its heaping quantities of sublime foie gras, frogs' legs, roast chicken, and incredible roast duck cooked over wood fires, L'Ami Louis is one of the most delightful and unpretentious dining experiences to be found in Paris; bring an appetite. The wine list has over three hundred selections, and dinner runs about 1,125F ($225) for two. You need to reserve far in advance, and note that it is closed Mondays and Tuesdays and from July 14 to August 25.

A time-honored bistro classic with a daily menu chalked on a slate, red-checkered linens on the tables, hams and sausages strung from the ceiling, and a thin layer of sawdust scattered on the tiled floors, **La Tour de Montlhéry** features massive salads and tasty meat and fish dishes served with lavish, old-fashioned sauces. This always bustling bistro is located on a tiny street near the former Les Halles market. Informal and inexpensive, about 475F ($95) for two, wine and tip included. Closed weekends and from July 15 to August 15.

L'Espadon. Hôtel Ritz, 15 place Vendôme, 75001 Paris, France. Tel: 011-33-1-43-16-30-30. Fax: 011-33-1-43-16-31-78. Credit cards accepted.

Les Ambassadeurs. The Crillon, 10 place de la Concorde, 75008 Paris, France. Tel: 011-33-1-44-71-16-16. Fax: 011-33-1-44-71-15-02. Credit cards accepted.

Lucas-Carton. 9 place de la Madeleine, 75008 Paris, France. Tel: 011-33-1-42-65-22-90. Fax: 011-33-1-42-65-06-23. Credit cards accepted.

L'Ami Louis. 32 rue Vertbois, 75003 Paris, France. Tel: 011-33-1-48-87-77-48. Credit cards accepted.

Le Tour de Montlhéry. 5 rue de Prouvaires, 75001 Paris, France. Tel: 011-33-1-42-36-21-82. Fax: 011-33-1-45-08-81-99. Credit cards accepted.

NON-GOLF ACTIVITIES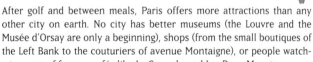

After golf and between meals, Paris offers more attractions than any other city on earth. No city has better museums (the Louvre and the Musée d'Orsay are only a beginning), shops (from the small boutiques of the Left Bank to the couturiers of avenue Montaigne), or people watching from the terraces of famous cafés like La Coupole and Les Deux Magots.

GETTING THERE: Most flights to Paris from the United States arrive at Charles de Gaulle Airport during morning rush hour. A taxicab to the center of the city will take a minimum of one hour and cost about 225F ($45). The concierge at your hotel will give you directions to the golf courses.

▶NORMANDY

GOLF IN AND AROUND DEAUVILLE—THE CITY OF KINGS

	The Golf	Golf Services	Lodging	Restaurants	Non-Golf Activities	Total
Rating	**17**	**15**	**17**	**18**	**19**	**86**

Although not a winegrowing region, Normandy is one of the most picturesque, friendly, and fascinating areas of France and a very good golfing destination. A Nor-

Ferme Saint-Siméon

man resident would be quick to point out that, true, virtually no wine is grown in Normandy, yet no other French province can boast the creation of what most of its denizens consider to be the nectar of the gods—Calvados, the heavenly, potent liqueur made from the region's omnipresent apples. As we walked among the lovely, flowered apple trees while playing the entire twenty-seven holes of spectacular golf at Omaha Beach recently, we could not help but be seduced by Normandy's many magical components.

Little known to American golfers, Normandy provides an excellent golfing adventure, as well as superb restaurants, wonderful sights, and, in the Hôtel Normandy, a fine base from which to explore the region. With the Hôtel Normandy, located in Deauville, as your headquarters, all the golf courses and sites are within relatively easy reach.

Deauville, of course, is one of the world's legendary *Town & Country* destinations, right up there with Saint-Moritz, Biarritz, Palm Beach, Marbella, and Saint-Tropez. In season (July, August, and September) its lustrous attractions lure the nobility, the socialites, the stars, and the gawkers. In addition to the Hôtel Normandy, Deauville offers horse racing, polo games, racehorse sales, an international film festival, glamorous gaming right out of a James Bond movie, and all the smart shopping you would expect to find on avenue Montaigne in Paris. A shopping fanatic can revel in a feeding frenzy here with Hermès, Ferragamo, Cartier, Louis Vuitton, Lancel, Longchamp, and on and on. The raison d'être of Deauville is pleasure, and the town leaders are determined to keep it that way, as well as safe, clean, and appealing.

For all its international appeal, Deauville is a town of only 4,000 full-time residents. Founded in 1859 by Napoleon III's brother-in-law the Duc de Morny, Deauville is a young town by European standards, and consequently it lacks a real sense of history or soul. It is, however, a place of ostentation where glitzy Ferraris, Porsches, Bentleys, and Mercedes prowl the streets, stars with sparkling smiles sit at the next table, and oil-glistening, nubile bodies fill the white sand beaches under the midafternoon Norman sun. Although it still maintains a real cachet, Deauville no longer exudes the undiluted style that it did up until the late 1980s. A major shift occurred in 1988 when the casino installed its first slot machines in an attempt to attract the masses. It worked, and at the same time it also altered the mix of the town; supported by a strong, blue-collar presence in the casino, today Deauville is a much more democratic town.

THE GOLF

The centerpiece of a golfing foray into Normandy has to be the magnificent **Golf de Bayeux Omaha Beach,** just forty-five minutes south of Deauville and five miles west of the city of Bayeux. Designed in 1986 by French native Yves Bureau, Omaha Beach well deserves its reputation as one of Europe's outstanding courses. Like all the great courses of the world, Omaha Beach has a charismatic personality that creates a very unique golfing experience. Augusta carries with it the aura of the Masters, Pine Valley and Cypress Point enjoy their removed exclusivity, and St. Andrews exudes history and nobility. At Omaha Beach, the associations stirred by the site of America's most memorable invasion form the distinguishing imprint of this golfing experience. The course takes you right to the cliffs overlooking the ominous German bunkers and the beaches where the Allied troops stormed ashore on D-Day just over fifty years ago. With quiet—yet over-whelming—awe, you feel the sobering power, the gravity, the heroism, the sorrow, and the glory of this hallowed site where the fate of free and democratic civilization was held in the offing.

We at GOLF TRAVEL had never before heard of Yves Bureau, but after having played Omaha Beach we know that he has succeeded in creating at least one truly memorable and outstanding golf course. A great course must offer an intriguing de-sign that does not punish the golfer unfairly, yet it must challenge the player to think and to play to the best of his or her abilities. It ought to honor its landscape or set-ting, and on a great course every well-played hole should be an achievement rather than a gift. All of this is true of Omaha Beach.

Omaha Beach actually consists of three nines: the rugged **La Mer,** which is Scottish in feel and constantly refreshed and occasionally beaten by sea breezes; **Le Bocage** (meaning a copse of trees), a more tranquil and pas-toral course that plays inland through orchards and giant oaks; and **L'Etang,** a course not to be underestimated, but a step down compared to the other two. We played all three, but if you are pressed to play just two, opt for the La Mer and Le Bocage loop. Together, they measure 6,851 yards from the back; par is sev-enty-two. Each hole is named for a

La Mer, Omaha Beach

historical figure associated with the invasion, including Eisenhower, Patton, Bradley, De Gaulle, Montgomery, and Colonel Rudder of the Rangers, to name just a few. A stately plaque next to the tee box on each hole describes the heroic con-tributions these men made to the D-Day invasion and the Allied cause in the war.

On the La Mer Course you will find virtually no trees, just dense shrubs in spots and heather rough. The first hole, appropriately named for General Eisenhower, is an inspirational 521-yard, dogleg-left par five. From this elevated hole you take in a visual panorama of what lies ahead on the front nine. Number two, a 150-yard par three from an elevated tee, provides an extraordinary view of not only the green be-low but also of the surrounding cliffs, the English Channel in the distance, and the small town of Port-en-Bessin with its church tower. Monsieur Bureau's design in-cludes an inspired use of bunkering. This is especially evident on number two, where the traps guarding the green necessitate a precise tee shot.

At Omaha, three straight holes win your heart—five, six, and seven. Five, a 521-yard par five, wondrously begins your trip out to the cliffs and the sea. The wind in-variably picks up, the air takes on a salty freshness, and it is difficult not to feel a surging sense of exhilaration. Five, bordered by heather rough, lies flat and straight, yet a diagonal, offshore wind against you the length of the hole and the strategically placed bunkers make it a memorable par five. With the wind blowing, five plays like a hole of well over six hundred yards—under such conditions even Tiger Woods would be challenged to reach the green in two. Six, a 427-yard par four, is Omaha's signature hole and a glorious memorial to General Omar N. Bradley, the hole's namesake. Since six plays out in the same direction as five, the same prevailing breeze lengthens the hole significantly. Protected by eight sand traps, the sixth green is dramatically perched out on the cliffs of Normandy stretching north and south, with an actual German bunker just a few feet to the left of the green.

Number seven heads away from the beach, meaning the wind is now behind you on this 398-yard par four lined by heather rough. Number eight, a 166-yard par three, is the only unattractive hole on the La Mer and Le Bocage loop; a homely steep bank flanks the whole right side, and the green lies gracelessly in bottomland surrounded by underbrush. Regrettably for General George Patton's memory, this hole bears his name.

The back nine of our round at Omaha, Le Bocage, leaves the sea, the cliffs, and most of the wind of the front nine behind, yet because of its variety and unique, scenic beauty, it is an inspired complement to La Mer. Where La Mer enjoys rolling terrain with interesting contour, Le Bocage is a relatively flat nine with plenty of trees and its own share of fine holes. La Mer's excellent sequence of three outstanding holes is nearly matched by holes thirteen, fourteen, and fifteen on Le Bocage. Thirteen, a well-trapped, 495-yard par five lined by apple trees and oaks, is a superb hole. Fourteen, our favorite hole on the back nine, is a 322-yard, slight dogleg-left par four capped by a challenging, undulating green. The walk down the fourteenth fairway opens up a visual feast of a rich, luxuriant valley dotted with a number of old Norman châteaux in the distance. Fifteen, a 146-yard par three across a swale, is guarded by a huge bunker ready to inhale any tee shots that fall short of the two-tiered green. Our only complaint of this back nine is that numbers ten and eighteen of Bocage and one of Etang are all wide open and run parallel to one another, offering very limited interest. La Mer and Le Bocage are both in excellent condition, with the added plus that no homes border either course.

The third nine at Omaha Beach, L'Etang is less interesting and not as well-maintained as the other two. Its design is quite lackluster; all but three holes run parallel to one another up and down the same very steep hill. When making reservations, be sure to reserve La Mer and Le Bocage, and play L'Etang only if the urge strikes you to play twenty-seven holes.

At Omaha Beach, a charming courtyard opens up to the clubhouse which is attached to an old Norman farmhouse. Facilities include the pro shop, a very pleasant bar, and the restaurant. The pro shop and restaurant personnel could not be more helpful and friendly. Unlike many of our local country clubs in the United States, where we are happy to get a good burger from the grill, the food at Omaha Beach, as at most clubhouses in France, is very good.

Founded in 1929, the inappropriately named **New Golf de Deauville** is owned by the Lucien Barrière family, proprietors of the Hôtel Normandy, the casino in Deauville, thirteen other hotels, and ten other casinos in France, as well as numerous restaurants throughout the country. New Golf de Deauville is only ten minutes east of the Hôtel Normandy, situated up in the hills on Mont Canisy overlooking Deauville, the beaches, and the ocean, making it a magnificent site for a golf club. The first eighteen, comprised of the Red and White nine-hole layouts, was designed by famed architect Tom Simpson in 1929; the Blue Course, designed by Henry Cotton, was finished in 1964. The course to play is the original **Red and White,** a lovely, mature course that at 6,546 yards is filled with interesting and challenging shots. In short, it is a very good golf course. Simpson imbedded more than seventy bunkers on the course, many of them the sadistic, British Isles–type pot bunkers that can turn a fairly good drive into a nightmare if the ball finds one of these devilish, little cauldrons. Number two, for example, is a 482-yard par five from an elevated tee that can play pretty gently if the bunkers are avoided, but if the second shot is played straight yet short you will be in a bunker and in serious trouble, and suddenly very busy trying to salvage a bogey. Fourteen, a 392-yard par four from an elevated tee, is a memorable hole. The drive funnels out of a long shoot of trees and brings joyful rewards if you stay straight or somewhat left, but fade your drive and you are in significant trouble. Because of the much elevated tee, a good drive on fourteen can give you a manageable iron to the green. The eighteenth is a first-rate finishing hole that plays 349 yards uphill to a green just below the Norman-style hotel.

Located about fifteen minutes northeast of Deauville, **Golf de Deauville Saint-Gatien** is a refreshingly unpretentious club surrounded by working farms and pastureland. We had serious doubts initially about what lay ahead on the course when we saw the ordinary sign at the entrance, a driving range that looked more like a cow pasture, and encountered rustic waiters and pro shop personnel who seemed like they were just off the farm. But after playing the course and spending some time around the clubhouse, we fully agree with the French golf guide that describes Saint-Gatien as "the most typical and most welcoming of the region's golf courses." This golf club is the French counterpart of the nonlegendary, yet wonderfully simple and infinitely appealing courses of rural Ireland.

As rustic as Golf de Deauville is, the course has a delightful, simple charm about it. Although not manicured, the course is kept in better than average condition and the greens are in particularly good shape. The front nine of this 6,899 yard layout is relatively flat, while the contour on the back nine affords striking views of an estuary of the Seine and the city of Le Havre in the distance. Lovely, mature trees line many of the holes and water comes into play occasionally. French golf course architect Olivier Brizon's intelligent placement of traps puts a decided premium on shot accuracy.

Number ten, a 530-yard par five, captures the true spirit of Saint-Gatien as it plays right down an elevated ridge with trouble on both sides. An old stone wall runs tight down the right side of the hole, separating the course from a contiguous farm, while to the left a steep slope means real trouble. You will find no bulldozed mounds on the course, just the natural terrain with which the architect worked.

One final word on Golf de Deauville Saint-Gatien. Although we have accurately marked golf services down considerably, we were ultimately charmed by the atmospheric clubhouse, a converted, eighteenth-century apple cider mill with giant, hand-hewn beams, a pleasant dining room, and welcoming terrace facing the course.

Golf de Bayeux Omaha Beach. Ferme Saint-Sauveur, 14520 Port-en-Bessin, France. Tel: 011-33-2-31-21-72-94. Fax: 011-33-2-31-51-79-61. Credit cards accepted.

- *Mer-Bocage Course.* 1986. Designer: Yves Bureau. Par 72. 6,851 yards.
- *L'Étang nine.* 1986. Designer: Yves Bureau. Par 35. 3,144 yards.
- Greens fees: 150F to 250F ($30 to $50). Walking permitted. Caddies can be arranged. Carts available. Restrictions: handicap limit: 35; current handicap card is required. Season: year-round.

New Golf de Deauville. 14800 Saint-Arnoult, France. Tel: 011-33-2-31-14-24-24. Fax: 011-33-2-31-14-24-25. Credit cards accepted.

- *Red and White Course.* 1929. Designer: Tom Simpson. Par 71. 6,546 yards. Greens fees: high season: 250F to 350F ($50 to $70), low high season: 150F to 250F ($30 to $50). Walking permitted. Caddies can be arranged. Carts available. Season: year-round.

Golf de Deauville Saint-Gatien. La Ferme du Mont Saint-Jean, 14130 Saint-Gatien-des-Bois, France. Tel: 011-33-2-31-65-19-99. Fax: 011-33-2-31-65-11-24. Credit cards accepted.

• 1988. Designer: Olivier Brizon. Par 72. 6,899 yards. Greens fees: high season: 220F to 300F ($45 to $60), low season: 180F to 220F ($36 to $45). Walking permitted. Caddies can be arranged. Carts available. Season: year-round.

GOLF SERVICES

Golf services at the courses in the Normandy region are uneven. At Golf de Bayeux Omaha Beach the staff is responsive and the driving range is above average for French standards (albeit with terrible range balls). The electric carts are fine, yet the pull carts are terrible and the putting green is exceedingly steep and slanted. Fortunately, the putting green is not a portent of what is to come.

Golf services at New Golf de Deauville are the best we found in Normandy, with a stylish clubhouse housing a well-stocked pro shop, a handsome bar, and a good restaurant. The driving range and putting green are well above average.

Regrettably, the same high standard does not apply to Golf de Deauville Saint-Gatien. Although we enjoyed the clubhouse atmosphere, the driving range and other facilities are almost primitive.

LODGING

Because of its central location and generally efficient services, we suggest you stay at the **Hôtel Normandy.** At the outset, however, we must qualify this recommendation. This is a very commercial hotel catering to many business and tours groups, so service can be frantic and impersonal at times; bellmen, in particular, seem harried and cold. In spite of this caveat, we hasten to add that even during periods of commotion, the concierge desk always set up our tee times and made our dinner reservations in a prompt and extremely friendly manner.

Another caveat is that not all the rooms have benefited from the hotel's recent renovation, and the unrenovated rooms are infinitely ordinary. Be sure to reserve one of the renovated, oceanfront rooms. Even from these rooms, with their wide, expansive water views, it is important to realize that "oceanfront" means the beach is some three to four hundred yards away. A number of red clay tennis courts and two streets with clusters of shops and restaurants stand between the hotel and the beach. The casino is right next door, and the beach is as close as it is to any other hotel in Deauville.

A most glamorous alternative to the Hôtel Normandy, the **Ferme Saint-Siméon** is truly one of the most endearing and luxurious places to stay in all France. Although not as convenient to the golf in Normandy, the Ferme Saint-Siméon, fourteen kilometers (8.4 miles) northeast of Deauville on the D513, deserves serious consideration because of its excellent food, luxurious rooms, wondrous setting, and charming seventeenth-century Norman building. Dinner in the hotel's lovely restaurant, looking into the garden and across the water at the lights of Le Havre, is quite expensive but more than worth it!

Hôtel Normandy. Rue Jean Mermoz, 14800 Deauville, France. Tel: 011-33-2-31-98-66-22. Fax: 011-33-2-31-98-66-23. 300 rooms and suites from 1,500F to 7,500F ($300 to $1,500) in high season, 980F to 3,500F ($196 to $700) in low season. Breakfast: 90F ($18). Credit cards accepted.

Ferme Saint-Siméon. Rue Adolphe Marais, 14600 Honfleur, France. Tel: 011-33-2-31-89-23-61. Fax: 011-33-2-31-89-48-48. 34 rooms and suites. Doubles from 790F to 2,300F ($158 to $460). Credit cards accepted.

 R E S T A U R A N T S   **18**

By French standards, Deauville, for all its panache, is something of a desert wasteland when it comes to good places to dine. Your best bet is the Hôtel Normandy's high-profile restaurant, **La Belle Époque** which delivers a deluxe meal with friendly service. The saffron-scented red mullet was superb, as was our dessert, the *croustillant Normand,* a terrific apple pastry with an orange and honey sauce. Prix fixe dinners cost 180F ($36) and 250F ($50).

With its beachfront setting and "in" status, **Ciro's** is the place to people watch, particularly given the large, glass partitions through which you can watch folks parading up and down the boardwalk. The food and service, however, are only marginal, although Ciro's is all right (though overpriced) for a light meal or a drink. **Le Spinnaker,** one of Deauville's best-known restaurants, has recently been demoted from one star to starless status by Michelin, the bible of French guidebooks. We also found that Le Spinnaker has declined precipitously in quality. Prix fixe meals cost 320F ($64).

To experience the real dining treats available in this part of Normandy, however, one has to travel out of Deauville. We highly recommend two dining excursions—Gill, the two-star restaurant in the cathedral town of Rouen, located roughly an hour east of Deauville, and the above-noted Ferme Saint-Siméon in the quaint town of Honfleur, just a thirty-minute drive up the coast.

A visit to Rouen is worth the hour drive for two reasons. First, Rouen is the home of the Cathédrale Notre-Dame, one of France's truly inspired cathedrals. The cathedral so captivated Claude Monet that he painted it at least thirty times, at different hours of the day and various times of the year. But another of France's treasures is located here as well—the sublime culinary shrine of the two-star restaurant Gill stands in the center of the city.

Just as the memory of the cathedral towers will be emblazoned forever upon your memory, so, too, will the wonderful recollection of enjoying one of the best meals of your life at **Gill.** Chef Gilles Tournadre is unquestionably one of the rising meteoric stars on the French culinary scene. Be sure to order the curried oysters, the red mullet with sprigs of thyme, the crayfish with tomato chutney, and the celestial Calvados soufflé. A five-course meal costs 400F ($80).

The beguiling town of Honfleur lies just up the beach from Deauville. Here you will find our other favorite restaurant in the area—the extraordinarily romantic **Ferme Saint-Siméon.** This idyllic, seventeenth-century hotel and restaurant, with its lovely grounds and setting overlooking the estuary of the Seine, is a most appealing alternative to the bigger, more commercial Hôtel Normandy. To dine in the stylish, heavily beamed restaurant is a must stop during your week in Normandy. À la carte dinners cost 530F to 760F ($106 to $134) without drinks. In addition to superb food, the Ferme Saint-Siméon has a very fine wine list. At our dinner we had a golden, luscious 1993 Chablis Vaudésir and one incredible, memorably elegant 1989 Château Calon-Ségur.

La Belle Epoque. Hôtel Normandy, rue Jean Mermoz, 14800 Deauville, France. Tel: 011-33-2-31-98-66-22. Fax: 011-33-2-31-98-66-23. Credit cards accepted.

Ciro's. Promenade Planches, 14800 Deauville, France. Tel: 011-33-2-31-88-18-10. Fax: 011-33-2-31-98-66-71. Credit cards accepted.

Le Spinnaker. 52 rue Mirabeau, 14800 Deauville, France. Tel: 011-33-2-88-24-40. Fax: 011-33-2-31-88-43-58. Credit cards accepted.

Gill. 9 quay de la Bourse, 76000 Rouen, France. Tel: 011-33-2-35-71-16-14. Fax: 011-33-2-35-71-96-91. Credit cards accepted.

Ferme Saint-Siméon. Rue Adolphe Marais, 14600 Honfleur, France. Tel: 011-33-2-31-89-23-61. Fax: 011-33-2-31-89-48-48. Credit cards accepted.

NON-GOLF ACTIVITIES   19

Non-golfing activities and sightseeing in this area of Normandy are limitless. From Deauville it's no more than an hour's drive to the Normandy Beach cemeteries. To walk among the graves of the thousands of young men who lost their lives during those bloody, world-changing days is a moving experience that will stay with you forever. The sight of the vast, symmetrical, marble gravestone markers stretching across the verdant lawn is most sobering.

The town of Bayeux boasts a dazzling collection of beautifully preserved, centuries-old tapestries depicting another invasion, the Norman invasion of England in 1066. And, of course, just a bit further down the coast is the magical Mont-Saint-Michel. Also worth a visit is the Peace Museum in Caen, the colorful Impressionist town of Honfleur, and the Pays-d'Auge. In addition, you will find a pleasant spa at the Hôtel Normandy, numerous clay tennis courts, the casino, the beach, the BMW and Honda speedways, horseback riding, horse racing, and polo matches.

GETTING THERE: Deauville is 198 kilometers from Paris on the A13 autoroute. There are frequent train connections from Paris's Gare Saint-Lazare with a change in Lisieux. The trip takes three hours and costs about $60 round-trip. Deauville/St. Gatien is also served by a small, international airport.

▶ BIARRITZ

	The Golf	Golf Services	Lodging	Restaurants	Non-Golf Activities	Total
Rating	18	14	19	18	19	88

Golf d'Arcangues

The illustrious Hôtel du Palais stands in the center of what was once one of the most fashionable resort towns in the world—Biarritz. From the mid-nineteenth century to the mid-twentieth century, Biarritz was called "the resort of kings." In its day, Biarritz was the place to be and the palais served as the epicenter of chic social activity.

By the mid-1980s, however, when we made our first visit, Biarritz had been passé for more than twenty years. Since the sixties, when, following the phenomenal Brigitte Bardot, the pulsating, hedonistic center of the French social scene shifted some two hundred miles to the east—to the Riviera and St. Tropez—Biarritz had been relegated to the status of a social relic. No place epitomized Biarritz's decline more than the Hôtel du Palais. Tired and tarnished, overrun by chipped paint and shoddy service—this beautiful hotel, built by Napoleon III's wife, Eugenie, in 1855, with its striking setting on a beach bluff facing the sparkling Atlantic, had become, like her city, a forgotten grande dame. The only notoriety left to Biarritz was its distinction as the surfing mecca of all Europe. Teenage surfers, however, do not oil the tourist machine much. Biarritz did have eight or ten quality golf courses (fully 10 percent of all the courses in France up until the early 1980s), but the French simply did not play much golf.

In our numerous returns since the mid-1980s, we found Biarritz a changed city. The joie de vivre is back! Today Biarritz is filled with vitality, fine restaurants, all the right shops, a beautifully renovated Hôtel du Palais, and some fine golf courses humming with action. Biarritz is the sister city of Augusta, Georgia, and it is now unquestionably the golfing mecca of France, a country that has recently undergone an absolute golfing craze. Less than a decade ago there were fewer than one hundred golf courses in all France; now the country is home to nearly five hundred. It is fair to say that golf, along with the local business and political leaders' real commitment to revitalizing the city, has made Biarritz a dynamic travel destination once again.

Of course, Biarritz has always had stunning scenic beauty—miles of magnificent Atlantic coastline with cliffs plunging into the sea, protected bays, coves, beautiful beaches, and the best waves in Europe. The Pyrenees, snowcapped much of the year, loom majestically to the south and southeast, and Biarritz itself is a lovely coastal town, a city of contour and hills, with lovely parks and gracious red tile-roofed villas. And then there is the Basque influence. Biarritz is a Basque city, rich in the fascinating color of that culture's joyous holidays, hearty and delectable cuisine, and language. The Basque language sounds like nothing you have heard in your life, but don't worry—many of the local residents are, in fact, quadrilingual, speaking French, Spanish, Basque, and English.

Biarritz makes for a perfect golfing destination, with great and varied golf courses and superb sightseeing. Where else can you play eighteen holes in the day, dine that night at possibly the best restaurant in France (which means the world!), and stay at one of the finest hotels in Europe? More on that later. First, let's play golf.

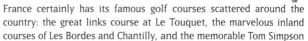

THE GOLF ⑱

France certainly has its famous golf courses scattered around the country: the great links course at Le Touquet, the marvelous inland courses of Les Bordes and Chantilly, and the memorable Tom Simpson inland valley course Morfontaine. Yet no region of France boasts more fine courses than the area within thirty miles of Biarritz. Like Pinehurst, Pebble Beach, and Hilton Head, Biarritz is a destination that offers great golfing diversity—from quasi-links courses like Moliets, to the venerable Chantaco, to an inland valley course like Arcangues, to the wonderfully forested Seignosse and Makila courses.

Twenty miles north of Biarritz and just a mile out of the small town of Seignosse lies **Golf de Seignosse,** a magical, 6,736-yard golf course designed by Robert von Hagge. Although it is not yet ten years old, the Seignosse course, having been carved out of the surrounding tree-filled hills, feels as if it has been there forever. Despite its location only a few miles from the ocean, the course yields only a few views of the Atlantic; nonetheless, the sea breezes make the air fresh and exhilarating. On the front nine, attractive Mediterranean villas form a tasteful border along the edges of the course, while on the back nine you enter a world of seclusion and tranquillity in a verdant setting. Because of the hills, the pines, the cork trees and oaks, the villas, and the six small lakes, every hole is a visual feast. Tight fairways lined with trees and water undulate to the well-bunkered greens. From the lush tees boxes to the beautifully kept fairways and true greens, the course is in ideal condition and the maintenance of the whole is flawless.

Like all other great golf courses, Seignosse rewards patience, course management, and accurate shot making. Number eleven, a 580-yard par five, epitomizes our memories of the glories of Seignosse. From the elevated tee you look upon a breathtaking vista with a small lake on the right and a lush, carpeted fairway bordered by pines and cork trees rolling out in front of you to the distant green, and behind it, the Bay of Biscay. When we played, a bright-colored cock pheasant slowly strutted before us as we approached the green.

As its fame spreads, Seignosse is fast becoming referred to as one of Europe's finest, most beautiful golf courses. Von Hagge has already made his reputation in France with his lovely course at Les Bordes in the heart of Sologne. The great Spanish golfer José Maria Olazabal, a golf course architect himself, considers Seignosse one of his three favorite courses. Greens fees are 330F ($66) on weekends and 250F ($50) during the week. Carts are available for 200F ($40).

The small but adequately equipped pro shop here shares a large room with a casual bar and a restaurant. The woman who coordinated the golf was helpful and engaging. Do not dream of renting clubs here—they are makeshift and horrible. This is true of the whole Biarritz area. Although most courses rent clubs, bring your own. And be sure to bring golf balls—in most shops they run approximately $5 a ball! Seignosse has a putting green, practice chipping green, and driving range.

Golf d'Arcangues

Golf d'Arcangues, only two and a half miles from Biarritz in the picturesque town of Arcangues, was designed by the American architect Ronald Fream. Although it is much too open in places and its young trees are still several years away from becoming a formidable factor, the course is as lush and well maintained as you will find. Unlike Seignosse, which was carved out of a forest, Arcangues was created out of 198 acres of hilly pastureland surrounding the château of the Marquis d'Arcangues. What a spectacular site it is—high in the hills with a distant view of the ocean and an unbelievably panoramic vista of the Pyrenees. When you play at Arcangues, you feel the presence of these majestic mountains.

Despite the forgiving openness of the course, Arcangues is no cakewalk. From the back tees it measures approximately 6,700 yards; it is well bunkered, and earth mounds crop up throughout to add interest and challenge. Most important, because of the terrain, you never seem to have a level lie. This is a very hilly course, and we suggest walking only for the particularly fit. Four small lakes have been created to enhance the aesthetics and make shots more demanding. We were particularly taken by holes thirteen, fourteen, and fifteen, all of which play around the lovely château and benefit from the mature planting of the grounds. We recommend Arcangues as one of your Biarritz courses. The course maintenance and the views make it a memorable golfing experience.

The clubhouse is very pleasant and has an engaging "English bar," a simple but fine restaurant with a lovely terrace facing the Pyrenees. Greens fees are 230F ($46) except during July and August, when they rise to 300F ($60). Golf carts are available for 200F ($40). The golf shop is small, but the driving range, practice green, and putting green are excellent.

The very Basque seaport town of Saint-Jean-de-Luz lies twelve miles to the south of Biarritz, and just southeast of Saint-Jean-de-Luz you'll find the lovely course **Golf de Chantaco.** The grand homes of some of the wealthiest people in France surround the course and the charming, tasteful, and luxurious Hôtel de Chantaco that adjoins it. The Chantaco course, which winds through mature woods and lies in the shadows of the Pyrenees, dates back to 1928. Although not a long (6,294 yards) or a difficult course, it charms you with its patina, maturity, great natural beauty, and perfect maintenance. Katherine Lacoste, of Lacoste fame and the last amateur to win the U.S. Women's Open (1967), is the club's current president. Golf services at Chantaco are good. Greens fees, which include a pull cart and balls at the driving range, are 260F ($52) except during July and August, when they rise to 340F ($68).

Designed by Robert Trent Jones, Sr., **Golf de Moliets (Golf de la Côte d'Argent)** ranks at or near the top of the best of the courses in the Biarritz area. Moliets, sixty kilometers (36 miles) north of Biarritz, is a real sports complex boasting eleven great tennis courts (this has been a Davis Cup site), archery fields that have hosted the world championships, and a golf course consistently considered one of Europe's finest and home to numerous European tour events over the years. The beautifully maintained course offers a combination of holes cut through pines and cork trees, although several follow along the sea. Yet do not count on leaving behind the water and wind when you leave the beach since there are several small lakes on the inland part of the course and the fresh breezes from the Atlantic find you wherever you are. Four exhilarating holes—thirteen, fourteen, fifteen, and sixteen—are right on the water. Although it is not as hilly as Seignosse, the Moliets track still provides plenty of contour and ridges, which add to its visual beauty. You can warm up on Moliets' driving range and putting green, and, overall, the golf services are fair. Here, as at most other courses in this region, do not expect to find a caddie—they simply do not exist. A very detailed brochure, another feature at most Biarritz courses, provides much-needed information on the course.

Although we also played the rather dull and confusing Golf de Biarritz, let us now go to an interesting new golf course—the **Makila Golf Club** in the tiny Basque town of Bassussarry. The Makila course was designed by American architect Rocky Roquemore and opened for play in the early winter of 1992. Because much of the course is cut deep into the woods, the layout has a lovely, mature feeling. In addition, the gentle, rolling countryside around Biarritz provides the ideal contour for a course—not too hilly, not too flat.

From the opening hole, with its elevated tee right in front of the clubhouse, to the eighteenth hole, the Bassussarry course is a wonder of interest and challenge. On clear days—there are many from April through September—the views from the Makila Club, highlighted by the majestic Pyrenees looming to the south and southeast, are spellbinding. The course is well bunkered, and water comes into play on ten of the holes. The only marginal hole is number eight, a par four with an ugly hazard flanking the hole to the left. Number five is a 529-yard dogleg par five where you hit from an eagle's nest tee down to the lush, tree-lined fairway far below. Your shot to the green is protected by a lovely lake on the right. This is a magnificent and spectacularly beautiful golf hole.

When we first played Makila a few years ago, we described the course maintenance as perfect. After our recent return we regrettably report this is no longer the case. The condition has slipped considerably, and now tacky real estate signs spread across the back of some of the greens. Makila's putting green and driving range are excellent, a real exception in France. The carts and cart paths are first-rate. In the extraordinary clubhouse, the men's and ladies' locker rooms are spaciously deluxe, the pro shop is fine, and the bar and restaurant are very nice. Greens fees are 200F ($40) in season and 100F ($20) off season.

Real Golf de San Sebastián, a special club, also referred to as Golf de Fontarrabie, is the real hidden links secret in the Biarritz area. Located in the small town of Hondarribia, in Spain, it is about twenty kilometers from the summer resort town of San Sebastián and is worth every bit of the forty-five-minute trip from Biarritz. This is the home course of Spain's second most famous golfer, José Maria Olazabal. In fact, José Maria's father is to this day the greenskeeper at Real San Sebastián. Olazabal's home is on the seventh green, one of the great holes on this memorable course. The clubhouse and course, built in 1910, exude a rich character. Nestled in the shadows and grandeur of the Pyrenees, this is a course that brings together all the elements of a great golfing experience—history, setting, intriguing layout, and very friendly members and staff. Be forewarned that very little English is spoken here. Call ahead to reserve a caddie, and be ready to have an eighteen-hole Spanish lesson in Iberian golf parlance. The course is kept in excellent condition; fairways are lush, and greens are superb. Good job, Señor Olazabal! Be sure to have lunch here, too. The Basque cuisine, served in a most handsome dining room, is very, very good.

Golf de Chiberta is a private club just a few miles up the coast from the Hôtel du Palais. Right on the ocean, this 1926-vintage Tom Simpson course has been wonderfully refurbished in the last three years. When we played it four years ago, it was in miserable condition. Now with a significant commitment from the membership, the masterpiece has reclaimed its past glories. The clubhouse and locker rooms, however, remain quite unimpressive, though not nearly as grim as the high-rise hotel on the property. The fourteenth, a links hole, gives you a view of one of the best surfing spots in Europe.

Golf de Seignosse. Avenue du Belvédère, 40510 Seignosse, France. Tel: 011-33-5-58-41-68-30. Fax: 011-33-5-58-41-68-31. Credit cards accepted.

• 1989. Designer: Robert von Hagge. Par 72. 6,736 yards. Greens fees: 250F ($50) weekdays, 330F ($66) weekends. Walking permitted. No caddies. Carts available. Season: year-round.

Golf d'Arcangues. 64200 Arcangues, France. Tel: 011-33-5-59-43-10-56. Fax: 011-33-5-59-43-12-60. Credit cards accepted.

• 1991. Designer: Ronald Fream. Par 69. 6,680 yards. Greens fees: 230F ($46), 300F ($60) in July and August. Walking permitted. No caddies. Carts available (200F/$40). Restrictions: closed Mondays during winter. Season: year-round.

Golf de Chantaco. Route d'Ascain, 64500 St. Jean-de-Luz, France. Tel: 011-33-5-59-26-14-22. Fax: 011-33-5-59-26-48-37. Credit cards accepted.

• 1928. Designer: H. S. Colt. Par 70. 6,294 yards. Greens fees: 260F ($52) weekdays, 340F ($68) in July and August. Walking permitted. Caddies and carts available. Season: year-round.

Golf de Moliets. Club House, 40660 Moliets, France. Tel: 011-33-5-58-43-54. Fax: 011-33-5-58-48-54-88. Credit cards accepted.

• 1989. Designer: Robert Trent Jones, Sr. Par 72. 6,790 yards. Greens fees: 300F ($60) high season, 230F ($46) low season. Walking permitted. No caddies. Carts available. Season: year-round.

Makila Golf Club. Route de Cambo, 64200 Bassussarry, France. Tel: 011-33-5-59-58-42-62. Fax: 011-33-5-59-58-42-48. Credit cards accepted.

• 1992. Designer: Rocky Roquemore. Par 72. 6,793 yards. Greens fees: 200F ($40) high season, 100F ($20) low season. Walking permitted. No caddies. Carts available. Season: year-round.

Real Golf Club de San Sebastián. Apartado 6, Hondarribia, Guipuzcoa, Spain. Tel: 011-34-43-61-68-45. Fax: 011-34-43-61-14-91. Credit cards and French francs accepted.

• 1910. Designer: Pevro Irigoyen. Par 71. 6,558 yards. Greens fees: October to June: 6,000 Pesetas ($41); July to September: 8,000 Pesetas ($55) weekends. Walking permitted. No carts. Caddies (3,000 Pesetas/$20) available. Restrictions: public access weekdays only. Season: year-round.

Golf de Chiberta. 104 boulevard des Plages, 64600 Anglet, France. Tel: 011-33-5-59-63-83-20. Fax: 011-33-5-59-63-30-56. Credit cards accepted.

• 1926. Designer: Tom Simpson. Par 71. 5,510 yards. Greens fees: 240F ($48) weekdays, 520F ($104) weekends. Walking permitted. No caddies or carts. Season: year-round.

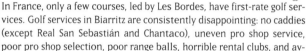

GOLF SERVICES (14)

In France, only a few courses, led by Les Bordes, have first-rate golf services. Golf services in Biarritz are consistently disappointing: no caddies (except Real San Sebastián and Chantaco), uneven pro shop service, poor pro shop selection, poor range balls, horrible rental clubs, and average driving ranges. This is one location where you are better off bringing your own golf supplies. The best golf services of the lot may be found at Makila and Arcangues, followed by Chantaco. Real Golf de San Sebastián offers the best lunch.

LODGING (19)

In the mid-1980s the **Hôtel du Palais** was fading fast. No longer. It now shines with new paint, glistening mirrors, highly polished antiques, sparkling chandeliers, and bright, happy faces. There are a number of very comfortable hotels in Biarritz, but none can approach the "new" Palais. The 126-room **Miramar,** situated very close to the Palais on avenue Impératrice, is a viable second choice and, like its exalted neighbor, features a one-star dining room. But in reality, the Miramar doesn't compare. We now consider the Hôtel du Palais to be one of the finest hotels in all of Europe.

Not all of the rooms at the Hôtel du Palais have been renovated, but the updated rooms are opulent and spacious. Although you'll pay a dearer price, by all means request a renovated room with an ocean view. In room 132, which faces the ocean, we loved watching the sunsets and drifting off to sleep to the sound of the breaking waves. Service throughout the hotel is flawless. We were grateful to the concierge desk for arranging all our tee times and dinner reservations. Lovely grounds surround the hotel, capped by the glamorous pool that overlooks the beach. The hotel location is perfect—right in town on the beach, a few minutes' walk to the casino, all the shops, and most of the fine restaurants. Room rates range from 1,325F to 2,750F ($265 to $550). The Hôtel du Palais does offer a seven-night, six-day golf package that includes breakfast and all greens fees. The low-season cost of this package is 6,585F ($1,317) per person, and the high-season rate, from June 1 to September 30, is 8,285F ($1,657) per person.

The **Hôtel du Chantaco,** with twenty-four very handsome rooms and suites, is an idyllic, intimate, Spanish-style hotel that serves excellent food. We have stayed there previously and loved it, but for playing the diversity of courses in the French Basque country, Biarritz is much more centrally located. Room rates at the Hôtel du Chantaco range from 850F to 1,740F ($170 to $340). The gardens, terraces, pool, and breathtaking mountain views make it a nice base from which to explore the western Pyrenees (Spanish and French) and the fascinating coastal town of Saint-Jean-de-Luz.

Miramar. 13 rue Louison-Bobet, 64200 Biarritz, France. Tel: 011-33-5-59-41-30-00. Fax: 011-33-5-59-24-77-20. 126 rooms. Doubles range from 1,550F to 2,650F ($310 to $530). Credit cards accepted.

Hôtel du Palais. 1 avenue Impératrice, 64200 Biarritz, France. Tel: 011-33-5-59-41-64-00. Fax: 011-33-5-59-41-67-99. 134 rooms and 22 suites. Room rates range from 1,325F to 2,750F ($265 to $550). Credit cards accepted.

Hôtel du Chantaco. 64500 Saint-Jean-de-Luz, France. Tel: 011-33-5-59-26-14-76. Fax: 011-33-5-59-26-35-97. 24 rooms. Doubles from 850F to 1,740F ($170 to $348). Credit cards accepted.

R E S T A U R A N T S

Prepare to relish the abundant culinary diversity within an hour-and-a-half radius of Biarritz—from celestial, one-star *gastronomique* dining at the Café de Paris to one of the many simple but festive Basque restaurants.

Chef Jean-Marie Gaiter has earned his Michelin star at the **Hôtel du Palais.** In addition to featuring one of the most stunning dining rooms on the entire French coast, the hotel restaurant boasts first-rate cuisine, a fine wine list, and gracious and unpretentious service. Two menus are offered: one, a *menu gastronomique* with more elaborate choices and prices that will bring your dinner for two, including wine and service, to about 1,250F ($250), and the other, a simple menu featuring regional dishes like *salade Landaise* and fabulous pigs' feet. A pianist plays soft American jazz and show tunes throughout dinner. Highly recommended.

To spend any time in the Basque country and not sample a good, hearty Basque meal would be a real shame, for an evening spent in a Basque restaurant is more than just a dining experience, it is a real night out on the town. With the help of the concierge at the Hôtel du Palais we found just the right place in **La Tantina de Burgos,** in the southern part of Biarritz toward Saint-Jean-de-Luz. At the front of the restaurant you will find a traditional Spanish tapas bar, while the back features a simple, friendly dining area. As the informal rustic wooden tables and benches, blue-and-white oilcloth, and blackboard with the day's specials suggest, this is the kind of place for boisterous laughing and loud singing. We heard a lot of both the night we were there. La Tantina features excellent calamari, grilled prawns, stuffed peppers, milk-fed lamb, and mutton with good Rioja wines at reasonable prices. We did not see another American; this is an extremely popular place for locals. Be sure to make reservations, but do not go before 8:45 P.M., when the first diners begin to arrive. Try the excellent crème brûlée. Dinner for two will cost approximately 300F ($60) plus wine and tip.

Just eighteen miles northeast of Biarritz in the tiny Basque river town of Urt, the **Auberge de la Galupe** is one of the best two-star Michelin restaurants in all France. Right on the Adour River, this quaint little inn serves delectable food. We are delighted that Monsieur Parra has come out of retirement to showcase his considerable culinary talent.

In addition to the superb dining room at the Hôtel du Palais and the charming Basque flavor of Tantina de Burgos, we strongly recommend four other restaurants in Biarritz itself:

Didier Oudill, one of France's hottest chefs, moved several years ago from the tiny, uncommercial town of Grenade-sur-l'Adour to the glitzier ambience of Biarritz to purchase the classic, elegant restaurant **Café de Paris,** which is now an esteemed Michelin one-star restaurant that serves some of the best cuisine in Biarritz. We thoroughly enjoyed our lobster salad with thin slices of mushrooms, chives, and vinaigrette, as well as the terrine of salmon with a gelatin of lobster and scallops. Dinner for two with wine and tip will run approximately 970F ($194).

La Table des Frères Ibarboure, in the tiny town of Bidart, just a few miles southeast of Biarritz, is lovely, tranquil, and very good. Lunch here will cost about 200F ($40) with wine and tip, and dinners average from 240F to 340F ($48 to $68).

L'Operne, just a block from the Hôtel du Palais, has a wonderful view of the ocean and serves some of the best seafood in town. With a beamed ceiling and dark paneling, L'Operne is handsome but casual and engaging with very polite, professional service. Dinner for two with wine will cost approximately 500F ($100).

San Sebastián Dining. Since the Spanish resort town of San Sebastián is only thirty miles south of Biarritz, it is worth a trip for lunch or dinner. The old section of town, in an area called Fontarrabie, is laden with tapas bars. These are colorful spots where you stand at the bar, enjoy a glass of wine, and have a small samplings of dishes from the kitchen. As tempting as it may be to stay in one great place, the trick in the tapas tradition is to remain in one establishment only until you've finished your wine, then move down the street to the next place. Don't worry, in this section of San Sebastián, the tapas bars are all great and equally friendly. Get directions from the Hôtel du Palais concierge, who can also arrange for a car and driver for the day for approximately $100.

The best restaurant in this entire section of the Basque country is in San Sebastián. **Restaurante Arzak,** one of only two Michelin three-star restaurants in all of Spain, is celestial in every way—excellent food, fine service, charming decor, and a superb wine cellar of both Spanish and French wines. We had fresh hake, crayfish, and veal tornedos. To accompany our dinner we had a Castillo de Monjardin chardonnay from the Basque province of Navarra, which we still dream about. Not inexpensive. Dinner for two with wine and tip will run 21,750 pesetas ($150).

Restaurants at the Hôtel du Palais. 1 avenue Impératrice, 64200 Biarritz, France. Tel: 011-33-5-59-41-64-00. Fax: 011-33-5-59-41-67-99. Credit cards accepted.

La Tantina de Burgos. 2 place Beau-Rivage, 64200 Biarritz, France. Tel: 011-33-5-59-23-24-47. No Fax. Credit cards accepted.

Auberge de la Galupe. Au port de l'Adour. 64270 Urt, France. Tel: 011-33-5-59-56-21-84. Fax: 011-33-5-59-56-28-66. Credit cards accepted.

Café de Paris. 5 place Bellevue, 64200 Biarritz, France. Tel: 011-33-5-59-24-19-53. Fax: 011-33-5-59-24-18-20. Credit cards accepted.

La Table des Frères Ibarboure. Chemin de Talinania, 64210 Bidart, France. Tel: 011-33-5-59-54-81-64. Fax: 011-33-5-59-54-75-65. Credit cards accepted.

L'Operne. 7 avenue Edouard VII, 64200 Biarritz, France. Tel: 011-33-5-59-24-30-30. Fax: 011-33-5-59-24-37-89. Credit cards accepted.

Restaurante Arzak. Alto de Miracruz 21, 20015 San Sebastián, Spain. Tel: 011-34-27-84-65. Fax: 011-34-27-27-53. Credit cards and French francs accepted.

NON-GOLF ACTIVITIES 19

Biarritz is the type of town where the fanatical golfers as well as the shoppers and sightseers in your travel party can meet up after a full day and exchange stories with equally broad smiles. These glowing feelings may well turn to horror a month later, however, when the credit card bills arrive! The itemized bills will reveal two things: one, how expensive the golf is; and two, that Biarritz has all the fashionable, sleek shops that anyone could want, including Cartier, Hermès, Sonia Rykiel, Escada, Chaumet, Louis Féraud, Cerruti, and Cacharel, to name only a few. The shopping in Biarritz is terrific and terrifically expensive.

To walk the promenades along the beaches and cliffs in Biarritz is an absolute joy. The beaches themselves are superb, and if your desire is seclusion you can drive north or south and find long stretches of uncrowded beaches. Spain—the land of bullfights, colorful cuisine, and Iberian culture—is less than an hour away. From Biarritz you can be in the Pyrenees in less than an hour; here the peaks are snow-capped, the rushing rivers are pristine, and the Basque mountain villages unspoiled. Those who like to engage in a game of chance will enjoy the famous casino of Biarritz, which lacks the vitality of Monte Carlo's but is a grand casino nonetheless. If you really want to pamper yourself, head to the spa at Eugénie-les-Bains (home of the famous, three-star restaurant Les Prés d'Eugénie), where you can enjoy a superb massage and mud bath and relax in the therapeutic waters. In short, the Biarritz area offers myriad activities for everyone.

GETTING THERE: By air, Biarritz is one hour from Paris. Air France and other carriers increase their service during July and August. The TGV rapid train makes the trip from Paris to Biarritz in about five hours and costs approximately 600F ($120) one-way.

▶LES BORDES

ROYAL GOLF IN THE LOIRE VALLEY

	The Golf	Golf Services	Lodging	Restaurants	Non-Golf Activities	Total
Rating	**19**	**17**	**17**	**17**	**20**	**90**

In the mid-eighties, Baron Marcel Bich (Bich of Bic pens) invited the esteemed golf course architect Robert von Hagge to Paris to talk about the baron's dream of building a golf course on his massive hunting estate in the Sologne, one and a half hours southwest of Paris. Over cognac after dinner, Baron Bich, a recent convert to golf in his late sixties, enthusiastically described his vision for a world-class golf course on this pristine site.

After having viewed the hunting preserve—fabulous though it was for ducks, pheasants, wild boar, and deer—von Hagge deemed the project infeasible because the inhospitable marshland and thick forest setting would eat up millions and millions of dollars in drainage work alone. His aristocratic and not-to-be-daunted host did not blink: "Build the course. I'll commit all the capital it takes to solve the drainage problems and make it a wonderful course." And so, buoyed by Baron Bich's open checkbook, von Hagge built Les Bordes.

When Les Bordes opened to the public in 1987, the extraordinary vision of Baron Bich, Robert von Hagge, and Jim Shirley, the on-site director, was realized beyond expectation. Today, Les Bordes is not only one of the great courses in Europe, it is one of the world's finest. What started out as a drainage nightmare eventually resulted in the creation of eleven lakes and ponds with numerous connecting, gurgling streams. Water comes into play on twelve of Les Bordes' eighteen holes.

Remarkably, the course fulfills another of Baron Bich's commitments—that it be harmonious with its natural surroundings. No gimmicks, no villas, no town houses, and no condos line the fairways at Les Bordes. So committed was Bich to maintaining the natural ecosystem here that he instantly ordered the removal of a single small willow tree introduced from the United States because it was not indigenous to the area. Mallards, loons, herons, and smaller ducks alight first on one lake and then another, the cackle of cock pheasants echoes throughout the course, and deer browse on the course in early evening. When playing Les Bordes, you cannot help but feel that you are in the heart of Sologne hunting country—this is a course carved out of mature forests of oak, fir, and birch. Indeed, the moment you start out from the first tee you enter a delightful wilderness world on each and every hole.

At Bich's direction, Les Bordes was to be a grand golf course with an understated aura—no flashy resort or heavy advertising promotion, just twenty simple but very tasteful rooms for guests, and only two members in the private club (Baron Bich and his 50 percent partner from Japan). Bich died in June of 1994 at age seventy-nine, but he must be pleased to look down from the heavens on a golf course that has become an oasis of tranquillity. During our visit, only six other guests were staying at Les Bordes and the course seemed virtually unplayed upon. We reveled in the magical golf out our back door (we stayed in room 2, which faces the eighteenth green), and we used Les Bordes as a perfect base from which to explore the lovely châteaux of the eastern Loire.

Ideal months to visit the Loire are May, June, and September, when the weather is unusually good and the crowds are not horrendous at the châteaux. July and August are ideal months at Les Bordes for weather, but the châteaux are overrun with tourists. May and September are usually pleasant during the day and cool in the evening. Rain can come anytime in May, June, and July, so be sure to take rain suits. Umbrellas are available at the course. July and August are much more predictable weather months for golf—usually short-sleeve weather. April and October can have beautiful sunny days but also raw, rainy days.

THE GOLF 19

Of the many golf courses we have played, **Les Bordes** is perhaps the most memorable—even now we yearn to tee it up on the first hole, that long, lovely par four, birches flanking the right side of the fairway, emerald-green in the early morning sun, and the green, ringed by white sand, gently inviting us on an unparalleled aesthetic adventure. What a golf course! What a *difficult* golf course! Jim Shirley says that "it's damn close to being a mean course without being mean."

Les Bordes, of course, is too exhilarating to be mean, but it presents hundreds and hundreds of opportunities for trouble if you are not as precise as a neurosurgeon. You must carry over water on ten of the holes, and two of those—the four-teenth and eighteenth—require a carry over water on both your tee shot and your approach. Number fourteen, measuring more than 550 yards from the back tees, is especially noteworthy for its picturesque island green. All but one of the four par threes plays over substantial water. Where water does not get you, tight tree-lined fairways and beguiling white sand bunkers will. Golfers whose errant shots find the deep rough run the risk not only of ballooning their scores but also of en-countering poisonous vipers! In fact, you are advised to make considerable noise when looking for balls in the high grass to scare off the snakes. Oh, to have the ball concession at Les Bordes! Quality balls cost $15 for three, forever presenting the dilemma of how much time to spend looking for your $5 Titleist in the snake-ridden tall grass.

While the first nine is tucked deep in the woods, halfway up the par five tenth hole the terrain opens up so that the vantage point from the elevated tenth green provides a breathtaking view of the next five holes. Of the many memorable holes at Les Bordes, the sixth, seventh, and eighteenth stand above the rest. Six is a lovely, long par four with a massive sand trap that is crested forbiddingly by an eighteenth-century stone cross. Von Hagge's signature hole, the five-hundred-yard, par five sev-enth, requires a layup to a lake off the tee, then an exciting shot over the water to the landing area for your approach shot to the green. Number eighteen is another particularly stunning hole—your approach shot soars over water to a beautiful green as the clubhouse forms a final backdrop. From the back tees Les Bordes mea-sures just over 7,000 yards with a par rating of seventy-two.

Maintenance on the course is, in a word, perfect! Each hole presents golfers with five superbly conditioned tee boxes. The fairways, thanks to limited play and the meticulous care of the greenskeepers, are some of the lushest you will find any-where in the world. And although the greens putt quite fast, they are eminently fair. Our only complaint, and we have to search to come up with this, is that with seven doglegs, Les Bordes, in our opinion, has two doglegs too many. But it's a marvelous golf course nonetheless.

Les Bordes. 41220 Saint-Laurent-Nouan, Loir et Cher, France. Tel: 011-33-2-54-87-72-13. Fax: 011-33-2-54-87-78-61. Credit cards accepted.

• 1987. Designer: Robert von Hagge. Par 72. 7,007 yards. Greens fees: 350F ($70) weekdays, 550F ($110) weekends. Walking permitted. No caddies. Carts available. Season: year-round.

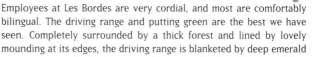

GOLF SERVICES (17)

Employees at Les Bordes are very cordial, and most are comfortably bilingual. The driving range and putting green are the best we have seen. Completely surrounded by a thick forest and lined by lovely mounding at its edges, the driving range is blanketed by deep emerald grass. The putting green, easily the largest we have visited, offers fifty-four differ-ent holes and features a raised mound in the center upon which stands a spectacu-lar sculpture of a wild boar. Les Bordes is obviously proud of its range and putting green as both are highly visible, one in front of the clubhouse and one behind. Range balls are virtually new, brilliantly white, and free for guests. The pro shop has a small, handsome, and very expensive selection of equipment and apparel. Golf carts are top quality with roll-down zippered sides; quality pull carts are also avail-able, but there are no caddies. Brand-new Daiwa graphite and steel clubs are avail-able for rent. Astoundingly, guest golf clubs are not cleaned overnight, nor are clubs put on carts for guests. However, we did appreciate the discretion of the maintenance crews, who have obviously been instructed to turn their backs when players are hitting or on the greens. We regret to report that no rest-room facilities are available on the course after leaving the clubhouse. The clubhouse, with its thirty-foot beamed ceiling, giant hearth, handsome bar, and spacious terrace, is stylish and inviting; massive windows face the driving range on one side and the putting green and first tee on the other. The locker rooms, as well as the ladies' and men's rest rooms, are tasteful and stylish. If clubs were cleaned and put on carts, golf services would be a perfect 20—as is, a remarkable 17.

 L O D G I N G

Anyone who has traveled to France in the last five years is aware that the French travel scene is outrageously expensive. Rooms at fancy Right Bank hotels in Paris and luxury rooms in the French countryside can easily top $500 per night, and three-star meals for two can run close to $300. With this in mind, the charm-ing, spacious, and elegantly functional rooms at **Les Bordes** are a remarkable bargain at 700F, or just over $140 per night. All twenty rooms are beautifully and unobtrusively located right off the eighteenth green, within easy walking distance of the pro shop, golf club, and dining room.

Les Bordes. 41220 Saint-Laurent-Nouan, Loir et Cher, France. Tel: 011-33-2-54-87-72-13. Fax: 011-33-2-54-87-78-61. 20 rooms at 700F ($140). Hotel closed December through February. Credit cards accepted.

R E S T A U R A N T S

Baron Bich wanted the culinary experience at **Les Bordes** to embody traditional dining *à la ferme* (at the farm), which translates into a hearty breakfast of homemade breads, croissants, omelettes, yogurt, and delicious fresh juices. Lunches are a buffet (60F/$12) with trays and platters laden with pâtés, fresh vegetables, seafood terrines, vegetable terrines, fresh poached salmon, pheasant, chicken, fresh fruits, and a cornucopia of delectable, homemade desserts (40F/$8). Each evening a single menu from 160F to 200F ($32 to $40) is offered. The evening we dined began with excellent smoked salmon, followed by sliced steak cooked to perfection and served with braised leeks and a heaping bowl of *haricots verts* (green beans), a delicious green salad, and local cheeses. One of France's best crème brûlées completed our most enjoyable and peaceful evening. There is a limited choice of five or six reasonably priced wines. Jackets are preferred at dinner.

The dining room, like the adjoining clubhouse room, is very comfortable; it features a great cathedral beamed ceiling, a massive hearth with cozy fires crackling on all cool nights, and, mounted over the hearth, a large European stag with wild boars to either side.

For additional dining in the area, the two-star cuisine at the **Grand Hôtel Lion d'Or** in Romorantin-Lanthenay is extremely fine; the restaurant boasts one of the great wine lists in the Loire. Skip famous Jean Bardet in Tours, as the service has become apathetic and rude and the cuisine no longer matches its earlier sparkle. There are several good restaurants in the château-filled city of Blois, most notably the renowned seafood restaurant **Rendez-vous des Pêcheurs.** The fillet of pickerel is a house specialty.

Les Bordes. 41220 Saint-Laurent-Nouan, Loir et Cher, France. Tel: 011-33-2-54-87-72-13. Fax: 011-33-2-54-87-78-61. Credit cards accepted.

Grand Hôtel Lion d'Or. 69 rue Clemenceau, 41200 Romorantin-Lanthenay, France. Tel: 011-33-2-54-94-15-15. Fax: 011-33-2-54-88-24-87. Credit cards accepted.

Rendez-vous des Pêcheurs. 27 rue Foix, 41000 Blois, France. Tel: 011-33-2-54-74-67-48. Fax: 011-33-2-54-74-47-67. Credit cards accepted.

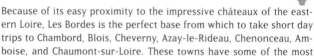

NON-GOLF ACTIVITIES

Because of its easy proximity to the impressive châteaux of the eastern Loire, Les Bordes is the perfect base from which to take short day trips to Chambord, Blois, Cheverny, Azay-le-Rideau, Chenonceau, Amboise, and Chaumont-sur-Loire. These towns have some of the most beautiful and inspiring architectural glories of the Middle Ages and Renaissance, and they are all within an hour's drive of Les Bordes! We can think of no more peaceful way to spend five days in the Loire than staying at Les Bordes, playing eighteen holes in the morning, and then touring a château each afternoon. These châteaux are so grand, so filled with history, that each easily merits a three-hour visit. We have enjoyed these châteaux a number of times and would prioritize visits in this way:

Chenonceau, built out into the Cher river, still in private hands, is the most perfectly beautiful of all the Loire châteaux. Although Chambord is more colossal, the graceful romantic architecture and exquisite fairy tale–like grounds of Chenonceau will win your heart.

Chambord, the extraordinary creation of François I with advice from Leonardo da Vinci, is the center of a massive hunting estate. This is the Loire Valley's largest château. Its double spiral staircase and roofline are awe-inspiring. Horseback riding offering unique perspectives of the Château is available.

Château de Blois, in the heart of the medieval city of Blois, boasts some of the most intriguing and bloody history of any of the French châteaux. Following a complete renovation, the château is a marvel of architecture spanning centuries. When you are in the area, don't miss the exquisite seafood at Rendez-vous des Pêcheurs.

Cheverny, Chaumont-sur-Loire, Azay-le Rideau, and Amboise are also must-see châteaux.

GETTING THERE: Les Bordes is about a ninety-minute drive from Paris. Take the Autoroute A10 toward Bordeaux. Get off the highway at the Meung-sur-Loire exit. Follow the Itinéraire Bis Châteauroux for sixteen kilometers (3.2 miles). Les Bordes will be on the left.

Portugal

▶THE ALGARVE

QUINTA DO LAGO, VALE DO LOBO, VILAMOURA, AND PENINA

	The Golf	Golf Services	Lodging	Restaurants	Non-Golf Activities	Total
Rating	18	13	16	17	17	81

For the British, who virtually invented the Algarve as a warm-weather golf colony during the 1930s, a trip to Portugal's sandy southern shore is not an especially exotic journey. A golfer from London flying down to the Algarve for a long weekend is about as commonplace as a New Yorker getting on a plane with clubs in tow for a few days of golf in the sunshine of Florida.

Hotel Quinta do Lago

For Americans, however, a golfing expedition of some 8,000 miles round-trip—with all the planning and expenses that such a long journey entails—can carry expectations that are enormously high, perhaps unreasonably so.

Just how well does the Algarve meet these expectations for the golfer traveling all the way from America? Is it worth the time and money to go there? And how, in all honesty, do the best Portuguese courses and resorts compare with those in the United States and elsewhere in the world? These were just a few of the important details GOLF TRAVEL set out to learn when we recently traveled to the Algarve.

British wine shippers first introduced golf to Portugal and the Algarve in 1890. The year-round temperate climate, the region's almost constant sunshine—the Algarve enjoys more hours of sunny weather each year on average than any other resort destination in Western Europe—and the spectacular combination of rugged Atlantic shoreline and gorgeous beaches make this a natural haven for golf. Yet until rather recently, the Algarve lagged far behind Spain's Costa del Sol as a golf getaway destination. That, however, has now changed. A recent golf course building boom, catalyzed by designs from America's top course architects, has now given the Algarve claim to being a true golf mecca. Players from all over the world flock to the numerous luxury tourist hotels and resort courses. And while the courses of Spain's Costa del Sol remain more popular (and, frustratingly, more crowded), the Algarve now boasts more top-rated courses than its Spanish rival.

The Algarve, from a Moorish word meaning "the West," attempts to maintain a peaceful and serene aura of days gone by. Its contemporary reality, however, is quite different from that carefully nurtured image of rustic simplicity and relaxed seaside flavor. The Algarve today is a bustling and highly commercial center for European tourism with only a few remaining vestiges of old Portugal. Like Hilton Head, the Algarve features one gated resort community after another and thousands of condos (called "villas" in this part of the world) hidden behind the eucalyptus trees.

There are several beautiful old fishing villages on the coast, like Lagos, Portimao, and Carvoeiro, but for a taste of the real Algarve before the advent of mass tourism you must head inland five or six miles, where you will still see peasant families dressed all in black driving donkey-drawn carts.

The Algarve's distinct vegetation includes wonderful, white-barked cork trees, gray olive trees, fig and almond trees, and the incredibly aromatic umbrella pines that line many fairways on the Algarve's nineteen golf courses. The busy Algarve Airport is located at Faro, about twenty minutes east of the Quinta do Lago hotel and about thirty-five minutes west of the Spanish border. The flight from Lisbon to Faro Airport takes just thirty minutes, but the automobile trip from Lisbon takes four hours or more because of the rugged terrain. British Airways offers nonstop flights from London to Faro. English is spoken at all the Algarve hotels and golf courses. The Algarve's location on the southern tip of Europe means that golf can be played comfortably here year-round.

THE GOLF

18

The best courses on the Algarve, in descending order of quality, include the Quinta do Lago Course and the Ria Formosa Course at Quinta do Lago, Sir Henry Cotton's Orange-Green Course at Vale do Lobo (with its par three seventh, the most famous hole in Portugal), the Donald Steel course at Vilasol, Sir Henry Cotton's Championship Course at Penina, and Frank Pennick's original layout at Vilamoura. Two other excellent eighteen-hole courses—San Lorenzo and Pinheiros Altos (each restricted to members only, but occasionally open to visitors)—are also located within the well-planned, 2,000-acre Quinta do Lago compound. With seventy-two quality holes of golf, therefore, Quinta do Lago is the natural place to stay on the Algarve. We played the courses at Quinta do Lago, Vale do Lobo, Vilamoura, and Penina, all operated as part of adjoining hotel facilities and villa rentals, although the lodging standards are highest at Quinta do Lago.

The **Quinta do Lago Course** and the **Ria Formosa Course** at **Quinta do Lago** are the best courses on the Algarve because they are broad, majestic layouts that offer a true taste of the beautiful Algarve landscape. The resort's two courses have not been destroyed or defaced by greedy developers building villas right on top of the fairways—increasingly the sad case at many top Algarve golf resorts. The Portuguese Open has been held at Quinta do Lago seven times, and on each occasion it has been played on the Quinta do Lago Course, which measures a combined 6,488 meters (7,095 yards) versus 6,205 meters (6,786 yards) for the slightly easier Ria Formosa Course. The Quinta do Lago Course provides a challenging but very enjoyable game as it winds through umbrella pines and water hazards. The fairways are lush, and the greens are kept in excellent condition. Ria Formosa is almost the equal of the Quinta do Lago Course, which, club members told us, is used for tournament action only because of its additional length, which makes it marginally more difficult than Ria Formosa. All thirty-six holes, with their incredibly rich scent of fresh pine, exude a remarkable sense of uniqueness and provide a truly unspoiled look at the Algarve. Playable for golfers of every ability, the very walkable Quinta do Lago tracks were designed by Americans William F. Mitchell, Joe Lee, and William Roquemore. The greens fees at Quinta do Lago are 10,000 escudo/$67 for resort guests and 13,000 escudo/$87 for the general public.

The Cotton-designed layout at **Vale do Lobo,** about twenty minutes west of Quinta do Lago, is perhaps the most famous course on the Algarve and is still worth playing despite the fact that Cotton's masterpiece has actually been reconfigured by real estate developers intent on squeezing in as many villas as possible. For example, in Cotton's day the sixth hole on the Yellow course played as a par five. Six is still a magnificent hole, but it has been shortened into a 296-meter (323-yard) par four in order to create more golf-view homesites. Now, obtrusive villas cling dangerously to the very edge of the fairway. Unlike the sensitively planned Quinta do Lago development, which utilizes a great deal of open space and admits absolutely no homes on its courses, the Vale do Lobo resort looks and feels cramped and congested, and you can easily detect this from a morning round on the golf course. We can only wonder how much more congested Vale do Lobo will be when a new nine is opened sometime in 1997 to join the current twenty-seven holes.

The first three nines at Vale do Lobo were all designed by Sir Henry—the Yellow, Orange, and Green—and in the planned configuration the **Orange** and the **Green** will be paired to form one course and the Yellow and the new Blue nine will form a second eighteen. Strategic thinking is more important than big hitting at Vale do Lobo given the narrowness of the fairways. Thick forests of pine, water, and private homes on certain holes are all real hazards to play. The seventh hole on the Yellow course— the celebrated 210-meter par three that requires a big drive over two deep chasms— truly lives up to its billing as one of the best golf holes anywhere in Europe. Overall, however, the Orange nine is more spectacular still than the Yellow. The first hole on the Orange is a great downhill par five with a creek protecting the green, the par-three eighth plays into the teeth of the prevailing winds (take two extra clubs), and the final hole is a long, tight, uphill par five. Despite its flaws, Vale do Lobo is worth the journey. Given its dramatic uphill/downhill nature, we suspect that even the most energetic golfers will prefer riding to walking. Greens fees are 13,200 escudo ($88).

The **Vilamoura Golf Club** consists of two traditional parkland courses and a third course that comprises three nines featuring large fairways and greens but also heavy bunkering and lots of water. Of the three courses, **Vilamoura I,** designed by Frank Pennick, is the best. The course has recently undergone major renovation and improvement; the narrow, undulating fairways of this hilly track wind through tall pines and frame the sea as a spectacular backdrop. Robert Trent Jones, Sr., has updated Pennick's original design of **Vilamoura II.** Three lakes add to the challenge of the open fairways on the front nine, while the back nine is tighter and several holes play uphill. Each of the three nines on **Vilamoura III** stretches about 3,000 meters (3,280 yards). Despite wide fairways, the course requires accurate shot making to avoid the numerous water hazards and the large greenside sand traps.

Sir Henry Cotton's design for the **Penina Golf Club** makes the most of the site's flat marshland. Cotton planted thousands of trees when the course was built in 1966, and now many huge trees loom as severe obstacles on tee shots and approaches. The **Championship Course** measures 6,439 meters (7,042 yards) and plays to a par of seventy-three; the **Monchique Course,** an accompanying nine-hole, par thirty-five course makes a nice outing if you are pressed for time.

Quinta do Lago Golf Club. Quinta do Lago. Almancil, Algarve, Portugal. Tel: 011-351-89-396002. Fax: 011-351-89-394013. Credit cards accepted.

- *Quinta do Lago Course.* Par 72. 6,488 meters (7,095 yards).
- *Ria Formosa Course.* Par 72. 6,205 meters (6,785 yards).
- Both courses: 1971. Designers: William F. Mitchell, Joe Lee, William Roquemore. Greens fees: resort guests: 10,000 escudo ($67); public: 13,000 escudo ($87). Walking permitted. Caddies and carts (7,000 escudo/$47) available. Handicap restrictions: twenty-eight men, thirty-six women. Season: year-round.

Vale do Lobo Golf Club. Vale do Lobo, 8125 Almancil, Algarve, Portugal. Tel: 011-351-89-39-39-39. Fax: 011-351-89-39-47-42. Credit cards accepted.

• *Orange-Green Course*. 1966, 1975. Designer: Sir Henry Cotton. Par 71. 5,650 meters (6,179 yards). Greens fees: resort guests: 10,000 escudo ($67); public: 13,200 escudo ($88). Walking permitted. No caddies. Carts (6,500 escudo/$43) available. Season: year-round.

Vilamoura Golf Club. Vilamoura, 8125 Quarteira, Algarve, Portugal. Tel: 011-351-89-380-722, 011-351-89-321-562, or 011-351-89-380-724. Fax: 011-351-89-380-726. Credit cards accepted.

• *Vilamoura I*. 1969. Designer: Frank Pennick. Par 73. 6,331 meters (6,924 yards). Greens fees: resort guests: 12,000 escudo ($81), public: 15,000 escudo ($100). Walking permitted. Caddies can be arranged. Carts available. Season: year-round.
• *Vilamoura II*. 1976/1985. Designers: Frank Pennick/Robert Trent Jones, Sr. Par 72. 6,256 meters (6,842 yards). Greens fees: resort guests: 8,000 escudo ($54), public: 10,500 escudo ($71). Walking permitted. Caddies can be arranged. Carts available. Season: year-round.
• *Vilamoura III*. 1990. Designer: Joseph Lee. 27 holes. Greens fees: resort guests: 6,500 escudo ($44), public: 8,500 escudo ($58). Walking permitted. Caddies can be arranged. Carts available. Season: year-round.

Penina Golf Club. PO Box 146, 8502 Portimao, Algarve, Portugal. Tel: 011-351-82-41-5500. Fax: 011-351-82-41-50-00. Credit cards accepted.

• *Championship Course*. 1966. Designer: Henry Cotton. Par 73. 6,439 meters (7,042 yards). Greens fee: 10,500 escudo ($71). Walking permitted. No caddies. Carts available. Season: year-round.
• *Monchique Course*. 1966. Henry Cotton. Par 35. 2,842 meters (3,108 yards). Greens fee: 8,000 escudo ($54). Walking permitted. No caddies. Carts available. Season: year-round.

GOLF SERVICES

We have to say up front that an otherwise delightful trip was temporarily marred because Quinta do Lago lost all of our carefully booked tee times. We did finally manage our way onto the golf course twenty-four hours later, but in all our years of traveling anonymously from one resort to another, this experience was a regrettable first for us. Could the same thing happen to you? We certainly hope not, but if it does, you may not receive much sympathy from the hotel and golf staff at Quinta do Lago. We left messages for the head pro to call us in our room, but to no avail. Due to this snafu, we lost out on an entire day of play. We at GOLF TRAVEL report our experiences precisely as they occur. Well, this was how our trip to the Algarve got started.

Had Quinta do Lago not lost our tee times, or had management made amends for the dilemma, we would rate its golf services a score of 18 because its facilities—from the practice range to the pro shop—are simply superb and truly the best on the Algarve. But a lost tee time and an unsympathetic attitude are negatives of the first rank. Vale do Lobo, Vilamoura, and Penina all have fine services, however, with helpful staffs to go with good facilities.

LODGING

Separated from the beach by an unusual saltwater lagoon filled with wildlife, the **Hotel Quinta do Lago** has a lovely, windswept setting on the most beautiful stretch of the Algarve coast.

Rooms are large, luxurious, and equipped with amenities like spacious bathrooms, stocked minibars, and English-language cable channels (BBC and CNN). We were very comfortable in our ocean-view room, which also featured a lovely, private, outdoor balcony overlooking the sea. Hotel facilities include a well-equipped exercise area and gym with spa, very nice indoor and outdoor swimming pools, beach access, tennis, a large horseback-riding complex with miles of trails, a pleasant bar that opens up to an outdoor terrace, and two good restaurants. The public areas on the ground floor are merely functional; the gift shop is tiny and the reception desk frequently inundated with guests checking in and out. Room rates range from 38,000 to 54,000 escudo ($262 to $379) per night, breakfast included.

Hotel Quinta do Lago. 8135 Almancil, Algarve, Portugal. Tel: 800-223-6800 or 800-745-8883 or 011-351-89-396666. Fax: 011-351-89-396393. 150 rooms and suites. Doubles cost 38,000 to 54,000 escudo ($262 to $379), breakfast included. Credit cards accepted.

RESTAURANTS ⑰

The cuisine of the Algarve is a wonderful delight. The top floor of the Hotel Quinta do Lago plays host to two fine restaurants: **Navegadores,** a traditional Portuguese restaurant with an emphasis on fresh seafood, and **Ca d'Oro,** which specializes in Italian cuisine. In addition, all of the Algarve golf clubs mentioned above have pleasant clubhouse facilities that include very agreeable restaurants for lunch.

The best bet for lunch on the Algarve is the extraordinary **Gigi Beach,** where you will experience the real Portugal without having to leave the Algarve. Accessible only by foot—you must walk across the narrow wood-plank bridge over the saltwater lagoon—Gigi Beach is no more than a beachfront shack located directly across from the Quinta do Lago hotel (you can charge your meal to your room). Run by the always welcoming Gigi, a former Lisbon real estate agent, and an equally friendly waiter named Josef wearing a T-shirt and swimming trunks, Gigi Beach is the kind of place where Pavarotti is played full-blast on the sound system and all the guests—including the smartest visitors—leave tipsy and laughing. There is no menu; just take your pick from the platters of fresh seafood arrayed in front of you and it will be grilled over a wood fire. The whole deal will come to about 5,000 escudo ($33) per person. Gigi Beach is open only for lunch and only between March and October. Do not miss it.

The restaurants at Hotel Quinta do Lago. 8135 Almancil, Algarve, Portugal. Tel: 011-351-89-396-666. Fax: 011-351-89-396-393. Credit cards accepted.

Gigi Beach. Quinta do Lago, 8135 Almancil, Algarve, Portugal. Tel: 0936-44-51-78. No credit cards.

NON-GOLF ACTIVITIES ⑰

Other activities at Quinta do Lago include riding, tennis, swimming, beachcombing, and windsurfing. Sightseeing should include the fishing villages noted above. Sit back at a café down by the wharf and watch all the boats sail up to the docks. The Algarve can be a shopper's delight, especially for hand-painted tiles and ceramics; for a good selection try a shop called Porches Pottery near Penina. If you are searching for high-quality leather goods, you will find rewarding shopping in the market town of Loule. The villages in the hills away from the sea allow you to step back into time, and the residents are wonderfully friendly and hospitable. If glitz rather than tradition is your preference, try the grand Vilamoura casino.

GETTING THERE: To reach the Algarve, take one of the frequent thirty-minute flights from Lisbon to the sparkling new Faro Airport. The Hotel Quinta do Lago is twenty-five minutes by car from the airport. Upon leaving the airport, follow the signs to Portimao and Almancil. At the first traffic light in Almancil you will see a small sign for Quinta do Lago. Follow the signs; when you come to the resort you will go through five roundabouts. The hotel is at the very end of the drive. Cab fare from the airport is 4,600 escudo ($31).

Italy

►LAKE COMO

LUXURIOUS HEDONISM AND SUPERB GOLF

	The Golf	Golf Services	Lodging	Restaurants	Non-Golf Activities	Total
Rating	**18**	**17**	**19**	**17**	**19**	**90**

Golf Club Villa d'Este

The area around Lake Como is *the* mecca for Italian golf. The fact that more than two thirds of all the Italian Opens have been played in the Lake Como/Milan area is solid testimony to the high level of golf in the area, and to match the quality of golf are accommodations that rank among the very best in Europe. The Hotel Villa d'Este should, without question, be your address while staying in the area, not only because of its amenities but also because within thirty minutes of the hotel you will find at least six first-rate golf courses that, although private, welcome outside guests during the week. We recommend that you play the following five, each of which is a true jewel—Golf Club Villa d'Este, Menaggio e Cadenabbia Golf Club, La Pinetina Golf Club, and Golf Club Monticello (the Red and Blue courses). Although Milan has some fine courses, the "forty-five-minute trip" there can turn into a two-hour nightmare because of the very heavy traffic around the city.

 THE GOLF

Twenty-five minutes southeast of the Hotel Villa d'Este is the wondrous and exclusive **Golf Club Villa d'Este.** Passing through the private, understated entrance, you enter a world of Italian refinement at every level. The club was owned by the hotel until 1981, when it was purchased by its members. Construction on the club's golf course, unquestionably one of the very best in Europe, began in 1926 under the creative eye of English architect Peter Gannon, and just two years later, in 1928, it hosted its first Italian Open. To date, the Villa d'Este has been the site of twelve Italian Opens, and for good reason: it has all the components of a top course, including a challenging design and many breathtaking holes. In addition, what makes the Villa d'Este course and others around the Lake Como area so memorable is the remarkable absence of residential development. In sharp contrast with the many new courses being built in the United States, which are first and foremost real estate plays, the golf course at Villa d'Este is miraculously unlittered with homes, making it a most peaceful and relaxing golf venue.

Villa d'Este is not, however, without its flaws. Holes three, four, six, and seven, for example, come together like a busy Roman intersection—the greens and tees are simply too close to one another. Excepting a few such design glitches, the course is truly inspirational, with lots of lovely oaks, birches, and a great variety of evergreens lining the fairways.

Course maintenance and conditions are excellent. The greens are fast, the fairways are lush, and the rough is high. Because Lake Como is six or seven miles away, it is not visible from the course, although a smaller lake can be seen from a number of holes. The course also offers nice views of the nearby mountains, which, although lovely, do not compare with the dramatic mountain panoramas of Menaggio (see below).

The beauty of Villa d'Este stems from the magical world of the course itself. Thickly lined with mature trees, the narrow fairways put a real premium on shot accuracy. Not one hole is truly wide open. Our favorite holes, numbers one and thirteen, are both par fives with elevated tees. On the first hole, you look down a lush corridor of fir, birch, and oak trees; 540 meters (590 yards) away, in a tranquil amphitheater of trees, the green awaits your approach. What an inspirational opening hole and a real harbinger of the enticing holes to come! Thirteen is thrilling because you tee off out of a shoot of trees, with a slight dogleg-left to the pin 492 meters (538 yards) away. Eighteen, though somewhat short at 314 meters (343 yards) from the tips, is an ideal finishing hole; it plays slightly uphill and slopes left, with the green right at the base of the club. Having played Villa d'Este once, we can't wait to get out again on this refined and scenic course—one that reflects the very best of the Italian style.

Menaggio, a small town on the western side of Lake Como, is halfway up the lake from Cernobbio, yet because of the narrow, tortuous roads around the lake, the drive takes at least an hour. We recommend putting your car on the ferry and taking the approximately one-hour ride over to Menaggio, where en route you will be able to enjoy the absolutely breathtaking views of the lake and lakefront villas. Once you arrive, the drive from the dock in Menaggio up the hill to the old, refined **Menaggio e Cadenabbia Golf Club** will take another ten minutes. Perhaps it sounds like an excess of travel time and effort to enjoy a single round of golf, but after playing the course at Menaggio, you will feel that the trip is more than worth it.

High above the lake, Menaggio is an alpine wonderland surrounded by dramatic mountains. The second oldest course in Italy (only Aquasanta, near Rome, is older), Menaggio was designed and built in 1907 by what management calls a "group of Englishmen." Although reworked in 1967 by John Harris, the course is basically the same beautiful layout devised in 1907 by that skilled, but now unknown, team of Englishmen.

A fine course in top condition, Menaggio's hilly contours will challenge every aspect of your game. At the center of this mountain wonderland is the pleasant old clubhouse, which, although nothing fancy, exudes a rustic charm and elegance. A handsome bar welcomes you inside, while just outside terraces on both the front and the back lure you back outdoors. Perhaps the more appealing of the two, the front terrace is protected by a canopy of trees and offers a nice view of the eighteenth fairway and green just below. No watering system on the fairways can mean hard, burned-out grass in the middle of a dry summer, but since we played during a period of considerable rain, the fairways were lush. The greens, as you would expect, are watered and in good shape.

With its *extremely* hilly terrain, we expected plenty of doglegs, but in actuality few exist. The first hole, a glorious par five with an elevated tee, is superb as it stretches out before you with a slight dogleg to the right. Eleven, a 369-meter par four (404-yard), and twelve, a 296-meter par four (324-yard), are two stunning holes with elevated tees offering breathtaking views. Twelve features a giant oak in the middle of the fairway, which adds considerable interest to your second shot as you hit up to the elevated green. Seventeen and eighteen, both very short par fours that seem squeezed in to round out an eighteen-hole track, are the only holes that really disappoint. Of the two, seventeen is the most unsuccessful, with a hodgepodge of elements—planted trees in the middle of the fairway, a dirt road crossing the fairway fifty yards in front of the green, and a small pond in front of the green.

Like other courses in the Lake Como area, Menaggio enjoys an absence of residential development. You need not worry about mis-hitting a shot into someone's hot tub or bay windows, nor is the view marred by giant nets protecting swimming pools or terraces. With no homes in view, you are left to enjoy the undiluted, untainted beauty of a course nestled in the foothills and surrounded by dramatic mountains reaching a 5,000-foot elevation. This course has great interest; the contours, design, panoramic views, and maturity lend it abundant character.

Located approximately twenty minutes southwest of the Villa d'Este, **La Pinetina Golf Club** is a new club that caters to the Milan market for the majority of its membership. Facilities include a new, rather nondescript clubhouse with a restaurant, a nice outdoor terrace overlooking the first and tenth holes, a pleasant bar, and perfectly clean and functional men's and women's locker rooms.

The course has been carefully and beautifully carved out of the forests of this part of Lombardy. With its gently rolling terrain, La Pinetina is a first-rate course whose lush fairways, superb greens, and fine tee boxes are beautifully maintained. The eighteenth, a long par five lined with evergreens, birch, and oak trees, was our favorite hole, with a slight uphill climb to the green by the clubhouse. It is a fine, tough finishing hole that almost makes a player forget La Pinetina's most significant flaw, a massive power line that dominates much of the front nine's visual panorama. Both the power lines traversing some fairways and the giant concrete towers that support the lines make for truly regrettable intrusions. Carts and pull carts are available.

Set in a residential area approximately twenty minutes south of Como and roughly a half hour from the Villa d'Este, the clubhouse at **Golf Club Monticello** gives one pause. With its modern, circular design, this golf complex is more reminiscent of the Doral in Miami than a golf club in the Como area. Although a long way from the rustic charm of Menaggio and the Old World refinement of the Villa d'Este Club, you will nonetheless be won over by Monticello's two eighteen-hole courses, the practice facilities, the efficient staff, and the clubhouse's functionality.

The two courses Raffaele Buratti and Jim Fazio designed in 1974 were quickly recognized as excellent golf venues and hosted the Italian Open in 1975, 1977, 1979, 1987, 1988, 1989, and 1992. These opens were played on the **Red Course,** which, at 6,286 meters (6,874 yards), is the longer and more difficult of the two courses. Golfing stars like Greg Norman, Sandy Lyle, Billy Casper, and Sam Torrance have won the Italian Open here. The **Blue Course,** although shorter at 5,904 meters (6,457 yards), is also a fine course. Conditions on both courses are superb, with excellent fairways and fast greens. Though set in a residential area, golf at Monticello is not compromised by homes, condominiums, and town houses lining the holes. Both courses are beautifully laid out—water comes into play on nine out of the thirty-six holes, mature fir trees are sprinkled liberally across the terrain, and a creative array of bunkers puts a high premium on accuracy. Although close to the mountainous region of Lake Como, the courses at Monticello are relatively flat and have views of the distant mountains.

The creative layout and length of these courses—especially the Red—will more than challenge your skills as a golfer. We especially liked two holes on the Red Course: number eight, a demanding, 397-meter (434-yard) hole that plays along the water on the right, and number sixteen, another difficult, 388-meter (424-yard) par four with a slight dogleg-left and water guarding the green on the left. On the Blue Course, the par three number fourteen is an intriguing hole at 143 meters (156 yards), with a long carry over the water. Number eighteen struck us as somewhat flawed; a par five, 438-meter (479-yard) dogleg-left that, unless you play over the dogleg with a driver, forces you to play your drive with a four or five iron in order to avoid playing through the dogleg. We suggest playing Monticello twice—the Blue Course the first day and the Red on the second.

Golf Club Villa d'Este. Via Cantù no. 13, 22030 Montorfano (Como), Italy. Tel: 011-39-31-200-200. Fax: 011-39-31-200-786. Credit cards accepted.

• 1926. Designer: Peter Gannon. Par 69. 5,727 meters (6,296 yards). 71 par rating. Greens fees: L95,700 ($59) weekdays, L142,700 ($88) weekends. No carts. Caddies can be arranged. Restrictions: closed Tuesdays, except in August. Season: February–December.

Menaggio e Cadenabbia Golf Club. Via Golf no. 12, 22010 Grandola ed Uniti (Como), Italy. Tel: 011-39-34-432-103. Fax: 011-39-34-430-780. Credit cards accepted.

• 1907/1967. Designers: unknown/John Harris. Par 69. 5,277 meters (5,771 yards). 69 par rating. Greens fees: L89,200 ($55) weekdays, L120,000 ($74) weekends. Caddies. No carts. Restrictions: closed Tuesdays. Season: March–November.

La Pinetina Golf Club. Via Golf no. 4, 22070 Appiano Gentile (Como), Italy. Tel: 011-39-31-933-202. Fax: 011-39-31-890-342. Credit cards accepted.

• 1971. Designers: John Harris, M. Albertini. Par 71. 5,928 meters (6,483 yards). 71 par rating. Greens fees: L69,750 ($43) weekdays, L110,300 ($68) weekends. Walking permitted. Caddies can be arranged. Carts available. Restrictions: closed Tuesdays. Season: year-round.

Golf Club Monticello. Via Volta no. 4, 22070 Cassina Rizzardi (Como), Italy. Tel: 011-39-31-928-055. Fax: 011-39-31-880-207. No credit cards.

• *Red Course.* 1974. Designer: Raffaele Buratti/Jim Fazio. Par 72. 6,286 meters (6,874 yards). 73 par rating.
• *Blue Course.* 1974. Designer: Raffaele Buratti/Jim Fazio. Par 72. 5,904 meters (6,457 yards). 71 par rating.
• Greens fee: $67. Walking permitted. Caddies can be arranged. Carts available. Restrictions: closed Mondays. Season: February–December.

 GOLF SERVICES

Golf services at the Golf Club Villa d'Este are a major step up from those at most courses on the Continent. Services include good caddies, a terrific caddie master, fine pull carts, a nice putting green, and a good driving range. Unfortunately, there are no rest rooms on the course. The clubhouse is elegant and has a refined bar, a very good dining room that stays busy and animated, and a verandah overlooking the eighteenth hole, the perfect place to take a drink after your round. A cozy little snack bar with remarkably good food is on the lower level near the caddie master's office. Club members dress with great refinement; our guess is that most hail from Milan or own summer homes on Lake Como. Here you can observe the great style of Italy's upper echelons, people who could not be more friendly and hospitable. Be sure to have dinner one night in the club's handsome dining room; the food and service are excellent.

Menaggio has only fair golf services. The range balls look as if they are from the fifties, the caddies look like casting rejects from the film *Caddyshack,* and there are no rest rooms on the course. The locker rooms are nice enough, although nothing plush, but members and staff at the club are extremely friendly. Compared to venerable Menaggio, La Pinetina Golf Club presents more pleasant golf services. You'll find a driving range, pitching green, and putting green, but overall golf services here are rather basic.

At Monticello you will find two pleasant dining rooms at the club: one casual and the other more formal. Locker rooms are clean and spacious, and the pro shop, while small, is filled with merchandise. Service throughout the club is pleasant and helpful, especially at the front desk.

LODGING

No one should come to Lake Como on a golf holiday and not stay at the **Villa d'Este,** certainly one of the top five hotels in the world! And, yes, we know it is also one of the most expensive. Double rooms in high season (from May to October) average roughly $500, but this does include breakfast in your room or the sumptuous buffet in the formal Verandah, with choices of omelettes, cheeses, ham, fruit, fresh pastries, yogurt, cereals, champagne, and other beverages.

Truly a *grand* hotel in the Old World style, the Villa d'Este has been beautifully maintained and updated to the most modern standards. A warning: our use of superlatives becomes a bit unrestrained when describing the Villa d'Este. Its location right on the lake in the tiny town of Cernobbio, just outside Como, is unforgettable; the gardens and grounds epitomize all the lovely elements of inspired Italian garden design with its combination of textures—trees, spired cedars, parasol pines, explosions of flowers, and a virtual cornucopia of fragrances, highlighted by the luxuriant panels of jasmine that seem to be in every romantic spot.

There is certainly a formality about the whole Villa d'Este experience, but it is a tranquil formality that does not intimidate or discomfort. A walk in the Villa d'Este gardens is a walk in history, where before you have strolled princes and princesses, dukes, poets, authors, and movie stars. One wonders how many affairs were begun here, inspired by kisses stolen beneath the clear Italian night. The Villa d'Este is much more than a hotel, it is a legend whose narrative stretches back over five hundred years and includes Lord Byron, Percy Shelley, Mark Twain, Franz Liszt, and Stendhal, who wrote, "Here everything speaks of love." It is Clark Gable, Napoleon, the Empress Maria Fedorovna of Russia, and more.

When you come through the Villa d'Este gates you enter a special world, a world where the service is flawless, the activities first-rate and inexhaustible, the public rooms stunning, and all the guest rooms luxurious and spacious. The inside rooms looking across the gardens and up into the hills are perfectly adequate, but the junior suites facing the lake, starting at just over $700, are magnificent.

Front desk personnel and the concierge desk were models of efficiency. The concierge provided thorough and faultless assistance in setting up tee times, arranging tours, making restaurant reservations, and giving expert advice on the sights in the Lake Como area. If you ask the concierge to do a number of things, we would certainly advise tipping $20 to $30 for a two- or three-day stay and $50 for a week-long stay. The maid service and room service are all a guest could ask for.

Villa d'Este Grand Hotel and Sporting Club. Via Regina no. 40, 22012 Cernobbio (Como), Italy. Tel: 011-39-31-34-81. Fax: 011-39-31-348-844. 156 rooms and suites from L475,000 to L2,575,000 ($293 to $1,589) from May to October and L375,000 to L2,375,000 ($231 to $1,464) in March, April, and November. Closed December and January. Credit cards accepted.

R E S T A U R A N T S   17

Dinner at the **Villa d'Este** is superb, with excellent service and a fine wine list. Captains could not be more helpful and professional. As one would expect of a hotel of this stature, the wine list offers an extraordinary selection of Italy's finest wines—from Sicily and Sardinia to Trentino–Alto Adige and Lombardy in the north. Trying to understand the Italian wine world is like negotiating a byzantine maze, but the treasures along the way are sure to delight the most discriminating oenophile, with both reds and whites that rival the best of France in finesse and refinement. The sommelier at the Villa d'Este is most competent and, given price parameters, will guide you to some superb wines. You can pay L300,000 ($185) for an extraordinary 1990 Angelo Gaja Barbaresco Sorì Tilden or just L35,675 ($22) for a delightful 1994 Chardonnay Collio by Eno Friulia of Friuli–Venezia Giulia. The dining room is glamorous and serves the best food on Lake Como. The hotel's other restaurant, the casual **Grill Room** is open only for dinner.

Aside from the hotel and the clubhouse restaurant at the Golf Club Villa d'Este, the culinary scene in the Lake Como area is rather limited. We can, however, recommend the following restaurants:

Although it refers to itself as a trattoria, **Trattoria del Navedano** is as much a trattoria as Lucas-Carton in Paris is a bistro. Romantic, yes, but also very expensive, Navedano serves very good *haut* Italian cuisine in a lovely setting on the eastern outskirts of the town of Como, fifteen minutes from Villa d'Este. Be sure to reserve a table outside on the terrace if visiting in early June through the first half of September, when the weather is generally perfect for outside dining in the evening. Service at Navedano, though somewhat obsequious, is professional, prompt, and cordial. Although not exhaustive, the wine list has some excellent selections from all the primary winegrowing regions of Italy. Superb lamb and veal dishes, along with terrific pasta selections, are on the menu. Expect to pay anywhere from L180,000 ($111) to L340,000 ($210) for dinner with wine and tip.

Although touristy, the **Locanda dell'Isola Comancina** delivers both good food and a delightful experience. Because the restaurant is located on the only island in Lake Como, a lovely boat ride becomes your only mode of transportation. Ask the concierge at the Villa d'Este to make the boat arrangements, and make sure to leave for dinner while it is still light in order to enjoy the ride to the fullest. There is only one menu at the Comancina, which includes wine, a great assortment of antipasti, a delectable trout (boned and served at your table), a selection of *twelve* superb vegetables, a chicken dish, cheese selection, dessert, and a specially brewed coffee served with an exotic liqueur, the preparation of which becomes the nightly floor show. The fixed price dinner costs L90,000 ($55).

Villa d'Este. Via Regina no. 40, 22012 Cernobbio (Como), Italy. Tel: 011-39-31-34-81. Fax: 011-39-31-348-844. Credit cards accepted.

Trattoria del Navedano. Via G. Velzi no. 4, 22100 Como, Italy. Tel: 011-39-31-308-080. Fax: 011-39-31-308-080. Credit cards accepted.

Locanda dell'Isola Comancina. Commune di Ossuccio (Como), Italy. Tel: 011-39-34-455-083. Fax: 011-39-34-457-022. No credit cards.

NON-GOLF ACTIVITIES

Non-golfing activities at the Villa d'Este abound: both indoor and outdoor pools, a squash court, an exercise room, lovely grounds, a spa, windsurfing, water skiing, sailing, a putting green, and, finally, eight tennis courts, six of which are fine, red, European clay courts. The courts are overseen by the hotel's tennis pro, a distinguished man in his mid-fifties who effortlessly wins the hearts of all the women who come near him. Of course, one of the real Villa d'Este delights is to take leisurely strolls around the grounds and feast upon one of the most beautiful and idyllic places on earth. After dinner, be sure to visit the outdoor terrace fronting the lake for after-dinner drinks and dancing to the romantic music of the pianist, who plays every night. We also encourage you to take a boat tour of the lake, absorbing all the extraordinary scenery that one would never see in a car. Also visit the lovely lakeside villas of Balbianello and Carlotta. Lake Como is within a couple of miles of Switzerland, and, if the gaming impulse moves you, go to the Swiss town of Campione d'Italia, twenty-two kilometers (13.2 miles) from Como.

As you leave the Villa d'Este, admittedly with a considerably lighter wallet, you will be struck by how memorable your stay has been and how much you enjoyed the fine food, elegant surroundings, and fascinating golf. Immediately, the desire to return proves to be keen and persistent.

GETTING THERE: As you leave Milan's Linate Airport, turn left and follow directions to Bologna-Varese-Como-Chiasso. After ten kilometers (6 miles) turn right and proceed toward Varese-Como-Chiasso (Highways A8-A9). Drive thirty kilometers (18 miles) on the Tangenziale Ovest up to the tollgate. About five kilometers (3 miles) from the first toll gate turn right and follow the signs to Como-Chiasso (Highway 9). Proceed thirty kilometers (18 miles) to the next toll gate. After ten kilometers (6 miles) take the exit Como Nord (the last exit before the Swiss border) and follow the signs to Cernobbio. The Villa d'Este is located three kilometers (1.8 miles) from this exit.

►THE COSTA SMERALDA, SARDINIA

PARADISE IN THE MEDITERRANEAN

	The Golf	Golf Services	Lodging	Restaurants	Non-Golf Activities	Total
Rating	18	18	19	17	18	90

We have been aware of the resort development on the Costa Smeralda since the mid-sixties. From the very beginning, this resort area has enjoyed extraordinary cachet, mostly because it was bought and developed by the irresistible Aga Khan, a dark, dashing, billionaire bachelor of infinite charm who dazzled some of the world's most beautiful women. Wherever he went became the instant hot spot. No wonder that, when he announced his plans for the Costa Smeralda, interest became intense. Travelers could not wait to make the exotic sojourn to this alluring, unspoiled island, the second largest in the Mediterranean, after Sicily. Within a few years of the announcement, big cover stories on the Costa Smeralda began to appear in the pages of *Vogue*, *Bazaar*, and *Town & Country*, replete with big, glossy photos of sleek yachts moored in quiet, azure coves; beautiful, tanned people luxuriating in the Sardinian sun;

Cala di Volpe

and bejeweled European nobility bathing in one another's admiration. What we do not recall are any articles featuring golf on Sardinia, a common oversight at most resort destinations until golf became popular seven or eight years ago.

For years, in fact, the Pevero Golf Club, with its Robert Trent Jones, Sr., course that opened in 1972, was a terrifically well kept secret. Cut out of the rocky terrain of a ridgelike peninsula overlooking Cala di Volpe (Fox Bay), the Pevero Golf Club has slowly emerged from its shroud of secrecy to become recognized as one of the finest golf courses in all Europe. In addition to an intriguing design, this course is one of the most scenic, and certainly one of the best conditioned, you will ever play. Talk circulates about building another course on the Costa Smeralda, but we feel one is enough; a second course would only contribute to the acceleration of Sardinia's development.

Sardinia is ruggedly beautiful, with mountains rising to more than 6,000 feet in elevation, sunbaked boulder outcroppings, and countless groves of olive trees. Situated 125 miles off the Italian coast to the south of Corsica, Sardinia is 170 miles long and 80 miles wide with a road system that is, shall we say, refreshingly rustic. Because of the narrowness and circuitousness of the roads, a trip from north to south will take at least four or, more comfortably, five hours. By European standards, Sardinia is not a densely populated place; it has just 1.6 million inhabitants, who are evenly distributed between the towns and countryside. Until the relatively recent advent of tourism, Sardinia's economy was driven by agriculture, primarily sheep raising, complemented by the production of wine and olive oil. Although boasting hundreds of miles of miraculous coastline and myriad protected coves and bays, Sardinia was never an island of fishermen but instead a terrain for shepherds. Until recently there were very few roads going down to the water.

While in Sardinia be sure to travel inland to view a culture that has not changed for hundreds of years. Driving about the island you will notice strange, conelike stone structures. There are more than 7,000 of these distinctive towers on the island, dating from the second century B.C. They are called *nuraghi*, and they were built to protect against marauders. To this day, in fact, bandits still roam some of the island's remote enclaves, but, rather than posing any real risk for the tourist, their presence only adds to Sardinia's romantic allure.

The Costa Smeralda, a thirty-three-mile stretch of coastline in northeastern Sardinia that the Aga Khan and his consortium purchased, certainly could not be described as rustic now. Although the developer showed enormous respect for the region's rugged terrain and native architecture, the homes and hotels are opulent, elegant, and infinitely refined. To his credit, the Aga Khan imposed strong, environmentally sensitive restrictions on the Costa Smeralda from the very beginning. For example, buildings may not exceed three stories in height; consequently, there are none of the horrid high-rises like those that litter the Costa del Sol in southern Spain. In addition, a very strong architectural review board ensures that all structures retain a certain Sardinian flavor. Costa Smeralda's main town is Porto Cervo, a newly constructed town on a protected cove that offers an extensive marina, restaurants, and a number of stylish shops. Porto Cervo, a delightful little town with buildings of red tile and whitewashed walls, blends into its natural surroundings as if it were an old fishing village.

THE GOLF

The construction of the **Pevero Golf Course** is legendary. Although in many ways not typical of a Robert Trent Jones, Sr., course, it repre-
sents one of his greatest accomplishments. At Pevero, Jones had to work with what nature provided him, which generously included a glorious setting offering magnificent views of the mountains in the distance and won-drous, panoramic vistas of the Mediter-ranean, yet also one of the rockiest terrains imaginable, with boulders so large that they simply could not be moved with even mega-earthmoving equipment. The course is narrow, not by human choice but by nature's insistence.

Pevero Golf Course

In his fascinating book *Golf's Mag-nificent Challenge*, Jones talks about the extraordinary obstacles his design team had to face on this formidable ridge. In one anecdote, he describes a meeting between himself, the Aga Khan, and a group of Italian agronomists. On the basis of their soil analysis, the agronomists declared that, considering the condition of the terrain, grass would be impossible to grow. They proposed importing thousands of tons of topsoil from the mainland to layer the whole course with a foot of this multimillion-dollar commodity. In his infinite Yankee wisdom, Jones came up with another proposal, which, if success-ful, would cost a fraction of the cost. He had observed that there was an abun-dance of crushed granite on the property and suggested adding grass seed and the necessary grass-growing nutrients to the crushed granite and then hope for the best. It worked, and within months Pevero had—and still has—some of the lushest fairways in Europe.

The course has one quirk. Each morning a few potholes appear on the fairways, apparently having been dug the evening before. One would guess that repairs were being made on the watering system, but, actually, the excavations do not represent the work of human beings at all; rather, they are the handiwork of wild boars, who clearly revel in their nightly fairway forages. Each morning the maintenance people do the best they can do, and the Sardinian world goes on.

Under very specific instructions from the Aga Khan, this whole setting was to re-main as natural as possible; fences were not to be put up around the golf club to keep the boars out—period. The course is well conditioned, but if you stray into the rough, it's just you and the elements. The course begins with an inspirational, 410-yard, downhill par four that presents a breathtaking view of the Bay of Pevero. Num-ber two, a dogleg-left par four, is the only uninteresting hole on the course, but it is immediately followed by the grandest hole on all Pevero—a tight, 520-yard, uphill par five that is both exhilarating and tough. The third green has the course's highest vantage point; from here you begin a two-hole descent down to number five. Both the fourth (a par four) and fifth (a par three) are dramatic holes, played from spectacular elevated tees. Number nine, a 510-yard par five, provides a fine conclusion to the front side as it climbs back up to the clubhouse.

No momentum is lost on the back nine, which in many ways is more stunning and intricate than the front. Number thirteen, a 395-yard par four, tees off as if right into the sea and the distant, majestic mountains; it is the most beautiful hole on the course.

Pevero Golf Club: 07020 Porto Cervo, Arzachena Costa Smeralda, Sardinia, Italy. Tel: 011-39-789-96210. Fax: 011-39-789-96572. Credit cards accepted.

• 1972. Designer: Robert Trent Jones, Sr. Par 72. 6,799 yards. Greens fee: L138,000 ($85). Walking permitted. Caddies upon request. Carts available. Season: year-round.

GOLF SERVICES

Golf services at Pevero are some of the finest in Europe. The pro shop is very well stocked; the dining and locker rooms are quite plush. The golf carts are spiffy, and there is an unusually fine driving range. Staff is especially helpful with your golf bags, and with club cleaning. Dining at the club is excellent. Carts and caddies are available upon request.

LODGING

Several years ago, the Aga Khan's Sardinian hotel properties were purchased by ITT Sheraton. Three of these properties—the Cala di Volpe, Hotel Romazzino, and Hotel Pitrizza—were added to the ITT Sheraton group's Luxury Collection. All three are very fine hotels offering spectacular views and settings. We opted to stay at Cala di Volpe and were delighted with what we found.

Quite simply, the **Cala di Volpe** is one of the most magical hotel creations in the world, incorporating a stunning design created by the imaginative mind of French architect Jacques Coulle. Conjuring up images of medieval castles and Moorish nights with its turrets, porticoes, terraces, and roofs

Cala di Volpe

pitched at a myriad of levels and angles, the Cala di Volpe transports its guests to another world, full of romance and enchantment.

The interior, highlighted by a handsome bar, lobby, and dining room, is equally fascinating and engaging. Guest rooms exhibit a certain rustic Sardinian elegance, in addition to being spacious and comfortable. The 125 rooms feature balconies with varying views of the sea, the lagoon in front of the hotel, and the mountains in the distance. The most stylish hotel on the Costa Smeralda, the Cala di Volpe offers superb service provided primarily by the island's professional and friendly residents. In addition, you will find a few chic shops, a pristine beach, tennis courts, and a magnificent seawater pool to enjoy. Another plus, the Cala di Volpe is the hotel closest to the Pevero Golf Club.

Cala di Volpe. 07020 Porto Cervo, Costa Smeralda, Sardinia, Italy. Tel: 011-39-789-976111. Fax: 011-39-789-976617. 123 rooms from L335,000 to L740,000 ($210 to $460), including full board, depending on the season. Credit cards accepted.

RESTAURANTS 17

Along the Costa Smeralda, the **Cala di Volpe** is our favorite dining spot. Whether indoors or out on the terrace, dining is an elegant affair, made even more memorable with the marvelous selection of fresh fish offered daily. Lamb raised on the island is another excellent choice. The kitchen revels in using fresh, local ingredients. The wine selection is fine, but

Hotel Romazzino

we were especially partial to the local varieties, particularly the Vermentino, a white wine that proved to be refreshing, fruity, and well balanced. Guests of the Cala di Volpe who are on the full board plan have the option of dining at any of the hotel's sister properties—the Hotel Cervo, the Hotel Pitrizza, the Hotel Romazzino, and the Pescatore restaurant. We especially enjoyed a dinner at the **Pescatore,** right on the water in Porto Cervo. Here, as the sun goes down, diners can take in the port activity, the highlight of which is watching dinner being served on the sleek yachts moored nearby. Meals are also consistently good at the **Pitrizza** and the **Romazzino.** Lunch is typically served outside in a barbecue buffet highlighted by local and regional seafood and pasta; dinners feature Continental and international fare. Menus change daily and offer a variety of exquisite selections. For diners who are not on the full board plan, the prix fixe is about $100 per person before wine and tip.

Cala di Volpe. 07020 Porto Cervo, Costa Smeralda, Sardinia, Italy. Tel: 011-39-789-976111. Fax: 011-39-789-976617. Credit cards accepted.

Pescatore. 07020 Porto Cervo, Costa Smeralda, Sardinia. Italy. Tel: 011-39-789-92296. Credit cards accepted.

Hotel Pitrizza. 07020 Porto Cervo, Costa Smeralda, Sardinia, Italy. Tel: 011-39-789-930111. Fax: 011-39-789-930611. Credit cards accepted.

Hotel Romazzino. 07020 Porto Cervo, Costa Smeralda, Sardinia. Italy. Tel: 011-39-789-977111. Fax: 011-39-789-96292. Credit cards accepted.

NON-GOLF ACTIVITIES 18

Most of the best non-golf activities on Sardinia follow the gentle rhythm of the sun as it moves across the azure Mediterranean sky. We strongly recommend renting a car while in Sardinia so that you can freely tour the countryside. The operative mood in Sardinia is tranquillity; the pace is slow. Drive through the little country villages, go up into the mountains, leave the Costa Smeralda, and head west along the undeveloped west coast. You will find that most of the Sardinian coastline is unspoiled and magnificent, with intermittent coves and beaches often bordered by rocky cliffs that plunge into clear, emerald-green water. Scuba diving can be arranged through the hotel. Having been fished very hard for centuries and centuries, the undersea world of the Mediterranean is no scenic wonderland. Rather, it is interesting in its barrenness—you will come upon very few fish and virtually no coral.

Another day charter a boat from the hotel, with or without a captain, and explore the miles of fascinating coastline. You will find many isolated coves and small beaches that provide perfect spots to set anchor in order to take a swim or just bask in the sun. Because Sardinia is so utterly peaceful—this relaxed environment will calm you like few other places—we have to rate non-golf activities a solid 18.

GETTING THERE: The Cala di Volpe is thirty kilometers from the airport. Leaving the airport, take the road to Costa Smeralda and look for signs for the Cala di Volpe. The hotel also provides a minibus pickup for L40,000 ($25); arrange for this at least twenty-four hours in advance. A taxicab will cost L130,000 ($70).

APPENDIX

GOLF TRAVEL'S TOP 20 DESTINATIONS BY TOTAL SCORE

Rating	The Golf	Golf Services	Lodging	Restaurants	Non-Golf Activities	Total
The Greenbrier (WV)	19	20	18	17	20	94
Hong Kong (China)	17	16	19	20	20	92
Spanish Bay (CA)	19	17	19	18	19	92
Mauna Kea (HI)	19	17	18	18	20	92
London Golf (England)	18	18	19	17	20	92
Paris (France)	18	15	19	20	20	92
The American Club (WI)	19	19	18	18	18	92
St. Andrews (Scotland)	20	18	18	18	18	92
Phuket (Thailand)	17	17	20	19	18	91
Sydney (Australia)	18	17	18	19	19	91
The Broadmoor (CO)	19	19	17	17	19	91
The Boulders (AZ)	18	19	18	18	18	91
Melbourne (Australia)	20	17	17	18	18	90
Pebble Beach (CA)	20	16	19	16	19	90
Mauna Lani (HI)	18	20	18	15	19	90
Les Bordes (France)	19	17	17	17	20	90
Villa d'Este (Italy)	18	16	19	17	19	90
Cala di Volpe & Pevero Golf Club (Italy)	18	18	19	17	18	90
Grand Cypress (FL)	18	18	17	17	20	90
Four Seasons Nevis (Caribbean)	17	17	20	17	19	90

GOLF TRAVEL'S TOP 20 DESTINATIONS BY THE GOLF SCORE

Rating	The Golf	Golf Services	Lodging	Restaurants	Non-Golf Activities	Total
St. Andrews (Scotland)	20	18	18	18	18	92
Melbourne (Australia)	20	17	17	18	18	90
Pebble Beach (CA)	20	16	19	16	19	90
The Scottish Highlands & Royal Dornoch (Scotland)	20	18	16	16	18	88
Central England	20	17	17	17	16	87
The Aberdeen Coast (Scotland)	20	16	17	16	17	86
Northern Ireland	20	19	16	16	14	85
The Greenbrier (WV)	19	20	18	17	20	94
Spanish Bay (CA)	19	17	19	18	19	92
Mauna Kea (HI)	19	17	18	18	20	92
The American Club (WI)	19	19	18	18	18	92
The Broadmoor (CO)	19	19	17	17	19	91
Les Bordes (France)	19	17	17	17	20	90
Gleneagles (Scotland)	19	18	18	15	20	90
Los Cabos (Mexico)	19	18	19	16	18	90
Ireland's West Coast (Ireland)	19	17	18	16	18	88
Jasper Park Lodge (Canada)	19	17	16	19	17	88
Southeast England (England)	19	17	16	16	18	86
Bermuda	19	16	17	16	18	86
Royal Troon & Prestwick (Scotland)	19	18	17	16	16	86

GOLF TRAVEL'S TOP 20 DESTINATIONS BY GOLF SERVICES SCORE

Rating	The Golf	Golf Services	Lodging	Restaurants	Non-Golf Activities	Total
The Greenbrier (WV)	19	20	18	17	20	94
Mauna Lani (HI)	18	20	18	15	19	90
Grayhawk (AZ)	18	19	18	18	18	91
The American Club (WI)	19	19	18	18	18	92
The Broadmoor (CO)	19	19	17	17	19	91
The Boulders (AZ)	18	19	18	18	18	91
Four Seasons Las Colinas (TX)	17	19	18	17	19	90
The Cloister (GA)	18	19	16	17	18	88
Northern Ireland	20	19	16	16	14	85
PGA National (FL)	17	19	14	13	16	79
Pasatiempo (CA)	18	18	17	17	17	87
London Golf (England)	18	18	19	17	20	92
St. Andrews (Scotland)	20	18	18	18	18	92
Gleneagles (Scotland)	19	18	18	15	20	90
Grand Cypress (FL)	18	18	17	17	20	90
Cala di Volpe & Pevero Golf Club (Italy)	18	18	19	17	18	90
Los Cabos (Mexico)	19	18	19	16	18	90
Chicago (IL)	18	18	19	18	17	90
Bay Hill (FL)	18	18	14	16	20	86

GOLF TRAVEL'S TOP 20 DESTINATIONS BY RESTAURANT SCORE

Rating	The Golf	Golf Services	Lodging	Restaurants	Non-Golf Activities	Total
Paris (France)	18	15	19	20	20	92
Hong Kong (China)	17	16	19	20	20	92
Jasper Park Lodge (Canada)	19	17	16	19	17	88
Sydney (Australia)	18	17	18	19	19	91
Phuket (Thailand)	17	17	20	19	18	91
St. Andrews (Scotland)	20	18	18	18	18	92
Melbourne (Australia)	20	17	17	18	18	90
Spanish Bay (CA)	19	17	19	18	19	92
Mauna Kea (HI)	19	17	18	18	20	92
The American Club (WI)	19	19	18	18	18	92
The Boulders (AZ)	18	19	18	18	18	91
Chicago (IL)	18	18	19	18	17	90
Biarritz (France)	18	19	19	18	14	88
Normandy (France)	17	15	17	18	19	86
Balsams (NH)	18	16	14	18	17	83
Bali (Indonesia)	17	15	20	18	19	89
Arizona Biltmore (AZ)	17	17	19	18	18	89
Ventana Canyon (AZ)	17	18	17	18	19	89
Sun Valley (ID)	17	17	18	18	18	88
Seattle (WA)	17	16	18	18	19	88

GOLF TRAVEL'S TOP 20 DESTINATIONS BY LODGING SCORE

Rating	The Golf	Golf Services	Lodging	Restaurants	Non-Golf Activities	Total
Phuket (Thailand)	17	17	20	19	18	91
Bali (Indonesia)	17	15	20	18	19	89
Four Seasons Nevis (Nevis)	17	17	20	17	19	90
Paris (France)	18	15	19	20	20	92
Hong Kong (China)	17	16	19	20	20	92
Spanish Bay (CA)	19	17	19	18	19	92
Chicago (IL)	18	18	19	18	17	90
Biarritz (France)	18	14	19	18	19	88
Arizona Biltmore (AZ)	17	17	19	18	18	89
London Golf (England)	18	18	19	17	20	92
Villa d'Este (Italy)	18	16	19	17	19	90
Cala di Volpe & Pevero Golf Club (Italy)	18	18	19	17	18	90
Pebble Beach (CA)	20	16	19	16	19	90
Los Cabos (Mexico)	19	18	19	16	18	90
Turnberry (Scotland)	18	17	19	16	18	88
Sydney (Australia)	18	17	18	19	19	91
St. Andrews (Scotland)	20	18	18	18	18	92
Mauna Kea (HI)	19	17	18	18	20	92
The American Club (WI)	19	19	18	18	18	92
The Boulders (AZ)	18	19	18	18	18	91

GOLF TRAVEL'S TOP 20 DESTINATIONS BY NON-GOLFING ACTIVITIES SCORE

Rating	The Golf	Golf Services	Lodging	Restaurants	Non-Golf Activities	Total
Paris (France)	18	15	19	20	20	92
Hong Kong (China)	17	16	19	20	20	92
London Golf (England)	18	18	19	17	20	92
Mauna Kea (HI)	19	17	18	18	20	92
The Greenbrier (WV)	19	20	18	17	20	94
Gleneagles (Scotland)	19	18	18	15	20	90
Les Bordes (France)	19	17	17	17	20	90
Grand Cypress (FL)	18	18	17	17	20	90
Disney World (FL)	17	18	17	16	20	88
Bay Hill (FL)	18	18	14	16	20	86
Bali (Indonesia)	17	15	20	18	19	89
Four Seasons Nevis (Nevis)	17	17	20	17	19	90
Spanish Bay (CA)	19	17	19	18	19	92
Villa d'Este (Italy)	18	16	19	17	19	90
Pebble Beach (CA)	20	16	19	16	19	90
Sydney (Australia)	18	17	18	19	19	91
Seattle (WA)	17	16	18	18	19	88
Torrey Pines (CA)	18	16	18	17	19	88
Four Seasons Las Colinas (TX)	19	17	17	19	19	91
The Broadmoor	19	19	17	17	19	91

INDEX

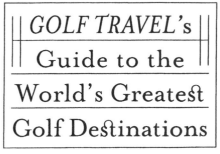